From

D0725613

POSTCARDS

FROM

ALASKA

A Native girl with Alaskan husky puppies in Kotzebue, 26 miles north of the Arctic Circle near the Bering Strait. See chapter 10. © Clark James Mishler/Alaska Stock Images.

The Starr Hill neighborhood in downtown Juneau. Built up a mountain on the side of the Gastineau Channel and surrounded by the Juneau Icefield, the city is the only state capital in the U.S. that cannot be reached by road. See chapter 5. © Mark Kelley/Alaska Stock Images.

Chilkat dancer Charles Jimmie, Sr., in front of the Tlingit tribal house at Fort William Seward in Haines. The Chilkat Dancers, formed in 1957, perform regularly in town and have toured all over the world. See chapter 5. © Kim Heacox Photography/Ken Graham Agency.

Denali State Park borders the southeast corner of Denali National Park, and provides wonderful views of the south side of Mt. McKinley. See chapter 8. © Mike Jones/Ken Graham Agency.

A kayaker exploring near icebergs in Tracy Arm. The South Sawyer Glacier, located at the end of the Arm, calves off many tons of ice daily, giving the channel an otherworldly look. See chapter 5. © Jeff Foott/Alaska Stock Images.

A sled dog race in Fairbanks. The city and the surrounding area host the Yukon Quest International Sled Dog Race in February and the North American Sled Dog Championships in March. See chapter 9. © Gary Schultz/Alaska Stock Images.

Glaciers flow down from Mt. McKinley, the tallest peak in North America. The dark streaks in the glacial ice are called moraine, and are accumulations of rock pushed to the side as the glacier flows slowly downhill. Those in the center of the flow are called median moraine, and are produced when two glaciers flow together. See chapter 8. © Ken Graham/Ken Graham Agency.

A baby Arctic ground squirrel shopping for groceries. See the appendix for a guide to Alaska's wildlife. © Paul McCormick/The Image Bank.

Visitors at Denali National Park encounter one of the locals. Though some complain about the buses, which are the only way to traverse the park in a vehicle, it's a system that keeps visitors from overwhelming the ecosystem, so the animals are still there to watch and their behavior remains essentially normal. It may be the only $20 safari in the world. See chapter 8. © Kim Heacox Photography/Ken Graham Agency.

A totem pole in Juneau. One of the most distinctive representations of Native culture in Southeast Alaska, totems are carved to depict the genealogy and history of their people. You'll see them throughout the region, particularly at Ketchikan's several totem parks and heritage centers and at the Sitka National Historic Park, which has a totem trail and a workshop where Native artists craft new poles. See chapter 5. © Randy Brandon/Alaska Stock Images.

In the summer, moose are most often seen standing in forest ponds eating the weeds from the bottom or pruning streamside willows, their all-time favorite food; at Denali, moose most often show up along the first few miles of the park road, in the willowy forest. See chapter 8. © Ken Graham/Ken Graham Agency.

Though Anchorage is Alaska's largest city, where 40% of the state's population resides, it sits so close to wild areas that anyone with a few hundred dollars for a float plane can be on a lake or river with the bears and salmon in a matter of minutes. See chapter 6. © Ken Graham/Ken Graham Agency.

Harry Gaines showing off his 80-pound trophy King salmon, caught in the Kenai River, home of the world's largest salmon. Kings come in two runs on the Kenai: The early run, from mid-May to the end of June, usually produces smaller fish in the 20- to 40-pound range; the second run comes during the month of July and includes massive fish that range up to 90 pounds. See chapters 2 and 7. © Ken Graham/Ken Graham Agency.

Dall sheep rams at Polychrome Mountain in Denali National Park. The Dall sheep's habitat is the high, rocky places, where their incredible agility makes them safe from predators. In Denali you'll typically see them from a great distance, using binoculars. Often the sheep move in herds of a dozen or more animals. See chapter 8. © Craig Blacklock/Larry Ulrich Stock.

A brown bear catching his dinner. In coastal areas where salmon are plentiful, such as Southeast Alaska or Katmai National Park, brown bears (also known as grizzlies) can grow to well over 1,000 pounds, and even approach the one-ton mark. The largest of all are found on salmon-rich Kodiak Island. See chapter 10. © Galen Rowell/Mountain Light.

A humpback whale breaching in Frederick Sound. No one knows for sure why they leap from the water like this—it may just be because they enjoy it. Humpbacks are easy to recognize by their huge, mottled tails; by the hump on their backs; and by their arm-like flippers, which can grow to be 14 feet long. See the appendix. © David Hoffmann/ Ken Graham Agency.

A bald eagle swoops down and makes off with its prey. Eagles are so common in Alaska that in most coastal towns a pigeon would cause a bigger stir among bird fanciers. In Southeast, Haines is a prime eagle-spotting area, where thousands congregate in the fall, and Sitka and Ketchikan both have raptor centers where you can see eagles up close. See chapter 5. © Dan Parrett/Alaska Stock Images.

Cruises are a popular way to see Alaska's coast, and the small cruise ships in particular—such as those operated by Alaska's Glacier Bay, Cruise West, American Safari Cruises, Clipper, and Special Expeditions—can really give you an up-close feeling for the rhythm of life in the region. *Left:* A Zodiac landing craft ferries passengers from the Yorktown Clipper (© Wolfgang Kaehler Photography). *Below:* Passengers on the Spirit of '98 *witness glacial calving at the South Sawyer Glacier in Tracy Arm* (© Dave G. Houser Photography). *See chapter 4.*

View of the Chigmit Mountains in Lake Clark National Park, located on the west side of the Cook Inlet at the north end of the Alaska Peninsula. The Chigmits include two active volcanoes, Mt. Redoubt and Mt. Iliamna, and the park's lakes and rivers are crucial salmon habitat to the Bristol Bay salmon fishery, one of the largest sockeye salmon fishing grounds in the world. See chapter 10. © Fred Hirschmann Wilderness Photography.

A pair of tufted puffins at the Walrus Islands State Game Sanctuary in the Bering Sea. Puffins favor the cracks of rugged granite islands and cliffs for nesting and laying their eggs, and they fly better underwater than in the air—something you can see at the Alaska SeaLife Center in Seward. See chapter 7. © Fred Hirschmann Wilderness Photography.

An Alaskan moose up close and personal. They're as big as a large horse and their flanks look like a worn-out shag carpet draped over a sawhorse, but moose are survivors, thriving in land that no one else wants. In the summer, they disperse and are not easily seen in thick vegetation. In the winter, they gather where walking is easy, along roads and in lowlands where people also like to live. See the appendix. © Dorothy Keeler/Ken Graham Agency.

Fields of Nootka lupine along the shores of Turnagain Arm, at the foot of the Chugach Mountains. One of the world's great drives follows the Seward Highway roughly 50 miles from Anchorage south to Portage Glacier, passing through a magnificent, ever-changing, mostly untouched landscape full of wildlife. See chapter 6. © Allen Prier/Ken Graham Agency.

Lone canoeist on Lower Summit Lake on the Kenai Peninsula, just south of Anchorage. See chapter 7. © Jeff Schultz/Alaska Stock Images.

Alaska

by Charles P. Wohlforth

with Online Directory by Michael Shapiro

IDG Books Worldwide, Inc.
An International Data Group Company
Foster City, CA • Chicago, IL • Indianapolis, IN • New York, NY

ABOUT THE AUTHOR

Charles P. Wohlforth is a lifelong Alaskan who has been a writer and journalist since 1986. After graduating from Princeton University, he worked as a newspaper reporter in the small town of Homer, Alaska, and then for the *Anchorage Daily News,* where he covered the *Exxon Valdez* oil spill. In 1992, Wohlforth went on his own as a freelance writer for various regional and national magazines and as the author of books such as this one. His *Frommer's Family Vacations in the National Parks* covers parks all over the United States based on insights from the Wohlforth family's own camping experiences. Wohlforth lives in Anchorage with his wife, Barbara, sons Robin and Joseph, and daughter, Julia.

Cruise chapter: Introductory comments by **Matt Hannafin** and Charles Wohlforth; cruise-planning information and big-ship reviews excerpted from *Frommer's Alaska Cruises,* by **Fran Wenograd Golden** and **Jerry Brown;** small-ship reviews by Matt Hannafin. Thanks to Lisa Renaud and Dan Glover for additional information.

IDG BOOKS WORLDWIDE, INC.

An International Data Group Company
919 E. Hillsdale Blvd.
Suite 400
Foster City, CA 94404

Find us online at **www.frommers.com**

Copyright © 2000 by Macmillan General Reference USA, Inc., a wholly owned
    subsidiary of IDG Books Worldwide, Inc.
Maps © by Macmillan General Reference USA, Inc., a wholly owned subsidiary of
    IDG Books Worldwide, Inc.

All rights reserved. No part of this book may be reproduced or transmitted in any form or by any means, electronic or mechanical, including photocopying, recording, or by any information storage and retrieval system, without permission in writing from the Publisher.

MACMILLAN is a registered trademark of Macmillan, Inc.
FROMMER'S is a registered trademark of Arthur Frommer. Used under license.

ISBN 0-02-862991-4
ISSN 1042-8283

Editor: Matt Hannafin
Production Editor: Suzanne Snyder
Design by Michele Laseau
Digital Cartography by John Decamillis, Roberta Stockwell
Page creation by Melissa Auciello-Brogan, Linda Quigley

The map on page 77 was adapted from maps belonging to Geosystems Global Corporation, copyright © 1995. Unauthorized use, including copying by technical means, is expressly prohibited.

SPECIAL SALES

For general information on IDG Books Worldwide's books in the U.S., please call our Consumer Customer Service department at 1-800-762-2974. For reseller information, including discounts, bulk sales, customized editions, and premium sales, please call our Reseller Customer Service department at 1-800-434-3422.

Manufactured in the United States of America

Contents

8 The Denali Park Region   310

9 The Alaskan Interior   342

10 The Bush   399

Appendix: Alaska in Depth 434

Frommer's Online Directory 463

Index 473

List of Maps

ACKNOWLEDGMENTS

I couldn't put together a book such as this one without a lot of help in covering Alaska's great distances and tracking its fast-changing visitor businesses. Friends all over Alaska show me around when I drop in for one of my visits as a "professional tourist," but a few people in particular do much more. My wife, Barbara, almost a coauthor, visits sights and hotels and keeps our family in order and happy as we travel together. My children, Robin, Julia, and Joseph, always are good sports and provide unique perspectives for "our travel book," making the discoveries of travel a joy, as only children can. My assistants in Anchorage and journalistic colleagues all over Alaska enabled me to make this book as up-to-date as any you'll find: Kathryn Gerlek, Lynn Englishbee, Carolyn Minor, Tom Begich, Brian O'Donohue, Alex DeMarben, Kathleen Tassaro, Robin Mackey Hill, Barbara O'Brien, Sydney D'Oro, and Eliot Peterson. Others, who helped build previous editions, included Wendy Feuer, Eric and Caroline Wohlforth, Eric Troyer, Mark Handley, Catherine Reardon, Dean Mitchell, and Laura Mathews. Many other friends offered help and advice, and I'm grateful to all of them.

—Charles P. Wohlforth

AN INVITATION TO THE READER

In researching this book, we discovered many wonderful places—hotels, restaurants, shops, and more. We're sure you'll find others. Please tell us about them, so we can share the information with your fellow travelers in upcoming editions. If you were disappointed with a recommendation, we'd love to know that, too. Please write to:

Frommer's Alaska 2000
IDG Travel
1633 Broadway
New York, NY 100019

AN ADDITIONAL NOTE

Please be advised that travel information is subject to change at any time—and this is especially true of prices. We therefore suggest that you write or call ahead for confirmation when making your travel plans. The authors, editors, and Publisher cannot be held responsible for the experiences of readers while traveling. Your safety is important to us, however, so we encourage you to stay alert and be aware of your surroundings. Keep a close eye on cameras, purses, and wallets, all favorite targets of thieves and pickpockets.

WHAT THE SYMBOLS MEAN

❏ Frommer's Favorites

Hotels, restaurants, attractions, and entertainment you should not miss.

The following abbreviations are used for credit cards:

AE	American Express	EURO	Eurocard
CB	Carte Blanche	JCB	Japan Credit Bank
DC	Diners Club	MC	MasterCard
DISC	Discover	V	Visa
ER	EnRoute		

FIND FROMMER'S ONLINE

Arthur Frommer's Budget Travel Online (www.frommers.com) offers more than 6,000 pages of up-to-the-minute travel information—including the latest bargains and candid, personal articles updated daily by Arthur Frommer himself. No other Web site offers such comprehensive and timely coverage.

The Best of Alaska

As a child, when my family traveled outside Alaska for vacations, I often met other children who asked, "Wow, you live in Alaska? What's it like?" I never did well with that question. To me, the place I was visiting was far simpler and easier to describe than the one I was from. The Lower 48 seemed a fairly homogeneous land of freeways and fast food, a well-mapped network of established places. Alaska, on the other hand, wasn't—and isn't—even completely explored. Natural forces of vast scale and subtlety still were shaping the land in their own way, inscribing a different story on each of an infinite number of unexpected places. Each region, whether populated or not, was unique far beyond my ability to explain. Unlike the built environment where human endeavor held sway, Alaska was so large and new, unconquered and exquisitely real, as to defy summation.

In contrast to many places you might choose to visit, it's Alaska's unformed newness that makes it so interesting and fun. Despite the best efforts of tour planners and the like, the most memorable parts of a visit are unpredictable and often unexpected: a humpback whale leaping clear of the water, the face of a glacier releasing huge ice chunks, a bear feasting on salmon in a river, a huge salmon chomping onto your own line. You can look at totem poles and see Alaska Native cultural demonstrations, and you can also get to know living indigenous people who still know and live by many of the traditional ways. And sometimes grand, quiet moments endure most deeply.

As the writer of this guidebook, I aim to help you get to places where you may encounter what's new, real, and unexpected. Opening yourself to those experiences is your job, but it's an effort that's likely to pay off. Although I have lived here all my life, I often envy the stories visitors tell me about the Alaskan places they have gone to and what happened there. No one owns Alaska, and most of us are newcomers here. In all this immensity, a visitor fresh off the boat is as likely as a lifelong resident to see or do something amazing.

The structure of the book is intended to make it a useful tool in your exploration. This first chapter gives broad-brush ideas about some of the best Alaska has to offer (the entries aren't in any particular order). Chapter 2 has practical information for planning a trip, including guidance on how to set up an outdoor vacation fishing, sea kayaking, hiking or staying at a wilderness lodge. Chapter 3 contains advice for foreign travelers. Chapter 4, by Frommer's cruise experts, is a guide to voyaging to Alaska by cruise ship. Chapters 5 through 10 cover each of the state's regions in detail, broken down into subregions or towns. And in the appendix, where it's easy to cross-reference, you'll find an overview of the people, social history, and natural history of the state.

1 The Best Views

You can find your own best views almost anywhere in Alaska. But here are some of the sorts of visions you may have:

- **From the Chugach Mountains Over Anchorage, at Sunset:** The city sparkles below, on the edge of an orange-reflecting Cook Inlet, far below the mountainside where you stand. Beyond the pink and purple silhouettes of mountains on the other side of the Inlet, the sun is spraying warm, dying light into puffs of clouds. It's midnight. See chapter 6.
- **Polychrome Pass, Denali National Park:** Riding in a bus rising up the narrow park road on a cliff face, you're too nervous to notice the horizon. And then, there it is—a great valley of green tundra, mountain peaks receding in every direction, and, on either side of the valley, mountains of colored rock standing like gates. See chapter 8.
- **Punchbowl Cove, Misty Fjords National Monument:** A sheer granite cliff rises smooth and implacable 3,150 feet straight up from the water. A pair of bald eagles wheel and soar across its face, providing the only sense of scale. They look the size of gnats. See chapter 5.
- **The Northern Lights, Alaska's Interior or Southcentral Region:** Blue, purple, green, and red lines spin from the center of the sky, draping long tendrils of slow-moving light. Bright, flashing, sky-covering waves wash across the dome of stars like ripples driven by a gust of wind on a pond. Looking around, your companions' faces are rosy in a silver, snowy night, all gazing straight up with their mouths open. See chapter 9.
- **A First Sight of Alaska:** Flying north from Seattle, you're in clouds, so you concentrate on a book. When you look up, the light from the window has changed. Down below, the clouds are gone, and under the wing, where you're used to seeing roads, cities, and farms on most flights, instead you see only high, snowy mountain peaks, without the slightest mark of human presence, stretching as far as the horizon. Welcome to Alaska.

2 The Best of Cruising Alaska

Cruises provide comfortable, leisurely access to the Inside Passage and the Gulf of Alaska. Here are some of the best bets. See chapter 4 for details.

- **Best Up-Close Alaska Experience:** Alaska's Glacier Bay Tours and Cruises' *Wilderness Adventurer* and *Wilderness Explorer* sail itineraries that shun overcrowded port towns in favor of wilderness areas and small fishing villages. Both carry sea-kayaks for off-ship exploration, and both feature naturalist-led hikes as central features of the experience. The line is owned by an Alaska Native corporation and the ships are small (carrying 74 and 36 passengers, respectively) and very casual. They're not fancy, but that's the point—it's where they take you that counts.
- **Best Itinerary:** World Explorer Cruises' *Universe Explorer* is unmatched, offering a 14-day round-trip itinerary from Vancouver that includes all the major ports of

call and a few others, too. They also offer a 9-night round trip out of Vancouver, featuring the best of the Inside Passage, including Haines and an overnight stop at Metlakatla, a Tsimshian Indian village on Annette Island, just south of Ketchikan. The ship is large, though not huge, and stresses education rather than the typical big-ship cruise diversions.

- **Most Comfortable Small Ships:** Cruise West's *Spirit of Endeavor* and *Spirit of '98* (a 19th-century coastal steamer recreation) and Clipper's *Yorktown Clipper* offer a higher level of comfort than the other small ships in Alaska while still giving you an intimate, casual, up-close small-ship experience.

- **Most Luxurious Big Ships:** The *Crystal Harmony* is the top-of-the-line ship in the Alaska market, with superb cuisine, elegant service, lovely surroundings, great cabins, and sparkling entertainment. If you want a more casual kind of luxury, Radisson Seven Seas' *Seven Seas Navigator* (which had just debuted at press time, and is slightly smaller than the *Harmony*) offers just that. Among the mainstream cruise ships, Celebrity's *Mercury* and *Galaxy* are the big winners, offering cutting-edge modern ships with great service, dining, and design.

- **Best Cruisetours:** Holland America Line and Princess are the leaders in linking cruises with land tours into the interior, either before or after your cruise. They own their own hotels, deluxe motor coaches, and railcars, and after many years in the business, they both really know what they're doing. Princess concentrates more on the Anchorage/Denali/Fairbanks routes, while Holland America has many itineraries that get you to the Yukon territory's Dawson City and Whitehorse.

3 The Best Glaciers

More of Alaska—more than 100 times more—is covered by glacier ice than is settled by human beings. Here are some favorite glaciers.

- **Grand Pacific Glacier, Glacier Bay National Park:** Two vast glaciers of deep blue meet at the top of an utterly barren fjord. They rubbed and creased the gray rock for thousands of years before just recently releasing it to the air again. Boats that pull close to the glaciers seem surrounded by the intimidating walls of ice on three sides. See chapters 4 and 5.

- **Childs Glacier, Cordova:** Out the Copper River Highway from Cordova, this is a participatory glacier-viewing experience. The glacier is cut by the Copper River, a quarter mile broad; standing on the opposite shore (unless you're up in the viewing tower), you have to be ready to run like hell when the creaking, popping ice gives way and a huge berg falls into the river, potentially swamping the picnic area. Even when the glacier isn't calving, you can feel the ice groaning in your gut. See chapter 7.

- **Exit Glacier, Seward:** You can drive near the glacier and walk the rest of the way on a gravel path. Then it towers above like a huge blue sculpture, the spires of broken ice close enough to breathe a freezer-door chill down on watchers. See chapter 7.

- **College Fjords, Prince William Sound:** In this area of western Prince William Sound, you can see a couple of dozen glaciers in a day. Some of these are the amazing tidewater glaciers that dump huge, office-building-sized spires of ice into the ocean, each setting off a terrific splash and outward-radiating sea wave. See chapters 4 and 7.

4   The Most Beautiful Drives & Train Rides

There aren't many highways in Alaska, but all are worth exploring. You'll find a description of each in chapters 6 through 9. Here are some highlights:

- **White Pass and Yukon Route Railway, Skagway to Summit:** The narrow-gauge excursion train, sometimes pulled by vintage steam engines, climbs the steep grade chiseled into the granite mountains by stampeders to the Klondike gold rush. The train is a sort of mechanical mountain goat, balancing on trestles and steep rock walls far above deep gorges. See chapter 5.

- **Seward Highway, Turnagain Arm:** Just south of Anchorage, the highway has been chipped into the side of the Chugach Mountains over the surging gray water of Turnagain Arm. Above, Dall sheep pick their way along the cliffs, within easy sight. Below, white beluga whales chase salmon through the turbid water. See chapter 7.

- **Alaska Railroad, Anchorage to Seward:** The line follows the same stretch of Turnagain Arm as the Seward Highway, then splits off as it rises into the mountains of the Kenai Peninsula, rumbling close along the face of a glacier and clinging to the edge of a vertically walled gorge with a roaring river at bottom. See chapter 7.

- **Denali Highway:** Leading east-west through the Alaska Range, the Denali Highway crosses terrain that could be another Denali National Park, full of wildlife and with views so huge and grand, they seem impossible. See chapter 8.

- **Richardson Highway:** Just out of Valdez heading north, the Richardson Highway rises quickly from sea level to more than 2,600 feet, switching back and forth on the side of a mountain. With each turn, the drop down the impassable slope becomes more amazing. North of Glennallen, the highway rises again, through a low boreal forest of black spruce, past small lakes and roaring rivers, and suddenly bursts through the tree line between a series of mountains. Then for miles it traces the edge of long alpine lakes, before descending, parallel with the silver skein of the Alaska Pipeline, to Delta Junction. See chapter 9.

- **Top of the World and Taylor Highways:** Leading over the top of rounded, tundra-clothed mountains from Dawson City, Yukon Territory, to the Alaska Highway near Tok, this gravel route floats on a waving sea of terrain, with mountains receding to the infinite horizon in every direction, then traces steep canyons in uninhabited territory. See chapter 9.

- **The Roads Around Nome:** You can't drive to Nome, but 250 miles of gravel roads radiate from the Arctic community into tundra populated only by musk oxen, bears, reindeer, birds, and other wildlife. See chapter 10.

5   The Best Fishing

The quality of salmon fishing in Alaska isn't so much a function of place as of time. See chapter 2 for how to find out where the fish will be when you arrive.

- **Copper River Valley, Cordova:** The Copper itself is silty with glacial runoff, but feeder streams and rivers are rich with trout, Dolly Varden, and salmon. See chapter 7.

- **Gustavus:** Via charter boat from Gustavus, you can get big halibut without long trips in the area of Icy Strait, and can see humpback whales feeding on the same afternoon, off Point Adolphus. See chapter 5.

- **Prince of Wales Island:** Fly-in trips or roadside streams yield some of the most prolific salmon fishing anywhere. See chapter 5.

- **The Kenai River:** The biggest king salmon—up to 98 pounds—come from the swift Kenai River. Big fish are so common in the second run of kings that there's a special, higher standard for what makes a trophy from this river. Silvers and reds add to a mad, summer-long fishing frenzy. See chapter 7.
- **Homer:** One of the state's largest charter fishing fleets goes for halibut ranging into the hundreds of pounds, accessible on the road network. See chapter 7.
- **Kodiak Island:** The bears are so big because they live on an island that's crammed with spawning salmon in the summer. Kodiak has the best roadside salmon fishing in Alaska, and the remote fishing, at lodges or fly-in stream banks, is legendary. See chapter 10.
- **Bristol Bay:** This is the world's richest salmon fishery; lodges on the remote rivers of the region are a fisher's paradise. See chapter 10.

6 The Best Tips for Cooking Salmon

Now that you've caught a Pacific salmon, you need to know how to cook it—or order it in a restaurant—to avoid spoiling the rich flavor.

- **Freeze As Little As Possible:** It's a sad fact that salmon loses some of its richness and gets more "fishy" as soon as it's frozen. Eat as much as you can fresh, because it'll never be better. Most fishing towns also have sport-fish processors who will flash-freeze or smoke the rest. Don't overlook smoking, the traditional Native way of preserving fish for the winter.
- **Choose the Best Fish:** The finest restaurants advertise where their salmon comes from on the menu—in early summer, Copper River kings and reds are the richest in flavor; later in the summer, Yukon River salmon are best. King, red, and silver are the only species you should find in a restaurant. The oil in the salmon gives it the rich, meaty flavor; the fish from the Copper and Yukon are high in oil.
- **Keep It Simple:** When ordering salmon or halibut in a restaurant, avoid anything with cheese, heavy sauces, or brown sugar. When salmon is fresh, it's best with light seasoning, perhaps just a little lemon, dill weed, and pepper and salt—or without anything on it, grilled over alder coals.
- **Don't Overcook It:** Salmon should be cooked just until the moment the meat changes color through to the bone, or slightly before. A few minutes more, and some of the texture and flavor are lost. That's why those huge barbecue salmon bakes often are not as good as they should be—it's too hard to cook hundreds of pieces of fish just right and serve them all hot.
- **Fillets, Not Steaks:** Salmon is cut two ways in Alaska—lengthwise fillets or crosswise steaks. The fillet is cut with the grain of the flesh, keeping the oil and moisture in the fish. Do not remove the skin before cooking—it holds in the oils, and will fall off easily when the fish is done.

7 The Best Bear Viewing

There are many places to see bears in Alaska, but if your goal is to make *sure* you see a bear—and potentially lots of bears—these are the best places:

- **Katmai National Park:** During the July and September salmon runs, dozens of giant brown bears congregate around Brooks Camp, where, from wooden platforms a few yards away, you can watch the full range of their behaviors. Flight services from Homer and Kodiak also bring guests to see bears in lesser-used areas of the park. See chapters 7 and 10.

- **Anan Bear Observatory:** When the fish are running, you see black and brown bears here feeding in a salmon stream from close at hand. Access is easiest from Wrangell. See chapter 5.
- **Pack Creek, Admiralty Island:** The brown bears of the island, which is more thickly populated with them than anywhere else on earth, have learned to ignore the daily visitors who stand on the platforms at Pack Creek. Access is by air from Juneau. See chapter 5.
- **Denali National Park:** The park is the best and least expensive wildlife-viewing safari in the state. Passengers on the buses that drive the park road as far as the Eielson Visitor Center usually see at least some grizzlies. See chapter 8.
- **Kodiak and Homer:** Air-taxi operators based in both towns take passengers to streams and beaches where bears congregate, offering a virtual guarantee of seeing one. If you're lucky enough to win a permit for the McNeil River State Game Sanctuary, you can live for a while among dozens of feeding bears. See chapters 7 and 10.

8 The Best Marine Mammal Viewing

You've got a good chance of seeing marine mammals almost anywhere you go boating in Alaska, but in some places it's almost guaranteed.

- **Frederick Sound, Petersburg:** A humpback jumped right into the boat with whale-watchers here in 1995. Petersburg boats also see otters and baby seals sitting on icebergs floating in front of LeConte Glacier. See chapter 5.
- **Point Adolphus, Gustavus:** Humpback whales show up almost on schedule off the point in Icy Strait, just a few miles from little Gustavus, a town of luxurious country inns. See chapter 5.
- **Sitka Sound:** Lots of otters and humpback whales show up in the waters near Sitka. In fall, when the town holds its Whale Fest, you can spot them from a city park built for the purpose. See chapter 5.
- **Kenai Fjords National Park, Seward:** You don't have to go all the way into the park—you're pretty well assured of sea otters and sea lions in Resurrection Bay, near Seward, and humpbacks and killer whales often show up, too. See chapter 7.
- **Prince William Sound:** Otters, seals, and sea lions are easy—you'll see them on most trips out of Valdez, Whittier, or Cordova—but you also have a good chance of seeing both humpback and killer whales in the Sound. See chapter 7.

9 The Best Encounters with Native Culture

An Alaska Native cultural renaissance is going on, so there's never been a better time for visitors to encounter Native culture.

- **Alaska Native Heritage Center, Anchorage:** All Alaska's Native groups joined together to build this grand new living museum and gathering place, where dance and music performances, storytelling, art and craft demonstrations, and simple meetings of people happen every day. See chapter 6.
- **Chilkat Dancers, Haines:** The Tlingit dances of Haines are authentically loose—children learn their new parts by being thrown into the dance and picking it up. The totem-carving studio is wonderfully casual, standing open for visitors to wander in and meet the artists. See chapter 5.
- **Saxman Totem Park:** Just south of Ketchikan, a Tlingit Native corporation owns a major totem pole collection and clan house, and provides tours and cultural

demonstrations for visitors. The informal part of the experience is the best part, because in the workshop you can meet the carvers. See chapter 5.

- **Alutiiq Museum, Kodiak:** The Koniag people are recovering their culture from the ground and from artifacts repatriated from the world's museums. A major exhibit will be held in May 2000. Visitors can even join in archaeological field work. See chapter 10.
- **Museum of the Aleutians, Unalaska:** Built by Aleuts to preserve and exhibit their own heritage, the brand new museum stands right beside a major dig still in progress. See chapter 10.
- **Inupiat Heritage Center, Barrow:** Another brand new living museum, this is a place to meet and enjoy performances by the Native people who built the place, and to see extraordinary artifacts they have made and recovered from frozen digs. See chapter 10.
- **NANA Museum of the Arctic, Kotzebue:** Eskimos of this still traditional city/village proudly show off their Inupiat way of life with a combination of high-tech and age-old entertainment. See chapter 10.

10 The Best Community Museums & Historic Sites

- **Anchorage Museum of History and Art:** Alaska's largest museum has the room and expertise to tell the story of Native and white history in Alaska, and to show-case contemporary Alaskan art and culture. See chapter 6.
- **Pratt Museum, Homer:** The Pratt explains the life of the ocean in an intimate and clear way you'll find nowhere else in Alaska. See chapter 7.
- **Sitka National Historical Park:** The site of the 1804 battle between the Tlingits and Russians, in a totem pole park and seaside stand of old-growth forest, allows you to really appreciate what the Native people were fighting for. Inside the visitor center, Native craftspeople carry on their traditional work and talk with visitors. See chapter 5.
- **The Alaska State Museum, Juneau:** This richly endowed museum doesn't just show off its wealth of objects, it also uses them to teach about the state, and a visit will put Alaska's Native cultures and pioneer history entirely in context. See chapter 5.
- **University of Alaska Museum, Fairbanks:** The wealth of the university's study of Alaska, in all its forms, is put on display in galleries and daily shows, from equipment used to study the aurora borealis to the petrified bison that stands above everything. See chapter 9.

11 The Best Gold Rush Sites

The Klondike Gold Rush of 1898 transformed Alaska from a blank map at the periphery of America's consciousness to a fast-growing frontier and magnet for thousands of dreamers with visions of wealth. A century later, Alaska's best historic sites preserve that extraordinary time.

- **Dawson City, Yukon Territory:** A group of prospectors made the Klondike gold strike in 1896 and returned to tell of it in 1897, and in 1898 tens of thousands of greedy gold seekers arrived after an arduous stampede. Dawson City is ground zero, and the town is dedicated to preserving and sharing the history of the gold rush phenomenon. See chapter 9.
- **Skagway:** The little town at the top of Lynn Canal was where most of the gold rush stampeders got off the boat to head over the mountains to the Klondike.

Spared from fire, flood, or even much significant economic development other than tourism, Skagway contains a large collection of gold rush–era buildings protected by the National Park Service. See chapter 5.

- **Eagle:** Unlike the other tourist-thronged gold rush towns, Eagle is a forgotten backwater where the gold rush was the last significant thing to happen. It's real and unspoiled, with lots to see but few other people to see it with. See chapter 9.
- **Nome:** The great Nome gold rush came next after the Klondike. Although few buildings remain from the gold rush period, the spirit and industry of that time remain authentically alive in Nome. See chapter 10.
- **Fairbanks:** The gold rush in Fairbanks, just after the turn of the century, is not entirely done yet—there's a big new mine north of town. The city is large enough to provide lots of interesting and fun activities that exploit gold rush history. See chapter 9.

12 The Best Winter Destinations

- **Sitka:** Much of historic Sitka is just as good in winter as at any other time of year, but with fewer crowds and lower prices. The humpback whale watching is exceptional in the late fall and early winter, as the whales stop off here on their migration. See chapter 5.
- **Alyeska Resort, Girdwood:** Alaska's premier downhill skiing area has lots of snow over a long season, fantastic views, new lifts, and a luxurious hotel. See "The Best Hotels," below, and chapter 6.
- **Anchorage:** The Fur Rendezvous and Iditarod sled dog races keep a winter-carnival atmosphere going through much of February and March, but those who enjoy participatory winter sports will enjoy Anchorage most, with some of the best Nordic and telemark skiing anywhere, close access to three downhill skiing areas, dog mushing, and lake skating. See chapter 6.
- **Chena Hot Springs Resort:** A 90-minute ride from Fairbanks and you're out in the country, where the northern lights are clear on a starry winter afternoon and night. The resort has lots of activities to get you out into the snowy countryside, or you can just relax in the hot mineral springs. See chapter 9.

13 The Best Unspoiled Small Towns

- **Gustavus:** It's a lovely little town near Glacier Bay National Park, except it isn't really a town. There's no local government or town center, just a collection of luxurious country inns and lodges in a setting of great scenic beauty, close to some of the best fishing, whale watching, and sea kayaking in Alaska. See chapter 5.
- **Petersburg:** The town is so easy to get to, right on the Inside Passage ferry route, it's incredible it has kept its quaint, small-town identity as perfectly as it has. Out of town, there's a wonderfully diverse choice of outdoor activities. See chapter 5.
- **Cordova:** This fishing town off the beaten track is a forgotten treasure, caught at some mythical point in the past when Norman Rockwell's paintings were relevant. That atmosphere combines with the best bird watching, fishing, scenic grandeur, and other outdoor activities to make Cordova one of Alaska's most charming and attractive destinations. See chapter 7.
- **Halibut Cove:** Halibut Cove has no roads, only the calm green water in an ocean channel between docks and floats and houses on boardwalks. There are three art galleries, but the main activities are slowing down, paddling around, and walking in the woods. See chapter 7.

- **Kodiak:** This hub for an area with the biggest bears, most plentiful salmon, richest wilderness sea kayaking waters, and much other natural beauty is virtually untouched by visitors. In town there are narrow, winding streets, Russian and Native historic sites, and wonderfully hospitable people. See chapter 10.

14 The Strangest Community Events

- **Cordova Ice Worm Festival:** The truth is, ice worms do exist. Really. This winter carnival celebrates them in February. The highlight is the traditional annual march of the ice worm (a costume with dozens of feet sticking out) down the main street. See chapter 7.
- **Snow Man Festival, Valdez:** A community that counts its winter snowfall by the yard makes the most of it in March, with a winter carnival that includes ice bowling, snowman building, and a drive-in movie projected on a snow bank. See chapter 7.
- **Midnight Sun Baseball Game, Fairbanks:** The semipro baseball game, without lights, doesn't begin until 10:30pm on the longest day of the year. See chapter 9.
- **Bering Sea Ice Golf Classic, Nome:** The greens are Astroturf, as the sea ice won't support a decent lawn in mid-March. Hook a drive and you could end up spending hours wandering among the pressure ridges, but you must play the ball as it lies. See chapter 10.
- **Nome Polar Bear Swim/Bathtub Race:** Nome has so *many* strange community events. Memorial Day is marked by the polar bear swim, sea ice permitting. Labor Day is celebrated by a bathtub race down Front Street, with water and a bather in each tub. See chapter 10.
- **Pillar Mountain Golf Classic, Kodiak:** The course is one hole, par is 70, and elevation gain is 1,400 feet. Having a spotter in the deep snow of late March is helpful, but use of two-way radios, dogs, and chain saws is prohibited. Also, no cutting down power poles, and cursing tournament officials carries a $25 fine. See chapter 10.
- **Community Softball, Barrow:** Play in the Arctic requires some special considerations. Spectators watch from their cars, and if a ball disappears in a puddle so that no part of it is showing, runners can advance no more than two bases. See chapter 10.

15 The Best Hotels

- **Westmark Cape Fox Lodge, Ketchikan** (☎ 907/225-8001): Standing in its own little forest atop a rocky promontory that dominates downtown Ketchikan, this cleanly luxurious hotel has the feel of a mountain lodge or resort. A funicular tram carries visitors to the Creek Street boardwalks, or you can take the wooded cliff-side path. The rooms and common areas, accented with masterpieces of Tlingit art, have exceptional views of the city and Tongass Narrows through the trees. See chapter 5.
- **Alyeska Prince Hotel, Girdwood** (☎ 800/880-3880): The first sight of this new ski resort hotel—designed in a château style and standing in an undeveloped mountain valley—is enough to make you catch your breath. Wait till you get inside and see the starscape and polar bear diorama in the lobby atrium, or the large swimming pool, with its high-beamed ceiling and wall of windows looking out on the mountain. The cozy rooms are full of cherry wood. A tram carries skiers and diners to the top of the mountain. See chapter 6.

- **Hotel Captain Cook, Anchorage** (☎ 907/276-6000): This is the grand old hotel of downtown Anchorage, with a heavy nautical theme, teak paneling, and furniture that carries through to the smallest detail in the rooms. It also remains the state's standard of service and luxury. See chapter 6.
- **Land's End, Homer** (☎ 907/235-2500): The hotel itself has some nice touches, but it wouldn't be in a class with the others on this list if not for the location. The low, wood buildings lie like a string of driftwood beached on the tip of Homer Spit, out in the middle of Kachemak Bay. Nothing stands between the rooms or restaurant and the ocean, across the beach. Sometimes whales and otters swim along the shore, just outside the windows. See chapter 7.
- **The Grand Aleutian Hotel, Unalaska/Dutch Harbor** (☎ 800/891-1194): Not long ago, it wasn't much of a distinction to be the best hotel in the Alaska Bush. Then the UniSea fish company built this large, lodge-style luxury hotel, which is competitive with the best in the state and gets extra points for the sheer audacity of building it on this remote, volcanic island. The hotel's existence creates a unique opportunity for those who want to stay in a fine hotel and see the Bush, with the best unexploited fishing and wildlife and bird watching. See chapter 10.
- **River's Edge Resort Cottages, Fairbanks** (☎ 800/770-3343 or 907/474-0286): A village of trim little cottages with nicely appointed rooms watches the Chena River flow by from patios with sliding glass doors. The owners thought of building the place when they saw how guests in their RV park enjoyed socializing. You feel like you've moved into a friendly neighborhood. Guests can fish and canoe right from their front yards. See chapter 9.
- **Fairbanks Exploration Inn** (☎ 907/451-1920): Alaska's best historic inn doesn't look so exciting from the outside—it's just a group of bungalows under the birch trees—but the bedrooms and common sitting rooms, full of light on bare wood floors, have a cool elegance and authenticity that make them that much more luxurious. See chapter 9.

16 The Best Moderately Priced Lodgings

- **Colony Inn, Palmer** (☎ 907/745-3330): A perfect country inn in a historic building with luxurious features and a great bargain price. See chapter 6.
- **Harborview Inn, Seward** (☎ 907/224-3217): A family's dedication to its guests at its bed-and-breakfast grew the business into this beautifully simple inn. The family continues to take pride in offering better lodgings for less money than the others in town. See chapter 7.
- **The New York Hotel, Ketchikan** (☎ 907/225-0246): An old building right on the water has been lovingly restored into just a few charming rooms, decorated with antiques and with views out on the town's most attractive historic district. See chapter 5.
- **The Northern Nights Inn, Cordova** (☎ 907/424-5356): Located in a historic hillside house with just a few rooms, the inn is operated by an old Cordova family with lots of energy and hospitality. The upstairs rooms have every amenity and are furnished with antiques, but rent for very low rates. See chapter 7.

17 The Best Bed & Breakfasts

- **Alaska Ocean View Bed and Breakfast, Sitka** (☎ 907/747-8310): Here, a family has set out to turn its home into perfect accommodations. Among other details, the elaborate decor in each room matches a unique packet of souvenir wildflower seeds given to each guest. See chapter 5.

- **Captain's Quarters Bed & Breakfast, Ketchikan** (☎ **907/225-4912**): On a hill where some of the streets are staircases, the ocean-facing rooms have unbelievable views of Tongass Narrows. The decor matches—a nautical theme, all in oak, lovingly crafted by the hands of the meticulous proprietor. See chapter 5.
- **Pearson's Pond Luxury Inn and Garden Spa, Juneau** (☎ **907/789-3772**): Diane Pearson takes the prize for the most obsessive attention to detail at any B&B in Alaska. Not only are the bathrooms stocked with condoms, but the private pond, with a spraying fountain, is stocked with fish. See chapter 5.
- **Glacier Trail Bed & Breakfast, Juneau** (☎ **907/789-5646**): The hosts built their house to be the perfect B&B, with Jacuzzi tubs, stunning glacier views from the bedrooms, and many amenities. Others could have done that, but only this fascinating and very Alaskan couple could make their guests feel so welcome. See chapter 5.
- **Aurora Winds Inn B&B Resort, Anchorage** (☎ **907/346-2533**): An enormous house on the hillside above Anchorage has rooms so completely and theatrically decorated you'll feel as if you're sleeping in a movie set. See chapter 6.
- **The Oscar Gill House Bed and Breakfast, Anchorage** (☎ **907/258-1717**): It's no longer hard to find beautifully restored historic B&Bs, but I've found no others like this one, where, despite being overwhelmed with business, the hosts keep their rates low just because they're decent people who know how it feels to be overcharged when you're traveling. See chapter 6.
- **Forget-Me-Not Lodge and the Aurora Express Bed & Breakfast, Fairbanks** (☎ **907/474-0949**): The owners bought an old-fashioned railroad train, hauled it up the side of a mountain above Fairbanks, and remodeled the cars in luxurious theme decor as a bed-and-breakfast. See chapter 9.

18 The Best Wilderness Lodges

- **Ultima Thule Lodge, Wrangell–St. Elias National Park** (☎ **907/258-0636**): The rugged surroundings in the park and the enthusiasm of the proprietors provide a seemingly limitless range of outdoor activities on mountains, glaciers, and rivers. Once back in the lodge, you're surrounded by comfort. See chapter 2.
- **Gustavus Inn at Glacier Bay** (☎ **907/697-2254**): Gustavus has several exceptional country inns, all similar to wilderness lodges, and this is the best of that superb collection. The rooms are charming, the grounds lovely, the meals incomparable, and the hospitality warm and welcoming. See chapter 5.
- **Kachemak Bay Wilderness Lodge, Near Homer** (☎ **907/235-8910**): This is the state's original ecotourism lodge, and still one of the best. The lodgings are completely comfortable while also fitting in with their rich maritime wilderness surroundings, the food is famous, and the hosts are expert at sharing their deep knowledge of the area and its natural history. See chapter 7.
- **Camp Denali, Kantishna, Denali National Park** (☎ **907/683-2290**): This lodge, on private land at the end of the national park road, is more than a place to relax and get into the wilderness; it also has a highly regarded program of natural-history education. See chapter 8.

2 Planning a Trip to Alaska

Planning a trip to Alaska can be a bit more complicated than traveling in the rest of the United States. Besides the vast distances and range of climatic conditions, Alaska travel in the high summer season can require long advance preparations and reservations. This chapter provides the general information you'll need to get started.

1 The Regions in Brief

SOUTHEAST ALASKA   The Southeast Panhandle is the relatively narrow strip of mountains and islands that lies between Canada and the Gulf of Alaska. To Alaskans, it's the Southeast, but to the rest of the country, it's more like the northernmost extension of the lush Pacific Northwest. It's a land of huge rain-forest trees, glacier-garbed mountains, and countless islands ranging in size from the nation's third largest to tiny, one-tree islets strewn like confetti along the channels and fjords. The water is the highway of Southeast Alaska, as the land is generally too steep and rugged to build roads, but there are lots of towns and villages reachable by the ferry system or cruise ships. Southeast contains **Juneau,** Alaska's capital and third-largest city, and **Ketchikan,** next in size to Juneau. Southeast's towns are as quaint and historic as any in Alaska, especially **Sitka,** which preserves the story of Russian America and its conflict with the indigenous Native people. Alaska Native culture—Tlingit and Haida—is rich and close to hand. No other region is richer in opportunities for boating or seeing marine wildlife. The weather is wet and temperate.

SOUTHCENTRAL ALASKA   As a region, Southcentral is something of a catchall. The area is roughly defined by the arc of the Gulf of Alaska from the Canadian border on the east to Cook Inlet and the end of the road network to the west. It's a microcosm of the state, containing **Prince William Sound,** which is similar to the wooded island habitat of Southeast; the **Kenai Peninsula,** a roaded fishing, boating, and outdoor mecca; **Anchorage,** the state's modern, major city; and the **Matanuska and Susitna Valleys,** an agricultural and suburban region of broad flatlands between steep mountains. Southcentral dominates Alaska, with most of the state's population and a more highly developed transportation system than elsewhere, including a network of highways and the Alaska Railroad. Southcentral's weather is influenced by the ocean, keeping it from being very hot or very cold. The coastal areas are wet, while just behind the coastal mountains the weather is drier.

Alaska by the Numbers

This chart shows some comparative indicators for 17 of Alaska's most popular destinations. The first column is the name of the destination; next is population. The third column is the season when there's enough going on and weather is suitable for a good visit (including for winter sports). The "Transportation" column shows ways of getting to each destination (see more on this in "Getting There," later in this chapter). The fifth column is average annual precipitation, in water equivalent (in inches), and the final column is average annual snowfall (in inches).

Place	Population	Season	Transportation	Precipitation (inches)	Snow (inches)
Anchorage	258,782	May–Sept/ Feb–Mar	Road, air, rail	15.4	69
Barrow	4,397	June–Aug	Air	4.7	28
Denali National Park	184	June–Sept	Road, rail	15.0	54.8
Fairbanks	83,928	May–Sept/ Feb–Mar	Road, air, rail	10.4	68
Glacier Bay National Park	368	May–Sept	Air	53.9	70.2
Homer	4,155	May–Sept	Road, air, ferry	24.9	58
Juneau	30,236	May–Sept	Air, ferry	52.9	100
Kenai	7,058	May–Oct	Road, air	18.9	59.3
Ketchikan	14,231	May–Sept	Air, ferry	155.2	37
Kodiak Island	12,145	May–Sept	Air, ferry	74.3	80
Kotzebue	2,964	June–Aug	Air	9.0	47.6
Nome	3,706	June–Aug/ Mar	Air	15.6	56
Petersburg	3,398	May–Sept	Air, ferry	105.8	102
Seward	3,040	May–Sept	Road, rail, ferry, air	67.7	79.9
Sitka	8,779	May–Sept/ Nov	Air, ferry	86.8	40.7
Skagway	814	May–Sept	Road, ferry, air	23.0	35.7
Valdez	4,155	May–Sept/ Mar	Road, air, ferry	61.5	32.0

THE INTERIOR   The vast central part of the state is crossed by highways and by rivers that act as highways. There are huge, generally flat areas lying between the Alaska Range, which contains **Mount McKinley,** North America's tallest peak, and the Brooks Range, a continental divide between the Interior's great rivers and the Arctic. The region's dominant city is **Fairbanks,** Alaska's second largest, which lies on the Chena River in the middle of the state. The natural environment is drier and less

Alaska

MILEAGE CHART — Approximate driving distances in miles between cities.	Anchorage	Circle	Dawson City	Eagle	Fairbanks	Haines	Homer	Prudhoe Bay	Seattle	Seward	Skagway	Tok	Valdez
Anchorage		520	494	501	358	775	226	847	2234	126	832	328	304
Circle	520		530	541	162	815	746	1972	2271	646	872	368	526
Dawson City	494	530		131	379	548	713	868	1843	619	430	189	428
Eagle	501	541	131		379	620	727	868	1974	627	579	173	427
Fairbanks	358	162	379	379		653	584	489	2121	484	710	206	364
Haines	775	815	548	620	653		1001	1142	1774	901	359	447	701
Homer	226	746	713	727	584	1001		1073	2455	173	1058	554	530
Prudhoe Bay	847	1972	868	868	489	1142	1073		2610	973	1199	695	853
Seattle	2243	2271	1843	1974	2121	1774	2455	2610		1361	1577	1931	2169
Seward	126	646	619	627	484	901	173	973	1361		958	454	430
Skagway	832	872	430	579	710	359	1058	1199	1577	958		504	758
Tok	328	368	189	173	206	447	554	695	1931	454	504		254
Valdez	304	526	428	427	364	701	530	853	2169	430	758	254	

Chukchi Sea

Little Diomede Island

Nome

Norton Sound

Yukon Delta National Wildlife Refuge

Bering Sea

Nunivak Island

Bethel

Yukon Delta National Wildlife Refuge

Bristol Bay

Attu Island

Pribilof Islands

Cape St. Stephen

Rat Islands

Adak

Adak Island

Atka Island

Atka

Fort Glen

Dutch Harbor

Unalaska

Unimak Island

Cold Bay

Unimak

Alaska Peninsula

Aleutian Islands

PACIFIC

Arctic Ocean

Barrow

Prudhoe
Bay

Beaufort Sea

Deadhorse

ape Krusenstern
ational Monument

Brooks Range

Arctic National
Wildlife Refuge

United States
Canada

8

Noatak National
Preserve

Anaktuvuk
Pass

Brooks Range

Kobuk Valley
National Park

Gates of the Arctic
National Park and Preserve

Kotzebue

Bettles

Land Bridge
al Preserve

Fort Yukon

Yukon Flats
National Wildlife
Refuge

Arctic Circle

5

Dempster Hwy

C A N A D A

Galena

Chena
Hot Springs

Circle

6

Yukon-Charley Rivers
National Preserve

YUKON

5

Manley
Hot Springs

2

Fairbanks

North Pole

Eagle

Unalakleet

Nenana

Delta
Junction

5

Dawson City,
Yukon

McGrath

Denali
National Park

Mt. McKinley

Alaska Range

9

Tok

6

muskokwim River

8

4

1

4

3

Talkeetna

Willow

1

Glennallen

Wasilla

Palmer

Wrangell Mts.

2

Whitehorse,
Yukon

4

ANCHORAGE

Valdez

10

McCarthy

1

Wrangell-St. Elias
National Park and Preserve

ke Clark National
ark and Preserve

Kenai

Soldotna

Cordova

7

Skagway

1

BRITISH
COLUMBIA

4

Homer

Whittier

Seward

ngham

Prince
William
Sound

Yakutat

Cook Inlet

Halibut Cove

King
Salmon

Seldovia

Kenai Fjords
National Park

Glacier Bay National
Park and Preserve

Haines

Juneau

Katmai National
Park and Preserve

Alaska
Marine
Highway

Gulf of Alaska

Gustavus

Admiralty Island
National Monument

Chichagof Island

Kodiak

Admiralty Island

Petersburg

Baranof Island

Sitka

Wrangell

Kodiak Island

Prince of Wales Island

kchak National
ument and Preserve

Craig
Ketchikan

Misty Fjords
National Monument

Prince Rupert,
B.C.

O C E A N

To Seattle ↘

Legend

—— Paved Road
—①— State or Provincial Route
—— Dirt Road

0   100 Miles

0   100 Kilometers

15

abundant than Southeast or Southcentral. Consequently, the Athabascans, the Interior's first people, are less numerous and traditionally lacked the rich natural endowments of Southeast's Native peoples. Summers can be hot and winters very cold in the Interior, because of the distance from the ocean.

THE BUSH   Bush Alaska is linked by lifestyle rather than by geography. One good definition would be that the Bush is that part of the state that's closer to the wilderness than to civilization. It's also the only part of the state where Native people outnumber whites and other relative newcomers. In many Bush villages, readily accessible to the outside world only by small plane, people still live according to age-old subsistence hunting-and-gathering traditions. The Bush region includes the majority of Alaska outside the road network, ranging from the north end of the Canadian border all the way around the coast, out the Aleutians, and the Alaska Peninsula and Kodiak Island, south of Anchorage. But some towns in each of the other regions also could be called "Bush villages." The Bush contains many regions, including the Arctic, Northwest, and Southwest Alaska.

2 Visitor Information

The **Alaska Division of Tourism,** P.O. Box 110801, Juneau, AK 99811-0801 (☎ **907/465-2010;** www.commerce.state.ak.us/tourism/), provides an *Official State Guide and Vacation Planner* with information on traveling to all parts of Alaska, including advertising from many tourism-related businesses. The booklet is sent free to domestic addresses and costs $10 to be sent internationally, payable by Visa or MasterCard, check, or money order. The Web site is even more useful, with links to all the community sites around Alaska.

For outdoor recreation, the **Alaska Public Lands Information Centers** are centralized sources of information on all government lands, which include more than 85% of the state. The centers, in Anchorage, Fairbanks, Ketchikan, and Tok, are operated cooperatively by many land agencies. The Anchorage center is at 605 W. Fourth Ave., Suite 105, Anchorage, AK 99501 (☎ **907/271-2737;** fax 907/271-2744; www.nps.gov/aplic). See the Fairbanks and Tok listings in chapter 9 for the centers there. Information on the facility in Ketchikan, called the Southeast Alaska Visitor Center, is in chapter 5.

The Alaska Department of Transportation provides an updated recording with **weather and road information** for various regions of the state (☎ **800/478-7675**).

ON THE NET

The Internet has revolutionized travel planning. Even the tiniest bed-and-breakfasts and outdoor guides have Web sites now; some are even relying on it to the exclusion of printed information. I've listed Web sites for the great majority of businesses and attractions in the book, included an appendix of useful sites for planning your travel, and provided directions for finding public Internet access in as many towns as it currently exists—which is almost all. Many Alaska towns also have a main Internet provider or community Web site that links to many local sites: those are listed under "Visitor Information" in each section. One warning: Web sites disappear or change URLs rapidly, so despite my checking the links, you may find duds. I've excluded those that appeared useless or misleading. Be careful about undated sites, as some people put them up and forget about them, distributing long-outdated information.

Here are some of the best Web sites with statewide information. See **Frommer's Online Directory** at the back of the book for more.

GOVERNMENT SITES

- **State of Alaska** (www.state.ak.us). The state's home page is the easiest starting point for navigating to some extremely useful sites, including the exceptional Alaska Department of Fish and Game site, the Division of State Parks site (within the Department of Natural Resources), and the Alaska Marine Highway System (within the Department of Transportation).
- **Alaska Division of Tourism** (www.commerce.state.ak.us/tourism/). Links to many communities on the Web, lots of other information, and a place to ask general questions.
- **National Park Service** (www.nps.gov). I use this one a lot. Each park has its own site, with much helpful information.
- **Bureau of Land Management** (wwwndo.ak.blm.gov/). This Department of the Interior agency manages much of Alaska, and has an excellent Web site.
- **National Weather Service Alaska Region Headquarters** (www.alaska. net/~nwsar/). This page has links to every conceivable forecast, weather map, and historical climate summary.

COMMERCIAL TRAVEL PLANNING SITES

- **Alcanseek** (www.alcanseek.com). This is a sort of Yahoo! of the north, with links organized by topic channels and for convenient travel planning; the name Alcan is a nickname for the Alaska Highway, which runs from British Columbia through the Yukon to Alaska.
- **Alaska Internet Travel Guide** (www.AlaskaOne.com/travel). As with a traditional tourist guide, find information (and links) on advertisers all over the state.
- **The Great Alaskan Mall** (www.alaskan.com). This ISP maintains an index of thousands of links to Alaska businesses by category.
- **The Alaska Information Cache** (www.akcache.com/akhome.html). Lots of well-organized links for travel and the outdoors, especially for fishing.
- **Great Alaskan Tour Saver** (TourSaver.com). This link will take you to the home-page for a potentially money-saving Alaska travel coupon book, and access to Anchorage travel expert Scott McMurren.

OTHER SITES OF INTEREST

- **University of Alaska Geophysical Institute** (www.gi.alaska.edu). Check here for lots of cool earth science about Alaska, including aurora forecasts, volcanic eruptions, and earthquakes.
- **Alaska Webcams** (camera.touchngo.com). Just for fun, here's a live image of downtown Anchorage. Links to other Alaska Web cams are at camera.touchngo. com/otherakcams.htm.
- **Anchorage Daily News** (www.adn.com). Find out what's going on in the news before you come, and read travel and outdoor features.

E-Mail the Author

I welcome your comments. Drop an e-mail to my personal account (wohlforth@ compuserve.com) telling me about your best or worst experiences in Alaska, or any errors or outdated material you find in the book. I'll answer questions to the extent that I have time, but I'm not in the trip-planning business, so please contact the many professional sources listed elsewhere in the book for that kind of advice.

3 Money

HOW MUCH MONEY YOU'LL NEED   Alaska is an expensive place to get to, to get around in, and to stay in. In popular spots, a good, standard motel double room is rarely available for less than $100 in the high season, and is more often over $120. Airfare from Seattle to Anchorage fluctuates wildly with competition among the airlines, but a $350 round-trip, with advance purchase, is a fair deal. You can easily pay twice that to fly to an Alaska Bush community. Even the train is expensive, with a one-way fare from Anchorage to Fairbanks (a 350-mile trip) costing $154 on the least luxurious of three choices of cars.

A couple ordering a good salmon dinner, appetizers, and wine will likely pay $90 to $100 in a fine restaurant, including tip. One reason cruise ships have become such a popular way to visit Alaska is that, for the same quality level they offer, they're less expensive on a daily basis than independent travel, and offer the chance to see remote coastal areas that can be quite costly to get to for land-based visitors. (See chapter 4 for details on cruising.)

To travel at a standard American comfort level, a couple should allow $120 per person, per day, for room and board. The cost of an activity such as "flightseeing," wildlife cruises, or guided fishing typically is $75 to $250 per person. Also add ground transportation—you may need to rent a car, the best way to see much of the state. An economy car rents for around $55 a day (weekly rentals generally cost the same as renting for 5 individual days, and be sure to check for sales). You also will likely need train and ferry tickets.

Of course, you also can trim down your costs by cutting your demands. You'll learn more about the real Alaska staying in bed-and-breakfast accommodations than in a standard hotel room. Expect to pay $85 to $95 for a decent room with a shared bathroom, $90 to $110 for a private bathroom. The free breakfast cuts down on your food costs, too. And there are plenty of family restaurants where you can eat a modest dinner for two for $30, with a tip and a glass of beer. Traveling in that style will bring the cost of room and board down to about $70 per person, per day, for a couple.

Another way to save money is to travel in the shoulder season, before and after the peak summer season. Hotel and guided activity prices drop significantly, typically 25% or more. May and September are solidly in the shoulder season, and sometimes you get bargains as late as June 15 or as early as August 15. Traveling in the winter is a whole different experience, but certainly saves a lot of money—where hotels are open, rates are typically half of peak. For other considerations on off-season and shoulder-season travel, see "When to Go," later in this chapter.

You can save the most money by giving up a private room every night and cooking some of your own meals. Camping is a fun way to really see Alaska and costs only $10 to $12 a night in state and federal government campgrounds. Hostels are available in most towns, typically for around $12 a night. Thousands of young people come to Alaska each summer and spend almost nothing, replenishing their funds when necessary with stints working at a fish cannery or restaurant—low-wage, long-hour jobs are usually available in the summer (see "For Students" under "Tips for Travelers with Special Needs," later in this chapter). People who own recreational vehicles travel for a cost little greater than staying at home, except for the fuel to navigate the beast down the road. A family can have the experience of a lifetime by driving the Alaska Highway or taking the family car up the Inside Passage on a state ferry, and camping at night. Unfortunately, most people don't have the time for these options. It adds up to a week

Native Art—Finding the Real Thing

In a gift shop in Southeast Alaska, a woman who said she was an artist's assistant was sanding a Tlingit-style carving. When I asked who made the carving, the artist said, "It's my work." At the time, that seemed like an odd way of putting it. Only later did I learn from one of the artist's former assistants that his "work" involved ordering the carvings from Southeast Asia and shipping them to Alaska, where he hired locals to pretend to be working on them in the shop. A journalist friend of mine met a boy in the alley behind a gift store in Ketchikan removing "Made in Taiwan" stickers from merchandise with a razor blade. Several years ago, the Federal Trade Commission fined an art dealer for peddling fake Native art. He was able to go on selling carvings signed by a person with a made-up, Native-sounding name along with the name of an Alaskan village. The artist was Cambodian and had spent only a few months in the village.

You may not care if the gifts and souvenirs you buy in Alaska really come from Alaska. But if you do, especially if you plan to spend a lot of money on authentic Alaska Native art, you need to take some care.

The most serious kind of counterfeit is fake Alaska Native fine art. Pieces sell for $500 or more, and the scam both defrauds the buyer and takes food off the tables of Alaska's village artists, who can't compete in price with Indonesian carvers. In 1995, *Anchorage Daily News* reporter Bruce Melzer documented that copying original Native art is a widespread practice. He found villages in Bali where hundreds of workers were turning out Eskimo masks and moose, otter, and sheep carvings from fossilized walrus ivory, whalebone, and other Alaskan materials, using designs taken from books sent from Alaska. (I am indebted to Melzer for much of the information in this essay.)

Ask some questions before you buy. Any reputable art dealer will provide you with a biography of the artist who created an expensive work. Ask specifically if that artist actually carved the piece: Some Native artists have sold their names and designs to wholesalers who produce knockoffs. Price is another tip-off: An elaborate mask is more likely to cost $3,000 than $300. Another indicator is the choice of materials: Most soapstone carvings are not made in Alaska.

A state program validates Native art and crafts with a **silver hand** label, which assures you it is a 100% Alaska Native product. But the program isn't universally used, so the absence of the label doesn't mean the work definitely isn't authentic. Other labels aren't worth much—an item could say **Alaska Made** even if only insignificant assembly work happened here. Of course, in Bush Alaska, and in some urban shops, you can buy authentic work directly from craftspeople.

For gifts that don't claim to be made by Natives but do at least purport to originate in the state, a symbol of two bears that says **Made in Alaska** validates that the item was at least substantially made here. Non-Natives produce Alaskan crafts of ceramics, wood, or fabric, but not plastic—if it's plastic, it probably was not made in Alaska. Again, price is an indicator: As with anywhere else in the United States, the cheapest products come from Asia.

Mostly, finding something real is up to you. When Melzer interviewed dealers selling fake Alaska Native arts and crafts, they said they tell customers where the work comes from if asked. But most people don't ask.

to each end of your trip to drive to Alaska, and puts thousands of miles and heavy wear and tear on your vehicle. Depending on where you start from, I wouldn't attempt it with less than 4 to 6 weeks for the trip.

HOW TO CARRY YOUR MONEY   There are few special warnings to be given about money in Alaska other than the caution you'd use in any other part of the United States. Don't carry enough cash to tempt a criminal, or to ruin your trip if it's lost. Even the small Bush communities now have ATMs; the main exceptions these days are remote outdoor destinations. In the "Fast Facts" section for each town in this book I'll tell you if there's an ATM and where to find it; there's even a Web site where you can locate the nearest Plus Network ATM wherever you are in the world: www.visa.com/pd/atm/. Alaska ATMs generally are on the Cirrus, Plus, or MAC networks, and other major ATM networks. Alaska banks generally charge no or very low ATM use fees, but your own bank and the network may. In larger towns, you'll find that every business you'd expect to take credit, charge, or debit cards at home will accept them. Even bed-and-breakfasts and inexpensive restaurants usually take cards now. Few businesses of any kind will take an out-of-state personal check. Traveler's checks are good just about anywhere, but there's no reason to go through the hassle and expense anymore.

When I travel around Alaska, I carry at least $100 in cash, plus a couple of different kinds of credit/charge cards and an ATM card. I use a credit or charge card (preferably earning frequent-flier miles) whenever I can, and stop at an ATM whenever my emergency cash falls under $100. If I'm going to a small village for a while, I load up on cash first.

4 When to Go

CLIMATE & SEASONS

The weather in Alaska can be extreme and unpredictable. We're the first to get whatever Arctic Siberia or the void of the North Pacific have to throw at North America. The extremes of recorded temperatures are a high of 100°F and low of -80°F. Statistics give means and averages of the climate, but that doesn't mean your vacation couldn't be made perfect by weeks of unbroken sunny weather or marred by weeks of unbroken rain. All you can do is play the averages, hope for the best, and, if you do get bad weather, get out and have fun anyway—that's what Alaskans do. My own subjective summary of the visitor season in various Alaska places is found below in the chart "Alaska's Climate, by Months & Regions."

JUNE, JULY & AUGUST   Summer in Alaska is a miraculous time, when the sun refuses to set, the salmon run up river, and people are energized with limitless energy. The sun dips below the horizon in Anchorage for only about 4 hours on June 21, the longest day of the year, and the sky is light all night. The state fills with people coming to visit and to work in the seasonal fishing, timber, and construction industries. Weather gets warmer, although how warm depends on where you go (see the chart below). June is the driest of the 3 summer months, July the warmest, and August generally the rainiest month of the brief summer, but warmer than June. In most respects, June is the best summer month to make a visit, but it does have some drawbacks to consider: In the Arctic, snow doesn't all melt till mid-June; in Southcentral Alaska, trails at high elevation or in the shade may be too muddy or snowy; and not all activities or facilities at Denali National Park open until late June. It's also the worst time for mosquitoes.

Alaska's Climate, by Months & Regions

	Jan	Feb	Mar	Apr	May	June	July	Aug	Sept	Oct	Nov	Dec
Anchorage: Southcentral Alaska												
Average high/low**	21/8	26/12	33/18	43/29	54/39	62/47	65/52	63/50	55/42	41/29	27/15	23/10
Hours of light*	6:30	9:15	12:00	15:00	17:45	19:30	18:15	15:30	12:00	9:15	7:00	5:30
Sunny days†	12	10	13	12	11	10	9	9	9	10	10	10
Rainy or snowy days	8	8	8	6	7	8	11	13	14	12	10	11
Precipitation‡	0.8	0.8	0.7	0.7	0.7	1.1	1.7	2.4	2.7	2	1.1	1.1
Barrow: Arctic Alaska												
Average high/low**	-7/-19	-12/-24	-9/-21	5/-9	24/14	38/30	45/34	42/33	34/27	18/9	3/-7	-5/-17
Hours of light*	0:00	7:30	12:00	17:00	24:00	24:00	24:00	18:00	12:00	8:00	0:00	0:00
Sunny days†	7	18	21	18	8	9	11	5	4	6	8	4
Rainy or snowy days	4	4	4	4	4	5	9	11	11	11	6	5
Precipitation‡	0.2	0.2	0.2	0.2	0.2	0.3	1	1	0.6	0.5	0.3	0.2
Cold Bay: Aleutian Archipelago												
Average high/low**	33/24	32/23	35/25	38/29	44/35	50/41	55/46	56/47	52/43	44/35	39/30	35/27
Hours of light*	8:00	10:00	12:00	14:30	16:30	17:30	16:30	14:30	12:00	10:00	8:00	7:00
Sunny days†	8	6	8	4	3	3	3	2	4	6	6	7
Rainy or snowy days	19	17	18	16	17	16	17	20	21	23	22	21
Precipitation‡	2.8	2.3	2.2	2	2.3	2.1	2.5	3.2	4.4	4.3	4.2	3.7
Fairbanks: Interior Alaska												
Average high/low**	-2/-18	7/-14	24/-2	41/20	59/38	70/50	72/53	66/47	55/36	32/18	11/-6	2/-15
Hours of light*	5:15	9:00	12:00	15:45	19:00	22:00	20:00	16:00	12:00	9:00	5:30	3:45
Sunny days†	15	14	17	14	16	13	12	10	10	9	12	12
Rainy or snowy days	8	7	6	5	7	11	12	12	10	11	11	9
Precipitation‡	0.5	0.4	0.4	0.3	0.6	1.4	1.9	2	0.9	0.9	0.8	0.8
Juneau: Southeast Alaska												
Average high/low**	29/19	34/23	39/27	47/32	55/39	61/45	64/48	63/47	56/43	47/37	37/27	32/23
Hours of light*	7:30	9:30	12:00	14:45	17:00	18:15	17:30	15:00	12:00	10:00	7:30	6:30
Sunny days†	8	7	7	8	8	8	8	9	6	4	6	5
Rainy or snowy days	18	17	18	17	17	15	17	17	20	24	20	21
Precipitation‡	4.5	3.7	3.3	2.8	3.4	3.1	4.2	5.3	6.7	7.8	4.9	4.4
Valdez: Prince William Sound												
Average high/low**	26/15	30/18	36/22	44/30	52/38	59/44	62/48	61/46	54/40	43/33	32/22	28/18
Hours of light*	7:00	9:15	12:00	15:00	17:45	19:30	18:00	15:30	12:00	9:15	7:00	5:30
Sunny days†	9	9	11	11	9	8	8	10	8	8	10	7
Rainy or snowy days	17	14	16	14	17	15	17	17	20	20	16	18
Precipitation‡	5.6	5.1	4.7	3.2	3.8	3.1	3.8	6	8.4	8	5.5	6.8

*Hours of light is an approximation of the possible daylight on the 20th day of each month.
**All temperatures are given in degrees Fahrenheit.
†Sunny days includes the average observed clear and partly cloudy days per month.
‡Precipitation is the average water equivalent of rain or snow.

Summer also is the season of high prices. Most operators in the visitor industry have only these 90 days to make their year's income, and they charge whatever the market will bear. July is the absolute peak of the tourist season, when you must book well ahead and crowds are most prevalent. (Of course, crowding is relative. With a population density of roughly one person per square mile, Alaska is never really crowded.) Before June 15 and after August 15, the season begins to decline, providing occasional bargains and more elbow room. But the length and intensity of the visitor season vary widely in different areas, and in some places it stays quite busy from Memorial Day to Labor Day.

MAY & SEPTEMBER   More and more visitors are coming to Alaska during these shoulder months to take advantage of the lower prices, absence of crowds, and special beauty.

May is the drier of the 2 months and can be as warm as summer, if you're lucky, but as you go farther north and earlier in the month, your chances increase of finding cold, mud, and even snow. In Alaska, we don't have spring—the melt of snow and resultant seas of mud are called **break up.** Flowers show up with the start of summer. Many outdoor activities aren't possible during break up, which can extend well into May. Before May 15, most tourist-oriented activities and facilities are still closed, and a few don't open until Memorial Day or June 1. Where visitor facilities are open, they often have significantly lower prices. Also, the first visitors of the year always receive an especially warm welcome. The very earliest salmon runs start in May, but for a fishing-oriented trip it's better to come later.

Sometime from late August to mid-September, weather patterns change, bringing clouds, frequent rainstorms, and cooling weather, and signaling the trees and tundra to turn bright, vivid colors. For a week or two (what week it is depends on your latitude), the bright-yellow birches of the boreal forest and rich red of the heathery tundra make September the most lovely time of year. But the rain and the nip in the air, similar to late October or November in New England, mean you'll likely have to bundle up; and September is generally the wettest month of the year. Most tourist-oriented businesses stay open, with lower prices, till September 15, except in the Arctic. After September 15, it's potluck. Some areas close up tight, but the silver salmon fishing hits prime time on the Kenai Peninsula, and the season stays active until the end of the month. A lucky visitor can come in September and hit a month of crisp, sunny, perfect weather, and have the state relatively to him- or herself. Or, it can be cold and rainy all month.

WINTER   One of the most spectacular trips I ever took was a train ride from Fairbanks to Anchorage in January. Outside the windows, Mount McKinley stood clear and so vivid in a vast, smooth landscape of pale blue and rich orange that I felt as if I could reach out and touch it. A young woman from South Africa was on the train. When I asked her why she came to Alaska in January, she only had to point out the window.

She was right, but visitors and the people who serve them generally haven't figured that out yet. Some towns—such as Skagway and Dawson City—close down almost completely. In others—most places on the ocean, for example—nearly all activities and attractions are closed for the season, but services remain open for business travelers. Where facilities are open, hotel prices are often less than half of what you'd pay in the high season. Quite luxurious rooms sometimes go for the cost of a budget motel. Visitors who seek out places of interest can have an exceptional and memorable time, enjoying some of the best alpine, Nordic, and backcountry skiing, outdoor ice-skating, dog mushing, and aurora and wildlife watching available anywhere, at any time. The best time to come is late winter, from mid-February through March, when the sun is up longer and winter carnivals and competitive dog mushing hit their peak.

WHAT TO WEAR

SUMMER   You're not going to the North Pole, and you don't need a down parka or winter boots weighing down your luggage. But you do need to be ready for a variety of weather, from sunny, 80° days to windy, rainy, 50° outings on the water. The way Alaskans prepare for such a range is with **layers.** The content of the layers depends on what you'll be doing, but everyone should bring at least this: warm-weather clothes, long-sleeved shirts and pants, a wool sweater, a warm jacket, and a raincoat. Gloves and wool hats are a good idea, too. Combining these items, you'll be ready for any summer conditions. If you will do any hiking, bring sturdy shoes or cross trainers.

WINTER   Normal alpine and Nordic skiing garb is adequate for skiing in South-central Alaska. Cross-country skiing in the Interior may require you to dress more warmly than you're accustomed to. Snowmobiling or dog mushing in winter requires the warmest possible clothing—you'll need the stoutest Sorel or Air Force bunny boots, insulated snow pants, thermal underwear, a heavy down parka with a hood, thick mittens (not gloves), and a wool hat or face-covering mask. Expect to spend $500 on a full outfit adequate for backcountry winter travel. You can buy what you need in Anchorage or Fairbanks when you arrive.

If you're not planning anything so rugged, you can get by in a city with a normal greatcoat, hat, gloves, and wool socks; if you're like most Alaskans, you'll just make a quick dash from car to heated building when really cold weather hits.

Alaska Calendar of Events

Here are some of the biggest community events of the year in Alaska's cities and towns. You'll also find fishing derbies going on all summer almost anywhere you go in Alaska. The dates, in many cases, are estimates: Don't plan a vacation around them; instead, call the organizers or visitor information centers listed in each of the towns for up-to-date details.

January

- **Russian Orthodox Christmas,** Kodiak and Sitka. Celebrated with solemn services and the starring ceremony, in which a star is carried through the streets from house to house, with song and prayer at each door. It falls about 2 weeks after Roman Catholic and Protestant Christmas. In Kodiak, call Father John Zabinko, ☎ **907/486-3854;** in Sitka, St. Michael's Cathedral, ☎ **907/747-8120.**

February

- **The Cordova Ice Worm Festival,** a winter carnival in Cordova on Prince William Sound; the big ice worm—or, to be precise, ice centipede—marches in a parade. Call ☎ **907/424-6665** for information. First full weekend of the month.
- **The Yukon Quest International Sled Dog Race** starts or finishes in Fairbanks. (Fairbanks has the start in even-numbered years; Whitehorse, Yukon Territory, in odd years.) The challenge of the 1,000-mile race is equal to the Iditarod. Call ☎ **907/452-7954** for information. Midmonth.
- ✪ **The Anchorage Fur Rendezvous,** a huge, citywide winter carnival, over 10 days. The main event is the **World Championship Sled Dog Race,** a 3-day sprint event of about 25 miles per heat. Call ☎ **907/277-8615** for information. Second and third weekends of the month.

March

- **The Nenana Ice Classic** starts with a weekend celebration early in the month. The Classic is a sweepstakes on who can guess closest to the exact date and time ice will go out on the Tanana River. You can buy tickets all over Alaska. Call ☎ **907/832-5446** for information.
- ✪ **The Iditarod Trail Sled Dog Race.** The famous race starts the first Saturday in March with much fanfare from **Anchorage,** then the teams are loaded in trucks for the **Iditarod Restart,** in **Wasilla,** which is the real beginning of the race. Here the historic gold rush trail becomes continuous for the dogs' 1,000-mile run to Nome. The event enlivens Wasilla at the end of a long winter. The finish in Nome is the biggest event of the year in the Arctic, drawing world media attention and turning Nome into a huge party for a few days. The race solicits volunteers to help, which is a much better way to experience it than just watching. Call ☎ **907/376-5155** for information.
- **The Bering Sea Ice Golf Classic,** during the Iditarod festivities, showcases Nome's well-developed sense of humor—six holes are set up on the sea ice. Call ☎ **907/443-5162** for information. Various similar silly events take place all year—you can get a list from the visitors center (☎ **907/443-5535**). Midmonth.
- ✪ **World Ice Art Championships,** in Fairbanks, brings carvers from all over the world to create spectacular sculptures out of immense chunks cut from Fairbanks lakes. Call ☎ **907/452-8250** for information. Mid-March.
- **World Extreme Skiing Championships** (☎ **907/835-2108;** www.wesc.com) is held on the faces of mountains north of Valdez, where invited professional skiers from North America and Europe hurl themselves down near-vertical, powder-filled chutes competing in speed and style. It's a daredevil competition, with one death and many injuries in its history. Late March or early April.

April

- **The Alaska Folk Festival,** Juneau. A community-wide celebration drawing musicians, whether on the bill or not, from all over the state. Call ☎ **907/ 364-2658** for information. April 10 to April 16, 2000.
- **The Garnet Festival,** the third week of April, marks the arrival of the sea lions, hooligans, shorebirds, and bald eagles on the Stikine River Delta, a spring tornado of wildlife in the region's largest coastal marshes. Community activities take place in town while jet boat tours traverse the delta. Call ☎ **800/367-9745** or 907/874-3901 for information.

May

- **Copper River Delta Shorebird Festival** (☎ **907/424-7260;** www.ptialaska. net/~midtown) revolves around the coming of dizzying swarms of shorebirds—estimates range from 5 to 22 million—that use the delta and beaches near the town as a migratory stopover in early May. The whole community gets involved to host bird-watchers and put on a full schedule of educational and outdoor activities.
- **Kachemak Bay Shorebird Festival** (☎ **907/235-7740;** www.xyz.net/~homer) includes guided bird-watching hikes and boat excursions, natural history workshops, art shows, and performances, activities, and other events in Homer, marking the return of the annual migration in early May.
- **The Kachemak Bay Wooden Boat Festival** (☎ **907/235-2141**), coinciding with Homer's shorebird festival, the Kachemak Bay Wooden Boat Society displays handmade boats from around the region and presents workshops and films.

- **Little Norway Festival,** Petersburg (☎ **907/772-4636;** www.petersburg.org), celebrating the May 17, 1814, declaration of independence of Norway from Sweden. The town goes wild, and 4 days of community events are planned the third full weekend of the month.
- ✪ **The Crab Festival,** Kodiak. Lasting 5 days, the festival includes a carnival, fleet parade, and various competitions, as well as a solemn service for lost fishermen, which occurs at the fishermen's memorial by the boat harbor. Call ☎ **907/486-5557** for information. Memorial Day weekend.
- **The Polar Bear Swim,** Nome, occurs in the Bering Sea on Memorial Day, ice permitting. Call ☎ **907/443-5535** for information.

June

- ✪ **The Sitka Summer Music Festival,** a chamber music series that began in 1972, is one of Alaska's most important cultural events, drawing musicians from all over the world. Call ☎ **907/747-6774** for information. All month.
- **Midnight Sun Baseball Game,** Fairbanks. A summer-solstice event—the local semipro baseball team, the Fairbanks Goldpanners, plays a game under the midnight sun, beginning at 10:30pm. Call ☎ **907/451-0095** for information. June 20 and 21.
- **Midnight Sun Festival,** Nome. Celebrates the summer solstice, when Nome gets more than 22 hours of direct sunlight, with a parade, softball tournament, bank holdup, raft race, and similar events. Call ☎ **907/443-5535** for information. June 21.
- ✪ **Prince William Sound Community College Theater Conference,** Valdez. Brings famous playwrights and directors to the community for seminars and performances. Call ☎ **907/835-2678** for information.

July

- **The Yukon Gold Panning Championships and Canada Day Celebrations,** Dawson City. The Canadian equivalent of the Fourth of July. Call ☎ **867/993-7228** for information. July 1.
- ✪ **Independence Day.** Most of the small towns in Alaska make a big deal of the Fourth of July. Seward always has a huge celebration, exploding with visitors, primarily from Anchorage. Besides the parade and many small town festivities, the main attraction is the **Mount Marathon Race,** from the middle of town straight up rocky Mount Marathon to its 3,022-foot peak and down again. **Seldovia, Kenai, Ketchikan,** and **Juneau** also have exceptional Fourth of July events. See the individual town write-ups for more information.
- **The Fairbanks Summer Arts Festival.** Artists of international reputation appear and offer workshops in music, dance, theater, opera, and the visual arts. Call ☎ **907/474-8869** for information. Late July and early August.
- **Concert on the Lawn,** Homer. Put on by KBBI radio (☎ **907/235-7721**), this is a daylong outdoor music, craft, and food festival that brings together the whole town for a day in late July.

August

- ✪ **Southeast Alaska State Fair** and **Bald Eagle Music Festival,** Haines. The area's biggest summer event, it's a regional small-town get-together, with livestock, cooking, a logging show, a parade, music, and other entertainment. Buildings constructed for the filming of the movie *White Fang* were donated to the fair, and now form the nucleus of a retail area there. Call ☎ **907/766-2476** for information. Early August.

✪ **Alaska State Fair,** Palmer. The biggest event of the year for the Matanuska Valley, and one of the biggest for Anchorage. It's a typical state fair, except for the huge vegetables. The good soil and long days in the Valley grow cabbages the size of a beanbag chair. A mere beach-ball-sized cabbage wouldn't even make it into competition. Call ☎ **907/745-2880** for information. The 11 days before Labor Day.

October

- **Alaska Day Festival,** Sitka. Alaska Day, commemorating the Alaska purchase on October 18, 1867, is a big deal in this former Russian and U.S. territorial capital city. Call ☎ **907/747-5940** for information. October 14 to October 18, 2000.

November

- **Athabascan Fiddling Festival,** Fairbanks. Draws together musicians and dancers from the Interior region for performances and workshops. Call ☎ **907/ 452-1825** for information. Early in the month.

- **Sitka WhaleFest.** Over a weekend during the fall and early winter period when humpback whales congregate in Sitka Sound and can be viewed from shore, the town offers workshops, whale-watching tours, and other community events. Held early in the month. Call ☎ **907/747-5940** for info.

- **Alaska Bald Eagle Festival,** Haines. Seminars and special events to mark the annual eagle congregation in early November. (☎ **800/246-6268;** Web site www.haines.ak.us/eaglefest/.)

- **Great Alaska Shootout Men's Basketball Tournament,** Anchorage. The University of Alaska Seawolves host a roster of the nation's top-ranked NCAA Division I teams at the Sullivan Arena. See chapter 7 for more information. Thanksgiving weekend.

- **Christmas Tree Lighting,** Anchorage. Takes place in town square, with Santa arriving behind a team of real reindeer. It's usually followed by a performance of *The Nutcracker* in the Alaska Center for the Performing Arts. Call ☎ **907/ 276-5015** for information. The Saturday after Thanksgiving.

5 Package Tour or Do-It-Yourself?

Hundreds of thousands of visitors come to Alaska each year on package tours, leaving virtually all their travel arrangements in the hands of a single company that takes responsibility for ushering them through the state for a single, lump-sum fee. But more and more visitors are cutting the apron strings and exploring Alaska on their own, and finding a more relaxed, spontaneous experience. There are advantages and disadvantages to each approach, and which way you choose to visit depends on how you value those pros and cons. Unfortunately, some people make the choice based on expectations that aren't valid, so it's important to know what you're getting into.

A package provides security. You'll know in advance how much everything will cost, you don't have to worry about making hotel and ground transportation reservations, you're guaranteed to see the highlights of each town you visit, and you'll have someone telling you what you're looking at. If there are weather delays or other travel problems, it's the tour company's problem, not yours. Everything happens on schedule, and you never have to touch your baggage other than to unpack when it magically shows up in your room. If you sometimes feel like you're a member of a herd on a package tour, you'll also meet new people, a big advantage if you're traveling on your own. Most passengers on these trips are retired, over age 65.

If you're short on time, packages make the most of it, often traveling at an exhausting pace. Passengers get up early and cover a lot of ground, with sights and activities scheduled solidly through the day. Stops last only long enough to get a taste of what the sight is about, not to dig in and learn about a place you're especially interested in. On a package, you'll meet few if any Alaska residents, since most tour companies hire college students from Outside to fill summer jobs. For visiting wilderness, such as Denali National Park, the quick and superficial approach can, in my opinion, spoil the whole point of going to a destination that's about an experience, not just seeing a particular object or place.

Studies by Alaska tourism experts have found that many people choose packages to avoid risks that don't really exist. Alaska may still be untamed, but that doesn't mean it's a dangerous or uncomfortable place to travel. Visitors who sign up for a tour to avoid having to spend the night in an igloo or use an outhouse may wish they'd been a bit more adventurous when they arrive and find that Alaska has the same facilities found in any other state. Except for tiny Bush villages that you're unlikely to visit anyway, you can find the standard American hotel room anywhere you go. The tourism infrastructure is well developed even in small towns—you're never far from help unless you want to be.

It's also possible for an independent traveler to obtain some of the predictability a package tour provides. You can reserve accommodations and activities and control your expenses by using a good travel agent experienced in Alaska travel. Some even offer fixed-price itineraries you do on your own (see " Independent Travel Planning" at the end of this section). But independent travelers never have the complete security of those on package tours. Once you're on the road, you'll be on your own to take care of the details, and weather delays and other cancellations confound the best-laid plans. If you can't relax and enjoy a trip knowing unforeseen difficulties could happen, then a package tour is the way to go.

LARGE TOUR COMPANIES

Three major tour and cruise-ship companies dominate the Alaska package-tour market with "vertically integrated" operations that allow them to take care of everything you do while in Alaska with tight quality control. Each also offers tours as short as a couple of hours to independent travelers who want to combine their own exploring with a more structured experience. All can be booked through any travel agent.

Holland America Westours/Gray Line of Alaska. 300 Elliot Ave. West, Seattle, WA 98119. ☎ **800/544-2206.**

The Holland America cruise line became the giant of Alaska tourism by buying local tour companies such as Gray Line and Westours to carry visitors in buses, trains, and boats, and the Westmark hotel chain to put them up for the night. Most clients arrive in the state on one of the company's ships (see chapter 4), but even within Alaska, chances are any tour you sign up for other than Princess or Alaska Sightseeing (see below) will put you on a Gray Line coach and exclusively in Westmark hotels. Descriptions of Westmark hotels are in each of the towns where they're found. The quality is not consistent—the Westmark Cape Fox in Ketchikan is among the best hotels in the state while the hotel in Skagway is below usually accepted standards. Most are adequate properties with standard American rooms. On a package, you don't spend much time in the room, as schedules generally are tightly planned and daily departures early. You'll find a description of the company's rail cars on the Anchorage-Denali-Fairbanks run in chapter 8. Gray Line coaches are first rate, especially several superluxurious, extralong vehicles that bend in the middle and have a lounge in the back. And the company goes more places than any other, and its catalog covers just about anything in the state that could possibly be done with a group. Some of its boat and tour excursions—on the Yukon River between Dawson City and Eagle, for example—are entirely unique. Prices depend on a variety of factors, but in general a tour of a week is about $1,500 per person.

Princess Cruises and Tours. 2815 Second Ave., Suite 400, Seattle, WA 98121-1299. ☎ **800/835-8907;** www.princesstours.com.

The Princess cruise line has built its land-tour operation from the ground up instead of buying it (as Holland America did), and the result is a smaller but consistently top-quality collection of properties. The four Princess hotels—two near Denali National Park, and one each in Fairbanks and Cooper Landing, on the Kenai Peninsula—all are exceptionally good. Princess operates its own coaches and has the best rail cars on the Alaska Railroad route to Denali. Descriptions of each hostelry can be found in the appropriate chapter. Most people on the tours come to Alaska on a cruise ship, but tours are for sale separately, too. The company's network of tours is less extensive than Holland America's but visit the places most people want to go.

Alaska Sightseeing/Cruise West. Fourth and Battery Bldg., Suite 700, Seattle, WA 98121. ☎ **800/888-9378.** Website www.cruisewest.com.

This relatively small company, started by Alaska-based tourism pioneers, offers a more intimate experience compared to the Princess and Holland America giants. Its ships, which carry around 100 passengers each compared to Holland America's and Princess's 1,500-plus, can navigate into more interesting places, and the company has taken the trouble to contract with some of the most knowledgeable small-town companies for tours rather than trying to do everything with their own hired college students. The land tours are marketed primarily as add-ons to small-vessel cruises, but are available separately, and cover most of the state. The company doesn't own its own hotels and uses the Alaska Railroad's cars on the train ride to Denali National Park.

INDEPENDENT TRAVEL PLANNING

Using this guide, you can book everything yourself, but for a long trip it can get quite complicated to keep track of all your dates and deposits. If you use a travel agency from home, bring them as detailed a plan as possible, derived from your own research, and just have them do the bookings. Most local travel agents are aware of only the biggest attractions and best marketed companies. Another option is to use a travel agency or trip planner based in Alaska. They'll know much more about the place and can help you more in picking out what you want to do. I've listed a few below.

Unfortunately, there are cautions to be offered in using the agencies. They work on commission, which means they're being paid by the establishments you're buying from. Of course, a good agent will disregard the size of the commission and really look out for you, but I've encountered too many visitors on a certain kind of itinerary—itineraries that take visitors to far-flung corners of the state in quick succession, staying only briefly in expensive places and then zooming off somewhere else, all with little relevance to the visitors' true interests—not to advise caution. Your best defense is to do enough research so you can actively participate in the planning.

Here I've gathered the names of some agencies that, by all reports, maintain good reputations here in Alaska.

Alaska Bound. 321 East Lake St., Petoskey, MI 49770. ☎ **888/ALASKA-7** or 616/ 439-3000. Fax 616/439-3004. www.alaskabound.com.

This Michigan-based agency started as a cruise planner, working primarily with Holland America, but now plans many independent trips, too, charging $150 per person per week. Although they don't take credit cards, they will use yours to book your stays, so you get the security and frequent flier mileage.

All Ways Travel. 302 G St., Anchorage, AK 99501. ☎ **800/676-2946** or 907/276-3644. Fax 907/258-2211. E-mail: allways@alaska.net.

This is a solid old travel agency in downtown Anchorage, with many years of experience in arranging Alaska trips. Owner Anna Mae Rocker is a respected community volunteer.

Sport Fishing Alaska. 1401 Shore Dr., Anchorage, AK 99515. ☎ **907/344-8674.** Fax 907/349-4330. E-mail: sfa@alaska.net.

Choose this company for a fishing vacation. The owner, a retired fisheries biologist, knows where the fish will be week-to-week. They charge a $95 up-front fee. (See "Fishing," below.)

Viking Travel. P.O. Box 787, Petersburg, AK 99833 ☎ **800/327-2571** or 907/772-3818. Fax 907/772-3940. alaska-ala-carte.com.

An entrepreneur in the small Southeast Alaska town of Petersburg built this travel agency, initially specializing in independent trips emphasizing the outdoors but now a leading trip planner for the whole state.

6 Sample Itineraries

Many visitors to Alaska feel compelled to cover the whole state, traveling to each region, and planning everything around seeing certain famous wilderness parks. By doing so, they spend a lot more time and money than is necessary. Each of Alaska's regions, by itself, has most of what you're coming to Alaska for—wildlife, mountains, glaciers, historic sites, cute little towns—and you can have a better trip touring one or two regions than spending precious time going from region to region.

The other mistake some people make is traveling only to the largest and most famous destinations. I think half the joy of traveling independently is discovering places off the beaten track where most tourists don't go. If you follow a set itinerary of places you're "supposed" to go see, you don't get that pleasure.

I've set up a series of itineraries in 1-week loops or tours. For 2- or 3-week itineraries, link these together, spend more time in each place, or add trips to the many places I haven't mentioned, which include some of my favorites. If you're driving to Alaska, add a week to each end of your trip.

Northern Southeast Alaska

Day 1: Fly to Juneau. **Day 2:** Take a look at the State Museum and other sights in town and Mendenhall Glacier, or take a 1-day hike or sea-kayaking excursion. **Day 3:** Take the *Auk Nu* passenger ferry to Gustavus, with a whale-watching excursion on the way. Spend the night at one of the charming inns there. **Day 4:** See Glacier Bay National Park on a boat tour. Spend another night in Gustavus. **Day 5:** Fly on a small plane to Haines, spending the day there seeing the eagles and attending the Native dancing and totem carving studio. **Day 6:** Take the passenger ferry to Skagway to see the historic sites and take the train excursion. **Day 7:** Take the Alaska ferry back to Juneau and fly home.

Southern Southeast Alaska

Day 1: Arrive in Ketchikan by ferry from Prince Rupert. **Day 2:** Tour the cultural sites in Ketchikan or take a hike in the rain forest. **Day 3:** Take a boat tour and flight day trip from Ketchikan to Misty Fjords National Monument, or take a charter fishing or sea kayaking excursion. **Day 4:** Take the ferry to Sitka. **Day 5:** See the historic sites and museums in Sitka. **Day 6:** Get outdoors in Sitka, hiking, fishing, sea kayaking, or on a whale and sea otter cruise. **Day 7:** Take the ferry or fly to Juneau, then fly out.

Kenai Fjords & Denali National Parks

Day 1: Fly to Anchorage. **Day 2:** Spend a day taking in the city, with a visit to the museum, zoo, or Native cultural center; or, outdoors, ride a bike on the coastal trail or hike in Chugach State Park. **Day 3:** Next day, take the train to Seward and take a boat ride into Kenai Fjords National Park. Spend the night in Seward. **Day 4:** Enjoy Seward and Exit Glacier, perhaps taking a hike or a sea kayak paddle, returning to Anchorage on the evening train. **Day 5:** Rent a car and drive to Denali National Park, taking an afternoon hike or raft ride in the entrance area. **Day 6:** Take a shuttle bus into the park for wildlife viewing and day hiking. **Day 7:** Drive back to Anchorage and fly out.

Prince William Sound Loop

Day 1: Fly to Anchorage. **Day 2:** Rent a car and drive all day to Wrangell–St. Elias National Park (make sure you're covered for driving on a gravel road). Stay at a lodge in McCarthy or Kennicott. **Day 3:** See Kennicott and take a hike near the glacier. **Day 4:** Drive to Valdez and see the sights in town. **Day 5:** Take the car ferry to Cordova. **Day 6:** Drive to the Childs Glacier; hike, canoe, and bird-watch on the Copper River Delta; or go sea kayaking. **Day 7:** Take the ferry to Whittier, drive back to Anchorage, and fly home.

Fairbanks Interior Loop

Day 1: Fly to Fairbanks and rent a car. **Day 2:** Spend a day in Fairbanks exploring the city and its attractions. **Day 3:** Drive to Denali National Park, taking an afternoon hike or raft ride in the entrance area. **Day 4:** Take a shuttle bus into the park for wildlife viewing and day hiking. **Day 5:** Drive via the Denali Highway and Richardson Highway back to Fairbanks, then drive out Chena Hot Springs Road to the resort, or to camp in the Chena Hot Springs State Recreation Area. **Day 6:** Swim at the Hot Springs and hike in the recreation area. **Day 7:** Return to Fairbanks and fly out.

Juneau to Fairbanks Via Klondike Loop

Day 1: Fly to Juneau and take a ferry to Skagway. **Day 2:** Spend the day seeing Skagway's historic sites and taking a rail or bike excursion. **Day 3:** Drive to Dawson City. **Day 4:** Spend the day seeing the historic sites in Dawson City. **Day 5:** Drive to Eagle and visit historic sites there. **Day 6:** Drive all day to Fairbanks. **Day 7:** Drop the car and fly home.

Wintertime Choices

Arrive in Anchorage in February, during the **Fur Rendezvous sled dog races,** or in March, to see the start of the **Iditarod.** If you're a Nordic skier, enjoy Kincaid Park. After checking on avalanche conditions, rent a car and make a day trip into **Chugach State Park** or to Turnagain Pass, south of Anchorage, or ski into one of many public cabins in Chugach National Forest. Alpine or Nordic skiers will want to spend at least a few days in Girdwood at the Alyeska Resort. Besides exceptional skiing, this is a good place for a **sled dog ride,** and there are others at each stop on the itinerary. After Girdwood, catch the train from Anchorage to Fairbanks, spending the night in Fairbanks and catching the sled dog races or ice-carving festivals in February or March. The following day, take the van out to the **Chena Hot Springs Resort,** for outdoor explorations, swimming, and aurora watching, returning and flying out of Fairbanks when your trip is over.

7 Planning an Outdoor Vacation

Alaska is full of museums, gold rush historical sites, and Native cultural events, but I bet that's not why you're coming—nor should it be. Alaska is unique for its scenery and wildlife, and for something about the outdoors that goes beyond either: the opportunity to be alone in truly natural places. It's ironic, then, that so many visitors spend their time in crowded ships, buses, trains, and airplanes, all of which are the antithesis of wilderness. You do need technology to get to the wilderness of Alaska, but unless you at least partly let loose of that umbilical cord, you'll never really arrive at your destination.

Every town in Alaska is a threshold to the wild. There's always a way to go hiking, biking, or sea kayaking, or to get on the bank of a stream or the deck of a boat to hook into a furiously fighting wild salmon. In the evening, you can be back in a comfortable hotel room. Or take a step further, and plan to go out overnight, perhaps with a friendly local guide at first, and then on your own. I've included lots of details on how to do this throughout the book. Too scary? If it weren't a little scary it would be Disneyland, and it's not. It's real, and that's why it's worth doing.

ACTIVITIES

BACKPACKING   Alaska's best backpacking country for trail hikes is in **Chugach State Park** near Anchorage (chapter 6), on Chena Hot Springs Road and on the Steese Highway near Fairbanks (chapter 9), and in the **Chugach National Forest** on the Kenai Peninsula (chapter 7). For hiking beyond trails, go to **Denali** and **Wrangell–St. Elias** national parks (chapters 8 and 9). Alaska trail hikes require the same skills as backpacking anywhere else, so long as you are prepared for cold and damp. Hiking beyond the trails is a glorious experience, but you need to know how to cross rivers and find your way—it's best if you have some outdoor experience first. For guided backpacking at Wrangell–St. Elias, see the listing in chapter 9 under "Getting Outside" in the "Wrangell–St. Elias National Park & the Copper River Balley" for St. Elias Alpine Guides. Other backpacking outfitters are listed below.

BIKING   Most every town in Alaska has a bike rental agency. You're on your own in most places, but there are excellent biking trails all over the state, and few restrictions on where you can ride. **Sockeye Cycles,** in Haines and Skagway (see chapter 5), leads mountain biking tours.

Alaska Bicycle Adventures, 907 Dowling Rd. no. 29, Anchorage, AK 99518 (☎ **800/770-7242** or 907/243-2329; fax 907/243-4985; www.alaskabike.com), leads bike tours over Alaska's rural highways. They provide everything, including the van that follows and ferries bicyclists over the dangerous or boring patches of road. Choose from many itineraries; one that's very appealing to me lasts a week, looping from Anchorage, over the Denali Highway, down the Richardson Highway, a little bit into Wrangell–St.Elias National Park, then to Valdez and across Prince William Sound (by boat) and back to Anchorage. It costs $2,345.

CAR CAMPING   Campgrounds are almost everywhere in Alaska, many in extraordinarily beautiful natural places. Public campgrounds far outnumber commercial ones. They're usually where they are because there's something special about the place: a great view or beach, an exceptional fishing stream or trailhead. Rarely will you find running water or flush toilets; most are seasonal, with hand pumps for water. I've mentioned some great campgrounds throughout the book. A map that lists all the public campgrounds is available from the Alaska Public Lands Information Centers (see "Visitor Information," above) for 25¢.

Traveling in a van with only 12 adults and camping at night, **Camp Alaska Tours,** P.O. Box 872247, Wasilla, AK 99687 (☎ **800/376-9438** or 907/376-9438; e-mail: campak@alaska.net), offers trips lasting 6 days to 2 weeks, with hiking, rafting, kayaking, and an opportunity to see the outdoors with a new group of outdoors-oriented friends. Prices are around $125 per day, and trips are available for families with children as young as age 10.

FISHING   Given the number of salmon in the state, fishing in Alaska is almost a must (see "Salmon Fishing Tips & Info," below). There's no room here to tell you *how* to fish in Alaska—the best way is to pick it up from other fishermen, most conveniently by going with a guide on your first outing. You can also study up by getting a detailed guidebook, *Alaska Fishing,* by Rene Limeres and Gunnar Pederson, published by Foghorn Press (☎ **800/364-4676;** www.foghorn.com). The *Anchorage Daily News* also has fish features on its Web site, at www.adn.com; one travel information Web site specializes in fish, **Alaska Information Cache,** at www.akcache.com/akhome.html. To find out when and where to go, the best resources are offered on the web, in printed guides, and on recorded messages by the **Alaska Department of Fish and Game Sport Fish Division** (☎ **800/874-8202** or 907/465-4180; www.state.ak.us/local.akpages/FISH.GAME/sportf/st_home.htm). The Web site is indispensable; if you don't want to type in that long URL, just go to www.state.ak.us and navigate from there. If you're not an avid fisher but just want to give it a try, you should be able to find salmon running somewhere along your way during a summer visit, and visitor centers can always direct you where to go locally.

If fishing is the primary goal of your trip, think about booking time at a fishing lodge. The remote rivers of the Bristol Bay region have Alaska's most prolific salmon fishing, and the only way out there is to take a floatplane to a remote site. You'll be all alone on streams jammed with salmon. But you'll waste your money if you book a date that's not near the peak of the local salmon run. For that reason, I haven't listed fishing lodges here (some are listed in the Prince of Wales Island section of chapter 5). Instead, I recommend booking through **Sport Fishing Alaska,** 1401 Shore Dr., Anchorage, AK 99515 (☎ **907/344-8674;** fax 907/349-4330; www.alaska.net/~sfa). The business is run by Russ Redick, a retired fisheries biologist who supervised sport fishing in the Southcentral region for 13 years. After receiving a $95 advance fee, Redick will plan a fishing vacation tailored to your budget that puts you right where fishing is hot at the time when you can travel.

LAKE CANOEING   Paddling a canoe on a remote Alaska lake may be the best way for novice outdoors people to get into the wilderness without a guide. In Southeast Alaska, Prince of Wales Island has some beautiful canoe routes with public-use cabins, and a canoe rental agency (chapter 5), and in the Southcentral region the Kenai National Wildlife Refuge and the Copper River Delta near Cordova both have placid waters for wilderness canoeing. For guided lake canoeing, see the section on the wildlife refuge (chapter 7).

RIVER FLOATING   Letting an Alaskan river pull you through untouched wild country in a raft, canoe or kayak provides a unique perspective without the sweat and toil of backpacking. Alaska has many great rivers. I've mentioned easy waters for self-guided floats in chapter 9, in and near Fairbanks, and between Dawson City and Eagle, and on the **Swanson River** in the Kenai National Wildlife Refuge, in chapter 7.

Salmon Fishing Tips & Info

In Alaska, it's not so much where you wet your line, but when. Our primary catch, Pacific salmon, lives in saltwater but spawns in freshwater, returning to certain streams during certain, narrow windows of time called *runs*. When the salmon are running, fishing is hot; when they're not running, it's dead. And the runs change day-to-day, typically lasting only a few weeks. (Halibut, on the other hand, are bottom-dwelling ocean fish; you can fish them from a boat every day when the tide is right.) There's salmon fishing all over the state, but the closer you are to the ocean, the better the fish are; salmon flesh softens in fresh water and their skin turns dull and red. Salmon right from salt water are called silver bright—when you see one, you'll understand why.

There are five species of Pacific salmon, each preferring its own habitat, and, even when the habitat overlaps, each timing its run differently. Each species has two names. **King** (or chinook) are the most coveted, best-fighting fish, as large as 50 pounds all over the state and up to 90 on the Kenai River. It takes a lot of effort to find and land a big king, but it's the ultimate in Alaska fishing. You also need a special king stamp from the Alaska Department of Fish and Game, in addition to your fishing license. King runs come mostly in June and July. The **silver** (or coho) is smaller than the king, typically topping out around 15 pounds, but fights and jumps ferociously. Silvers run mostly in the fall, beginning in August. **Red** (or sockeye) salmon, so named for their tasty red flesh, are the trickiest to catch. They feed on plankton at sea, and when they strike a fly, it's out of an instinct that no one really understands; you need perfect river conditions to get reds to strike. **Pinks** (or humpies) and **chum** (or dog) salmon grow to only a few pounds and aren't as tasty as the other three species. They are so plentiful that Alaska fishers usually view them as a nuisance to get off the line, but visitors often enjoy catching them: There's nothing wrong with a hard-fighting 4-pound fish. Alaska streams and lakes also have abundant steelhead, cutthroat, and rainbow trout and Dolly Varden char.

River day trips with guides go from around Anchorage, Denali National Park, Valdez, and Haines. Outfitters who lead trips deep in Alaska can help you access many more remote rivers for longer journeys (see the section on Wrangell–St. Elias National Park in chapter 9 and on Kotzebue in chapter 10). The **Tatshenshini** and **Alsek** rivers have been called the world's wildest, flowing from the Yukon Territory through vast mountains to Glacier Bay National Park. Among the companies offering floats are Alaska Discovery and Mountain Travel-Sobek, mentioned below. The rivers of the Arctic National Wildlife Refuge, flowing north to the Arctic Ocean, open vast stretches of open caribou habitat. Alaska Discovery and Equinox Wilderness Expeditions offer these trips, among others, also listed below.

SEA KAYAKING   Kayakers love the waters of Prince William Sound, of Homer's Kachemak Bay, of Kenai Fjords National Park (chapter 7), and Kodiak (chapter 10), and around all the little islands and deep fjords of Southeast Alaska (chapter 5). Just about every coastal town has a kayak outfitter taking visitors on day trips or expeditions. Among the best is Jim and Nancy Lethcoe's **Alaskan Wilderness Sailing & Kayaking Safaris,** listed in the Valdez section of chapter 7. Based on an island near Prince William Sound's Columbia Glacier, they lead kayak and sailing trips through waters about which they've written books. Other firms offer trips in many places around the state, including those listed below. You can set up voyages of a week or more, camping each night on the shoreline and hiking or paddling during the day.

OUTFITTERS & OUTDOOR PACKAGE TRIPS

Besides the outfitters listed below, I've noted other operators in the towns where they primarily operate. Browse through those destination chapters before deciding on a trip, because the local guides often know their own areas best, and the small towns are often the most interesting.

Alaska Discovery. 5449 Shaune Dr., Suite 4, Juneau, AK 99801. ☎ **800/586-1911** or 907/780-6226. Fax 907/780-4220. www.akdiscovery.com.

A homegrown ecotourism pioneer that's grown to national renown, Alaska Discovery still offers some of the best sea kayaking trips in Southeast Alaska, including Glacier Bay and Amiralty Island, catering both to beginners and the truly rugged. Their river trips float in the Arctic and on the Tatshenshini and Alsek rivers. They also offer outdoor packages for complete vacations. A 3-day kayak expedition near Juneau is $495, while 10 days in the Arctic is around $3,000.

Alaska Wildland Adventures. P.O. Box 389, Girdwood, AK 99586. ☎ **800/334-8730** or 907/783-2928. Fax 907/783-2130. www.alaskawildland.com.

This Alaska-based company specializes in trips for regular folks who may not have done a lot of arduous outdoor activities before. Concentrating in the area from Denali National Park to the Kenai Peninsula, where they operate three wilderness lodges, most of the company's trips link together a series of outdoor day activities, such as rafting, hiking, or wildlife watching, with beds and indoor plumbing in the evening. A 10-day safari is $3,700.

Alaska Worldwide Adventures. P.O. Box 220204, Anchorage, AK 99522. ☎ **888/842-6877** or 907/349-2964. Fax 907/344-6877. www.alaska.net/~akwildj.

Steven Weller's trips include backpacking in the Talkeetna Mountains and kayaking and hiking in the remote Wood-Tikchik State Park, as well as expeditions to the Russian Far East, Africa, and Australia. A 3-day trek is $795.

Equinox Wilderness Expeditions. 618 W. 14th Ave., Anchorage, AK 99501. ☎ **907/274-9087.** www.equinoxexpeditions.com.

Karen Jettmar, author of *The Alaska River Guide,* the most complete guidebook on floating Alaska's rivers, leads challenging rafting, sea kayaking, and hiking trips each summer in some of the wildest and most exotic places around the state. She specializes in trips for women and lesbians, but also has co-ed expeditions. A 10-day Arctic float trips costs around $2,600.

Mountain Travel–Sobek. 6420 Farimount Ave., El Cerrito, CA 94530. ☎ **888/687-6235.** Fax 510/525-7710. www.mtsobek.com.

Alaska is only part of a chapter in the mind-blowing international adventure catalog of this 30-year-old trip leader, but they've hit some of the highlights, including a 9-day sea kayak paddle in Prince William Sound and Tatshenshini and Alsek river floats. They charge around $3,000 for 10 days on the rivers. Going with such a large and established company may give an added sense of security, but these are still wild and rugged trips.

WILDERNESS LODGES

Wilderness lodges are sprinkled through the book. Some of the best are near in Gustavus (chapter 5), across Kachemak Bay from Homer (chapter 7), and in or near

Booking Your Trip Online

For more information about using the Internet to book your trip, see the **Frommer's Online Directory** at the back of this book.

Denali National Park or Talkeetna (chapter 8). I've excluded the majority of lodges, which cater mostly to fishers, for the reasons explained above under "Fishing."

8 Getting There & Getting Around

BY PLANE   Anchorage is the main entry hub for Alaska. It's served by several major carriers to the rest of the United States, primarily through Seattle, including **United Airlines** (☎ 800/241-6522; www.ual.com), **Northwest Airlines** (☎ 800/225-2525; www.nwa.com), **Delta Air Lines** (☎ 800/221-1212; www.delta-air.com), and **Alaska Airlines** (☎ 800/426-0333, TDD 800/682-2221; www.alaskaair.com). The route is competitive and prices are volatile, so use a travel agent or a Web site such as **Travelocity** (www.travelocity.com) or **Microsoft Expedia** (www.expedia.com) to get the best price. There usually is a charter or seat wholesaler in operation with below-market deals on economy seats. If you can make a last-minute purchase, sign up for Web specials on the Alaska Airlines site and other Web sites, as there usually are bargains to be had. Most airlines also continue to Fairbanks. **Alaska Airlines** is the only jet carrier to Southeast Alaska and most of Alaska's small towns. It also has arrangements with commuter lines that fan out from its network to smaller communities.

To fly to the smallest villages, or to fly between some small towns without returning to a hub, you take a **Bush plane.** The legendary Alaska Bush pilot is alive and well, connecting Alaska's villages by small plane and flying air-taxi routes to fishing sites, lodges, remote cabins, or just about anywhere else you might want to go. An authentic Alaskan adventure is to be had from many small towns by taking a **Bush mail plane** round-trip to a village and back. The ticket price is generally much less than a flight-seeing trip, and you'll have at least a brief chance to look around a Native village. Cordova, Kodiak, Nome, Kotzebue, Barrow, and Fairbanks are places from which you can do this.

BY SHIP   The most popular way to get to Alaska is on a **cruise ship.** Chapter 4, "Cruising Alaska's Coast," provides an in-depth look at coming to the state that way. The **Alaska Marine Highway System,** P.O. Box 25535, Juneau, AK 99802-5535 (☎ 800/642-0066; TDD 800/764-3779; fax 907/277-4829; www.dot.state.ak.us/external/amhs/home.html), is the lowest-cost way to get to Alaska. The big blue, white, and gold ferries ply the Inside Passage from Bellingham, Washington, and Prince Rupert, B.C., to the towns of Southeast Alaska, with road links to the rest of the state at Haines and Skagway. On long runs, the savings over flying aren't huge, but the ferry has an enormous advantage in flexibility and cost savings on shorter hops. For a complete discussion of using the ferries in Southeast, see chapter 5, "Southeast Alaska." One ferry a month connects Southeast Alaska across the Gulf of Alaska to the central part of the state. Smaller ferries also connect towns in Prince William Sound and the Ke36nai Peninsula, in Southcentral Alaska, to Kodiak Island and the Aleutian Archipelago. I've described that service in the sections on individual towns served.

BY RAIL   You can't get to Alaska by train, but you can get close. **Amtrak** (☎ 800/872-7245; www.amtrak.com) runs from Seattle to Vancouver, B.C., with stops in Bellingham, Washington, where you can catch the Alaska ferry north at a dock near the depot. From the east, it makes more sense to catch the ferry in Prince Rupert, B.C.

Travel Tip: Cheap One-Way Car Rentals

A little-known trick is that you can often get great rates on one-way rentals late in the season, when the car-rental companies ship most of their cars back to the Lower 48 and need to get them all back to the dock in Anchorage.

Get there from the east on Canada's **Via Rail** (☎ **800/561-3949;** www.viarail.ca/), from the south on **B.C. Rail** (☎ **800/663-8238;** www.bcrail.com/bcr/). Within Alaska, you can travel the **Alaska Railroad** (☎ **800/544-0552;** www.akrr.com) from Seward north through Anchorage, Denali National Park, and Fairbanks. Winter service is severely limited. For a full description of the Alaska Railroad's service, see chapters 6 and 7.

BY CAR OR RV Driving to Alaska is a great adventure, but it requires thousands of miles on the road, and you have to be ready to spend plenty of time. Anchorage is almost 2,500 miles from Seattle by car, 3,700 miles from Los Angeles, and 4,650 miles from New York City. Some of the 1,400-mile **Alaska Highway** is dull, but there are spectacular sections of the route, too, and few experiences give you a better feel for the size and personality of Alaska. Putting your car on the ferry cuts the length of the trip considerably but raises the cost; you could rent a car for 2 weeks for the same price as carrying an economy car on the ferry from Bellingham to Haines. I love riding the ferry up the Inside Passage, but I usually rent a car or bike to get around in the towns on the way. Details on the Alaska section of the Alaska Highway, and other highways, are contained in chapter 9. *The Milepost,* published by Morris Communications (☎ **800/726-4707** or 907/272-6070), contains mile-by-mile logs of all Alaska highways and approaches, but its commercial listings are sold as advertisements and thus are not objective. Inexpensive road maps also are widely available.

Renting a car in Alaska is the easiest way to see the Interior and Southcentral part of the state. All major car-rental companies are represented in Anchorage; to get the best deal, go through a travel agent or use a Web site such as **Travelocity** (www.travelocity.com) or **Microsoft Expedia** (www.expedia.com). In smaller cities and towns, you can usually rent from one of the majors or save by renting from a small, local company—individual town listings provide details on which firms are in each town. Base rates for major rental companies are in the range of $55 a day for an economy car. You can save by reserving far in advance, renting by the week, or using a down-market franchise or independent company that rents older cars. One-way rentals between Alaska towns are an attractive way to travel, but you generally pay steep drop-off charges, so a more popular plan is to fly into and out of Anchorage and use it as a base to pick up and return the car. There are two popular circular routes from Anchorage: to Fairbanks on the Parks Highway and back on the Richardson and Glenn Highways, or to Valdez by ferry from Whittier and back on another part of the Richardson Highway and the Glenn Highway.

Families will enjoy traveling by rented motor home RV. Rentals don't really save much money over traveling with a rental car and renting hotel rooms, as a week's rental in the high season starts around $1,400, plus gas, food, and incidentals. But if you don't mind driving that huge beast, it's a great way to see the country while saving you from reserving everything far in advance and schlepping in and out of hotels or setting up tents. A further advantage is that the RV insulates you better than a car from rainy weather—and is certainly better than a tent. I've listed two major rental agencies in the Anchorage section of chapter 6. There are big savings to be had in the spring and fall.

9 Tips for Travelers with Special Needs

FOR TRAVELERS WITH DISABILITIES   The Americans with Disabilities Act along with economic competition have sped the process of retrofitting hotels and even bed-and-breakfasts to be accessible for people with disabilities. They're often the best rooms in the house. Hotels without such facilities now are the exception; however, check when making reservations.

Nationally, **The Society for the Advancement of Travel for the Handicapped,** 347 Fifth Ave. Suite 610, New York, NY 10016 (☎ **212/447-7284;** fax 212/725-8253; www.sath.org), offers members access to a vast network of connections in the travel industry, information sheets on travel destinations, and referrals to tour operators that specialize in traveling with disabilities. Memberships cost $45 annually, $30 for seniors and students.

There are several Alaska agencies for people with disabilities. **Challenge Alaska,** P.O. Box 110065, Anchorage, AK 99511 (☎ **907/344-7399**), is a nonprofit organization dedicated to providing accessible outdoor activities. They have a skiing center on Mount Alyeska (☎ **907/783-2925**), in Girdwood, and also offer summer camping, sea kayaking, fishing, and other trips. **Alaska Welcomes You! Inc.,** 7321 Branche Dr., P.O. Box 91333, Anchorage, AK 99509-1333 (☎ or TTY **800/349-6301** or 907/349-6301; fax 907/344-3259; http://alaskan.com/vendors/welcome.html), offers a variety of accessible tours in Southcentral Alaska, extended travel packages to Denali National Park and the Kenai Peninsula, and trip planning for independent travelers with special needs. Trips include rafting, boating, flightseeing, fishing, and accessible self-driven tours. **Alaska Snail Trails,** P.O. Box 210894, Anchorage, AK 99521-0894 (☎ **800/348-4532,** phone or fax 907/337-7517), operates 5- and 10-day tours to Seward and Denali National Park for people with disabilities and anyone who is interested in a slower pace of guided travel. A 10-day trip covering these areas is $2,362 per person, double occupancy.

FOR SENIORS   People over age 65 get reduced admission prices to most Alaska attractions, and many accommodations have special senior rates. National parks offer free admission and special camping rates for people over 62 with a Golden Age Passport, which you can obtain at any of the parks for $10. Most towns have a senior citizens center where you'll find activities and help with any special needs. The **Anchorage Seniors Center** (☎ **907/258-7823**) offers guidance for visitors, as well as use of the restaurant, showers, gift shop, and fitness room; a big band plays Friday nights for dancing. **Elderhostel,** 75 Federal St., Boston, MA 02110-1941 (☎ **877/426-8056** or 617/426-8056; fax 617/426-8351; www.elderhostel.org), operates many weeklong Alaska learning vacations for groups of people 55 and older.

FOR GAY & LESBIAN TRAVELERS   Anchorage and Juneau have active gay and lesbian communities. In Anchorage, **Identity Inc.** (☎ **907/258-4777**) offers referrals, publishes a newsletter called *NorthView,* sponsors potluck dinners, and holds a gay pride picnic the last Sunday in June on the Delaney Park Strip. The **S.E. Alaska Gay/Lesbian Alliance** (☎ **907/586-4297**) is a similar organization in Juneau. **Apollo Travel Agency,** 1207 W. 47th Ave., Anchorage, AK 99503 (☎ **907/561-0661**), is a member of the International Gay Travel Agencies Association and can guide you to businesses, such as bed-and-breakfast accommodations and tours, that cater specifically to gays and lesbians. **Equinox Wilderness Expeditions,** listed above under "Outfitters & Outdoor Package Trips," is a small company offering co-ed trips, trips for groups of women or men only, and trips exclusively for lesbians.

Nationally, **The International Gay & Lesbian Travel Association** (☎ **800/448-8550** or 954/776-2626; fax 954/776-3303; www.iglta.org) links travelers up with the appropriate gay-friendly service organization or tour specialist. Members are kept informed of gay and gay-friendly hoteliers, tour operators, and airline and cruise-line representatives.

FOR STUDENTS   Most museums offer free or greatly reduced admission for students and anyone under 18, although sometimes you have to ask. Make sure to bring a student ID card. There are hostels in most major towns in Alaska, mostly open in the summer only. You'll find them listed in the text for each town, and most are listed in the directory published by **Hostelling International/American Youth Hostels,** 733 15th St. NW, Suite 840, Washington, DC 20005 (☎ **800/444-6111** or 202/783-6161; www.hiayh.org). Membership gives you discounts at member hostels, and is free for youths 17 and under. For age 18 to 54, membership is $25, 55 and over $15.

Many students travel to Alaska for summer work. It's usually possible to get a job in a fish cannery in most coastal towns. Work on the "slime line" is hard and unpleasant, and the pay is low; but if the season is good, you can work long hours, camp, and keep your expenses low (most canneries have tent cities of summer workers nearby), and take home decent money for your summer's work—more than you'd earn for a normal summer job. Hillary Rodham Clinton worked an Alaska slime line when she was in school, and you can, too. Stay onshore, however, as offshore fish-processing ships are a truly miserable and dangerous place to work; and if the ship doesn't get any fish, you don't make any money. Don't come north expecting to make fabulous wages. The stories of college students making huge crew shares on fishing boats are legends— there are plenty of experienced fishers to take those jobs before boats hire raw hands they have to train. Jobs are often available in the tourism industry, too. The **Alaska Department of Labor Job Service** posts job openings and advice on its Web site, **www.labor.state.ak.us/esjobs/jobs**. A search function allows you to narrow it down by area and field—just point your Web browser to seafood processing.

FOR FAMILIES   I researched most of this book while traveling with my wife, Barbara, 7-year-old boy, Robin, and 4-year-old girl, Julia. They made many of the best discoveries, and I've tried to include my advice for families throughout the text.

Alaska is a great place to take a family. The magnificent scenery is something even young children can understand and appreciate. Also, an Alaska vacation is largely spent outdoors, which is where kids like to be. Robin never gets enough ferry riding, even after we've been doing it for weeks, and both children enjoy camping immensely. We started camping with Julia at 6 months and never had a serious problem. When she realized everyone was going to sleep in the tent with her, on her level, her face lit up. The children taught the adults to slow down and find joy in new discoveries.

There are drawbacks to Alaska as a family destination. The primary one is the expense. Airlines offer significant discounts (generally 50%) only for infants young enough to ride in a parent's lap. Activities like flightseeing and tour boat cruises tend to have less-than-generous children's discounts and cost too much for most families. Often bed-and-breakfasts have rooms too small for a family. Hotel rooms are expensive in Alaska. Restaurants that aren't too fancy to take the kids may be too smoky (any listed in this volume should be okay unless noted). Car camping solves many of those problems, with stops in a hotel every few days to get everyone cleaned up. But the highways in Alaska are long, and children will require a gradual approach to covering ground.

You must be careful in choosing your itinerary and activities with children. There are the obvious things, like allowing time to play, to explore, and to rest, but also remember that children often don't enjoy activities like **wildlife watching.** It takes a long time to find the animals, and when you do, they're usually off in the distance—kids often don't have the visual skills to pick out the animals from the landscape. Don't overtax children with walks and **hiking** trips; it'll just make everyone miserable. We keep track of the longest hike we've managed without excessive whining, then try to extend that record just a little each time out. Short **sea-kayaking** excursions, on the other hand, are great for children who are old enough, riding in the front of a double-seat boat with a parent in back. Age limits depend on the outfitter and your child's responsibility level and ability to endure bad weather without complaining too much.

If you're flawed mortals like us, after the end of a few weeks on the road, you'll be getting on each other's nerves. We found success by leaving time for low-key kid activities, like **beachcombing** and playing in the park, while one grown-up would split off for a museum or special, more expensive activity. Of course, if you want to save your marriage, you'll have to be scrupulously fair about who gets to go flightseeing and who has to stay behind and change diapers, as you won't have my all-purpose excuse—research.

If you're interested in a package tour with your family, most of the companies listed below will take children. Some wilderness outfitters offer special trips for families, too (full addresses are listed below, under " Outfitters & Outdoor Package Trips"). **Alaska Wildland Adventures** (☎ **800/334-8730**), has various trips for kids as young as 12, and even offers a "Family Safari" for families with children ages 6 through 11 that strings together day trips in various places with stays at wilderness lodges, including a float trip on the Kenai River and several days in Denali National Park. The 8-day trip costs $3,495 for adults and $3,295 for kids, exclusive of air travel to Anchorage. **Alaska Discovery** (☎ **800/586-1911**), listed in the Juneau section in chapter 5, takes children as young as 10 on some of its extended Southeast Alaska sea kayaking trips, which start at $495 for 3 days and 2 nights.

10 Health, Safety & Traveler's Insurance

HEALTH & SAFETY

You'll find modern, full-service hospitals in each of Alaska's larger cities, and even in some small towns that act as regional centers. There's some kind of clinic even in the smallest towns, although they often are staffed by physicians' assistants rather than medical doctors. I've listed the address and phone numbers for medical facilities in each destination under "Fast Facts." Call those numbers, too, for referrals for a dentist or other health professional.

Travelers who don't plan to spend time in the outdoors need take no health precautions beyond what they'd do when traveling anywhere else in the United States. If you'll be doing any hiking, boating, camping, or other outdoor activities, the tips below may be more relevant.

BEARS & OTHER WILDLIFE   Being eaten by a bear is probably the least likely way for your vacation to end. Deaths from dog bites are much more common, for example. But it's still wise to be prepared for bears, and know how to avoid being trampled by moose. The first rule of defense is simple: Don't attract bears. All food and trash must be kept in airtight containers when you're camping (when car camping, the trunk of the vehicle will do), and be careful when you're cooking and cleaning up not to spread food odors. Never keep food in your tent. When walking through brush or thick trees, make lots of noise to avoid surprising a bear or moose—bells you can hang on your belt are for sale at sporting good shops, or you can sing or carry on loud conversation. At all costs, avoid coming between a bear and its cubs or a bear and food. Moose are strongly defensive of their young, too, and can attack if they feel you're getting too close. If you see a bear, stop, wave your arms, make noise, and (if you're with others) group together so you look larger to the bear. Don't tempt the bear to chase; depart by slowly backing away, at an angle. If the bear follows, stop. Once in a great while, the bear may bluff a charge; even less often, it may attack. Fall and play dead, rolling into a ball face down with your hands behind your neck. The bear should lose interest, but you have to stay still util it's gone. In extremely rare instances, a bear may not lose interest, because it's planning to make a meal of you. If this happens, fight back for all you're worth. Many Alaskans carry a gun for protection in bear country, while some carry pepper spray that's available in sporting-goods stores. In either case, you have to hold back the weapon as a last resort, when the bear is quite close and in the process of an attack. If you take a gun, it had better be a big one. Even a .45-caliber handgun won't stop a bear in time if you don't get off a precise shot. A .300-Magnum rifle or 12-gauge shotgun loaded with rifled slugs is the weapon of choice.

BOATING SAFETY   Going out on the water is more hazardous in Alaska than in most other places, and you should go only with an experienced, licensed operator unless you really know what you're doing. The weather can be severe and unpredictable, and there's no margin for error if you fall into the water or capsize—you have only minutes to get out and get warm before hypothermia and death. A life jacket will keep you afloat, but it won't keep you alive in 40°F water. If sea kayaking, stay close to shore and take along everything you need to quickly warm a person who gets wet (see "Hypothermia," below).

CRIME   Sadly, crime rates are not low in Alaska's major cities, although muggings are rare. Take the normal precautions you'd take at home. You're safe in daylight hours anywhere tourists commonly go, less so late at night leaving a bar or on a wooded bike trail. Women need to be especially careful on their own, as Alaska has a disproportionately high rate of rape. Most women I know avoid walking by themselves at night in Alaskan towns and cities, especially in wooded or out-of-the-way areas. The late-night sunlight can be deceiving—just because it's light doesn't mean it's safe. Assaults occur in towns big and small. Women should never hitchhike alone.

HYPOTHERMIA   Sometimes known as exposure, hypothermia is a potentially fatal lowering of core body temperature. It can sneak up on you, and it's most dangerous when you don't realize how cold you are, on a damp mountain hike or wet boating trip. The weather doesn't have to be very cold if you're damp and not adequately dressed in a material (whether wool or synthetic) that keeps its warmth when wet. Among the symptoms are cold extremities, shivering, being uncommunicative, poor judgment or coordination, and sleepiness. The cure is to warm the victim up—getting indoors, forcing him or her to drink hot liquids, and, if shelter is unavailable, applying body heat from another person, skin on skin, in a sleeping bag.

INSECT BITES   The good news is that Alaska has no snakes or poisonous spiders. The bad news is the mosquitoes and other biting insects. They're not dangerous, but they *can* ruin a trip. Insect repellent is a necessity, as is having a place where you can get away from them. Hikers in the Interior, where mosquitoes are worst, sometimes use head nets. Mosquitoes can bite through light fabric, which is why people in the Bush wear heavy Carhart pants and jackets even on the hottest days.

DANGEROUS PLANTS   Two shrubs common in Alaska can cause skin irritation, but we've got nothing as bad as poison ivy or poison oak. **Pushki,** also called cow parsnip, is a large-leafed plant growing primarily in open areas, up to shoulder height by late summer, with white flowers. The celerylike stalks break easily, and the sap has the quality of intensifying the burning power of the sun on skin. Wash it off quickly.

Devil's Club, a more obviously dangerous plant, grows on steep slopes and has ferocious spines that can pierce through clothing.

RIVER CROSSINGS   Hiking in Alaska's backcountry often requires crossing rivers without bridges. Use great caution: It's easy to get in trouble. Often, the water is glacial melt, barely above freezing and heavy with silt that makes it opaque and can quickly fill your pockets and drag you down. If in doubt, don't do it. If you do decide to cross, unbuckle your pack, keep your shoes on, face upstream, use a heavy walking stick if possible, and rig a safety line. Children should go in the eddy behind a larger person, or be carried.

SHELLFISH   Don't eat mussels or clams you pick or dig from the seashore unless the local office of the **Alaska Department of Fish and Game** (Cook Inlet, ☎ **907/ 267-2100;** Southeast ☎ **907/465-4270;** Kodiak **907/486-1840;** Prince William Sound **907/459-7207**) indicates that the area is safe. Most of Alaska's remote beaches are not tested and so are not safe. The risk is paralytic shellfish poisoning, a fatal malady caused by a naturally occurring toxin. It causes total paralysis, including breathing. A victim may be kept alive with mouth-to-mouth respiration until medical help is obtained.

SWIMMING   Ask about lake water before swimming in it. In recent years, some lakes have been infested with a bug that causes an itchy rash.

WATER   Authorities advise against drinking unpurified river or lake water. Hand-held filtration devices available from sporting-goods stores are the most practical way of dealing with the problem, but iodine kits and boiling also work. The danger is giardia, a bug that causes diarrhea. It may not show up until a couple of weeks after exposure and could last up to 6 weeks. If you get symptoms on getting home, tell your doctor you were exposed so you can get tested and cured.

DRIVING SAFETY

SUMMER   Keep your headlights on for safety on the highway. Drivers are required to pull over at the next pull-out whenever five or more cars are trailing on a two-lane highway, regardless of how fast they're going. This saves the lives of people who otherwise will try to pass. When passing a truck going the other way on a gravel highway, slow down or stop and pull as far as possible to the opposite side of the road to avoid losing your windshield to a flying rock. Always think about the path of rocks you're kicking up toward others' vehicles. Make sure you've got a good, full-sized spare tire and jack if driving a gravel highway. For remote driving, take a first-aid kit, emergency food, a tow rope, and jumper cables.

WINTER   Drivers on Alaska's highways in winter should be prepared for cold-weather emergencies far from help. Take all the items listed for rural summer driving, plus a flashlight, matches and materials to light a fire, chains, a shovel, and an ice scraper. A camp stove to make hot beverages also is a good idea. If you're driving a remote highway such as the Alaska Highway between November and April, take along gear adequate to keep you safe from the cold even if you have to wait 24 hours with a dead car at -40°F—parkas, boots, hats, mittens, blankets, and sleeping bags. Never drive a road marked "Closed" or "Unmaintained in Winter." Even on maintained rural roads, other vehicles come by rarely. All Alaska roads are icy all winter. Studded tires are a necessity—nonstudded snow tires or so-called "all-weather" tires aren't adequate. Also, never leave your car's engine stopped for more than 4 hours in extreme cold (-10°F or colder). Alaskans generally have electrical head-bolt heaters installed to keep the engine warm overnight; you'll find electrical outlets everywhere on rural highways.

TRAVEL INSURANCE

There are three kinds of travel insurance: trip cancellation, medical, and lost-luggage coverage. **Trip cancellation insurance** is a good idea if you have paid a large portion of your vacation expenses up front, as is often the case in Alaska. The other two types of insurance, however, don't make sense for most travelers. Rule number one: Check your existing policies before you buy any additional coverage.

Your existing health insurance should cover you if you get sick while on vacation (though if you belong to an HMO, you should check to see whether you are fully covered when away from home). For independent travel health-insurance providers, see below. Your homeowner's insurance should cover stolen luggage. The airlines are responsible for $1,250 on domestic flights if they lose your luggage; if you plan to carry anything more valuable than that, keep it in your carry-on bag.

The differences between travel assistance and insurance are often blurred, but in general the former offers on-the-spot assistance and 24-hour hot lines (mostly oriented toward medical problems), while the latter reimburses you for travel problems (medical, travel, or otherwise) after you have filed the paperwork. The coverage you should consider will depend on how much protection is already contained in your existing health insurance or other policies. Some credit- and charge-card companies may insure you against travel accidents if you buy plane, train, or bus tickets with their cards. Before purchasing additional insurance, read your policies and agreements over carefully. Call your insurers or credit/charge-card companies if you have any questions.

Some credit cards (American Express and certain gold and platinum Visa and MasterCards, for example) offer automatic flight insurance against death or dismemberment in case of an airplane crash.

If you do require additional insurance, try one of the companies listed below. But don't pay for more than you need. For example, if you need only trip-cancellation insurance, don't purchase coverage for lost or stolen property. Trip-cancellation insurance costs approximately 6% to 8% of the total value of your vacation.

Among the reputable issuers of travel insurance are: **Access America,** 6600 W. Broad St., Richmond, VA 23230 (☎ 800/284-8300); **Travel Guard International,** 1145 Clark St., Stevens Point, WI 54481 (☎ 800/826-1300); **Travel Insured International,** P.O. Box 280568, East Hartford, CT 06128 (☎ 800/243-3174); and **Travelex Insurance Services,** P.O. Box 9408, Garden City, NY 11530-9408 (☎ 800/228-9792).

Fast Facts: Alaska

American Express   There are eight American Express offices in Alaska. Four are in Anchorage, with the downtown location at 700 G St., Anchorage, AK 99501 (☎ **907/274-5588**). Other offices around the state are: 400 Cushman St., Fairbanks, AK 99701 (☎ **907/452-7636**); 202 Center St., Suite 103, Kodiak, AK 99615 (☎ **907/486-6084**); 8745 Glacier Hwy., Suite 328, Juneau, AK 99801 (☎ **907/789-0999**); and Front Street and Federal Way (P.O. Box 1769), Nome, AK 99762 (☎ **907/443-2211**).

Area Code   All of Alaska is in area code **907.** In the Yukon Territory, the area code is **867.** When placing a toll call within the state, you must dial 1, the area code, and the number. See "Telephone," below, for important tips.

Banks & ATM Networks   There are Alaska-based banks in most towns, as noted in the listings for each, but national chains are little represented. Automatic-teller machines are widely available, except in the tiniest towns. They generally are connected to the Plus and Cirrus networks, as well as other networks.

Business Hours   In the larger cities, major grocery stores are open 24 hours a day and carry a wide range of products in addition to food. At a minimum, **stores** are open Monday through Friday from 10am to 6pm, on Saturday afternoon, and often are closed on Sunday, but many are open much longer hours, especially in summer. **Banks** may close an hour earlier and, if open on Saturday, usually are open only in the morning. Under state law, **bars** don't have to close until 5am, but many communities have an earlier closing, generally around 2am.

Cellular Phone Coverage   Most towns have cellular coverage, including in some remote areas where it is used primarily for backcountry safety. Your cell phone provider should be able to give you a "Roaming Guide" detailing coverage and charges.

Emergencies   Generally, you can call ☎ **911** for medical, police, or fire emergencies. On remote highways, there sometimes are gaps in 911 coverage. A widely available brochure called **"Help Along the Way"** provides emergency phone numbers on most highways and the location of emergency phone boxes. It contains a lot of other useful information for motorists, too. You can write for a free copy from the state Emergency Medical Services Program, P.O. Box 110616, Juneau, AK 99811-0616 (☎ **907/465-3027**; health.hss.state.ak.us/dph/ems/ems_home.htm). Dialing 0 will generally get an operator, who can connect you to emergency services. CB channels 9 and 11 are monitored for emergencies on most highways, as are channels 14 and 19 in some areas.

Holidays   Besides the normal national holidays, banks and state and government offices close on two state holidays: Seward's Day (the last Monday in March) and Alaska Day (October 18, or the nearest Friday or Monday if it falls on a weekend). See chapter 3 for a listing of national holidays.

Internet/E-mail Access   The easiest way to connect is to go to the local Internet cafe or public library. Even small towns now have such services, which I've listed under Fast Facts in each town write-up. If you want to dial up the Internet from your laptop, you may have to call long distance to your home access number; as long distance phone lines in Alaska's smaller towns can be poor, you may not succeed. Major networks have local numbers in Anchorage and Fairbanks (where the phone connections are crystal clear).

Liquor Laws   The minimum drinking age in Alaska is 21. Some rural communities have laws prohibiting the importation and possession of alcohol (this is known as being "dry") or only the sale but not possession of alcohol (known as being "damp"). With a few exceptions, these are Bush communities off the road network. (Urban areas are all "wet.") Check the listings for the towns you'll visit for details. If in doubt, ask, as bootlegging is a serious crime.

Maps   The **Alaska Public Lands Information Centers** have maps with outdoor information. I've noted the best trail maps in each applicable section. For some of the most popular areas, I recommend the excellent trail maps published by **Trails Illustrated**, P.O. Box 4357, Evergreen, CO 80437-4357 (☎ **800/962-1643** or 303/670-3457; fax 800/626-8676; www.trailsillustrated.com). They're sold in park visitor centers, too. The maps are printed on plastic, so they don't get spoiled by rain; however, they don't cover the whole state. **Official topographic maps** from the U.S. Geological Survey are sold at the public lands centers or directly from USGS-ESIC, 4230 University Dr., Anchorage, AK

99508 (☎ **907/786-7011**), open Monday through Friday, 8:30am to 4:30pm. *The Alaska Atlas and Gazetteer,* published by DeLorme Mapping, 2 DeLorme Dr., Yarmouth, ME 04096 (☎ **207/846-7000;** www.delorme.com), contains topographical maps of the entire state, most at 1:300,000 scale. It's widely available in Alaska.

Newspapers   The state's dominant newspaper is the *Anchorage Daily News* (www.adn.com); it's available everywhere but is not easy to find in Southeast Alaska. Seattle newspapers and *USA Today* are often available, and in Anchorage you can get virtually any newspaper.

Taxes   There is no state sales tax, but most local governments have a sales tax and a bed tax on accommodations. The tax rates are listed in each town section under "Fast Facts."

Telephone   Making toll calls can be a headache for visitors. Before you leave for Alaska, contact your long-distance company for instructions on how to use your phone card and charges. AT&T calling cards should work, but you may not be able to use some other carriers. One solution is to buy one of the privately issued, by-the-minute cards. (For further information, see "Fast Facts: For the Foreign Traveler" in chapter 3.)

Time Zone   Although the state naturally spans five time zones, in the 1980s Alaska's central time zone was stretched so almost the entire state would lie all in one zone, known as Alaska time. It's 1 hour earlier than the U.S. West Coast's Pacific time. Crossing over the border from Alaska to Canada adds an hour and puts you at the same time as the West Coast. As with almost everywhere else in the United States, daylight saving time is in effect from 1am on the first Sunday in April (turn your clocks ahead 1 hour) until 2am on the last Sunday in October (turn 'em back again).

For Foreign Visitors

3

The pervasiveness of American culture around the world may make you feel that you know the U.S.A. pretty well, but leaving your own country still requires an additional degree of planning. This chapter will help prepare you for the more common problems that visitors may encounter.

Information on border crossings between the United States and Canada on the Alaska Highway is contained in chapter 9.

1 Entry Requirements

Immigration laws are a hot political issue in the United States these days, and the following requirements may have changed somewhat by the time you plan your trip. Check at any U.S. embassy or consulate for current information and requirements. You can also plug into the **U.S. State Department's** Internet site at **http://state.gov**.

VISAS Canadian citizens may enter the United States without visas; they need only proof of residence. The U.S. State Department has a **Visa Waiver Pilot Program** allowing citizens of certain countries to enter the United States without a visa for stays of up to 90 days. At press time these included Andorra, Argentina, Australia, Austria, Belgium, Brunei, Denmark, Finland, France, Germany, Iceland, Ireland, Italy, Japan, Liechtenstein, Luxembourg, Monaco, the Netherlands, New Zealand, Norway, San Marino, Slovenia, Spain, Sweden, Switzerland, and the United Kingdom. Citizens of these countries need only a valid passport and a round-trip air or cruise ticket in their possession upon arrival. If they first enter the United States, they may also visit Mexico, Canada, Bermuda, and/or the Caribbean islands and return to the United States without a visa. Further information is available from any U.S. embassy or consulate.

Citizens of all other countries must have (1) a valid passport that expires at least 6 months later than the scheduled end of their visit to the United States, and (2) a tourist visa, which may be obtained without charge from any U.S. consulate.

OBTAINING A VISA To obtain a visa, the traveler must submit a completed application form (either in person or by mail) with a 1 ½-inch-square photo, and must demonstrate binding ties to a residence abroad. Usually you can obtain a visa at once or within 24 hours, but it may take longer during the summer rush from June through August. If you cannot go in person, contact the nearest U.S.

Travel Tip

Be sure to keep a copy of all your travel papers separate from your wallet or purse, and leave a copy with someone at home should you need it faxed in an emergency.

embassy or consulate for directions on applying by mail. Your travel agent or airline office may also be able to provide you with visa applications and instructions. The U.S. consulate or embassy that issues your visa will determine whether you will be issued a multiple- or single-entry visa and any restrictions regarding the length of your stay.

British subjects can obtain up-to-date passport and visa information by calling the **U.S. Embassy Visa Information Line** (☎ **0891/200-290**) or the **London Passport Office** (☎ **0990/210-410** for recorded information).

IMMIGRATION QUESTIONS   Telephone operators will answer your inquiries regarding U.S. immigration policies or laws at the **Immigration and Naturalization Service's Customer Information Center** (☎ **800/375-5283**). Representatives are available from 9am to 3pm, Monday through Friday. The INS also runs a 24-hour automated information service, for commonly asked questions, at ☎ **800/755-0777.**

MEDICAL REQUIREMENTS   Unless you're arriving from an area known to be suffering from an epidemic (particularly cholera or yellow fever), inoculations or vaccinations are not required for entry into the United States. If you have a disease that requires treatment with narcotics or syringe-administered medications, carry a valid signed prescription from your physician to allay any suspicions that you may be smuggling narcotics.

For HIV-positive visitors, requirements for entering the United States are somewhat vague and change frequently. For up-to-the-minute information concerning HIV-positive travelers, contact the Center for Disease Control's **National Center for HIV** (☎ **404/332-4559;** www.hivatis.org) or the **Gay Men's Health Crisis** (☎ **212/367-1000;** www.gmhc.org).

DRIVERS' LICENSES   Foreign driver's licenses are mostly recognized in the United States, although you may want to get an international driver's license if your home license is not written in English.

2 Passport Information

Safeguard your passport in an inconspicuous, inaccessible place like a money belt. If you lose it, visit the nearest consulate of your native country as soon as possible for a replacement. Passport applications are downloadable from the Internet sites listed below.

UNITED KINGDOM   To pick up an application for a regular 10-year passport, visit your nearest passport office, major post office, or travel agency. You can also contact the London Passport Office at ☎ **0171/271-3000** or search its Web site at www.open.gov.uk/ukpass/ukpass.htm. Passports are £21 for adults and £11 for children under 16.

IRELAND   You can apply for a 10-year passport, costing IR£45, at the Passport Office, Setanta Centre, Molesworth Street, Dublin 2 (☎ **01/671-1633;** www.irlgov.ie/iveagh/foreignaffairs/services). Those under age 18 and over 65 must apply for a IR£10 3-year passport. You can also apply at 1A South Mall, Cork (☎ **021/272-525**) or over the counter at most main post offices.

AUSTRALIA   Apply at your local post office or passport office or search the government Web site at www.dfat.gov.au/passports/. Passports for adults are A$126 and for those under 18 A$63.

NEW ZEALAND   You can pick up a passport application at any travel agency or Link Centre. For more info, contact the Passport Office, P.O. Box 805, Wellington (☎ **0800/225-050**). Passports for adults are NZ$80 and for those under 16 NZ$40.

3 Customs

WHAT YOU CAN BRING IN

Every visitor over 21 years of age may bring in, free of duty, the following: (1) 1 liter of wine or hard liquor; (2) 200 cigarettes, 100 cigars (but not from Cuba), or 3 pounds of smoking tobacco; and (3) $100 worth of gifts. These exemptions are offered to travelers who spend at least 72 hours in the United States and who have not claimed them within the preceding 6 months. It is altogether forbidden to bring into the country foodstuffs (particularly fruit, cooked meats, and canned goods) and plants (vegetables, seeds, tropical plants, and the like). Foreign tourists may bring in or take out up to $10,000 in U.S. or foreign currency with no formalities; larger sums must be declared to U.S. Customs on entering or leaving, which includes filing form CM 4790. For more specific information regarding U.S. Customs, call your nearest U.S. embassy or consulate, or the **U.S. Customs** office at ☎ **202/927-1770;** www.customs.ustreas.gov.

WHAT YOU CAN BRING HOME

WILDLIFE PRODUCTS   Alaska Native art and crafts made from protected marine mammals are perfectly legal (even though possessing the raw animal pelts would not be for non-Natives), but you do need to get permits to take these items out of the country. Permits also are required to export products made from brown or black bear, bobcat, wolf, lynx, or river otter. The best solution is to have the shop where you buy the item mail it to you insured, and have them take care of the paperwork. If you carry it with you, or buy from a shop that can't handle the paperwork, you'll need to get your own permits. To go into or through Canada, get a Personal Effects Exemption Certificate for the item by calling the **U.S. Fish and Wildlife Service** in Anchorage (☎ **907/271-6198**). They can handle it in a few days. Call them also for permits for products made of nonmarine mammals. To take **marine mammal products** to a country other than Canada, you have to get a permit from the **Fish and Wildlife Service** in Washington D.C. (☎ **800/358-2104**). It can take a month to get these permits. There may be other regulations for bringing walrus ivory into your home country because of the international ban on elephant ivory. It's important to note that Alaska Natives have used these materials for thousands of years, and their harvest poses no threat to the species.

OTHER GOODS   Rules governing what you can bring back duty-free vary from country to country. For a clear summary of **Canadian** rules, write for the booklet *I Declare*, issued by Revenue Canada, 2265 St. Laurent Blvd., Ottawa K1G 4KE (☎ **613/993-0534**). **British** citizens should contact HM Customs & Excise, Passenger Enquiry Point, 2nd Floor Wayfarer House, Great South West Road, Feltham, Middlesex, TW14 8NP (☎ **0181/910-3744;** from outside the U.K. 44/181-910-3744; www.open.gov.uk). **Australian** citizens should contact Australian Customs Services, GPO Box 8, Sydney NSW 2001 (☎ **02/9213-2000**). **New Zealand** citizens should contact New Zealand Customs, 50 Anzac Ave., P.O. Box 29, Auckland (☎ **09/359-6655**).

4 Insurance

Travel insurance policies can cover everything from the loss or theft of your baggage and trip cancellation to health coverage and the guarantee of bail in case you're arrested. Good policies will also cover the costs of an accident, repatriation, or death. See "Health, Safety & Traveler's Insurance" in chapter 2 for more information. Packages such as **Europ Assistance** in Europe are sold by automobile clubs and travel agencies at attractive rates. **Worldwide Assistance Services** (☎ 800/821-2828) is the agent for Europ Assistance in the United States.

Although it's not required of travelers, **health insurance** is highly recommended. Unlike many European countries, the United States does not usually offer free or low-cost medical care to its citizens or visitors. Doctors and hospitals are expensive, and, except in emergencies, usually require advance payment or proof of coverage before they render their services. Though lack of health insurance may prevent you from being admitted to a hospital in nonemergencies, don't worry about being left on a street corner to die: The American way is to fix you now and bill the living daylights out of you later.

5 Money

The U.S. monetary system is simple: The most common **bills** (all ugly, all green) are the $1 (colloquially, a "buck"), $5, $10, and $20 denominations. There are also $2 bills (seldom encountered), $50 bills, and $100 bills (the last two are usually not welcome as payment for small purchases). Note that a newly redesigned $100 and $50 bill were introduced in 1996, and a redesigned $20 bill in 1998. Expect to see redesigned $10 and $5 notes in the year 2000. Despite rumors to the contrary, the old-style bills are still legal tender.

There are six denominations of **coins:** 1¢ (1 cent, or a penny); 5¢ (5 cents, or a nickel); 10¢ (10 cents, or a dime); 25¢ (25 cents, or a quarter); 50¢ (50 cents, or a half dollar); and the uncommon $1 piece (the older, large silver dollar and the newer, small Susan B. Anthony coin). A new gold-colored $1 piece will be introduced by the year 2000.

See chapter 2 for a discussion of **credit cards, ATMs, traveler's checks,** and other payment methods in Alaska.

6 Safety

Robberies (like muggings) are quite rare in Alaska, even in Anchorage, but the incidence of rape is quite high. Precautions are covered in chapter 2. Of course, thefts can happen anywhere; the only time anyone has tried to steal from me in a life in Alaska was in a tiny village. Keep control of your belongings and lock your car and hotel doors. Don't leave valuables in sight in the car.

With the ubiquity of guns in Alaska, it's wise to avoid late nights in rough bars or other situations where you could get into an argument.

7 Getting to the United States

Almost all flights to Alaska come from domestic airports, requiring trips from overseas to pass through Seattle or another major city. Carriers serving Anchorage are listed in chapter 2. Canadians can drive to Alaska over the Alaska or Top of the World highways, covered in chapter 9, or on an Alaska Marine Highway System ferry from Prince Rupert, B.C., covered in chapter 5.

Currency Exchange Tips

The "foreign-exchange bureaus" so common in Europe are rare even at airports in the United States, and nonexistent outside major cities. It's best not to change foreign money (or traveler's checks denominated in a currency other than U.S. dollars) at a small-town bank, or even a branch in a big city; in fact, leave any currency other than U.S. dollars at home—it may prove a greater nuisance to you than it's worth.

AIRLINE DISCOUNTS   The idea of traveling abroad on a budget is something of an oxymoron, but travelers can reduce the price of a plane ticket by several hundred dollars if they take the time to shop around. For example, overseas visitors can take advantage of the APEX (advance purchase excursion) reductions offered by all major U.S. and European carriers.

IMMIGRATION & CUSTOMS CLEARANCE   Visitors arriving by air, no matter what the port of entry, should cultivate patience and resignation before setting foot on U.S. soil. Getting through immigration control may take as long as 2 hours on some days, especially on summer weekends, so be sure to have this guidebook or something else to read. Add the time it takes to clear Customs, and you'll see that you should make a 2- to 3-hour allowance for delays when you plan your connections between international and domestic flights.

In contrast, for the traveler arriving by car from Canada, the border-crossing formalities have been streamlined to the vanishing point.

Fast Facts: For the Foreign Traveler

See "Fast Facts" in chapter 2 for information not listed here.

Currency & Currency Exchange   See "Entry Requirements" and "Money," above.

Electricity   Like Canada, the United States uses 110 to 120 volts AC (60 cycles), compared to 220 to 240 volts AC (50 cycles) in most of Europe, Australia, and New Zealand. If your small appliances use 220 to 240 volts, you'll need a 110-volt transformer and a plug adapter with two flat parallel pins to operate them here. Downward converters that change 220 to 240 volts to 110 to 120 volts are difficult to find in the United States, so bring one with you.

Embassies & Consulates   All embassies are located in the nation's capital, Washington, D.C. Some consulates are located in major U.S. cities, and most nations have a mission to the United Nations in New York City. If your country isn't listed below, call for directory information in Washington, D.C. (☎ 202/ 555-1212) for the number of your national embassy.

Australia: 1601 Massachusetts Ave. NW, Washington, DC 20036 (☎ 202/ 797-3000; www.austemb.org). There are consulates in New York, Honolulu, Houston, Los Angeles, and San Francisco.

Canada: 501 Pennsylvania Ave. NW, Washington, DC 20001 (☎ 202/ 682-1740; www.cdnemb-washdc.org). Other Canadian consulates are in Buffalo (New York), Detroit, Los Angeles, New York, and Seattle.

Ireland: 2234 Massachusetts Ave. NW, Washington, DC 20008 (☎ 202/ 462-3939). Irish consulates are in Boston, Chicago, New York, and San Francisco.

Japan: 2520 Massachusetts Ave. NW, Washington, DC 20008 (☎ 202/ 238-6700; www.embjapan.org). Japanese consulates are located in Atlanta, Kansas City, San Francisco, and Washington D.C.

New Zealand: 37 Observatory Circle NW, Washington, DC 20008 (☎ 202/328-4800; www.emb.com/nzemb). New Zealand consulates are in Los Angeles, Salt Lake City, San Francisco, and Seattle.

United Kingdom: 3100 Massachusetts Ave. NW, Washington, DC 20008 (☎ 202/462-1340). Other British consulates are in Atlanta, Boston, Chicago, Cleveland, Houston, Los Angeles, New York, San Francisco, and Seattle.

Emergencies   Call ☎ 911 to report a fire, call the police, or get an ambulance almost anywhere in the United States. This is a toll-free call (no coins are required at public telephones).

Gasoline (Petrol)   Petrol/gasoline stations are known as both gas stations and service stations. Gasoline costs about half as much here as it does in Europe (about $1.30 per gallon at press time), and taxes are already included in the printed price. One U.S. gallon equals 3.8 liters or .85 Imperial gallons.

Holidays   Banks, government offices, post offices, and many stores, restaurants, and museums are closed on the following legal national holidays: January 1 (New Year's Day), the third Monday in January (Martin Luther King Day), the third Monday in February (Presidents' Day, Washington's Birthday), the last Monday in May (Memorial Day), July 4 (Independence Day), the first Monday in September (Labor Day), the second Monday in October (Columbus Day), November 11 (Veterans' Day/Armistice Day), the fourth Thursday in November (Thanksgiving Day), and December 25 (Christmas). Also, the Tuesday following the first Monday in November is Election Day and is a federal government holiday in presidential-election years (held every 4 years, and next in 2000). Additionally, banks and state government offices in Alaska close on 2 state holidays: the last Monday in March (Seward's Day) and October 18 (Alaska Day, which is celebrated on the nearest Friday or Monday if the 18th falls on a weekend).

Legal Aid   The foreign tourist will probably never become involved with the American legal system. If you are "pulled over" for a minor traffic infraction (such as speeding), never attempt to pay the fine directly to a police officer; this could be construed as attempted bribery, a much more serious crime. Pay fines by mail, or directly into the hands of the clerk of the court. If accused of a more serious offense, say and do nothing before consulting a lawyer. Here the burden is on the state to prove a person's guilt beyond a reasonable doubt, and everyone has the right to remain silent, whether he or she is suspected of a crime or actually arrested. Once arrested, a person can make one telephone call to a party of his or her choice. Call your embassy or consulate.

Mail   If you aren't sure what your address will be in the United States, mail can be sent to you, in your name, c/o General Delivery at the main post office of the city or region where you expect to be (call ☎ 800/275-8777 for information on the nearest post office). The addressee must pick mail up in person and must produce proof of identity (driver's license, passport). Most post offices are open Monday to Friday from 8am to 6pm, and Saturday from 9am to 3pm, and will hold your mail for up to 1 month.

Generally found at intersections, **mailboxes** are blue with a red-and-white stripe and carry the inscription "U.S. Mail." If your mail is addressed to a U.S. destination, don't forget to add the five-digit postal code (or ZIP code), after the two-letter abbreviation of the state to which the mail is addressed.

At press time domestic postage rates were 20¢ for a postcard and 33¢ for a letter. For international mail, a first-class letter of up to one-half ounce costs 60¢

Telephone Dialing Info at a Glance

Most long-distance and international calls can be dialed directly from any phone.

- **To call the United States from another country using direct dial,** dial the international access code (0011 in Australia, 00 in the U.K., Ireland, and New Zealand), then the country code (**1**), the area code (**907** for Alaska, **867** for the Yukon Territory), and the seven-digit local number.

- **For calls within the United States and to Canada,** dial 1 followed by the area code and the seven-digit number (for example, 1-212/000-0000).

- **For international calls (other than to Canada),** dial the international access code (**011**) followed by the country code (U.K. 44, Ireland 353, Australia 61, New Zealand 64), city code, and the local number.

- **For reversed-charge or collect calls,** and for person-to-person calls, dial 0 (zero, not the letter O) followed by the area code and number you want; an operator will then come on the line, and you should specify that you are calling collect, or person-to-person, or both. If your operator-assisted call is international, ask for the overseas operator.

- **For local directory assistance** ("information"), dial 411; for long-distance information, dial 1, then the appropriate area code and 555-1212.

(46¢ to Canada and 40¢ to Mexico), a first-class postcard costs 50¢ (40¢ to Canada and 35¢ Mexico), and a preprinted postal aerogramme costs 50¢.

Taxes   In the United States there is no value-added tax (VAT) or other indirect tax at the national level. Every state, county, and city has the right to levy its own local tax on all purchases, including hotel and restaurant checks, airline tickets, and so on.

Telephone, Telegraph, Telex & Fax   The telephone system in the United States is run by private corporations, so rates, especially for long-distance service and operator-assisted calls, can vary widely. Generally, hotel surcharges on long-distance and local calls are astronomical, so you're usually better off using a **public pay telephone,** which you'll find clearly marked in most public buildings and private establishments as well as on the street. Convenience grocery stores and gas stations always have them. Many convenience groceries and packaging services sell **prepaid calling cards** in denominations up to $50; these can be the least expensive way to call home. Many public phones at airports now accept American Express, MasterCard, and Visa credit cards. **Local calls** made from public pay phones in most locales cost either 25¢ or 35¢. Pay phones do not accept pennies, and few will take anything larger than a quarter

Calls to area codes **800, 888,** and **877** are toll-free.

Telegraph and telex services are provided primarily by Western Union. You can bring your telegram into the nearest Western Union office (there are hundreds across the country) or dictate it over the phone (☎ 800/325-6000). You can also telegraph money or have it telegraphed to you very quickly over the Western Union system, but this service can cost as much as 15% to 20% of the amount sent.

Most hotels have **fax machines** available for guest use (be sure to ask about the charge to use it), and many hotel rooms are even wired for guests' fax machines. A less expensive way to send and receive faxes may be at establishments listed as

"Business Services" in the "Fast Facts" section of the larger cities and towns in this book.

There are two kinds of **telephone directories** in the United States. The so-called **White Pages** list private households and business subscribers in alphabetical order. The inside front cover lists emergency numbers for police, fire, ambulance, the Coast Guard, poison-control center, crime-victims hot line, and so on. The first few pages will tell you how to make long-distance and international calls, complete with country codes and area codes. Government numbers are usually printed on blue-trimmed within the White Pages. Printed on yellow paper, the so-called **Yellow Pages** list all local services, businesses, industries, and houses of worship according to activity with an index at the front or back. (Drugstores/pharmacies and restaurants are also listed by geographic location.) The Yellow Pages also include city plans or detailed area maps, postal ZIP codes, and public transportation routes.

Time   The continental United States is divided into **four time zones:** eastern standard time (EST), central standard time (CST), mountain standard time (MST), and Pacific standard time (PST). Alaska and Hawaii have their own zones. For example, noon in New York City (EST) is 11am in Chicago (CST), 10am in Denver (MST), 9am in Los Angeles (PST), 8am in Anchorage (AST), and 7am in Honolulu (HST).

Daylight saving time is in effect from 1am on the first Sunday in April through 1am the last Sunday in October, except in Arizona, Hawaii, part of Indiana, and Puerto Rico. Daylight saving time moves the clock 1 hour ahead of standard time.

Tipping   In hotels, tip **bellhops** at least $1 per bag ($2 to $3 if you have a lot of luggage) and tip the **chamber staff** $1 per day. Tip the **doorman** or **concierge** only if he or she has provided you with some specific service (for example, calling a cab for you or obtaining hard-to-get theater tickets). Tip the **valet parking attendant** $1 every time you get your car.

In restaurants, bars, and nightclubs, tip **service staff** 15% to 20% of the check, tip **bartenders** 10% to 15%, tip **checkroom attendants** $1 per garment, and tip **valet-parking attendants** $1 per vehicle. Tip the **doorman** only if he has provided you with some specific service (such as calling a cab for you). Tipping is not expected in cafeterias and fast-food restaurants.

Tip **cab drivers** 15% of the fare.

As for other service personnel, tip **skycaps** at airports at least $1 per bag ($2 to $3 if you have a lot of luggage) and tip **hairdressers** and **barbers** 15% to 20%.

Tipping gas-station attendants and ushers at movies and theaters is not expected.

Toilets   You won't find public toilets (or "rest rooms") on the streets in most U.S. cities, but they can be found in hotel lobbies, bars, restaurants, museums, department stores, railway and bus stations, or service stations. Note, however, that restaurants and bars in resorts or heavily visited areas may reserve their rest rooms for the use of their patrons. Some establishments display a notice that toilets are for the use of patrons only. You can ignore this sign or, better yet, avoid arguments by paying for a cup of coffee or a soft drink, which will qualify you as a patron. Large hotels and fast-food restaurants are probably the best bet for good, clean facilities. If possible, avoid the toilets at parks and beaches, which tend to be dirty.

Cruising Alaska's Coast 4

Alaska is one of the top cruise destinations in the world, with almost three quarters of a million people sailing the state's coast annually, visiting the towns and wilderness areas of Southeast and the Gulf of Alaska by day and allowing the ship to do the traveling for them by night. This element of cruise travel—the fact that it's *easy*—is one of its main drawing cards for visitors to Southeast, where the lack of roads between towns makes the waters of the Inside Passage the region's de facto highway. You could do the same routes on the Alaska State Ferry, but you'd have to be willing to invest more time, both for the actual traveling and for the planning. If all you've got is a week yet you're dead set on seeing Alaska, the cruise ship option may be a solution.

For a more in-depth examination of Alaska cruises, pick up a copy of *Frommer's Alaska Cruises & Ports of Call.*

1 Weighing Your Cruise Options

Your two main questions in choosing a cruise in Alaska are "Where do I want to go?" and "How big a ship?"

INSIDE PASSAGE OR THE GULF OF ALASKA?

Typically, the cruise lines offer two basic weeklong itineraries. **Inside Passage cruises** generally sail round-trip from Vancouver (British Columbia), visiting three or four port towns along the Inside Passage, spending a day in Glacier Bay or one of the other glacier areas, and spending 2 days "at sea," meaning they just cruise along, allowing you to relax and enjoy the scenery.

Gulf of Alaska cruises generally sail north- and southbound between Vancouver and Seward (the port for Anchorage) in alternating weeks, visiting many of the same towns and attractions as the Inside Passage cruises but—since they don't have to turn around and sail back to Vancouver—also tagging on a visit to Valdez, Hubbard Glacier, College Fjord, or one or more of the other Gulf towns or natural attractions.

Though most of the major operators stick pretty closely to these two basic routes, the small-ship cruise lines tend to offer more **variations**—some sailing round-trip from Juneau or Sitka, some sailing between Juneau and Ketchikan, and one even sailing between Juneau and Glacier Bay.

Cruisetours: Alaska by Land & Sea

Since many of the people who make the effort to get all the way to Alaska for their cruise want to stick around a while after (or before) the cruise, the cruise lines all offer land tours that can be added onto their cruise itineraries, bookable as a package with your cruise. Typical packages include cruise plus a 3- to 5-day **Anchorage/Denali/Fairbanks** tour, a 7-day **Yukon** tour (which visits Anchorage, Denali, and Fairbanks on the way), or a 5- to 7-day tour of the **Canadian Rockies.** Holland America–Westours (with their subsidiary, Gray Line of Alaska) and Princess are the two big leaders in the cruisetour market, with Princess possibly having the edge in the Anchorage/Denali/Fairbanks corridor and Holland America definitely on top in the Yukon. Cruise West is the third major operator. Even if you book with another cruise line, chances are your land tour will be through one of these operators.

BIG SHIP OR SMALL?

Imagine an elephant. Now imagine your pet pug dog, Sparky. That's about the size difference between your options in the Alaska market: behemoth modern megaships and small, more exploratory coastal vessels.

The **big ships** offer you heated pools, theatrical productions, organized activities, spas, jogging tracks, discos, generally spacious accommodations, fine dining, and more—but their size comes with three major drawbacks: (a) they can't sail into narrow passages or shallow-water ports, (b) their size and inflexible schedules limit their ability to stop or even slow down when wildlife is spotted, and (c) when their passengers disembark in a town, they tend to overwhelm that town, limiting your ability to see the real Alaska.

The **small ships** offer little in terms of amenities: They usually have small cabins, only one lounge/bar and dining room, and no exercise facilities, entertainment, or organized activities. Despite all of this, they're slightly more expensive than the big ships, and offer fewer discounts. That's the minus side. On the plus side, (a) they can sail almost anywhere (including far into Misty Fjords, where no large ship can penetrate), (b) since they tend to have more flexibility in their schedules than the large ships, they can usually take time to linger if a pod of whales is sighted nearby, and (c) their small size doesn't scare off wildlife as easily as the big ships, and the fact that you're at or near the waterline (rather than 10 stories up, as on the large ships) means you get a more close-up view. Additionally, all these ships except Clipper Cruise Line's *Yorktown Clipper* are 100% casual—no dressing up for dinner here, and even on the Clipper ship all you need is a sports jacket.

On a more philosophical level, the small ships seem to be much more sensitive to Alaska. The big ships are becoming disliked among many Alaskans because they overload communities and waterways, whereas the smaller ships tend to be owned by smaller, private companies (the best example, Alaska's Glacier Bay Tours and Cruises, is owned by Goldbelt, a Native corporation based in Juneau) that are more clued in to local social and environmental concerns.

Some travelers may be disappointed by the small ships, however, especially those sold on the "Love Boat" image or those who expect little more from Alaska than a few souvenir shops in port and a pretty picture outside the window while they hit the slots. For these travelers, a big ship is the way to go. Those who want to really immerse themselves in the local spirit, though, will opt for the smaller ships—which is why we're devoting much of this chapter to them.

2 Booking Your Cruise

Almost all cruises are booked through travel agents. Why? For one, it's easier that way: The agent worries about the details. Most cruise lines are happy with this system— among other things, it saves them the expense of having to employ huge reservations staffs. Some of the small-ship operators do accept direct bookings, but often if you try to call the large-ship companies directly you'll be referred to a travel agent.

Don't fight it. Working with an agent doesn't cost you anything and can in fact save you money, since agents are the most knowledgeable about current discounts being offered by the cruise lines. If you don't have an agent you trust, you can often get the name of one near you by calling the cruise line or lines you're interested in and asking for one near you. (Note that not all agents represent all cruise lines. In order to be experts on what they sell, and to maximize the commissions the lines pay them, some agents may limit their product to, say, one luxury line, one midpriced line, one mass-market line, and so on.) Another option is to check the Web site of the **Cruise Lines International Association** (www.cruising.org), which maintains a list of cruise-savvy agents by region.

CRUISE PRICES

For the most part, the advertised prices of cruises are a fiction—they're like new-car prices: what the dealer would *like* to get, in a perfect world where there was no law of supply and demand. In reality, the cruise lines—especially the big-ship lines— discount their prices by almost whatever it takes to fill their open berths, so you'll commonly see deep discounts off these published rates, sometimes up to 40% off. Small-ship lines tend to stick closer to their published rates.

In the cruise line reviews below we've listed the typical upper- and lower-end prices for cabins (both inside and outside) and suites. **Note that these are the line's brochure rates,** so depending on how early you book and on any special deals the lines are offering, the actual price may be much less. Rates listed are per person, based on double occupancy.

BOOKING AHEAD

The best way to save on an Alaska cruise is to **book in advance.** Typically, lines offer early-bird rates to those who book their Alaska cruise before February 14 of the year of the cruise. If the cabins do not fill up by the cutoff date, the early-bird rate may be extended, and it may be slightly lower. If the cabins are still not full as the season begins, the cruise line may start marketing special deals, usually through its top-producing travel agents. Due to the popularity of Alaska cruises, it's rare to find true last-minute deals, and where these deals do exist they are for a very limited selection of cabins. Planning your Alaska cruise well in advance is the best way to save.

MONEY-SAVING STRATEGIES
SHOULDER SEASON DISCOUNTS

You can think of the Alaska cruise season as three distinct periods: **(1) peak season,** late June, July, and early to mid-August; **(2) value/standard season,** early June and late August; and **(3) budget season,** May and September. You can save by booking a cruise during this last period, in the **shoulder months** of May or September, when cruise pricing is lower. The weather might be a little chillier, and September is known for rain, but a lot fewer people visit during those months, allowing you a bit more pristine view of the place, especially if you're sailing on a small ship. We took an early May sailing with Glacier Bay Tours and Cruises in 1998 and felt like we had the state all to ourselves.

DISCOUNTS FOR THIRD & FOURTH PASSENGERS & GROUPS

Most ships offer highly discounted rates for third and fourth passengers sharing a cabin with two full-fare passengers, even if the latter two have booked at a discounted rate. It may mean a tight squeeze, but it'll save you a bundle. Some lines offer **special rates for kids,** usually on a seasonal or select-sailings basis, that may include free or discounted airfare. Those under age 2 generally cruise free.

One of the best ways to get a cruise deal is to book as a **group,** so you may want to gather family together for a family reunion or convince your friends or colleagues they need a vacation, too. A group is generally at least 16 people in at least eight cabins. The savings include not only a discounted rate, but at least the cruise portion of the 16th ticket will be free (on some upscale ships you can negotiate a free ticket for groups of eight or more).

SENIOR-CITIZEN DISCOUNTS

Senior citizens may be able to get extra savings on their cruise. Some lines will take 5% off the top for those 55 and up, and the senior rate applies even if the second person in the cabin is younger. Membership in groups such as AARP is not required, but such membership may bring additional savings.

BOOKING YOUR AIR TRAVEL THOUGH THE CRUISE LINE

As a general rule, if you are offered air transportation from the cruise line, it's best to take it. Why? First of all, as big customers of the airlines, the cruise lines tend to get very good (if not the best) discounted airfare rates, which they pass on to their customers. Secondly, booking air with the cruise line also allows the line to keep track of you. If your plane is late, for instance, they might even hold the boat. And most cruise lines include **transfers** from the airport to the ship, saving you the hassle of getting a cab (if you do book on your own, you may still be able to get the transfers separately— ask your agent about this).

While airlines may offer attractive sale fares in the newspapers, keep in mind cruises tend to depart on the peak travel days of Friday or Saturday, so the discounted airfares you read about may not even apply.

The only time it may pay to book your own air transportation is if you are using frequent-flyer miles and can get the air for free, or if you are fussy about which carrier you fly or route you take (you are more or less at the mercy of the cruise line to make these choices if you take their air offers, and may even end up on chartered aircraft).

CHOOSING YOUR CABIN

Cruise ship cabins run from tiny boxes with accordion doors and bunk beds to palatial multiroom suites with hot tubs on the balcony. Which is right for you? Price will likely be a big factor here, but so should the vacation style you prefer. If, for instance, you plan to spend a lot of quiet time in your cabin, you should probably consider booking the biggest room you can afford. If, conversely, you plan to be out on deck all the time checking out the glaciers and wildlife, you might be just as happy with a smaller (and cheaper) cabin to crash in at the end of the day. Cabins are either **inside** (without a window or porthole) or **outside** (with), with the latter being more expensive. On the big ships, the more deluxe outside cabins may also come with **private verandas.**

SPECIAL MENU REQUESTS

The cruise line should be informed at the time you make your reservations about any special dietary requests you have. Some lines offer kosher menus, and all will have vegetarian, low-fat, low-salt, and sugar-free options available.

EXTRA COSTS TO CONSIDER

It's important when figuring out what your cruise will cost to remember what extras are *not* included in your cruise fare. The most pricey addition to your cruise fare, particularly in Alaska, will likely be **shore excursions.** Ranging from about $29 for a bus tour to $250 or more for a helicopter or fixed-wing flightseeing excursion, these sightseeing tours are designed to help cruise passengers make the most of their time at the ports the ship visits, but they can add a hefty sum to your vacation costs.

You'll also want to add to your calculations **tips for the ship's crew.** Tips are given at the end of the cruise, and passengers should reserve at least $9 per person, per day ($63 per passenger for the week) for tips for the room steward, waiter, and bus boy. (In practice, we find that most people tend to give a little more.) Additional tips to other personnel, such as the head waiter or maître d', are at your discretion. If you have a fancy room with a butler, slip him or her about $14 (or $2 a day). Most lines automatically add 15% to bar bills, so you don't have to tip your bartender. On the small ships, all tips often go into one pot, which the crew divides up after the cruise.

All but a very few ships charge extra for **alcoholic beverages** (including wine at dinner) and for soda. Nonbubbly soft drinks such as lemonade and iced tea are included in your cruise fare.

Port charges, taxes, and other fees are usually included in your cruise fare but not always, and these charges can add as much as $175 per person onto the price of a 7-day Alaska cruise. Make sure you know whether these are included in the cruise fare when you are comparing rates. We've included information on port charges in the ship reviews in chapters 5 and 6.

3 The Small-Ship Cruise Lines

Whereas big ships allow you to see Alaska while immersed in a vibrant, resortlike atmosphere, small ships allow you to see it from ground level, without distraction from anything un-Alaskan—no glitzy interiors, no big shows or loud music, no casinos, no spas, and no crowds, as the largest of these ships carries only 138 passengers. You're immersed in the 49th state from the minute you wake up to the minute you fall asleep, and for the most part left alone to form your own opinions. Personally, we feel this is by far the better cruise experience for those who really want to get the feel of Alaska.

Small ships also allow you to visit more isolated parts of the coast. Thanks to their smaller size and **shallow draft** (the amount of hull below the waterline), these ships can go places where larger ships can't, and they have the flexibility to change their itineraries as opportunities arise—say, to go where whales have been sighted. Depending on the itinerary, ports of call might include popular stops like Sitka or Ketchikan, tiny towns like Elfin Cove or Warm Springs Harbor, or a Tlingit village like Kake, and all itineraries include **glacier and whale watching.** Most of them also build in time to explore the wilder parts of Alaska, either ferrying passengers ashore for **hikes in wilderness areas** or carrying **sea kayaks** that passengers can launch right from the ship.

The alternative ship experience tends toward adventure, although it's usually of a soft rather than rugged sort. Rather than glitzy entertainment, you'll likely get

informal lectures and sometimes video presentations on Alaskan wildlife, history, and Native culture. Meals are served in open seatings, so you can sit where and with whom you like, and time spent huddled on the outside decks scanning for whales fosters great camaraderie among passengers.

Cabins on these ships don't generally offer TVs or telephones and tend to be very small and sometimes spartan (see the individual reviews for exceptions). There are no stabilizers on most of these smaller ships, so the ride can be bumpy in rough seas.

Except in the case of Cruise West's *Spirit of '98,* there are no elevators on any of these small ships, so they're not ideal choices for travelers with disabilities or mobility problems. These small ships may also not be the best choice for families with children, unless those kids are avid nature buffs and are able to keep themselves entertained without a lot of outside stimuli.

ALASKA'S GLACIER BAY TOURS AND CRUISES
226 2nd Ave. W, Seattle, WA 98119. ☎ **800/451-5952** or 206/623-7110. Fax 206/ 623-7809. www.glacierbaytours.com.

Alaska's Glacier Bay Tours and Cruises—the only **Native-owned** cruise line in Alaska—offers three types of cruises: adventure (both soft and active) and port-to-port sailings, with the balance weighted far toward the adventure side.

The adventure sailings are for a particular type of traveler, one interested in exploring Alaska's wilds rather than its towns. On the average soft-adventure cruise, the biggest town you're likely to encounter after departing Juneau is tiny little Elfin Cove, population around 30 to 35 (as least in the summer). Other than this, days are spent kayaking, hiking in remote regions, exploring the glaciers, and cruising the waterways looking for whales and other wildlife. On board, the atmosphere is casual and friendly, with the staff providing just enough attention while leaving you the space to enjoy your vacation however you want.

BEST FEATURES The line's two adventure ships (the *Wilderness Adventurer* and *Wilderness Explorer*) carry a fleet of stable two-person **sea kayaks,** which are launched from dry platforms at the ships' sterns. A weeklong sailing typically includes three kayak treks. Other big pluses include the extreme **informality** of the onboard atmosphere, the extent to which respect and understanding of the natural environment and **Native culture** are emphasized, the fact that all off-ship excursions on the adventure cruises are included in the cruise price, and the friendly, casual rapport between passengers and crew—it's all one big happy family with this line.

TYPICAL PASSENGERS On the line's **soft-adventure and active-adventure vessels,** passengers tend to be on the youngish side, with as many couples in their 40s and 50s as in their 60s and 70s, and a scattering of 30-somethings (and a few 80- or 90-somethings) filling out the list. Whatever their age, passengers tend to be active and interested in nature and wildlife. On the *Executive Explorer,* the line's upscale **port-to-port** ship, passengers tend to be older (60 and up) and less active and adventurous, though they still enjoy the same informality as aboard the line's other vessels.

ACTIVITIES & ENTERTAINMENT **Naturalists** sail with every cruise to point out natural features and lead off-ship expeditions. One naturalist on a recent sailing was a native Aleut who had taken it upon herself to learn a number of Tlingit legends, which she told to the passengers in a traditional manner. It was a big, big highlight of the trip. Entertainment facilities on all ships are minimal: board games, books, and a TV/VCR in the lounge, on which passengers can view tapes on wildlife, Alaska history, Native culture, and a few feature films.

DINING   Meals are pretty standard middle-American fare (plus the requisite Alaska salmon) and are served in single open seatings. Special diets (vegetarian, kosher, low-fat, low-salt) can be accommodated with some advance warning.

SHIPS

EXECUTIVE EXPLORER   Glacier Bay's most luxurious ship, sailing port-to-port itineraries and featuring larger, cushier public areas than the line's other ships. It's an odd-looking vessel—a very wide, tall catamaran—but streamlined and powerful, and able to get between ports faster than its competition. It has one lounge, one dining room, and outside observation decks. **Itineraries:** 7-night Inside Passage cruises between Juneau and Ketchikan visit Haines, Skagway, Sitka, Glacier Bay, Tracy Arm, Wrangell Narrows, Misty Fjords, and the Native village of Kake. **Rates:** $2,680–$3,580 outside. No inside cabins or suites. Rates include a precruise hotel stay in Juneau or Ketchikan, all shore excursions, and port charges. **Specifications:** Built 1986; passenger capacity 49; crew 18; tonnage 98; length 98.5 feet; cabins 25, all outside.

WILDERNESS ADVENTURER   Glacier Bay's soft-adventure ship, outfitted with sea kayaks and a kayak dry-launch platform in the stern. The ship itself is spartan—basic unfancy cabins, one lounge, one dining room, and outside viewing decks—but passengers who book aboard are more interested in what's outside than in. The ship was constructed to sail in tough-to-navigate waters, and is low slung, maneuverable, and quiet, with an incredibly shallow draft and a bow ramp that allows it to nose right up onto dockless shoreline to allow passengers to explore. **Itineraries:** Six-night Inside Passage wilderness cruises round-trip from Juneau visit Glacier Bay, Tracy Arm, Admiralty Island, and other wild areas, avoiding busy ports and staying entirely in wilderness areas for kayaking, hiking, and wildlife watching—in a week's sail on this ship you might only see a couple of dozen other people, so far does it stay from well-traveled routes. **Rates:** $1,990–$2,215 inside, $2,280–$2,775 outside. No suites. Rates include a precruise hotel stay in Juneau, all shore excursions, and port charges. **Specifications:** Built 1984; passengers 74; crew 22; tonnage 89; length 156.6 feet; cabins, 30 outside, 5 inside.

WILDERNESS DISCOVERER   This ship is almost identical to the *Wilderness Adventurer,* above, though it sails port-to-port itineraries and so is not outfitted with kayaks or a launch platform. **Itineraries:** Six-night Inside Passage cruises round-trip from Juneau visit Skagway, Sitka, Glacier Bay, and Icy Strait. **Rates:** $1,980–$2,180 inside, $2,180–$2,780 outside. No suites. Rates include a precruise hotel stay in Juneau, all shore excursions (including a tramway ride and river float trip), and port charges. **Specifications:** Built 1992; passengers 86; crew 22; tonnage 95; length 169 feet; cabins, 37 outside, 6 inside.

WILDERNESS EXPLORER   The *Wilderness Explorer* offers the most active cruise experience available in Alaska, with cruises structured so passengers are out kayaking and hiking most of each day and only use the vessel to eat, sleep, and get from place to place. It's the line's most basic ship, with tiny cabins with bunk beds, one lounge/bar, one dining room, and an observation deck. You'll really feel like you're exploring on this one. **Itineraries:** 5-night Inside Passage adventure cruises between Juneau and Glacier Bay spend 2 full days in Glacier Bay and 2 in Icy Strait. The itinerary visits no ports; days are spent kayaking, hiking, and wildlife watching. **Rates:** $1,530–$1,690 outside. No inside cabins or suites. Rates include transport between Juneau and Glacier Bay, all shore excursions, and port charges. **Specifications:** Built 1969; passengers 36; crew 13; tonnage 98; length 112 feet; 18 cabins, all outside.

AMERICAN SAFARI CRUISES

1724 W. Marine View Dr., Seattle, WA 98201. ☎ **800/325-6722** or 425/252-6800. Fax 425/252-6038. www.americansafaricruises.com.

Directed to the slightly jaded high-end traveler, American Safari Cruises (formerly Alaska Yacht Safaris) promises an intimate, all-inclusive yacht cruise to some of the more out-of-the-way stretches of the Inside Passage. The price is considerable, as is the pampering. A crew-to-passenger ratio of one to two ensures that a cold drink, a clever meal, or a sharp eagle-spotting eye is always nearby on the line's 120-foot ships.

BEST FEATURES   The company books only 12 to 22 people per cruise, guaranteeing unparalleled flexibility, intimacy, and privacy. Black-bear aficionados can chug off in a Zodiac boat for a better look, active adventurers can explore the shoreline in one of the yacht's four kayaks, and lazier travelers can relax aboard ship. Another big plus: All off-ship excursions—including a flightseeing trip—are included in the cruise fare, as are drinks.

TYPICAL PASSENGERS   Passengers—almost always couples—tend to be more than comfortably wealthy and range from 45 to 65 years of age. Most hope to get close to nature without sacrificing luxury.

ACTIVITIES & ENTERTAINMENT   Off-vessel expeditions include trips to boardwalked cannery villages and to Tlingit villages. Activities throughout the day are well spaced, with many opportunities to see wildlife. A big-screen TV in the main lounge forms a natural center for impromptu lectures during the day and movie-watching at night.

DINING   A shipboard chef assails guests with multiple-course meals and creative snacks, barters with nearby fishing boats for the catch of the day, and raids local markets for the freshest fruits and vegetables. Between meals, snacks are set out, and guests may always serve themselves from the ludicrously well-stocked bar.

SHIPS
SAFARI QUEST

More private yacht than cruise ship, the *Safari Quest* looks like a Ferrari, all sleek, contoured lines and dark glass. One old tar we met called it "the Tupperware ship." Inside, there are very few areas out of bounds, lending to the feel that you're vacationing on an impossibly rich friend's space-age yacht. Cabins are comfortable, and sitting rooms are intimate and luxurious, almost as if they had been transported whole from a spacious suburban home. Four or five prime vantages for spotting wildlife (one is a hot tub!) ensure as little or as much privacy as you desire. **Itineraries:** Two different itineraries: (1) 7-night Inside Passage cruises between Juneau and Sitka visit Tracy Arm, Frederick Sound, Petersburg, Kake, and Warm Springs Bay. (2)10-night shoulder-season Inside Passage cruises between Juneau and Vancouver visit Tracy Arm, Petersburg, Ketchikan, Lowe Inlet, Prince Rupert, Bishops Bay, Alert Bay, and Seymour Narrows. **Rates:** 7-night $4,695–$6,495 outside (includes a pre-cruise overnight in a Juneau or Sitka hotel); 10-night $3,695–$5,495. No inside cabins or suites. Rates include port charges. **Specifications:** Built 1992; passengers 22; crew 9; tonnage n/a; length 120 feet; 11 cabins, all outside.

SAFARI SPIRIT   Almost identical to the *Safari Quest,* above, except more so, catering to only 12 passengers—by far the smallest passenger capacity of any cruise ship in Alaska. **Itineraries:** Two different itineraries. 7-night Inside Passage cruises between Juneau and Prince Rupert (BC) visit Tracy Arm, Petersburg, Anan Creek, Yes Bay, Misty Fjords, and Ketchikan. 10-night shoulder-season Inside Passage cruises follow the same route as the *Safari Quest,* above. **Rates:** 7-night $5,195–$7,395 outside (includes a pre-cruise overnight in a Juneau or Rupert Bay hotel); 10-night $3,895–$$6,595 outside. No inside cabins or suites. Rates include port charges. **Specifications:** Built 1981; passengers 12; crew 7; tonnage n/a; length 105 feet; 6 cabins, all outside.

CLIPPER CRUISE LINE

7711 Bonhomme Ave., St. Louis, MO 63105. ☎ **800/325-0010.** Fax 314/727-6576. www.clippercruise.com.

Honored by *Condé Nast Traveller* as one of the top-10 cruise lines in the world, Clipper's operation is more sophisticated and service-oriented than most other lines with ships this size, and the fact that its cruises are led by professional naturalists means passengers also get a full-on experience of natural Alaska in the bargain. As aboard Alaska's other small-ship lines, the onboard atmosphere is casual, the organized activities are few (mostly lectures), and what lies out there beyond the ship's rail is most passengers' real focus.

BEST FEATURES   Along with Cruise West's *Spirit of Endeavor* and *Spirit of '98,* and Glacier Bay's *Executive Explorer,* the *Yorktown Clipper* is one of the best choices in Alaska for someone who wants small-ship intimacy and flexibility but doesn't want to skimp on comfort. Its staff is friendly, and its **itineraries** mix the more popular ports with out-of-the-way destinations.

TYPICAL PASSENGERS   Passengers are generally over 55, educated, and financially sound, with relatively high expectations when it comes to food, comfort, and overall experience. While they want to experience Alaska's natural wonders—whales, glaciers, woodlands—they're not necessarily run-the-rapids types.

ACTIVITIES & ENTERTAINMENT   Lectures and videos on Alaska make up the bulk of the entertainment program, and a nightly **social hour** encourages passengers to mix and mingle. Motorized landing craft, carried aboard the ship, ferry passengers to remote beaches, pristine forests, small villages, and wildlife refuges, where naturalists and/or historians and other experts may conduct walking tours. As with other small ships, there are no special facilities or activities for children.

DINING   Meals are a cut above the average fare served on other small-ship cruise lines. Fresh salmon, Alaska king crab, and other regional specialties are highlighted. There are two dressy evenings on each cruise, but they don't require formal attire, just a sports jacket for men and a skirt or pantsuit for women—though only about half the passengers dress up.

SHIP

YORKTOWN CLIPPER   Rising four decks above the water, the 138-passenger *Yorktown Clipper* is dominated by big picture windows that ensure bright interior public spaces and allow comfortable areas for viewing passing scenery. Shipboard life is easygoing, centered around wildlife watching, conversation, and enjoyment of naturalist lectures and informal talks. All cabins are outside, and except for those at the lowest level, most have picture windows. They're modern and pleasantly decorated. Public areas are larger and more inviting than most ships of comparable size, but remain cozy enough to engender camaraderie among crew and passengers. **Itineraries:** 7-night Inside Passage cruises north- and southbound between Juneau and Ketchikan visit Tracy Arm, the Inian Islands, Elfin Cove, Sitka, Chatham Strait, Petersburg, and Misty Fjords. **Rates:** Outside cabins $2,200–$3,800. No inside cabins, no suites. Rates include port charges. **Specifications:** Built 1988; passengers 138; crew 40; tonnage 97; length 257 feet; 69 cabins, all outside.

CRUISE WEST

4th and Battery Building, Suite 700, Seattle, WA 98121. ☎ **800/426-7702** or 206/441-8687. Fax 206/441-4757. www.smallship.com.

The operative words here are *casual, relaxed,* and *friendly.* At sea, the lack of organized activities leaves you free to scan for wildlife, peruse the natural sights, or read a book. In port—whether one of the large, popular ports or a less-visited one—the line arranges some novel, intimate shore excursions, such as a visit with local artists at their home outside Haines, or an educational walking tour led by Native guide Joe Williams in Ketchikan. These trips are for people who want to visit Alaska's port towns and see its wilderness areas up close and in a relaxed, comfortable, small-scale environment without big-ship distractions; they're not for people who want to spend their days hiking and kayaking.

BEST FEATURES   The line's friendly, enthusiastic staffs are a big, big plus, making guests feel right at home, and its list of **shore excursions** includes some real gems. Also, a couple of the line's ships—the *Spirit of Endeavor,* a sleek, yachtlike vessel, and *Spirit of '98,* a re-creation of a late 19th-century coastal steamer—offer **snazzier surroundings** than most of their small-ship competitors.

TYPICAL PASSENGERS   Passengers with Cruise West tend to be older (typically around 60 to 75), financially stable, and well educated, and consider themselves adventuresome.

ACTIVITIES & ENTERTAINMENT   As with other small ships, Cruise West vessels don't offer much in the way of diversion. A cheerful and knowledgeable **cruise coordinator** accompanies each trip to answer passengers' questions about Alaska's flora, fauna, geology, and history; and Forest Service rangers, local fishers, and Native Alaskans sometimes come aboard to give **informal talks** about the culture and industry of the state. Binoculars are provided for onboard use. Videos are available on some ships for in-cabin use. Onboard fitness options are limited to the exercise bike and/or Stairmaster each ship carries.

DINING   Breakfast, lunch, and dinner are served at set times at one unassigned seating. At all meals the fare is primarily home-style American—not overly fancy, but tasty and varied. Chefs make a point of stocking up on fresh salmon and crabs while in port. The galley can accommodate special diets (vegetarian, kosher, low-salt, low-fat), but be sure to make special arrangements for this when you book your cruise.

SHIPS

SHELTERED SEAS   This is an odd one—like a road trip, but by boat, cruising Alaska's waterways by day and depositing you at a hotel in one of the ports at night. Additional travel by rail or motor coach allows visits to Fairbanks and Denali National Park, and the timing of your arrival in ports—generally in the early evening—means that you'll be hitting the town after the crowds from larger cruise ships have left. If you can't decide between cruising Alaska and seeing it by land, this is an option worth exploring. **Itineraries:** 4- and 5-night cruises between Ketchikan and Juneau visit Wrangell, Petersburg, Tracy Arm, and LeConte Glacier (5-night adds Misty Fjords and a second night in Ketchikan). **Rates:** 4-night cruises from $995; 5-night cruises from $1,395, including all shore-side accommodation, port charges, and all meals aboard ship.

SPIRIT OF '98   The *Spirit of '98* is a time machine. Built as a replica 19th-century steamship in 1984 and extensively refurbished in 1995, it carries its Victorian flavor so well that fully two-thirds of the people we met on board thought the ship had been a private yacht at the turn of the century. Cabins are comfortable and of decent size, and feature TV/VCR combos. The lounge and dining room are both lovely, and the outside viewing decks include an exceptionally large open bow. Note: The *'98* is the only small ship in Alaska that has an elevator and a cabin that's wheelchair friendly. **Itineraries:** 7-night Inside Passage cruises between Seattle and Juneau visit Ketchikan, Frederick Sound, Misty Fjords, Glacier Bay, and either Sitka or Skagway and Haines. **Rates:** $2,565–$4,385 outside, $5,145–$5,695 suite. No inside cabins. Rates include a pre- or postcruise hotel stay in Juneau. **Specifications:** Built 1984; passengers 96; crew 23; tonnage 96; length 192 feet; 49 cabins, all outside.

SPIRIT OF ALASKA   Less fancy than the *Spirit of Endeavor* and *'98* (and, in fact, very similar to Glacier Bay's *Wilderness Adventurer* and *Discoverer* and Special Expeditions' *Sea Bird* and *Sea Lion*). Cabins are very snug, but comfortable, with light, airy decor. There's one dining room, a lounge that can get a little tight when all passengers try to squeeze in, a couple of exercise machines, and a video library. **Itineraries:** Seven-night Inside Passage cruises between Ketchikan and Juneau visit Glacier Bay, Misty Fjords, LeConte Bay, Tracy Arm, Metlakatla, Petersburg, Sitka, Haines, and Skagway. **Rates:** $2,315–$2,645 inside, $3,065–$3,995 outside. No suites. Rates include a pre- or postcruise hotel stay in Juneau. **Specifications:** Built 1980; passengers 78; crew 21; tonnage 97; length 143 feet; cabins, 27 outside, 12 inside.

SPIRIT OF COLUMBIA   This ship is almost identical to the *Spirit of Alaska*, discussed above. **Itineraries:** 3- and 4-night Prince William Sound cruises round-trip from Whittier (near Anchorage) visit Blackstone Bay, King's Bay, College and Harriman fjords, Esther Passage, Columbia Glacier, and Valdez (4-night cruise adds a call at Cordova). **Rates:** 3-night cruises $875–$955 inside, $1,255–$1,475 outside, $1,615–$1,665 suite; 4-night cruises $1,045–$1,155 inside, $1,495–$1,775 outside, $1,945–$2,015 suite. Rates include port charges. **Specifications:** Built 1979; passengers 78; crew 21; tonnage 97; length 143 feet; cabins, 27 outside, 12 inside.

SPIRIT OF DISCOVERY   This ship is almost identical to the *Spirit of Alaska*, discussed above, though it's slightly larger and has all outside cabins. **Itineraries:** Two different itineraries: (1) 7-night Inside Passage cruises between Seattle and Juneau (same as 7-night *Spirit of '98*, above). (2) 7-night Inside Passage cruises between Ketchikan and Juneau (same as *Spirit of Alaska*, above). **Rates:** Seattle-Juneau, $2,625–$3,815 outside. Ketchikan-Juneau, $2,815–$4,445 outside. No suites. Rates include a pre- or postcruise hotel stay in Juneau and all port charges. **Specifications:** Built 1976; passengers 84; crew 21; tonnage 94; length 166 feet; 43 cabins . . . all outside.

SPIRIT OF GLACIER BAY   Almost identical to the *Spirit of Alaska, Columbia,* and *Discovery,* discussed above, though it's smaller. **Itineraries:** 3- and 4-night Prince William Sound cruises round-trip from Whittier (same as *Spirit of Columbia,* above). **Rates:** 3-night cruises $775–$895 inside, $1,225–$1,345 outside; 4-night cruises $935–$1,075 inside, $1,465–1,595 outside. No suites. Rates include port charges. **Specifications:** Built 1971; passengers 52; crew 16; tonnage 97; length 125 feet; cabins, 14 outside, 13 inside.

SPIRIT OF ENDEAVOR   The flagship of Cruise West, this stealthy, quiet, nicely decorated vessel offers a higher level of small-ship comfort than the other Cruise West ships, and among the highest of all small ships in Alaska. Cabins are well appointed. There's one dining room, a piano lounge/bar decorated with considerable style, and outside viewing decks. **Itineraries:** Seven-night Inside Passage cruises between Seattle and Juneau (same as *Spirit of '98,* above). **Rates:** $2,565–$4,385 outside. No suites. Rates include a pre- or postcruise hotel stay in Juneau. **Specifications:** Built 1983; passengers 102; crew 25; tonnage 99; length 217 feet; 51 cabins, all outside.

SPECIAL EXPEDITIONS

720 Fifth Ave., New York, NY 10019. ☎ **800/762-0003** or 212/765-7740. Fax 212/265-3770. www.specialexpeditions.com.

Special Expeditions specializes in environmentally sensitive, soft-adventure vacations to remote places in the world. The trips are explorative and informal in nature, designed to appeal to the intellectually curious traveler seeking a vacation that's educational as well as relaxing. Days aboard are spent learning about the Alaskan outdoors from high-caliber expedition leaders trained in botany, anthropology, biology, and geology, and observing the world around you either from the ship or on shore excursions, which are included in the cruise package. (*Tip:* Bring your own binoculars.) Educational films and slide presentations aboard ship precede nature hikes and quick jaunts aboard Zodiac boats.

BEST FEATURES   Rather than relying on **shore excursions** run by outside concessionaires—which can get mighty touristy—Special Expeditions runs theirs as an integral part of their cruises (costs of which are included in the cruise fare). Add in the guidance provided by onboard **expedition leaders** and you have a really personal Alaskan adventure.

TYPICAL PASSENGERS   Passengers tend to be over 55, educated, relatively well off, and physically active (even so, the ships become very quiet not long after dinner; everyone crashes early to store up energy for the next day's adventures). As there are no facilities for children, these ships are not really suitable for families.

ACTIVITIES & ENTERTAINMENT   Aboard ship, there are no organized activities aside from talks and film presentations from onboard naturalists. Off the ship, naturalists lead guests on frequent trips ashore in Zodiac boats. Like other small-ship lines, Special Expeditions builds plenty of flexibility into its cruise schedules to allow its ships to search for whales or stop for a cookout in a quiet cove.

DINING   Meals feature hearty but basic American fare at single open seatings.

SHIPS

SEA BIRD/SEA LION   The shallow-draft *Sea Lion* and *Sea Bird* are identical twins, right down to their decor schemes and furniture. Unfancy, with just two public rooms and utilitarian cabins, they're very similar to other "expedition style" small ships, such as Glacier Bay's *Wilderness Adventurer* and Cruse West's *Spirit of Alaska* (as a matter of fact, the *Spirit of Alaska* and the two Special Expedition ships all sailed at one time for the now-defunct Exploration Cruise Lines). Cabins are small and functional, and public space is limited to the open sundeck and bow areas, the dining room, and an observation lounge that serves as the nerve center for activities. **Itineraries:** 7-night Inside Passage cruises between Juneau and Sitka visit Tracy Arm, Le Conte Bay, Haines, Glacier Bay, and Point Adolphus. **Rates:** $3,580 "portlight" cabins (portlights provide some light, but no view), $4,280–$5,120 outside. No suites. Rates include port charges. **Specifications:** Built 1981/1982; passengers 70; crew 22; tonnage 100; length 152 feet; 37 cabins, all outside.

4 Midsized Educational Cruising

WORLD EXPLORER CRUISES

555 Montgomery St., San Francisco, CA 94111-2544. ☎ **800/854-3835** or 415/393-1565. Fax 415/391-1145. www.wecruise.com.

This is a real one-of-a-kind Alaska cruise experience that combines a relatively large ship (the dowdy, 740-passenger *Universe Explorer*) with an education-oriented approach more typical of a small-ship line. The ship offers an incredible itinerary, an educational lecture series, an atmosphere of friendly informality, and some truly high-caliber shore excursions. You'll find chamber music, lectures by people who know their subject, and more ports (and lots of time in them) than aboard any other ship sailing Alaska.

BEST FEATURES   The **itinerary** wins in this category, hands down. The *Universe Explorer* specializes in 14-night round-trip cruises out of Vancouver—the only round-trips of that length out of the British Columbia gateway—that offer all of the popular ports of call along with a few extra for good measure—Haines, for instance, and also Wrangell, Valdez, and Seward. As an alternative, the company will repeat a 9-night round-trip introduced last year, again out of Vancouver, featuring the best of the Inside Passage, including Haines and an overnight stop at Metlakatla, a Tsimshian Native village on Annette Island, just south of Ketchikan. For 2000, there will be three of these shorter voyages (in May, August, and September), and seven of the line's bread-and-butter 2-weekers, which the company bills as "The Uncommon Route."

Honorable mention in the "Best Features" department has to go to the ship's 16,000-volume **library** and its **onboard lecture** schedule.

TYPICAL PASSENGERS   The *Universe Explorer* tends to attract an older clientele, though the average age of its passengers is declining, mostly due to bike/hike-and-cruise options that allow passengers to bike or hike their way through the ports of call. These more active shore excursions appeal to a family market. It's not unusual for the ship to sail with between, say, 15 and 30 teens and preteens on board. There is a youth program and a team of counselors.

ACTIVITIES & ENTERTAINMENT   The ecology and the cultures of Alaska are big on the ship's **lecture circuit** log, and there is a 150-seat cinema for movie watching, as well as a 16-terminal **computer learning center** operated by a company called SeniorNet. With regard to entertainment, one night it might be a string quartet, the next a cello soloist, a classical pianist, or an operatic soprano or cabaret singer.

DINING   The food is good and nobody leaves the table hungry, but, again, it could never be mistaken for gourmet cuisine.

SHIP

UNIVERSE EXPLORER   Since the *Universe Explorer* is World Explorer Cruises' only vessel, the company takes *really* good care of it. The ship has nice but not spectacular public spaces and adequate if not palatial cabins. It's a good buy for those who don't want frills and fripperies or too much dressing up and who don't expect the last word in pampering. The bulk of the ship is taken up with double-occupancy rooms with twin beds (convertible to queen-size). Some also are capable of accommodating a third passenger in a foldaway sofa bed. Public areas are fairly spartan. It has a functional reception area, lounge/bar facilities, a comfortable but not glamorous show room, and a huge library, with many selections on nature and wildlife. **Itineraries:** Two different itineraries: (1) 14-night Inside Passage/Gulf itinerary round-trip from Vancouver visits Ketchikan, Metlakatla, Sitka, Haines, Seward, Valdez, Hubbard Glacier, Skagway, Juneau, Wrangell, Victoria, Glacier Bay, and Yakutat Bay/Hubbard Glacier. $1,445–$3,550 cabins, $3,395–$3,850 suites. (2) 9-night Inside Passage itinerary round-trip from Vancouver visits Ketchikan, Juneau, Haines, Glacier Bay, Metlakatla, and Victoria. **Rates:** $1,145–$2,265 cabins, $2,095–$2,465 suites. Port charges on the 14-night cruise are an additional $175; on the 9-night cruise, $115. **Specifications:** Built 1958; passengers 739; crew 330; tonnage 23,500; length 617 feet; cabins, 290 outside, 78 inside.

5 The Big-Ship Cruise Lines

The ships featured in this section vary in size, age, and offerings, but share the common thread of having all the facilities you can imagine on a cruise ship, and sometimes more. You will not be roughing it. On these ships you'll find swimming pools, health clubs, spas, nightclubs, movie theaters, shops, casinos, multiple restaurants, bars, and special kids' playrooms, and in some cases sports decks, virtual golf, computer rooms, and cigar clubs, as well as quiet spaces where you can get away from it all. In most cases, you'll find lots and lots of onboard activities including games, contests, classes, and lectures, plus a variety of entertainment options and show productions, some very sophisticated.

CARNIVAL CRUISE LINES

3655 NW 87th Ave., Miami, FL 33178-2428. ☎ **800/CARNIVAL.** Fax 305/471-4740. www.carnival.com.

Carnival is the Big Kahuna of the cruise industry, but translating the line's warm-weather "24-hour orgy of good times" philosophy to Alaska's "look at the bears and whales!" temperament isn't an easy trick. Do passengers really belly up to the rail with a multicolored party drink to gawk at a glacier? In its Alaska brochure, the line says that, like the prospectors, you might find yourself shouting "Eureka"—but in the ship's casino, not at a gold rush site.

BEST FEATURES **Entertainment** is among the industry's best, with each ship boasting a dozen dancers, a 12-piece orchestra, comedians, jugglers, and numerous live bands, as well as a big casino. For kids, the line offers **Camp Carnival,** an expertly run children's program with activities that include Native arts and crafts sessions, lectures conducted by wildlife experts, and special shore excursions for teens.

TYPICAL PASSENGERS Overall, Carnival has some of the youngest demographics in the industry: mostly under 50, including couples, lots of singles, and a good share of families. It's the same middle America crowd that can be found in Las Vegas and Atlantic City and at Florida's megaresorts.

ACTIVITIES & ENTERTAINMENT *Nonstop* is the key word. Cocktails begin to flow before lunch, and through the course of the day you can learn to country line dance or ballroom dance, take cooking lessons, learn to play bridge, watch first-run movies, practice your golf swing by smashing balls into a net, join in a knobby-knee contest, or just eat, drink, shop, and then eat again. Alaska-specific naturalist lectures are delivered daily. In port, Carnival offers **more than 60 shore excursions,** divided into categories of easy, moderate, and adventure.

DINING Food is bountiful, geared toward a middle-American audience. Red meat is a popular item on these ships. Carnival bans smoking in its dining rooms.

SHIP

JUBILEE The *Jubilee* is one of the older ships in the Carnival fleet, but still offers a good variety of public spaces and a creative interior design. Cabins are larger than many others you'll find in the same price category; all offer TV and telephone. Among the ship's public rooms, the *Wizard of Oz*–themed Oz Dance Club is a standout, and there are about a dozen bars and lounges. **Itineraries:** Three different itineraries. (1) 7-night northbound itinerary between Vancouver and Seward/Anchorage visits College Fjord, Skagway, Juneau, Ketchikan, and Sitka, and cruises Endicott or Tracy Arm. (2) 7-night southbound itinerary between Seward and Vancouver visits Valdez, Skagway, Juneau, and Ketchikan, and cruises Yakutat Bay (to view Hubbard Glacier).

(3) 7-night Glacier Bay itinerary, round-trip from Vancouver, visits Juneau, Skagway, Ketchikan, the Inside Passage and Glacier Bay. **Rates:** $1,559–$2,309 cabins, $2,659–$2,959 suites, per person, double occupancy. Rates include port charges. **Specifications:** Built 1986; passengers 1,486; crew 670; tonnage 47,262; length 733 feet; cabins, 453 outside (10 with verandas), 290 inside.

CELEBRITY CRUISES

5201 Blue Lagoon Dr., Miami, Fl 33126. ☎ **800/437-3111** or 305/262-8322. Fax 800/ 437-5111. www.celebrity-cruises.com.

Celebrity Cruises offers a great combination: a classy, tasteful, and luxurious cruise experience at a moderate price. The line's ships are beautiful; its cuisine outstanding; its service first-class, friendly, and unobtrusive; and its spa facilities among the best in the business. The line has its two newest ships, 1995's *Galaxy* and 1997's *Mercury,* in Alaskan waters.

BEST FEATURES   These ships are real works of art and definitely the **best in the midpriced category.** Particularly high marks go to **food** and **spas.**

TYPICAL PASSENGERS   The typical guest is less party-oriented, more sophisticated, and more independent-minded than aboard a lot of other megaships. You'll find everyone from kids to retirees.

ACTIVITIES & ENTERTAINMENT   A typical day might offer bridge, darts, a culinary art demonstration, a trapshooting competition, a fitness fashion show, an art auction, a volleyball tournament, and a none-too-shabby stage show. **Lectures** on the various ports of call, the Alaskan environment, glaciers, and Alaskan culture are given by resident experts. Celebrity ships also employ a group of counselors who direct and supervise a camp-style **children's program.** Activities are geared toward different age groups. There's an impressive kids' play area and a separate lounge area for teens.

DINING   Celebrity's dining experience is meticulously guided by Michel Roux, the line's celebrity culinary consultant and one of the top French chefs in Britain. Cuisine is extraspecial, and tends to lean toward the French (which also means it's not generally low fat, although healthy alternatives are always available). Alaska cruises offer an array of **Pacific Northwest regional specialties,** and vegetarian dishes are offered at both lunch and dinner.

SHIPS

GALAXY / MERCURY   Sleek, modern, and stunningly designed, these sister ships have a lot of open deck space, and lots of large windows provide access to the wide skies and the grand Alaskan vistas. Overall, there are no really bad cabins on these ships—inside cabins are about par for the industry standard, outside cabins are larger than usual, and suites (which come with butler service) are particularly spacious. Startlingly modern art—by the likes of Robert Rauschenberg, Jasper Johns, David Hockney, Pablo Picasso, Andy Warhol, or Richard Serra—is scattered throughout both vessels. Both ships feature incredible spas with hydrotherapy pools, steam rooms, and saunas, plus health and beauty services and exceptionally large fitness areas. **Itineraries:** *Galaxy:* Seven-night round-trip cruises from Vancouver visit Juneau, Skagway, Haines, Hubbard Glacier, and Ketchikan. *Mercury* sails two different itineraries: (1) Seven-night north- and southbound Gulf of Alaska cruises between Vancouver and Seward/Anchorage (northbound cruises visit Ketchikan, Juneau, Skagway, Hubbard Glacier, Valdez, and College Fjord; southbound visit Hubbard Glacier, Juneau, Skagway, Sitka, and Ketchikan). (2) 7-night round-trip Inside Passage cruises from Vancouver visit Juneau, Skagway, Hubbard Glacier, and Ketchikan. **Rates:** *Galaxy:*

$1,299–$5,895 cabins, $3,949–$9,195 suites; *Mercury:* $1,399–$5,995 cabins, $4,949–$6,849 suites. Rates include port charges. **Specifications:** Built 1996/1997; passengers 1,870; crew 909; tonnage 77,713; length 866 feet; cabins, 639 outside (220 with verandas), 296 inside.

CRYSTAL CRUISES

2049 Century Park East, Suite 1400, Los Angeles, CA 90067. ☎ **800/446-6620** or 310/785-9300. Fax 310/785-3891. www.crystalcruises.com.

Luxury all the way. Crystal offers all the amenities of much bigger ships, but in a more luxurious and intimate atmosphere, with only 940 passengers. Everything is first class, with fine attention paid to detail and to making guests feel comfortable. Service on the ship is nothing short of superb.

BEST FEATURES Excellent cuisine, elegant service, handsome public areas, sparkling entertainment, impressive guest quarters—the *Crystal Harmony* has it all. Another of the *Harmony*'s selling points is its itinerary: It will be one of only two ships this year (with Princess's *Sky Princess*) to offer of Alaska cruises out of San Francisco.

TYPICAL PASSENGERS Passengers aboard Crystal tend to be successful business-people who can afford to pay for the best. Many are under 50, with the average age probably closer to 60 than 70. Whatever their age, they'll tend to be people who like to dress up rather than down. "Casual night" doesn't mean the same thing to Crystal guests as it means to other people.

ACTIVITIES & ENTERTAINMENT *Crystal Harmony* carries a battery of Alaska naturalists, environmentalists, and National Park Service rangers to educate and entertain passengers in the wilderness areas of the 49th state. The line's **food-and-wine series** presents well-known chefs and wine experts who put on food preparation demonstrations, lecture on the art of cookery, and prepare dinner one night during the cruise. A **PGA-approved golf pro** accompanies practically every *Harmony* cruise, conducting clinics along the way. The *Harmony* also has a flourishing **computer room** on board, with training for the uninitiated. There's dazzling show-lounge entertainment, first-run movies, and a casino operated by Caesar's World, parent company of Caesar's Palace.

DINING Cuisine aboard the *Harmony* is superbly prepared and professionally served, with a choice of at least four entrees, health-conscious vegetarian dishes, and a pasta offering nightly.

SHIP

CRYSTAL HARMONY A handsome ship by any standard, *Crystal Harmony* has one of the highest passenger-space ratios of any cruise ship. Its cabins are large, well appointed, and tastefully decorated with quality fittings and in agreeable color tones. Almost half of them have private verandas. Public rooms are classy throughout. Two alternative restaurants, Prego (Italian, mostly northern) and Kyoto (Asian/Japanese), introduce variety to the dining experience. **Itineraries:** Four different itineraries. (1) Twelve-night round-trips departing from San Francisco visit Victoria, Ketchikan, Juneau, Skagway, Sitka, and Glacier Bay. (2) 12-night cruises between San Francisco and Vancouver visit Sitka, Skagway, the Gulf of Alaska, Hubbard Glacier, Juneau, Ketchikan, and Glacier Bay. (3) 10-night round-trip from Vancouver visit Sitka, Skagway, Juneau, Ketchikan, Victoria, Glacier Bay, and Tracy Arm. (4) 11-night Vancouver to San Francisco sailing visits Sitka, Skagway, Juneau, Ketchikan, the Gulf, Hubbard Glacier, and Glacier Bay. **Rates:** 12-night, $2,575–$7,605 cabins, $6,965–$17,510 suites; 11-night, $4,400–$8,580 cabins, $10,380–$21,535 suites;

10-night, $3,435–$6,335 cabins, $7,995–$14,590 suites. All rates include port charges. **Specifications:** Built 1990; passengers 940; crew 545; tonnage 49,400; length 791 feet; cabins, 461 outside (260 with verandas), 19 inside.

HOLLAND AMERICA LINE–WESTOURS

300 Elliott Ave. W., Seattle, WA 98119. ☎ **800/426-0327** or 206/281-3535. Fax 206/286-7110. www.hollandamerica.com.

Holland America (HAL) can be summed up in one word: *tradition.* The company was formed way back in 1873 as the Netherlands-America Steamship Company, and its ships today strive to present an aura of history and dignity, like a European hotel where they never let rock stars register. Though most of the line's Alaskan fleet is relatively young, the ships are designed with a decidedly "classic" feel—no flashing neon lights need apply. As for service, the line employs primarily Filipino and Indonesian staff members who are uniformly fantastic—gracious and friendly without being cloying.

BEST FEATURES The expertise that comes with having a lot of tradition. Also, HAL includes a lot of little extras in its cruise fare (no extra charge, for instance, for a latte or cappuccino).

TYPICAL PASSENGERS Though it still caters mostly to the older crowd that's long been its bread and butter, the average age is dropping, partly thanks to an increased emphasis on its children's program.

ACTIVITIES & ENTERTAINMENT Holland America's ships are heavy on more mature, less frenetic kinds of activities. You'll find good bridge programs and music to dance (or just listen) to in the bars and lounges, plus health spas and the other amenities found on most large ships. The line has improved its nightly **show-lounge entertainment,** which was once, frankly, not so hot. Each week includes a **crew talent show** in which the Indonesian and Filipino staff members perform their countries' songs and dances. Club HAL is one of the industry's more creative children's programs, though the children's playrooms are no match for what you find on the latest Princess or Celebrity megaships.

DINING Years ago, HAL's meals were about as traditional as its architecture and its itineraries. In the last few years, though, it's become a lot more adventurous in all three areas, and the quality is generally high throughout the fleet.

SHIPS

NIEUW AMSTERDAM The smallest and oldest ship in the Holland America fleet this summer, *Nieuw Amsterdam* is traditional in design, with no private verandas. Cabins are comfortably sized. Public rooms are low-key, tasteful, and appealing, with very little glitz and absolutely nothing jarring. **Itineraries:** Two itineraries. (1) 7-night northbound/southbound Gulf of Alaska cruises between Vancouver and Seward visit Ketchikan, Juneau, Sitka, Hubbard Glacier, Valdez, and College Fjord. (2) 7-night round-trip Inside Passage cruises from Vancouver (offered only twice, in May) visit Juneau, Skagway, Haines, Glacier Bay, and Ketchikan. **Rates:** $899–$2,510 cabins, $2,165–$3,020 suites, per person, double occupancy. Rates include port charges. **Specifications:** Built 1983; passengers 1,214; crew 566; tonnage 33,390; length 704 feet; cabins, 411 outside, 194 inside.

STATENDAM / RYNDAM / VEENDAM These three are identical to one another and a lot bigger and more spacious than the *Nieuw Amsterdam.* All cabins have a sitting area and lots of closet and drawer space, and even the least expensive inside cabins run almost 190 square feet, quite large by industry standards. Outside doubles have either picture windows or verandas. The striking dining rooms, two-tiered show-rooms, and Crow's Nest forward bar/lounges are among these ships' best features. **Itineraries:** The *Statendam* and *Ryndam* follow the same route as *Nieuw Amsterdam,* above. The *Veendam* sails 7-night Inside Passage cruises, round-trip from Vancouver, visiting Juneau, Skagway, Glacier Bay, and Ketchikan. **Rates:** *Statendam/Ryndam:* $1,099–$2,660 cabins, $2,769–$4,970 suites; *Veendam:* $1,249–$2,810 cabins, $2,881–$5,120 suites. Rates include port charges. **Specifications:** Built 1993/1994/ 1996; passengers 1,266; crew 571; tonnage 69,130; length 720 feet; cabins, 485 out-side (149 with verandas), 148 inside.

VOLENDAM   Holland America pulled out all the stops on its newest ship: The cen-terpiece of the striking triple-decked oval atrium, for instance, is a glass sculpture by Luciano Vistosi, one of Italy's leading practitioners of the art. The 197 suites and deluxe staterooms have private verandas, and the smallest of the remaining 523 is a comfortable 190 square feet. The ship has five showrooms and lounges, and an alter-native restaurant designed as an artist's bistro, featuring drawings and etchings. Throughout, the *Volendam*'s art collection and interior motif is themed around flowers. **Itinerary:** Follows the same route as *Veendam,* above. **Rates:** $1,299–$2,885 cabins, $2,938–$5,195 suites, per person, double occupancy. Rates include port charges. **Specifications:** Built 1999; passengers 1,440; crew 647; tonnage 63,130; length 781 feet; cabins, 384 outside (197 with verandas), 139 inside.

WESTERDAM   This very long, comfortable, stately vessel is reminiscent of an old-time ocean liner, with portholes on some decks, a wide wraparound promenade, a truly lovely showroom, and spacious cabins and lounges. Cabins are large, and many are appointed in stately dark woods. None have verandas. Most public rooms are located on the spacious Promenade Deck, including several lounges/bars, a low-key disco, shops, a library, casino, and the Admiral's Lounge showroom, a truly lovely space which, with the lights dimmed, takes on a rich, dark, burgundy glow. Through-out the ship, artwork reflects the theme of Dutch exploration, with large-scale antique ship models and a salvaged cannon being standout display items. **Itinerary:** Follows same route as *Veendam,* above. **Rates:** $999–$3,320 cabins, $2,900–$4,370 suites, per person, double occupancy. Rates include port charges. **Specifications:** Built 1986; passengers 1,494; crew 639; tonnage 53,872; length 798 feet; cabins, 495 outside, 252 inside.

NORWEGIAN CRUISE LINE

7665 Corporate Center Dr., Miami, FL. 33126. ☎ **800/327-7030.** Fax 305/448-7936. www.ncl.com.

Norwegian Cruise Line (NCL) offers an informal and upbeat onboard atmosphere on medium-sized ships and a new megaship, the *Norwegian Sky,* that debuts in Alaska this year, inaugurating cruises for the line from Seattle. The line excels at activities. Recre-ational and fitness programs are among the best in the industry.

BEST FEATURES   Weekend sports games are broadcast in cabins and at the sports bars. And the line's **scuba program,** which includes snorkeling and scuba diving in Ketchikan (offered on the *Norwegian Wind* only), can't be beat.

TYPICAL PASSENGERS   In Alaska, the demographic tends more toward retirees than on the line's warmer-climate sailings, but you'll find families as well, including grandparents bringing along the grandkids.

ACTIVITIES & ENTERTAINMENT   In Alaska the line offers an Alaskan lecturer, wine tastings, art auctions, trap shooting, cooking demonstrations, craft and dance classes, incentive fitness program, and bingo, among other activities. Passengers can choose from over **65 shore excursions,** including snorkeling or scuba in Ketchikan and a good selection of soft-adventure shore excursions (including hiking, biking, and kayaking). **Entertainment** is generally strong, and includes Broadway-style musical productions. For kids, there's an activity room, video games, an ice-cream bar, and guaranteed baby-sitting aboard, plus a Polar Bear Pajama Party, sessions with park rangers, and escorted shore excursions.

DINING   In addition to the dining room, both ships have a Le Bistro alternative venue serving very good Italian food in a romantic setting. There's a recommended cover charge at Le Bistro of $5 per person. A chocolate midnight buffet, offered once during the cruise, has become an NCL standard.

SHIPS

NORWEGIAN SKY   The newest and biggest ship in the NCL fleet, with the industry's first Internet cafe at sea (with 10 computers) and photographers snapping digital photos on board that guests can e-mail home. Web access is also available from every cabin, for a fee. Other fun extras include a huge sundeck (complete with a driver in a golf cart delivering drinks), a basketball court and batting cage, and a wedding chapel (for in-port ceremonies only). The ship feels spacious and features a contemporary design that includes a glass-domed atrium midship that rises impressively for seven decks. Standard cabins average around 154 square feet (not particularly large). **Itineraries:** 7-night round-trip Inside Passage cruises from Seattle visit Glacier Bay or Sawyer Glacier, Haines, Skagway, Juneau, and Vancouver. **Rates:** $1,039–$6,839 cabins, $1,639–$6,839 suites. Rates include port charges. **Specifications:** Built 1999; passengers 2,002; crew 800; tonnage 80,000; length 848 feet; cabins, 574 outside (279 with verandas), 427 inside.

NORWEGIAN WIND   Formerly known as the *Windward,* this ship was literally cut in two and then stitched back together in 1998 with a new 130-foot midsection added. The addition increased its capacity by 500 berths and allowed for the addition of many new public rooms. For the sports-minded, the *Wind* has a fitness center, two heated pools, an unobstructed rubberized jogging/walking track, a sports bar with walls of TV screens showing ESPN, and a good selection of sports facilities. Cabins are fairly standard in size and vary little. Closet and drawer space is quite limited, so pack lightly. **Itineraries:** 7-night round-trip Inside Passage cruises from Vancouver visit Skagway, Haines, Juneau, Ketchikan, and Glacier Bay or Sawyer Glacier. **Rates:** $989–$3,139 cabins, $1,439–$5,439 suites. Rates include port charges. **Specifications:** Built 1993; passengers 1,726; crew 614; tonnage 46,000; length 758 feet; cabins, 651 outside (74 with verandas), 212 inside.

PRINCESS CRUISES

10100 Santa Monica Blvd., Los Angeles, CA 90067. ☎ **800/LOVE-BOAT** (568-3262) or 310/553-1770. Fax 310/277-6175. www.princesscruises.com.

Consistency is Princess's strength. With new ships joining its fleet like so many cars off a Detroit assembly line you'd think that maintaining acceptable service standards could be a problem. All things considered, though, Princess does this rather well.

BEST FEATURES   Throughout the fleet, the service in all areas—dining room, lounge, cabin maintenance, and so on—tends to be of consistently high quality. On shore, the line's shore-excursion staffs get big points for efficiency.

TYPICAL PASSENGERS   Typical Princess passengers are likely to be between, say, 50 and 65. Recent additional emphasis on its youth and children's facilities has begun to attract a bigger share of the **family market,** resulting in the passenger list becoming more active overall.

ACTIVITIES & ENTERTAINMENT Princess passengers can expect enough onboard activity to keep them going morning to night, if they've a mind to, and enough nooks and crannies to allow them to do absolutely nothing, if that's their thing. Kids are well taken care of, with especially large **children's playrooms** on the *Dawn, Ocean, Sea,* and *Sun.*

DINING The meals in general are good, if hardly gourmet. In the dining rooms, **pastas** are prepared table-side several times during each cruise.

SHIPS

DAWN PRINCESS / SEA PRINCESS / OCEAN PRINCESS / SUN PRINCESS

These four ships are virtually indistinguishable from one another except for cosmetics. Despite their size, you'll probably never feel crowded; there always seems to be lots of space on deck, in the buffet dining areas, and in the lounges. There are beautiful libraries, patisseries for pastries and cappuccino, and pizzerias for good made-to-order Italian fast food. The ships have extensive children's playrooms with ball drop, castles, computer games, puppet theatres, and more. As for cabins, even the smallest are a spacious 175 square feet, and more than 400 have private verandas. **Itineraries:** 7-night Gulf of Alaska cruises between Vancouver and Anchorage/Seward visit Ketchikan, Juneau, Skagway, Glacier Bay, and College Fjord. **Rates:** $1,549–$4,109 cabins, $4,259–$5,699 suites, per person, double occupancy. Rates include port charges. **Specifications:** Built 1995/1997/1998/2000; passengers 1,950; crew 900; tonnage 77,000; length 856 feet; cabins, 603 outside (411 with verandas), 372 inside.

REGAL PRINCESS The *Regal* is warm and inviting inside, and on the outside looks like—what? a spaceship? a *Star Wars* storm trooper's helmet? Spacious, well-furnished cabins are one of the ship's better features (standard dimensions about 190 square feet), and there are some interesting public rooms, like the huge observation lounge/casino/bar. **Itineraries:** 7-night Inside Passage cruises depart Vancouver, visiting Juneau, Skagway, Glacier Bay (or Hubbard Glacier on certain sailings) and Sitka. **Rates:** $1,649–$4,129 cabins, $3,999–$5,249 suites, per person, double occupancy. Rates include port charges. **Specifications:** Built 1991; passengers 1,590; crew 696; tonnage 70,000; length 811 feet; cabins, 614 outside (184 with verandas), 181 inside.

SKY PRINCESS Now about 16 years old, the *Sky Princess* is singing its Alaska swan song—after its 2000 season it will be renamed *Pacific Sky* and will take up a new position based in Sydney, Australia, operating South Pacific cruises for P&O, Princess's parent company. Because the ship was built before verandas became the vogue, only its top-10 suite accommodations have that feature. The standard cabins are relatively small, at 140 to 160 square feet. **Itineraries:** 11-night round-trips depart San Francisco, visiting Victoria, Vancouver, Juneau, Ketchikan, Skagway, and Hubbard Glacier. **Rates:** $2,799–$5,029 cabins, $5,899–$7,549 suites, per person, double occupancy. Rates include port charges. **Specifications:** Built 1984; passengers 1,200; crew 535; tonnage 46,000; length 789 feet; cabins, 383 outside (10 with verandas), 217 inside.

RADISSON SEVEN SEAS CRUISES

600 Corporate Dr., Suite 410, Fort Lauderdale, FL 33334. ☎ **800/477-7500.** www.rssc.com.

Radisson offers the best in food, service, and accommodations in an environment that's a little more casual and small shiplike than Crystal's. This year marks the first year the line has done a full season in Alaska, and it make its entrance with a brand new all-suite ship, the *Seven Seas Navigator,* and brand new itineraries.

BEST FEATURES   The line has a no-tipping policy; excellent food, service, and accommodations; and creative shore excursions.

TYPICAL PASSENGERS   Radisson tends to attract high-income passengers aged 50 and up who don't like to flaunt their wealth. The typical passenger is well educated, well traveled, and inquisitive.

ACTIVITIES & ENTERTAINMENT   The line assumes for the most part passengers want to entertain themselves on board, so organized activities are limited; but they do include lectures by local experts, well-known authors, and the like, plus facilities for card and board games and the occasional dance lesson. There are three computers in the library of the *Seven Seas Navigator* to allow guests to send e-mail and view CD-ROMS. Entertainment includes production shows, cabaret acts, and local acts that come on board at ports. The library stocks books and movies guests can play on their in-cabin VCRs.

DINING   Radisson's cuisine is excellent, and would gain high marks even if it were on land. Service by professional waiters adds to the experience, as do little touches like fresh flowers on the tables. Complimentary wines are served at dinner. The main dining room is open seating (you can eat when and with whom you like). Seating is by reservation only in the alternative restaurant. There is also an outdoor grill, open on a weather-permitting basis during the day and on select evenings.

SHIP

SEVEN SEAS NAVIGATOR   Cabins on this Italian-built ship are all ocean-view suites, most with private verandas. The standard suite is a large 301 square feet; some suites can interconnect if you want to book two for additional space. In the public areas, the show lounge is designed to resemble a 1930s nightclub. There are two additional lounges plus a casino and the Connoisseur Club, a cushy venue for predinner drink and after-dinner fine brandy and cigars. The ship's spa offers Judith Jackson European spa treatments using a variety of herbal and water-based therapies. **Itineraries:** Four different itineraries. (1) 7-night round-trip Inside Passage cruises from Vancouver visit Tracy Arm, Juneau, Skagway, and Ketchikan. (2) 7-night Inside Passage/Gulf cruises between Vancouver and Seward visit Ketchikan, Juneau, Skagway, Sitka, Hubbard Glacier, and either Misty Fjords or Tracy Arm. (3) 11-night Inside Passage/Gulf Cruises from Vancouver to Seward visit Victoria, Misty Fjords, Ketchikan, Skagway, Juneau, Tracy Arm, Valdez and College Fjord. (4) 10-night Inside Passage/Gulf cruises from Seward to Vancouver visit College Fjord, Valdez, Hubbard Glacier, Sitka, Tracy Arm, Skagway, Haines, Juneau, Ketchikan, and Victoria. **Rates:** $2,995–$7,895 suites (7-night); $3,995–$10,495 (10-night); $4,395–$11,395 (11-night). **Specifications:** Built 1999; passengers 490; crew 313; tonnage 30,000; length 560 feet; cabins, 250 outside (214 with verandas), no inside.

ROYAL CARIBBEAN INTERNATIONAL

1050 Caribbean Way, Miami, FL 33132. ☎ **800/327-6700** or 305/379-4731. www.rccl. com.

Royal Caribbean sells a mass-market style of cruising that's reasonably priced and offered aboard enormous ships with every diversion imaginable. The ships are well run and tend to be informal—dress is informal most evenings.

BEST FEATURES   The *Vision* and *Rhapsody of the Seas* have elaborate health clubs and spas, covered swimming pools, and large open sundeck areas. The Viking Crown

Lounge and other glassed-in areas make excellent **observation rooms** to see the Alaska sights. Royal Caribbean spends big bucks on **entertainment,** which includes high-tech show productions. Headliners are often featured.

TYPICAL PASSENGERS The crowd on Royal Caribbean ships, like the decor, tends to be a notch down on the whoopee scale from what you find on Carnival. Passengers represent an age mix from 30 to 60, and a good number of families are attracted by the line's well-established and fine-tuned **kids' programs.**

ACTIVITIES & ENTERTAINMENT On the activity front, Royal Caribbean offers plenty of the standard cruise line fare—craft classes, horse racing, bingo, shuffleboard, deck games, line-dancing lessons, wine-and-cheese tastings, cooking demonstrations, art auctions, and the like. Port lectures are offered on topics such as Alaska wildlife, and the line offers some **65 shore excursions. Children's activities** are some of the most extensive afloat. In terms of entertainment, the line doesn't skimp, incorporating sprawling, high-tech cabaret stages into each of its ships.

DINING The food is okay, but not gourmet. Every menu contains selections designed for low-fat, low-cholesterol, and low-salt dining, as well as vegetarian and children's dishes.

SHIPS

RHAPSODY OF THE SEAS / VISION OF THE SEAS Almost identical, these huge ships are true floating cities. Plenty of nice touches—sumptuous, big-windowed health club/spas and loads of fine shopping, dining, and entertainment options—give them the feel of top-flight shore resorts. Cabins are not large, but do have small sitting areas. All outside cabins on both ships' Bridge and Commodore decks have balconies and can sleep up to four quite comfortably. The Viking Crown Lounge atop each ship affords a 360° view of the passing scenery. Glass windbreaks shelter an observatory (complete with stargazing equipment), a cushioned jogging/walking track, a pool bar, whirlpools, and an outdoor swimming pool. **Itineraries:** *Rhapsody:* 7-night Inside Passage cruises visit Juneau, Skagway, Haines, Hubbard Glacier/Yakutat Bay, and Ketchikan. *Vision:* 7-night Inside Passage cruises visit Hubbard Glacier, Skagway, Haines, Juneau, Ketchikan, and Misty Fjords. **Rates:** *Rhapsody:* $1,099–$3,429, cabins, $3,099–$7,679, suites; *Vision:* $1,199–$3,529, cabins, $3,199–$7,779, suites. Rates include port charges. **Specifications:** Built 1998/1997; passengers 2,000; crew 834; tonnage 78,491; length 915 feet; cabins, 593 outside (229 with verandas), 407 inside.

Southeast Alaska

Rich, proud people have lived in Southeast Alaska for thousands of years, fishing its salmon and hunting all through its primeval forests, where the tree trunks grow up to 10 feet thick. In canoes, they explored the hundreds of misty, mossy, enchanted islands where the animals, trees, and even the ice had living spirits. The salmon lived under the sea in human form, becoming fish in the spring and summer to swim in seething masses up the rivers and streams as a gift of food to feed their kin, the people. In return, the people treated the salmon with respect and ceremony, allowing their spirits to return to human form under the sea to live another year. So blessed, the Tlingit and Haida built great, carved houses and poles, fought wars, owned slaves, traded with faraway tribes, and told stories in their potlatch celebrations (rich contests of giving) that live on today as powerful explanations of their mysterious world. Even for a modern non-Native walking in the grand quiet of the old-growth rain forest, it's easy to forget you don't believe in the spirits of the trees. Life there is so abundant, it sometimes seems to speak.

Incredibly, after all those thousands of years of exploration of Southeast Alaska, the region still is being discovered—literally. In 1987, an amateur caver looking at a map speculated that the limestone of Prince of Wales Island would be a likely place to find caves. On his vacation, he went out to look and discovered what was then the deepest known vertical cave in the United States, in a place where no modern explorer had bothered to look before. In the annual explorations that followed, expeditions mapped miles and miles of caverns, finding the bones of extinct animals and prehistoric people, bear dens, strange eyeless shrimp that live nowhere else, and even underground streams that host spawning salmon. Inside, the honeycomb of caves networks at every step into passages that lead straight up or down or off to either side, some only large enough to carry a cool wind. The unfathomable intricacy is exhilarating but also a bit disquieting, like a breath of the supernatural, for it is proof of the unknowable.

That unknowable intricacy, lying below the tree roots and footsteps of Southeast Alaska, is a perfect metaphor for the region. This land of ice and forest may not look as large on the map as other parts of Alaska, but it keeps unfolding as you visit until you have to give up in its immensity. The Prince of Wales caves offer another illustration of this: Upon finding them, geologists realized that the same cave-making conditions prevail elsewhere—that many of Southeast's islands are composed of limestone dripping with rain forest acids to carve the rock. They're still finding new caves, but you can be quite sure no one will come close to finding them all.

You're probably not planning a caving vacation, but you don't need to go underground to experience the fractal geometry of the endlessly folded, rocky shoreline. The discoveries you make depend only on how closely you look. On a ship passing through the **Inside Passage,** you'll marvel at all the little beaches and rocky outcroppings you pass—hundreds of inviting spots each day you steam through. If you were to stop at random on any one of those uninhabited beaches in a skiff or kayak, you'd find you could spend a day surveying just a few acres of rocks, the overhanging forest, and the tiny pools of water left behind by the tide. And if you gazed down into any one of those pools, you'd find a complex world all its own, with tiny predators and prey living out their own drama of life in the space of a few square feet.

If Alaska sometimes feels like a different country from the rest of the United States, Southeast certainly feels like a different state from the rest of Alaska. The area stands apart, and not only because most of it can't be reached by road. No other part of the state shares the mysterious, spirit-ridden quality of the coastal **rain forest.** No other area has **weather** that, though so wet (no other area in Alaska gets so much rain— precious few places anywhere on earth do, for that matter), is also so mild: The climate is more akin to the Pacific Northwest than to the heart of Alaska.

The area's **Native heritage** is rich—the Tlingit, Haida, and Tsimshian exploited the wealth nature gave them and amplified it by being successful traders with tribes to the south and over the mountains in today's British Columbia and Yukon Territory. In their early contact, the Tlingits even briefly defeated the Russian invaders in the Battle of Sitka, and after white dominance was established, managed to save many of their cultural artifacts and stories.

Along with its other riches and complexity, Southeast Alaska also has many charming **small towns and villages** that seem to have grown organically from mountainsides bordering the fjords and channels of the islands. With economies that predate Alaska's oil boom, they developed slowly, their fishermen building houses to hand on to their children. The smaller towns remain completely free of America's blight of retail chains. Instead, the real, old-fashioned main streets are prosperous with family businesses where the proprietors know their customers by first name.

Mystery-laden forests, rich Native culture, old-time small-town life: It all awaits your discovery, within the endless folds of Southeast's islands.

1 Exploring Southeast Alaska

A unique and inviting aspect of traveling in Southeast Alaska is that no roads connect most of the communities. People are forced to get out of their speeding cars and get on boats, where they can meet their fellow travelers and see what's passing by—slowly. The islands of the region form a protected waterway called the **Inside Passage,** along which almost all of the region's towns are arrayed. Thanks to the **Alaska Marine Highway** ferry system, it's inexpensive to travel the entire passage, hopping from town to town and spending as much time in each place as you like. And if you're short on time, air service is frequent, with jets to the major towns and commuter planes to the villages.

Why are there no roads? A tectonic plate that underlies the Pacific Ocean brought the islands of the Southeast Alaska Panhandle from far afield and squished them up against the plate that carries the land mass of Canada. Along the line of this glancing collision, large glacial mountains thrust up, and the islands themselves were stretched

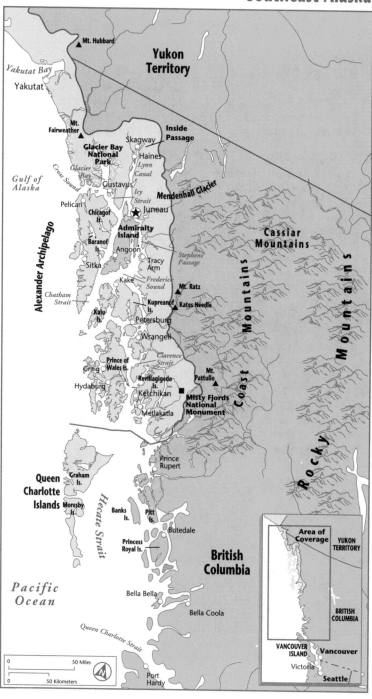

Mt. Hubbard

Yukon Territory

Yakutat Bay

Yakutat

Mt. Fairweather

Glacier Bay National Park

Skagway

Inside Passage

Haines

Lynn Canal

Glacier Bay

Cross Sound

Gustavus

Gulf of Alaska

Icy Strait

Mendenhall Glacier

Pelican

Chicagof Is.

Juneau

Cassiar Mountains

Admiralty Island

Baranof Is.

Angoon

Sitka

Tracy Arm

Stephens Passage

Alexander Archipelago

Kake

Frederick Sound

Mt. Ratz

Kates Needle

Chatham Strait

Kupreanof Is.

Kulu Is.

Petersburg

Wrangell

Coast Mountains

R o c k y   M o u n t a i n s

Prince of Wales Is.

Clarence Strait

Craig

Revillagigedo Is.

Mt. Pattullo

Hydaburg

Ketchikan

Misty Fjords National Monument

Metlakatla

Prince Rupert

Queen Charlotte Islands

Graham Is.

Moresby Is.

Hecate Strait

Banks Is.

Pitt Is.

Butedale

Princess Royal Is.

British Columbia

Pacific Ocean

Bella Bella

Bella Coola

Queen Charlotte Strait

Port Hardy

0   50 Miles

0   50 Kilometers

Area of Coverage

YUKON TERRITORY

BRITISH COLUMBIA

VANCOUVER ISLAND

Vancouver

Victoria

Seattle

and torn into the fractured geography that makes the area so interesting. In short, it's just too difficult to build roads through those icy mountains and across the steep, jumbled terrain of the islands.

VISITOR INFORMATION

Before you come to the region, contact the **Southeast Alaska Tourism Council,** P.O. Box 20710, Juneau, AK 99802-0710 (☎ **800-423-0568,** 907/586-4777; fax 907/463-4961; www.AlaskaInfo.org). Covering all the communities, this organization can send you an attractive guide. More useful yet, they have a good Web site.

GETTING AROUND BY FERRY: THE ALASKA MARINE HIGHWAY

The state-run **Alaska Marine Highway System,** P.O. Box 25535, Juneau, AK 99802-5535 (☎ **800/642-0066;** fax 907/277-4829; www.dot.state.ak.us/external/amhs/home.html), founded in 1963, is a subsidized fleet of blue-hulled, ocean-going ferries whose mission is to connect the roadless coastal towns of Alaska for roughly the same kind of cost you'd pay if there were roads and you were driving. Call for a free schedule or download it from the Web site. A new ferry, the *Kennicott,* links Southeast Alaska to Prince William Sound and the Kenai Peninsula, crossing the open ocean of the Gulf of Alaska once a month. From there, ferries run out to Kodiak Island and all the way to the Aleutian Archipelago (see chapters 7 and 10).

PROS & CONS   The ferry system's strengths are its low cost, frequent summer sailings, exceptional safety, and the fact that it's about the most fun form of family travel I can imagine—kids love it. In the summer, Forest Service guides offer interpretive talks on board. Its weaknesses are crowding during the July peak season, sometimes many hour delays, generally lackluster food, and a shortage of cabins, which means that most people camp on deck or in chairs during overnight passages.

SERVICE ROUTES & FARES   To the south, the ferry system calls on Prince Rupert, British Columbia, and Bellingham, Washington, running north to Haines and Skagway. Each of these towns is connected to the rest of the world by roads, but none of the towns in between are (with the negligible exception of Hyder, covered below). The voyage from Prince Rupert to Haines is about 35 hours if you never get off to visit any of the towns in between (which would be an act of sheer lunacy, in my view). The foot-passenger, or walk-on, fare for that route is $122 for adults. As on all ferry routes, the fare for children 11 and under is half price, while children 2 and under ride free.

The **B.C. Ferries** system, 1112 Fort St., Victoria, B.C., Canada V8V 4V2 (☎ **250/386-3431;** fax 250/381-5452; www.bcferries.bc.ca), docks right next to the Alaska ferry in Prince Rupert, so you can easily connect to wonderful places such as Vancouver Island and British Columbia's portion of the Inside Passage.

The Alaska ferry *Columbia* goes all the way south to Bellingham, Washington, taking 37 hours in a nonstop run to Ketchikan, then continuing up to Haines. The walk-on fare is $164 to Ketchikan, $244 to Haines. The Bellingham trips, running only once a week, get booked early, so even foot passengers should make reservations during the summer. Other large ferries stop roughly six times a week in Prince Rupert, connecting the highway there to points north. In the summer, large ships make daily stops (although sometimes in the middle of the night) in Ketchikan, Wrangell, Petersburg, Haines, and Skagway. Juneau is a hub, and you may need to change ferries there to continue north to Haines and Skagway. Sitka, which lies to the west of the Inside Passage, is bypassed by some ferries, receiving port calls from a main-line ferry twice a week and from a smaller, connecting ferry, the *LeConte,* three times a week.

Ferry Tip

The Alaska Marine Highway ferries are crowded northbound in June and southbound in August. If you're planning to fly one way and take the ferry the other, go against the flow (southbound in June and northbound in August) and you'll have the ship more to yourself.

The two smaller ferries, the *LeConte* and *Aurora*, connect the larger towns to small towns and villages up and down the coast. These are **commuter ferries,** and if you have the time, taking one to the tiny towns they serve is a lot of fun. You can jump off and explore for an hour or so during port calls, or plan a longer visit to one of the quiet Bush communities, catching the next ferry or a scheduled Bush plane. The smaller boats mostly take local residents back and forth to their villages, so they're rarely crowded, and they are the definition of "off the beaten track." They have restaurants but no cabins. The risk of planning to visit towns during port calls, whether on the main line or the smaller ferries, is that if the ship falls behind its schedule, you might not be able to get off as the crew does a quick turnaround to pick up time.

While touring the region, **combining flying and the ferry** can save time and reduce the chance of you having to spend the night sleeping in a chair on board. There are, however, some runs I wouldn't miss. Going to Sitka through Peril Straits, the ferry fits through extraordinarily narrow passages where no other vessel of its size ventures; the smooth, reflective water is lovely, and you may see deer along the shore. This is where the ferries can lose time—they can go through only when the current isn't running, so if they miss the tide, they have to wait 6 hours. The Wrangell Narrows, between Petersburg and Wrangell, also are an incredible ride, day or night, as the ship accomplishes a slalom between shores that seem so close you could touch them, in water so shallow the schedules must be timed for high tide. Approaching Skagway through the towering mountains of the Lynn Canal fjord also is especially impressive.

BRINGING VEHICLES & RESERVING CABINS If you're bringing a vehicle or definitely need a cabin on the ferry system during the June-through-August high season, you *must* reserve well in advance. That doesn't mean that you can't get a car on board or pick up a cabin on stand-by, but you'd be counting on a lot of luck. Cabins on the Bellingham run book up more than 6 months in advance. Obviously, fares for taking vehicles vary according to the size of the car and how far you're going; a passage from Prince Rupert to Haines for a typical 15-foot car is $283, or $578 from Bellingham. You also have to buy a ticket for each person, including the driver. Compare the cost of **renting a car** at your destination, as it could cost the same or less and save the inconvenience and wear-and-tear of bringing your own. You can bring a kayak, canoe, or bike on the ferry for around 25% of the cost of an adult ticket.

An overnight, two-berth **outside cabin** (one with a window) is around $50 on most sailings, or $121 from Prince Rupert to Haines, $271 from Bellingham to Haines, plus the cost of your ticket. The great majority of the cabins are small and spartan, coming in two- and four-bunk configurations, but for a premium you can reserve a more comfortable unit (called a "stateroom" in the ferry literature) with a sitting room attached. Most have tiny private bathrooms with showers. Try to get an outside cabin so you can watch the world go by. Cabins can be stuffy, and the windowless units can be claustrophobic as well. The staterooms don't cost that much more and provide your own private observation lounge.

DO YOU NEED A CABIN? If you do a lot of layovers to see Southeast's towns, you can time most of your passages during the day, but you're likely to have to sleep on board at least once. One of the adventures of ferry travel is finding a chair to sleep in or **setting up a tent on deck** with everyone else. The solarium, on the top deck, is the best sleeping spot on board, in part because the noise of the ship covers other sounds. The recliner lounges are comfortable, too. If the ship looks crowded, grab your spot fast to get a choice location. **Showers** are available, although there may be lines. Lock the valuables and luggage you don't need in the **coin-operated lockers.** If you're tenting, the best place is behind the solarium, where it's not too windy. On the *Columbia,* that space is small, so grab it early. And bring duct tape to secure your tent to the deck in case you don't have a sheltered spot—using exposed deck space can be like camping in an endless gale. If all that sounds too rugged, or if you have small children and no tent, reserve a cabin. It offers a safe and private home base and a good night's rest, and there's a certain romance to having your own compartment on a public conveyance.

FERRY FOOD   If you can, bring your own food on the ferry. Ferry food isn't positively bad, but it's quite inconsistent from one ship to the next, it's often greasy, and you can get awfully tired of it after several meals in a row. Also, during peak season, the food lines are sometimes unreasonably long. We usually bring a cooler or picnic basket. Even if you're traveling light, you can pick up some bagels and deli sandwiches on a stopover or long port call.

GETTING AROUND BY AIR & ROAD

BY AIR   Air travel is the primary link between Southeast's towns and the rest of the world. Major towns without road access have jet service, provided by **Alaska Airlines** (☎ **800/426-0333;** www.alaskaair.com), currently the region's only major airline. Juneau is Southeast Alaska's travel hub. Ketchikan and Sitka each have a few flights a day, while Wrangell, Petersburg, and Yakutat each have one flight going each direction daily. Gustavus is served from Juneau once daily during the summer. Some of these "milk runs" never get very far off the ground on hops between small towns: On the 31-mile Wrangell-to-Petersburg flight, the cabin attendants never have time to unbuckle. Haines and Skagway, which have highway connections, don't receive visits from jets, but all the towns and even the tiniest villages have scheduled prop service.

If you can possibly afford it, you'll want to take a **"flightseeing" trip** at some point during your trip. The poor man's way of doing this is to fly a small prop plane on a scheduled run between two of your destinations instead of taking the ferry. If you ask, the pilot may even go out of his or her way to show you the sights; even if not, you'll gain an appreciation for the richness and extreme topography of the region. Each operator also offers flightseeing tours, which cost as little as $50 for a brief spin. In the northern Panhandle, try **L.A.B. Flying Service** (☎ 800/426-0543 or 907/ 789-9160), which goes as far south as Petersburg. **Wings of Alaska** (☎ **907/ 789-0790)** also covers the northern area around Juneau. In the southern Panhandle, **Taquan Air** (☎ **800/770-8800** or 907/225-8800; www.taquanair.com) is the largest carrier.

Like the ferries, the planes can be quite late. Each of the airports in Southeast has its own challenges caused by the steep, mountainous terrain and the water. In bad weather, even jet flights are delayed or they "overhead"—they can't land at all at the intended destination and leave their passengers somewhere else. Your only protection against these contingencies are travel insurance, a schedule that allows plenty of slack in case you're significantly delayed, and low blood pressure.

BY ROAD   Three Southeast Alaska communities are accessible by road: Haines, Skagway, and the village of Hyder, which lies on the British Columbia border east of Ketchikan and is accessible from the gravel Cassiar Highway through Canada. If you're driving the Alaska Highway, passing through Haines and Skagway adds 250 miles of very scenic driving to the trip. Take the ferry the 15 miles between the two towns (they're separated by 362 road miles). This ferry route is not as heavily booked as the routes heading between either town and Juneau, but it's a good idea to reserve ahead anyway. It's possible to take a bus or rent a car from Haines or Skagway for travel to the rest of the state at the end of a ferry journey (Haines will save you only 60 miles over Skagway); details are listed in the sections on each of those towns. If you're driving the highway in winter, you should be prepared for weather as cold as 40°F below zero. Alaska winter driving information is under "Health, Safety & Traveler's Insurance" in chapter 2.

2 Outside in Southeast

TONGASS NATIONAL FOREST

Nearly all of Southeast Alaska, stretching 500 miles from Ketchikan to Yakutat, is in Tongass National Forest. The towns sit in small pockets of private land surrounded by 17 million acres of land controlled by the U.S. Forest Service—an area nearly as large as the state of Maine, and considerably larger than any other national forest or any national park in the United States. The great majority of this land has never been logged, and the rate of logging has dropped dramatically in recent years, preserving one of the world's great temperate rain forests in its virgin state. It's an intact ecosystem full of wildlife, and mostly free of human development. Indeed, you quickly forget it *is* the Tongass National Forest. Since it always surrounds you when you're in this region, it's simply the land.

I've covered outdoor recreation in the National Forest in the sections that follow. In a place this big, it makes little sense to generalize. For **visitor information,** the Forest Service maintains centers in Ketchikan, Juneau, and Petersburg, and staffs ranger offices in Sitka and Wrangell, and, on Prince of Wales Island, in Craig and Thorne Bay. Each of those centers and offices is listed in the appropriate town section, below. In addition, there are ranger offices in Hoonah (☎ **907/945-3631**) and Yakutat (☎ **907/784-3359**), towns I haven't covered in this book.

You can get to remote parts of the National Forest through various thresholds: to **Misty Fjords National Monument** through Ketchikan, to the **Kootznoowoo Wilderness** of Admiratly Island through Juneau, and to the **Anan Bear Observatory** through Wrangell, to name but a few. Each is covered below. Guides also offer extended trips by kayak to places few people have ever heard of. I recommend **Alaska Discovery,** described in full in the Juneau section.

FOREST SERVICE CABINS

One of the best ways to get into Southeast's wilderness is by staying at one of the scores of remote Forest Service Public Recreation Cabins. These are simple cabins, generally without electricity or running water, where you can lay your sleeping bag on a bunk and sit by a warm wood stove, out of the rain. You need to bring everything with you, as if camping, but it's a good deal more comfortable than a tent. And you will probably find yourself in a stunningly beautiful spot, perhaps with your own lake and a boat for fishing. Cabins are along canoe trails, on beaches best reached by sea kayak, on high mountain lakes accessible only by floatplane, and along hiking trails.

CABIN INFORMATION I've listed details about some of the cabins in the text with the towns they're nearest, but the most complete sources of information are the **Public Recreation Cabin catalogs** published by the Forest Service. A free booklet is distributed for each of the three major areas in the national forest: the Ketchikan Area,

Jobs & Trees: The Tongass Battleground

A friend described this scene: a forest of tall, straight spruce and hemlock trees, widely spaced, the sunlight streaming down through the branches into a green, mossy glade. He stood on the soft forest floor beside the owner of the land, breathing deeply the fragrant air that seemed to cling to the trees all around him. He couldn't help smiling at such beauty, and he noticed his host was smiling broadly, too. But when the landowner opened his mouth to speak, my friend realized that this man saw something entirely different. His joy was that these trees, worth several thousand dollars apiece, would soon be logged to provide him with an ample retirement.

That scene occurred in the Prince William Sound area, but the conflict it represents is Alaska's fundamental political and social conflict—between exploiting resources and preserving them. The vast majority of Southeast is in the Tongass National Forest, a land used for many different ends—including providing for a timber harvest. Of course, cutting down trees isn't compatible with looking at them, appreciating the wildlife that relies on them, or harvesting fish from the streams they protect from heat and erosion. And there are jobs and retirement incomes tied up in those uses, too.

The heavy rain and temperate climate of Southeast Alaska create perfect conditions for growing huge trees. The main commercial species in Southeast are western hemlock, cedar (western red and Alaska yellow), and Sitka spruce, Alaska's state tree. It's a rain forest. There are tree trunks up to 10 feet across. And the forest has another unique feature—millions of acres that have never been cut, some of the last major tracts of old-growth forest in the United States. Once logged, those ecosystems are gone virtually forever, for the succession of forest development to maturity in this region takes longer than the span of a human life, and much longer than the duration of human patience.

The timber industry sustained itself for many years under 50-year contracts the federal government signed with U.S. and Japanese companies after World War II to stimulate economic growth in Japan and Alaska. They were guaranteed lots of wood at subsidized prices. Cutting was accelerated further in the 1980s by Native corporations that liquidated much of their timber assets quickly for business and tax reasons. Mills to turn the trees into lumber and pulp developed in towns all over the region, and other logs went overseas in the round.

With 17 million acres of sparsely populated land—Tongass is the largest national forest—you might think there would be enough for everyone. But in recent years, the Forest Service concluded that the cut rates of the past were unsustainable: The trees here grow large, but they grow slow. Despite the immense area, trees were being cut faster than they could grow back. Moreover, wildlife such as bears and wolves need big blocks of intact ecosystem, not little fragments of habitat left behind by clear-cuts. And the high-value timber that the loggers want grows in river valleys and other areas that are valuable to animals and people, not the mountaintops that make up much of the national forest.

The decisions to slow down were made in Washington, D.C.—far away from the Alaska communities that would suffer the economic consequences. In 1990, Congress set aside more land for conservation. Within a few years, the U.S. Forest Service, under President Clinton, offered less wood in timber sales. At the same time, severe environmental problems at some of the mills dragged down their economic viability with high cleanup costs. When the big Sitka pulp mill shut down, the federal government eagerly canceled the 50-year contract that went with it. Locals realized the timber jobs that were going weren't coming back. From 1989 to 1999, timber employment in the region dropped from 3,500 to around 1,200, falling heaviest on Wrangell, Ketchikan, and Sitka.

With 1994's national elections and the Republican takeover of Congress, loggers pinned their hope on Alaska's all-Republican, three-member congressional delegation. They took the chairs of the resource committees in both the House and the Senate, placing them in charge of these issues for the whole country. All three are adamantly prodevelopment. But when these members of Congress tried to use their new muscle, it didn't bring more timber jobs to Southeast. The rest of the country had other priorities. The issue of timber supply became a sticking point in the budget stalemate between Congress and the president that shut down the government at the end of 1995. Alaska senator Ted Stevens used the opportunity to demand more trees for Southeast Alaska's mills. Instead, Clinton agreed to a $110 million payment to help communities transition to an economy not so dependent on large-scale logging.

In 1996, Louisiana Pacific threatened that it would close its Ketchikan pulp mill unless it received a contract extension from the Forest Service to guarantee timber well into the next century—otherwise, environmental plant upgrades couldn't be financed. Neither the Clinton administration nor Congress would accept the deal, and the mill closed in 1997 as promised, eliminating about 7% of the jobs in town. At about the same time, the Forest Service announced a new, even more restrictive timber sale program that would cancel many timber sales and slow down others that had been in the planning process for many years. Yet the news wasn't as bad as it first appeared for Southeast communities. The sawmill in Wrangell that closed in 1994, taking a third of the town's total payroll, reopened on a smaller scale. The site of the Ketchikan plant became a new, smaller operation that will produce high-quality lumber products, no longer grinding trees into pulp. It won't employ as many people, but will make better use of the more limited timber supply the government is offering. The town of Sitka took over the mill there after environmental cleanup was complete, hoping it will become the site of a new plant. The economic collapse expected when the plants shut down never arrived. Individual workers suffered, but many of them had lived outside the state anyway and just came north for seasonal jobs. The fast growth of the tourism industry cushioned the drop in the industrial work for the merchants and town governments. Population in Southeast Alaska as a whole managed slow, steady growth through the 1990s.

Wrangell is quieter now; the bars aren't as rowdy at night. It was hit especially hard because the town was so small compared to its mill. But you don't see boarded up houses here—I'm told there are a lot fewer mobile homes, and nice houses sell cheap, but it's not a ghost town. The town has developed the tourist potential of the surrounding forests and Stikine River, and they're building a big new museum. The anger has started to die, too.

Today, it appears that prodevelopment Alaskans have lost the battle for the Tongass. The fight goes on, and probably always will, but with the economic transition easier than expected and the big plants gone, the noise level has abated. The battles of the 1990s saved much of this primeval forest. In the Tongass, they cut down jobs instead of trees, and the jobs are growing back.

which includes Prince of Wales Island and Misty Fjords; the Stikine Area, around Petersburg and Wrangell; and the Chatham Area, around Juneau, Sitka, and Admiralty Island. Each cabin is briefly described. You can get the booklets from the visitor centers and ranger offices listed with each town, or write ahead to the **Southeast Alaska Visitor Center,** 50 Main St., Ketchikan, AK 99901 (☎ **907/228-6220** or TTY 907/228-6237), or the Forest Service Information Center, Centennial Hall, 101 Egan Dr., Juneau, AK 99801 (☎ **907/586-8751;** TTY 907/586-7894). Much of this information is also on the Web, at **www.fs.fed.us/r10/tongass/.**

You'll need a good map to figure out where the cabins are, and an idea of how to get there and how much travel will cost—generally, this will be many times the cabin rental of $25 or $35 a night. Often, a flight service can help you choose according to your interests and how far you can afford to fly. You may be able to rent the gear you need, but you'll have to reserve that ahead, too. The solution to all those puzzles is different for each town; I've listed where to find help for each problem in the town sections later in this chapter.

RESERVING A CABIN   The cabins are reserved through a new national system. (The locals aren't too happy about that, because now outsiders can grab their favorite spots just as easily as they can.) Don't rely on the reservation operators or Web site for cabin information—they're in upstate New York—but pose your questions instead to the ranger station nearest where you plan to go. The rangers are friendly and have probably stayed in the cabin you're interested in. The reservation concessionaire is **Reserve USA** (☎ **877/444-6777;** TDD 877/833-6777; or with toll from overseas, 518/885-3639; reserveusa.com). The phone lines are open summer daily 8am to midnight EST, winter daily 10am to 7pm. You can also reserve online, and the site lists what's available, allowing some shopping according to your itinerary. They take American Express, Discover, MasterCard and Visa, or you can reserve on the phone and then pay within ten days by check or money order. Cabins are available for reservation on a first-come, first-served basis, starting 180 days ahead.

A note: Don't get fooled by the ease of the reservations process into choosing carelessly—if you can't actually pull off the trip, you'll only be wasting your money and, more important, depriving someone else of the use of the cabin.

ACTIVITIES

Generally, each town serves as a base for outdoor activities in the surrounding area, so this section serves as a reference to direct you to the town sections, below.

BEAR VIEWING   You might see bears a lot of places in Southeast—small-town garbage dumps in the region are plagued with black bears, and almost anyone living near the edge of town has encountered them. Running into bears in more natural surroundings means going where bears congregate for natural food sources. Salmon is their most important food, so when salmon are spawning in streams confined by a waterfall or other barrier, you can be sure of many bears. Pack Creek, on Admiralty Island, 25 miles from Juneau by floatplane or boat, is a prime brown-bear viewing area in July and August. Access is limited by the U.S. Forest Service; you can reserve a spot with a guided tour, or enter a lottery (explained in the Juneau section). Anan Wildlife Observatory, on the mainland about 30 miles from Wrangell, gathers black bear and some browns in July and August. Permits aren't needed, but it's easier and safer to go with a guided trip by boat or floatplane from Wrangell or by air from Ketchikan. There's also an uncontrolled and relatively little-visited bear viewing area near Hyder.

BIKING   Bikes make a lot of sense for getting around Southeast's small towns, which tend to be compact. You can rent one almost anywhere you go (bike rental operators are listed in the town sections, below), or bring your own on the ferry. The networks of abandoned or little-used logging roads on some islands offer limitless routes for mountain biking. Prince of Wales Island alone has more than 1,000 miles of logging roads, although some of this mileage is quite dull. Wrangell and Petersburg also have lots of remote dirt road mileage, and more you can get to by boat if you really want to be by yourself. Skagway and Haines have good bike shops with folks who help find routes and guide trips.

DIVING   You'll find dive shops in several towns. The Inside Passage is not as clear or as biologically productive as Gulf of Alaska waters, so Sitka and Prince of Wales Island, facing the ocean side, are better for diving. Summer, when most people come, is likely to be plagued by algae blooms that obscure visibility. Dry suit diving helps cope with the very cold water, but in the summer you can get by with a wet suit, if that's what you're familiar with.

FISHING   Almost anywhere you happen to be, you can find great fishing in Southeast Alaska. Before whites arrived, the Natives of the region ate an estimated 526 pounds of salmon a year per capita. As always, the best fishing is away from the roads. The Forest Service's lake cabins and the wilderness lodges around Ketchikan provide some of the best opportunities for remote, all-alone fly-fishing. Sea charters for salmon or halibut are great all over, but you can combine them with whale watching in Gustavus, Sitka, Petersburg, and Juneau. Gustavus is known for huge halibut relatively near town. For details on runs, seasons, regulations, and licenses, contact the **Alaska Department of Fish and Game,** Division of Sport Fish, 1255 W. Eighth St. (P.O. Box 25526), Juneau, AK 99802-5526 (☎ **907/465-4180;** www.state.ak.us/local/akpages/FISH.GAME/adfghome.htm). They produce detailed fishing guides for each of several areas in Southeast that any angler would find useful. The Web site is exceptionally good, and includes a guide to when salmon runs happen around Alaska, a place to order publications, and other data that will put you way ahead of other fishers. I've included more fishing guidance in chapter 2.

HIKING   The **Chilkoot Trail,** near Skagway, is a 33-mile-long museum, and a challenging 3-day hike. Petersburg is a good starting point for more remote hiking, but there are excellent choices of trails in Juneau, Ketchikan, and Haines. Trails long enough for overnights are the exception in the mountainous country, where people traditionally get around by boat. Gustavus has long beach walks.

SEA KAYAKING   Ketchikan, Sitka, Wrangell, Petersburg, Juneau, Haines, and Glacier Bay all have kayaking guides and great places to kayak. Each little town has a kayak business run by people who know the area by heart. Going out with these little operations can really be a treat. **Alaska Discovery,** listed in the Juneau section, offers extended kayak trips in various wilderness areas even for beginners. It's a great way to backpack without having to carry anything, and perhaps the best way to see the nature of the region. Most towns also have someone offering kayak rental. Experienced paddlers sometimes tour the region by kayak. Few places in the world are as conducive to that kind of travel. The tariff to take a kayak on the ferry is about 25% of the passenger fare.

TIDE POOLING   Locals almost always know a good spot nearby to find tide pools, where you can climb over the rocks and inspect the strange animals and plants that make their home underwater. Get a tide table (usually available free at any hardware store, grocery store, or boat harbor) to find out when you can expect the next deep low tide. The number by the date and tide indicates how many feet above or below mean low tide the water will come on the shore; a lower number means more tide pooling territory is uncovered and more unusual animals will be evident. Go a couple of hours before dead low, and head back soon after the tide starts coming back in, to avoid getting wet or worse. Wear rugged shoes with good traction; rubber boots are best.

WHALE WATCHING   Humpback whale-feeding patterns determine where and when you can see them, and the best feeding grounds can change from year to year. In recent years, the whale watching has been entirely reliable near Gustavus, in Icy Strait, and near Petersburg, in Frederick Sound. July and August are best. Juneau and Sitka also offer good possibilities, with sighting possible from shore in Sitka, especially in the fall during the migration. For more information on whales, with illustrations, see the appendix.

WINTER SPORTS   Few visitors come to Southeast in the winter, as they would miss out on the boating and other watery activities. But for those who do come, it's not terribly cold, crowds are gone, and skating and Nordic skiing are available in a lot of places. Some towns close down entirely, however, including Skagway and Gustavus/Glacier Bay. **Eaglecrest**, in Juneau, is the region's only significant alpine skiing area.

3 Ketchikan: On the Waterfront

Had they known about it, the film noir directors of the 1950s would have chosen the Ketchikan (*ketch*-e-kan) waterfront for Humphrey Bogart to sleuth. One can picture the black-and-white montage: A pelting rain drains from the brim of his hat, suspicious figures dart through saloon doors and into the lobbies of concrete-faced hotels, a forest of workboat masts fades into the midsummer twilight along a shore where the sea and land seem to merge in miles of floating docks. Along Creek Street, salmon on their way to spawn swim under houses chaotically perched on pilings beside a narrow boardwalk; inside, men are spawning, too, in the arms of legal prostitutes. Meanwhile, the faces of totem poles gaze down on the scene disapprovingly, mute holders of their own ancient secrets.

Today, the director hoping to re-create that scene would have his work cut out for him removing the T-shirt shops and bright street-front signs that seek to draw throngs of cruise passengers in to buy plastic gewgaws. Not so long ago, Ketchikan was a rugged and exotic intersection of cultures built on the profits of logging Southeast's rain forest, but in just a few years it has transformed into a tourist center, softening its rough edges while selling their charm to visitors. And the changes can only accelerate. More and bigger ships are coming, and Southeast Alaska's last major timber mill—the Louisiana Pacific–owned pulp plant in Ward's Cove, north of town—closed in 1997 due, in part, to environmental concerns, and was blown up in 1999. They sold tickets to see who would get to press the button on the explosives, but the occasion was less than festive, as former employees saw the scene of their work lives disappear into dust. Locals hope for a smaller, more labor-intensive wood-products operation to take the place of Louisiana Pacific, but in the meantime the economy is moving on.

On summer days, the white cruise ships tower above the town like huge new buildings on the dock facing Front Street, the downtown's main drag. Each morning their gangways disgorge thousands of visitors, clogging the streets and, for a few hours, transforming the town into a teeming carnival. With only a few hours to spend, the passengers explore the closest of the twisting streets, see the museum at the Southeast Alaska Visitor Information Center, or take a tour to one of the totem pole parks. Then evening comes, the streets empty, and the cruise ships slide off quietly on the way to their next port.

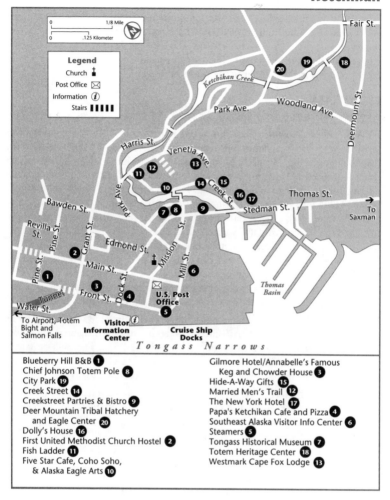

That is when a sense of the old, misty, mysterious Ketchikan starts to return. Visitors with a little more time to spend, and the willingness to explore beyond the core tourist areas, can drink fully of the history and atmosphere of the place, staying in a quaint old hotel, hiking a boardwalk path through the primeval rain forest, and making unique discoveries.

There certainly is plenty to see. Ketchikan is a center of Tlingit and Haida culture, and there are two replica **clan houses** and **totem pole parks,** as well as the only museum dedicated solely to preserving the old, original poles from the days when the Tlingit and Haida peoples' cultural traditions were more intact. Two other museums preserve and explain the broader culture and natural history of the area. There are several art galleries that feature serious local work.

Ketchikan also makes a great jumping-off point for getting into some spectacular outdoor experiences, including **Misty Fjords National Monument** (see section 4, later in this chapter). As the state's fourth-largest city, Ketchikan is the transportation hub for the southern portion of Southeast Alaska. (The nickname "Gateway City" refers to its geographical location and transportation function.) Seaplanes based on docks along the waterfront are the taxis of the region, and a big interagency visitor center can get you started. Ketchikan also is one of the wettest spots on earth, with rain measured in the hundreds of inches; consequently, quality rain gear is requisite for any activity, in the wilds or in the streets of town.

ESSENTIALS
GETTING THERE
BY AIR   Alaska Airlines (☎ 800/426-0333 or 907/225-2145; www.alaskaair.com) provides Ketchikan with nonstop jet service from Seattle and with flights to the north, including Petersburg, Wrangell, Sitka, Juneau, and Anchorage. Commuter lines run float- and wheeled planes from Ketchikan to the neighboring communities, as well as offering fishing packages and flightseeing. **Taquan Air Service** (☎ 907/800-8800 or 907/225-8800; www.AlaskaOne.com/TaquanAir) has a desk at the airport as well as at 1007 Water St., on the waterfront. The airport is on a different island from the town and can be reached only by a ferry that runs each way every half hour. It leaves the airport on the hour and half hour, and leaves the Ketchikan side on quarter hours. Believe the airline when it tells you when to catch the ferry for your plane. The fare is $2.50 for adults, $1.50 ages 6 to 11, and free under 6. Returning the same day is free. The fare for cars is $5 each way, no matter how soon you come back. You'll need a vehicle to get to town from the airport ferry. (See "Getting Around," below.)

BY FERRY   The dock is 2½ miles north out of town. **Alaska Marine Highway** ferries (see listing under "Getting Around" at the beginning of this chapter) run 6 hours north to Wrangell and 6 hours south to Prince Rupert, B.C. The walk-on fare for Prince Rupert is $38, Wrangell is $24, children under 12 go half price. For updated arrival and departure times, call the local terminal at ☎ 907/225-6181.

GETTING TO TOWN   A shuttle, taxi, or city bus can get you into town from the ferry terminal or the airport ferry. The **Airporter Shuttle** (☎ 907/225-5429) meets each flight and picks up at the major hotels according to a schedule you can get at the front desk. They'll pick up anywhere else by arrangement. The $15 fare downtown is comparable to what you'd pay for a taxi, and includes the airport ferry fare.

The local taxis, mostly minivans, charge reasonable prices compared to some Alaska communities. Try **Yellow Taxi** (☎ 907/225-5555) or **Sourdough Cab** (☎ 907/225-5544). Take the cab just to the airport ferry dock and walk on to avoid an expensive added cost.

A **bus** operated by the Ketchikan Gateway Borough (☎ 907/225-6800) runs roughly every half hour from the airport ferry parking lot and state ferry terminal downtown from 5:15am to 9:45pm Monday through Saturday and once an hour Sunday 8:45am to 3:45pm.

GETTING AROUND
Ketchikan is on huge **Revillagigedo Island.** The downtown area with most of the attractions is quite compact and walkable, but the whole of Ketchikan is long, strung out between the Tongass Narrows and the mountains. A waterfront road goes under various names through town, becoming North Tongass Highway as it stretches about 16 miles to the north. A tunnel divides the downtown and northwestern section of town. Saxman is 2½ miles to the south on the 14-mile South Tongass Highway. A good map, available at either visitor center (see below), is a necessity, as the layout of the streets is quite confusing at first.

Once you've arrived in town and found the downtown area, you can spend a day seeing the sights on foot, but to get to the totem pole parks and other interesting places you'll need a rented car or a guided tour.

BY RENTAL CAR   Alaska Car Rental (☎ **800/662-0007** or 907/225-5000) has offices at the airport and at Third Avenue and Tongass, or will pick up or deliver the car for free. **Southeast Auto Rental** (☎ **800/770-8778** or 907/225-8778) is a budget agency and also delivers. **Avis** (☎ **800/831-2847** or 907/225-4515) has a desk at the airport, too.

BY GUIDED TOUR   Schoolteacher Lois Munch, of **Classic Tours** (☎ **907/ 225-3091;** www.classictours.com), makes her tours fun: She wears a poodle skirt to drive visitors around in her '55 Chevy. A 2-hour tour is $43, and a 3-hour tour is $57. **Sourdough Tours** (☎ **907/225-4081**) is a family business offering set or custom tours.

BY BIKE   A bike is a good way to see Ketchikan, and there is a 2½-mile bike trail along the water to Saxman and the totem pole park there, described below. **The Pedalers,** on Spruce Mill Way, near the visitors center (☎ **907/225-0440**), rents bikes for $6 an hour or $25 a day.

BY BOAT & SEA KAYAK   Waterfront boat cruises are available from **Alaska Cruises** (☎ **800/228-1905** or 907/225-6044) at $49 for a ride lasting just under 2 hours. I'd recommend taking a sea kayak and getting a closer look at the watery part of the city and the marine life of the surrounding area. **Southeast Exposure** (☎ **907/ 225-8829**) offers a 3-hour tour, no experience necessary, for $50.

VISITOR INFORMATION

Much more than a visitor center, the **Southeast Alaska Visitor Center,** 50 Main St., Ketchikan, AK 99901 (☎ **907/228-6220;** TDD 907/288-6237; fax 907/228-6234; www.nps.gov/aplic/), housed in a large, attractive building of log and concrete on the waterfront near the cruise-ship dock, contains an exceptional museum of the region's natural and cultural history and contemporary society. Curators have managed to tell the truth without offending either side in the community's hot debate over logging and the environment. There's also an auditorium showing a high-tech slide slow. Without paying, you can get guidance for your time in the outdoors. An information kiosk and bookstore are located near the entrance, and downstairs you'll find a trip-planning room, a luxurious library of material in various media, and an information desk where you can ask questions and get help on the details. Like the interagency Alaska Public Lands Information Centers in Anchorage, Fairbanks, and Tok, the trip-planning room provides guidance for enjoying the outdoors in all areas of the state. The center is open May to September daily 8:30am to 4:30pm, October to April Tuesday to Saturday from 8:30am to 4:30pm. Admission to the museum and slide show is $4.

You can reach the Forest Service through the **Ketchikan Ranger District,** at 3031 North Tongass Ave., Ketchikan, AK 99901 (☎ **907/225-2148;** www.fs.fed.us/ r10/tongass/).

The small **Ketchikan Visitors Bureau,** 131 Front St. (at Mission Street), Ketchikan, AK 99901 (☎ **800/770-2200** or 907/225-6166; fax 907/225-4250; www.visit-ketchikan.com), sits right on the cruise-ship dock and is open daily in the summer from 8am to 5pm and when cruise ships are in town; winter weekdays only. Their Web site contains links to an extraordinary number of local businesses, and allows you to order a Travel Guide to Ketchikan.

This local **Ketchikan Internet Service** maintains a page with links to many businesses and services at **www.ktn.net/**.

SPECIAL EVENTS

Celebration of the Sea, a 10-day event beginning around the first of May, includes a variety of art, music, and community events; you can get a schedule from the Ketchikan Visitors Bureau. **The King Salmon Derby,** almost 50 years old and run by the Greater Ketchikan Chamber of Commerce (☎ **907/225-3184**), takes place at the end of May and the beginning of June. **The Fourth of July** celebration will give you a true sense of the meaning of the holiday, with a long parade watched on Front Street by mobs of locals and cruise-ship passengers; after the parade, there's a **Timber Carnival** with an all-afternoon loggers' competition at the baseball field near City Park on Park Avenue; admission free. **The Blueberry Arts Festival,** held the second Saturday of August, has booths, music, and food, and is put on by the Ketchikan Area Arts and Humanities Council, 338 Main St. (☎ **907/225-2211**). **The Winter Arts Faire,** also hosted by the Council, is held the first Saturday and Sunday after Thanksgiving.

Fast Facts: Ketchikan

Banks   Several banks have ATMs, including National Bank of Alaska, at 306 Main St., and Bank of America, at 2417 Tongass Ave.

Hospital   Ketchikan General Hospital is at 3100 Tongass Ave. (☎ 907/225-5171).

Internet/E-mail   Cyber-by-the-Sea (☎ 907/247-6904; www.cyberbythesea.com), at 5 Salmon Landing, is a bookstore with access via Mac, PC, or WebTV. There's a $6 minimum, or $10 per hour. The bookstore has an extensive Alaska section and many off-the-mainstream magazines. They're open summer Monday through Saturday 9am to 6pm, Sunday noon to 6pm; winter Monday through Saturday 10am to 6pm.

Police   Call ☎ 907/225-6631 for nonemergencies.

Post Office   The main post office is at 3609 Tongass Ave.

Taxes   Sales tax is 5.5%. Room taxes for accommodations total 11.5%.

EXPLORING KETCHIKAN
TLINGIT, HAIDA & TSIMSHIAN CULTURAL HERITAGE

The Ketchikan area has two totem pole parks and a totem pole museum, as well as a wealth of contemporary Native art displayed all over town. Notable pieces stand at Whale Park at Mission and Bawden streets and at the Westmark Cape Fox Lodge. Most of what you see in Southeast Alaska is Tlingit—the Haida and Tsimshian generally live to the south and east in British Columbia—but Ketchikan is near the boundary between the three peoples, and here their similar cultures mix.

Totem Heritage Center. 601 Deermount St. ☎ **907/225-5900.** Admission $4 in summer or $5 for a combination ticket that also gets you into the Tongass Historical Museum (see below). Free in winter. Open daily 8am–5pm summer; Tues–Fri 1–5pm winter.

Located near City Park, the center contains the largest collection of original 19th-century totem poles in existence. The poles are displayed indoors, mostly unpainted, many with the grass and moss still attached where it was when they were rescued from the elements in villages where they had been mounted up to 160 years ago. Totem poles were never meant to be maintained or repainted, instead disintegrating after about 70 years and being constantly replaced, but these were preserved to help keep the culture alive. A high ceiling and muted lighting lend to the spiritual grandeur of the art. Well-trained guides are on hand to explain what you're looking at, and there are good interpretive signs. The gift shop carries authentic Native crafts in the summer.

Totem Bight State Historical Park. 10 miles out of town on North Tongass Highway. City Tour (☎ **800/652-8687** or 907/225-9465) offers a 2½-hour Totem Bight and rain-forest tour for $25, leaving at 10am daily. A number of other companies have guided tours, available through the Ketchikan Visitors Bureau.

The park, a New Deal–era work project to save disappearing Tlingit cultural artifacts by replicating them in an authentic setting, stands out among the clan houses and outdoor totem pole collections in Southeast for having excellent interpretive signs and a printed guide that explains what you're looking at. It sits at a peaceful spot on the edge of Tongass Narrows, at the end of a short walk through the woods, and provides an experience that's both aesthetic and educational.

Saxman Native Village Totem Pole Park. On a lawn above the Tlingit town of Saxman, 2½ miles south of Ketchikan on the South Tongass Highway. Call the Village Store in Saxman at ☎ **907/225-4421** for tour times and information. Admission $30 adults, $15 children 12 and under.

Saxman's park has artifacts similar to those at Totem Bight park, but an added resource: Accomplished carvers are still at work here in the small building to the right of the park. The drawback of the site for independent travelers is that Cape Fox Corp., the Native corporation that owns it, caters mainly to cruise-ship passengers, and no interpretive material is available other than its 2-hour tour, which includes art demonstrations, a slide show, and, during the week, dancing. The timing of the tour is different each day, depending on the ships.

A STROLL THROUGH TOWN

Get the clearly presented *Official Historic Ketchikan Walking Tour Map* free from the visitor center; its three routes cover everything of interest downtown. Here are the highlights.

Creek Street was Ketchikan's red-light district until fairly recently. Now its quaint, meandering boardwalks are a tourist attraction thronged with visitors. Prostitution was semilegal in Alaska until 1952, recently enough to survive in local memories but distant enough from life today to have made Creek Street historic and to transform the women who worked there from outcasts to icons. Dolly Arthur, who started in business for herself on the creek in 1919 and died in 1975, touched both periods, and her home became a commercial museum not long after her death. **Dolly's House** is amusing, mildly racy, and a little sad. Admission is $4; it's open 9am to 4pm during the summer and when cruise ships are in town.

Creek Street has some interesting shops and a couple of good restaurants, described below. It's fun just to walk the creek-side boardwalk into the forest above, and over the "Married Men's Trail" that leads through the woods from the street to the Westmark Cape Fox Lodge (or, for those married men of the old red-light days, in the other direction).

The Cape Fox Hill–Creek Street Funicular, a sort of diagonal elevator, runs 211 feet from the boardwalk up to the Westmark Cape Fox Lodge on top of the hill. Take it up and then enjoy the walk down through the woods. The summertime fare is $1, but if no one is around, just press the "up" button and go.

If you need a place to recharge, stop at the attractively situated **Ketchikan Public Library.** Its big windows look out on the foaming rapids, and the children's section downstairs has a play area with lots of toys. On the same site is the **Tongass Historical Museum,** 629 Dock St. (☎ **907/225-5600**), a one-room museum that presents the history and Native heritage of Ketchikan, along with an annually revolving exhibit. Although it's too small to hold your attention for long, what the museum has is informatively displayed. (It's open daily 8am to 5pm in the summer; Wednesday to Saturday afternoons in the winter. Admission is $3. The library is open Monday through Wednesday from 10am to 8pm, Thursday through Saturday from 10am to 6pm, and on Sunday from 1 to 5pm.)

Following the creek upstream, take a look at the **fish ladder** at the Park Avenue bridge, then continue to the **Deer Mountain Tribal Hatchery,** 1158 Salmon Rd. (☎ **907/225-6760**), a small king and silver salmon hatchery where you can see fry swimming in large tubs and even feed them. The hatchery is combined with the educational **Eagle Center,** exhibiting captive bald eagles and other raptors. Besides the indoor cages, there's a large outdoor eagle enclosure that takes in some trees and a section of the salmon stream. Visitors can go inside, a perfect setting for photos; when we visited, an eagle perched just 10 feet away. The birds are flightless or otherwise injured, some of them from Sitka's Alaska Raptor Rehabilitation Center, which is a sort of bird hospital. Unfortunately, the eagle center here is open only on days when cruise ships land (most days in the summer, and usually 8:30am to 4:30pm), or by arrangement. Admission is $6.95.

Beyond the hatchery is **City Park,** where Ketchikan Creek splits into a maze of ornamental pools and streams once used as a hatchery; my young son and I found it a magical place. The Totem Heritage Center, listed above, opens on the park.

Continuing to Deermount Street, you round the hill back to the waterfront. Turn right on Stedman, past the Thomas Basin boat harbor, to the starting point.

GETTING OUTSIDE

There's lots to do outdoors from Ketchikan, but most of it will require a boat or plane; the opportunities right on the road system are limited. See section 4 on Misty Fjords National Monument and section 5 on Prince of Wales Island (both later in this chapter) for more. In any event, your first stop should be the trip-planning room at the Southeast Alaska Visitor Information Center (see address above), where a forest ranger can provide detailed information on trails, fishing, and dozens of available U.S. Forest Service cabins.

SPECIAL PLACES

REMOTE CABINS   The U.S. Forest Service maintains more than 50 **cabins** around Ketchikan; all are remote and primitive, but at $25 to $35 a night, you can't beat the price or the settings. This is a chance to be utterly alone in the wilderness, and many of the lake cabins come with a boat for fishing and exploring. For details and descriptions of all the cabins, contact the Southeast Alaska Visitor Information Center (☎ **907/228-6214**). The reservation system is described above, in the "Outside in Southeast" section. You'll need all your camping gear except a tent, including sleeping bags, a camp stove and your own cooking outfit, a lantern, and so on. **Alaska Wilderness Outfitting and Camping Rentals,** 3857 Fairview St., Ketchikan, AK 99901 (☎ **907/225-7335**), rents the gear, as well as small outboards for the skiffs, and will even take care of your grocery shopping. (The same folks have a water taxi, kayak delivery, and charter service called Experience One Charters, listed below in the Misty Fjords section.)

As the cabins are remote, it takes a plane, a boat, or a hike to get to all of them—most are accessible only by floatplane. That's where the money comes in. A good rule of thumb is that a floatplane charter will cost roughly $300 an hour, and you'll have to pay for the plane to get out there and back twice. **Taquan Air Service,** 1007 Water St., Ketchikan, AK 99901 (☎ **800/770-8800** or 907/225-8800; www.AlaskaOne. com/TaquanAir), has round-trip charter rates for the closest cabins of $360 for a two-passenger Cessna 185 or $600 for a four-passenger DeHavilland Beaver. They sell a cabin planning package for $8.95 including the Forest Service maps and other information. **Promech Air,** 1515 Tongass Ave., Ketchikan, AK 99901 (☎ **800/860-3845** within Alaska only, or 907/225-3845), also operates these charters, among others.

SCENIC TRAILS   The **Ward Lake Nature Trail** circles 1.3 miles around a smooth lake among old-growth Sitka spruce large enough to put you in your place. Ward Creek has trout and salmon. To reach the trail, lakeside campground, and picnic area, travel about 7 miles out North Tongass Highway and turn right on Revilla Road just before the defunct pulp mill. For a slightly more challenging hike, **Perseverance Lake Trail** climbs up boardwalks with steps from the 3C's campground, 1.4 miles up the road, to another lake 2.3 miles away.

   Deer Mountain Trail is a challenging overnight trek, starting only half a mile from Ketchikan, but you don't have to go all the way for dramatic views, 1 mile up the trail and at the summit, after a 2½-mile, 3,000-foot climb; the trail continues through the mountains from there, to a Forest Service cabin, across another summit, through some summer snow and ice, and ends at another trailhead 10 miles away. The main trailhead is ½ mile up Ketchikan Lakes Road. Pick up a trail guide sheet from the Forest Service at the Southeast Alaska Visitor Information Center.

OUTDOOR ACTIVITIES

○ **FISHING**   The **Alaska Department of Fish and Game** produces a 24-page fishing guide to Ketchikan, with details on where to find fish in both fresh and salt water, listing 17 spots accessible from the roads. You can pick up a copy at the Southeast Alaska Visitor Information Center or from the department's Juneau office (see section 2, "Outside in Southeast," above). For licenses and other help, the local **Fish and Game office** is at 2030 Sea Level Dr., Suite 205, Ketchikan, AK 99901 (☎ **907/225-2859**). There are plenty of charters available to get out on the water for salmon and halibut. The Ketchikan Visitors Bureau can provide you with a list. For even more remote fishing, you can fly out to meet a charter boat or fish a remote lake or stream all by yourself. See the flight services above under "Special Places." If you want to devote your time in Ketchikan to fishing, check out the fishing lodges listed below.

SEA KAYAKING   The islands, coves, and channels around Ketchikan seem infinite in complexity, creating protected waters rich with life and welcoming for exploration by kayak. Any reasonably fit adult can enjoy a kayak paddle, and your appreciation of the area's beauty will expand greatly. **Southeast Exposure,** 515 Water St. (P.O. Box 9143), Ketchikan, AK 99901 (☎ **907/225-8829;** fax 907/225-8849), rents kayaks and guides trips from 1 to 6 days long. A 6-hour day trip is $80 per person; a 6-day trip is $950 per person. They'll put together a special trip for groups of three or more.

Indoor Recreation in Ketchikan

   Ketchikan's wet weather prompted the locals to build a large **Indoor Recreation Center** at 601 Schoenbar Rd. (☎ **907/225-9579**), with three racquetball courts, one of which converts to squash, gymnasiums, a running track, weights, and drop-in classes. It is open Monday through Saturday 5am to 10pm, Sunday noon to 5pm.

WILDLIFE VIEWING   You're likely see eagles, otters, and much other wildlife in the area without really trying. You're also a short flight away from one of Alaska's best bear viewing areas, the Anan Wildlife Observatory. (See the section on Wrangell, below, for a full description.) Taquan Air Service offers daily tours to Anan during the bear-viewing season for $225 per person (see above for contact information).

ACCOMMODATIONS

In addition to the hotels and B&Bs listed below, the **Ketchikan Reservation Service,** 412 D-1 Loop Rd., Ketchikan, AK 99901 (☎ **800/987-5337** or fax/phone 907/ 247-5337; www.ketchikan-lodging.com), books more than 20 bed-and-breakfasts and outfitted apartments. Also, some of the higher quality B&Bs in town have developed their own network, which you can reach through Blueberry Hill B&B below, or at www.ptialaska.net/~bestbnbs.

EXPENSIVE

Best Western Landing. 3434 Tongass Ave., Ketchikan, AK 99901. ☎ **907/225-5166.** Fax 907/225-6900. www.landinghotel.com. 75 units, 1 2-bedroom apt. TV TEL. High season, $125–$148 double; $160 suite. Low season, $85–$95 double; $120 suite. Apt. $200 year-round. AE, CB, DC, DISC, MC, V.

A well-run, regularly remodeled establishment with a wide variety of different types of rooms: simple hotel rooms; suites with sitting rooms, microwave ovens, refrigerators, and balconies; and a two-bedroom apartment. The new wing has the best rooms. The location, right across from the ferry dock, is distant from the downtown sights, so you'll need to rent a car or use the courtesy van, which runs back and forth regularly. The hotel's restaurant is popular with locals checking up on the day's gossip. It serves family meals for reasonable prices in a dining room with a 1950s motif. Kids are well treated. Hours are 6am to 9pm off-season, until 10pm in summer. Drinks are available from Jeremiah's bar, upstairs, which serves an excellent pub menu and has live music Wednesday through Saturday. Smoking and no-smoking areas each have their own fireplace, and there's a deck overlooking the water across the highway.

Salmon Falls Resort. 16707 N. Tongass Hwy. (P.O. Box 5700), Ketchikan, AK 99901. ☎ **800/247-9059** (reservations) or 907/225-2752. Fax 907/225-2710. www.ktn.net/sfalls. 52 units. TEL. $139 double. Additional person in room $10 extra. MC, V. Closed Sept 15– May 15.

This huge fishing lodge has its own waterfall where silvers spawn in August, as well as a dock on Clover Passage with boats for all the guests. Inclusive fishing packages start at $900 per person, double occupancy, for a 3-day stay with 2 days on the water, self-guided. With a guide, the price is $1,300 per person. The lodge is on the Tongass Highway 16½ miles north of town, so you save the cost of flying to a comparable lodge off the island. The rooms are comfortable and well decorated; the new building is best. But it's the restaurant and bar that are really amazing: a massive log octagon held up in the center by a section of the Alaska pipeline, with great views from all tables and a well-prepared menu of steak or seafood ranging from $18 to $29. Non-fishers will enjoy a drive out the road for dinner, even if they aren't staying here.

✪ **Westmark Cape Fox Lodge.** 800 Venetia Way, Ketchikan, AK 99901. ☎ **800/ 544-0970** (central reservations) or 907/225-8001. Fax 907/225-8286. www.westmarkhotels. com. 72 units. TV TEL. High season, $159–$169 double; Low season, $119–$129 double; $200 suite. AE, DC, DISC, MC, V.

This is the most beautiful hotel in Southeast Alaska. Owned by the Native Cape Fox Corporation and run by the Westmark chain, the hotel's understated but inspired design and masterpieces of Tlingit art lend a sense of the peace and spirit of the rain forest. All but a dozen rooms share Ketchikan's most spectacular view, looking out among huge trees over the edge of a cliff that dominates the city and waterfront (rooms on the opposite side are $10 less). To get down the cliff merely requires stepping aboard the Creek Street funicular, which drops you in the middle of the town's most charming and popular tourist area. Even if you can't afford to stay, the elegance and view are worth a visit. Rooms have coffeemakers, clock radios, and double phone jacks, and suites are furnished with quilts and other homey features. A reader complained recently of losing a reservation due to overbooking—arriving early would avoid that situation.

The **Heen Kahidi restaurant** shares the wonderful view, and the food is generally good, placing it among the best in the less than stellar field of Ketchikan's restaurants. Lunch entrees are around $10 ($8 for a burger), and dinner $18 to $32.

MODERATE

The Cedars. 1471 Tongass Ave. (P.O. Box 8331), Ketchikan, AK 99901. ☎ **907/225-1900.** Fax 907/225-8604. E-mail: TheCedars@ptialaska.net. 13 units, 2 without tubs. TV TEL. $110 double; $140 studio with spa; $215 suite. Fishing packages available. AE, CB, DC, DISC, MC, V.

The Cedars is hard against the sidewalk of a busy street, but the whole building is on pilings over the water, with a dock where floatplanes tie up for fishing trips. It combines being near downtown with a sense of being out of town on the water. The palatial waterfront suites with Jacuzzis and full kitchens surpass anything else in town. Some have second bedrooms up spiral staircases. They serve breakfast and dinner as part of the fishing packages, and pack and ship your catch, starting around $600 for 2 nights and 1 day of fishing. All rooms house smokers.

The Narrows Inn. 4871 N. Tongass Hwy. (P.O. Box 8296), Ketchikan, AK 99901. ☎ **888/686-2600** or 907/247-2600. Fax 907/247-2602. www.narrowsinn.com. 44 units. TV TEL. High season $95–$115 double. Low season $69 double. Additional person in room $10 extra. AE, DISC, MC, V.

It's on the water near a boat dock 1½ miles north of the ferry terminal, so you'll want to rent a car if staying here, but the reasonable prices on these fresh, new accommodations could make staying here worthwhile. The rooms and bathrooms are small and entered from the outside, as at a motel, but they're immaculately clean and have natural woodwork, and some have private decks. The inn offers free coffee and a courtesy van, and sets up fishing packages for guests.

The **Narrows Inn Restaurant** serves an extensive steak and seafood menu, with dinner entrees generally near $20, and all the usual American choices for lunch. Meals are hearty and consistently good. The dining room is spacious and bright with a ocean frontage, but doesn't have the character or style fitting the fine dining menu and prices.

INEXPENSIVE

Blueberry Hill B&B. 500 Upper Front St. (P.O. Box 9508), Ketchikan, AK 99901. ☎ **907/247-2583.** Fax 907/247-2584. www.ptialaska.net/~blubrry. 4 units. TEL. High season, $85–$95 double, $105 suite. Low season $75–$85 double, $95 suite. Additional person in room $15 extra. AE, DISC, MC, V.

This gracious 1917 house, once a residence for nuns, stands atop the rocky cliff that bounds the north side of the downtown waterfront, above the tunnel. It's a short drive, or 115 steps down a public stairway, to the center of the action; but up here all is peaceful, with soothing New Age music playing under the high ceiling of Elson Zimmerly and Hank Newhouse's stately living room. Each of the guest rooms is large and light, with handmade quilts and elegant furniture. The hosts try to make friends with guests and serve a full breakfast. Newhouse also operates charters on his sailboat; Zimmerly is an accomplished fine art photographer and does weekly slide shows. Smoking is not allowed.

✪ **Captain's Quarters Bed & Breakfast.** 325 Lund St., Ketchikan, AK 99901. ☎ **907/ 225-4912.** www.ptialaska.net/~captbnb. 3 units. TV TEL. High season, $80 double. Low season, $65 double. Additional person in room $20 extra. MC, V.

These large, quiet, immaculate rooms, with a sweeping view of the city and ocean, private telephone lines, and a self-contained, self-service breakfast room, rival the best hotel rooms in Ketchikan but cost half as much. Marv Wendeborn custom-built the B&B with his own hands, carrying the nautical theme through oak woodwork. The family interacts with guests only at their request, and the business is completely separate from their home, with its own entrance. One room has a full kitchen. The house perches a reasonable walk from downtown, in a mountainside neighborhood just north of the tunnel where half the streets are stairs. Children aren't allowed, and there's no smoking in the house.

Gilmore Hotel. 326 Front St., Ketchikan, AK 99901. ☎ **800/275-9423** or 907/225-9423. Fax 907/225-7442. www.gilmorehotel.com. 38 units. TV TEL. High season, $68–$82 double, $129 suite. Low season, $50–$60 double, $104 suite. Additional person in room $5 extra. AE, CB, DC, DISC, MC, V.

This 1927 concrete structure on the waterfront tries for a historic feel to match the high ceilings, dignified facade, and views over the cruise-ship dock. The front rooms are the most desirable, while some others are tiny nearly to the point of claustrophobia. About two thirds have shower stalls in the bathrooms, while the balance have shower-tub combinations. The service and style—including the courtesy van, room service, and free coffee in the lobby—suggest a more expensive place.

Annabelle's Famous Keg and Chowder House, the hotel restaurant, serves lots of shellfish, salads, sandwiches, and pasta, with many items around $10, amid turn-of-the-century tavern decor with much brass and mahogany.

✪ **New York Hotel.** 207 Stedman St., Ketchikan, AK 99901. ☎ **907/225-0246.** 8 units. TV TEL. High season $79 double. Low season $49 double. AE, MC, V.

This funny little 1924 building, in a perfect central location just off Creek Street, contains charming, antique-furnished rooms that look out on a small boat harbor. The rooms have more attractive amenities than other hotels in town that cost much more, and when we visited, they were sparkling clean. The tasteful restoration of the New York was a family project, and the owners still meet guests in the tiny lobby with casual small-town hospitality. A continental breakfast is included in the bargain rates. The attached cafe is described below.

A HOSTEL

First United Methodist Church. 400 Main St. (P.O. Box 8515), Ketchikan, AK 99901. ☎ **907/225-3319.** 25 beds. $11 per person. Closed Sept–May.

Open only June through August, this church-run hostel, affiliated with Hostelling International (members get a $3 discount), is just up from the tunnel in the downtown area. Free pastries and hot drinks are provided, and guests have use of the church kitchen. Bring a sleeping bag. The office is open from 7 to 9am and 6 to 11pm.

CAMPING

Three Forest Service campgrounds with a total of 47 sites are located at **Ward Lake** (see "Special Places," above). Eighteen miles out North Tongass Highway, the **Settler's Cove State Park** includes a sandy beach—a good place to watch whales, beach-comb, or even swim—and the 1-mile Lunch Falls Loop Trail, a handicapped-accessible path to a spectacular waterfall. There are 14 campsites, half of which will take rigs of up to 30 feet, without hookups. For information, contact the Alaska Division of Parks (☎ 907/247-8574), 9883 N. Tongass Hwy.

If you need hookups for an RV, try **Clover Pass Resort,** about 13 miles north of the ferry terminal on North Point Higgins Road (☎ **800/410-2234** outside Alaska only, or 907/247-2234). They charge $26 a night.

DINING

Ketchikan isn't a place for great dining, but there is a selection of decent places to eat. The hotels house some of the best restaurants, which I've described under "Accommodations," above, in the Westmark Cape Fox Lodge, Gilmore Hotel, Salmon Falls Resort, The Narrows Inn, and Best Western Landing listings. An Internet cafe is listed under "Fast Facts." If you're interested in pizza, try **Papa's Ketchikan Cafe and Pizza,** on the third floor at 316 Front St. (☎ **907/247-7272**). They deliver their fancy, Italian-style pizza free. The pesto and artichoke is a local favorite.

New York Cafe. 207 Stedman St. ☎ **907/225-0246.** Lunch $5–$8; dinner $15–$20. MC, V. 7am–9pm. STEAK/SEAFOOD/SANDWICHES.

The food here is good and inexpensive and the decor a perfectly realized restoration of an old-fashioned lunch counter, in a bright little room on the street across from the boat harbor. Huge windows and a high ceiling pour light into a room with a black-and-white tiled floor and a lot of old woodwork. It can be smoky in the small dining room.

Ocean View Restaurante. 3159 Tongass Ave. ☎ **907/225-7566.** Lunch $6–$9; dinner $8–$17. MC, V. Daily 11am–11pm. MEXICAN/ITALIAN.

Off the usual tourist path, ¼ mile south of the ferry terminal, this bustling family restaurant packs in the locals by doing many things well: steak and seafood, sizzling fajitas and other Mexican dishes, submarine sandwiches, pizza, pasta, and even Greek appetizers. The smoke-free dining rooms are small, making reservations a wise move during rush hours, but there's nothing fancy about the place—bowls of chips and salsa hit the Formica table as soon you sit down. The reasonable prices make meals here the best deal in town, with few entrees over $15. At this writing, they did not have a liquor license, but were planning to get one.

Polar Treats. 410 Mission St. ☎ **907/247-6527.** Lunch $5–$7. MC, V. High season 8am–7pm. Low season Mon–Sat 11am–4pm. DELI/WRAPS

The chairs are plastic and the tableware disposable, but if you're looking for a quick, inexpensive, and delicious lunch break while sightseeing, you'll do no better. The wraps are huge, messy, and flavorful, with wonderfully exotic combinations of ingredients. The panini and other sandwiches are good, too. At the least, stop in for the hand-packed ice cream. There are only four tables and a lunch counter, so much of the business is takeout or delivered.

Steamers. 76 Front St. ☎ **907/225-1600.** Lunch and dinner $5–$50. AE, DC, DISC, MC, V. 11am–11pm daily. STEAK/SEAFOOD.

On the third floor right on the dock (take the corner elevator to the top), this huge bar and grill tries for a Seattle feel, with 20 beers on tap and a long menu of seafood and some beef, available as full dinners or à la carte. Prices demand this be a place for a special meal—a fish-and-chips dinner is $17, and you can easily spend more than $50 per diner. My soup was well seasoned and the fish grilled not a moment too long. The bright dining room of light oak has towering ceilings and huge windows, with tables well separated; service was professional. They have live music during the day in the visitor season.

SHOPPING

Ketchikan has become a shopping and art destination thanks to the explosion of visitors. If you want something authentically Alaskan, however, you have to be careful. For some important tips, see "Native Art—Finding the Real Thing," in chapter 2.

☼ **Soho Coho,** at 5 Creek St., is worth a visit even if you aren't a shopper. Owner Ray Troll is Alaska's leading fish-obsessed artist. His gallery shows his work and that of other Ketchikan artists from the same school of surreal rain forest humor. In Troll's art, subtle ironies and silly puns coexist in a solidly decorated interior world. His popular T-shirts allow people to clothe themselves in Troll's strange metaphors linking mankind and lower evolutionary forms. "Spawn Till You Die" is a classic. Troll displays his art on a gorgeous Web site at www.trollart.com. The gallery is open summer daily from 9am to 5pm, winter Tuesday through Saturday 11 to 5. Down the hall in the same building, **Alaska Eagle Arts** is a serious gallery featuring the bold yet traditional work of Native artist Marvin Oliver. Upstairs, stop in at **Parnassus Books,** a cubbyhole with a broad and sophisticated selection of Alaskana, great for browsing. Down the boardwalk at 18 Creek St., expert craftsmen create indigenous art and interact with visitors at **Hide-A-Way Gifts,** which carries carvings and Native crafts. At 123 Stedman St., near the bridge over the creek, **Blue Heron Gallery and Gifts** (☎ **907/225-1982**) carries Alaskan arts and crafts that appeal to locals as well as visitors: jewelry, stained glass, clothing, jam, prints, and so on. **The Wood Shop,** at 632 Park, on the way to the hatchery and City Park, sells wonderful wooden toys, jewelry, and other underpriced crafts made and sold by participants in a program for the mentally ill.

Don't miss the open-air **Salmon Landing Market,** on Spruce Mill Way between the Southeast Alaska Visitor Center and the cruise ship dock. Local artists and craftspeople market their output in covered booths—prints, clothing, cards, and so on. The adjacent two-story wood and metal mall contains **Fairweather Prints,** an outdoor gear store, an Internet cafe, and other shops of potential interest.

On the city streets near the cruise-ship dock, check out **Scanlon Gallery,** at 318 Mission St., which carries Alaska contemporary art, Alaska Native art, and affordable prints and other items in various media. **Finzel's Books and Gifts,** at 633 Mission St., carries local Native and contemporary art, books about Alaska, and ordinary paperbacks for your next ferry ride. The **Ketchikan Arts and Humanities Council,** at 338 Main St., maintains a gallery of regional work. **KetchiCandies,** at 315 Mission St., caters to visitors and the many locals addicted to their homemade chocolates and other candies.

KETCHIKAN IN THE EVENING

First City Players (☎ **907/225-4792**) puts on a popular summer melodrama, *Fish Pirate's Daughter,* in the small Main Street Theater. Tickets are $10, and reservations are recommended.

Historically, Ketchikan has been a hard-drinking town. Trap doors remain in the floors of some Creek Street buildings where bootleggers would pass booze up from boats underneath. The bars on Front Street are generally authentic waterfront places: dark gritty rooms where you can meet commercial fishermen and locals. **Annabelle's** is a more genteel, refurbished version of an old-fashioned Front Street bar. On the more aesthetic side, the **Kingfisher Bar** is probably the most attractive place for a drink, located in the Salmon Landing Market with a sweeping waterfront view over the cruise-ship dock. The barroom has cathedral ceilings and wood floors. A variety of regional microbrews are on tap and live music plays every night, year-round. Bowling, live music, and ball games on TV, as well as meals and drinks, are available at the **Roller Bay Cafe,** at 2050 Sealevel Dr. **Jeremiah's,** at the Best Western Landing Hotel, 3434 Tongass Ave., often has live music.

4 Misty Fjords National Monument: Granite & Water

Among the vast, uninhabited islands, bottomless bays and fjords, massive trees, and inconceivably towering cliffs of the southern Alaska Panhandle are 2.3 million acres of inviolate wilderness Pres. Jimmy Carter set aside as a national monument with a stroke of his pen in 1978. It's still waiting to be discovered. There are cliffs comparable to (and higher than) Yosemite Valley's, but they rise straight from remote Punchbowl Cove, where only those fortunate enough to explore by boat, kayak, or floatplane are likely to see them. There's no question this land, larger than Yellowstone National Park, qualifies scenically as among America's greatest wild places, but without roads or trails it feel more like a great national park a century ago than the busy places we know now. Here, a seemingly endless untouched wilderness forces you to admit that your own imagination is sadly puny by comparison with its huge trees and extraordinary geology.

As with all uncrowded places, access to Misty Fjords is rationed, in this case by cost. The only practical way to get there is by boat or floatplane—there's no cheap way to see the bulk of the monument. The only places to stay are 14 rustic **U.S. Forest Service cabins.** One can get to the edge of the monument on an 18-mile trail from the little town of **Hyder,** which can be reached either by road from British Columbia or by a long ferry ride from Ketchikan, but that's a rare and challenging route. The most popular way to see the monument is on a **tour boat from Ketchikan.** The monument is also a good place for sea kayaking—that's how the four backcountry Forest Service rangers get around.

There are several noteworthy places to see. **New Eddystone Rock,** standing in the middle of Behm Canal, is a 237-foot-tall exclamation point of weathered rock, the remaining lava plug from an eroded volcano. **Rudyerd Bay** is like a place where the earth shattered open: The cliffs in its Punchbowl Cove rise vertically 3,150 feet from the surface of water that's 900 feet deep—topography in a league with the Grand Canyon. Waterfalls pound down out of the bay's granite. The glaciers of the northern part of the monument also are impressive, although they require a plane to visit.

But don't go to Misty Fjords to see animals. You may see harbor seals, but here the attraction is the land itself and its outrageous geology. Also, the name is accurate: It's misty. Or it could be pouring rain. This is among the rainiest spots on earth.

ESSENTIALS
GETTING THERE
BY BOAT Charters are available from Ketchikan, but it's 50 miles to Rudyerd Bay, an expensive ride. A better choice is to go on one of the tour boat excursions offered by Ketchikan operators. The largest and most experienced of these is **Alaska Cruises,** 220 Front St. (P.O. Box 7815), Ketchikan, AK 99901 (☎ **800/228-1905** or 907/ 225-6044; www.ptialaska.net/~akcruise). They run a high-speed, 92-passenger cata-maran on daily trips that take 6½ hours out and back. Most passengers take the boat 3 hours one way, then fly 20 minutes back to Ketchikan on a floatplane, seeing the same amazing scenery from the air. The tour travels up the Behm Canal, past New Eddystone Rock, then drifts through Punchbowl Cove before finally coming to a

floating dock at the head of Rudyerd Bay, where passengers board the floatplanes. The fare is $198 for adults, $160 for children 2 to 11. If you choose to stay on the boat back to Ketchikan, hearing the narration twice, the adult fare is $145 and the child fare $115. Snacks and chowder are served on board. If you're susceptible to seasickness, try to have an alternative date to go in case of bad weather; the water is generally smooth in the fjords but more exposed on the way there.

Among other charter operators, **Experience One Charters,** 3857 Fairview, Ketchikan, AK 99901 (☎ **907/225-8886;** visit.ktn.net/aae), can take you to Misty Fjords on a vessel and itinerary you control. Their vessel can handle groups of up to 12. They also haul kayaks and specialize in outfitting visits to Forest Service cabins.

BY KAYAK   **Southeast Exposure,** 507 Stedman St. (P.O. Box 9143), Ketchikan, AK 99901 (☎ **907/225-8829;** fax 907/225-8849), offers guided trips to the monument, starting at 4 days for $700 per person. They also have kayaks for rent for $30 to $50 a day; a 90-minute training class is mandatory, and an unguided trip deep into the fjords isn't advisable for first-timers, although it's hard to imagine a more appealing destination for experienced paddlers. The Forest Service produces a good kayaker's map showing camping spots, rip tides, and dangerous waters, available for $4 from the Southeast Alaska Visitor Information Center (see "Visitor Information," below). Alaska Cruises (see "By Boat," above) drops off or picks up kayakers at Rudyerd Bay for $200. Experience One Charters does drop-offs at the spot of your choosing, and rents camping equipment.

BY PLANE   You can cover a lot more ground a lot faster this way, and flying over the cliffs, trees, and glaciers is an experience all its own. Several air-taxi operators in Ketchikan take trips; **Taquan Air Service,** 1007 Water St., Ketchikan, AK 99901 (☎ **800/770-8800** or 907/225-8800; www.AlaskaOne.com/TaquanAir), for example, offers a 90-minute flight leaving at 10:30am daily that costs $149 per person. You can also use them to get to a remote cabin (see below) or other outings in the area. They also can help you figure out what you want to do.

ON FOOT   Hyder is 18 miles by trail from the monument, but it's at the end of the long Portland Canal, so most of the monument is not readily accessible from there. There's an opportunity to watch black and brown bears feeding from a Forest Service platform on Fish Creek—the most unregulated, accessible bear viewing in the state—and the area has good birding. Hyder can be reached by the Cassiar Highway from British Columbia or by ferry once every 2 weeks from Ketchikan, a 12-hour run that costs $40.

Visitor Information

The **Southeast Alaska Visitor Center,** 50 Main St., Ketchikan, AK 99901 (☎ **907/ 228-6220**), can give you a packet about Misty Fjords in the trip-planning room downstairs. The **Ketchikan Visitors Bureau,** 131 Front St., Ketchikan, AK 99901 (☎ **907/225-6166**), can provide the names of charter operators. The monument is part of the Tongass National Forest. **Misty Fiords National Monument offices** are at the U.S. Forest Service Ketchikan Ranger District, 3031 Tongass Ave., Ketchikan, AK 99901 (☎ **907/225-2148;** www.fs.fed.us/r10/tongass/).

ACCOMMODATIONS

The only lodgings are 14 **U.S. Forest Service cabins** and several three-sided shelters. Many are little used and extremely remote, and all those on lakes have rowboats.

The cabins cost $25 to $45 per night, but that's only a small part of the cost of using them. You also have to pay for a floatplane to get there. I've listed the names of some of the air-taxi and gear-rental operators in "Special Places" under "Getting Outside," in the Ketchikan section, earlier in this chapter. While $300 to $400 an hour for flight time may seem steep, remember that in town or at a wilderness lodge, you'd be paying for a hotel room and meals. A group of three could do 3 days at a Forest Service cabin for under $600.

Winstanley Island Cabin is a good destination for kayakers, and there's a chance of seeing bears. **Big Goat Lake Cabin** sits on a point on an alpine lake near a 1,700-foot waterfall; it's accessible only by plane, and because it's so beautiful, a lot of plane traffic comes by. **Ella Lake** is relatively near Ketchikan, so the cost of the trip isn't as high as some others, but it's very secluded. You can fly to it, or take a boat to the 2.3-mile trail to the lake, then row across the lake to the cabin. Right off Rudyerd Bay, beautiful **Nooya Lake** has a three-sided shelter. These are just highlights; for a complete listing of cabins, contact the Forest Service at the Southeast Alaska Visitor Center or the Misty Fjords National Monument offices, listed above. For reservation information, see "Outside in Southeast," earlier in this chapter.

5 Prince of Wales Island

If you have plenty of time, the Alaska Bush is just a short ferry or small-plane ride from Ketchikan, ready to be explored by car. Prince of Wales Island, known locally as "POW," is 135 miles long and 45 miles wide, making it the third-largest island in the United States (after Alaska's Kodiak Island and Hawaii's Big Island), yet it is populated by only a few tiny towns and Native villages. What makes the island unique in Alaska is that it's traversed by a network of more than 1,000 miles of gravel roads, built and maintained by the U.S. Forest Service to facilitate logging. That means you can get out on your own to beautiful places rich with fish, exploring without the expense of an airplane or boat, but rarely seeing another person. It can be a strange feeling to drive for hours without seeing a building or another car. Unfortunately, this accessibility also means that many of the beautiful places are not as beautiful as they once were, as the island is scarred by many large clear-cuts.

Fishing, in both salt- and freshwater, is by far the biggest reason to visit the island. The Forest Service lists 32 good fishing streams and maintains some 20 public cabins, mainly built for their access to remote fishing lakes and streams. Many **fishing lodges** operate on the island, mostly taking guests out on boats to fish salmon in the ocean; most visitors to the island have booked inclusive packages at one of the lodges well in advance.

Some people discover more of the island, though. **Divers** find clear water and a rich profusion of life in these waters; two **canoe routes** cross wilderness areas of the island; and few other places offer families the same opportunities for solitude and discovery along the road and trails. Plus, POW contains hundreds of barely explored **caves,** two of which casual visitors can safely enter, albeit with some effort.

ESSENTIALS
ORIENTATION

The largest town is **Craig,** on the west side of the island. Here you'll find three good hotels, restaurants, a bank with an ATM, various stores, and a floatplane base. Seven miles east is Klawock, a large Native village with the island's major paved landing strip, a shopping center, more restaurants and accommodations, and a rotting totem pole park built under the New Deal in the 1930s. The other towns and villages on the island are quite small and have limited services. **Hollis,** where the ferry lands on the east side of the island, is just a collection of houses.

GETTING THERE & GETTING AROUND

You can fly to Prince of Wales on a float- or wheeled plane with any of the air-taxi operators in Ketchikan. **Taquan Air Service,** 1007 Water St., Ketchikan, AK 99901 (☎ **800/770-8800** or 907/225-8800; www.AlaskaOne.com/TaquanAir), has frequent flights to Craig or Klawock, as well as packages and tours of the island's highlights, including the caves. If you fly, and you're not at a lodge or on a package, you'll need to rent a car. **Wilderness Rent-a-Car,** at Log Cabin Sporting Goods in Craig (☎ **800/949-2205** or 907/826-2205), charges $79 a day plus 30¢ a mile after 100 miles, which can add up fast if you explore the whole island. Depending on your plans, you may do better to rent a car in Ketchikan and take the ferry over. The **Alaska Marine Highway** fare for a small car from Ketchikan to Hollis is $41, and each passenger is $20 more (see listing in section 1, "Exploring Southeast Alaska," at the beginning of this chapter).

VISITOR INFORMATION

Before going to Prince of Wales, stop at the trip-planning room in the **Southeast Alaska Visitor Information Center** in Ketchikan (☎ **907/228-6220;** see "Visitor Information" in section 3, above) and pick up the Forest Service recreation guides and the $4 road guide, which is a large map showing the roads and topography and listing the cabins and facilities available around the island. Fishermen will also want to get a copy of the Alaska Department of Fish and Game's *Sport Fishing Guide* for the island, as well as other guidance they can provide at their Ketchikan Division of Sport Fish office, at 2030 Sealevel Dr., Suite 207, Ketchikan, AK 99901 (☎ **907/ 225-2859**). The **Prince of Wales Chamber of Commerce,** P.O. Box 497, Craig, AK 99921 (☎ **907/826-3870;** fax 907/826-5467; princeofwalescoc.org), distributes listings of accommodations and businesses in the various communities.

GETTING OUTSIDE

FISHING   The fishing opportunities on Prince of Wales are legendary. I'm not a fly-fisherman myself, but I know some, and when they come back from POW they look like they've been yanked back from a near-death visit to paradise. They talk of rain forest surrounding streams and lakes that are seemingly virgin to the fishhook and yield steelhead, cutthroat, and other trout by the dozen in a day's fishing. The ethic of this externally pointless sport demands, of course, that the fish are photographed and released. Meat-eating fishers tend to go instead for the big, plentiful salmon, which you can fish in streams or, with greater predictability, trolling from a boat. Many lodges on the island offer river or ocean trips, and guides are booked up many months in advance. Some are described below.

You can also go on your own, of course, using the Forest Service cabins or camping (see "Accommodations & Dining," below). Some cabins come with boats that allow access away from the road, or you can rent a canoe (see below). Even without a boat, there are enough roads and enough good fishing that a car can take you to no-fail fishing spots by the dozen. The Alaska Department of Fish and Game's *Sport Fishing Guide* lists many of these (it's mentioned above).

CAVING   The limestone of Prince of Wales Island contains a honeycomb of miles of caves. Though they're wet, cold, and challenging, advanced cavers consider these to be among the world's most exciting caves, for their complexity and for the wonder of exploring areas that have never been seen by mankind. The caves originally were explored only in 1987, and there's still plenty left to be mapped by explorers led by the Forest Service.

Two caves have been developed for the public. Forest Service guides lead visitors on 2-hour treks into **El Capitan** cave four times a day during the summer. Although the tour goes only about 600 feet into the 12,000-foot cave, it feels like you've been to the center of the earth in these incredibly complex, twisting chambers known in the caving business as a "spongework maze." The hike is only for the fit and starts with a climb up 350 steps to the mountainside cave opening. Visitors can wade into the grotto-like **Cavern Lake Cave** on their own—you never lose daylight in this broad crack in the earth. Tall rubber boots or other preparations for the flowing cavern stream will help. You'll need the Forest Service's road guide map mentioned above to find the caves after a 3-hour drive from Craig, and reservations are required for a tour in the El Capitan Cave; contact the **Thorne Bay Ranger District,** 1312 USFS Dr. (P.O. Bos 19001), Thorne Bay, AK 99919 (☎ **907/828-3304;** www.fs.fed.us/r10/ tongass/). El Capitan Cave is blocked by a gate a couple of hundred feet in, so I strongly recommend going on the tour.

DIVING   Craig Sempert's **Craig Dive Center,** 107 Main St. (P.O. Box 796), Craig, AK 99921 (☎ **907/826-3481** or 800/380-DIVE in Alaska only; www.diveguideint. com/p0089.htm), offers rentals and fully guided diving packages to the island. The water here is clearer and the invertebrate and marine mammal life even richer than in the Inside Passage part of Southeast Alaska. Plankton blooms can cloud things up in the summer, but winter is always clear. Sempert dives in wet and dry suits, and tailors packages to visitors' interests, diving in unexplored areas, and even in caves. He also rents out a pair of attractive kitchenette apartment units by the night, for $85 double—a great place for families to stay, whether divers or not.

CANOEING   A couple of lovely backwoods canoe routes cross parts of the island, on Sarkar Lake and through the Honker Divide, each with Forest Service cabins along the way. Here's an inexpensive way into deep wilderness, with the relative comfort of a roof over your head at night. You can bring your own canoe or rent one from **Log Cabin Sporting Goods** in Craig (☎ **800/949-2205** or 907/826-2205). They charge $20 a day for a canoe and rent camping packages, as well as carry anything else you might need to buy.

ACCOMMODATIONS & DINING
IN CRAIG

In addition to the rooms at Craig's Dive Shop, mentioned above, Craig has three good hotels. In each case, however, most of their rooms are booked far in advance of the summer season by fishing packages.

Haida Way Lodge. P.O. Box 90, Craig, AK 99921. ☎ **800/347-4625** or 907/826-3268. $90–$100 double in summer.

A good hotel on the island renting nice standard rooms to people not on fishing packages. *Note:* They book up by early winter for the summer season. The same owners operate **Sunnahae Lodge,** also in Craig (☎ **907/826-4000**), with comfortable, smoke-free rooms available with packages.

Ruth Ann's Hotel. P.O. Box 645, Craig, AK 99921. ☎ **907/826-3377.** Big, luxurious rooms $115.50–$131.50 double; cozy, well-appointed rooms $78.75 double. 3-day, all-inclusive fishing packages $1,650 (roughly the going rate).

No rooms are reserved for nonsmokers, and noise from a bar can be a problem in the better rooms. **Ruth Ann's Restaurant** has the fanciest dining room on POW, overlooking the placid Craig harbor, but I've never found a restaurant on the island that served better than adequate food.

In Klawock

Try **Fireweed Lodge,** P.O. Box 116, Klawock, AK 99925 (☎ **907/755-2930**), which has its own dock and a wilderness feel, but is near the airport and shopping center. **Papa's Pizza** (☎ **907/755-2244**), in the shopping center in Klawock, has some of the island's best food and free delivery.

On the Northern End of POW

McFarland's Floatel. P.O. Box 19149, Thorne Bay, AK 99919. ☎ **888/828-3335** or 907/828-3335. 4 large, 2-bedroom cabins with bathrooms and kitchens, $200 per night.

You can fly in or drive to Thorne Bay and cross the 2 miles over on a boat, but once there, you're mostly on your own, cooking your own meals. The proprietors charter guided fishing trips and rent skiffs for $65 a day ($80 if you're not a guest). As with all POW lodges, reserve well ahead.

Waterfall Resort. P.O. Box 6440, Ketchikan, AK 99901. ☎ **800/544-5125** outside Alaska only, or 907/225-9461. 4-day, 3-night trips, including the ride over from Ketchikan, start at $2,960 per person.

One of the state's best-known luxury lodges, Waterfall is reached only by floatplane, and is located on the western side of the island.

Camping

To me, one of the most appealing stays on POW is renting a primitive **Forest Service cabin** on a remote lake. Several of the cabins on Prince of Wales are reached by skiffs that the Forest Service leaves tied up at the bank by the road—you load your gear and row to your lodgings. The cabins must be reserved, up to 180 days in advance, with **Reserve USA** (☎ **877/444-6777,** TDD 877/833-6777; or with toll from overseas, ☎ 518/885-3639, reserveusa.com). Read about this system in section 2, "Outside in Southeast." It's only a step from camping, so you'll need to bring or rent gear.

If you don't need a solid roof, you can camp almost anywhere on the island. The **Eagles Nest Campground,** near the intersection of the Thorne Bay Road, has 11 well-separated sites among huge trees by the edge of Balls Lake. A ½-mile boardwalk along the edge of the lake ends at Control Creek among a grove of Sitka spruce of staggering girth and height.

6 Wrangell: An Old-Fashioned Small Town

Wrangell, valuable for its position near the mouth of the Stikine River, began as a fur-trading post and was the site of a Russian fort built in 1834. The British leased the area from the Russians in 1840, and their flag flew until the U.S. purchase of Alaska in 1867. Over the balance of the 19th century, Wrangell experienced three gold rushes and the construction of a cannery and the sawmill.

Then time pretty much stopped.

While the world outside changed, Wrangell stayed the same from the mid–20th century on. It even moved backward. Elsewhere, Wal-Mart and shopping malls were invented and small town main streets deflated, then people noticed what they had lost and tried to bring back their communities. Not out here, beyond the road system. With little incentive for anyone to visit, Wrangell stayed as it was, a burly, blue collar American logging town from the 1950s, simple and conservative. Petersburg, 50 miles away up the twisting Wrangell Narrows, with its fishing fleet and government workers, was more sophisticated. It's boardwalks and clapboard houses had more charm, it had bigger hotels, more "to do." Wrangell cut trees, processed them, shipped them. The bars stayed busy; no one thought of opening a health food restaurant. The whole town

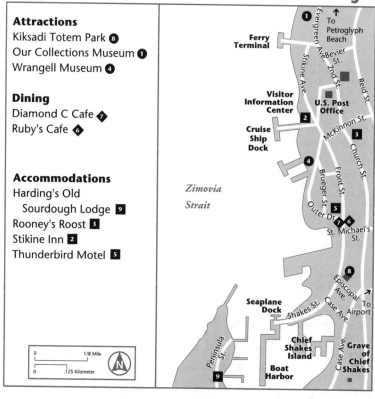

Attractions
Kiksadi Totem Park **8**
Our Collections Museum **1**
Wrangell Museum **4**

Dining
Diamond C Cafe **7**
Ruby's Cafe **6**

Accommodations
Harding's Old
 Sourdough Lodge **9**
Rooney's Roost **3**
Stikine Inn **2**
Thunderbird Motel **5**

laid itself out, simple and straightforward, on the steep side of the island that bore its name as it had for more than 150 years. As long as there were trees to saw into lumber, the future was safe in the past.

Then, a few years ago, the sawmill shut down and a third of the jobs in town went away. People were forced to sell out and leave the place where they'd been born and raised. Today, more than 5 years later, a more modest logging operation is back in operation and a solid core of 2,500 residents have stayed behind, and Wrangell may be an even better place to visit. The town has a nonthreatening, small-scale feel that allows a family to wander comfortably and make friends. Each time my family's gone, we've met new people and enjoyed what the town has to offer: playing in the two totem pole parks, hiking in the rain forest, and looking for the ancient art strewn across Petroglyph Beach.

In its new incarnation, Wrangell is improving on its positive qualities, and the residents show an endearing eagerness to please. Turn-of-the-century buildings that survived the big downtown fire of 1952 can be found with the help of the minimal *Wrangell Historic Building Walking Tour* map available at the visitor center or museum (see below). A big new museum is planned, and two ecotourism operators are offering kayaking, hiking, and the like. They have plenty to draw on: Wrangell sits near the wild **Stikine River,** has Southeast's great **ocean salmon fishing,** and is the jump-off for the **Anan Bear Observatory.** There's most of a day's worth of sightseeing within walking distance, and the U.S. Forest Service maintains gravel roads that lead to some spectacular places. They even built a **golf course** called Muskeg Meadows—leave it to

Wrangell to name a golf course for a hummocky swamp. Wrangell can't change its stripes—it's still a muscular town with narrow horizons—but that's part of the attraction.

ESSENTIALS
GETTING THERE
BY AIR Alaska Airlines (☎ 800/426-0333; www.alaskaair.com) serves Wrangell once daily with a jet flying 28 minutes south to Ketchikan and another 19 minutes north to Petersburg, a flight that skims low over the treetops the entire way. **Taquan Air Service** (☎ 800/770-8800 or 907/874-8800; www.AlaskaOne.com/TaquanAir) connects Wrangell to the same cities with prop-driven service.

BY FERRY Wrangell is on the main line of the Alaska Marine Highway System (see "Getting Around" at the beginning of this chapter), with landings six times a week in the summer. The voyage through the narrow, winding **Wrangell Narrows** north to Petersburg is one of the most beautiful and fascinating in Southeast Alaska. It's quite a navigational feat to watch as the 300-foot ships squeeze through a passage so slender and shallow the vessel's own displacement changes the water level on shore as it passes. The route, not taken by cruise ships (which approach through larger waterways), is also a source of delays, as the water in the narrows is deep enough only at high tide. The walk-on fare is $24 to Ketchikan, $18 to Petersburg.

GETTING AROUND
For the town of Wrangell, you can go on foot. The main part of town is laid out north to south along the waterfront at the northern point of the Wrangell Island. **Front Street** is the main business street, leading from the small-boat harbor and **Chief Shakes Island** at the south to the city dock and the ferry dock at the north. Most of the rest of the town is along **Church Street,** which runs parallel a block higher up the hill. **Evergreen Avenue** and **Bennett Street** form a loop to the north which goes to the airport. The only road to the rest of the island, the **Zimovia Highway,** heads out of town to the south, paved for about 12 miles, then connects to over 100 miles of gravel logging roads built and maintained by the Forest Service, most of which are usable for two-wheel-drive vehicles in the summer.

BY CAR If you're going to get out of town for a hike or camping, a car is necessary. The guys at **Practical Rent A Car** are friendly; they're at the airport (☎ 907/874-3975; fax 907/874-3911), or you can have them deliver the car to you.

BY TAXI For a taxi, try **Porky's Cab Company** (☎ 907/874-3603), or **Star Cab Company** (☎ 907/874-3622).

BY BIKE Bikes are for rent from **Solo Cat Sports** (☎ 907/874-2920), described in more detail below.

VISITOR INFORMATION
The small office of the **Wrangell Chamber of Commerce Visitor Center** is located in the Stikine Inn (P.O. Box 49), Wrangell, AK 99929 (☎ 800/367-9745 or 907/874-3901; www.wrangell.com/Chamber), facing the city dock, where cruise ships tie up. It's a place to pick up information on local businesses and get ideas on what to do. The Web site is quite useful, as is the city's page at www.wrangell.com. The center is open Monday to Friday 10am to 4pm in summer, and other hours when a cruise ship is in town.

The U.S. Forest Service also has an information desk at the **Wrangell Ranger District** office, 525 Bennett St. (P.O. Box 51), Wrangell, AK 99929 (☎ 907/

874-2323; www.fs.fed.us/r10/tongass/), located on the hill behind town. Here you can draw on local knowledge of the logging roads and fishing holes, obtain two-page guides to each Forest Service cabin and path, and, for $4, buy a detailed Wrangell Island Road Guide topographic map that shows and describes the island's outdoor attractions. The office is open Monday to Friday 8am to 5pm in summer and Monday to Friday 7:30am to 4:30pm in winter.

SPECIAL EVENTS

The Garnet Festival, the third week of April, marks the arrival of the sea lions, hooligans, shorebirds, and bald eagles on the Stikine River Delta, a spring tornado of wildlife in the region's largest coastal marshes. Community activities take place in town while jet boat tours traverse the delta. **The Wrangell King Salmon Derby,** the last 2 weeks of May and first part of June, started in 1953; in 1999, prizes totaled $17,000. Contact the Wrangell Chamber of Commerce (listed above under "Visitor Information"), or check their Web site for details on these events.

Fast Facts: Wrangell

Banks   The National Bank of Alaska, at 115 Front St., has an ATM.

Hospital   Wrangell General Hospital, at 310 Bennett St. (☎ 907/874-3356), has a walk-in clinic.

Internet/E-mail   A cybercafe called SeaPac.net is on Main Street (☎ 907/874-4010).

Police   For nonemergency calls, dial ☎ 907/874-3304.

Post Office   At 105 Federal Way, near the ferry dock.

Taxes   Sales tax is 7%. There's a $4 per room bed tax on top of the 7% sales tax when you rent a room.

EXPLORING WRANGELL & ENVIRONS

Before whites arrived, Tlingits had already warred over this strategic trading location near the mouth of the Stikine River for centuries. The first Chief Shakes was a successful conqueror who enslaved his enemies, then handed down power through the female line, in the Tlingit way, for seven generations. Charlie Jones was recognized as the last of the line, Chief Shakes VII, at a potlatch in 1940, but the position had long since lost most of its status. The decline began after the Alaska purchase, in 1867. Word came of the Emancipation Proclamation, which theoretically freed a third of the residents of the coast's Tlingit villages. Chief Shakes VI sent his slaves in canoes to dry halibut; they kept paddling home to Puget Sound, never looking back. (An excellent pamphlet, "Authentic History of Shakes Island and Clan" by E. L. Keithhahn, sells for $4 at the Wrangell Museum, described below.)

✪ **Chief Shakes Island,** a tiny islet in the middle of the small-boat harbor, is the site of a Tlingit clan house and collection of totem poles constructed by Native workers, using traditional tools, in the Civilian Conservation Corps during the 1930s. Unlike some CCC clan house replicas in the region, which mix Tlingit styles, this house is an exact, scaled-down copy of the 1834 house in which Chief Shakes VI lay in state in 1916. The inside of the clan house is fascinating, both in the sense it gives of the people's ways, and for some extraordinary artifacts. Unfortunately, it takes some effort to get inside if you're not traveling on a cruise ship. The tribal association opens the house regularly only when ships are in town, when you can enter for $2 and hear an explanatory talk. If there's no cruise ship, call Nora Rinehart at ☎ 907/874-2023, or, if you can't reach Nora, Margret Sturdevant at ☎ 907/874-3747. For a $20 minimum fee, they'll come down and open the house and give you the talk. Even if you can't manage that, visit the island to see the rotting totem poles and the charming setting, and the **grave of Chief Shakes V,** on Case Avenue just across the harbor. There's a resident otter that you can often see near the island's footbridge, sometimes feeding its young.

The carved house posts in the clan house are replicas of the mid-18th-century originals that now stand in the ✪ **Wrangell Museum** (☎ **907/874-3770**). These are probably the oldest and certainly the best preserved Tlingit house posts in existence, still bearing the original fish egg and mineral paints, and a gash where, during a potlatch, a chief hacked off an image that a visitor admired and gave it to him—a gesture that, as intended, still demonstrates the extent of his wealth even today. The museum has many other important Alaska Native pieces, and a lot of other just plain old stuff that tells the story of Wrangell, one of Alaska's most historic towns. As director Theresa Thibalt told me, "We were the economic center of Alaska at one time—for a short time—believe it or not."

A new $4.5 million home for the museum is being built by the town and a local foundation and will help recover some of the history. They hope to finish in time for the 2000 visitor season, with a building on the waterfront near the city dock that will serve as an exhibit space and as a cultural and civic center for the town. (If they don't make it in time for your visit, the old museum is at 318 Church St.) Even in its old quarters, in a gymnasium basement, this is a special museum, connecting visitors and locals in many ways other than just showing off artifacts. In the new building, it should be the town's centerpiece. Admission is $3 for adults, free ages 16 and under. Summer hours are Monday through Friday 10am to 5pm, Saturday 1pm to 5pm, and when the ships are in. Winter, they're open Tuesday through Friday 10am to 4pm.

One of the museum's projects has been the preservation of an impressive set of petroglyphs that lie on the beach a mile north of town. The 50 carvings of **Wrangell Petroglyph Beach State Historic Park** probably represent the work of forgotten indigenous people predating the Tlingit, and were made over a long period of time. The images, chipped into rocks, are of animals and geometric forms. Their purpose is lost to time. Walk north on Evergreen Avenue and follow the signs down to the beach (don't go within an hour of high tide). Replicas of the petroglyphs were recently carved so that visitors who want to take rubbings will not destroy the originals; also try not to step on them. The great pleasure here is simply to search for the carvings—they're just lying out there, and it takes some looking—and to wonder at their meaning and age. It's a fine place for a family to spend an afternoon, in good weather.

Wrangell has one more museum, a good place to stop on the way back from the Petroglyph Beach, meet a delightful old lady, and see her favorite things. Elva Bigelow maintains her **Our Collections Museum** in a big old boat shed on Evergreen Avenue (☎ **907/874-3646**). It's an all-inclusive gathering of her family's 60 years in Wrangell. There are old tools, nautical equipment, and sewing machines, a collection of 60 dolls, bottles, a large diorama of the town assembled for the 1967 centennial celebration, old typewriters, local wildflowers, and anything else you can imagine. Mrs. Bigelow's museum is open when cruise ships are in town, or you can reach her by phone and she'll gladly show it to you—she loves visitors. Donations are appreciated, and genuine, Mrs. Bigelow–made crochet work and other crafts are for sale.

On Front Street near the center of town, the **Kiksadi Totem Park** was built by the Sealaska regional Native corporation in the mid-1980s on the former site of a clan house. The grass is a comfortable place to sit, and the totem poles truly beautiful.

GETTING OUTSIDE: ON WRANGELL ISLAND

Wrangell Island's network of gravel roads, maintained by the Forest Service, leads to places of awesome beauty rarely visited by anyone but the many active outdoors people from town. There are a few day-hike trails, some lovely camp sites, and paths to remote cabins and fishing lakes you can have to yourself. Kayak paddles begin from the boat harbor, or from remote Earl West Cove, on the opposite side of the island.

There's only one way out of town, heading south on the Zimovia Highway along narrow Zimovia Strait. The Forest Service map mentioned above under "Visitor Information" is helpful for anything you might want to do along this route.

The first stop is **City Park,** just south of town. Besides having a picnic area on the shore among big trees, it's a fine tide pooling spot. Go a couple of hours before a good, low tide. Five miles out Zimovia Highway you reach the **Shoemaker Bay Recreation Area,** with a small boat harbor, campground, and picnic sites (see "Camping," below). Continuing south, **Eight Mile Beach** is a good stop for a ramble, and don't miss **Nemo Point,** a high, ocean-side overlook from which you can see more than 13 miles along Zimovia Strait all the way back to town. The campsites here are gorgeous. All the way across the island, about 45 minutes from town, **Earl West Cove** gives access to the protected wilderness waters on the Eastern Passage. There's a good campground there, too.

HIKING   Across the road from the Shoemaker Recreation Area, mentioned above, the **Rainbow Falls Trail** climbs steeply on a boardwalk with steps .8 of a mile (and 500 feet in elevation gain) up a ridge between two creeks, forested with big, mossy Sitka spruce and western hemlock. The falls seem to tumble down between the branches. From that point, you can continue another 2.7 miles and another 1,100 feet higher into open alpine terrain on the **Institute Creek Trail** to the Shoemaker Overlook, where there are great views, a picnic area, and a shelter. **Rainwalker Expeditions** (☎ **907/874-2549**) leads nature walks on the lower part of the trail, and longer hikes all over the island. The Rainbow Falls Trail is the island's busiest, especially when cruise ships are in town. If you want to assure you won't see anyone, take one of the less developed walks you can reach along the logging roads—the Forest Service can point the way. One good choice is the **Salamander Ridge Trail,** which leads a mile to subalpine terrain, where you can take off for off-trail hiking. The trail begins 27 miles from Wrangell on Salamander Road, also known as Forest Road 50050.

BIKING   A paved bike trail leads all the way from town, between the Zimovia Highway and the water, to the Shoemaker Recreation Area, 5 miles south. There are many more miles of appealing mountain bike routes, on Forest Service roads and single-track trails, all over the island. **Solo Cat Sports** (☎ **907/874-2920;** fax 907/874-2923; www.thetongass.com/solocat.htm), owned by the warm and enthusiastic Steve Prysunka, leads backcountry tours and rents quality mountain bikes and other gear out of his home at 441 Church St. (P.O. Box 2294), Wrangell, AK 99929. Prices range from $30 a day for a standard bike to $56 for a tandem.

SEA KAYAKING   **Solo Cat Sports,** mentioned above, and **Alaska Vistas,** P.O. Box 2245, Wrangell, AK 99929 (☎ **907/874-2429;** fax or message 907/874-3006; www.alaskavistas.com), both offer guided sea kayaking and rentals from Wrangell. Solo Cat aims to make independent sea kayakers of beginners; Alaska Vistas offers a wide variety of ecotourism services and has been around longer. Either will do day trips starting from the boat harbor, or guided trips of many days. An interesting longer day trip starts from Earl West Cove, on the east side of the island. Solo Cat uses it as a launch point. Among the destinations is Berg Bay, where there's a Forest Service cabin for rent, excellent bird watching, and an old mining trail for hiking. Alaska

Vistas leads trips to the South Etolin Wilderness Area. You can rent all the equipment you need in Wrangell, including boats and camping gear, or bring it on the ferry. Water taxis cost $90 to $120 an hour.

FISHING   Wrangell Island allows fishers access to rarely visited streams and lakes, some with public cabins, that you can reach by car or a drive and short hike. The Forest Service provides a list, and the Alaska Department of Fish and Game publishes a 20-page *Petersburg Wrangell Sport Fishing Guide* (contact them at the address listed in section 2, "Outside in Southeast"), or go with a guide. **Marlin Benedict,** P.O. Box 301, Wrangell, AK 99929 (☎ **907/874-2590;** e-mail: fishing@seapac.net), guides fly-fishing outings on shore. Or get out on the water for salmon or halibut. May and June are the prime months for king salmon fishing, and halibut are available all summer. The well-run **Alaska Waters,** listed below under "Stikine River," offers a long day of saltwater fishing for $195 per person. You can probably arrange to take part of the day for sightseeing and wildlife watching, too. Many other charter boats are available at the harbor—pick up information about them at the visitor center. Among the unique choices, Alaska Vistas (see "Sea Kayaking," above), offers a commercial fishing experience.

GETTING OUTSIDE: OFF THE ISLAND

Wrangell is in an extraordinary place, surrounded by vast, rich wild lands for fishing, rafting, sea kayaking, or simply enjoying. I've described two of the main off-island destinations below—the Stikine River and the Anan Wildlife Observatory—but there are many more, too many to mention. The services I've listed can give ideas, or contact the Forest Service to get a list of the cabins they rent to the public, many of which provide exclusive access to exceptional fishing.

To get anywhere, you need a boat or floatplane. You can go independently, hiring a water taxi for $90 to $120 an hour; it costs about $400, one-way, to get to a remote Forest Service cabin. That service is offered by various operators, including the impressive, Native-owned **Alaska Waters,** 241 Berger St. (P.O. Box 1978), Wrangell, AK 99929 (☎ **800/347-4462** or 907/874-2378; fax 907/874-3138; www.alaskawaters.com). They also rent all the outdoor stuff you'll need, including camping equipment and canoes, and offer guided fishing, Stikine River jet boat tours and expeditions, and trips to the Anan Bear Observatory. Commentary includes natural history and Tlingit cultural traditions and legends.

Todd Harding's **Stikeen Wilderness Adventures,** P.O. Box 934, Wrangell, AK 99929 (☎ **800/874-2085** or 907/874-2085; www.akgetaway.com), helped pioneer jet boat tours up the Stikine River and also offers Anan trips. The emphasis here is on the thrills of the jet-boat ride. The 600-horsepower vessels are capable of 60 miles per hour and can run in 4 inches of water; Harding has films of incredible rides in wild rapids.

If going by air, **Sunrise Aviation,** P.O. Box 432, Wrangell, AK 99929 (☎ **907/ 874-2319;** fax 907/874-2546), is a Wrangell-based operator. Taquan Air flies tours and outings from Ketchikan (see "Getting There," above).

THE STIKINE RIVER

The Stikine is unique. Rushing with gray, glacial water, it descends all the way from the dry Interior of British Columbia to a broad, shallow delta in the rain forest a few miles from Wrangell. It's among the fastest navigable rivers anywhere, and in early gold rush years was a route over the mountains. Tours that sometimes go as far as Telegraph Creek, B.C., use high-powered jet boats that can accelerate like a hot rod. (Two major operators for such tours are described just above.)

The shallow delta is an exceptionally rich **wildlife viewing** area, with sea lions, eagles, and many other species of birds. When the salmon are running, you can see them thrashing in their spawning pools. Farther up river, tours see Sitka black tailed deer, moose, brown and black bears, mountain goats, river otters, beavers, and occasional otters.

The Garnet Ledge, near the river's mount, still yields gems 130 years after its discovery. It's probably not worth the somewhat arduous visit for most travelers, but the story is interesting. The ledge was exploited from 1907 to 1936 by the first all-woman corporation in the nation, a group of investors from Minneapolis. Today, only children have the right to remove the stones since the deposit's last owner deeded the mine to the Boy Scouts and the children of Wrangell in 1962. Information on the history and recreational mining of the ledge is available at the Wrangell Museum and the visitor center, and you can buy garnets from the ledge from children who set up card tables at the ferry and cruise-ship docks when the ships are in, and often elsewhere, too.

Traveling upriver, tours usually stop at the **Shakes Glacier** and **Shakes Lake,** where there are 3,000-foot cliffs and some 50 waterfalls. Bring a swim suit for a dip in the Forest Service–owned **Chief Shakes Hot Springs,** where there's an indoor and an outdoor tub for public bathing. The temperature is adjustable up to 120°F. Some tours go all the way to Telegraph, B.C., 160 miles upriver, where the operator Alaska Waters (see above) brings travelers to a remote homestead lodge. A 3-day, 2-night package is $575. The going rate for a 6-hour jet boat tour from Wrangell is around $145.

Rafting the Stikine offers fast water, expansive scenery, and the potential for a many-day journey. The two firms listed above under "Sea Kayaking," Alaska Vista and Solo Cat Sports, offer these guided trips, lasting about 8 days, for a price of around $2,200 per person. Solo Cat also takes kayakers down the river. Alaska Waters and Solo Cat rent rafts and other gear for floating the Stikine. A raft is about $100 a day.

ANAN WILDLIFE OBSERVATORY

Here you can see lots of black bears and some brown bears close up as they feed on spawning pink salmon trying to make it up a waterfall in Anan Creek, on the mainland southeast of Wrangell Island. When the fish are running in July and August (peak is mid-July to August 20), more than 40 bears use the creek, sometimes walking close to the platform where people stand watching. Outside the season, you probably would see no bears—don't be deceived into thinking otherwise. Forest Service guides are on duty during the bear months; visitors must also take care of themselves by observing safe bear behavior (they'll brief you when you arrive; also, see "Safety" in chapter 2). Most visitors will enjoy a **guided day trip from Wrangell** more than going on their own. Alaska Waters and Stikeen Wilderness Adventures (see above) go by boat, charging about $145 per person for the hour-long run from Wrangell and a few hours with the bears. Sunrise Air flies the 29 miles. It's also possible to go without a guide, and no permit is needed; there's even a Forest Service cabin for rent, although it's in high demand during the bear season. The walk to the observatory is half a mile from the shore where you land, on a good trail.

ACCOMMODATIONS

Besides the accommodations listed here, the **Thunderbird Motel,** 223 Front St. (P.O. Box 110), Wrangell, AK 99929 (☎ **907/874-3322**), offers decent economy lodgings right downtown. There are also several other bed-and-breakfasts in town. A list is available from the visitor center.

Buness Bed and Breakfast. 327 First St. (P.O. Box 66), Wrangell, AK 99929. ☎ **907/874-2036.** E-mail: buness@seapac.net. Summer, $65; winter, $50.

This B&B has just one fresh, attractively decorated room with a VCR, coffeemaker, microwave, refrigerator, telephone, and claw-footed tub with shower, and a nearby sauna. The owner is the town fire chief and a lifelong resident.

Harding's Old Sourdough Lodge. 1104 Peninsula (P.O. Box 1062), Wrangell, AK 99929. ☎ **800/874-3613** or 907/874-3613. Fax 907/874-3455. www.akgetaway.com. 16 units. TEL. $85 double, $135 triple or quad, $150–$195 suite. AE, DC, DISC, MC, V.

The energetic Bruce Harding, a large dog, and a cat run the hotel in the style of a fishing lodge—he rents the rooms alone or as part of fishing or jet-boat tour packages with his brother, Todd, who owns Stikeen Wilderness Adventures, and other local guide services for kayaking, rafting, flightseeing, and so on. The attractive building with a wraparound porch is about a mile from the center of town in a waterfront area, but Harding will drive you where you want to go. Some rooms are small, and most have only shower stalls, not tubs. Decoration is on an outdoors theme. The suites are huge. All rooms have access to a central sauna and steam bath, and a self-service laundry. Breakfast comes with the room, and dinners of fresh seafood are served nightly, family style—you eat what they cook. Dinner prices are $16 to $24 per person, and nonguests can partake with reservations.

Rooney's Roost Bed and Breakfast. 206 McKinnon (P.O. Box 552), Wrangell, AK 99929. ☎ 907/874-2026. $55 double.

It's not so grand, but Rooney's Roost provides good, inexpensive lodgings—two nice rooms with dormer windows and private baths in an old house downtown—and a hostess, Gertrude Rooney, who is a character.

Stikine Inn. 107 Front St. (P.O. Box 990), Wrangell, AK 99929. ☎ **888/874-3388** or 907/874-3388. Fax 907/874-3923. www.stikine.com. 34 units. TV TEL. High season, $80 double, $90 suite. Low season, $70 double, $90 suite. Additional person in room $5 extra. AE, DISC, MC, V.

The town's main hotel is close to the ferry dock and stands right on the water's edge. It's a bustling place, a center of community activity. The visitor center is in the same building. Rooms are spacious, comfortable, and clean, but somewhat worn and generally outdated. The more modern units have only one bed. The suites are well worth the price. We could hear the water lapping the shore outside the window as we fell asleep, and had a view of the sunset over the ocean. The restaurant is described under "Dining," below. The art gallery and gift shop on the ground floor, **River's Edge Fine Arts & Gifts,** is the largest in town, with fine art, pottery, and inexpensive gifts. Sometimes artists give demonstrations there.

HOSTELLING & CAMPING

Wrangell Hostel is at the First Presbyterian Church, 220 Church St., Wrangell, AK 99929 (☎ **907/874-3534**). It's a rudimentary hostel, run by the young minister and his wife. They're open mid-June to Labor Day, and the rate is $10 a night.

There are several attractive campgrounds in Wrangell. I've never seen a campground in a spot like the mountaintop **Nemo Point Forest Service Campground** described above under "Getting Outside," but it's more than a dozen miles out of town. Five miles south of town, the **Shoemaker Bay Recreation Area** has sites by the road overlooking the boat harbor, right across from the Rainbow Falls Trail. There are water and electric hookups for RVs. Contact the **Wrangell Recreation and Parks Department** at ☎ **907/874-2444** for information. They also manage **City Park,** right at the edge of town on Zimovia Highway, where camping is permitted. For a full hookup RV site, try **Alaska Waters'** small park, at 241 Berger St. (☎ **907/874-2378**). They charge

$15 a night, and $3 for access to the shower room. Showers also are available for $3 at the town swimming pool, at the school

DINING

You don't go to Wrangell for the dining, but you can get an adequate meal there. The best restaurant in town is the **Waterfront Grill** at the Stikine Inn (see "Accommodations," above). It's a typical family restaurant serving three meals a day. When you sit down for dinner, they bring two menus, one for fine dining and another for the less expensive fare favored by the locals. Nothing is terribly expensive or terribly exciting among the steak, seafood, sandwiches, or pizza. The dining room is trim and bright, with superb ocean views.

Harding's Old Sourdough Lodge (see "Accommodations," above) serves meals to guests, and to others by reservation. It's a family-style dinner without a menu. The **Diamond C Cafe,** at 215 Front St. (☎ **907/874-3677**), is a comfortable small town coffee shop open 6am to 3pm daily in summer, closing at 1pm Sundays in the winter. It's lighter, cleaner, and better decorated than these places usually are, and the service is fast and friendly. Besides the hearty breakfasts, they serve burgers and sandwiches in the $4 to $8 range. **Ruby's Restaurant,** at 316 Front St. (☎ **907/874-2002**), is a friendly little sandwich shop with smoke-free air and a clean, relaxed atmosphere. Lunch consists of good, light food: mostly sandwiches and salads. Dinner, served only in the summer, is steak, seafood, and pasta in the $12 to $20 range. Summer hours are Monday through Saturday 11:30am to 4pm and 5 to 9pm.

7 Petersburg: Unvarnished Threshold to the Outdoors

Petersburg is the perfect small town, the sort of prosperous, picturesque, quirky place that used to be mythologized in Disney films. Except that Petersburg never would have let Disney in the door. People here are too smart for that, and too protective of a place they know would be spoiled by too much attention. For the same reason, Petersburg is just as glad the big cruise ships can't enter their narrow harbor. They've got something too good going here to spoil it with throngs of tourists and seasonal gift shops. Instead, locals spend the money that keeps Nordic Drive, the main street, thriving with family-owned grocery and hardware stores, restaurants, a fish market, a cybercafe, and other businesses. Wooden streets over **Hammer Slough** still serve utilitarian purposes, making them far more appealing than if they were prettied up as tourist areas. When you walk along Sing Lee Alley and check out the stylish little bookstore, you rarely see others like yourselves—instead, you see Norwegian fishermen in pickup trucks and blond-haired kids on bikes.

Keeping Petersburg insular and authentic also means the **outdoor opportunities** to which it provides an entryway are sublime but little used. There are wonderful trails, mountain biking routes, and secret places. On the water, the humpback whale watching is as reliable as anywhere in Alaska, and still undiscovered. There's a glacier to visit, terrific fishing, and limitless sea kayaking waters. The in-town attractions are few—a day is plenty for simple sightseeing—and little attempt has been made to accommodate lazy gawkers. But Alaska's best is waiting for those willing to spend the effort to look.

Petersburg is named for its founder, Peter Buschmann, who killed himself after living here for only 4 years. But that shouldn't be a reflection on the town, which is in an ideal location and has flourished since that inauspicious beginning. In 1898, or thereabouts (historians differ), Buschmann founded a cannery on Mitkof Island facing the slender, peaceful Wrangell Narrows in what was to become Petersburg. The stunning abundance of salmon and halibut and a nearby source of ice—the LeConte Glacier—made the site a natural. Buschmann had emigrated from Norway in 1891 and, as a proud old Son of Norway told me, he always hired Norwegians. Any Norwegian who came to him, he hired. In a few years, the cannery failed. Perhaps an excessive payroll? My suggestion was met with an icy glance and a change of subject. Teasing aside, Buschmann's mistake was merging his cannery with a firm trying to challenge a monopolistic Alaska operation, and they went down together. His suicide followed his financial reverses, but the promise of Peterburg remained. The Norwegians stayed, including the ancestors of my friend, and slowly built a charming town of white clapboard houses with steeply pitched roofs, hugging the water. Their living came from the sea, as it still does. Appropriately, the downtown area doesn't stop at water's edge. Roads, boardwalks, and buildings continue over the smooth waters of Wrangell Narrows, out to the cannery buildings that survive on long wooden piers, and into the boat harbors, which stretch out in a network that far surpasses the city streets.

Today the town's economy, based on fishing and government work—the Stikine Ranger District of the Tongass National Forest is headquartered here—makes for a wealthy, sophisticated, and stable population.

ESSENTIALS
GETTING THERE

BY FERRY   Petersburg has the most welcoming ferry terminal in the system (☎ **907/772-3855**), with a grassy lawn and a pier from which to watch the boats and marine animals. It's about a mile to the town center. To the north, the **Alaska Marine Highway** (see listing under "Getting Around" at the beginning of this chapter) can take you to Juneau direct, or by way of Sitka. The fare is $18 to Wrangell, $26 to Sitka, and $44 to Juneau.

BY AIR   Petersburg is served by **Alaska Airlines'** jets (☎ **800/426-0333;** www. alaskaair.com) once north and once south each day, with the nearest stops on the puddle jumper being Sitka and Wrangell. Scheduled prop service goes south with **Taquan Air Service** (☎ **800/770-8800** or 907/772-8800; www.AlaskaOne.com/ TaquanAir), or north with **L.A.B. Flying Service** (☎ **800/426-0543** or 907/ 772-4300).

GETTING AROUND

Petersburg is on Mitkof Island, divided from the much larger Kupreanof Island by the long, slender channel of the Wrangell Narrows. There are three small-boat harbors—the north, south, and middle—and so many docks, boardwalks, and wooden streets that the town seems to sit on the ocean. **Nordic Drive** is the main street, running from the ferry dock through town, then becoming **Sandy Beach Road** as it rounds Hungry Point to the north. At Sandy Beach, you can circle back, past the cannery worker's tent city and the airport, which stands above the town, to **Haugen Drive,** which meets Nordic again near **Hammer Slough,** right in town. To the south, Nordic becomes the **Mitkof Highway,** which runs to the undeveloped balance of the island. You need some mode of transportation to really enjoy Petersburg because the best of the place is the outdoors.

BY RENTAL CAR   The **Tides Inn Motel** and **Scandia House** (see "Accommodations," below) both rent cars, but not many are available in town, so book well in advance for summer.

Petersburg

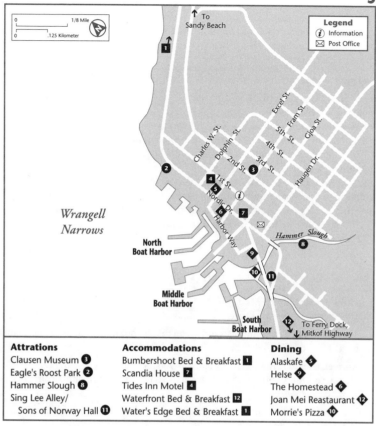

Attrations

Clausen Museum ❸
Eagle's Roost Park ❷
Hammer Slough ❽
Sing Lee Alley/
  Sons of Norway Hall ⑪

Accommodations

Bumbershoot Bed & Breakfast ▮
Scandia House ▧
Tides Inn Motel ▮
Waterfront Bed & Breakfast ⑫
Water's Edge Bed & Breakfast ▮

Dining

Alaskafe ❺
Helse ❾
The Homestead ❻
Joan Mei Reastaurant ⑫
Morrie's Pizza ❿

BY BIKE   Biking is a great way to see Petersburg. You can rent a bike for $4 to $5 an hour or $20 a day from **Northern Bikes,** located in the Scandia House Hotel (☎ 907/772-3978). They're open 11am to 5pm Monday through Saturday in the summer.

BY BOAT   The Scandia House rents small boats, a wonderful way to explore Wrangell Narrows and get to trails across on the other side, or go fishing inexpensively. An 18-footer with a 40-horse outboard rents for $150 a day, gas included, $25 less for guests of the hotel. They don't provide fishing gear.

VISITOR INFORMATION

The Petersburg Chamber of Commerce and the U.S. Forest Service jointly operate the informative **Visitor Information Center,** corner of First and Fram streets (P.O. Box 649), Petersburg, AK 99833 (☎ 907/772-4636; www.petersburg.org), where a ranger can give you detailed guidance on the outdoor opportunities that really make Petersburg fun (plus trail guides and natural history publications) and a chamber person can help you hire a boat, get lodgings, and make other arrangements to make it happen. This also is the place for details on Forest Service cabins in the ranger district, which you can reserve through national system described above under "Outside in Southeast." The center is open in summer daily from 9am to 5pm, winter Monday to Friday 10am to 2pm.

In a new building, the full-service **Viking Travel agency,** corner of Nordic Drive and Sing Lee Alley (P.O. Box 787), Petersburg, AK 99833 (☎ 800/327-2571 or

907/772-3818; fax 907/772-3940; http://alaska-ala-carte.com), also specializes in booking local guides for tours, kayaks, whale watching, flights, fishing charters, and other activities. Owner David Berg is knowledgeable and helpful. They also sell custom Alaska tour packages.

SPECIAL EVENTS

The Little Norway Festival, which celebrates the May 17, 1814, declaration of independence of Norway from Sweden, is an occasion for Petersburg to go wild. The 4-day schedule of events is the third full weekend of the month, with a street fair, parade, beauty pageant, seafood feast, and so on. **The King Salmon Derby** offers a $30,000 purse over Memorial Day weekend. **The Canned Salmon Classic** lasts June 1 through August 15, with a first prize of up to $4,000 going to the person who guesses how many cans of salmon will be packed in Petersburg during the season. **Julebukking,** a Norwegian tradition, happens on Christmas Eve, when merchants offer food and drink to their customers and the streets fill with people. For information on any of the above events, contact the **Petersburg Chamber of Commerce** (☎ **907/ 772-4636**).

Fast Facts: Petersburg

Banks There are ATMs at the National Bank of Alaska and First Bank, both at the corner of Nordic Drive and Fram Street.

Hospital The Petersburg Medical Center is the hospital, at Second and Fram streets (☎ 907/772-4291).

Internet/E-mail AlasKafe, upstairs at 306 N. Nordic (☎ 907/772-5282), offers access for $2.50 for 15 minutes, and you can get lunch and a haircut (see "Dining," below).

Police The police and fire station is on Nordic Drive near Haugen. Call ☎ 907/772-3838 for nonemergencies.

Post Office At 12 N. Nordic Dr., at the corner of Haugen Drive.

Taxes Sales tax is 6%. The room tax on accommodations totals 10%.

EXPLORING PETERSBURG

A walk around Petersburg should include the boardwalk streets of **Hammer Slough,** the tidal mouth of a creek that feeds into the waterfront. **Sing Lee Alley** leads from North Nordic Drive at the charming center of town, passing by several interesting little shops, including **Sing Lee Alley Books,** at no. 11 (☎ **907/772-4440**), where there's a good collection on natural history and local culture. Petersburg has so many thriving little shops because of its isolation and healthy economy—so far, its been too small to attract the predation of Wal-Mart and other chains. Sing Lee Alley turns from solid ground to wooden dock before you reach the **Sons of Norway Hall,** a town center where a large model Viking ship used in the Little Norway Festival is often parked. Next door, also on pilings, is a large plaza with flags and plaques memorializing Petersburg residents. Across the street, on the outboard side, **Tonka Seafoods** (☎ **907/772-3662**) is a specialty fish processor offering tours during the summer, 1 to 3pm Monday through Saturday. Call ahead if you're really interested, as times can change. The charge is $3. Continue on to Nordic Drive, then turn left, crossing back over the slough to **Birch Street,** which follows the slough's bank on pilings upstream past old, weathered houses (many with one door for the road and another for the water) that hang over the placid channel. It's one of Alaska's most charming and authentic places. Step out of the way of cars on the one-lane dock/street.

Back down at the waterfront, stroll the harbor floats to see the frenetic activity of the huge commercial fishing fleet in the summer, then continue north on Nordic Drive to **Eagle's Roost Park,** where there is a grassy area to sit and a stairway that leads down to the water. At low tide there's an interesting if rugged beach walk. You're almost guaranteed to see eagles, which congregate here for the fish waste from the nearby cannery. Look in the tops of the trees. (In fact, you can see eagles almost anytime and anywhere along the water in Petersburg.)

The **Clausen Memorial Museum,** at Second and Fram streets (☎ 907/ 772-3598), interprets Petersburg and its history for the people who live here. It has a living, community feel. When I last visited, a portfolio of old photographs was on display with sticky notes for visitors to write down the names of anyone they could identify and other memories. The office of a leading fish packer is displayed just as he left it in the 1970s, a time capsule of the ordinary that says much about the town. No doubt the local fishermen are fascinated by the obsolete fishing gear, rugged old nautical equipment, and a model fish trap, outlawed in 1959 when Alaska became a state. It's like being invited into the town's collective memory. If such things peak your interest, buy for $8 a copy of *From Fish Camps to Cold Storages; A Brief History of the Petersburg Area to 1927,* by Pat Ellis, published by the museum. The hardships of pioneer life are told with quiet pride. The museum is open in summer Monday through Saturday from 10am to 4:30pm; winter Wednesday and Saturday 12:30 to 4pm. Admission is $2 for adults, free for children 11 and under.

GETTING OUTSIDE

There are so many great outdoor activities in Petersburg, I have listed only a few highlights. For other choices, many of which are as good as those I've written about here, or for the detailed trail and backcountry information you'll need, call or visit the U.S. Forest Service at either of two locations in Petersburg—the visitor center, listed above, or the **Petersburg Ranger District** offices at Nordic and Haugen drives (P.O. Box 1328), Petersburg, AK 99833 (☎ **907/772-3871;** www.fs.fed.us/r10/tongass/), above the post office.

The best places to go around Petersburg require the use of a boat. Viking Travel, listed above under "Visitor Information," books most of the dozen or so small charter boats that are operating from the harbor at any one time, allowing them to consolidate small groups into six-person boatloads for whale watching, sightseeing, or fishing. Some operators have made a specialty of natural history tours and nonconsumptive use of the outdoors. Barry Bracken, a retired marine fish biologist, offers these types of trips on his 28-foot vessel. Contact **Kaleidoscope Cruises** at P.O. Box 1201, Petersburg, AK 99833 (☎ **800/TO-THE-SEA** or 907/772-3736; www.alaska.net/~bbsea). Ron Compton's **Alaska Scenic Waterways,** 114 Harbor Way (P.O. Box 943), Petersburg, AK 99833 (☎ **800/ASW-1176** or 907/772-3777; akscenic.com) also specializes in natural history cruises.

SPECIAL PLACES

SANDY BEACH   It's an easy bike ride or a long walk 1.6 miles up Nordic Drive, around Hungry Point, at the northern tip of the island, then along Sandy Beach Road, to the beach and picnic area. Return the same distance back by way of the airport, coming back into town on Haugen Drive. The beach itself is coarse sand and fine gravel, and you wouldn't swim in the frigid water, but it's a lovely spot, facing Frederick Sound on the east side of Mitkof Island. If you go at high tide, you can beach-comb and bird watch—a great blue heron was hanging out last time I visited—but a better choice is to time your visit at a low tide, preferably one of one foot or lower (free tide books are widely available, or ask at the visitor center). At such a low tide, you can see the outlines of ancient fish traps built on the beach beginning 2,000 years ago. They look like V-shaped rows of rocks, and at times you can see stakes. The indigenous people who built them knew how to create channels that would corral salmon at high tide, leaving them stranded to be gathered up when the water receded. These ancient people presumably also created the petroglyphs on rocks near the traps, which some theorize depict the traps, and others believe have something to do with the sun. Finding the traps and petroglyphs isn't easy—it's best if you can get someone to lead you, such as on the occasional Forest Service walks that you can find out about at the visitor center. Or, if you have the time and inclination to explore, walk out to the left from the picnic area, to the edge of the lagoon near the house with the greenhouse. A major petroglyph is on a black bedrock face, visible when you are looking back toward the picnic area, and the traps are just offshore from there.

RAVEN TRAIL & RAVEN'S ROOST CABIN   About 4 miles up the steep but spectacular Raven Trail, which begins behind the airport off Haugen Drive near the water tower (roughly a mile from town), the Raven's Roost Forest Service cabin sits atop a mountain with a sweeping view of the town and surrounding waters and islands. It's the sort of place that inspires artists and poets. Allow 3 hours for the climb along a boardwalk, then up a steep muddy slope, then along a ridge, with an elevation gain of over 1,000 feet. It's possible to continue hiking over the steep, subalpine terrain of the Twin Ridge Ski Trail another 4.9 miles to the Twin Creek Road, and then get a ride 11 miles back to town. Check with the visitor center for trail conditions. Reserve the cabin through the national system listed under "Outside in Southeast," at the start of this chapter. You'll need sleeping bags, cooking gear, lights, and food.

MITKOF ISLAND   The Mitkof Highway, leading south from Petersburg, opens most of Mitkof Island, with its king salmon fishing; views of swans, fish, and glaciers; salmon hatchery; hiking trails; lakes; and many miles of remote roads for mountain biking. The town's swimming hole and ice-skating pond are out the road, too. Anyone can enjoy a day's sightseeing drive over the island, and if you enjoy hiking and the outdoors, you'll find days of fun. Pick up the $4 *Forest Service Mitkof Island Road Guide* map at the visitor center; it shows what you'll find along the way.

Ten and 20 miles from Petersburg, the Three Lakes Loop Road meets the highway and traverses over the top of the island to the east side. Fifteen miles from the north end of the loop, the level, 4.5-mile boardwalk **Three Lakes Trail** circles four small lakes, each of which contains trout, and three of which have Forest Service rowboats for public use. Besides the fish, it's a place of abundant wildflowers and berries, where you may see deer, beavers, bears, and many birds, including seasonal sandhill cranes.

Thirteen miles out Mitkof Highway, you come to **The Dip,** a declivity in the road where high school seniors have long painted their names and classes on the road. A mile farther, a quarter-mile boardwalk leads across the damp, hummocky ground of the rain forest muskeg to **Blind River Rapids,** a peaceful spot with a three-sided shelter where you can watch and fish for king salmon in June and silvers in September, and sometimes watch eagles and bears feeding on the fish.

At 17 miles, somewhat hidden in the trees on the right, a bird-watching blind looks out on **Blind Slough,** where trumpeter swans winter. Swans normally will be gone by mid-March.

At 18 miles, at the end of the pavement, you'll reach the **Blind Slough Recreation Area,** where locals go to swim in the amber water in the summer and, in the winter, much of the town congregates for ice-skating and bonfires. Water warms in the narrow slough here, more than 5 miles from Wrangell Narrows. These are appealing canoeing or sea-kayaking waters, too.

A branch road at the recreation area leads over the slough to the **Crystal Lake Hatchery** (☎ 907/772-4772), which raises king and silver salmon. I've toured a lot of hatcheries, but never enjoyed one as much as this place, simply because it's so informal—they get so few visitors that you just wander through on your own and ask questions of the friendly technicians. A guy who was using a machine to count millions of fish let us watch and help.

At 22 miles from Petersburg, you reach the **Ohmer Creek campground,** with a 1-mile trail, a floating bridge over a beaver pond, and access to king salmon in June and July and trout and some salmon in late summer. The road continues from here along the south shore of Mitkof Island, with great ocean views, to its end at mile 32. Many Forest Service roads branch off, and there are more picnic and camping areas than I can list here.

PETERSBURG CREEK   The lovely, grassy Petersburg Creek area can be an afternoon's family frolic among the meadows of wildflowers that meet the water, or the start to a challenging 21-mile, multiday hike into the **Petersburg Creek–Duncan Salt Chuck Wilderness.** You'll need a skiff or sea kayak, or get a charter to drop you off, as the creek is on Kupreanof Island, across Wrangell Narrows from town; the state maintains a dock there. **Guided sea kayak day trips** go up the creek (see "Sea Kayaking," below), which contains four species of salmon and two species of trout. The trail is maintained by the Forest Service and has miles of boardwalks and two cabins, one at Petersburg Lake and one at East Salt Chuck, each with a boat for public use. (Reservations are required, as noted above.) Petersburg Lake has trout, and odds are good you'll see ducks, geese, loons, trumpeter swans, bald eagles, and black bears. The Kupreanof dock also provides access to the 3-mile, 3,000-foot trail that climbs Petersburg Mountain, a challenging hike that has spectacular views from the top.

LECONTE GLACIER / STIKINE RIVER DELTA   Ice calving from the glacier has choked the waters in front, making approach difficult, but in June you can see seal pups on the floating ice and possibly mountain goats. A bit farther on is the Stikine River Delta, a wildlife habitat of grasslands, braided channels, and marshes with excellent bird watching in late April and early May, when the hooligan run, more than 1,500 bald eagles congregate, and some 2 million other birds rest up on their west coast migration. The charter operators listed above can take you, or Viking Travel can book one of the others who offers these trips. Boat tours based in Wrangell specialize in going to the Delta—they're closer to the river. The going rate for a 4- to 5-hour tour to LeConte Glacier from Petersburg is about $90 per person. Going on to the delta would be more like $175 per person and take all day.

ACTIVITIES

WHALE WATCHING   Most summers, Frederick Sound is one of the best places in the state to see humpbacks when they're feeding. Whale-watching charters go every day from May 15 to September 15, but the height is July and August. You'll likely see stunning **bubble-net feeding,** when the whales confine a school of fish in a circle of bubbles, then lunge upward to scoop them up, bursting through the surface in a great swoosh. Whales have even been known to **spy-hop,** poking their heads as high above the surface as possible in order to look down into the boats that are watching them. In the summer of 1995, a humpback jumped right into one of these boats, presumably accidentally. (No one was injured, but a few people fell into the water.) Several charter operators offer trips in small, six-passenger boats. Some, including Kaleidoscope Cruises (under "Getting Outside" above), have hydrophones on board, so you may be able to hear the whales' vocalizations while waiting for them to surface, if their feeding behavior and the water conditions are right. Book through Viking Travel or directly with one of the operators I've mentioned above. Trips usually leave around 8am and stay out 8 to 10 hours, with several hours with the whales. Prices are $150 to $175 per person.

SEA KAYAKING   The waters along Wrangell Narrows are perfect for sea kayaking. The area is both protected and interesting, with plenty to see. On longer trips of 3 days to a week, you can get out among the glaciers, Stikine River Delta, and even the whales—there's as much variety here, among these rain forest islands, as anywhere in the region. It's possible to set up a trip linking some of the two dozen Forest Service cabins, too, or to use one as a base camp for a few days of exploration. **Tongass Kayak Adventures,** P.O. Box 787, Petersburg, AK 99833 (☎ **907/772-4600;** www.alaska. net/~tonkayak/), offers each of these options guided or, for experienced kayakers, with rental equipment. Their 4-hour paddle crosses Wrangell Narrows from the harbor and penetrates Petersburg Creek, where they stop for a snack and often see bears and deer. No experience is required, and they charge $55 for adults and $30 for children 11 and under. A 3-night base camp tour costs $575 per person, an 8-night explore $1,190.

MOUNTAIN BIKING   The largely abandoned logging roads on the island and on surrounding islands that can be reached by boat provide long bike rides without seeing cars or other people. **Northern Bikes,** listed under "Getting Around," rents gear and can give ideas on where to go.

A COMMERCIAL FISHING TOUR   Retired Petersburg high school principal Syd Wright runs a unique commercial fishing demonstration. Wright is a crusty and well-loved local institution, often called upon for knowledge about the area's natural history. He takes six passengers on his crude, crowded workboat, trawls for shrimp and sole, and pulls crab pots in Scow Bay, south of town; and then his crewman cooks it up with butter and garlic, and serves it with a glass of wine. Wright can identify all the weird creatures that come up in the trawl. The price is $100, with a three-passenger minimum, but it's usually booked way in advance. Wright can be reached direct at **Chan IV Charters,** P.O. Box 624, Petersburg, AK 99833 (☎ **907/772-4859**).

SPORTFISHING   There are many fishing streams and lakes you can reach on the roads—several are mentioned above, under "Mitkof Island." For more choices, check at the visitor center, or send away before you come for a *Petersburg/Wrangell Sport Fishing Guide* from the Alaska Department of Fish and Game, listed under "Outside in Southeast," at the beginning of this chapter. For expert advice and regulation information you also can contact the **Petersburg office of Fish and Game,** at ☎ **907/ 772-3801.** The boat harbor has a couple of dozen licensed charter fishing boats, mostly six-passenger vessels. As elsewhere, halibut and salmon are usually the target. You can get a list of operators at the visitor center, or book through **Viking Travel** (see "Visitor Information," above). Salmon charters usually last half a day and cost $100 per person, while halibut charters go all day and cost $165.

ACCOMMODATIONS

Among the places below I've listed three outstanding B&Bs, but the visitor center can direct you to other choices if these are booked up.

Bear Necessities Guesthouse. 18 Sing Lee Alley (P.O. Box 923), Petersburg, AK 99833. ☎ **907/772-2279.** www.alaska.net/~bearbnb. $90 double.

A nice one-bedroom apartment that's rented by the night. Although it lacks a view, the decoration is cute and the facilities perfect for a family, with a full kitchen, lots of beds, and all expected amenities—and it's right on Sing Lee Alley, up on pilings in the middle of things.

Bumbershoot Bed and Breakfast. 909 Sandy Beach Rd. (P.O. Box 372), Petersburg, AK 99833. ☎ **907/772-4682.** Fax 907/772-4627. E-mail: ohknigs@pobox.alaska.net. 4 units, shared bathroom. $80–$90 double. Additional person in room $10 extra. AE, DC, DISC, MC, V.

The industrious Gloria Ohmer, who owns the Tides Inn Motel (see below), has opened her extraordinary waterfront home on Frederick Sound to guests as well. The rooms are large, decorated with quilts she made—Gloria and her husband, Don Koenigs, also will share their bead work, wood work, sewing, stained glass, lapidary, music room, fish cleaning room, and deck barbecue with you. It's hard to come away without gaining a little of their enthusiasm for life. Rooms with water views—and the water is only barely beyond your reach—rent for $10 more. For $150 a night, you can rent the entire downstairs apartment, with two rooms, a kitchen, and a large living room with a fireplace.

Scandia House. 110 Nordic Dr. (P.O. Box 689), Petersburg, AK 99833. ☎ **800/722-5006** or 907/772-4281. Fax 907/772-4301. E-mail: scandia@alaska.net. 33 units. TV TEL. $90–$105 double, $130 double with kitchenette; $175 suite. Additional person in room $10 extra. AE, CB, DC, DISC, MC, V.

Rebuilt in the town's distinctive Norwegian style after a fire in 1995, this building is in a class by itself for its solid simplicity. White rooms with blond wood trim are pale with natural light. There's a choice of rooms: front rooms with king-size beds, eight kitchenettes, twins, or a magnificent fourth-floor suite with towering ceilings. Most rooms have only one bed, a few have shower stalls, not tubs, and none are reserved exclusively for nonsmokers, although I smelled no smoke during my tour—the place was immaculate. There's free coffee and continental breakfast, and a courtesy van is available. The hotel rents skiffs (see "Getting Around," above) and has four cars for rent for $50 a day. Book rooms well in advance for the busy summer season.

Tides Inn Motel. 307 N. First St. (P.O. Box 1048), Petersburg, AK 99833. ☎ **800/665-8433** or 907/772-4288. Fax 907/772-4286. E-mail: tidesinn@alaska.net. 48 units. TV TEL. $85 double. Additional person in room $10 extra. AE, DC, DISC, MC, V.

Few hotels in Alaska have rooms as good as these at such a bargain price. The kitchenette rooms, which rent for the same rate, are an incredible bargain. The large, dark-brown building has its flaws: Rooms in the older part face an air shaft instead of the sweeping view you get from the best, no-smoking rooms in the front of the new section. We watched bald eagles doing aerobatics less than 50 feet from our window there. The management is efficient and committed to quality, slowly remodeling rooms while keeping those that remain out-of-date in clean, attractive condition. A block above Nordic Drive, the hotel also rents cars, offers a free continental breakfast of muffins and juice, and keeps coffee on in the lobby around the clock. A courtesy van connects to the ferry or airport.

Waterfront Bed and Breakfast. Nordic Dr. near the ferry dock (P.O. Box 1364), Petersburg, AK 99833. ☎ **907/772-9300.** Fax 907/772-9308. www.alaska.net/~h20frbnb. 3 units. $95–$105 double. MC, V.

Built to be a bed-and-breakfast as well as a family home and located on pilings over the Wrangell Narrows near the ferry dock, the building combines supreme ocean views and the essential, watery sense of Petersburg. The kids' yard is on the wooden pier, and the canoe down below is free for guests to borrow. Rooms are decorated with oak furniture and comforters, and each has a private bathroom. Everything looks brand new. Two rooms have a single queen-size bed and the third, with two doubles, costs $10 more; the rate is the same no matter how many are in the room. Besides a hot breakfast, guests can use a microwave, fridge, coffeemaker, and the barbecue in the gazebo on the deck outside, as well as the washer and drier and a sitting room with a VCR.

Water's Edge Bed and Breakfast. 705 Sandy Beach Rd. (P.O. Box 1201), Petersburg, AK 99833. ☎ **800/TO-THE-SEA** (800/868-4373) or phone/fax 907/772-3736. www.alaska.net/ ~bbsea. 2 units. High season, $90 double. Low season, $80 double. Additional person in room $10 extra. 2-night minimum stay. No credit cards.

Barry and Kathy Bracken's house sits right on the beach on Frederick Sound, about a mile from town, with a creek running next to one room. You can sit in the large common room and bird-watch from there, or borrow the canoe for a paddle along the shore. Guests also get the use of bikes and laundry facilities, and Kathy picks them up at the airport or ferry terminal. Probably the best way to do it is to book a package in the B&B and on Barry's 28-foot boat; a retired state marine fish biologist, he leads natural history and whale-watching excursions. His knowledge of the area is deep and his enthusiasm infectious. Book well ahead, as it's a rare and popular opportunity. Children under 12 aren't allowed at the B&B, and there's no smoking in the house.

CAMPING

Petersburg's most famous campground is the **Tent City** at 1800 Haugen Dr. (P.O. Box 329), Petersburg, AK 99833 (☎ **907/772-4224**), where the summer's young cannery workers set up tents and plastic sheeting on 50 wooden platforms for $5 a night. It's a bit rowdy for most tourists, but young people looking to make friends and party should enjoy it. A central pavilion has coin-op showers, sinks, phones, cooking areas, and firewood.

The closest natural camping is found 22 miles out the Mitkof Highway at **Ohmer Creek** (see "Special Places: Mitkof Island," above). **Twin Creek RV Park** is 6.5 miles out the highway (☎ **907/772-3244**), charging $18.85 for full hookups.

DINING

Petersburg has several good, small-town restaurants, nothing you'd seek out for the food, but with enough character to make the experience memorable.

AlasKafe. Upstairs at 506 N. Nordic, at the corner of Excel St. ☎ **907/772-JAVA.** $6–$9.25. No credit cards. Sun–Fri 7:30am–5pm, Sat 8am–midnight. COFFEE HOUSE.

It's mostly a coffee shop, but they also serve delicious panini sandwiches, pasta, soup, and salad. You can log in on the Internet, talk or read on the couch, or get your hair cut—Glenn and Valerie Miller started the place as a hair salon, and their customers wouldn't let them shut down the salon in the back rooms when they decided to shift to selling coffee. Summer nights they sometimes stay open late for live music, poetry readings, and the like.

Helse. 17 Sing Lee Alley. ☎ **907/772-3444.** All meals $2.25–$7.25. No credit cards. Mon–Fri 7:30am–3pm, Sat 10am–3pm. SANDWICHES/HEALTH FOOD.

For a Good Take-Out Lunch

Stop in at **Coastal Cold Storage,** at Excel Street and Nordic Drive (☎ 907/ 772-4177), where they sell seafood from freezers and live from tanks. Order burgers, sandwiches, fish specials, and ice-cream cones at the counter.

This health-food store/restaurant serves hearty plates of food—mostly sandwiches plus daily specials—and I sure enjoyed my shrimp and cream cheese on grainy bread. The dining room is small and a little grubby, each table hanging at one end from a rope. The early '70s thing is wearing a bit thin.

The Homestead. 217 N. Nordic Dr. ☎ **907/772-3900.** Lunch $3.50–$10.50; dinner $10.50–$24. AE, MC, V. Mon–Sat 24 hours. DINER.

Your first clue that this is where the locals go is on the street front: There's no sign, because none is needed. The Homestead, open around the clock, is for commercial fishermen coming off the boat in the middle of the night and looking for a glorious, juicy burger or deep-fried fresh halibut and a pile of greasy fries, or to stop in for a delicious traditional breakfast and limitless coffee at the lunch counter to talk sports and fish. The counter would be a museum piece some places, with its swiveling, wooden-backed stools. Mercifully, they've banned smoking throughout. Kids are well treated.

Joan Mei Restaurant. 1103 S. Nordic, across from the ferry dock. ☎ **907/772-4222.** Lunch $6.25–$14.50, dinner $6.25–$20. MC, V. Daily 11am–8:30pm. CHINESE.

The whole family works together in this large, bright dining room, serving flaky egg rolls and entrees with vegetables that remain crisp and flavorful rather than being smothered or overcooked. Locals come here for nice dinner out, and we saw many happy faces.

Morrie's Pizza. 203 Sing Lee Alley. ☎ **907/772-3424.** Sandwiches $3.50–$6.75. Large pizza $17.55 one-topping. MC, V. Daily 11am–9pm. PIZZERIA.

You might find a family pizzeria like this anywhere, with video games (including some antiques) and a juke box, Alaska Amber beer on tap, and tasty pizza with a light, crispy crust. The big difference is the location: on pilings over the boat harbor along the dock/street of Sing Lee Alley, with views you won't forget. The business has changed hands frequently in past years, but in its current incarnation was quite good.

8 Sitka: Rich Prize of Russian Conquest

The history that Sitka preserves is interesting not only because of the Russian buildings that record Alaska's early white settlement, but more deeply for the story of the cultural conflict of Alaska Natives—and by extension, all aboriginal peoples—with the invaders, and their resistance and ultimate accommodation to the new ways. Here, 18th-century Russian conquerors who had successfully enslaved the Aleuts to the west (and whose culture they nearly extinguished, though it bounced back, to some extent), met their match in battle against the rich, powerful, and sophisticated Tlingit. A visit to Sitka teaches the story of that war, and also the cultural blending that occurred in the uneasy peace that followed under the influence of the Russian Orthodox church—an influence that remained after the Russians packed up and left upon the U.S. purchase of Alaska in 1867, and continues today.

   Sitka's history is Alaska's richest, and there's more of real interest in town than anywhere else you might visit. The fact is, most Alaska towns haven't been on the map long enough to have accumulated much history. Those that have been around for a while often have been wiped out a time or two, leaving little to remind you of the distant past. There's usually a small museum and a few gold rush sites, often no more than you can see in half a day. Not so in Sitka. Historic photographs bear a surprising resemblance to today's city. The National Park Service protects buildings and grounds of major historic significance—places where the pioneers spoke Russian, with ways so much more European than those of the rest of the American West. Even a superficial exploration of the attractions takes a day, and that without time for the out-of-the way points of interest or the outdoors.

In 1799, the Russians chose these protected waters on Sitka Sound, on the ocean side of Baranof Island, for a new fort as part of a strategy of pushing their fur operations and territorial claims east and south along the west coast of North America. The Tlingit understandably considered this to be an invasion, and in 1802 they attacked the Russian's redoubt and killed almost everyone inside. The Russians counterattacked in 1804 with the cannons of the ship *Neva* and a swarm of Aleut warriors, eventually forcing the Tlingit chief, Katlian, to withdraw.

The Russians never rested easy in their new capital (which they named New Archangel), however, as Tlingit hostility long remained. Some poor Russian laborers intermarried and essentially joined Tlingit culture, but many of the bureaucrats and naval officers sent to run the colony for the czar viewed Alaska as purgatory and left as soon as they could. Under their ineffective and uninterested control, the Russians made surprising little impression on the great mass of Alaska (aside from nearly wiping out the sea otters), building only three major towns—Unalaska, Kodiak, and Sitka, of which only Sitka retains any significant number of Russian buildings.

Besides its historic significance, Sitka also is fun to visit. Somehow it has retained a friendly, authentic feel, despite the crush of thousands of visitors. Perhaps because cruise-ship travelers must ride boats to shore, or because Sitka is a slightly inconvenient, out-of-the-way stop on the Alaska Marine Highway's main-line ferry routes, the city's streets haven't been choked by solid rows of seasonal gift shops, as has occurred in Ketchikan, Skagway, and a large part of Juneau. It remains picturesque, facing Sitka Sound, which is dotted with islands and populated by feeding eagles. Tourism is important here, but Sitka's community remains its center. The process of being "spoiled" hasn't even begun.

Even beyond the town and its history, Sitka is a gateway to a large, remote portion of Southeast Alaska, in the western coastal islands. This area contains some of Tongass National Forest's least-used outdoor opportunities. The ocean halibut and salmon fishing are excellent and not overexploited, the bird and wildlife watching exceptional.

If I could visit only one Alaska town, it would probably be Sitka.

ESSENTIALS
GETTING THERE

BY FERRY   Sitka sits on the west side of Baranof Island, a detour from the Inside Passage. The big, main-line ferries on the **Alaska Marine Highway System** (see listing under "Getting Around" at the beginning of this chapter) don't always stop here, but the small *LeConte* adds more connecting trips each week, often stopping at villages in the region. The ride through narrow Peril Straits into Sitka is definitely worth the trip. The shore seems close enough to touch, and if you look closely you can sometimes see deer. The fare to either Juneau or Petersburg is $26. The ferry dock is 7 miles out of town; see "Getting Around," below, regarding transfers.

BY AIR   Alaska Airlines (☎ **800/426-0333** or 907/966-2422 locally; www.alaskaair.com) links Sitka to Juneau and Ketchikan, flights that then continue nonstop to Seattle and Anchorage.

GETTING INTO TOWN FROM THE AIRPORT   Sitka Tours charges $3 to get to town from the ferry dock or airport, with buses meeting all arrivals.

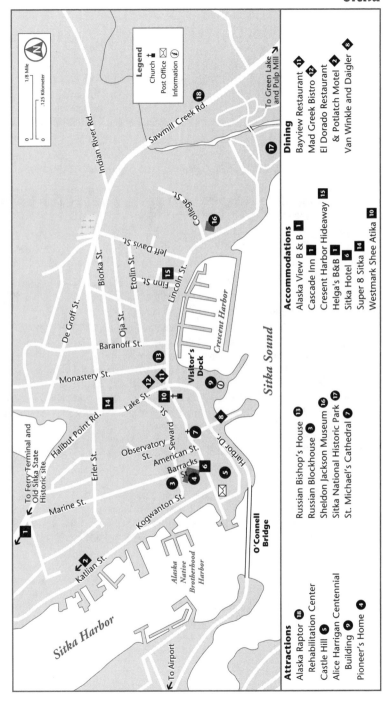

Sitka

Legend
Church
Post Office
Information

Attractions
Alaska Raptor Rehabilitation Center **18**
Castle Hill **5**
Alice Harrigan Centennial Building **9**
Pioneer's Home **4**
Russian Bishop's House **13**
Russian Blockhouse **3**
Sheldon Jackson Museum **16**
Sitka National Historic Park **17**
St. Michael's Cathedral **7**

Accommodations
Alaska View B & B **1**
Cascade Inn **1**
Cresent Harbor Hideaway **15**
Helga's B&B **1**
Sitka Hotel **6**
Super 8 Sitka **14**
Westmark Shee Atika **10**

Dining
Bayview Restaurant **11**
Mad Greek Bistro **12**
El Dorado Restaurant **8**
& Potlatch Motel **2**
Van Winkle and Daigler **8**

125

GETTING AROUND

Sitka, on the west side of Baranof Island, has only a few miles of road. The **ferry terminal** is located at its north end, 7 miles out, on **Halibut Point Road;** the abandoned pulp mill is at the south end, 5 miles out **Sawmill Creek Boulevard.** The town faces Sitka Sound. Across Sitka Channel is **Japonski Island** and the **airport** (don't worry, it only looks as if your plane is going to land in the water). **Lincoln Street** contains most of the tourist attractions. A free map provided by the Sitka Convention and Visitors Bureau at the visitor center will help you navigate the initially confusing downtown streets.

BY RENTAL CAR   Rental cars are available at the airport from **Avis** (☎ **800/ 331-1212** or 907/966-2404) and **Allstar/Practical** (☎ **800/722-6927** or 907/ 966-2552).

BY TAXI   **Sitka Cab** is available at ☎ **907/747-5001,** and the ride from the ferry dock is around $15.

BY BUS   The Visitor Transit Bus operated by **Sikta Tribal Tours,** 456 Katlian St. (☎ **888/270-8687** or 907/747-7290; www.sitkatribe.org), makes a continuous circuit of the sites Monday through Friday, 12:30p to 4:30pm, with added hours when cruise ships are in. The fare is $5 all day, and kids ride free.

BY BIKE   **S.E. Diving and Sports,** 329 Harbor St., Sitka, AK 99835 (☎ **800/ 824-3483** in Alaska only, or 907/747-8279), rents bikes for $5 an hour or $20 a day.

BY TOUR   **Sitka Tribal Tours** (see above) and **Sitka Tours** (☎ **907/747-8443**), which offers a more Russian perspective, offer a variety of town tours by bus and on foot, mostly serving cruise-ship passengers who are shorter on time than are independent travelers. Prices range from about $12 to tour the historical park to $33 for a longer town tour that includes most of the attractions, with admission to either the Native or Russian dancing, depending on which firm you go with. Or join **Sitka Walking Tours** (☎ **907/747-5354**) to find some of the lesser-known places—Jane Eidler does a great job, charging $9 for a 90-minute walk.

VISITOR INFORMATION

Although only a desk, the city-operated **Harrigan Centennial Hall Visitor Center,** 330 Harbor Dr., next to the Crescent Boat Harbor (☎ **907/747-3225**), provides refreshingly straightforward printed information. They're open daily 8am to 5pm in summer, Monday to Friday 8am to 5pm in winter. If you are writing ahead for information, instead contact the **Sitka Convention and Visitors Bureau,** at P.O. Box 1226, Dept. 122, Sitka, AK 99835 (☎ **907/747-5940;** fax 907/747-3739). They maintain an extensive and aesthetic Web site at **www.sitka.org**.

The **Sitka National Historical Park Visitor Center,** 106 Metlakatla St., Sitka, AK 99835 (☎ **907/747-6281;** www.nps.gov/sitk), run by the National Park Service, maintains the most important historic sites in Sitka, and is an essential stop where you can gather information and learn about what happened here. The *Historic Sites of Sitka* map produced by the Park Service and Sitka Historical Society is an indispensable guide to the buildings and parks around town. You can easily see Sitka's history on foot with one of these maps. The center is open daily 8am to 5pm in summer, Monday to Friday 8am to 5pm in winter.

SPECIAL EVENTS

The Starring Ceremony, in early January (with the exact date depending on the church calendar), marks Russian Orthodox Christmas with a procession through the streets and song and prayer at the doors of the faithful. **The Annual Gathering of the People** occurs in mid-April, when Alaska Natives from across Alaska come to Sitka for a cultural exchange (☎ 907/747-2579). **The Sitka Salmon Derby** occurs at the end of May and beginning of June, when the kings are running; contact the Convention and Visitors Bureau. **The Sitka Summer Music Festival,** a chamber-music series that began in 1972, is one of Alaska's biggest cultural events, drawing musicians from all over the world during June. Performances and other events take place all month. Rehearsals are free. Contact the festival office for info: P.O. Box 3333, Sitka, AK 99835 (☎ 907/747-6774). **Alaska Day,** October 18, commemorating the Alaska purchase, is a big deal in this former Russian capital city; the Alaska Day Festival lasts 4 days leading up to the big event. The Convention and Visitors Bureau has information. **The Sitka Grind,** a music and arts celebration at varying sites around town, takes place the third Saturday of each month from October to March. The **Sitka WhaleFest** takes place over a weekend in early November, during the fall and early winter period when humpback whales congregate in Sitka Sound. There are workshops, whale-watching tours, and other community events. Call ☎ **907/747-5940** for information.

Fast Facts: Sitka

Banks   There's an ATM at the National Bank of Alaska, 300 Lincoln St.

Hospital   The Sitka Community Hospital (☎ 907/747-3241) is at 209 Moller Dr.

Internet/E-mail   Highliner Cafe, in the Seward Square Mall (☎ 907/747-4924), offers access for $3 for the first half hour as well as serving food.

Police   Call ☎ 907/747-3245 for nonemergencies.

Post Office   At 1207 Sawmill Creek Hwy., on the south side of town.

Taxes   Sales tax is 5%. The bed tax in Sitka is 6%, in addition to the 5% sales tax.

EXPLORING SITKA
SITKA'S TLINGIT & RUSSIAN HERITAGE

✪ **Sitka National Historical Park.** 106 Metlakatla St. ☎ **907/747-6281.** Free admission. Visitor center open 8am–5pm daily summer; 8am–5pm Mon–Fri winter.

In 1799, the Russian America Company, led by Alexander Baranof, landed from their base in Kodiak, established Redoubt St. Michael (today the **Old Sitka State Historic Site,** 7½ miles north of town—just a grassy picnic area with interpretive signs), and claimed the Pacific Northwest of America for Russia. The Tlingit, who were sophisticated traders and already had acquired flintlocks, attacked with knives, spears, and guns, and destroyed the redoubt in mid-June 1802, killing almost all of the Russians. The Natives immediately began building fortifications on the site now within the national historic park, anticipating a Russian counterattack, which came in 1804. Baranof returned with an attacking force of a Russian gunship and a swarm of Aleut kayaks, which towed the becalmed vessel into position to begin the bombardment. The Tlingits withstood the siege for 6 days, then vacated their fort at night, after taking heavy losses from the shelling and from a bomb-laden canoe. Thereafter, the Russians founded and heavily fortified the town of New Archangel, and in 1808 it became their administrative capital. But the Tlingit name is the one that stuck: Shee Atika, since contracted to Sitka.

The historic significance of the battle site was recognized early, and Pres. Benjamin Harrison, a friend of Alaska missionary Sheldon Jackson, set it aside in 1890. In 1905, a collection of totem poles from around Southeast was brought here (the originals are in storage, and replicas are on display). The historic park emphasizes, as it should, the Native perspective. In the visitor center, a display explains the history, and Alaska Native artisans from the Southeast Alaska Indian Cultural Center work in a series of windowed workshops in wood, silver, and cloth, making traditional carvings, jewelry, drums, and regalia. You can watch them work; go in and ask questions. An auditorium shows films and other programs.

I found the totem park and battle site most impressive. The totems stand tall and forbidding along a pathway through massive spruce and hemlock, where misty rain wanders down from an unseen sky somewhere above the trees. The battle site is along the trail—only a grassy area now—but among the trees and totems, with the sound of the lapping sea and raven's call, one can feel deep down what the Tlingits were fighting for.

And, in fact, the park and center are full of evidence of the Tlingit's living heritage. In 1996, a gathering of clans erected a major new pole in front of the center, the Indian River Tlingit History Pole, to explain their story from before the Russians' arrival, back to mankind's beginnings in North America. It took quite a bit of debate to settle the story the pole would tell. For example, the crests of the eagle and raven tribal moieties are traditionally never shown on the same pole, but they had to be to tell the whole history of the Tlingits. The obvious success of the project speaks from the beauty of the pole, a strong symbol of cultural renewal.

The Russian Bishop's House. Lincoln and Monastery sts. No phone; call Sitka National Historical Park Visitor Center (☎ **907/747-6281;** see "Visitor Information," above). Free admission downstairs; $2 per person or $5 per family for upstairs tour. Daily 9am–1pm and 2–5pm summer; by appointment winter.

Father Ivan Veniaminov, born in 1797, translated the Bible into Tlingit and trained deacons to carry Russian Orthodoxy back to their Native villages. Unlike most of the later missionaries of other faiths, he allowed parishioners to use their own language, a key element to saving Native cultures. When the United States bought Alaska in 1867, few Russians remained, but the Russian Orthodox faith Veniaminov planted as a priest and later as Bishop Innocent remains strong in Native Alaska; there are 89 parishes, primarily in tiny Native villages. In 1977, Veniaminov was canonized as St. Innocent in the Orthodox faith.

In 1842, the Russian America Company retained Finnish shipbuilders to construct this extraordinary house, Sitka's oldest surviving Russian building, as a residence, school, and chapel for Bishop Innocent. It survived many years of neglect in part because its huge beams were fit together like a ship's. The National Park Service bought and began restoring the building in 1972, and today it makes for a fascinating visit. Downstairs is a self-guided museum; rangers lead frequent tours upstairs to the bishop's quarters, which are furnished with original and period pieces. The tour concludes with a visit to a tiny chapel with many of the original icons Innocent brought from Russia.

St. Michael's Cathedral. Lincoln and Cathedral sts. ☎ **907/747-8120.** $2 donation requested. Mon–Sat 1:30–5:30pm, Sun for services; 7:30am–5:30pm when cruise ships are in port.

The first Orthodox cathedral in the New World stands grandly in the middle of Sitka's principal street, where it was completed in 1848 by Father Veniaminov (see above). The cathedral contains icons dating from the 17th century, including the miraculous *Sitka Madonna.* The choirmaster or another knowledgeable guide is on hand to answer questions or give talks when large groups congregate. The original building burned down in a fire that took much of Sitka's downtown in 1966, but the icons were saved, and Orthodox Christians all over the United States raised the money to rebuild it exactly as it had been, completing the task in 1976.

✪ **Sheldon Jackson Museum.** 104 College Dr. ☎ **907/747-8981.** www.educ.state.ak. us/lam/museum/sjhome.html. Admission $3 for adults, free age 18 and under. Mid-May to mid-Sept, daily 8am–5pm; mid-Sept to mid-May, Tues–Sat 10am–4pm.

Among the best collections of Alaska Native artifacts on display anywhere is kept here in Alaska's first concrete building (circa 1895), now a state museum run by the Alaska Department of Education on the campus of Sheldon Jackson College. Jackson, a Presbyterian missionary and major figure in Alaska history, started the collection in 1888. Although his assimilationist views today appear tragically destructive to Native cultures, Jackson also advanced Native education and economic opportunity—for example, he first imported domesticated reindeer to Alaska. This museum's small octagonal building is like a jewel box, but the overwhelming wealth is displayed in such ingenious ways that it avoids feeling cluttered. Some of the drawers in the white cabinetry open to reveal more displays. Some of the artifacts, despite their antiquity, are as fresh as if they had just been made.

OTHER ATTRACTIONS IN TOWN

Performances by the **New Archangel Dancers** (☎ **907/747-5516**) are one of the most popular attractions in the state, and most cruise-ship passengers go to their crowd-pleasing shows in the Harrigan Centennial Hall. The all-woman troupe performs male and female roles in traditional Russian and Ukrainian dances commemorating Sitka's Russian heritage (although the performers aren't Russian—the Russians left on the first available boat upon the sale of Alaska to the United States in 1867). Shows are geared to ship arrivals—the times are posted at the hall, or phone for information. Admission is $6.

Also at the Centennial Hall, the free **Isabel Miller Museum** (☎ **907/747-6455**) shows exhibits on town history by the Sitka Historical Society, including a diorama of early Sitka. The one-room museum is open 8am to 6pm daily in the summer, 10am to 4pm Tuesday through Saturday in the winter.

The Sitka Tribe (☎ **888/270-8687** or 907/747-7290; www.sitkatribe.org) sponsors performances of **traditional Tlingit dance** daily at the Tribal Community House near the Pioneers' Home. The dancers explain the dances and interact with the audience; my son was entranced. The 45-minute show is $6 for adults, $4 for children. Call the numbers above for performance times.

Since 1980, injured eagles, hawks, owls, and other birds of prey have been brought to the **Alaska Raptor Rehabilitation Center,** 1101 Sawmill Creek Blvd. (take the dirt road up the hill to the left after the historical park), for veterinary treatment, convalescence, and release or transfer to a zoo. The main attraction for visitors is seeing these impressive birds close up in large enclosures with natural habitats, and to watch staff treating birds and teaching them to fly again. Admission is $10 for adults and $5 for children under 12, money which helps the nonprofit center in its work. They're open 8:30am to 4pm in summer, 10am to 2pm in winter.

I highly recommend the **Historic Sites of Sitka walking tour,** available at either of the visitor centers; but if you just want some of the high points, don't miss these:

The brick **Pioneers' Home,** a state-run residence for retired people who helped settle Alaska, stands on a grassy park at Lincoln and Katlian, where the Russians had their barracks and parade ground. Stop to talk to one of the old-timers rocking on the porch—each probably has more Alaska in his or her little finger than all the tour guides you'll meet all summer. Just north on Marine Street is a replica of a **Russian Blockhouse;** across Lincoln Street to the south and up the stairs is **Castle Hill,** a site of historic significance for the ancient Tlingits, for the Russians, and for Alaskans. The first American flag raised in Alaska was hoisted here in 1867. There are historic markers and cannons. Walking east past the cathedral and Crescent Harbor, several quaint historic buildings are on the left—my favorite is **St. Peter's by-the-Sea Episcopal Church,** a lovely stone-and-timber chapel with a pipe organ, consecrated in 1899. At the east end of the harbor is a **public playground;** continue down the street to **Sheldon Jackson College** and the national historical park.

GETTING OUTSIDE: ON THE WATER

The little islands and rocks that dot Sitka Sound are an invitation to the sea otter in all of us; you must get out on the water. Humpback whales tend to show up in large groups in the fall but are also sometimes seen in the summer. There are so many bald eagles that you're pretty well guaranteed of seeing them from shore. But the lowly sea otter is the most common and, in my experience, most amusing and endearing of marine mammals, and you'll certainly see them from a boat tour. Otters seem so friendly and happy it's hard not to anthropomorphize and envy them.

SIGHTSEEING & WILDLIFE TOURS

Tour boats visit ✪ **St. Lazaria Island,** a bird rookery where you can expect to see puffins, murres, and rhinoceros auklets; if you stay overnight on a boat, you can be there for the return of the storm petrels, back from the sea to feed their young. The volcanic rock drops off straight down into deep water, so even big boats can come close. The public tubs at **Goddard Hot Springs,** 17 miles south of town, are another possible stop for charters.

Many boats are available for **wildlife tours** or **saltwater fishing.** Sitka Convention and Visitors Bureau (see "Visitor Information," above) keeps a detailed charter boat list, including rates, that goes on for five pages. Their "Sitka Through Four Seasons" booklet includes a checklist of what birds and animals you can expect to see and when.

The **Sitka Wildlife Quest** operated by Allen Marine Tours (☎ **888/747-8101** or 907/747-8100; www.allenmarinetours.com) does a terrific job, with well-trained naturalists to explain the wildlife, at least some of which you are almost certain to see. You have a good chance of encountering humpback whales and sea otters. The 2-hour cruise costs $49 adults, $30 children, and leaves from the Crescent Harbor Visitors Dock Wednesday at 6pm and Saturday and Sunday at 9am. The Sunday excursion includes a visit to St. Lazaria Island. Buy tickets on board, or call ahead for reservations. These are different excursions from the ones offered to cruise ship passengers.

Raven's Fire Tour Connection, 403 Lincoln St. (P.O. Box 6112), Sitka, AK 99835 (☎ **907/747-5777;** www.ravensfire.com), is Barbara Bingham's 42-passenger natural history tour boat. It's equipped with hydrophones to eavesdrop on the whales, although they often keep mum. Although she does day trips in Sitka Sound and St. Lazaria Island, her specialty is longer natural history voyages—such as the uproarious nightly return of the storm petrels to St. Lazaria Island. Itineraries may last up to a week.

SAILING

Noel and Claire Johnson offer a $75 ecosightseeing cruise on their 56-foot gaff-rigged wooden cutter (a former commercial fishing vessel), as well as longer charters, commercial fishing outings, and sea kayak drop-off. Contact them at **Southeast Alaska Ocean Adventures,** 1705 Sawmill Creek Rd., Sitka, AK 99835 (☎ and fax **907/747-5078;** www.ptialaska.net/~jparker/saoa.htm).

SEA KAYAKING

Sitka's protected waters and intricate shorelines are perfect for sea kayaking, the closest thing to being a sea otter a human ever gets. Four companies offer sea kayaking in Sitka, but Larry Edwards has seniority—he's been doing it for 23 years. His **Baidarka Boats,** 201 Lincoln St. (P.O. Box 6001) Sitka, AK 99835 (☎ **907/747-8996;** www.kayaksite.com), rents the boats and offers instruction and guided paddles for every experience level, including raw beginners. The cost of the guided trips depends on the number in your group: A half-day trip is $95 for one alone, $180 for six together.

DIVING

These waters tend to be clear and biologically rich, making them appealing to divers. Winter is best, when plankton isn't blooming, but good periods come in summer, too. **S.E. Diving and Sports,** 329 Harbor St., Sitka, AK 99835 (☎ **800/824-3483** or 907/747-3483) is the dive shop in town.

GETTING OUTSIDE: ON SHORE
WHALE WATCHING

Humpback whales stop to feed in Sitka Sound on their way south in the winter migration. During the months of October, November, December, and March, you can watch from shore—the local government has even built a special park for the purpose. At **Whale Park,** 3½ miles south of town on Sawmill Creek Blvd., spotting scopes are mounted on platforms along a boardwalk and at the end of staircases that descend the dramatic, wooded cliffs. Excellent interpretive signs, located near a surfacing concrete whale in the parking lot, explain the whales.

TIDE POOLING & SHORE WALKS

Halibut Point State Recreation Area, 4.4 miles north of town on Halibut Point Road, is a great place for a picnic, ramble, and tide pooling. To find the best low tides, check a tide book, available all over town. It's best to go on the lowest tide possible, arriving on the shore an hour or 2 hours before the low. To identify the little creatures you'll see, buy a plastic-covered *Mac's Field Guide* at the National Park Service visitor center at the historical park.

FISHING

Fishermen should pick up the *Sitka Area Sport Fishing Guide,* which has lots of tips on places and methods in the area. You can write ahead for it from the Alaska Department of Fish and Game, listed in "Outside in Southeast," earlier in this chapter. The local Fish and Game office is at 304 Lake St., Room 103, Sitka, AK 99835 (☎ **907/ 747-5355**).

HIKING

There are a dozen U.S. Forest Service hiking trails accessible from the roads around Sitka and another twenty you can get to by plane or boat. *Sitka Trails,* a handy 78-page trail guide describing them, sells for $4 at the **Sitka Ranger District,** 201 Katlian St., Suite 109, Sitka, AK 99835 (☎ **907/747-4220;** www.fs.fed.us/r10/tongass/). Two trailheads are walking distance from downtown. The 5½-mile **Indian River Trail** is a relaxing rain-forest walk rising gradually up the river valley to a small waterfall. Take Indian River Road off Sawmill Creek Road east of the Alaska State Troopers Academy. For a steeper mountain-climbing trail to alpine terrain and great views, the **Gavan Hill–Harbor Mountain Trail** is just past the house at 508 Baranof St., near downtown. It gains 2,500 feet over 3 miles to the peak of Gavan Hill, then continues another 3 miles along a ridge to meet Harbor Mountain Road.

At the north end of Halibut Point Road, 7½ miles from downtown, a broad board-walk circles a grassy estuary, rich with birds and fish. The **Estuary Life Trail** and **Forest Muskeg Trail,** totaling about a mile, are exquisitely developed and accessible to anyone. It's a place of peaceful beauty. A new trail was under construction at this writing to loop through the old growth of Mosquito Cove. The Forest Service dis-tributes a superb guide map to this whole area at the end of the road.

FOREST SERVICE CABINS

The **Sitka Ranger District,** 201 Katlian St., Suite 109, Sitka, AK 99835 (☎ **907/ 747-4420;** www.fs.fed.us/r10/tongass/), maintains more than 20 wilderness cabins on Baranof, Chichagof, and Kruzof islands, in coves and on remote fishing lakes, where rowing skiffs generally are provided. The cabins and their facilities are described in a booklet titled *Public Recreation Cabins: Chatham Area Tongass National Forest,* which you can get from the Sitka Ranger District. Renting a cabin is $35 to $45 a night, but your major cost is getting to the cabin—for each, it takes either a floatplane, boat, or helicopter. **Taquan Air Service,** 485 Katlian St. (☎ **800/770-8800** or 907/ 747-8636; www.AlaskaOne.com/TaquanAir), can fly you out. They also offer a variety of flightseeing excursions from Sitka. Check "Outside in Southeast," at the beginning of this chapter, for information on reserving a cabin.

ACCOMMODATIONS

✪ **Alaska Ocean View Bed and Breakfast.** 1101 Edgecumbe Dr., Sitka, AK 99835. ☎ and fax **907/747-8310.** Fax 907/747-3440. 3 units. TV TEL. High season, $99–$139 double; additional person in room $15–$20 extra. Low season, $69–$89 double; additional person in room $10 extra. AE, MC, V.

Ebullient Carol Denkinger and her husband, Bill, have a passion for making their bed-and-breakfast one you'll remember. They've thought of everything—the covered out-door spa where you can watch the eagles, toys and games for the kids, thick robes and slippers, an open snack counter and big full breakfast, even wildflower seeds to take home. All rooms have coffee pots, refrigerators, microwaves, VCRs, CD players, clocks, phones, and modem jacks. They're located on a residential street with a view of the water about a mile from the historic district. The whole place is reserved for nonsmokers.

Crescent Harbor Hideaway. 709 Lincoln St., Sitka, AK 99835. ☎ and fax **907/747-4900.** www.ptialaska.net/~bareis. 2 units. TV. High season, $95–$125 double. Low season, $75–$95 double. Additional person in room $20 extra. No credit cards.

This stately 1897 house, one of Sitka's oldest, stands across a quiet street from Cres-cent Harbor and the lovely park at the harbor's edge, with a glassed-in porch to watch the world go by. One room is a large, one-bedroom apartment with a full kitchen and a private patio and phone line. The other nestles adorably under the eaves. Both have VCRs, clocks, radios, and hair dryers. Everything is clean and fresh. The operators, an artist and local radio host and a skipper of ecotours, love to tell stories of their life homesteading in Alaska's Bush. Breakfast is continental. The common areas are shared with an Australian shepherd, and no smoking is permitted, even outside.

Harborview Inn. 713 Katlian St., Sitka, AK 99835. ☎ **800/354-6017** or 907/747-8611. Fax 907/747-5810. 34 units. TV TEL. High season, $90 double, $185 suite. Low season, $60 double, $135 suite. AE, MC, V.

A clean, recently remodeled building of reasonably priced standard motel rooms located in a business district a mile from the historic area. There's a coin-op laundry and a fish-cleaning and -freezing facility in the hotel, and free coffee in the lobby. Seven kitchenette suites are available, and some of these have a good water view. The service is efficient and kid-friendly. A courtesy van will take you to the ferry dock, airport, or even downtown.

Helga's Bed and Breakfast. 2827 Halibut Point Rd. (P.O. Box 1885), Sitka, AK 99835. ☎ **907/747-5497.** 4 units. TV TEL. $75 double. Additional person in room $20 extra. AE, MC, V.

Helga Garrison offers three large, light rooms and a two-bedroom apartment overlooking Sitka Sound in a house several miles out Halibut Point Road. You'll need a car to stay here, but you have the advantage of close proximity to the Channel Club, an excellent restaurant. The rooms are a great bargain—modern and very clean, with all the comforts of home, including coffeemakers, microwave ovens, refrigerators, clocks, radios, TVs, and phones. Three rooms have large shower stalls, while the suite has a shower-tub combination.

Sitka Hotel. 118 Lincoln St., Sitka, AK 99835. ☎ **907/747-3288.** Fax 907/747-8499. 60 units, 45 with private bathroom. TV TEL. $55 double without bathroom, $70 double with bathroom. Additional person in room $7 extra. AE, MC, V.

If you choose carefully among these rooms, which vary greatly in size and quality, you could come up with a real bargain. Some, however, are not up to standards, none are reserved for nonsmokers, and I wouldn't recommend the 15 rooms with shared bathrooms. Common areas in the 1939 building are nicely done in heavy Victorian decor. The location is central, right among the sights, and many rooms have good views. A coin-op laundry is available.

Super 8 Sitka. 404 Sawmill Creek Blvd., Sitka, AK 99835. ☎ **800/800-8000** for reservations; ☎ and fax 907/747-8804. 35 units. TV TEL. High season, $108 double. Low season, $86 double. Additional adult in room $6 extra, 11 and under free. AE, CB, DC, DISC, JCB, MC, V.

The Super 8 is small, quiet, and centrally located to walk to the sights. A coin-op laundry and a large whirlpool are in the building. The rooms, in light standard hotel decor, are quite clean and have modem jacks, clocks, radios, and air-conditioning— perhaps you'll be in Sitka on one of the few days each year when it's needed. Free coffee, a toast bar, and a microwave oven are in the lobby.

Westmark Shee Atika. 330 Seward St., Sitka, AK 99835-7523. ☎ **800/544-0970** for reservations, or 907/747-6241. Fax 907/747-5486. www.westmarkhotels.com. 99 units. TV TEL. High season $129–$139 double, $175–$225 suite. Low season $119–$129 double, $152–$175 suite. Additional person in room $15 extra. AE, DC, DISC, MC, V.

This brown, four-story wood structure overlooking Crescent Harbor in the heart of the historic district is the community's main upscale hotel, where events and meetings take place. The restaurant, lounge, and most rooms have good waterfront views; rooms facing the harbor are $10 more. Rooms are clean and equipped with such extras

Additional Accommodations in Sitka

Besides those hotels listed under "Accommodations," I can recommend the **Cascade Inn,** 2035 Halibut Point Rd., Sitka, AK 99835 (☎ **800/532-0908** outside Alaska, or 907/747-6804; fax 907/747-6572), which has many amenities and waterfront balconies, but is 2.1 miles out of the downtown area. There's also the **Rockwell Lighthouse,** P.O. Box 277, Sitka, AK 99835 (☎ **907/747-3056**), which is a mock lighthouse on an island built to rent to guests.

To Find More B&Bs in Sitka

The Sitka Convention and Visitors Bureau (☎ 907/747-5940) produces a chart listing the town's B&Bs, with rates and facilities.

---

as coffeemakers and hair dryers; the furniture tends to be worn and out-of-date. In the summer you can book tours and activities in the lobby.

The restaurant is reliably good, its menu reasonably priced for all three meals a day, including everything you'd expect from an upscale hotel restaurant, plus a large variety of seafood entrees in the evening.

HOSTELLING & CAMPING

Hostelling International—Sitka is located at 303 Kimsham St. (P.O. Box 2645), Sitka, AK 99835 (☎ 907/747-8661), more than a mile from downtown. The 20 beds are $7 per night, no linens available. It's open June through August; office hours are 8 to 10am and 6 to 10pm.

The Forest Service's **Starrigavan Campground,** at the north end of Halibut Point Road, 7½ miles from town and ½ mile from the ferry dock, is one of the loveliest in Alaska. One loop of sites branches from the Estuary Life Trail, widely separated under huge trees. The other loop is at the water's edge, with some sites situated next to the ocean to make you feel like you're way out in the wilderness. The 28 sites, with pit toilets, are first-come, first-served, with an $8 fee, open May 1 through Labor Day.

RV parks are located near the ferry dock and on Japonski Island, close to downtown.

DINING

Bayview Restaurant. 407 Lincoln St. ☎ **907/747-5440.** All meals $5.50–$27. AE, DISC, MC, V. Spring–fall, Mon–Sat 5am–9pm, Sun 5am–8pm; winter, Mon–Sat 7am–8pm, Sun 8am–8pm. STEAKS/SANDWICHES/SEAFOOD.

Although sometimes noisy and a bit cramped, the view of the boat harbor, reasonable prices, and good food make this second-story restaurant popular year-round. The Russian dishes are for the tourists, but everything I've tried from the extensive menu has been well prepared and served. The clam chowder sings, and they've got a beer and wine license.

✪ **Channel Club.** 2906 Halibut Point Rd. ☎ **907/747-9916.** Dinner $12–$37. AE, DC, MC, V. Sun–Thurs 5–10pm, Fri–Sat 5–11pm. STEAK/SEAFOOD.

The dining room looked like a typical small-town bar and restaurant. A young guy in a baseball cap was grilling steaks against one wall, the menu was posted over the salad bar, and the service was casual to a fault. Imagine my surprise, then, to receive the best steak I've had in years and the most fascinating and delicious salads served anywhere in Alaska. In hindsight, I enjoyed having the Channel Club be a diamond in the rough. It's located several miles out Halibut Point Road, but a courtesy van will come get you and take you home at the end of the evening. They've got a full liquor license.

Mad Greek Bistro. 104 Lake St. ☎ **907/747-6818.** All items $6–$10, pizza to $19. MC, V. High season daily 11am–9pm. Low season daily 11am–10pm. GREEK/PIZZA.

The restaurant, situated in the historic area across from the Westmark Shee Atika, doesn't appear promising from outside, but once inside the small dining room you'll find large portions of delicious and authentic Greek entrees, served with home-baked bread and salad for prices that are an unreal bargain. You can get a standard pepperoni

You've Got a Friend in Sitka

Besides the restaurants recommended above & below, you'll find good, hearty Mexican food at **El Amigo,** 327 Seward St. (☎ **907/747-7968**). They're open daily for lunch and dinner, with prices that top out at $13.50 for the most expensive dinner entree.

pizza if you must, but the menu leads you to toppings like goat cheese, artichoke hearts, roasted red peppers, and garlic. The bar was smoky, but the very casual dining room was not.

Van Winkle and Daigler. 228 Harbor Dr. ☎ **907/747-3396.** Reservations required in summer, recommended off-season. Lunch $5–$9; dinner $16–$20. AE, MC, V. High season, Mon–Sat 11:30am–2:45pm, 5–9:45pm; Sun 5–9:45pm. Low season, Mon 11:30am–2pm, Tues–Sat 11:30am–2pm, 5–8:45pm, Sun 5–9pm. STEAK/SEAFOOD.

VanWinkle and Daigler are cousins—one tends the bar, the other the kitchen, and their place is a nice balance of the casual and fine; the dining room has shelves of old cookbooks but also tablecloths. The cuisine concentrates on Sitka-caught seafood, prepared with a well-informed simplicity: With fresh fish this good, it's important to know how to let the natural flavor shine through. A few creative dishes let the chef show off. Portions are huge and service quick, and the wine list and entrees are well priced. There's a full liquor license.

SHOPPING

There are some good shops and galleries in Sitka, mostly on Lincoln and Harbor streets. Several are across the street from St. Michael's Cathedral, on the uphill side, including **Sitka's Artist Cove Gallery** at 241 Lincoln St. (closed Jan to Mar), and **Impressions,** right next door at 239 Lincoln St.—contemporary Alaskan prints and originals. Just down the street is **Fairweather Prints,** at 209 Lincoln St., a T-shirt shop with a difference: original wearable art made in Sitka. A couple of doors down is a quaint bookstore, **Old Harbor Books,** at 201 Lincoln St., a good browsing store with an excellent selection of Alaska books. **The Backdoor** espresso shop, at 104 Barracks St., in the back of the bookstore, has a relaxing art scene atmosphere for reading the newspaper or playing chess. We enjoyed an inexpensive breakfast there. The **Sitka Rose Gallery** occupies a lovely Victorian house at 419 Lincoln St., featuring sculpture, painting, and jewelry. The **Sheldon Jackson Museum Gift Shop,** 104 College Dr., has authentic Native arts and crafts from all over the state. The output of Sitka's own **Theobroma Chocolate Company** is sold all over town.

9 Juneau: Forest Capital

Juneau (*June*-oh) hustles and bustles like no other city in Alaska. The steep downtown streets echo with the mad shopping sprees of cruise-ship passengers in the summer tourist season and the whispered intrigues of the politicians during the winter legislative session. Miners, loggers, and ecotourism operators come to lobby for their share of Southeast's forest. Lunch hour arrives, and well-to-do state and federal bureaucrats burst from the office buildings to try the latest trendy restaurant or brown bag on one of the waterfront wharves, the sparkling water before them and gift store malls behind. The center of town becomes an ad hoc pedestrian mall as the crush of people forces cars to creep.

My Juneau is close at hand, but very different. At a magical age as a child, I lived here with my family in a house on the side of the mountains above downtown. My

Juneau is up the 99 steps that lead from the cemetery to the bottom of Pine Street—the way I walked home from school—and then to the top of residential Evergreen Avenue, where the pavement gives way to a forest trail among fiddlehead ferns and massive rain-forest spruces. That trail leads to the flume—a wooden aqueduct that used to bring water down from the mountains—upon which we would walk into the land of bears and salmon, the rumbling water at our feet. It's still a short walk from the rackety downtown streets to a misty forest quiet, where one can listen for the voices of trees.

Juneau is Alaska's third-largest city, with a population of 30,000 (Anchorage and Fairbanks are larger), but it feels like a small town that's just been stuffed with people. Splattered on the sides of Mount Juneau and Mount Roberts along Gastineau Channel, where there really isn't room for much of a town, its setting is picturesque but impractical. Further development up the mountains is hemmed in by avalanche danger; beyond is the 1,500-square-mile **Juneau Icefield,** an impenetrable barrier. Gold-mine tailings dumped into the Gastineau created the flat land near the water where much of the downtown area now stands. The Native village that originally stood on the waterfront is today a little pocket of mobile homes several blocks from the shore. There's no road to the outside world, and the terrain forbids building one. Jets are the main way in and out, threading down through the mountains to the airport.

Gold was responsible for the location; it was found here in 1880 by Joe Juneau and Richard Harris, assisted by the Tlingit chief Kowee, who told them where to look. All three men are buried in the Evergreen Cemetery. Their find started Alaska's first modern development—the territory's first significant roads and bridges and its first electrical plant were built here, well before the Klondike Gold Rush. Hard-rock mining, which continued into the 1940s, in a few years removed more value in gold than the United States paid for all of Alaska, as a photograph in the State Museum attests. There's plenty of gold left, but getting it out is too expensive under modern environmental controls—a company tried and failed recently to get the mines started again. There are several interesting gold mining sites to see around town. The **Treadwell Mine** on Douglas Island gives the ghostly sense of a thriving city abandoned and overgrown by the rain forest.

In 1900, Congress moved the territorial capital here from Sitka, which had fallen behind in the rush of development. Alaskans have been fighting over whether or not to keep it here for many decades since, but Juneau's economy is heavily dependent on government jobs, and it has successfully fought off a number of challenges to its capital status, most recently in 1994. The closest the issue came was in the 1970s, when the voters approved moving the capital, but then balked at the cost of building a whole new city to house it—a necessity since neither Anchorage nor Fairbanks (which have their own rivalry) would support the move if it meant the other city got to have the capital nearby.

There's plenty to see in Juneau, and it's a good town to visit because the relatively sophisticated population of government workers supports good restaurants and amenities not found elsewhere in Southeast. Besides two good museums, Alaska's most accessible glacier (the Mendenhall) is in Juneau, and businesses ranging from the fish hatchery to the brewery have set up tours for visitors. Also, Juneau is a starting point for outdoor travel in the area, and all over the northern Panhandle. Because the city is a travel hub, you'll likely pass through on your way to Glacier Bay or virtually anywhere else you want to go in the region. But you don't have to go that far to get into the outdoors from Juneau: You can start from the capitol building for a hike to the top of the Mount Juneau or Mount Roberts, or up the Perseverance Trail that leads in

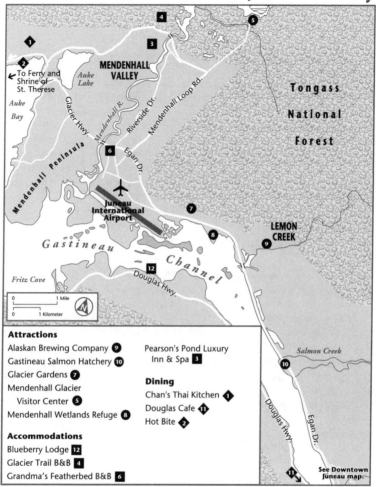

Attractions
Alaskan Brewing Company **9**
Gastineau Salmon Hatchery **10**
Glacier Gardens **7**
Mendenhall Glacier
  Visitor Center **5**
Mendenhall Wetlands Refuge **8**

Accommodations
Blueberry Lodge **12**
Glacier Trail B&B **4**
Grandma's Featherbed B&B **6**

Pearson's Pond Luxury
  Inn & Spa **3**

Dining
Chan's Thai Kitchen **1**
Douglas Cafe **11**
Hot Bite **2**

between. **Sea kayaking and whale watching excursions** are near at hand, as well as some of Alaska's most scenic tide pooling and beach walking.

Downtown, the crush of visitors can be overwhelming when many cruise ships are in port at once, and the streets around the docks have been entirely taken over by shops and other touristy businesses. Many of these are owned by people from outside who come to the state for the summer to sell gifts made outside to visitors. But only a few blocks away are quiet mountainside neighborhoods of houses with mossy roofs, and only a few blocks farther are the woods and the mountains.

ESSENTIALS
GETTING THERE

BY AIR Jet service is available only by **Alaska Airlines** (☎ **800/426-0333**; www.alaskaair.com), with several daily nonstop flights from Seattle and Anchorage and to the smaller Southeast Alaska towns. Most of the commuter and air-taxi operators in Southeast also maintain a desk at the airport and have flights out of Juneau,

Flying to Juneau

Don't schedule anything tightly around a flight to Juneau: The mist-shrouded airport, wedged between ocean and mountain, is tough to get into and can be a hair-raising place to land. It even has its own verb: *to overhead.* That means that when you fly to Juneau, you could end up somewhere else instead. The airline will put you on the next flight back to Juneau when the weather clears, but they won't pay for hotel rooms or give you a refund. Your only protection is travel insurance and a loose itinerary. This situation is such an ingrained part of Juneau's way of life that a channel on the cable TV system (the Channel Channel, 23 on the dial) broadcasts the view from the airport 24 hours a day, showing the weather over the Gastineau Channel; residents tune in to find out if they'll get out that day.

including **L.A.B. Flying Service** (☎ 907/789-9160) and **Wings of Alaska** (☎ 907/789-0790).

BY FERRY   All main-line **Alaska Marine Highway** ferries (see "Getting Around" at the beginning of this chapter) stop at the terminal in Auke Bay (☎ **907/465-3940**), 14 miles from downtown. The *Malaspina* runs daily up the Lynn Canal to Haines and Skagway and back in the summer, leaving Juneau at 7am, arriving Haines at 11:30am, arriving Skagway at 1:30pm, then going back to Haines and returning to Juneau at 10pm. The passenger fare is $24 to Haines, $32 to Skagway.

GETTING INTO TOWN FROM THE AIRPORT & FERRY TERMINAL   Capital Cab (☎ 907/586-2772 or 907/364-3349) offers taxi service (as well as tours by the hour). A cab in from the airport will cost you nearly $20, but the **Island Waterways van** (☎ **907/463-5321** or 907/321-1106) meets all the planes and picks up at the major hotels on a schedule; it costs $6 one-way, or $5 per person for parties of three or more. An express **Capital Transit** city bus (☎ **907/789-6901**) comes to the airport at 11 minutes past the hour on weekdays from 8:11am to 5:11pm and costs $1.25; however, your luggage has to fit under your seat or at your feet.

A cab to the ferry dock costs even more than to the airport, but **Mendenhall Glacier Transport (MGT)** (☎ **907/789-5460**) meets the boats with a blue school bus, and the price of $5 to town includes the driver's commentary. They'll also take you from the ferry to the airport, but won't take passengers from the airport downtown. Call between 6 and 8pm the night before your ferry leaves to arrange a pickup.

GETTING AROUND

Juneau has three main parts: downtown, the Mendenhall Valley, and Douglas. Downtown Juneau is a numbered grid of streets overlying the uneven topography like a patterned quilt over a pile of pillows. As you look at Juneau from the water, Mount Juneau is on the left and Mount Roberts on the right; Mount Roberts is a few hundred feet taller, at 3,819 feet. **Franklin Street** extends south of town 5½ miles to good hiking trails and the hamlet of Thane. When the city outgrew its original site downtown, housing spread to the suburban **Mendenhall Valley,** about a dozen miles out the Egan Expressway or the parallel, two-lane Glacier Highway to the north. The glacial valley also contains the Juneau International Airport, University of Alaska Southeast, and the **Auke Bay** area, where the ferry terminal is located. The road continues 40 miles, to a place generally called **"The End of the Road."** Across a bridge over the Gastineau Channel from downtown Juneau is Douglas Island. Turn left for the town of **Douglas,** mostly a bedroom community for Juneau, and turn right for the North Douglas Highway, which leads to some beautiful rocky beaches.

BY RENTAL CAR   You can get around downtown Juneau easily without a car, but if you're going to the Mendenhall Glacier or to any of the attractions out the road or on Douglas Island, renting a car for 1 or 2 days of your stay is a good idea. Major car-rental companies are based at the airport.

BY BIKE   Bikes make good sense in Juneau, where separated paths parallel many of the main roads and downtown traffic is slow. The 24-mile round-trip to Mendenhall Glacier keeps you on a bike path almost all the way. There are several bike shops. **Mountain Gears,** at 126 Front St. (☎ 907/586-4327), rents 21-speed mountain bikes for $6 an hour or $25 a day, full suspension for $35. A full-service bike shop, they can give you ideas for mountain biking rides and provide maps and directions with rentals. If you're staying in the valley, try **Adventure Sports,** in the Nugget Mall at 8757 Glacier Hwy. (☎ **907/789-5696**).

BY TOUR   Mendenhall Glacier Transport (☎ **907/789-5460**) does a 2-hour town and Mendenhall Glacier tour for $17.50. Also, a 90-minute mining-history tour, with gold panning, operates in the summer through **Alaska Travel Adventures** (☎ **800/ 323-5757** or 907/789-0052; www.alaskaadventures.com); the cost is $35 for adults and $23 for children 12 and under. Walking tours are covered below, under "Exploring Juneau."

VISITOR INFORMATION

The **Davis Log Cabin Visitor Center,** 134 Third Ave., Juneau, AK 99801 (☎ **888/ 581-2201** or 907/586-2201; fax 907/586-6304; www.traveljuneau.com), located at Seward Street, near the capitol building in the center of downtown, is a replica of Juneau's first school, a log cabin with a little log belfry. Operated by the Juneau Convention and Visitors Bureau, the center distributes the usual commercial visitor information but also hands out a readable Juneau map, a brochure called *Free Things to See and Do in Juneau,* and an informative Historic Downtown Juneau Guide, which you can use to create a walking tour of any length. Their *Juneau Travel Planner* contains handy comparative charts of hotels and B&Bs, charter boats, tours, and other services. The center is open Monday to Friday 8:30am to 5pm, Saturday and Sunday 9am to 5pm in summer; Monday to Friday 9am to 5pm in winter.

Volunteers also staff a **visitor information desk** at the airport, near the door in the baggage-claim area, during the summer. The Web URL listed above was not yet in operation at this writing, but you can reach them through Juneau Web at www. juneau.com.

Though it's just a modest alcove in the convention center lobby, the **U.S. Forest Service Visitor Information Center,** in the Centennial Hall, 101 Egan Dr. (mailing address Juneau Ranger District, 8465 Old Dairy Rd., Juneau, AK 99801; ☎ **907/ 586-8751;** fax 907/586-7928; www.fs.fed.us/r10/tongass/), is the main visitor center for the 17-million-acre Tongass National Forest. The rangers behind the desk are a critical link to the outdoors of the region, answering questions about trips and hikes; selling a fine collection of trail guides, field guides, and maps; distributing permits for Pack Creek bear viewing; and providing the lowdown on public recreation cabins around Juneau. They're open Monday to Friday 8am to 5pm.

Last Chance Tours, P.O. Box 22884, Juneau, AK 99802 (☎ **907/586-1890;** fax 907/586-9767; www.alaska.net/~suparna/last.htm), is a central booking agency for all kinds of local activities, especially boating charters.

Juneau Web (www.juneau.com) is a Web site with links to just about everything in town, including many travel-oriented sites.

SPECIAL EVENTS

The Alaska Folk Festival is an annual community-wide celebration drawing musicians (whether on the bill or not) from all over the state, April 10 to 16, 2000. **The Juneau Jazz and Classics Festival** (☎ 907/463-3378), May 19 to 28, 2000, includes concerts at various venues. **Gold Rush Days** (☎ 907/586-2497) at Riverside Park includes logging and mining events and competitions anyone can join, June 24 and 25, 2000. **The Golden North Salmon Derby** (☎ 907/789-2399; www.salmonderby.org) held annually since 1947, targets kings and silvers over a weekend in late August. Unlike some other such derbies around the state, this isn't just a tourist thing—it empties the town. They're hoping the 2000 derby will put them over the $1 million mark in scholarship funds raised for Juneau high school seniors over a half century.

Fast Facts: Juneau

Banks   There are numerous banks in Juneau, and ATMs are available in most grocery stores.

Business Services   Capital Copy, with fax and copying services, is located at 123 S. Seward St. (☎ 907/586-9696).

Hospital   Bartlett Regional Hospital, 3260 Hospital Dr. (☎ 907/586-2611), is 3 miles out the Glacier Highway.

Internet/E-mail   The organic Cafe Myriad, 230 Seward St. (☎ 907/586-3433), charges $12 an hour to use a computer, with a $10 minimum food purchase.

Police   The police department is at 210 Admiral Way. For nonemergency business, call ☎ 907/586-2780.

Post Office   The main post office downtown is in the federal building, 709 W. Ninth St., and in Mendenhall Valley at 9491 Vintage Blvd., by the airport.

Taxes   Sales tax is 5%. Juneau's room tax is 12%.

DOWNTOWN ATTRACTIONS & ACTIVITIES

✪ **Alaska State Museum.** 395 Whittier St. ☎ 907/465-2901. www.educ.state.ak.us/lam/museum/asmhome.html. Admission $4 adults, free age 18 and under. Winter discount $3. High season, Mon–Fri 9am–6pm, Sat–Sun 10am–6pm; winter, Tues–Sat 10am–4pm.

The museum contains a huge collection of Alaskan art and Alaska Native and historical artifacts, but it doesn't seem like a storehouse at all because the objects' presentation is based on their meaning, not their value. Come here to put the rest of your visit in context. A clan house in the Alaska Native Gallery contains authentic art you'd really find in its functional place. The Lincoln Pole is here, carved by an artist who used a picture of the president as his model to represent his clan's first encounter with whites. Native cultures from around the state contributed superb artifacts, presented to explain the lifestyle of those who made them. The ramp to the second floor wraps around the natural history display, with an eagle in a tree, and at the top a state history gallery uses significant pieces to tell Alaska's story. The children's area is among the best we've seen, with a ship they can play in—I just about needed a crowbar to get my son out. The gift store carries authentic Native arts and crafts, plus books, maps, and so on.

Travel Tip

Even if you don't choose to ride the **Mount Roberts Tramway** to the top, the visitor center at the base is worth a stop. Native artisans often are at work there—we visited with a master totem pole carver who was completing a major work.

The Juneau-Douglas City Museum. At the corner of Fourth and Main sts. ☎ **907/ 586-3572.** Admission $2 adults, free for students and children 18 and under. High season, Mon–Fri 9am–5pm, Sat–Sun 10am–5pm. Low season, Fri–Sat noon–4pm and by appointment.

This fun little museum displays artifacts and photographs from the city's pioneer and mining history in a meaningful way. The children's gallery lets kids learn about what it was like to grow up in Juneau in the old days by play-acting with real old things, like an old-fashioned desk, old clothes, and equipment. There's a gorgeous stained-glass window. The tiny book shop is stocked with handy information for your visit, including the historic hike guide booklet, historic walking-tour map, and maps of the Evergreen Cemetery and the old Treadwell Mine. The plaza in front is where the 49-star U.S. flag was first raised in 1959—they didn't make many of those, as Hawaii was admitted as the 50th within a year.

Mount Roberts Tramway. 490 South Franklin St., at the waterfront near the cruise-ship dock. ☎ **888/461-8726** or 907/463-3412. All-day pass $19.75 for adults, $10.50 for children 12 and under, tax included. Daily 9am–9pm. Closed Oct–Apr.

It takes only 6 minutes to carry 60 passengers at a time up a 1,760-foot slope with sweeping views that used to require a day of huffing and puffing to witness. Once there, you can explore the alpine environment above the tree line on a series of nature trails, or start a 6-mile round-trip to Mount Roberts's summit, at 3,819 feet. Or hike down—its 2.5 miles back downtown. The auditorium at the top of the tram has a film on Tlingit culture and a multimedia performance on wildlife put on by the Alaska Native owners of the attraction. A restaurant serves lunch and dinner, either as a package with the tram ride or à la carte. The restaurant hasn't gotten great reviews from the locals, but these things often change year to year.

The Last Chance Mining Museum. 1001 Basin Rd. (From downtown, take Gold St. to the top, then turn left, continuing up the valley to the end of Basin Rd.) ☎ **907/586-5338.** Admission $3. Daily 9:30am–12:30pm and 3:30–6:30pm. Closed Oct to mid-May.

The museum is in old mining buildings on forested Gold Creek, amid intact old mine shafts that penetrated many miles through the mountains—annually, the local historic society leads expeditions through them. The museum preserves the equipment and story of hard-rock gold mining in Juneau, once among the world's biggest centers of the industry. They have intricate, many layered glass maps of mines, a mock tunnel, and one of the world's largest air compressors.

A Juneau Walking Tour

Start: At the cruise-ship dock, or skip the first three paragraphs and start at the Capitol Building.
Finish: Gold Street
Time: 1 to 1½ hours for standard tour; 2½ hours for the extended tour (but times depend on how many places you stop)

1. The **Marine Park waterfront area** is thronged with cruise-ship passengers and tour operators selling their services on most summer days. Juneau's downtown attractions are within walking distance. There's a visitor information kiosk to ask questions and pick up a map.

☕ **TAKE A BREAK**   If you need a break from Juneau's bustle, **the Juneau Public Library,** atop the parking garage at the waterfront on South Franklin Street (☎ **907/586-5249**), has a large kids section, views of the water and Douglas Island, and impressive stained glass and art on Tlingit themes. Hours are Monday to Thursday 11am to 9pm and Friday to Sunday noon to 5pm.

Among the most popular sites in town is right at the dock, the statue of a small dog facing the ships as they come in. This is:

2. **Patsy Ann,** a bull terrier that in the 1930s always seemed to know when a steamer was arriving and faithfully stationed herself on the dock to meet the disembarking passengers.

Walk several blocks uphill on Franklin Street, to see some of the town's most interesting shops and turn 1 block left on Third Street to the:

3. **Log Cabin Visitor Center,** at Third and Seward streets. It's a replica of a log school house, and is described above under "Visitor Information." Stop in for the *Historic Downtown Juneau Guide* to learn more on your walk.

Another block upward brings you to the:

4. **Alaska State Capitol,** standing on Fourth Street between Main and Seward. The federal government built the nondescript brick building in 1931; it may be the least impressive state capitol in the most beautiful setting in the nation. Some of the old fashioned woodwork and decorative details are interesting, and the building is mostly without security that would block your wanderings. During the summer, free tours start every half hour, 9am to 4:30pm, except Saturdays; other times, pick up a self-guided tour brochure in the lobby. Call ☎ **907/465-3800** for information. The legislature is in session January to mid-May.

Across Fourth is the:

5. **Courthouse,** with a statue of a bear in front. This bear defines Alaskan taste in art: It replaced a hated abstract steel sculpture called *Nimbus* that was removed by an act of the legislature, finally coming to rest in front of the state museum.

On the opposite, northwest corner is the:

6. **Juneau Douglas City Museum,** described above. Stop in there now to buy the Evergreen Cemetery map if you plan to include that in your walk.

7. **The State Office Building** stands on the fourth corner, opposite the capitol. It's built into the edge of a cliff that forms a major barrier through the downtown area; if you're headed for the lower land where the state museum and Centennial Hall are located, you can avoid eight flights of steps in between by taking the building's elevator down. In any event, visit the towering atrium, with its great views and a 1928 movie theater pipe organ that's played on Fridays at noon (although the organist didn't show up last time we stopped in). The **state library historical collections** (☎ **907/465-2923**), off the lobby, contain a collection of historic photographs and artifacts, some of which are often on exhibit. They're open Monday to Friday 1 to 5pm. On sunny days, the patio off the atrium is a warm place for a picnic, with a fabulous view.

Returning out the door you entered, turn left and follow Calhoun Street around the curve. An outdoor staircase here leads down to the flat area of town down below (but you know about taking the elevator). Those lowlands originally were mostly underwater and this embankment stood just above the shoreline,

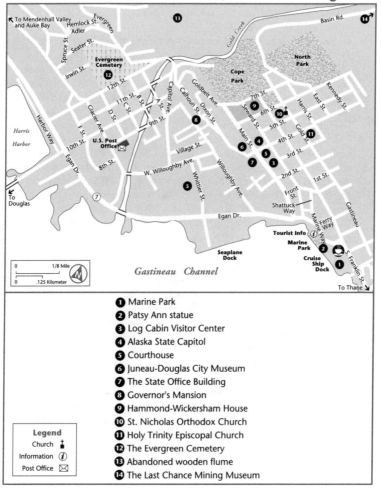

1. Marine Park
2. Patsy Ann statue
3. Log Cabin Visitor Center
4. Alaska State Capitol
5. Courthouse
6. Juneau-Douglas City Museum
7. The State Office Building
8. Governor's Mansion
9. Hammond-Wickersham House
10. St. Nicholas Orthodox Church
11. Holy Trinity Episcopal Church
12. The Evergreen Cemetery
13. Abandoned wooden flume
14. The Last Chance Mining Museum

Legend
Church
Information
Post Office

which continued along Front and South Franklin streets, before mine tailings created the fill that's now much of Juneau. The pedestrian overpass across Calhoun is used by the governor and his dog, a black lab, to get to the Capitol from the white, neoclassical:

8. **Governor's Mansion** that's on the left. It was built by the federal government in 1912. If you see a tall, slender man with dark hair running a dog in the yard, that's Gov. Tony Knowles.

Continuing down Calhoun, you'll come to Gold Creek, where you can turn right to peaceful **Cope Park,** which has tennis courts.

To continue this walk to Evergreen Cemetery and up to the top of the town and through the woods on the flume—a long, strenuous walk—continue straight ahead. That's covered below under "The Extended Walk." Otherwise, backtrack from Gold Creek to Goldbelt Street, which branches from Calhoun on a seemingly impossible upward slope and circles back to the interesting and historic neighborhood behind the capitol.

From Goldbelt, follow Seventh Avenue toward the mountains. On the right, you'll pass the well-marked:

9. Hammond-Wickersham House. A typical large frame house, it was built my a mine superintendent in 1899 and was bought in 1928 by Judge James Wickersham, revered by Alaskans for bringing the law to Interior Alaska in Eagle and Fairbanks, for exploring the Denali area and helping make it a national park, and for winning Alaska's right to make its own laws when he represented the territory in Congress. In the past, the house has been open at times, but no longer. Call the State Museum (see above) with inquiries.

If you were to continue on Seventh you would come to Basin Road, which leads to the left up Gold Creek to the **Last Chance Mining Museum,** described above under "Downtown Attractions & Activities". That's for a longer walk. For the shorter walk, turn right on Gold Street to Fifth and Gold, site of the tiny:

10. St. Nicholas Orthodox Church, a significant architectural landmark. The octagonal chapel was built in 1893 and 1894 by Slavic miners and Tlingits. Many Tlingits chose the Russian Orthodox faith in the 19th century when government-sponsored missionaries sought to convert Alaska Natives to Christianity, for it was the only faith that allowed them to worship in their own language. Father Ivan Veniaminov (see "Exploring Sitka" in section 8 of this chapter) had translated the Bible into Tlingit 50 years earlier when the Russians were still in Sitka. Today, Alaska Natives make up the bulk of the Russian Orthodox church in Alaska, and St. Nicholas still has an active Tlingit parish. Lengthy services are sung in English, Tlingit, and Slavic on Saturday evening at 6pm and on Sunday morning at 10am; the congregation stands throughout the service. Otherwise, A guide is on hand 9am to 6pm, May 15 through September, to answer questions, and excellent written guides are available, too. A $1 donations is requested.

11. Holy Trinity Episcopal Church, 1 block down Gold at Fourth, also is worth a stop for its peaceful turn-of-the-century sanctuary of dark wood under a steeply pitched roof; it's unlocked all day. The church was built in 1896 by Alaska's first Episcopal bishop, when he established their first mission in Juneau. A little-known piece of church history: As an undersized acolyte at age 8, I almost smashed the stained glass in the back of the church when I lost control of the heavy crucifix and had to run down the aisle to keep up with it.

The Extended Walk

This long walk will take most of an afternoon, and includes some steep stairways and streets. Follow the walking tour until you reach Gold Creek, then cross the creek and stay on the same road, bearing right as it becomes Martin Street.

12. The Evergreen Cemetery slopes toward the ocean, opening a wonderful vista over the clear green lawn. One reason it's so broad and open is that the markers are flush with the ground. The old Alaska Native graves are in the wooded portion on the far side. Joe Juneau and Richard Harris, the city's founders, are buried near the cross at this top end of the cemetery.

Across the road from the cross, Rheinhart Street reaches a little way into the mountainside. Follow the steep public stairs on the left up to the bottom of Pine Street. This is the walk I described in the introduction. The views get better and better as you rise to the top of Pine Street then go right on Evergreen Street, following to where it gives out among shadowy spruce and western hemlock. Continue on the peaceful forest trail among the ferns and evergreens up the valley from here, coming to the:

13. Abandoned wooden flume. Once the town's aqueduct, it now is maintained as a boardwalk for walks into the forest. Since it carried water, it's nearly level, but watch your step in wet weather, as it crosses some the high trestles over gullies.

At the end of the flume, cross over the valley to Basin Road. Stop here to see:

14. The Last Chance Mining Museum, described above under "Downtown Attractions & Activities".

To the left is the Perseverance Trail, described below, which continues up between the mountains, and the trailhead for a challenging hike up Mount Juneau. To get back to town, follow Basin Road back down the valley. It will leave you downtown, at the top of Gold Street, where you can complete the walking tour described above.

ATTRACTIONS BEYOND WALKING DISTANCE

Mendenhall Glacier. At the head of Glacier Spur Rd. (right from Egan Dr. on Mendenhall Loop to Glacier Spur). ☎ **907/586-6640** visitor center. Summer daily 8am–6pm; call for winter hours.

At the head of Mendenhall Valley the Mendenhall Glacier glows bluish white, looming above the suburbs like an ice age monster that missed the general extinction. Besides being a truly impressive sight, Mendenhall is the easiest glacier in Alaska to get to and one of the state's most visited attractions. The parking lot has a great view across the lake to the glacier's face, with several short paths and a covered viewing area. A wheelchair-accessible trail leads down to the lake. Atop a bedrock hill, reached by stairs or an elevator chipped out of the rock, the Forest Service visitor center was just remodeled, with exhibits on glaciers, rangers who can answer questions, and a video about the glacier and the Juneau Icefield. In late summer, you can watch red and silver salmon spawning in **Steep Creek,** just short of the visitor center on the road.

There are several trails at the glacier, ranging from a half-mile nature trail loop to two fairly steep, 3½-mile hikes approaching each side of the glacier. At the visitor center and a booth near the parking lot, the Forest Service distributes a brochure, "Mendenhall Glacier: Carver of a Landscape," which includes a trail map. The **East Glacier Loop Trail** is a beautiful day hike leading through the forest to a waterfall near the glacier's face and parts of an abandoned rail tram and an abandoned dam on Nugget Creek; the trail has steep parts but is okay for school-age children. The **West Glacier Trail** is more challenging, leaving from 300 yards beyond the skater's cabin and campground off Montana Creek Road and following the edge of the lake and glacier, providing access to the ice itself for experienced climbers with the right equipment.

Gastineau Salmon Hatchery. 2697 Channel Dr. (3 miles from downtown, turn left at the first group of buildings on Egan Dr.). ☎ **907/463-5114.** www.alaska.net/~dipac. $2.75 for adults, $1 for children 12 and under. Summer Mon–Fri 10am–6pm, Sat–Sun 10am–5pm. Sept 15 to May 15, call ahead.

The hatchery, commonly known as DIPAC (Douglas Island Pink and Chums), was ingeniously designed to allow visitors to watch from outdoor decks the whole process of harvesting eggs and fertilizing them with milt for hatching. From mid-June to October, salmon swim up a 450-foot fish ladder, visible through a window, into a sorting mechanism, then are "unzipped" by workers who remove the eggs. You can often see seals and other wildlife feeding on the returning salmon just offshore from the hatchery at these times. Inside, large saltwater aquariums show off the area's indigenous marine life as it looks in the natural environment. In May and June, before the fish are running, the tour includes the incubation area, where the fish eggs develop

---

Nordic Skiing at Mendenhall Glacier

In the winter, Mendenhall's lake and the surrounding paths in front of the glacier are groomed for Nordic skiing. A loop circles on the lake ice—flat skiing, but with a great view of the glacier. Don't go beyond the orange safety markers near the glacier's face. Other trails weave through the pothole lakes across from the glacier. Start at the Skater's Cabin—follow the loop road past the Glacier Spur Road, turn right on Montana Creek Road, and right again on Skater's Cabin Road. That's also the way to the lakeside and riverside Mendenhall Campground.

---

in racks of trays. The tour takes 45 minutes, including time to look around on your own.

Alaskan Brewery and Bottling Company. 5429 Shaune Dr. ☎ **907/780-5866.** May–Sept, Mon–Sat, 11am–4:30pm. Oct–Apr, Thurs–Sat 11am–4:30pm. Turn right from Egan Dr. on Vanderbilt Hill Rd., which becomes Glacier Hwy., then right on Anka St. and right again on Shaune Dr.

Beer lovers and aspiring capitalists will enjoy the tour of Alaska's most popular craft brewery. Now too big to still be called "micro," the brewery started in 1986 when 40 friends bet $5,000 each on Geoff and Marcy Larson's idea of bringing a local gold rush–era brew back to life. It worked, and now Alaskan Amber is everywhere in Alaska and in much of the Northwest, and the brewery has won more medals at the Great American Beer Festival than any other craft brewery. The short but informative free tour includes tasting of the Amber, Pale Ale, and Alaskan Frontier beers, and starts every half hour.

Glacier Gardens. 7600 Glacier Hwy. (1 mile from the airport, beyond the Fred Meyer store). ☎ **907/790-3377.** www.ptialaska.net/~ggardens. $14 adults, $8 ages 6–12. Summer daily 9am–6pm.

This recently developed botanical garden, built by a family with a greenhouse and landscaping business, shows off both the native rain forest and subalpine flora of Southeast Alaska and also the brilliant colors gardeners can draw from this climate with such plants as rhododendrons and azaleas. Trails weave through the wooded formal garden, then head up the mountainside to a level of 500 feet, with broad views and a different ecological community. Covered golf carts shuttle visitors through.

ATTRACTIONS & ACTIVITIES OUT THE ROAD

On sunny summer weekends, Juneau families get in the car and drive out the road (or the Glacier Highway, as it's officially known). The views of island-stippled water from the paved two-lane highway are worth the trip, but there also are several good places to stop—besides those mentioned here, there are others for you to discover.

The **Auke Village Recreation Area** is a mile beyond the ferry dock (which is 14 miles from downtown Juneau) and is a good place for picnics and beach walks. Less than a mile farther is a Forest Service campground.

The **Shrine of St. Therese** (☎ **907/780-6112),** 9 miles beyond the ferry dock, stands on a tiny island reached by a foot trail causeway. The wonderfully simple chapel of rounded beach stones, circled by markers of the 14 stations of the cross, stands peaceful and mysterious amid trees, rock, water, and the cries of the raven, seeming to be truly of another world. The setting help make it the most truly spiritual of churches. The vaguely Gothic structure was built in the 1930s of stone picked up from these shores and dedicated by Alaska's first Catholic bishop to a 20th-century saint,

Therese of Lisieux. Liturgy services are held June through August at 1pm. The Juneau Catholic Diocese maintains a log retreat hall on the shore facing the island; be quiet when descending the gravel driveway from the highway. The shrine's island is a good vantage from which to look around in the **Lynn Canal** for marine mammals or, at low tide, to go tide pooling among the rocks.

Eagle Beach, 5 miles beyond the shrine, makes a good picnic area in nice weather, when you can walk among the tall beach grass or out on the sandy tidal flats and look for eagles, or go north along the beach to look for fossils in the rock outcroppings. The road turns to gravel, then comes to **Point Bridget State Park,** at mile 38 (measured from Juneau)—the trail there is discussed under "Getting Outside," below. Two miles farther, the road comes to an end, 40 miles from Juneau at pretty **Echo Cove.**

GETTING OUTSIDE: ON LAND

BIRD WATCHING   Bald eagles are commoner than pigeons in Juneau. A few years ago, one of them made off with a tourist's Chihuahua, starting a statewide debate about whether it was funny or horrible. Eagles are most common on the shoreline, especially where fish are plentiful, such as at the hatchery. For more variety, the drive out the four-lane Egan Drive to the Mendenhall Valley crosses tidal flat bird habitat; there's a viewing platform as you near the airport.

The **Juneau Audubon Society,** P.O. Box 021725, Juneau, AK 99802-1725, leads weekly birding walks during the spring migration and most weeks in the summer. Check at the visitor center for up-to-date information on when and where the walks are planned, or visit the group's Web site at **www.juneau.com/audubon.**

HIKING   I've mentioned two good hikes above, under Mendenhall Glacier. A **trail guide** available from the Forest Service visitor center for $4 describes 27 more routes in the Juneau area. *In the Miner's Footsteps,* a guide to the history behind 14 Juneau trails, is available for $3 from the Juneau-Douglas City Museum. The Juneau city **Department of Parks and Recreation** (☎ 907/586-5226) leads hikes in summer and cross-country skiing in winter on Wednesdays for adults and on Saturdays for all ages. **Gastineau Guiding Company** (☎ 907/586-6421; www.ptialaska.net/~hikeak) also leads day hikes.

The **Perseverance Trail** climbs up the valley behind Juneau and into the mining history of the area it accesses. It can be quite crowded in summer. To reach the trailhead, go to the top of Gold Street and follow gravel Basin Road; the trailhead is about a mile from the capitol building. The trail is 3 miles of easy walking on the mountainside above Gold Creek to the Perseverance Mine, at the Silverbow Basin, which operated intermittently from 1885 to 1921. Be sure to pick up the well-documented $1 historic guide to the trail at the Juneau-Douglas City Museum.

Two trails start from points along the Perseverance. The challenging **Mount Juneau Trail** rises more than 3,500 feet in about 2 miles from a point 1 mile from the Perse-

---

Gearing Up for Juneau's Outdoors

You can rent all the equipment you'll need for outings somewhere in Juneau. **Mountain Gears,** listed above under "Getting Around," has mountain bikes and offers guidance on where to ride. **Adventure Sports,** in the Nugget Mall at 8757 Glacier Hwy. (☎ 907/789-5696), rents sea kayaks, mountain bikes, and camping gear, and they'll deliver to you. **Gearing Up,** at the Douglas Boat Harbor (☎ 907/586-2549), rents gear by appointment, including all kinds of camping supplies, rubber boots, and rain gear.

verance trailhead. Go only in dry weather. The **Granite Creek Trail,** starting 2 miles in, climbs 1,200 feet over 1.5 miles to an alpine basin. Either trail will allow escape from the crowds on the Perseverance Trail.

Another hike right from downtown climbs **Mount Roberts**—just follow the stairway from the top of Sixth Street, a neighborhood called Star Hill. The summit is 4½ miles and 3,819 vertical feet away, but you don't have to go all the way to the top for incredible views and alpine terrain. At the 1,760-foot level, you come to the restaurant at the top of the Mount Roberts tram, mentioned above. Of course, its easier to take the tram up and hike down, or start from the tram stop to hike to the summit.

The **Treadwell Mine Historic Trail,** on Douglas Island, is a fascinating hour's stroll through the ruins of a massive hard-rock mine complex that once employed and housed 2,000 men. Since its abandonment in 1922, big trees have grown up through the foundations, intertwining their roots with rails and machinery and adding to the site's exceptional power over the imagination. The well-written guide from the Juneau-Douglas City Museum is indispensable. This is a great hike for kids. To find the trailhead, drive over the bridge to Douglas, turn left, then continue, staying as close to the water as possible, until you reach Sandy Beach Park. Keep going the same way on foot, looking for the tall stamp mill.

Another great family outing is to the **Outer Point Trail,** 1.3 miles on a forest boardwalk to a beach with good tide pooling, lots of eagles, and possible whale sightings. Nowhere else I know are there so many kinds of lovely places in such a short walk: the mossy rain forest, the stunted muskeg swamp, a glassy little creek, and the pebbled beach and bedrock ocean pools. From there, on the western point of Douglas Island—the opposite side from Juneau—you can see Auke Bay and the airport back to the east, Admiralty Island to the west, and the tiny islands of Stephens Passage before you. The only drawback is crowding, especially when tour groups tromp through; avoid them by going early or late. To get there, drive over the bridge to Douglas, then right on North Douglas Highway 11½ miles to the trailhead.

Out the road at mile 38 on the Glacier Highway, **Point Bridget State Park** is less used but easy and beautiful, and from the beach toward the end of the trail you may see sea lions and possibly humpback whales. The flat 3½-mile trail leads through forest, meadow, marsh, and marine ecosystems. It's good for cross-country skiing, too. Pick up the free trail-guide brochure from the Forest Service visitor center in Centennial Hall.

U.S. FOREST SERVICE CABINS   Four U.S. Forest Service cabins are accessible from Juneau's road system by trails ranging from 3.3 to 5.5 miles. The **Peterson Lake** cabin has a skiff for Dolly Varden and cutthroat trout from the lake, and silver and pink salmon and steelhead trout run in the nearby stream. The **John Muir** cabin sits on a 1,500-foot ridge top above Auke Bay, up the Auk Nu Trail. The large **Dan Moller** cabin is located on Douglas Island right across from town. The **Eagle Glacier** cabin overlooks the glacier upriver from Eagle Beach, reached by the Amalga Trail. All the cabins are popular and must be reserved well in advance. Each rents for $35 a night, and generally there's a 2-night maximum stay. Many more cabins in the area require a boat or plane to get to them, which you can charter from one of the operators listed elsewhere in this section. Two are on **Turner Lake** in alpine terrain off Taku Inlet, each with a skiff and spectacular scenery. A bunch of cabins sit on trails and remote lakes and beaches on Admiralty Island, less than a half-hour floatplane ride from Juneau. The sea kayaking and canoe opportunities there are exceptional, and the island is mobbed with brown bears. It's described more below, under "On Admiralty Island." You'll need camping gear to stay at the primitive cabins—all that's definitely provided is a bunk for your sleeping bag and a roof over your head. Get information on cabins from the Forest Service visitor center in Centennial Hall, then reserve through the national system described under "Outside in Southeast," at the beginning of this chapter.

ALPINE SKIING   The city-owned **Eaglecrest Ski Area** (☎ **907/586-5284**) may not be Vail, but it was good enough to train Olympic silver medalist Hillary Lindh, Juneau's favorite daughter. A chair goes right to the top of Douglas Island, with 360° views that defy description. More than 30 trails have a total vertical drop of 1,400 feet. If the winter is snowy, these slopes 12 miles from downtown on North Douglas Highway are the locals' favorite place. An all-day lift ticket is $25 for adults; an adult equipment package rents for $20 a day. The views are incredible.

   Out of Bounds Adventures (☎ **800/HELL-YEA** or 907/789-7008) offers guided heli-skiing in four separate mountain ranges around Juneau, with unlimited choices of powder slopes and never-before-skied runs.

NORDIC SKIING   Juneau's warm, damp winters don't always provide enough snow for good cross-country skiing at the lower elevations, but many of the hiking trails into the mountains become winter backcountry routes, and snow does stick up there. Before going out, always check with the Forest Service for advice on your route and on avalanche conditions. Several of the Forest Service cabins also serve as winter warm-up houses during the day, and make good skiing destinations. If conditions permit, a network of trails is set around the Mendenhall Glacier (see above).

GETTING OUTSIDE: ON THE WATER

DIVING   The **Channel Dive Center,** 8365 Old Dairy Rd., Juneau, AK 99801 (☎ **907/790-4665;** fax 907/790-4668), offers instruction, rentals, and guiding for dry-suit diving. In the fall through spring, you can dive among sea lions. Diving is not as good in the summer, when plankton blooms tend to cloud the water.

RAFTING   The Mendenhall River isn't a wild or scary ride, so the guides on the Native-owned **Auk Ta Shaa Discovery,** 76 Egan Dr. (☎ **800/820-2628**), offer commentary on Native legends and natural history. Although the float starts at the Mendenhall Glacier, this is far from a wilderness area—the river flows through the Mendenhall Valley suburbs. Still, you are likely to see eagles, and the river will look natural, not built up. The 4-hour rides cost $89 for adults, $44.50 children 8 to 16.

SEA KAYAKING   The protected waters around Juneau welcome sea kayaking, and the city is a popular hub for trips on the water farther afield. Many operators offer sea kayaking excursions—five recently had brochures on display around town. Besides the sublime scenery, you'll almost certainly see eagles, sea birds, and seals, and possibly humpback whales.

   The area's most established ecotourism operator is **Alaska Discovery,** 5449 Shaune Dr., Suite 4, Juneau, AK 99801 (☎ **800/586-1911** or 907/780-6226; fax 907/ 780-4220; www.akdiscovery.com), with trips all over Southeast and beyond. Part of the company's ethic and reason for being is to build support for protecting Southeast's wild places. A multiday trip is your chance to really know the Alaska wilderness, and there's no better way to do it here than in a kayak. Alaska Discovery has lots of trips, or they'll design one for your group. A great introductory trip is the Coastal Escape, a 3-day, 2-night camping trip to Berner's Bay, on Lynn Canal north of the end of the road. Besides paddling, groups spend plenty of time exploring the beaches and rainforest shorelines. Fit beginners will do fine, with teens as young as 14 normally invited; trips may include kids as young as 10. The cost is $495 per person. If you haven't spent much time in the outdoors but would like to see real Alaska wilderness, I couldn't recommend a better way to go. No whiners, however: There's a good chance

A Day Trip to Tracy Arm

I receive more positive letters and e-mails from readers about the ✪ **boat tours to Tracy Arm,** south of Juneau, than about anything else. One reason, I suspect, is that the fjords of the Tracy Arm–Fords Terror Wilderness (part of Tongass National Forest), are relatively unknown outside the area, but the scenery and wildlife viewing easily rival Glacier Bay National Park, which is rated as the best national park to visit by the readers of *Consumer Reports.* For those not riding a cruise ship, Tracy Arm has a significant advantage over Glacier Bay: It's much easier and less expensive. Day trips to Tracy Arm from Juneau cost about $110; a day trip to Glacier Bay costs at least three times as much, and is really exhausting—you're much wiser to overnight there, though that just adds to the cost.

The Tracy Arm fjords is a long, narrow, twisting passageway into the coastal mountains, with peaks up to a mile high that jut straight out of the water, waterfalls tumbling thousands of feet down their sides. At its head, Sawyer Glacier and South Sawyer Glacier calve ice into the water with a rumble and a splash. Whales and other wildlife usually show up along the way. And, as at Glacier Bay, John Muir paid a visit. No second-best here!

The largest operator is the Native-owned **Auk Nu Tours,** 76 Egan Dr., Juneau, AK 99801 (☎ **800/820-2628** or 907/586-8687; www.auknutours.com), offering a day-long trip each morning in the summer, leaving at 9am, for $109 per person. A naturalist provides commentary on the high-speed catamaran. Light meals and the use of binoculars are included in the price. Other large boats compete, and you can shop around. The family operated **Adventure Bound Alaska,** at 215 Ferry Way (P.O. Box 23013) Juneau, AK 99802 (☎ **800/ 228-3875** or 907/463-2509), prides itself on slower tours that allow more time to soak up the sights. The total time on the water is 90 minutes more than Auk Nu. The 56-foot single-hull boat has deck space all the way around. Another way to go is on a six-passenger charter boat that you control. Although it may cost twice as much or more per person, you'll decide when to linger with the animals or ice, and whatever else you choose to do. Check with the visitor center for a referral, or **Juneau Sportfishing and Sightseeing** (☎ **907/586-1887**), listed in this section under "Fishing & Whale Watching."

of rain, you'll sleep in a two-man tent, and paddling is work. Alaska Discovery's other trips range up to 12 days and go some truly incredible places—best for those with some sea kayaking experience.

If you don't have that kind of time, Alaska Discovery and the Native-owned **Auk Ta Shaa Discovery** (☎ **800/820-2628** or 907/586-8687) jointly offer a wildlife-watching sea kayak day trip starting from Juneau for $95 per person, $47.50 ages 12 to 16. Other operators offer even shorter tours, often in waters closer to town or with larger groups. If you're very short of time, **Alaska Travel Adventures** (☎ **800/ 323-5757** or 907/789-0052; www.alaskaadventures.com) does a 3½-hour trip, with 90 minutes on the water, for $72 adults, $48 children. Their groups, mostly off the cruise ships, put in at a boat ramp on the North Douglas Highway.

Several businesses rent kayaks, including **Adventure Sports** (see "Getting Around: By Bike," above), and **Alaska Paddle Sports,** 800 6th Ave., Juneau, AK 99801 (☎ **907/789-2382**). A double rents for around $50 a day, a single for about $40, but of course you must first learn how to kayak. Peter Wright, whose business is called **Kayak Express and Auke Bay Landing Craft** (P.O. Box 210562, Auke Bay, AK 99821; ☎ **907/790-4591;** e-mail: peterb@ptialaska.net), specializes in supporting trips for experienced paddlers, setting up base camps and dropping off parties.

FISHING & WHALE WATCHING   The closest I ever saw a humpback whale— within a few yards—was on the way back from king salmon fishing out of Juneau on a friend's boat. More than two dozen charter companies offer fishing from Juneau and Auke Bay; you can go to **watch whales** or fish, or both. Juneau is well protected behind layers of islands, so the water generally is calm. The Juneau Convention and Visitors Bureau maintains a list of businesses with details on their services and prices; there's a lot of competition, so you can choose the kind of tour you want. **Juneau Sportfishing and Sightseeing,** 2 Marine Way, Suite 230 (P.O. Box 20438), Juneau, AK 99802 (☎ **907/586-1887;** fax 907/586-9769; www.ptialaska.net/~suparna), is one of the largest operators, exclusively booking 40 six-passenger boats. They charge $195 per person for a full day of fishing, $115 for 4 hours, or $85 for a 2½-hour whale-watching trip, and they'll pick you up at your hotel.

Juneau isn't known particularly for its stream fishing, but there are a few places on the roads where you can put in a line. The *Northern Southeast Alaska and Yakutat Sport Fishing Guide,* published by the Alaska Department of Fish and Game Division of Sport Fish, 1255 W. 8th Ave (P.O. Box 3-2000) Juneau, AK 99801 (☎ **907/ 465-4180;** www.state.ak.us/local/akpages/FISH.GAME/adfghome.htm), contains all the information you'll need. For a remote fly-in experience, contact **Alaska Fly'N'Fish Charters,** 9604 Kelly Ct., Juneau, AK 99801 (☎ **907/790-2120;** www.alaskabyair.com). A 3-hour trip is $250 per person.

CRUISING   A sailing or motor yacht can put you in the Inside Passage wilderness in perfect comfort, but with the freedom usually reserved only for hardy outdoors people. Imagine motoring up to a glacier or landing on a remote beach on an uninhabited island for a picnic, or catching your own salmon dinner and watching humpback whales from your own deck. Of course, it's also quite expensive to go this way.

Five Juneau operators offer multiday cruising charters on motor yachts, including **Adventures Afloat** (☎ **800/323-5628** or 907/789-0111), **Alaska Yacht Adventures** (☎ **907/789-1978;** www.alaskayacht.com), **Captain Cook Charters** (☎ **907/ 789-3811;** e-mail: captcook@ptialaska.net), and **Seawind Charters** (☎ **907/ 586-6641;** e-mail: seawind@aol.com), all operating a large boat with many comforts. The fifth is a company with a fleet of 32- to 110-foot vessels, **ABC Alaska Yacht Charters,** P.O. Box 33217, Juneau, AK 99801 (☎ **800/780-1239** or 907/780-1239; fax 907/789-1237; www.abcyacht.com). The all-inclusive prices for a cruise with a skipper range from $165 to $650 per person, per day. They also charter bareboat motor yachts, without skippers, starting at $2,150 for a 32-foot vessel. An 18-foot runabout for day trips rents for 3-day stretches at $225 a day.

Southeast's lone bareboat sailing charter operator operates from Juneau, **58° 22′–North Sailing Charters,** P.O. Box 32391, Juneau, AK 99803 (☎ and fax **907/789-7301;** alaskasailing.com), and they're busy enough that you should reserve the previous fall. They have two 36-foot Catalinas, for which they charge $356. Inside Passage wind can be weak and fluky, blowing through the narrow channels between the mountains, but sailing is a peaceful way to explore the wilderness.

GETTING OUTSIDE: ON THE ICE

The more than 36 major glaciers around Juneau flow from a single ocean of ice behind the mountains, the 1,500-square-mile **Juneau Icefield.** You can land on it in a helicopter and touch the ice, or even land for a nature hike or dog sled ride. It's expensive, but there are few other places to see, let alone explore, the kind of ice sheet that carved North America in the last ice age. From the air, glaciers look unreal, like creations by a graphic artist, their sinuous lines of blue and white ice striped with darker gray gravel debris. Only standing on the ice, which on closer inspection resembles the crusty compressed snow of springtime snow berms, do you get a clear sense of this entirely unfamiliar kind of terrain.

Era Helicopters (☎ 800/843-1947 or 907/586-2030; www.eraaviation.com/helicoptertours) is among Alaska's oldest and most respected operators. **Temsco Helicopters** (☎ 877/789-9501 or 907/789-9501; www.temscoair.com) started these tours almost 20 years ago, and offers a broad choice of tours. Both companies have a program of dog sled rides on the ice. This is a neat idea: A lot of visitors to Alaska want to ride a dog sled, but it's a winter sport that really can't be recreated with sleds on wheels, as most dog sled tours try to do. Here, you do it on snow, as it's meant to be done. With either company, expect to pay a minimum of $160 per person for a 50 minute tour, including 20 minutes on a glacier. A longer flight, perhaps with a couple of miles of glacier hiking, is around $250. A dog mushing excursion lasts around an hour with another 30 minutes in the air and costs about $340. Always wait for decent weather for an aerial sightseeing trip.

Another company with its own helicopters specializes in hiking and teaching about glaciers: **NorthStar Trekking,** P.O. Box 32540, Juneau, AK 99803 (☎ 907/790-4530; e-mail: trekking@ptialaska.net). Their small groups (a maximum of 11, with two guides) go on hiking excursions of up to a few miles, with the speed determined by the group. The 4-hour trip, which includes half an hour of flight time, costs $289 per person.

GETTING OUTSIDE: ON ADMIRALTY ISLAND

The 900,000 acres land mass beyond Douglas Island from Juneau, at the entrances to the Gastineau Channel, is Admiralty Island, one of the largest virgin blocks of old-growth forest in the country. The vast majority of the island is the protected **Kootznoowoo Wilderness.** Kootznoowoo, Tlingit for "fortress of bears," is said to have the highest concentration of bears on earth. Despite the town of Angoon on the western side of the island, there are more bears than people on Admiralty. The island's **Pack Creek Bear Viewing Area** is the most famous and surefire place to see bears in Southeast. The area has been managed for bear viewing since the 1930s, when hunting was outlawed. There's a platform for watching the bears up close as they feed on salmon spawning in the creek in July and August (with peak viewing in the middle of that period). They generally pay no attention to the people.

Only 25 miles from Juneau, **Pack Creek** is so popular that permits are allocated in a lottery for a maximum of 24 people to go during the day (from 9pm to 9am, no humans are allowed). There are no facilities in this wilderness area, but a platform allows safe bear viewing. Book early. The easiest way to go is with a tour operator who has permits. The Forest Service visitor center at the Centennial Hall can give you a list of guides. **Alaska Discovery,** listed above under "Sea Kayaking," has many permits for sea kayak trips. Their 1-day excursion flies out, then paddles to the creek; no experience is necessary, but you must be physically capable of hiking and paddling. It costs $450 per person. A 2-night campout and sea kayak near the creek offers more time to see the bears and appreciate the scenery. It costs $895 per person. **Alaska Fly 'N' Fish Charters,** 9604 Kelly Ct., Juneau, AK 99801 (☎ 907/790-2120; www.alaskabyair.com), also has permits for its 5½-hour fly-in visits, which cost $400 per person. Twelve permits per day go to the commercial operators and 12 to other people; 8 of those 12 can be booked in advance with the Forest Service, and the other 4 are held out to be distributed 3 days before they're good, or the previous Friday for Tuesday and Wednesday, at 9am at the Forest Service visitor center at the Centennial Hall. In the peak season, permits cost $50 for adults, $25 for those aged 16 or under or 62 and over. After you have the permit, you'll still need a way to get there, and it won't be cheap, so there's little cost savings over simply booking with a commercial operator that already has its own permits. Other than flying on an air taxi, the only practical route is by charter boat, which would allow you to combine the bear watching with other sightseeing.

Protected **Seymour Canal,** on the east side of the island, is popular for canoeing and kayaking, and has two other sites besides Pack where bears often show up: Swan Cove and Windfall Harbor. Outfitters are listed above. There are 15 Forest Service cabins on Admiralty, and the well-reputed **Thayer Lake Lodge** (P.O. Box 211614, Auke Bay, AK 99821; ☎ **907/789-5646;** fax 907/789-5697) is located on a wilderness inholding near Angoon. For information on the island, cabins, and an excellent $4 map, contact the Forest Service visitor center at the Centennial Hall in Juneau, listed above, or **Admiralty Island National Monument,** 8461 Old Dairy Rd., Juneau, AK 99801 (☎ **907/586-8790**; www.fs.fed.us/r10/chatham/anm/).

ACCOMMODATIONS

Hotel rooms are tight in the summer, so book ahead. Bed-and-breakfasts are really the way to go in Juneau—the best B&Bs I know are here. You'll get a better room and have more fun for less money. The *Juneau Travel Planner,* published by the Juneau Convention and Visitors Bureau (☎ **888/581-2201**) contains a chart showing many of the hotels and B&Bs, with their features and price ranges. **Bed & Breakfast Association Inside Passage,** P.O. Box 22800, Juneau, AK 99802 (☎ **907/789-8822;** www.wetpage.com/bbaaip/), represents more than 20 establishments, and publishes a brochure listing their attributes.

EXPENSIVE

Baranof Hotel. 127 N. Franklin St., Juneau, AK 99801. ☎ **800/544-0970** or 907/586-2660. Fax 907/586-8315. www.westmarkhotels.com. 193 units. TV TEL. High season, $145 double. AE, DC, DISC, MC, V.

In winter, the venerable old Baranof acts like a branch of the state capitol building for conferring legislators and lobbyists; in the summer, it's like a branch of the package-tour companies. The nine-story, 1939 concrete building has the feel of a grand hotel, although some rooms are on the small side. The upper-floor rooms have great views on the water side. Remodeling there has successfully added fresh, modern comforts while retaining the old fashioned opulence of the building. Rooms below the fifth floor hadn't gotten the same treatment, however, and are much less desirable. Phones have voice mail and modem jacks. There are many room configurations, so make sure you get what you want. Kitchenettes and large, multiroom suites are available. It belongs to the Westmark chain.

The art deco **Gold Room** restaurant is Juneau's most traditional fine-dining establishment. The dining room remarkably combines intimacy and grandeur, a real showplace of shining brass, frosted glass, and rich wood. The food varies in quality year to year, sometimes ranking as the best in Juneau, and at other times not living up to the high prices. The hotel cafe is popular and serves good basic meals.

Goldbelt Hotel Juneau. 51 W. Egan Dr., Juneau, AK 99802. ☎ **888/478-6909** or 907/586-6900. Fax 907/463-3567. www.goldbelthotel.com. 105 units. TV TEL. High season, $169 double. Low season, $139 double. Additional person in room $15 extra. AE, DC, DISC, JCB, MC, V.

The Goldbelt Native corporation bought this somewhat heartless upscale hotel near the water and brought its public spaces to life with masterpieces of Tlingit art, including a new totem pole out front and a huge yellow cedar bas-relief by Nathan Jackson in the lobby-restaurant area. The dreary Mediterranean theme restaurant was flooded with light from big windows, further lightened with light wood furniture, and renamed Chinooks, after the area's king salmon. The large bedrooms, with either two full-sized or one king bed, were upgraded with bold colors and new furniture in a wood finish like dark cherry. They're noticeably silent and immaculate. Some have exercise equipment, and all come with standard extras such as data ports, voice mail, and ironing boards and irons. The rooms on the front have good views of the Gastineau Channel. A courtesy van runs to the airport and ferry dock.

The restaurant serves three meals daily. Lunch ranges from $7 to $15, and includes items like sautéed veal as well as the usual sandwiches and salads. Dinner entrees are $13 to $36 on a short but varied menu that draws on continental and American regional cuisine.

Grandma's Feather Bed. 2348 Mendenhall Loop Rd. (mail: 9300 Glacier Hwy.) Juneau, AK 99801. ☎ **888/781-5005** or 907/789-5566. Fax 907/789-2818. TV TEL. 14 units. $160 double. Rates include breakfast. AE, CB, DC, DISC, EURO, MC, V.

Incongruously set on a busy highway near the airport, this is a ground-up re-creation of a luxurious New England country inn. Rooms have all imaginable amenities, including Jacuzzis and old-fashioned undressing screens; it's simply a building full of honeymoon suites, each an open invitation to lovemaking. Choose your room, however, as the luxurious effect is lost in the smaller rooms. There's a small restaurant in the lobby, where breakfast is served for guests and dinners are served to the guests and the public Tuesday through Saturday. There's a 24-hour courtesy car; no children and no smoking allowed.

✪ **Pearson's Pond Luxury Inn and Garden Spa.** 4541 Sawa Circle, Juneau, AK 99801. ☎ **888/658-6328** or 907/789-3772. Fax 907/789-6722. www.juneau.com/pearsons.pond. 3 units. TV TEL. High season, $169–$259 double. Low season, $89–$159 double. Additional person in room $30 extra. AE, CB, DISC, DC, MC, V.

Here's a mental game you can play: Imagine you're a slightly obsessed bed-and-breakfast host and you decide to give your guests every amenity you can possibly think of. Now go to Diane Pearson's house and count how many you missed. A refrigerator and coffee machine? Kid's stuff—Pearson also provides a kitchenette stocked with food, wine, and her own home-baked bread. Did you think of a private duck pond with a dock, a rowboat, and a fountain? How about stocking the pond with fish? How about VCRs, stereos, bicycles, fishing rods, massage, yoga, a Jacuzzi, and a separate hot tub in the garden (and maybe one in your room, too), and a business center, modem ports, e-mail accounts, and free laundry? There's more. To finish the game, you'll have to check in, but book far ahead. It's located in the Mendenhall Valley, 15 minutes from downtown.

MODERATE

Breakwater Inn. 1711 Glacier Ave., Juneau, AK 99801. ☎ **800/544-2250** or 907/586-6303. Fax 907/463-4820. E-mail: breakwtr@ptialaska.net. 48 units. TV TEL. High season, $120 double. Low season, $89 double. Additional person in room $10 extra. AE, DC, DISC, MC, V.

This two-story building near the small-boat harbor, a long walking distance to the central downtown area, has newly remodeled standard motel rooms. The water-side rooms, which cost $10 more, have balconies but also significant highway noise. On

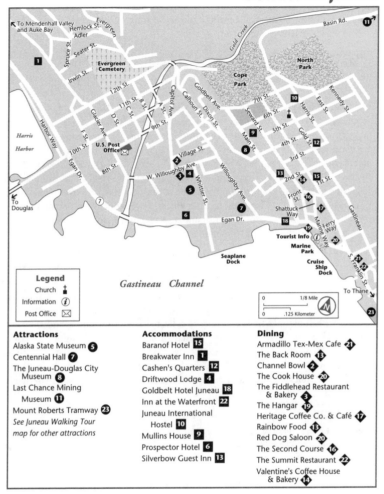

Legend
Church ✝
Information ⓘ
Post Office ✉

Attractions
Alaska State Museum ⑤
Centennial Hall ⑦
The Juneau-Douglas City Museum ⑧
Last Chance Mining Museum ⑪
Mount Roberts Tramway ㉓
See Juneau Walking Tour map for other attractions

Accommodations
Baranof Hotel 15
Breakwater Inn 1
Cashen's Quarters 12
Driftwood Lodge 4
Goldbelt Hotel Juneau 18
Inn at the Waterfront 22
Juneau International Hostel 10
Mullins House 9
Prospector Hotel 6
Silverbow Guest Inn 13

Dining
Armadillo Tex-Mex Cafe ㉑
The Back Room ⑬
Channel Bowl ②
The Cook House ⑳
The Fiddlehead Restaurant & Bakery ③
The Hangar ⑲
Heritage Coffee Co. & Café ⑰
Rainbow Food ⑬
Red Dog Saloon ⑳
The Second Course ⑯
The Summit Restaurant ㉒
Valentine's Coffee House & Bakery ⑭

the mountain side, all 20 rooms have kitchenettes with microwave ovens. Two rooms have two double beds and a set of bunk beds and a dining table. There's a nautical-theme restaurant on the second floor.

✪ **Glacier Trail Bed & Breakfast.** 1081 Arctic Circle, Juneau, AK 99801. ☎ **907/789-5646.** Fax 907/789-5697. www.wetpage.com/glacier. 3 units. TV TEL. High season, $110–$135 double. Low season, $85–$100 double. Additional person in room $20 extra. AE, MC, V.

You wake up to an expansive view of the Mendenhall Glacier filling a picture window in a big, quiet room decorated with infinite taste. Luke and Connie Nelson built the house with this moment in mind. Before beginning construction, they researched B&Bs all over the country, getting ideas for the soundproof rooms, microwaves, coffeemakers, and fridge in each room, and for the Jacuzzi bathtubs, free bicycles, private phone lines, and many other extras. They're fascinating, literate people with varied interests and lifelong Alaska outdoors experience who enjoy the relationships they develop with guests. Luke's family owns a lodge on Admiralty Island, and with them he does Pack Creek tours (see "Getting Outside"). A family apartment downstairs is a perfect choice for large groups, and has two bathrooms.

Prospector Hotel. 375 Whittier St., Juneau, AK 99801-1781. ☎ **800/331-2711** or 907/586-3737. Fax 907/586-1204. www.prospectorhotel.com. 58 units. TV TEL. High season, $100 double; $125–$130 double with kitchenette. Low season, $80–$85 double. AE, DC, DISC, MC, V.

This is a comfortable hotel right on the waterfront, with large, standard rooms in attractive pastel colors. More than two dozen rooms have kitchenettes, and some of the more expensive ones equate to a nice furnished apartment. Those facing the channel have good views, but suffer from highway noise. When I last visited, the carpet and wall coverings had recently been renewed, but the furniture was worn and out of date. The lower level, called the first floor, is a half-basement; it's somewhat dark and lacks an elevator. A parking garage takes care of the chronic shortage of downtown parking.

The restaurant, T. K. Maguire's, features an extensive dinner menu ranging in price from $11 to $22, with lots of fresh fish and a special prime rib. Lunch is sandwiches, salads, and fish in the $7 to $16 range.

Silverbow Guest Inn. 120 Second St., Juneau, AK 99801. ☎ **907/586-4146.** Fax 907/586-4242. www.wetpage.com/silverbow. 6 units. TV TEL. High season $109 double, low season $79 double. Additional person in room $10 extra. Rates include breakfast. AE, MC, V.

The young proprietors have found an original and oddly pleasing style in their little hotel. The lobby mixes the wood floors and stained glass of a real old Victorian building with funky plastic kitsch they've collected from junk shops and the Home Shopping Network. In the rooms, the overlay of new on old is a comfortable Pottery Barn style. These charming rooms are the right size for a couple, but small for more than two. Breakfast from the family bakery (famed for its authentic bagels) is included in the price. Phones are direct and the televisions are small. (See the restaurant description below.)

INEXPENSIVE

Blueberry Lodge. 9436 N. Douglas Hwy., Juneau, AK 99801. ☎ and fax **907/463-5886.** www.wetpage.com/bluberry. 5 units, all with shared bathroom. High season, $75–$85 double. Low season, $75 double. Additional person in room $10 extra. Rates include full breakfast. AE, DISC, MC, V.

Staying here is like visiting a first-class wilderness lodge, except you're only 6 miles from downtown Juneau. Jay and Judy Urquhart built the spectacular log building themselves in the woods of Douglas Island, looking out on an eagle's nest and the Gastineau Channel's Mendenhall Wetlands Refuge—they keep a spotting scope in the living room and will lend you binoculars and rubber boots for an exploration by the water. Rooms are large, contemporary, and very clean, with rich colors that contrast with the huge logs of the walls. It's possible to be alone and to enter without passing through the family's quarters, but the general atmosphere is social, with two teenagers and two dogs resident. Judy serves a big, luxurious breakfast and offers her laundry machines free for guests to use. You'll need to rent a car for the 10-minute drive to town.

Cashen's Quarters. 315 Gold St., Juneau, AK 99801. ☎ **907/586-9863.** Fax 907/586-9861. www.cashenquarters.com. 5 units. TV TEL. $89 double, $156 suite. Additional person in room $10 extra. DISC, MC, V.

I'm trying to think of any reasons not to stay here, and I can't come up with any. The 1914 guest house, right downtown, next door to Dan and Cindy Cashen's home, contains five large, self-contained units with full kitchens, satellite TV, telephones on their

Travel Tip

Generally, **smoking** is not permitted at bed-and-breakfasts; smokers should inquire before they register if smoking is allowed even outside.

own lines with answering machines, and homey decoration that shows a certain artistry on Cindy's part. For breakfast, they stock the refrigerator with everything you need for a heavy or light breakfast to make on your own—the only factor that puts the place in the bed-and-breakfast category, rather than being one of the best hotels in town. The front door opens with a combination lock to the only common room, a laundry with coin-op machines; guest rooms open from there with their own keyed locks.

The Driftwood Lodge. 435 Willoughby Ave., Juneau, AK 99801. ☎ **800/544-2239** or 907/586-2280. Fax 907/586-1034. driftwoodalaska.com. 63 units. TV TEL. High season, $78 double; $95 suite. Low season, $62 double; $87 suite. Additional person in room $7 extra. AE, DC, DISC, MC, V.

This three-story motel right downtown, next door to the State Museum is popular with families, and houses legislators and aides in the winter in its apartment-like kitchenette suites. Although the building can't hide its cinderblock construction and old-fashioned motel exterior, or its lack of elevators, the rooms were remarkably clean on my last visit and had received new carpets and wall coverings. They all have coffee machines and some other extras you would expect only in a more expensive hotel. The management is doing a good job keeping prices low while constantly improving the place. For the price of an ordinary room elsewhere, you can get a huge suite with a full kitchen here. A round-the-clock courtesy car saves guests money getting to the airport, and there's a coin-op laundry and coffee in the lobby.

Inn at the Waterfront. 455 S. Franklin, Juneau, AK 99801. ☎ **907/586-2050.** Fax 907/586-2999. 21 units, 12 with private bathroom. TEL. $86 double, $60–$72 with shared bathroom; $110 suite. Additional person in room $9 extra. Rates include breakfast. AE, CB, DC, DISC, MC, V.

Many people, especially those accustomed to quirky little European hotels, will enjoy and even treasure a stay in this gold rush–era former brothel, with its authentic Victorian woodwork, old-fashioned waterfront facade, and campy feel. Those who seek the standard American hotel room should look elsewhere, however, as the narrow stairs, oddly shaped rooms, worn bathrooms, and oddball collection of antiques and near antiques might be too much for them. The rooms are a bargain, and come with a substantial breakfast in the bar of The Summit, one of Juneau's best restaurants, which is downstairs (and described below).

A HOSTEL

Juneau International Hostel. 614 Harris St., Juneau, AK 99801. ☎ **907/586-9559.** 48 beds. $10 per person. Prepaid reservations required. June–Sept.

This exceptional hostel is conveniently located in a historic yellow house among the downtown sights. The office is open from 7 to 9am and 5 to 11pm in the summer, 8 to 9am and 5 to 10:30pm in the winter. Kitchen and laundry facilities are available. Hostelling International members get a $3 discount.

CAMPING

Juneau has two Forest Service campgrounds, each exceptional in its own way (for information on either campground, call the Juneau Ranger District at ☎ 907/

Other Juneau B&B

There are too many outstanding, inexpensive B&Bs in Juneau to review them all in detail. Aside from those I've listed, I also like **The Mullins House,** at 526 Seward St., Juneau, AK 99801 (☎ **907/586-3384**), a wonderfully traditional homestay B&B in a historic house a block from the Capitol, right downtown.

586-8800). **The Mendenhall Glacier Campground,** overlooking the lake and glacier and next to the Mendenhall River, has 68 sites, 18 of which offer full hookups to RVs. In 1999, new bathrooms with showers and flush toilets were being built. To get there, turn right on Montana Creek Road from Back Loop Road, also known as Mendenhall Loop Road. Tent sites are $8, RV sites $18; no reservations are accepted. **The Auke Village Campground,** 1.7 miles north of the ferry dock, lies along an ocean beach, with pit toilets and running water. Sites are $8 per night.

Auke Bay RV Park, less than 2 miles from the ferry terminal (P.O. Box 210215), Juneau, AK 99821 (☎ **907/789-9467**), has sites with full hookups for $22 a night, and showers and laundry facilities on-site. Reservations are recommended.

DINING
EXPENSIVE
The Hanger. 2 Marine Way. ☎ **907/586-5018.** Reservations recommended. Dinner $13–$27. AE, DISC, MC, V. Sun–Thurs 11am–1am, Fri–Sat 11am–3am. STEAK/SEAFOOD.

Situated in a converted airplane hanger on a wooden pier with large windows, this bar and grill has great views and a jolly atmosphere. It can be smoky, and the food can be pricey for what you get, but the atmosphere and camaraderie they're trying for—a Northwest thing—come off well. It's a great place to drink beer, with live music, pool, and darts on a mezzanine, and 28 brews on tap.

✪ **The Summit Restaurant.** 455 S. Franklin St. ☎ **907/586-2050.** Reservations recommended. Main courses $15–$28. AE, CB, DC, DISC, MC, V. Daily 5–11pm. STEAK/SEAFOOD.

An intimate dining room with only nine tables looks over the cruise-ship dock from big windows, making the wonderfully formal service seem only the more opulent. This air of easy, world-weary elegance can't be faked, and the Summit is the only restaurant in Alaska that really has it. If you're lucky enough to get a reservation during the summer season, you'll find the seafood and vegetables from the constantly changing, sometimes creative menu perfectly prepared. This is the best place in town for a romantic meal. Upstairs is the Inn at the Waterfront, listed above.

MODERATE
The Back Room. 120 Second Ave. ☎ **907/586-4146.** Lunch/dinner $6.50–$22. AE, MC, V. Mon–Thurs 11:30am–2pm, 5–11pm, Fri 11:30am–2pm, 5pm–midnight, Sat–Sun 10am–2pm, 5pm–midnight. SANDWICHES/ECLECTIC

An architect and an urban planner met in graduate school in Seattle, married, and took over the historic Silverbow Inn, with its bakery and restaurant. With them they brought a cosmopolitan sensibility new to Juneau: When we ate there, diners didn't start filtering in until after 8pm, and when we left at 9:30 it was finally full. The dining room, with its rough, redbrick walls, high ceilings, and faux Victorian details, is decorated with campy plastic toys and junk that the rock group Devo would have loved—ray guns and the like. The food, when it finally came, was well conceived but imperfectly executed: The cheese fondue solidified before we could finish it. With time, that should improve, and there's nothing wrong with the prices or broad selection, which includes a Philly cheese steak sandwich with cheese whiz, an Indonesian peanut pasta, and a teriyaki salmon kebab. Exotic beers are on tap.

⚫ **Douglas Cafe.** 916 Third St., Douglas (turn left after crossing the bridge from Juneau, then continue till you see the cafe on the left). ☎ **907/364-3307.** Lunch $6.50–$9. Dinner $8.25–$17. MC, V. Summer Tues–Fri 11am–8:30pm, Sat 9am–8:30pm, Sun 9am–1:30pm. Closed Mon. Winter closed Tues. ECLECTIC.

It's a great pleasure to find a place like this hiding in the guise of an ordinary small-town burger place. The key, I'm convinced, is the two owners working in the kitchen behind the counter, indistinguishable from the other young guys in baseball caps back there. They turn out creative seafood, meat, and vegetarian dinners, drawing on world cuisines and using some combinations rarely ever thought of before. The small dining room is lively, bright, and casual, but a bit cramped, and the wooden benches get hard by the end of a meal. Weekend breakfasts are an event, filling the place with towns-people. Service is quick and casual. Alaskan Amber and other craft brews are on tap.

The Fiddlehead Restaurant and Bakery. 429 W. Willoughby Ave. ☎ **907/586-3150.** Reservations recommended for the Fireweed Room. Main courses $8.25–$22; lunch $8–$13. 15% gratuity added for parties of 6 or more. AE, MC, V. Daily 6:30am–10pm. SEAFOOD/ECLECTIC.

A Juneau institution founded more than 20 years ago, the Fiddlehead is the definition of a ferny restaurant, serving, as they say, "Food close to the earth." In 1991 they published a successful cookbook. The downstairs dining room has butcher-block tables, knotty pine paneling, and stained glass of the delicious curled up ferns that are its namesake. The food is ambitious, and includes some beef and lots of fish as well as the many vegetarian dishes, but it's not always consistent. A portobello mushroom sandwich I ordered combined a nice variety of flavors and textures, but the smoked halibut chowder that went with it was dull and lacked halibut. The upstairs Fireweed Room, open from 5 to 9pm, Thursday through Monday, offers a more formal experience with huge picture windows and live music. Downstairs prices top out under $20. They have a full bar.

INEXPENSIVE

Armadillo Tex-Mex Cafe. 431 S. Franklin St. ☎ **907/586-1880.** Lunch/dinner $6–$16. MC, V. Daily 11am–10pm. TEX-MEX.

You order lunch at a counter and choose drinks from a cooler, but this casual, infectiously cheerful place is where Alaska's best Southwestern food comes from. Locals, who swear by it, know the restaurant merely as "Tex-Mex." Chicken is a specialty, and the homemade salsa is famous, served free with a basket of chips for each diner. The tiny dining room is located near the docks. They serve wine and beer, brewing their own brand periodically.

Chan's Thai Kitchen. 11820 Glacier Hwy. (in Auke Bay, across the boat harbor). ☎ **907/789-9777.** Lunch/dinner $8–$12. MC, V. Tues–Thus 11am–2pm, 5–8pm, Fri 11am–2pm, 5–8:30pm, Sat 4:30–8:30pm. Closed Sun–Mon.

The small, overlit dining room in the half-basement level of a steak house sees few tourists, but locals trade stories about how long they were willing to stand in the small entrance area to get a table. For a year after it opened, everyone I met would ask me, "Have you been to the Thai place yet?" When I did finally go, I became a believer, too—the authentic Thai food is that good, the service quick and professional, and the atmosphere, if lacking in polish, conducive to a good time. Reservations are not accepted and they do not have a liquor license.

Local Joints in Juneau

In addition to the restaurants listed here, the **Channel Bowl,** in the bowling alley at 608 W. Willoughby (☎ 907/586-6139), near the State Museum, is a classic (very) greasy spoon frequented by locals in search of a perfect breakfast. My friends drag me to its tiny, boisterous dining room every time I come to town. You can pick up a picnic at the deli at the **Rainbow Food** health-food grocery at the corner of Seward and Second streets (☎ 907/586-6476). **Hot Bite,** a stand at the Auke Bay boat harbor, is a local secret, serving charcoal-broiled burgers and mind-blowing milkshakes.

The Second Course, 213 Front St. (☎ 907/463-5533), one of Juneau's best restaurants, is open only for lunch (Monday through Friday noon to 2pm), except for private banquets in the evening. The lunch buffet is $10.45, including tax. The warm and cheerful Heidi Grimes prepares and presides over tasty and interesting "New Asian Cuisine."

There are several good coffee houses in downtown Juneau, with its young, professional population. My favorite is **Valentine's Coffee House and Bakery,** 111 Seward St. (☎ 907/463-5144), which serves delicious, inexpensive soups, salads, pizza, and calzone, as well as microbrews, in an authentic, old-fashioned store front. They're open for three meals a day in summer and often have music or other cultural events in the evening. **Heritage Coffee Co. and Café,** 174 S. Franklin St. (☎ 907/586-1087), also serves light meals and is a good people-watching place. Near the cruise-ship dock, **The Cookhouse,** 200 Admiral Way (☎ 907/463-3658), specializes in massive hamburgers and other big helpings, catering mainly to tourists in a pleasant dining room.

SHOPPING

Juneau, like Ketchikan and Skagway, has developed a shopping district catering primarily to the cruise ships. When the last of more than 500 port calls are over late in the summer, many of the shops close their doors. If you're looking for authentic Alaskan art and crafts, be warned that counterfeiting has become widespread. For buying tips, read the "Native Art—Finding the Real Thing" section in chapter 2.

For serious galleries, check out **Portfolio Arts,** 210 Ferry Way, Suite 101 (☎ 907/586-8111), a gallery of Native and contemporary Alaskan art. **The Raven's Journey,** 175 S. Franklin (☎ 907/463-4686), a brightly lit, museum-like gallery, shows Tlingit and other Northwest Indian carvings and masks; whalebone, ivory, and fossil ivory carvings and jewelry from the Yup'ik and Inupiat of western and northern Alaska; and other apparently authentic work by Alaska Natives.

Rie Muñoz paints in Juneau, and her prints and tapestries are shown downtown at the **Decker Gallery,** 233 S. Franklin (☎ 907/463-5536), and in the Mendenhall Valley at the **Rie Muñoz Gallery,** at 2101 Jordan Ave. (☎ 907/789-7411). Her simple, graphic watercolors represent coastal Alaska communities and Native people with a cheerful but observant sensibility.

For gifts, try **Annie Kaill's** fine arts and crafts gallery, 244 Front St. It's a little out of the cruise-ship shopping area and gets most of its business from locals. It has a rich, full, homey feeling, with local work at various price levels. The long-established **Ad Lib,** at 231 S. Franklin St., also is reliable and oriented to items made in Alaska, with a charming variety of things that look and feel real. **Galligaskins,** 207 and 219 S. Franklin St., features clothing with Alaska-theme designs. **Hearthside Books** is a cubbyhole of a bookstore, but has a good selection for its size, at the corner of Franklin and Front streets. (Their larger branch is in the Mendenhall Valley's Nugget Mall, at 8745 Glacier Hwy.) The pleasingly dusty **Observatory,** at 235 Second St. (☎ 907/586-9676), sells rare books, maps, and prints about Alaska.

Bill Spear sells his own brightly colored metal pins from his studio upstairs at 174 S. Franklin (☎ 907/586-2009). Alaskans collect the vividly executed fish, birds, and other natural subjects, and treasure Spear's witty, provocative, and special-issue pins, too. He's a local original.

Taku Smokeries, at 550 S. Franklin, across the parking lot from the tram station (☎ 907/463-4617), is worth a stop even if you're not in the market for the pricey delicacies in the case: It's interesting to watch workers fillet, smoke, and pack salmon through large windows, and to read the explanatory signs about what they're doing. They'll ship the smoked fish anywhere. An upscale restaurant was planned when I last visited, but had not opened yet. They're open in summer daily 8am to 8pm, winter Monday through Friday noon to 5pm and Saturday 3 to 5pm.

JUNEAU IN THE EVENING

Two **salmon bakes** take place nightly during the summer, each offering entertainment with the fish. Alaska Travel Adventures has offered its **Gold Creek Salmon Bake** for almost 30 years. It's touristy, yes, but fun, with marshmallow roasting, music, and other entertainment—great for families. (I'd avoid it in the rain, though.) The cost is $24 for adults, $16 for children. Call ☎ 907/789-0052 to arrange pickup by van. **The Gold Nugget Revue** plays summer nights at 7pm at the Thane Ore House, 4 miles out Thane Road, south of Juneau (☎ 907/586-1462). The show includes cancan dancing and a gold rush melodrama—corny, yes, but people go away smiling. The meal of salmon, halibut, or beef ribs costs $27, or skip the meal and pay $8.50 for the show alone. There is indoor or outdoor seating.

For more substantial performances, try to catch a show by Juneau's **Perseverance Theatre,** Alaska's largest professional theater. Theirs is a winter season, mainly for Juneau audiences, but occasionally they tour or put on summer shows. For information, contact the theater's office at 914 Third St., Douglas, AK 99824 (☎ 907/364-2421).

A political scandal or two have put a damper on some of the infamous legislative partying that once occurred in Juneau, far away from home districts, but there still are good places to go out drinking and dancing. The **Red Dog Saloon,** at 278 S. Franklin St., is the town's most famous bar, with a sawdust-strewn floor and slightly contrived but nonetheless infectious frontier atmosphere. It's a fun place, with walls covered with lots of Alaskan memorabilia. The nightly live music doesn't entail a cover charge. Across the street, **The Alaskan Bar,** 167 S. Franklin, is in an authentic gold rush hotel, with a two-story Victorian bar room that's the scene of boisterous parties and music all year. **The Hanger,** listed above under "Dining," is the place for beer drinkers, with 28 brews on tap. They have a big-screen TV and live music Friday and Saturday nights, as well as pool and darts.

10 Glacier Bay National Park: Ice, Whales & Wilderness

Glacier Bay is a work in progress; the boat ride to its head is a chance to see creation fresh. The bay John Muir discovered in a canoe in 1879 didn't exist a century earlier. Eighteenth-century explorers had found instead a wall of ice a mile thick where the entrance to the branching, 65-mile-long fjord now opens to the sea. Receding faster than any other glacier on earth, the ice melted into the ocean and opened a spectacular and still-unfinished land. The land itself is rising 1½ inches a year as it rebounds from the weight of now-melted glaciers. As your vessel retraces Muir's path—and then probes northward in deep water where ice stood in his day—the story of this new world unravels in reverse. The trees on the shore get smaller, then disappear, then all vegetation disappears, and finally, at the head of the bay, the ice stands at the water's edge surrounded by barren rock, rounded and scored by the passage of the ice but not yet marked by the waterfalls cascading down out of the clouds above. It's often windy and cold at the head of the bay, near the glaciers. Precipitation and cold add up to glaciers. Be prepared, and try to enjoy the beauty of the mist and rain—at times the smooth silver water, barren rock, white clouds, and ice create an ethereal study in white.

Glacier Bay, first set aside by President Calvin Coolidge in 1925, is managed by the National Park Service, which has the difficult job of protecting the wilderness while showing it to the public. This is a challenge, since this rugged land the size of Connecticut can be seen only by boat or plane, and the presence of too many boats threatens the park (plus, the whales appear to be sensitive to the noise of vessels). Since the 1970s, when in one year only a single whale returned, the Park Service has used a permit system to severely limit the number of ships that can enter the bay. With Alaska tourism booming, the state's powerful congressional delegation pushed for more cruise-ship permits for the bay. The Park Service agreed to an increase to take effect in 1997, and was sued by the National Parks and Conservation Association. While that case is pending, the increase is in effect, apparently without ill effect. Already, any tour boat sees several other ships on a day's journey up the bay, but how much it bothers the whales really can't be proved. As for the visitors, they seem happy: In 1996, *Consumer Reports* readers voted this the best of all the national parks to visit.

The uniqueness of the glaciers of Glacier Bay lies in their size and geological activity, in their number, and in the opportunity to see them fairly close up in a remote setting. On a Glacier Bay boat ride, you'll also see wildlife—sea lions and eagles almost certainly, and possibly humpback whales.

The drawback? Since you'll have to take a plane or boat, it's expensive. But there are other places in Southeast rich with marine wildlife, so don't feel compelled to go. If you're in Juneau, consider a day trip to **Tracy Arm** instead. In Southcentral Alaska, plan a day trip from Whittier to see the glaciers in **College Fjord.**

ESSENTIALS
GETTING THERE

Gustavus, described in the next section, is the gateway to Glacier Bay. Unless you're on a cruise ship, you'll fly or take a passenger ferry to Gustavus, then a van to the park headquarters. The vans meet the planes and boats and cost $10 one-way to make the 10-mile trip to the park, plus $2 for baggage.

BY TOUR BOAT   The *Spirit of Adventure* tour boat is the main way for independent travelers to see the park. It is operated by park concessionaire **Glacier Bay Tours and Cruises,** 520 Pike St., Suite 1400, Seattle, WA 98101 (☎ **800/451-5952** or 206/623-2417; fax 206/623-7809; www.glacierbaytours.com), or locally, in the summer only, P.O. Box 199, Gustavus, AK 99826 (☎ **907/697-2226;** fax 907/697-2408). Despite the address, the company is owned by Juneau's Goldbelt Native corporation; there's a light emphasis on Native culture in their offerings. The fast, quiet tour boat carries up to 250 passengers in upper and lower lounges in a comfortable, table-oriented seating configuration. Bring heavy rain gear, as the windows can fog up

and you'll want to spend as much time as possible outside. There's a snack bar, and a simple lunch is provided. Bring binoculars or rent them on board; they're a necessity. The boat leaves Bartlett Cove at 8am for a 9-hour cruise for $175 adults, $87.50 children. Glacier Bay Tours and Cruises offers a same-day trip from Juneau, Haines, or Skagway, but it makes for too long a day, and the schedule leaves no time in Glacier Bay, Gustavus, or anything else but the boat trip. The package fare from Juneau is $346.50, more from Haines or Skagway. A better choice is to take their 2-day package, riding from Juneau to Gustavus on the Auk Nu passenger ferry, including a whale-watching trip in Icy Strait (see the Gustavus section, below), then spend the night at Bartlett Cove and do the *Spirit of Adventure* tour the second day, and fly back to Juneau, Haine, or Skagway. That package costs $481 from Juneau. See the Gustavus section for even more choices. My preferred itinerary is to stay in Gustavus and make Glacier Bay a side trip, but that's potentially costly and will take more time.

BY SMALL CRUISE SHIP   If your budget allows, there may be no better way to see Glacier Bay than on a small cruise ship on an excursion of a couple of days or more. **Glacier Bay Tours and Cruises** has developed a whole small-ship cruise fleet around this idea, and the visitors I've talked to afterward—including my editor, who has sailed with the company twice—have been overjoyed with their experience. The four vessels—including the ***Wilderness Explorer*** and the larger ***Wilderness Adventurer,*** which carry racks of sea kayaks—carry only 36 to 86 passengers each, and offer a range of itineraries. See chapter 4 for a complete review.

Smaller operators based in Gustavus also do these trips. If you have a large group, you can have a boat and guide to yourself. Mike Nigro, a former backcountry ranger and 25-year resident, takes groups of four to six for $1,400 to $1,650 per day on a 42-foot yacht. **Gustavus Marine Charters** is reached at P.O. Box 81, Gustavus, AK 99826 (☎ **907/697-2233;** fax 907/697-2414; www.gustavusmarinecharters.com).

VISITOR INFORMATION

The Park Service's address is **Glacier Bay National Park and Preserve,** P.O. Box 140, Gustavus, AK 99826 (☎ **907/697-2230;** www.nps.gov/glba/). But the concession-aire, **Glacier Bay Tours,** listed above under "Getting There," operates most of the activities in the park. The Park Service interprets the park mainly by placing well-prepared rangers on board all cruise and tour vessels entering the bay. The park also maintains a modest visitor center with displays on the park in the concessionaire's lodge at Bartlett Cove. The park's offices, a free campground, a backcountry office, a few short hiking trails, a dock, and other park facilities also surround the lodge in a wooded setting.

ACTIVITIES AT THE PARK

AT BARTLETT COVE There are two short **hiking trails,** right at the Bartlett Cove compound, for an afternoon walk. A free trail guide is available at the visitor center. Rangers lead daily nature walks, and there are displays in the lodge. In the evening, the Park Service does a slide show.

KAYAKING IN THE PARK The great majority of people see the park on cruise ships or on one of the tour boats described above, but a sea kayak is the outdoor way. Most kayakers go to see the glaciers up the protected eastern fjords after being carried part of the way by the concessionaire-operated ship *Crystal Fjord,* or stay in the islands near the Bartlett Cove lodge, where there are no glaciers. Make sure you calibrate the length of your trip to your outdoors experience—this is remote territory, and you can't just leave once you're out there. Also, everyone going into the backcountry is required to check in with the backcountry office by the lodge for orientation. **Glacier Bay Sea Kayaks,** P.O. Box 26, Gustavus, AK 99826 (☎ **907/697-2257;** fax 907/697-3002; www.he.net/~kayakak/), is the Park Service concessionaire, operating May 1 to September 30. They offer instruction and rentals for $50 a day, and drop-offs up the bay are $167.50 round-trip.

For guided kayak trips, **Alaska Discovery,** 5449 Shaune Dr., Suite 4, Juneau, AK 99801 (☎ **800/586-1911** or 907/780-6226; fax 907/780-4220; www.akdiscovery. com), offers paddles ranging from 6 hours to 8 days. A 6-hour guided paddle around Bartlett Cove and the Beardslee Islands is a good choice for beginners, although it goes nowhere near the glaciers. It costs $119, including lunch and a ride from your lodgings or the airport. The longer tours also are well guided and outfitted, but I wouldn't recommend a week sea kayaking to anyone who hasn't tried it before—you have to cover the ground, even if you're sore—and you should have spent enough time in the outdoors to know you'll enjoy such a remote camping trip even if it rains the whole time, which is possible. If you're up to it, this is the most intimate and authentic way to experience this wilderness, with almost unlimited time to see the glaciers and wildlife. The 5-day trip to the bay's more visited west arm is $1,675; 8 days in the spectacular but forgotten east arm is $1,975. The company, which is described in more detail in the Juneau section, above, also has a bed-and-breakfast in Gustavus, which they use to offer traditional overnight and 2-night visits to the area.

FLIGHTSEEING The other way to get into the park is by flightseeing. **Frontier Air,** P.O. Box 1, Gustavus, AK 99826 (☎ **907/697-2386**), offers flights from the

Bartlett Cove visitor center. Other companies offer tours from various towns, Haines being the closest, served by **L.A.B. Flying Service** (☎ **800/426-0543** or 907/766-2222), for one. They charge $105 per person for a one-hour flight from Haines, with a two-person minimum. You'll see the incredible rivers of ice that flow down into the bay, and may even see wildlife. What you give up is a lingering, up-close look and the awesome sense of having all that ice and rock above you.

ACCOMMODATIONS & DINING

Glacier Bay Lodge. Bartlett Cove (P.O. Box 199), Gustavus, AK 99826. ☎ **800/451-5952** or 907/697-2226. Fax 206/623-7809 or 907/697-2408. www.glacierbaytours.com. 56 units. TEL. $165 double. Additional person in room $9 extra. Hostel bunks $28 per person. AE, DC, DISC, MC, V. Closed mid-Sept to mid-May.

Operated by park concessionaire Glacier Bay Tours and Cruises, this is the only place to stay in the park, although Gustavus, 10 miles down the road, has some of the most attractive accommodations in Alaska. The lodge rooms are comfortable but, for the price, nothing special. They're in buildings accessed from the main lodge by board-walks. Laundry facilities and bike rentals are available. The restaurant has a great view of Bartlett Cove. There are inexpensive main courses on the dinner menu, but mainly it's a fine-dining establishment with dishes in the $20 range. Breakfast is available as early as 5:45am and dinner as late as 10pm. There is no bar. For those on a budget, there are bunk rooms with six beds each for men and women. The lodge also provides showers for the free Park Service campground.

11 Gustavus: Country Inns & Quiet

The unincorporated town of Gustavus (gus-*tave*-us) remains an undiscovered treasure for visitors—or at least it succeeds in making itself feel that way. It's wonderfully remote, accessible for visitors only by air or a small passenger ferry, but has a selection of comfortable and even luxurious inns and lodges, plus several days' worth of outdoor activities, including excellent salmon and halibut fishing, nearly surefire whale watching, close access to Glacier Bay National Park with the sea kayaking and activities there, and places for casual hiking and bicycle outings. Neither large cruise ships nor the Alaska State Ferry land here, leaving the roads free of their throngs of shoppers and the development they bring. Miraculously, the 300 townspeople have been smart enough to value what they've got and build on it. Even the gas station is a work of art. Walking, biking, or driving down the quiet roads, everyone you pass—every single person—waves to you.

The buildings, mostly clapboard houses and log cabins, are scattered widely across an oceanfront alluvial plain. Several of the founding homesteads were farms, and the broad clearings of sandy soil wave with hay and wildflowers. The setting is unique in Alaska.

The bad news: Visitors need to be prepared to have their fun in the rain, well bundled up. Also, the remoteness and lack of tourist development means that Gustavus is expensive. Rooms aren't cheap and neither are meals. There's only one freestanding restaurant, and it can be inconsistently open, but you can buy a meal at the lodges and inns—for a price. Also, the most memorable activities in the outdoors all involve charters or rentals.

ESSENTIALS
GETTING THERE

BY BOAT The *Auk Nu* passenger ferry, a high-speed catamaran (☎ **800/820-2628** or 907/586-8687; www.auknutours.com), leaves Juneau's Auke Bay harbor from 11789 Glacier Highway, right next to the ferry terminal, at 11am daily May through September. The adult fare is $45 one-way, $85 round-trip; children 3 to 12 $30 and $60. The *Auk Nu* lands at the Gustavus dock at 1:15pm, goes on an afternoon whale-watching cruise, then leaves for Juneau at 5:45pm, arriving at 8pm. Adding the whale watch (which I recommend unless you are planning to see the whales of Icy Strait some other way) brings the adult round-trip fare to $139. The boat also carries kayaks and bikes, for an added fee.

BY AIR   During the summer, **Alaska Airlines** (☎ 800/426-0333) flies a jet once a day from Juneau to Gustavus and back. Various commuter carriers serve Gustavus from Juneau and other nearby towns, including **L.A.B. Flying Service** (☎ 800/ 426-0543 or 907/766-2222). Daily flights from Juneau are $70 one-way.

Visitor Information

There are no public buildings in Gustavus because there is no government: Only the informal community association and the state government hold sway. Generally, you contact a lodge, and once comfortable with them, allow them to advise you on what to do and to book your activities. Be certain you reserve a place to stay before showing up in Gustavus.

Getting Around

There are just a few roads. The main one starts at the airport and runs about 10 miles to **Bartlett Cove,** the Glacier Bay National Park base of operations. **Dock Road** branches off to the left, at the gas station, and leads to the ocean dock. Most businesses will give you a good free map, which shows everything in town, for exploring by bicycle. Many inns and B&Bs have courtesy vans and free bicycles. **TLC Taxi** (☎ 907/697-2239) also will carry you and your kayak.

EXPLORING GUSTAVUS

Everything to do in Gustavus involves the outdoors.

✪ **WHALE WATCHING**   Trips aboard the passenger ferry *Auk Nu* leave the town dock for Point Adolphus every day at 2pm. Icy Strait, where the vessel cruises, is the most reliable place in the state to see humpbacks in summer. They come here because a swirl of currents makes it a rich feeding ground. The fare for the 3-hour cruise is $78, and you get your money back if you don't see whales. If you're coming to Gustavus on the *Auk Nu* anyway, you'll save $24 by buying a combination ticket. Other smaller operators will provide a more intimate experience on smaller boats. They'll also combine the trip with superb halibut and salmon fishing. Your inn host can make the arrangements. A boat typically charters for $225 or more per person for a full day.

SEA KAYAKING   **Alaska Discovery,** 5449 Shaune Dr., Suite 4, Juneau, AK 99801 (☎ 800/586-1911 or 907/780-6226; fax 907/780-4220; www.akdiscovery.com), offers an easy 2½-day, 2-night kayaking expedition among the whales for $695 per person. They take a boat to a base camp, then kayak among the whales from there. They also lead more challenging 5-night trips with the whales and along the remote shores of Chichagof Island, for $1,625. Gustavus-based **Spirit Walker Expeditions,** P.O. Box 240, Gustavus, AK 99826 (☎ 800/KAY-AKER or 907/697-2266; fax

---

Be Prepared

Gustavus isn't formally a town; it has no bank and few other businesses. Bring cash and anything you may need.

907/697-2701; www.he.net/~kayak), leads guided 1- to 7-day trips to the whale-watching grounds and beyond. The 1-day trip is $115; 7-day trips, including itineraries linking wilderness lodges along the way, can go over $2,000. **Sea Otter Kayak,** P.O. Box 228, Gustavus, AK 99826 (☎ **907/697-3007;** www.he.net/~seaotter/) rents kayaks on Dock Road.

HIKING & BICYCLING   There are few cars in Gustavus (because they have to be hauled here on a barge), but most inns provide bikes. The roads are fun to explore, and the sandy beaches, accessed from the town dock, are great for a walk and a picnic. It's 14 miles from Good River Road along the shore around Point Gustavus to the Bartlett Cove national park center, 7 miles from the town dock along the beach to the airport.

There's also a primitive nine-hole **golf course** in the area, carved out of the meadows near the beach; inquire with your host for information, or just go to the first tee, paying your fee and borrowing clubs on the honor system at a shed there.

ACCOMMODATIONS & DINING

There are a surprising number of good places to stay in Gustavus. Besides those I've described below, I can also recommend the motel-style **Growley Bear Inn,** Dock Road (P.O. Box 246), Gustavus, AK 99826 (☎ **907/697-2730**).

There isn't much of a choice for food. The Gustavus concept is a **full-service inn or lodge,** with generous family-style meals included in the price; that makes it hard for a separate restaurant to survive. There's a small store, and a restaurant on Dock Road that's currently out of business; perhaps it will be operating when you visit, perhaps not. The full-service restaurant at the Glacier Bay Lodge (see "Accommodations & Dining" in section 10, earlier in this chapter) is open all summer, and the inns that serve meals to their guests will sometimes make room for another party if you call ahead. Most of the inns do not have licenses to serve alcohol; if that's a consideration, be sure to ask before you book your stay.

Annie Mae Lodge. 2 Grandpa's Farm Rd. (P.O. Box 80), Gustavus, AK 99826. ☎ **907/697-2346.** Fax 907/697-2211. E-mail: mnimaka@sprynet.com. 11 units, 9 with bathroom. $80 double without bathroom or meals, $215 double with bathroom and all meals. Additional person in room $90 extra. AE, DC, MC, V.

The lodge, run by three sisters, has a log porch that wraps around and is secluded down a dirt side road overlooking a field of wildflowers through which runs a little creek. The cozy decor is country style, with family pictures and memorabilia on the walls and a friendly dog. The set menu emphasizes seafood. They offer free transportation and bicycles, but have no liquor license.

Glacier Bay Country Inn. Tong Rd. (P.O. Box 5), Gustavus, AK 99826. ☎ **800/628-0912** or 907/697-2288. Fax 907/697-2289. www.glacierbayalaska.com. 6 units, 3 cabins. $322 double, $352 cabin. Additional adult in room $85 extra; additional child under 12 $50 extra. Rates include all meals. AE, DISC, MC, V. Closed Oct–Apr.

Set on a 160-acre former agricultural homestead well back in the woods, this inn is renowned for its food and service. The quaint and quirky lodge building has lots of places to sit and watch the passing wildlife. Ponch and Sandi Marchbanks and family also operate Grand Pacific Charters, with three boats for fishing and whale watching. They offer packages that cover everything you'll want to do in the area. The same family operates **Whalesong Lodge** (use the same address and phone; www.whalesonglodge.com), which has a three-bedroom apartment and B&B accommodations, as well as a lodge package with meals at the Glacier Bay Country Inn. It's not an impressive building, sitting on the road from the airport, but the rooms are comfortable and attractively decorated. Rates there are $140 double, with a continental breakfast; adding your other meals at the inn costs $40 per person. Nonguests are welcome for dinner, too, if there's room, but must call ahead. The inn also offers a van to the airport, laundry, and bicycles.

Glacier Bay's Bear Track Inn. 255 Rink Rd., Gustavus, AK 99826. ☎ **888/697-2284** or 907/697-3017. Fax 907/697-2284. www.BearTrackInn.com. 14 units. $393 per person, double occupancy; discounts for additional nights. Rates include round-trip air from Juneau and all meals. AE, DISC, MC, V. Closed Nov–Jan.

Recently built of native spruce logs by the proprietors, the lodge is a real showplace, with large rooms and a huge lobby with great views, a central fireplace, and a 28-foot vaulted ceiling. Everything is wood. Unlike other lodges and inns in Gustavus, where meals generally are served family style, guests' main courses for dinner are cooked to order—you can pick your cut of steak, seafood, caribou, or musk ox, then watch it being grilled. The menu also includes vegetarian choices.

✪ **Gustavus Inn at Glacier Bay.** Gustavus Rd. (P.O. Box 60), Gustavus, AK 99826 (in winter, 7920 Outlook, Prairie Village, KS 66208). ☎ **800/649-5220** or 907/697-2254. Fax 907/697-2255 in summer, 913/649-5220 in winter. 11 units. $270 double. Additional person in room $135 extra; children under 12 half price. AE, MC, V. Closed Sept 16–May 15.

This is the original and still the best of the Gustavus inns—my choice for its authenticity as well as the comforts that all the others have copied. The old homestead farmhouse stands at the center of the community, amid blowing grass and with a huge vegetable garden that provides much of the wonderful food they serve. The Lesh family has run the inn since 1965 and Dave, the chef, has published a cookbook—the seasonings he uses on seafood, which is served on big platters in the dining room, are a real revelation. There's also a bar serving guests beer and wine. That's unusual in this area. Talk over what you want to do with Dave or his father, Jack, and let them book everything; you pay through them. They drive their guests around and offer free bikes, fishing rods, and laundry service.

A Puffin's Bed and Breakfast. Rink Creek Rd. (P.O. Box 3), Gustavus, AK 99826. ☎ **800/ 478-2258** in Alaska, or 907/697-2260. Fax 907/697-2258. www.puffintravel.com. 3 cabins, 1 house. $85 cabin for two, $125 house for two. Additional adult in room $20 extra; additional child (up to 12 years old) in room $10 extra. No credit cards.

The cabins are set among the trees, connected by paths to a central building where breakfast is served in a big room with a cathedral ceiling. The two-bedroom house with a complete kitchen and laundry facilities is a good choice for families; it does not include breakfast. The proprietors also run a charter and tour business, offering a multitude of packages for visiting Gustavus and Glacier Bay. A courtesy car, bikes, and a coin-op laundry are available.

12 Haines: Eagles & the Unexpected

For years we always just passed through Haines on the way from the ferry up the highway. I didn't know what I was missing until I stopped and took a couple of days to really investigate. Now Haines is one of my favorite Alaska towns.

Haines is casual, happy, and slightly odd. It waits for one to find it, but once found, has wonderful charms. If you're looking for the mythical town of Cicely from television's *Northern Exposure,* you'll get closer in Haines than anyplace else I know. As I walked down a sidewalk, I saw a sign in a storefront that said to look in the big tree across the street. I looked, and there was an eagle peering back at me. At the Native

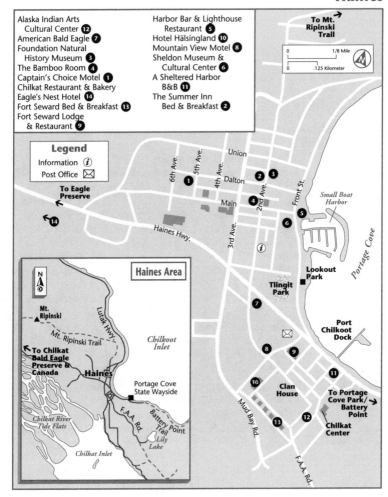

Alaska Indian Arts
  Cultural Center **12**
American Bald Eagle
  Foundation Natural
  History Museum **3**
The Bamboo Room **4**
Captain's Choice Motel **1**
Chilkat Restaurant & Bakery
Eagle's Nest Hotel **14**
Fort Seward Bed & Breakfast **13**
Fort Seward Lodge
  & Restaurant **9**

Harbor Bar & Lighthouse
  Restaurant **5**
Hotel Hälsingland **10**
Mountain View Motel **8**
Sheldon Museum &
  Cultural Center **6**
A Sheltered Harbor
  B&B **11**
The Summer Inn
  Bed & Breakfast **2**

Legend
Information **(i)**
Post Office **✉**

Haines Area

cultural center, seeking an office or a ticket window or someone in charge, I wandered into a totem pole studio where a carver was completing a major commission. He gladly stopped to talk. It turned out there wasn't anyone in charge.

The **Chilkat Dancers** have performed here for almost 40 years, and their efforts are among the most respected and authentic in carrying on the Tlingit cultural heritage. But their membership is undefined, and their performances, while impressive, are also funny and slightly strange. Whites dance beside Natives, and rehearsals are never held; the new generation learns by being thrown into the performances, sometimes before the age of 5. Issues that are a big deal in some other towns just aren't in Haines.

Haines's chief feature, **Fort William Seward,** gives the town a pastoral atmosphere. The fort is a collection of grand, white clapboard buildings arranged around a 9-acre parade ground, in the middle of which stands a Tlingit clan house—out of place, yes, but wonderfully symbolic of Haines. The town is a friendly, accessible center of Tlingit culture as well as a retired outpost of seemingly pointless military activity.

And Haines has **bald eagles**—always plenty of bald eagles, and in the fall, a ridiculous number of bald eagles. More, in fact, than anywhere else on earth. The chance to see the birds draws people into the outdoors here. There are well-established guides for any activity you might want to pursue, all cooperating and located together. There are some excellent hiking trails right from town, as well as protected sea kayaking waters. Also, it's well worth noting that due to its location in relation to the flow of weather, Haines is not as rainy as elsewhere in Southeast.

ESSENTIALS
GETTING THERE
BY WATER   The **Alaska Marine Highway System** (☎ **907/766-2111** locally; see "Getting Around" at the beginning of this chapter for a full listing) is how most people get to Haines, and the cruise on the Lynn Canal fjord from Juneau or Skagway is among the most beautiful in the Inside Passage. (The fare is $24 to Juneau and $17 to Skagway.) But there's a drawback: Since this is the northern highway connection where nearly all vehicles get off or on, there often are delays. The dock is 5 miles north of town. If you're just going to Skagway without a car, a good alternative is one of the privately operated passenger ferries. The **Haines-Skagway Shuttle Ferry,** operated by Chilkat Cruises (☎ **888/766-2103** or 907/766-2100; www.chilkatcruises.com), runs a new 150-passenger catamaran, the *Fairweather Explorer,* at least three round-trips a day on the 40-minute trip. It leaves from near the Port Chilkoot dock, below Fort William Seward. Adult round-trips are $35, one-way $21; children under 12 pay $19 and $13 respectively. **The Haines-Skagway Water Taxi and Scenic Cruise** (☎ **907/ 766-3395;** www.kcd.com/watertaxi) offers a similar service with an 80-passenger vessel, leaving from the small boat harbor and charging adults $32 round-trip, $20 one-way; children half price. Unlike the state ferry, these are summer-only shuttles.

BY CAR   The **Haines Highway** leads 155 miles to Haines Junction, Yukon Territory, an intersection with the Alaska Highway (you must pass through Canadian customs—see the "Alaska Highway" section in chapter 9 for rules). The road runs along the Chilkat River and the bald eagle preserve, then climbs into spectacular alpine terrain. Anchorage is 775 driving miles from Haines, 653 from Fairbanks. One-way car rentals to Anchorage, Fairbanks, and Skagway are available from **Avis,** at the Hotel Hälsingland (☎ **907/766-2733**) with a $300 drop-off charge plus the rental cost; you can sometimes get a special deal at the end of the season, when the rental companies are shuffling cars around and shipping many back to the Lower 48. You can also rent an RV one-way to Anchorage. **ABC Motorhome Rentals,** 3853 W. International Airport Rd., Anchorage, AK 99502 (☎ **800/421-7456** or 907/279-2000; fax 907/243-6363; www.abcmotorhome.com), charges $500 plus a 1-week rental, starting around $1,400 in the high season.

BY BUS   Gray Line's **Alaskon Express** bus (☎ **800/544-2206**) serves routes during the tourist season 3 days a week each to Skagway, Whitehorse, Anchorage, Fairbanks, and Beaver Creek. The fare to Anchorage is $195. The bus stops at the Hälsingland and the Captain's Choice Motel, where you can buy tickets.

BY AIR   L.A.B. Flying Service (☎ **800/426-0543** or 907/766-2222) has frequent flights, charging $65 one-way for the 30-minute trip from Juneau. It's $10 more if you use a credit card.

GETTING AROUND
Haines sits on the narrow Chilkat Peninsula near the north end of the Southeast Alaska Panhandle. Highways run north on either side of the peninsula; the one on the

east side goes to the ferry dock, 5 miles out, and ends after 11 miles at **Chilkoot Lake.** The other is the **Haines Highway,** which leads to the Canadian border, the Alaska Highway, and the rest of the world.

The town itself has two parts: the sparsely built downtown grid and, down Front Street or Second Avenue, a short walk to the west, the Fort William Seward area. Vans and buses that meet the ferry offer free or inexpensive transfers, seeking to take you on a town tour. Hotel Hälsingland books tours, too, but your feet or a bicycle will get you around.

BY BIKE & SCOOTER   Bikes are available from **Sockeye Cycle,** just uphill from the Port Chilkoot Dock on Portage Street in the Fort William Seward area (☎ and fax **907/766-2869;** www.haines.ak.us/sockeye/), for $6 an hour or $30 a day. Motorized scooters are for rent from the Portage Cove Adventure Center (see "Visitor Information," below) for $45 a day.

BY TAXI   **Haines Taxi** can be reached at ☎ **907/766-3138.**

BY RENTAL CAR   **Avis** car rental has an outlet at the Hotel Hälsingland, and **Affordable Cars** is at the Captain's Choice Motel (see "Accommodations," below).

Visitor Information

The small but well-staffed and -stocked **Haines Convention and Visitors Bureau Visitor Information Center,** Second Street near Willard (P.O. Box 530), Haines, AK 99827 (☎ **800/458-3579** or 907/766-2234; www.haines.ak.us), is operated by the city government, which also sends out a vacation-planning packet. It's open Monday to Friday 8am to 5pm, Saturday 9am to 6pm, Sunday 10am to 7pm in summer; normal business hours in winter.

The unique **Portage Cove Adventure Center,** 142 Beach Rd. (P.O. Box 509), Haines, AK 99827 (☎ **877/766-2800** or 907/766-3800; fax 907/766-3801; www. portage.klukwan.com), which sits on a dock below Fott William Seward, books all kinds of tours—outdoors, in Haines, and in the village of the Klukwan Native Corp. that owns the center—and serves coffee, halibut-and-chips, and other simple meals. You can also arrange fishing charters, a trip to Skagway or Glacier Bay, or most anything else to do in the area. The boat to Skagway docks here, too.

Alaska Mountain Flying and Travel, 132 2nd Ave. (P.O. Box 1404), Haines, AK 99827 (☎ **800/954-8747** or 907/766-2665; www.haines.ak.us/mtnfly/), offers flight service and also serves as a travel agency, booking fishing charters, ferry reservations, Glacier Bay excursions, and other local activities.

Special Events

The **Great Alaska Craftbeer and Homebrew Festival** (☎ 800/542-6363) takes place over 3 days in mid-May. **The Kluane to Chilkat International Bike Relay** (☎ 907/766-2869) is held on the summer Solstice, June 21, heading down the Haines Highway, with hundreds of entrants; it's quite a downhill. **The Southeast Alaska State Fair** and **Bald Eagle Music Festival** (☎ 907/766-2476) is the biggest event of the summer, held for a week in early August; it's a regional small-town get-together, with livestock, cooking, a logging show, a parade, music, and other entertainment. Buildings constructed for the filming of the movie *White Fang* were donated to the fair, and now form the nucleus of a retail area there. **The Alaska Bald Eagle Festival** (☎ 800/246-6268; www.haines.ak.us/eaglefest/) offers seminars and special events to mark the annual eagle congregation. It's held in mid-November.

Fast Facts: Haines

Banks   There are two ATMs, at the First National Bank of Anchorage, Main Street and Second Avenue; and at Howsers Supermarket, a few doors down Main.

Hospital   The Haines Medical Clinic is on First Avenue, near the visitor center (☎ 907/766-2521).

Police   The police can be reached in nonemergency situations at ☎ 907/766-2121.

Post Office   At 55 Haines Hwy.

Taxes   Sales tax is 5.5%.

EXPLORING HAINES

The main feature of Haines is **Fort William Seward,** a collection of large, white, wood-frame buildings around sloping parade grounds overlooking the magnificent Lynn Canal fjord. (Get the informative walking-tour map of the National Historic Site from the Haines Convention and Visitors Bureau.) The fort led a peaceful life, for a military installation. By the time the U.S. Army built it, in 1903, the Klondike gold rush was over, and there's no evidence it ever deterred any attack on this little peninsula at the north end of the Inside Passage. It was deactivated at the end of World War II, in which it played little part.

In 1947, a group of five veterans from the Lower 48 bought the fort as surplus, with the idea of forming a planned community. That idea didn't really work out, but one of the new white families helped spark a Chilkat Tlingit cultural renaissance in the 1950s. The Heinmillers, who still own a majority of the shares in the fort, were looking for something to do with all that property when someone suggested a Tlingit tribal house on the parade grounds. The project, led by a pair of elders, took on a life of its own, and the ✪ **Chilkat Dancers** and **Alaska Indian Arts** cultural center followed. Lee Heinmiller, a member of the second generation, still manages the dance troupe his father started in 1957 as a Boy Scout project and participates in the performances with his pale, spreading paunch gleaming in abbreviated traditional Native dress. He has been adopted as a member of the tribe and given a name that accords high respect.

The dancers, who have been all over the world, perform at the **Chilkat Center for the Arts** (☎ and fax **907/766-2160**), an auditorium just off the southeast corner of the parade grounds, and sometimes at the clan house. Times of the performances are geared to the arrival of cruise ships; check at the Visitor Information Center or the Alaska Indian Arts Cultural Center. Admission is $10 for adults, $5 for students, and free for children 4 and under. The cultural center is open from 1 to 5pm Monday through Friday and when cruise ships are in town. It is in the old fort hospital on the south side of the parade grounds and has a small gallery and a carvers' workshop where you may be able to see work in progress.

The Portage Cove Adventure Center (see "Visitor Information," above), which is owned by the Klukwan Native corporation, offers 3-hour cultural tours to the village of **Klukwan** for $75 per adult, $40 children 12 and under.

In the downtown area, the **Sheldon Museum and Cultural Center,** 11 Main St. (☎ **907/766-2366**; e-mail: sheldmus@seaknet.alaska.edu), contains an upstairs gallery of well-presented Tlingit art and cultural artifacts; downstairs is a collection on the white history of the town. There's a uniquely personal feel to the Tlingit objects, some of which are displayed with pictures of the artisans who made them and the history of their relationship with the Sheldons for whom the museum is named. It's open in summer, daily from 1 to 5pm, plus mornings and evenings that are posted weekly; in winter, on Sunday, Monday, and Wednesday from 1 to 4pm and Tuesday, Thursday, and Friday 3 to 5pm. Admission is $3 for adults, free for children 17 and under.

The entirely unique **American Bald Eagle Foundation Natural History Museum,** at 115 Haines Hwy. (☎ 907/766-3094), is essentially a huge, hair-raising diorama of more than a hundred eagles and other animal mounts. Dave Olerud sits in a wheelchair behind the desk and will talk your ear off about the museum if you want him to—he worked on it for 18 years and was paralyzed in a fall during construction. The museum is free, but donations are requested. It's open 10am to 6pm.

GETTING OUTSIDE

There's a lot to do in Haines—good hiking, biking, kayaking, climbing, and rafting—with a special advantage over the rest of Southeast: It's not as rainy. Also, there's a small fraternity of outdoor guides that has grown up in Haines, on Portage Street and Beach Road next to the Port Chilkoot cruise-ship dock, a kind of one-stop shop. On the water nearby, the Portage Cove Adventure Center (see "Visitor Information," above), has become a booking agency for anything there is to do in town, including the guided outdoor activities.

✪ **EAGLE VIEWING**   Haines is probably the best place on earth to see bald eagles. The **Chilkat Bald Eagle Preserve** protects 48,000 acres of river bottom along the Chilkat River. From October to January, some 3,000 eagles gather in the cottonwood trees (also known as western poplar) on a small section of the river, a phenomenon known as the Fall Congregation. (A healthy 200 to 400 are resident the rest of the year.) The eagles come for easy winter food: A very late salmon run spawns here into December in a 5-mile stretch of open water known as the Council Grounds.

During the Congregation, dozens of eagles stand in each of the gnarled, leafless cottonwoods on the riverbanks, occasionally diving for a fish. The best place to see them is from the bank just off miles 18 to 21 on the Haines Highway. Don't walk on the flats, as that disturbs the eagles. The preserve is managed by Alaska State Parks, 400 Willoughby, 3rd Floor, Juneau, AK 99801, but the Haines Convention and Visitors Bureau may be a better source of information for planning a visit.

Local guides offer trips to see the eagles by raft, bicycle, or bus—mostly in the summer, when the eagles are fewer but visitors more numerous. ✪ **Chilkat Guides,** on Beach Street on the waterfront below the fort; P.O. Box 170, Haines, AK 99827 (☎ 907/766-2491; www.raftalaska.com), does a rafting trip twice a day during the summer down the Chilkat to watch the eagles. The rapids aren't threatening—there's a chance you'll be asked to get out and push—and you'll see lots of eagles. The company is run by young people who create a sense of fellowship with their clients. The 4-hour trip, with a snack, costs $80 for adults, $40 for children.

Sockeye Cycle (see "Biking," below) has guided bike tours to see eagles and Fort Seward on a 90-minute trip that costs $42, and **Alaska Nature Tours** (☎ 907/766-2876; kcd.com/aknature) takes 3-hour bus and walking tours to the preserve for $50 per person in summer.

HIKING   There are several good trails near Haines, ranging from an easy beach walk to a 10-mile, 4,000-foot climb of **Mount Ripinsky,** north of town (it starts at the top of Young Street). Get the *Haines Is for Hikers* trail guide from the visitor center. The easiest for families is the **Battery Point Trail,** which goes 2.4 miles along the beach from the end of the shore road that leads southeast from the Port Chilkoot cruise-ship dock. **Mount Riley** is south of town, with three trail routes to a 1,760-foot summit that features great views and feels much higher than it is; get the trail guide or ask directions to one of the trailheads. **Seduction Point Trail** is 7 miles long, starting at Chilkat State Park at the end of Mud Bay Road south of town and leading to the end of the Chilkat Peninsula. It's a beach walk, so check the tides; they'll give you a tide table at the visitors bureau.

BIKING   **Sockeye Cycle,** P.O. Box 829, Haines, AK 99827 (☎ and fax **907/ 766-2869**), leads a variety of guided trips—a couple of hours, half or full day, or even a 9-day trek. A 3-hour ride along Chilkoot Lake costs $70. Or you can go on your own for $30 a day. The area is especially conducive to biking.

SEA KAYAKING   Next door to Chilkat Guides and Sockeye Cycle on Portage Street is **Deishu Expeditions,** P.O. Box 1406, Haines, AK 99827 (☎ **800/552-9257** or 907/766-2427; fax 907/766-2423; www.seakayaks.com), which offers instruction, short guided trips, longer expeditions, and rentals ($35 a day for a single, plus $20 for getting dropped off somewhere). A half-day guided paddle is $85, including a snack; a full day, including lunch, is $125.

FISHING   There are several charter operators in Haines, for halibut or salmon, or guided freshwater fishing for king and silver salmon, halibut, Dolly Varden, or cutthroat trout. The Haines Convention and Visitors Bureau can help you out, and they maintain a list of operators, their specialties, and how to contact them. Portage Cove Adventure Center (see "Visitor Information," above) offers salmon and halibut charters lasting 4 hours for $80 per person, about as low a price as you'll find in Alaska for an ocean charter. You also can book through **Alaska Mountain Flying and Travel,** also listed under "Visitor Information," above.

☻ FLIGHTSEEING   If you have money for just one flightseeing trip in Alaska, this is one of the best places to choose. The Inside Passage is beautiful, and one mountain away is Glacier Bay National Park; the ice field and the glaciers spilling through to the sea are the sort of sight you never forget. It's possible to land on an immense glacial ice field and see the sun slicing between the craggy peaks. **Alaska Mountain Flying and Travel,** listed above under "Visitor Information," offers these flights; the owner and pilot is known for his glacier and beach landings. Prices range from $89 to $249 per person, and reservations are recommended. **L.A.B. Flying Service,** Main Street and Fourth Avenue (P.O. Box 272), Haines, AK 99827 (☎ **800/426-0543** or 907/766-2222), is a larger operator, offering flights from Haines starting at $105 per person, with discounts for groups.

ACCOMMODATIONS

Many towns have a lot of chainlike hotels and only one or two unique places with character. In Haines, the situation is reversed.

Captain's Choice Motel. North Second Ave. and Dalton St. (P.O. Box 392), Haines, AK 99827. ☎ **800/478-2345** or 907/766-3111. Fax 907/766-3332. www.capchoice.com. 39 units. TV TEL. High season, $104 double, $145 suite. Low season, $76 double. Additional person in room $5 extra. AE, CB, DC, DISC, MC, V.

These trim, red-roofed buildings house the one standard chainlike motel in town, with all the amenities that entails—objectively, probably the best hotel in town, and with a certain amount of charm. The room decor is on the dark side, with paneling, and somewhat out-of-date, but quite clean, and many of the rooms have good views on a large sundeck. More than half are reserved for nonsmokers. Each has a coffeemaker and refrigerator, Showtime movies, a clock radio, and a telephone with a modem port. They offer a courtesy van and rent cars and pickup trucks.

Eagle's Nest Motel. Mile 1 Haines Hwy. (P.O. Box 250), Haines, AK 99827. ☎ **800/ 354-6009** or 907/766-2891. Fax 907/766-2848. 13 unit all with shower only. TV TEL. High season, $85 double, $100 suite. Low season, $60 double, $75 suite. AE, CB, DC, DISC, MC, V.

Although it doesn't look promising from the outside, this motel on the way into town has been recently remodeled inside into bright, modern, no-smoking rooms. The bathrooms lack tubs, with shower stalls instead, but the rooms have Showtime movies, clocks, and radios. They offer a courtesy van and coffee in the lobby.

✪ Fort Seward Bed and Breakfast. 1 Fort Seward Dr. (P.O. Box 5), Haines, AK 99827. ☎ **800/615-NORM** or phone/fax 907/766-2856. www.haines.ak.us/norm. 6 units, 2 with private bathroom. TV. High season, $84–$110 double, $193 suite. Low season, $70 double. Additional person in room $25 extra. Rates include full breakfast. MC, V. Closed Oct 15– Apr 7.

The fort surgeon's quarters overlook the parade grounds and the Lynn Canal with a big wraparound porch and an unspoiled historic feel. Norm Smith has lived in this house most his life and in 1981 started the B&B with his wife, Suzanne, a gifted hostess who instantly makes you feel like an old friend. The rooms have high ceilings, fireplaces, wonderful cabinetry—all kinds of authentic charm. An upstairs suite has a full kitchen and many other extras. It's a social place, with a barbecue on the porch, and guests are welcome to use the kitchen, where Norm produces a fine full breakfast. Smoking is not permitted. They'll pick you up where needed, and free bikes are available for guests.

Hotel Hälsingland. Fort William Seward parade grounds (P.O. Box 1589), Haines, AK 99827. ☎ **800/542-6363** or 907/766-2000. Fax 907/766-2445. www.haines.ak.us/halsingland. 50 units, 45 with private bathroom. TV. $93 double with private bathroom, $59 double without bathroom, $119 suite. AE, DC, DISC, MC, V. Closed mid-Nov to mid-Mar.

There was no need to bring back the historic character of this National Historic Landmark—it has been operating continuously as a hotel in the same family since 1947, a year after it stopped functioning as the commanding officer's quarters at Fort William Seward. Owner Arnie Olsson has worked hard to renew the rooms, however, and his work has paid off in upgrading the huge, white clapboard structure, although some of the furniture still looks not antique but just plain old. Every room is different, so it's wise to choose when you check in. Most, but not all, have telephones; some are priced for backpackers, with fewer amenities. When I stayed in a big, oddly shaped room with a nonworking fireplace and windows on the parade grounds, I felt like I could almost hear the commander walking across the floor in his spurs. A courtesy van and car rental are available, and the hotel serves as a center for tours, buses, and other arrangements.

The **Commander's Room** restaurant has a wide selection of fresh seafood with views of the ocean and parade grounds, and prompt service. It's open for breakfast and

---

Additional Accommodations in Haines

Besides the hotels I've listed, you'll find good economy rooms at **Mountain View Motel,** at Mud Bay Road and Second Avenue (P.O. Box 62), Haines, AK 99827 (☎ **907/766-2900**), in a low-slung, rectangular building, and at **Fort Seward Lodge, Restaurant & Saloon,** nearby in the fort (P.O. Box 307), Haines, AK 99827 (☎ **907/766-2009**), which is in the historic Post Exchange. I've listed three of the best and most centrally located **B&Bs;** for others, inquire at the visitor center.

dinner. The small bar has craft brews on tap. It's a friendly, low-key place in the evening.

A Sheltered Harbor B&B. 57 Beach Rd. (P.O. Box 806), Haines, AK 99827. ☎ or fax **907/766-2741.** E-mail: m_rettinger@yahoo.com. 5 units. TV TEL. High season, $85 double, $115 suite. Low season, $60 double, $115 suite. Rates include full breakfast. AE, MC, V.

Upstairs from a gift shop across the street from the cruise-ship dock, these small, inn-like rooms are a nice surprise once you get inside (the outside is a bit run-down). They're nicely decorated with matching reproduction furniture and all have telephones and TVs, private baths, and entrances—more like a hotel than a typical B&B. The hostess runs a courtesy van. Smoking is not allowed

The Summer Inn Bed and Breakfast. 117 Second Ave. (P.O. Box 1198), Haines, AK 99827. ☎ and fax **907/766-2970.** www.summerinn.wytbear.com. 5 units, none with private bathroom. High season, $80 double, $100 suite. Low season, $70 double, $90 suite. Additional person in room $10 extra. Rates include full breakfast. MC, V.

This lovely old clapboard house downtown has a big porch and living room, decorated in whites and pale, lacy fabrics, like grandma's house. The five rooms are cozy but small, and share three bathrooms among them (bathrooms were immaculate when we last visited). The house was built by a reputed former member of Soapy Smith's gang in 1912 (see Skagway section for more on Soapy). No smoking or drinking is allowed.

DINING

Haines doesn't have a great restaurant, but you can eat well at the Hotel Hälsingland during the summer season (see "Accommodations," above), and there are lots of places for a burger or a slice of pizza. Among the best lunch places is the **Mountain Market & Cafe,** a health-food store at Third Street and the Haines Highway (☎ 907/ 766-3340). A youthful hangout, they serve hearty and reasonably priced sandwiches, wraps, and soups—great for picnics, or stop by for coffee or breakfast. The **Chilkat Restaurant and Bakery,** on Fifth Avenue off Main Street (☎ 907/766-2920), is a bright family restaurant for inexpensive breakfasts and lunches and good bakery items.

The Bamboo Room. Second Ave. near Main St. ☎ **907/766-2800.** Lunch $5.75–$10.75. Dinner $5.75–$23. AE, DC, MC, V. Summer daily 6am–midnight. Winter daily 6am–9pm. DINER/SEAFOOD.

This small restaurant, in the same family for nearly 50 years, was recently rescued from being a smoky adjunct to the bar—it has been divided off by attractive etched glass and made into a first-class diner serving burgers, salads, pasta, and lots of seafood. Many light and healthy items are on the menu along with the solid fried food. This great new incarnation fits a building that started as a French restaurant in the gold rush and then became a brothel and speakeasy before the Teng family got it in 1953. The whole history is on the back of the menu.

Fort Seward Restaurant and Saloon. Mile 0 Haines Hwy., in Fort William Seward. ☎ **907/766-2009.** Lunch $8–$10. Dinner $8–$25. DISC, MC, V. Summer daily 5–10pm. Winter daily 5:30–9pm. STEAK/SEAFOOD.

A favorite of the locals, the restaurant resides in a tall room in the old Post Exchange of the historic fort, where patrons have long speared dollar bills to the ceiling. It's now papered with money. This is a fun place, with a friendly and gregarious staff and partying tradition (although the bar is in a separate room). The food—simple, fresh fish, meat, and vegetables—may be the best in town. The prime rib especially is famous. The full bar has Alaskan microbrews on tap.

The Lighthouse Restaurant and Harbor Bar. Front and Main sts. ☎ **907/766-2442.** Lunch $3.75–$21. Dinner $17.50–$35. AE, MC, V. Summer daily 6am–10pm. Winter daily 6am–9pm.

This is a traditional waterfront place, with better food—charcoal grilled steaks and fish—than you'd expect from the lackluster dining room. The dinner menu is short, but covers the essentials, while lunch includes everything you'd expect in a diner plus steaks and fish. The waterfront views are from the smoking section only.

Port Chilkoot Potlatch Salmon Bake. Fort William Seward parade grounds. ☎ **907/766-2000.** $21.75 per person. AE, DC, DISC, MC, V. Daily 5–8:30pm. Closed Oct–Apr. SALMON BAKE.

Salmon bakes are touristy by nature, but this long-established event is a *good* salmon bake. The sockeye is grilled on alder and not overcooked or ruined with overseasoning. Dining is at picnic tables, either in tents or in the clan house on the parade grounds. After you go through the line, waiters replenish your plate. One glass of beer or wine is included in the price.

SHOPPING

Haines has a few shops of interest, but you must be cautious to avoid counterfeit Native art—see "Native Art—Finding the Real Thing" in chapter 2. **Form and Function Art Gallery,** 211 Willard St., near the visitor center, carries contemporary Chilkat carvings, prints, photography, and beadwork. Artisans often demonstrate. Aside from some Eskimo ivory, **The Wild Iris,** in Fort Seward Building 22, sells only prints, jewelry, and clothing made by its owners, Fred and Madeleine Shields. Fred, a former mayor, also fixes eyeglasses and is good for an entertaining conversation. Madeline, we're told, designed the logo for the David Letterman Show. **Dejon Delights,** on Portage Street, sells excellent local smoked fish and salmon caviar. **King's Store,** at 104 Main St., offers 1-hour photo processing.

13 Skagway: After the Gold Rush

It is only 100 years since white civilization came to Alaska. There were a few scattered towns in Southeast before that—Juneau, Sitka, and Wrangell, for example—but until the Klondike Gold Rush, the great mass of Alaska was populated only by Natives who had never seen a white face, for only a few explorers and prospectors had ever ventured farther. Then, in a single year, 1898, the population exploded. (See "The Gold Rush in Context," in chapter 9.) It still stands as the biggest event in Alaska's short but eventful history, for the flow of people in a few short years set the patterns of development ever since. For Skagway, it created a long-term living based on showing off to visitors the wildest boom town of the era, a true Wild West outpost that in its biggest years was completely without law other than the survival of the meanest. And a good living it's been, for in today's Skagway, more money and more than 10 times as many visitors come through in a year as made the trip to the Klondike during the gold rush.

The tourist rush is the continuation of a 100-year-old phenomenon that's nearly as interesting as the gold rush itself. In 1896 there was a single log cabin in Skagway, in 1897 the word of the Klondike strike made it to the outside world, and in 1898 Skagway was a huge gold rush boomtown. In 1899 the gold rush was ending, and in 1903, 300 tourists arrived in a single day to do the same thing as the thousands who still come. By 1908 local businessmen had started developing their tourist attractions, moving picturesque gold rush buildings to Broadway, the main street, to create a more unified image when visitors arrived on the steamers. By 1920 tourism had become an important part of the economy. By 1933 historic preservation efforts had started. Today, you can see history in Skagway, and you can see the history of history.

With around 800 residents and nearly half a million visitors annually, the "real" town has all but disappeared, and most of the people you'll meet are either fellow visitors or summer workers brought north to serve them. Most of the tourists are from cruise ships—it's not unusual for several ships to hit town in a single morning, unleashing waves of people up the wharf and into the one historic street. But there are plenty of highway and ferry travelers, too, and outdoor enthusiasts come to do the Chilkoot Trail, just as the stampeders did.

Is it worth all those visits? Skagway, spared from fire and recognized so long ago for its history, is probably the best-preserved gold rush town in the United States. What happened here in a 2-year period was certainly extraordinary, even if the phenomenon the town celebrates is one of mass insanity based on greed, inhumanity, thuggery, prostitution, waste, and, for most, abject failure. In 1897 a group of prospectors showed up on the dock in Seattle with steamer trunks full of gold from the Yukon Territory's Klondike River, found the previous year. Even the mayor of Seattle joined the stampede. In the rush years of 1897 and 1898, Skagway or its ghost-town twin city of Dyea were the logical places to get off the boat to head off on the trek to the gold fields near the new city of Dawson. (That fascinating town is covered in chapter 9.) Skagway instantly grew from a single homestead to a population of between 15,000 and 25,000—no one knows exactly how many, in part because the people were flowing through so fast. Dawson City ended up with 30,000.

While Canada was well policed by the Mounties, in Skagway there was no law—a hell on earth, as one Mountie described it. **Soapy Smith,** a con artist turned organized crime boss, ruled the city; the governor offered to put him officially in charge as a territorial marshal and rode with him in the 1898 Independence Day parade. Four days later, Smith was shot dead in a gunfight with Frank Reid, who led a vigilante committee upset over one of Smith's thefts. Reid died of his wounds in the shoot-out, but Smith's gang was broken. Of course, the gold rush was about to end anyway.

In 1976 the National Park Service began buying many of Skagway's best old buildings for the **Klondike Gold Rush National Historic District,** and now it owns about 15. Broadway is a prosperous, freshly painted 6-block strip of gold rush–era buildings, a few of which look like real businesses but turn out to be displays showing how it was back then. Other buildings restored by the Park Service are under lease to real businesses, and still others are just now under restoration. Visitors also can ride the gold rush–era narrow-gauge **White Pass and Yukon Route railroad** into the White Pass, hike the **Chilkoot Trail,** or join in some other, limited outdoor activities.

ESSENTIALS
GETTING THERE
BY FERRY   The **Alaska Marine Highway System** (☎ **907/983-2941** locally, see "Getting Around" at the beginning of this chapter for a full listing), connects Skagway with Haines and Juneau. The fare is $17 to Haines, $30 to Juneau. Or take the more convenient privately operated passenger ferries. The **Haines-Skagway Water Taxi and Scenic Cruise** excursion boat goes to Haines a couple of times a day in summer for $20 one-way, $32 round-trip. In Skagway, the ticket office is at Dejon Delights, Fifth Avenue and Broadway (☎ **907/983-2083**), or you can buy them on board at the boat harbor. The **Chilkat Cruises Haines-Skagway Shuttle Ferry** (☎ **888/766-2103**)

Skagway

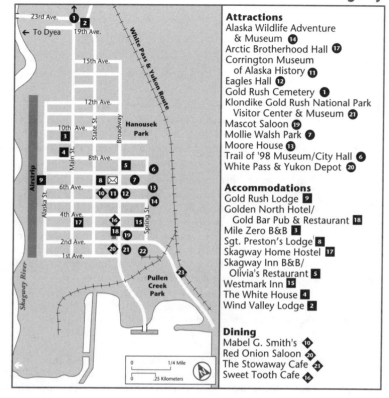

Attractions
Alaska Wildlife Adventure
   & Museum ⑭
Arctic Brotherhood Hall ⑰
Corrington Museum
   of Alaska History ⑪
Eagles Hall ⑫
Gold Rush Cemetery ①
Klondike Gold Rush National Park
   Visitor Center & Museum ㉑
Mascot Saloon ⑲
Mollie Walsh Park ⑦
Moore House ⑬
Trail of '98 Museum/City Hall ⑥
White Pass & Yukon Depot ⑳

Accommodations
Gold Rush Lodge ⑨
Golden North Hotel/
   Gold Bar Pub & Restaurant ⑱
Mile Zero B&B ③
Sgt. Preston's Lodge ⑧
Skagway Home Hostel ⑰
Skagway Inn B&B/
   Olivia's Restaurant ⑤
Westmark Inn ⑮
The White House ④
Wind Valley Lodge ②

Dining
Mabel G. Smith's ⑩
Red Onion Saloon ⑳
The Stowaway Cafe ㉓
Sweet Tooth Cafe ⑯

covers the same route for similar fares. Haines is 15 miles away by boat but more than 350 miles by road.

BY CAR   Since 1978, **Klondike Highway 2** has traced the route of the stampeders through the White Pass, a parallel route to the Chilkoot Trail, into Canada. The road runs 99 miles, then meets the Alaska Highway a dozen miles southeast of the Yukon capital of Whitehorse. The border is at the top of the pass, 14 miles from Skagway. (Information on customs is in chapter 9 in the Alaska Highway section.) This is one of the most spectacular drives anywhere in Alaska. The views are basically equivalent to the White Pass and Yukon Route railway, but a lot cheaper. Do it in clear weather, if possible, as in cloudy weather all you'll see is whiteout. Car rentals are available from **Avis** (☎ 800/331-1212 or 907/983-2247), with an office at the Westmark Inn Skagway, at Third and Spring streets. The **Gold Rush Lodge** (see "Accommodations," below) also has cars for rent. Recreational vehicles are available from **ABC Motorhome Rentals** (☎ 800/421-7456 or 907/279-2000; fax 907/243-6363; www.abcmotorhome.com). You can rent one-way to Anchorage for about $1,400 for a week, plus a $500 drop-off fee.

BY BUS   Two bus lines have daily summer service to Whitehorse, where you can make connections to Anchorage or Fairbanks 3 days a week. Gray Line's **Alaskon Express** (☎ 800/544-2206) stops at the Westmark Inn Skagway, at Third and Spring streets. The fare is $209 to Anchorage. **Alaska Direct Busline** (☎ 800/780-6652) operates the same route, charging $180.

BY AIR   Several air taxi operators serve Skagway. **L.A.B. Flying Service** (☎ 800/ 426-0543 or 907/983-2471) has scheduled flights to Juneau for $96 one-way.

GETTING AROUND

Skagway is laid out on a simple grid, with streets branching off from Broadway. All the main sights can be reached on foot.

BY BIKE   If you want to go to Dyea (2 miles up Klondike Hwy. 2, then 8 miles up a gravel road) or the gold rush graveyard, a bike is a fun way to do it. **Sockeye Cycle,** on Fifth Avenue off Broadway (☎ **907/983-2851;** www.haines.ak.us/sockeye/), rents good mountain bikes for $6 an hour and leads guided day trips (see "Getting Outside," below).

BY TOUR   Many companies offer car, van, or bus tours of Skagway, but none goes to greater lengths for a unique experience than Steve Hites, whose **Skagway Street Car Company,** 270 Second Ave. (P.O. Box 400), Skagway, AK 99840 (☎ **907/ 983-2908**), uses antique touring vehicles with costumed guides who consider their work "theater without walls." The very personal and amusing 2-hour streetcar tour, based on a tour originally given to President Harding, is $35 for adults. Hites also offers a 90-minute van ride up the highway to the White Pass Summit for $29 and a 5-hour tour into the Yukon Territory for $69; children are charged half fare. Hites operates out of his big gift shop with an espresso counter and a theater, where he completes his tour with a slide show—in character, of course. Book the tour at least 2 weeks in advance, as they're always sold out.

VISITOR INFORMATION

In the restored railroad depot, the **National Park Service Visitor Center,** Second Avenue and Broadway (P.O. Box 517), Skagway, AK 99840 (☎ **907/983-2921;** www.nps.gov/klgo), is the focal point for activities in Skagway. Rangers answer questions, give lectures, and show films, and four times a day lead an excellent guided walking tour. The building houses a small museum that lays the groundwork for the rest of what you'll see. Most of the Park Service's programs are free. It's open daily 8am to 6pm from June through August, 8am to 6pm in May and September. It's closed October to April except when ferries are in town, but the park headquarters in the same building is open normal business hours, and the staff there will gladly answer questions or show a film.

The relatively modest **Skagway Convention and Visitors Bureau Center,** 333 Fifth Ave., between Broadway and State Street (P.O. Box 1025), Skagway, AK 99840 (☎ **888/762-1898** or 907/983-2854; fax 907/983-3854; www.skagway.org), offers listings of hotels, restaurants, and activities and an exceptionally informative **Skagway Walking Tour Map** of historic sites. It's the single handiest and most informative historic resource available. The Web site is useful, too. It's open daily 8am to 5pm in the summer, Monday to Friday 8am to 5pm in the winter.

SPECIAL EVENTS

A Mini Folk Festival in April is sponsored by the Skagway Fine Arts Council (☎ 907/983-2276). **Skagway's July 4th Parade and Celebration,** organized by the city, has been a big deal since Soapy Smith led the parade in 1898. It includes an international softball tournament, involving teams from Canada. **The Klondike Road Relay,** a 110-mile overnight foot race over the pass, brings hundreds of runners in teams of 10 from all over the state. It's held in early September. Call the visitor center for information.

Fast Facts: Skagway

Banks   An ATM is at the National Bank of Alaska, on Broadway at Sixth Avenue.

Hospital   The local physicians assistant can be reached at ☎ 907/983-2255 during business hours, or ☎ 907/983-2418 after-hours.

Internet/E-mail   Try the library, at Eighth and State streets.

Police   For nonemergency police business, call ☎ 907/983-2232.

Post Office   On Broadway between Sixth and Seventh avenues.

Taxes   Sales tax is 4%. The bed tax is 8%.

EXPLORING SKAGWAY
TOURING THE HISTORIC PARK

The main thing to do in Skagway is to see the old buildings and historic gold rush places. Do it with the *Skagway Walking Tour Map* or join a fascinating National Park Service guided walking tours (see "Visitor Information" above). Commercial tours are covered above, under "Getting Around."

Start with a visit to the **museum** at the National Park Service Visitor Center and next door. It helps put everything else in context. Of greatest interest is a collection of food and gear similar to the ton of supplies each prospector was required to carry over the pass in order to gain entry into Canada, a requirement that prevented famine among the stampeders, but made the job of getting to Dawson City an epic struggle for each of them.

While they prepared to go over the pass, gold rush greenhorns spent their time in Skagway drinking and getting fleeced in the many gambling dens and brothels. Nothing was against the law in the town's heyday because there was no civil authority. It's at times hard to picture, because now everything looks so orderly, but the Park Service has tried. For example, the **Mascot Saloon,** at Broadway and Third Avenue, has statues bellying up to the bar. It's open daily from 8am to 5pm and admission is free.

The Park Service recently completed restoration of the 1897 **Moore House,** near Fifth Avenue and Spring Street, and leads free tours there on family life during the gold rush (1pm to 5pm during the summer). Ten years before it happened, Captain William Moore brilliantly predicted that the gold rush would occur, and so homesteaded the land Skagway would be built on, knowing that this would be a key staging area. He built a cabin in 1887, which stands nearby. But when the rush occurred, the stampeders simply ignored his property claims and built the city on his land without offering compensation. Years later, he won in court.

A block east, on Sixth Avenue, is **Mollie Walsh Park,** with a good children's play area, public rest rooms, and phones. A sign tells the sad story of Skagway's first respectable woman, who chose to marry the wrong man among two suitors and was killed by him in a drunken rage. The other suitor—who'd previously killed another rival for her affections—commissioned the bust of Walsh that stands at the park. Another block east is Skagway's most beautiful building, the 1900 granite city hall and jail. Outside is a display of railroad cars, with informative historical markers, and by the summer of 2000 the museum (above) should have moved into the building.

The **Gold Rush Cemetery** is 1½ miles from town, up State Street. Used until 1908, it's small and overgrown with spruce trees, but some of the charm and mystery of the place are lost because of the number of visitors and the shiny new paint and maintenance of the wooden markers. The graves of Soapy Smith and Frank Reid are the big attractions, but don't miss the short walk up to Reid Falls. A map is available at the visitor center. The closely spaced dates on many of the markers attest to the epidemics that swept through stampeders living in squalid conditions. Remember, there was no sanitation for the tens of thousands who passed this way in 1898.

About 9 miles north of Skagway (on a lovely drive or bike ride 2 miles up Klondike Highway 2 and then 8 miles on a gravel road) is the ghost town of **Dyea,** where stampeders started climbing the Chilkoot Trail. It's a lot more ghost than town—all that remains are a few boards, broken dock pilings, and miscellaneous iron trash. But on a sunny day, the protected historical site is a perfect place for a picnic, among beach grasses, wild iris, and the occasional reminder that a city once stood here. The National Park Service leads a guided history and nature walk once a week; check at the visitor center. (See "Getting Outside," below, for other ideas on going to Dyea.)

The little-visited **Slide Cemetery,** in the woods near Dyea, is the last resting place of many of the 60 to 70 men who died in an avalanche on the Chilkoot Trail on Palm Sunday, April 3, 1898. No one knows how many are here, or exactly who died, or how accurate the wooden markers are. In 1960, when the state reopened the Chilkoot Trail, the cemetery had been completely overgrown, and the markers were replaced. But somehow the mystery and forgetting make it an even more ghostly place, and the sense of anonymous, hopeless hardship and death it conveys is as authentic a gold rush souvenir as anything in Skagway.

MUSEUMS & ATTRACTIONS

The White Pass and Yukon Route. Second Ave. depot (P.O. Box 435, Dept. B), Skagway, AK 99840. ☎ **800/343-7373** or 907/983-2217. www.whitepassrailroad.com.

A narrow-gauge railroad line that originally ran to Whitehorse, the White Pass was completed after only 2 years in 1900. It's an engineering marvel and a fun way to see spectacular, historic scenery. Tickets are expensive, however, and I wouldn't recommend going in bad weather, when the pass is socked in and all you'll see out the window are white clouds. Also, they tell you not to get out of your seat (although many people do), and children may have a hard time sitting still that long. The ride begins at a depot with the spine-tingling sound of a working steam engine's whistle. The steamer pulls the train a couple of miles, then diesels take the cars—some of them originals more than 100 years old—up steep tracks that were chipped out of the side of the mountains. The summit excursion—which travels 20 miles with an elevation gain of 2,865 feet, then turns back—takes about 3 hours and costs $78. Children are charged half price. The biggest treat for train lovers is an 8-hour all-steam-powered round-trip to Lake Bennett, where the stampeders launched their boats for the trip to Dawson City. Only six departures are planned annually, and the fare is $156. Lunch at Lake Bennett is included. A Lake Bennett trip by diesel engine happens Thursday through Monday weekly for $128, and includes a walking tour at the lake. You can get all the way to Whitehorse on a train that meets a bus, for a $95 fare, one-way. These days, the line operates only as a tourist attraction, closing down mid-September through mid-May. Make reservations at least a month ahead.

Trail of '98 Historical Museum and Archives. On Broadway between Second and Third aves. (see note on location below). ☎ **907/983-2420.** Admission $2 adults, $1 students and children. Summer, daily 9am–5pm. Winter, by appointment only.

In the building with the driftwood facade on Broadway, the museum contains Skagway's best collection of gold rush artifacts, including Soapy Smith's bloody tie, worn on the day of his fatal gunfight. Most of it is well explained in labels. Although cramped in the historic Arctic Brotherhood Hall, the museum contains enough to hold your interest for an hour or two. If plans come about as hoped, the museum will move back to its former and more fitting quarters at Seventh and Spring streets by summer 2000.

Alaska Wildlife Adventure and Museum. Fourth and Spring sts. ☎ **907/983-3600.** Admission $9.50 adults, $8.50 seniors, $5 children under 12. Summer, daily 9am–6pm. Closed winter.

This unique business contains an amazing collection of miscellaneous memorabilia from the long Alaska lives of Bob and Anna Groff and an immense display of their animal mounts in a room built for the purpose. Bob shows you around, and he is a museum-quality example of the solid, friendly, old-time Alaskan type.

Corrington Museum of Alaska History. Fifth Ave. and Broadway, in Corrington's gift shop. Free admission. Mid-May to mid-Sept 9am–7pm. Closed winter. Admission free.

The eclectic and often impressive exhibit that leads into the gift shop is well worth a stop. Besides owning some interesting items, they've done a good job of putting it together in an understandable way.

GETTING OUTSIDE

BACKPACKING The National Park Service and Parks Canada jointly manage the famous **Chilkoot Pass Trail,** publishing a trail guide and offering information at their offices in Skagway and Whitehorse. Some 20,000 stampeders used the trail to get from Dyea—9 miles from Skagway—to Lake Bennett, 33 miles away, where they could launch boats bound for Dawson City. Today about 3,000 people a year make the challenging hike, taking 3 to 5 days. The Chilkoot is not so much a wilderness trail as an outdoor museum, but don't underestimate it, as so many did during the gold rush. To control the numbers, **Parks Canada,** 205-300 Main St., Whitehorse, Yukon Y1A 2B5 Canada (☎ **800/661-0486;** fax 867/393-6701), allows only 50 with permits hikers a day to cross the summit. To buy the $10 permits, call with a Visa or MasterCard and the date you plan to start. If you mail the money, your reservation isn't guaranteed till it arrives. Eight of the 50 daily permits are held for walk-ins, but I wouldn't count on getting one of those. Once over the pass, you're on Lake Bennett, on the rail line 8 miles short of the road. You can get back to Skagway on the White Pass and Yukon Route railway (see "Museums & Activities," above), which runs twice daily, 5 days a week June through August. The one-way fare for the scenic 3-hour ride is $65 adults, $32.50 children. Be certain to make your reservations in advance.

There are two **U.S. Forest Service cabins** near Skagway, and official access to both is by the White Pass and Yukon Route railway. Both are on trails described in the *Skagway Trail Map,* mentioned below. One cabin is an old White Pass caboose parked next to the tracks 6 miles up the line at the trailhead for the 4.5-mile **Denver Glacier Trail.** Another cabin is 1½ miles off the track, 14 miles up on the spectacular **Lawton Glacier Trail.** For either you need a $35 cabin permit (see "Outside in Southeast," at the start of this chapter, for reservations information) and a train ticket from the railroad. For details, contact the National Park Service visitor center (see above), or the **Juneau Ranger District,** 8465 Old Dairy Rd., Juneau, AK 99801 (☎ **907/ 586-8800;** www.fs.fed.us/r10/tongass/).

BIKING Sockeye Cycle, on Fifth Avenue off Broadway (☎ **907/983-2851**), leads bike tours, including one that takes clients to the top of the White Pass in a van and coasts down on bikes; the 2-hour trip is $69. They also lead a tour of the quiet townsite of Dyea for $69, going over in a van. I rode to Dyea from Skagway on my own over the hilly, 9-mile coastal road, one of the loveliest and most pleasant rides I can remember.

HIKING   A *Skagway Trail Map* is available from the visitor center, listing 11 hikes around Skagway. An easy evening walk starts at the suspension footbridge at the north end of First Avenue, crossing the Skagway River to **Yakutania Point Park,** where pine trees grow from cracks in the rounded granite of the shoreline. Across the park is a shortcut taking a couple of miles off the trip to Dyea and to the **Skyline Trail and A.B. Mountain,** a strenuous climb to a 3,500-foot summit with great views. On the southern side of town, across the railroad tracks, a network of trails heads up from Spring Street between Third and Fourth avenues to a series of mountain lakes, the closest of which is **Lower Dewey Lake,** less than a mile up the trail.

HORSEBACK RIDING   **Chilkoot Horseback Adventures** leads half-day horseback tours of Dyea and West Creek Glacier for $109, booked through Southeast Tours at Fifth Avenue and Broadway (☎ **800/478-2990** or 907/983-2990).

FLIGHTSEEING   Skagway, like Haines, is a good place to choose for a flightseeing trip, as Glacier Bay National Park is just to the west. **L.A.B. Flying Service,** listed above under "Getting There," is one of several companies offering fixed-wing service; **Mountain Flying Service** (☎ **800/954-8747** or ☎ and fax 907/766-2665; www. haines.ak.us/mtnfly/) is a good smaller operator. Expect to pay $120 to $280 per person. **Temsco Helicopters** (☎ **877/789-9501** or 907/983-2900; www.tescoair. com) takes 55-minute tours over the Chilkoot Trail and lands on a glacier for 25 minutes; those flights cost $160.

ACCOMMODATIONS

All the accommodations in Skagway are close walking distance to the historic district, except as noted. I cannot recommend the **Westmark Inn Skagway.** Although by far the largest and most expensive hotel in town, I found the rooms lacking.

Gold Rush Lodge. Sixth Ave. and Alaska St. (P.O. Box 514), Skagway, AK 99840. ☎ **877/ 983-3509** or 907/983-2831. Fax 907/983-2742. www.AlaskaOne.com/goldrush. 12 units, all with shower only. TV TEL. High season, $80–$105 double. Low season, $65–$75 double. Additional person in room $10 extra. AE, DISC, MC, V.

This is a clean, comfortable motel by the airstrip 3 blocks from the historic district, with a grassy picnic area out back. The rooms are on the small side but modern and attractively decorated in light colors, and have clocks, fans, coffeemakers, hair dryers, and HBO. Bathrooms have shower stalls, no tubs. The hosts provide fruit, coffee, and a cookie jar in the lobby, writing the guests' names and hometowns on an erasable board so they can get to know each other. They offer a courtesy car and rent cars for $50 a day. Smoking is prohibited.

Golden North Hotel. Third Ave. and Broadway (P.O. Box 343), Skagway, AK 99840. ☎ **888/222-1898** or 907/983-2294. Fax 907/983-2755. www.alaskan.com/goldenorth. 31 units, 27 with private bathroom. TEL. $100–$115 double, $75 double with shared bathroom. Additional person in room $15 extra. Rates include continental breakfast. AE, DISC, MC, V.

This big, yellow landmark on Broadway was built in 1898 and is Alaska's oldest operating hotel. It's a fun place to stay. New owners spent $1.6 million to restore the creaking wooden building while keeping its campy character intact, including the placards in each room about a different gold rush family and the big claw-footed tubs. Ask for the bathroom configuration you want, as eight rooms have showers only, two have shower-tub combinations, and the balance have only tubs. Four rooms share bathrooms. A courtesy car is available, and a continental breakfast comes with the price of the room. At street level, the **Gold Bar Pub & Restaurant/Skagway Brewing Company** is a good spot for lunch and dinner, with a diverse American menu and

---

Additional Accommodations in Skagway

In addition to the accommodations listed, you'll find good standard rooms, reasonably priced and about a mile from the sights, at **Wind Valley Lodge,** 22nd Avenue and State Street (P.O. Box 354), Skagway, AK 99840 (☎ **907/983-2236;** fax 907/983-2957).

---

tasteful, old-timey decor that makes it a good family choice, plus a raft of fine home-brewed beer that'll please the adults. In the summer, there's also a salmon bake.

Historic Skagway Inn Bed and Breakfast. Seventh Ave. and Broadway (P.O. Box 500), Skagway, AK 99840. ☎ **800/SKAGWAY** or 907/983-2289. Fax 907/983-2713. www. skagwayinn.com. 12 units, none with bathroom. High season, $95–$115 double. Low season, $75–$90 double. AE, DISC, MC, V.

Built in 1897, this cute little Victorian inn has frilly rooms ranging from small single bedrooms to a large front room, above the street, with a porch. There are six bathrooms for the 12 guest rooms, and they're kept immaculate. The lobby is a welcoming parlor full of books where guests visit over tea. A courtesy van and a kennel are available. A full breakfast is served in the windowed dining room, which at night becomes **Olivia's,** an intimate fine dining establishment. With only seven tables, guests can't help feeling special. The sometimes creative menu emphasizes fresh local seafood and garden produce. Reservations are required.

Mile Zero Bed & Breakfast. Ninth Ave. and Main St. (P.O. Box 165), Skagway, AK 99840. ☎ **907/983-3045.** Fax 907/983-3046. www.bbonline.com/ak/milezero. 7 units. TEL. High season, $105 double; additional person in room $25 extra. Low season, $70 double; additional person in room $20 extra. AE, MC, V.

In 1995, Howard and Judy Mallory specially built this place to be a B&B, and they thought of everything. The large, immaculate rooms all have private bathrooms, telephone lines, and two entrances, from an internal hall and through French doors that lead to a porch. It's an exceptional place, located a few blocks from the historic area. Continental breakfast is served in a large common room, and they'll pick you up at the ferry and lend you a bicycle free of charge. Smoking is not allowed, and there are no televisions.

Sgt. Preston's Lodge. Sixth Ave. and State St. (P.O. Box 538), Skagway, AK 99840. ☎ **907/ 983-2521.** Fax 907/983-3500. E-mail: sgt-prestons@usa.net. 30 units. TV TEL. High season, $75–$85 double. Low season, $50–$55. AE, CB, DC, DISC, MC, V.

Set in several motel-style buildings on a grassy compound, many of the rooms are large and clean; and eight of the newer rooms, reserved for nonsmokers, are huge and light with high ceilings—quite a bargain for the price. The smoking rooms, where pets are allowed, are less appealing. Seven rooms have shower stalls, and the balance of the rooms has tub-shower combinations or even in-room Jacuzzis. They offer a courtesy car.

The White House. Corner of Eighth and Main sts. (P.O. Box 41), Skagway, AK 99840-0041. ☎ **907/983-9000.** Fax 907/983-9010. www.skagway.com/whitehouse. 10 units. TV TEL. High season, $99–$120. Low season, $75–$85. Additional person in room $10 extra. AE, DISC, MC, V.

The Tronrud family essentially rebuilt a burned 1902 gable-roofed inn, which has dormer and bow windows and two porticos with small Doric columns. They made the rooms comfortable and modern while retaining the style of the original owner, the most successful saloon owner of the gold rush years. The inn has hardwood floors and fine woodwork. Bedrooms vary in size, but all have the owner's homemade quilts on the beds, TVs, phones with direct lines, clock-radios, and ceiling fans, and all but one has a shower-tub combination in the bathroom. A full breakfast is included in the price, as is the bottomless cookie jar, tea and coffee, and the courtesy van.

HOSTELS & CAMPSITES

There's a free **National Park Service campground** at Dyea, with well-separated sites near the water. For recreational vehicles, there are plenty of parks in Skagway; the city maintains one at the small-boat harbor.

Skagway Home Hostel. Third Ave. near Main St. (P.O. Box 231), Skagway, AK 99840. ☎ **907/983-2131.** 2 private rooms, neither with bathroom; 3 dorms. $15 per bunk; $40 double private room.

Frank Wasmer and Nancy Schave have really opened up their historic home to hostelers, sharing their meals, refrigerator, bathrooms, laundry machines, bicycles, and hospitality side by side with guests. The atmosphere is like off-campus shared housing at college, except the house is nicer and better kept. Bunks are in separate male and female dorm rooms. To reserve, you have to send the money ahead—they don't return long-distance calls. In winter, reservations are required, as Frank and Nancy might otherwise not be there. Summer registration hours are 5:30 to 10:30pm. No pets, alcohol, or smoking.

DINING

Restaurants go out of business and open up faster in Skagway's fully seasonal economy than anywhere else I know, so you may need ask around for a current recommendation. Among the places I can currently recommend, two are mentioned above (see "Accommodations"): the brew pub at **Golden North Hotel,** and **Olivia's,** in the Historic Skagway Inn.

Stop off for espresso and baked goods at **Mabel G. Smith's** (☎ **907/983-2609**), a bakery, card, and coffee shop on Fifth Avenue off Broadway.

The Stowaway Cafe. End of Second St. near the small boat harbor. ☎ **907/983-3463.** Reservations recommended. Dinner $7.75–$22.50. Summer daily 4–10pm; spring and fall Fri–Sun only. Closed winter. SEAFOOD/CAJUN

In a small, gray clapboard house overlooking the boat harbor; also a 5-minute walk from the historic sites, Jim and Kim Long's 20-seat restaurant is a labor of love—they met here, then married and bought the place. Jim expertly cooks the grilled and blackened salmon and halibut that anchor the menu; there's also beef, pasta, and all the usual waterfront restaurant items. Service is almost too fast. The tiny dining room is decorated with a miscellaneous collection of knickknacks that will keep your attention almost as well as the harbor view. Avoid the alcove in the back, however, where you're out of the flow and lose the view. Lunch is available as takeout only. They have a beer and wine license.

Sweet Tooth Cafe. 315 Broadway. ☎ **907/983-2405.** Lunch $5.75–$7. Dinner $7.50–$13.50. MC, V. Summer daily 6am–7pm. Winter 6am–2pm. DINER

One of Skagway's few year-round restaurants, the Sweet Tooth makes it through the winter with good, simple food, quick service, reasonable prices, and hearty portions. A salmon dinner is only $13.25, and comes with their exceptional homemade soup. The dining room is light and keeps with the town's quaint theme. It often stays open later than the posted hours in the summer. Alcoholic beverages are not available.

SHOPPING

With almost 100 years of experience, Skagway knows how to do gift shops, and now has more than 50. Of course, most are closed in winter, as the town has only about 800 year-round residents. And, as always, you must be cautious about counterfeits when buying Native artwork (see "Native Art—Finding the Real Thing," in chapter 2).

Corrington's, at Fifth and Broadway, is a large gift store with an entire free museum attached (see "Museums & Attractions," above). **Lynch and Kennedy,** at Fourth Avenue and Broadway, is in a building owned and restored by the National Park Service and leased to the current gift store; it carries fine art, jewelry, and high-quality gifts. **Inside Passage Arts,** on Broadway between Fourth and Fifth avenues, is a gallery of Alaska Native fine art.

SKAGWAY IN THE EVENING

Incredibly, the *Days of '98 Show* has been playing since 1927 in the Fraternal Order of Eagles Hall No. 25, at Sixth Avenue and Broadway (☎ **907/983-2545**). Jim Richards carries on the tradition each summer with actors imported from all over the United States. The evening shows begin at 7pm with mock gambling at a casino run by the actors. The performance, at 8:30pm, includes singing, cancan dancing, a Robert Service reading, and the story of the shooting of Soapy Smith. Matinees are $12, and evening shows are $14; senior citizens pay $2 less, and children are charged half price.

The **Red Onion Saloon,** at Second Avenue and Broadway, is an authentic-feeling old bar that often has terrific live jazz and other styles of music, but the players sometimes jump up suddenly and leave—they're cruise-ship musicians who enjoy coming here to stretch out and jam, and they can't afford to miss the boat. It was a brothel originally (what wasn't?); look in the upstairs windows. **Mel's Frontier Bar,** at Fifth Avenue and Broadway, is more of a gritty local hangout.

6 Anchorage & Environs

As teenagers living in Anchorage, my cousin and I got a job from a family friend painting his lake cabin. He flew us out on his floatplane and left us there, with paint, food, and a little beer. There was a creek that ran past the lake so full of salmon that we caught one on every cast until we got bored and started thinking of ways to make it more difficult. We cooked the salmon over a fire, then floated in a boat on the lake under the endless sunshine of a summer night, talking and diving naked into the clear, green water. We met some guys building another cabin one day, but otherwise we saw no other human beings. When the week was over, the cabin was painted—it didn't take long— and the floatplane came back to get us. As we lifted off and cleared the trees, Anchorage opened in front of us, barely 10 minutes away.

The state's largest city, Anchorage—where 40% of Alaska's population resides—is accused crushingly of being just like a city outside, not really part of Alaska at all. It's true that the closer you get to Anchorage, the more the human development reminds you of the outskirts of any town in the United States, with fast-food franchises, occasional traffic jams, and the ugly big-box retail development inflicted everywhere by relentless corporate logic. You often here the joke, "Anchorage isn't Alaska, but it's close," and writers piously warn visitors to land in Anchorage but move on as soon as possible, as if it's catching.

When I hear that advice, I think of the many great experiences I've had here—like painting that cabin, years ago. Anyone in Anchorage with a few hundred dollars for a floatplane can be on a lake or river with the bears and salmon in a matter of minutes, in wilderness deeper than any you could find in the Lower 48. **Chugach State Park** is largely within city limits—it's the size of Rocky Mountain National Park, and has similar alpine terrain, with the critical difference that most of it is virtually never visited. From a downtown hotel, you can be climbing those mountains in half an hour. **Chugach National Forest,** the nation's second largest, is less than an hour down the road. In downtown's **Ship Creek,** people catch 40-pound salmon from under a freeway bridge. Even within the city, you can bike dozens of miles along the coast or through wooded greenbelts, or ski in one of the nation's best Nordic skiing parks. Anchorage is indeed a big American city, with big city problems of crime and pollution, but it's also entirely unique for being surrounded by pristine and spectacular wild lands. Anywhere else, it would be an outdoors mecca.

A LITTLE HISTORY

Anchorage isn't old enough to have a sharp identity as a city—its first generation is just now passing away. Anchorage started as a tent camp for workers mobilized to build the Alaska Railroad in 1915. A grid was laid out north and south of Ship Creek, and lots were sold at auction. A few houses and businesses went up to serve the federal employees who were building and later running the railroad, as Steve McCutcheon's father did. McCutcheon, who died in 1998, remembered a remote, sleepy railroad town, enlivened by World War II and the construction of a couple of large military bases, but never more than strictly functional. As one visitor who came in the early 1940s wrote, the entire town looked like it was built on the wrong side of the tracks.

A couple of years ago, McCutcheon looked out the picture window from his living room on a placid lake surrounded by huge, half-million-dollar houses, each with a floatplane pulled up on the green front lawn, and he recalled the year people started to take Anchorage seriously. It was the year, he said, when they started thinking it would be a permanent city, not just an encampment where you went for a few years to make money before moving on—the year they started building Anchorage to last. That year was 1957. Oil was discovered on the Kenai Peninsula's Swanson River, south of here. It was around that time that McCutcheon built his own house, far out in the country with no neighbors anywhere in the area, all alone on a lake. At that time, you could homestead in the Anchorage bowl. Those who had the opportunity but chose not to—my wife's family, for example—gave it a pass only because it seemed improbable that the flat, wet acreage way out of town would ever be worth anything.

Oil grew Anchorage like nitrogen fertilizer poured on a shooting weed. Those homesteads that went begging in the 1950s and early 1960s now have shopping malls and high-rise office buildings on them. Fortunes came fast, development was haphazard, and a lot was built that we'd all soon regret. I had the bizarre experience of coming home from college to the town I'd grown up in and getting completely lost in a large area of the city that had been nothing but moose browse the last time I'd seen it. Visitors found a city full of life, but empty of charm.

In the last 15 years, that has started to change. Anchorage is slowly outgrowing its gawky adolescence. It's still young, prosperous, and vibrant—and exhausting, at times, when the summer sun refuses to set—but now it also has some excellent restaurants, a good museum, a new Native cultural center and a nice little zoo, and things to do in the evening besides the tourist melodramas you'll find in every Alaska town. People still complain that Anchorage isn't really Alaska—in Fairbanks, they call it "Los Anchorage" (and in Anchorage, Fairbanks is known as "Squarebanks")—yet the great wilderness around the city remains intertwined with its streets. Along with a quarter million people, Anchorage is full of moose—so many, they're becoming pests and wintertime hazards, inspiring debate on having a hunting season in city limits. Bears and bald eagles also show up in town, though less frequently, on the system of greenbelts and bike trails that brings the woods into almost every neighborhood.

Anchorage stands between the Chugach Mountains and the silt-laden waters of upper Cook Inlet. The site of the city is broad and flat; it's mostly built on sediment. At the water's edge, mud flats of the same material, not yet made into land, stretch far offshore when the tide is at its low point, up to 38 vertical feet below high water. There's a **downtown area** of about 8-by-20 blocks, near Ship Creek where it all started, but the rest of the city spreads some 5 miles east and 15 miles south along broad commercial strips and freeway frontages. Like many cities in the western United States built in the era of the car, the layout is not particularly conducive to any other form of transportation. But the city's boundaries go even farther, far beyond the reach

Anchorage

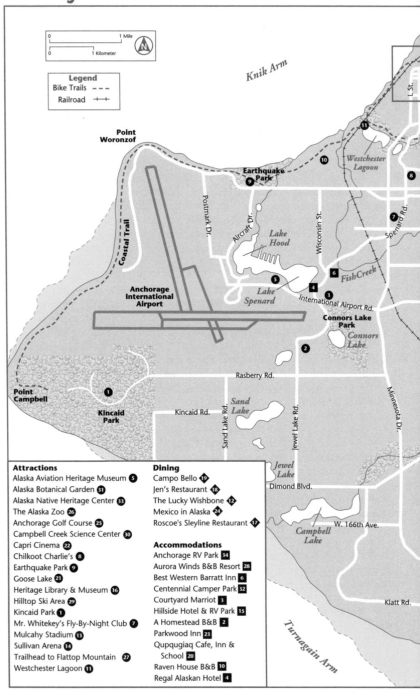

Legend
Bike Trails – – –
Railroad ┼┼┼

Attractions
Alaska Aviation Heritage Museum 5
Alaska Botanical Garden 31
Alaska Native Heritage Center 33
The Alaska Zoo 26
Anchorage Golf Course 25
Campbell Creek Science Center 30
Capri Cinema 22
Chilkoot Charlie's 8
Earthquake Park 9
Goose Lake 21
Heritage Library & Museum 16
Hilltop Ski Area 29
Kincaid Park 1
Mr. Whitekey's Fly-By-Night Club 7
Mulcahy Stadium 13
Sullivan Arena 14
Trailhead to Flattop Mountain 27
Westchester Lagoon 11

Dining
Campo Bello 19
Jen's Restaurant 18
The Lucky Wishbone 12
Mexico in Alaska 24
Roscoe's Sleyline Restaurant 17

Accommodations
Anchorage RV Park 34
Aurora Winds B&B Resort 28
Best Western Barratt Inn 6
Centennial Camper Park 32
Courtyard Marriot 3
Hillside Hotel & RV Park 15
A Homestead B&B 2
Parkwood Inn 23
Qupqugiaq Cafe, Inn & School 20
Raven House B&B 10
Regal Alaskan Hotel 4

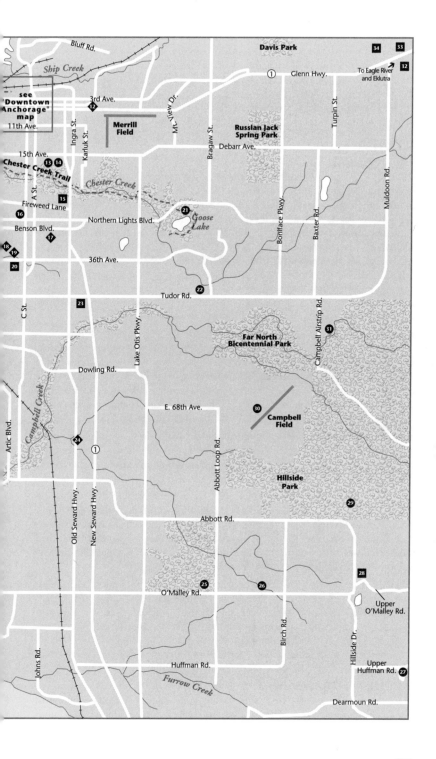

Bluff Rd.

Davis Park

34 33

Ship Creek

① Glenn Hwy. 32

To Eagle River and Eklutra

see "Downtown Anchorage" map

11th Ave.

3rd Ave. 12

Ingra St.

Karluk St.

Mt. View Dr.

Bragaw St.

Merrill Field

Russian Jack Spring Park

Turpin St.

Debarr Ave.

15th Ave. 13 14

Chester Creek Trail

A St.

Chester Creek

Muldoon Rd.

Fireweed Lane 15

16

Benson Blvd. 17

21 Goose Lake

Boniface Pkwy.

Baxter Rd.

Northern Lights Blvd.

18 19

20

36th Ave.

Tudor Rd. 22

C St.

23

Campbell Airstrip Rd.

31

Far North Bicentennial Park

Dowling Rd.

Campbell Creek

E. 68th Ave.

30 Campbell Field

Artic Blvd.

24

①

Old Seward Hwy.

New Seward Hwy.

Abbott Loop Rd.

Hillside Park

29

Abbott Rd.

28

25

26

O'Malley Rd.

Birch Rd.

Upper O'Malley Rd.

Hillside Dr.

Johns Rd.

Huffman Rd.

Furrow Creek

Upper Huffman Rd. 27

Dearmoun Rd.

191

of cars, taking in the Chugach, Turnagain Arm all the way to Portage, and even reaching over to Prince William Sound. Most of that land is there only to be explored. I can't say for sure if all the mountain peaks in the municipality have been climbed, and far from all have been named.

This chapter also includes coverage of the suburbs in the Matanuska and Susitna valleys and beyond.

ESSENTIALS
GETTING THERE
BY AIR   You'll probably get to Anchorage at the start of your trip by air, as it has by far the most flights linking Alaska to the rest of the world on many airlines. The **Anchorage International Airport** is a major hub. Flights connect the city to Asia and the Russian Far East, but Seattle has the most frequent flights, with numerous domestic carriers flying nonstop all day. Within Alaska, most flights route through Anchorage, even for communities that are much closer to each other than either is to Anchorage. **Alaska Airlines** (☎ **800/426-0333;** www.alaskaair.com) is the dominant carrier for Alaska destinations, and the only jet operator to most Alaska cities. Various commuter carriers link Anchorage to rural destinations not served by jet. **Era Aviation** (☎ **800/866-8394** or 907/266-8394) is one of the largest for Southcentral Alaska destinations and can be booked through Alaska Airlines.

GETTING INTO TOWN FROM THE AIRPORT   The **Borealis Shuttle** charge $6 to go downtown from the airport (☎ **907/276-3600**), picking up frequently at the domestic terminal; they drop off and pick up passengers anywhere in town. The **People Mover** city bus system (☎ **907/343-6543**) goes to the airport weekdays only, and on most runs you have to transfer to get downtown; it takes quite a while. Taxis are expensive in Anchorage because of the spread-out urban design. A ride downtown from the airport runs about $14. Try **Alaska Cab** (☎ **907/563-5353**).

BY CAR   There's only one road to the rest of the world: the Glenn Highway, which reaches an intersection with the Parks Highway 30 miles out of town. The Glenn continues to Glennallen, Tok, and the Alaska Highway, 330 miles from Anchorage (see chapter 9). The Parks Highway goes to Denali National Park and Fairbanks. The other road out of town, the Seward Highway, leads south to the Kenai Peninsula.

BY BUS   Gray Line's **Alaskon Express** (☎ **800/544-2206** or 907/277-5581) links Anchorage to Seward, Valdez, Denali National Park, and down the Alaska Highway to Haines and Skagway. The fare is about $200 to Haines or Skagway. Other small vans and buses go to Seward, Homer, Fairbanks, and Denali National Park; see the sections on each of those places for details.

BY RV   A recreational vehicle is a popular way to explore the region, and you can rent one-way from the ferry in Skagway or Haines with a $500 drop-off fee. High-season rates are around $1,400 a week, plus the large amount of fuel you use. Major agencies include **ABC Motorhome Rentals,** 3853 W. International Airport Rd., Anchorage, AK 99502 (☎ **800/421-7456** or 907/279-2000; fax 907/243-6363; www.alaskan.com/abcmotorhomes/), and **Cruise America,** 10560 Old Seward Hwy., Anchorage, AK 99515 (☎ **800/327-7799** or 907/349-0499).

BY RAIL   The **Alaska Railroad** (☎ **800/544-0552** or 907/265-2494; www.akrr. com) connects Anchorage to Seward to the south and to Fairbanks and Denali National Park to the north. The run to Seward, which operates only in the summer, is incredibly spectacular; the fare is $50 one-way, $86 round-trip, children ages 2 to 11 half off. Heading north, you can ride the Alaska Railroad cars year-round 12 hours to Fairbanks (the summer fare is $154 one-way), and in the summer to Denali ($102), or take full-dome cars with Princess Tours or Holland America–Westours. For details, see chapter 8 on Denali National Park.

ORIENTATION

Navigating Anchorage is easy if you just remember that the mountains are to the east. Maps are available at the visitor centers or in any grocery store.

Many visitors never make it beyond the **downtown** area, the old-fashioned grid of streets at the northwest corner of town where the large hotels and the gift shops are located. Street numbers and letters work on a simple pattern. Beyond downtown, most of Anchorage is oriented to commercial strips. Three major north-south thoroughfares run from downtown, through the **midtown** commercial area, to the shopping malls and residential districts of **South Anchorage.** These are **Minnesota Drive,** which becomes I and L streets downtown; **C Street** and **A Street;** and the **New Seward Highway,** which is Ingra and Gambell streets downtown and heads out of town to the south. Major east-west roads in the grid are Fifth and Sixth avenues, becoming the **Glenn Highway** and leading out of town to the north; **Northern Lights Boulevard** and **Benson Boulevard** running across the city in midtown; and **Dimond Boulevard,** in South Anchorage. Some parts of Anchorage are outside the bowl defined by the Chugach Mountains. The communities of **Eagle River** and **Eklutna** are out the Glenn Highway, to the northeast; go a little farther that way and you reach the **Matanuska Valley. Girdwood** and **Portage** are on the Seward Highway, to the south.

GETTING AROUND

BY RENTAL CAR   Most major car-rental companies operate in Anchorage, at the airport or at other locations in town. An economy car costs about $55 a day, with unlimited mileage. Book well in advance in the summer high season.

BY BUS   Bus fare all over town on the People Mover city bus system (☎ **907/ 343-6543**) is $1, but there is a free zone in the downtown core. The transit center bus depot is at Sixth Avenue and G Street. Buses generally come every half hour but are less frequent on weekends.

BY BIKE   A bike is a great way to explore, using the network of bike trails. The **Tony Knowles Coastal Trail** comes right downtown (see "Special Places" under "Getting Outside," below). Bikes are for rent 2 blocks away from **Adventure Café,** at 414 K St. (☎ **907/276-8282**), a couple of blocks east (they also serve espresso, vegetarian soups, and sandwiches). They charge $15 for 3 hours. **The Bicycle Shop,** in midtown at 1035 W. Northern Lights Blvd. (☎ **907/272-5219**), rents and services a wide selection of bikes, with weekly rentals available.

BY TOUR   City tours are available from many operators; check with the visitor center to take your choice. The best downtown tour is the historic walking tour described below under "A Stroll Around Downtown Anchorage." **Anchorage City Trolley Tours** (☎ **907/257-5603**) offers hourly tours in buses that have been made to look like San Francisco streetcars from 612 W. Fourth Ave., near the Fourth Avenue Theater, charging only $10. They leave every hour from 9am to 6pm during the summer. Their David and Goliath conflict with the owner of the theater, who built an identical trolley to compete with them, has fascinated Anchorage for several years.

VISITOR INFORMATION

The **Anchorage Convention and Visitor Bureau,** 524 W. Fourth Ave., Anchorage, AK 99501-2212 (☎ **907/276-4118;** fax 907/278-5559; www.anchorage.net), operates five visitor information centers, distributing brochures and providing guidance for the whole state. The main location is the **Log Cabin Visitor Information Center,** downtown at Fourth Avenue and F Street (☎ 907/274-3531; fax 907/272-9564). It's open June to August daily 7:30am to 7pm, May and Sept daily 8am to 6pm, October to April daily 9am to 4pm. If it's crowded, go to the storefront office right behind it. You'll also find a visitor center on the way into town by car, staffed in the summer only, in Eagle River, in the Parkgate Building on the Old Glenn Highway at Easy Street, and three at the airport—one in the baggage-claim area in the domestic terminal and two in the international terminal: in the lobby and in the transit area.

The ✪ **Alaska Public Lands Information Center,** located at 605 W. Fourth Ave. (in the 1930s concrete federal building across the intersection from the log cabin at Fourth and F), Suite 105, Anchorage, AK 99501 (☎ **907/271-2737;** www.nps.gov/ aplic), has guidance for anyone planning to spend time in the outdoors anywhere in Alaska, as well as exhibits of interest even for those who aren't. The center occupies a grand room with high ceilings in the former post office and federal courthouse. All the land agencies are represented, you can buy ferry tickets from the Alaska Marine Highway System, there's an excellent selection of trail and field guides, and the rangers behind the desk know what they're talking about. Similar centers are in Ketchikan, Tok, and Fairbanks. They're open daily in summer 9am to 5:30pm; winters Monday to Friday 10am to 5:30pm.

The **Chugach State Park Headquarters,** in the Potter Section House on the Seward Highway at the south end of town (☎ **907/345-5014**), is open normal business hours all year. The *Anchorage Daily News* maintains a free voice-mail **Daily Newsline** (☎ **907/277-1500**) with hundreds of recorded topics, including fishing, hiking, skiing, and snowmobiling conditions, as well as basic visitor guidance, such as the Airport Information Line, at extension 5252. For information on the considerable recreation opportunities in city parks, including Kincaid Park and the bike trails, contact the **Division of Parks and Recreation** (☎ **907/343-4474;** www.ci.anchorage. ak.us/). The Web site contains abundant Anchorage information.

SPECIAL EVENTS

The Fur Rendezvous Winter Carnival, over 2 weekends in mid-February (☎ **907/ 277-8615**), is a huge, citywide winter celebration, with many community events, craft fairs, snowshoe softball, dog sled rides, and other fun. The main event is the **World Champion Sled Dog Race** (☎ **907/562-2235**), a 3-day sprint event of about 25 miles per heat. **The Iditarod Trail Sled Dog Race** (☎ **907/376-5155**) starts from Anchorage the first Saturday in March at 10am, but the teams are loaded in trucks a few miles out of town and restarted in Wasilla for the 1,000-mile run to Nome (see the section on the Matanuska and Susitna Valleys, later in this chapter). **The International Ice Carving Competition** (☎ **907/279-5650**) takes place that same weekend as the Iditarod in town square, at Fifth Avenue and E Street.

The Native Youth Olympics, in April at the University of Alaska Sports Center, is a tough competition in traditional Native sports (☎ **907/265-5900**). **The Saturday Market** is a big street fair farmer's market held during the summer at Third Avenue and E Street; a **Wednesday Market** happens a block over, on Fourth Avenue. **The Mayor's Midnight Sun Marathon** (☎ **907/343-4474**) brings more than 2,000 runners for a race near the time of the summer solstice. **The Chugiak–Eagle River Bear Paw Festival** (☎ **907/694-4702**) is a community celebration in July with a parade, rodeo, carnival, and other festivities.

The Alaska Federation of Natives Convention, held in October, brings villagers from all over the state, and with them dance celebrations and an exceptional opportunity to buy Native crafts at a fair. **The Great Alaska Shootout Men's Basketball**

Tournament brings top-ranked college teams to the Sullivan Arena over Thanksgiving weekend (see "Spectator Sports," below). **The Christmas Tree Lighting** (☎ 907/276-5015) takes place in town square the Saturday after Thanksgiving, with Santa usually arriving behind a team of real reindeer. A performance of *The Nutcracker* often follows in the Alaska Center for the Performing Arts.

Check for up-to-date information on any of these events on the Anchorage Convention and Visitor Bureau Web site, www.anchorage.org.

Fast Facts: Anchorage

Banks A bank is rarely far away, and grocery stores also have ATMs. Downtown, Key Bank is at the corner of Fifth Avenue and F Street.

Business Services Kinko's Copies is at 2210 E. Northern Lights Blvd. (☎ 907/276-4228.

Hospital There are two hospitals in Anchorage serving the general public: Alaska Regional Hospital, at 2801 DeBarr Rd. (☎ 907/276-1131), and Providence Alaska Medical Center, at 3200 Providence Dr. (☎ 907/562-2211).

Internet/E-mail Surf City, an Internet cafe, is at 415 L St. (☎ 907/279-7877). The Z. J. Loussac Library, at 3600 Denali St. (☎ 907/343-2975), also offers free Web access.

Police The Anchorage Police Department has main offices at 4501 S. Bragaw Rd., south of Tudor Road (☎ 907/786-8500). For police business outside the city, call the Alaska State Troopers (☎ 907/269-5511).

Post Office There are many branches in town; in the downtown area, it's downstairs in the brown building at Fourth Avenue and D Street.

Taxes There's no sales tax in Anchorage. The bed tax is 8%.

1 Attractions & Activities

I've arranged this section starting with a walking tour through downtown Anchorage, followed by details on the downtown museums and attractions that are farther afield.

Walking Tour: Downtown Anchorage

Start & Finish: Fourth Avenue and F Street.

Time: About 90 minutes (though add more time if you plan to linger at any of the stops).

Start at the **Log Cabin Visitor Information Center** at Fourth Avenue and F Street. Outside is a sign that shows the distance to various cities, a popular spot for pictures. Walking east, toward the mountains, the:

1. **Old City Hall (1936)**, at Fourth Avenue and E Street, is on the right. Recently renovated, its lobby contains an interesting display on city history, including dioramas of the early streetscape.

Crossing E Street, notice on the left side of Fourth Avenue that all the buildings are modern—everything on that side from E Street east for several blocks collapsed in the 1964 earthquake. The street split in half, lengthwise, with the left side ending up a dozen feet lower than the right. That land was later reinforced with a gravel buttress by the U.S. Army Corps of Engineers and the slope below forever set aside from new construction because of the earth-quake risk. This stretch of Fourth Avenue is where the **Iditarod Trail Sled Dog Race** and the **Anchorage Fur Rendezvous World Championship Sled Dog Race** start each year in March and February, respectively.

At Fourth Avenue and D Street, the:

2. **Wendler Building,** the old Club 25, is among the oldest buildings in Anchorage, but no longer the very oldest. (See the Oscar Gill House Bed and Breakfast, in "Accommodations," below, for an explanation of that conundrum.) The bronze statue of the dog commemorates the sled-dog races that start here. Across D Street is a mural that depicts a relief map of Alaska, with the Iditarod Trail marked.

Turn right, walking a block south on D Street to Fifth Avenue. There are several interesting little businesses and restaurants on this block, the chief of which is:

3. **Cyrano's Off-Center Playhouse** (☎ 907/274-2599) with its Eccentric Theater Company and Bistro Bergerac. It's a cultural ground zero that's also a fun meeting place, with great food from an ever-changing menu.

4. **The 5th Avenue Mall,** a grand, four-story shopping center, is across Fifth; it includes Alaska's finest upscale shopping.

On the opposite side of the building—turn left on Fifth Avenue and right on C Street to Sixth Avenue—is:

5. **Wolf Song of Alaska** (☎ 907/346-3073; www.alaska.net/~wolfsong), a museum and gift shop. This nonprofit organization aims to educate and elevate the public about Alaska's most controversial mammal. Inside you'll find dioramas, exhibits, artwork, videos, and eager volunteers. Admission is $3 for adults, $1.50 ages 6 to 18. Unless your interest in wolves is strong, you'll spend only 10 or 15 minutes. Hours vary, but in summer they're usually open at least 10am to 6pm Monday through Saturday.

A door or two west (away from the mountains) is the free:

6. **Alaska State Troopers Museum** (☎ 907/279-5050). I don't know why I so enjoy this trove of law enforcement insignia, equipment, a 1952 Hudson Hornet, photographs, and other memorabilia—maybe it's the way these things convey the positive spirit of pioneer Alaska combined with the troopers' obvious pride. It's open year-round Monday through Friday, 10am to 5pm, Saturday noon to 4pm.

A side trip down C to 7th Avenue will bring you to the:

6a. **Anchorage Museum of History and Art** (see under "Downtown Museums," below). You probably don't want to break up your walking tour to visit it now, but note the location for later.

Back by the State Trooper Museum, walk west, past the mall, to Sixth Avenue and E Street, one corner of the beautifully planted:

7. **Town square.** The community raised money for the improvements by collecting donations of $40 each for the granite bricks, with an inscription of the contributor's choosing. There are 13,344 (bet you can't find mine). The building on the north side that looks like a rolltop desk is the acclaimed:

8. **William A. Egan Civic and Convention Center.** Inside you'll find a pleasant atrium, public rest rooms, and whatever's going on in the ballrooms. On the east side of the square, the huge whale mural was painted freehand by Wyland in 1994. He painted similar whale murals in cities all along the West Coast. On the west side of the square, the massive, highly decorated:

Downtown Anchorage Walking Tour

0 ____ 1/8 Mile
0 ____ .125 Kilometer

Rail Depot ■ 🔼 17a 🔼 17b
Warehouse Ave.

Christiansen Dr. \
W. 1st Ave.
Knik Arm
W. 2nd Ave. · 17
W. 3rd Ave.
Post Office
E. 2nd Ave.
15
16
18
19 1 2 3
W. 4th Ave.
12
W. 5th Ave.
14
13
11 10 8
4 5
W. 6th Ave.
7 6
6a
W. 7th Ave.
W. 8th Ave.
W. 9th Ave.
Delaney Park
W. 10th Ave.
28

K St., I St., M St., L St., H St., G St., F St., E St., D St., C St., B St., A St., P St., N St., M St., Barrow St., Cordova St.

1 Old City Hall
2 Wendler Building
3 Cyrano's Off-Center Playhouse
4 The 5th Avenue Mall
5 Wolf Song of Alaska
6 Alaska State Troopers Museum
6a Anchorage Museum of History and Art
7 Town square

8 William A. Egan Civic and Convention Center
9 Alaska Center for the Performing Arts
10 City hall
11 The Alaska Experience Center
12 Off-beat businesses
13 Holy Family Cathedral
14 Elderberry Park
14 Oscar Anderson House

14 Coastal Trail
15 Resolution Park
16 Totem poles
17 Alaska Union monument
17a Old depot
17b Fairbanks Gold Company Mining Museum and Gold Works
18 Old federal building
19 4th Avenue Theater

9. Alaska Center for the Performing Arts dominates; it's Anchorage's most controversial building, completed in 1988 at a cost of over $70 million. The lobby is usually open, and whatever your opinion of the decor, a look inside will spark a discussion. Tours are Wednesday at 1pm; a $1 donation is requested. Thespians believe the building is haunted by the ghost of painter Sydney Lawrence, who makes lights mysteriously vary and elevators go up and down with no one in them. An auditorium demolished to make room for the center was named for Lawrence. Check the box office (☎ **907/263-2787**) also for current performances in the three theaters—this is Alaska's premier performance venue.

☕ **TAKE A BREAK**   From the Alaska Center, cross Sixth Avenue at the light by the center's door. Continuing west, **Humpy's,** the tavern on the left side of Sixth, has a huge selection of microbrews, in case you're already thirsty, and good casual meals.

The square green office building next door is:

10. City hall. Turn left through the pedestrian walkway between Humpy's and city hall. A mural showing a timeline of the history of Anchorage faces the parking lot. A much better mural is on the wall in Humpy's outdoor seating area. It is by Duke Russell, whose work depicts Anchorage's seedier side with humor and insight.

| Big State, Big Movies |

In the summer, films for visitors often play on a large screen in the concert hall of the **Alaska Center for the Performing Arts**. Whether or not they're Imax films seems to be a matter of dispute, but they're certainly huge and impressive. Recently they've shown *Alaska: Spirit of the Wild,* and *Whales, An Unforgettable Journey,* with one or the other on the screen hourly from 9am to 9pm. Tickets are $9.75, adults, $7.75 children, at the center box office.

Walk west, past city hall to G Street, turn right, and proceed to Sixth Avenue and G. (If you're up for a longer walk, you can turn left on G Street instead and explore the Delaney Park strip and lovely South Addition residential neighborhood south of 9th Avenue.) On the northwest corner of Sixth Avenue and G Street, in the dome tent is:

11. **The Alaska Experience Center** (☎ 907/276-3730) is on the northwest corner of Sixth Avenue and G Street, in the dome tent. A 40-minute Omnivision wraparound movie about Alaska costs $7 for adults, $4 for children, showing hourly. It's certainly spectacular—too much so for some people, who get motion sickness. Sit toward the center at the back. An Alaska Earthquake display that really shakes is $5 for adults and $4 for children. They're open daily from 9am to 9pm in summer, and from 11am to 6pm in winter. On the southwest corner is the transit center, for city buses. The **Decker/Morris Gallery,** one of Alaska's best and most uncompromising, is on the northeast corner.

Walk a block north, back to Fifth Avenue. The west side of G Street between Fourth and Fifth avenues contains some of the downtown's best:

12. **Offbeat businesses: Side Street Espresso,** where you can get into a lively political discussion; **Denali Wear,** which is Tracy Anna Bader's studio and shop of wearable art; **Darwin's Theory,** a friendly, old-fashioned bar with character that shows up in an Indigo Girls song; and **The Great Alaska Train Company,** a retired couple's labor of love, which sells nothing but model trains and train memorabilia. There are others, too—it's a great little block. (If you're tired, you can stop the walk here, 1 block from the starting point.)

Going west (away from the mountains) on Fifth, **Aurora Fine Arts** is on the right, **The Imaginarium,** described under "Downtown Museums," below, is next, and finally **The Glacier Brewhouse,** a brew pub restaurant described under "Dining" below. Continuing west on Fifth Avenue and crossing H Street, the:

13. **Holy Family Cathedral,** a concrete, art deco church, is the seat of the Roman Catholic archbishop.

Keep going toward the water, crossing L Street and down the hill to:

14. **Elderberry Park.** The yellow-and-brown house is the **Oscar Anderson House,** described under "Downtown Museums," below. There's good playground equipment here, public rest rooms, and comfortable places where you can sit and watch the kids and Cook Inlet at the same time and meet other parents. This also is the easiest access point to the **Coastal Trail** (see "Special Places" under "Getting Outside," below), where it tunnels under the Alaska Railroad tracks. Even if you don't have time to go far on the trail, you may want to walk through the tunnel and see the ducks paddling around and, at low tide, see the vast mud flats, and walk through the rock garden of **Hannah Cove Park.**

Now hike back up the hill to L Street and turn left, going north 2 blocks to:

15. **Resolution Park,** with the bronze **Captain Cook Monument.** Capt. James Cook stands on a large, wooden deck, but he's gazing out to sea—which certainly

---

Historic Downtown Anchorage Walking Tour

Anchorage Historic Properties, 645 W. Third Ave. (☎ **907/274-3600**), a city-endowed historical preservation group, offers a 2-hour/2-mile guided walking tour of historic downtown Anchorage June to August, Monday through Friday at 1pm. The volunteer guides are fun and knowledgeable. Meet at the lobby of old city hall, 524 W. Fourth Ave., next door to the Log Cabin Visitor Information Center. Tickets cost $5 for adults, $4 for seniors over age 65, and $1 for children. If you can't do the guided tour, pick up their brochure at the visitor center, which tells a little about the buildings and directs you to 11 sequential historical sign kiosks.

---

wouldn't have been the way he was facing when he discovered Cook Inlet in 1778 aboard HMS *Resolution.*

Follow Fourth Avenue east (back toward the mountains), passing a couple of good coffee houses and restaurants, and the courthouse plaza on the left between I and K streets (for a reason I've never understood, there is no J Street). Across I street, in front of the **Nesbett State Courthouse,** take a look at the two:

16. Totem poles. Erected in 1997, they represent the eagle and raven moieties of the Tlingit people, intended to symbolize the balance of justice.

Go 1 block east, then turn left around the courthouse on H Street, continuing north across Third Avenue, then down the hill where H becomes Christensen Drive, and turn right again on Second Avenue, toward the mountains. Many of the **old houses** that line Second are marked, their historic significance carefully catalogued—80-year-old houses may not be "historic" where you come from, but here we have to take what we can get. If you imagine houses like this over much of downtown, you'll know what Anchorage looked like before oil.

Continue east to E Street. At Second Avenue and E:

17. A monument to Alaska's 1959 admission to the Union honors President Eisenhower. You overlook the Alaska Railroad yards from here, and see part of the port of Anchorage and the neighborhood of Government Hill across the Ship Creek river bottom. This is where the tent city of Knik Anchorage, later shortened to Anchorage, was set up in 1914.

If you have the energy, there are several interesting sites down the hill in **Ship Creek.** (Otherwise, skip to the paragraph following number 17b.) Walking down

17a. the stairs that lead down the earthquake buttress area hillside, take a look inside the:

Old depot and the beautifully restored steam engine on the pedestal in front. It was used on construction of the Panama Canal, then worked in the yard here as a switch engine.

Continue to the creek, then follow the path east, toward the mountains. Ship

17b. Creek yields good-sized salmon all summer (see "Fishing" below). The covered bridge contains the:

Fairbanks Gold Company Mining Museum and Gold Works (☎ **907/457-6058**), a gold-panning tourist attraction. Gold mining occurred along Turnagain Arm, south of Anchorage, but never in this area. Farther upstream, a path crosses the creek atop a dam, where there is a plaza to watch the ducks and possibly the fish. Now retrace your steps back to the Eisenhower Monument at Second Avenue and E Street.

Walk up the hill on E Street to Third Avenue. The extensively landscaped parking lot on the left becomes the ✪ **Saturday Market** every weekend in the summer, a street fair drawing hundreds of vendors and thousands of shoppers.

You can buy everything from local vegetables to handmade crafts to somebody's old record collection. There are food booths and music, too.

Turn right and walk a block west (away from the mountains) on Third Avenue, then turn left on F Street. **F Street Station,** on the left, is a fun bar with an after-work crowd. Proceed to Fourth Avenue, and you're back at the Log Cabin Visitor Information Center, but don't stop. Turn right on Fourth Avenue. On the right side is the:

18. **Old federal building,** a grand, white, Depression-era structure that now contains the Alaska Public Lands Information Center, with interesting displays and lots of information about the outdoors. Across the street is Anchorage's most attractive historic building, the restored:

19. **4th Avenue Theater.** It was built by Cap Lathrop, Alaska's first business magnate, who created it as a monument to the territory and the permanence of its new society. Today it's a gift store. Don't miss going in and looking at the bas-relief murals and the blinking big dipper on the ceiling, which during many a movie over the years was more entertaining than whatever was on the screen.

DOWNTOWN MUSEUMS

✪ **Anchorage Museum of History and Art.** 121 W. Seventh Ave. ☎ **907/343-4326.** www.ci.anchorage.ak.us. Admission $5 adults, $4.50 seniors 65 and older, free for children 17 and under. High season, Sun–Fri 9am–9pm, Sat 9am–6pm; low season, Tues–Sat 10am–6pm, Sun 1–5pm.

The state's largest museum doesn't have its largest collection, but unlike the Alaska State Museum in Juneau or the University of Alaska Museum in Fairbanks, the Anchorage museum has the room and staff both to teach and to serve as a center of contemporary culture of a regional caliber. Most visitors tour the Alaska Gallery, an informative and enjoyable walk through the history and anthropology of the state. In the art galleries, you can see what's happening in art in Alaska today; Alaska art isn't all scenery and walrus ivory, but the grandeur of the place does influence almost every work. The Anchorage museum also gets the best touring shows. It's the only museum in Alaska that could require more than one visit. The cafe, covered below under "Dining," serves some of the best lunches to be had downtown. Lectures, openings, and jazz happen many summer evenings.

The Imaginarium. 737 W. Fifth Ave., Suite G. ☎ **907/276-3179.** Admission $5 adults, $4 seniors 65 and older and children 2–12. Mon–Sat 10am–6pm, Sun noon–5pm.

This is a science museum geared to children, with not many words and lots of fun learning experiences. The idea is that while they're running around having a great time, the kids may accidentally learn something; at least, the displays will excite a sense of wonder that is the start of science. There's a strong Alaska theme to many of the displays. The saltwater touch tank is like an indoor tide pool. This is one of our children's favorite places to go for a treat.

The Oscar Anderson House Museum. 420 M St. ☎ **907/274-2336** or 907/274-3600. www.customcpu.com/np/ahpi. Admission $3 adults, $1 children 5–12. Summer only Tues–Sat 11am–4pm. Closed in winter.

This house museum, moved to a beautiful site in Elderberry Park over the water, shows how an early Swedish butcher lived. Although far from grand, the house is quaint, surrounded by a lovely little garden. The tour provides a good explanation of Anchorage's short history. Anderson died in 1974, and the house contains many of the family's original belongings, including a working 1909 player piano around which the structure was built. If you come at Christmas, don't miss the Swedish Christmas tours, the first two weekends in December.

SIGHTS BEYOND DOWNTOWN

Alaska Native Heritage Center. Near the intersection of the Glenn Highway and Muldoon Rd. ☎ **800/315-6608** or 907/263-5170. www.alaskanative.net. Admission $19.95 adults, $14.95 children 5–12. Open summer daily 9am–9pm.

Completed in 1999 by a consortium of Alaska Native groups after many years of planning and effort, this $15 million center aims to teach visitors about their cultures and to serve as a gathering place where traditions can be passed on. Here you get the real thing—Natives demonstrating the art and ways of their own peoples—but it's all presented to please and interest large groups passing through. Dance, storytelling, and music performances take place all day in the entry atrium; next you watch a film; then the wall opens on a gallery that introduces the five main Native cultural groupings. Craftsmen from each of the five demonstrate their work in open workshops. Finally, walk around a pond that's surrounded by traditional structures of each of the peoples, with Natives to explain what you're seeing.

Alaska Aviation Heritage Museum. 4721 Aircraft Dr. ☎ **907/248-5325.** Admission $5.75 adults, $4.50 active military and seniors over age 62, $2.75 children under 12. High season, daily 9am–6pm; low season call ahead. Take International Airport Rd. toward the airport to the Lake Hood exit, then follow the signs.

Hangers house restored classic aircraft and wrecks, with detailed explanatory placards, photographs, and memorabilia of Alaska's Bush pilots posted around. An old advertising sign for the Kantishna-based McGee Airways tells the story: "Fly an Hour or Walk a Week." Aviation was and is the only practical way to most of the state, and pilots are among our greatest heroes. Not being an expert on old planes, however, I found the living parts of the museum of most interest: the dock on the Lake Hood floatplane base (it's the world's busiest), where you can join a $50 air tour; and the restoration shop, where visitors wander among the works in progress and converse with the volunteers painting, grinding, and putting back together old aircraft. Mechanics and tinkerers will feel at home. Call ahead, as the museum is chronically in financial trouble.

Alaska Botanical Garden. Campbell Airstrip Rd. (off Tudor Rd.). ☎ **907/265-3165.** E-mail: garden@alaska.net. Free admission. Summer, daily 9am–9pm. From downtown, drive out New Seward Hwy. (Gambell St.) to Tudor Rd., exit to the east (left), turn right off Tudor onto Campbell Airstrip Rd., and park at the Benny Benson School. It's 20 minutes from downtown.

It's young and the volunteer staff still has a long way to go to fill out the 110-acre wooded site, but the garden already is a restful place to learn about native flora and see what else grows here while sitting in peaceful shade on benches and watching birds and squirrels. They've done a good job of integrating the garden into its forest setting while adding a formal herb garden and other lovely alcoves. I don't know of many other botanical gardens where you're warned to watch out for moose and bear. Kids love the paths and secluded spots. A fine nature trail with explanatory signs leaves from the garden down to Campbell Creek, where you may see salmon swimming.

✪ **The Alaska Zoo.** 4731 O'Malley Rd. ☎ **907/346-3242.** Admission $7 adults, $6 seniors, $5 children 12–17, $4 children 3–12. MC, V. Opens daily at 10am; closing time varies by season. Drive out the New Seward Hwy. to O'Malley Rd., then turn left and go 2 miles; it's 25 minutes from downtown, without traffic.

If you're expecting a big-city zoo, you'll be disappointed, but the Alaska Zoo has a charm all its own. Anchorage residents have developed personal relationships with the animals, many of which are named, in their campy little Eden. Gravel paths wander through the woods past large enclosures with natural flora for bears, seals and otters, musk oxen, mountain goats, moose, caribou, waterfowl—all the animals you were supposed to see in Alaska but may have missed. (Don't get the elephant or Siberian tigers in your snapshots—they'll blow your story.) A snack bar serves basic meals and there is a large gift shop.

Earthquake Park. West end of Northern Lights Blvd. Drive west on Northern Lights from Minnesota Dr. (L St. downtown), looking on the right after Lakeshore Dr.

The 1964 Good Friday earthquake was the biggest ever in North America, registering at 9.2 on the Richter Scale, killing 131 people, and flattening much of the region. Downtown Anchorage and the Turnagain residential area, near the park, suffered enormous slides that turned neighborhoods into chaotic ruins. A sculpture and excellent interpretive signs commemorate and explain the event and point out its few remaining marks on the land. This also is a good access point to the Coastal Trail.

Heritage Library and Museum. C St. and Northern Lights Blvd. ☎ **907/265-2834.** Free admission. High season, Mon–Fri noon–5pm; low season, noon–4pm.

This well-endowed little museum, in a room off the lobby of the white National Bank of Alaska building, houses a collection of paintings and Alaska Native cultural artifacts and a reference library of 2,500 volumes on Alaska-related topics.

Eklutna Tribe Historic Park. About 25 miles out the Glenn Hwy. ☎ **907/688-6026** or 907/696-2828. Tour $3.50. Summer, daily 8am to 6pm. Take the Glenn Hwy. to the Eklutna exit, then go left over the overpass.

The Native village of Eklutna has a fascinating old cemetery in which each grave is enclosed by a highly decorated spirit house, the size of a large doll house. They excite the imagination in a way no ordinary marker would. The tribe leads a 30-minute tour of the cemetery, two Russian Orthodox churches (including the **St. Nicholas Orthodox Church,** which is on the National Register of Historic Places), and a museum. Those not on a tour have to stay outside the cemetery fence. If you come out this far, don't miss the Thunderbird Falls, described below under "Hiking."

2 Getting Outside

Anchorage is unique in Alaska (and anywhere else I know) for the number of places right near town to hike, bike, ski, and otherwise get into the wild. I've broken the options down by activities below. In town, the city's bike trails connect through greenbelts that span the noisy, asphalt urban core with soothing creek-side woods. Kincaid Park and Far North Bicentennial Park are both on the trail system within the city, and encompass scores of miles of trails for Nordic skiing, mountain biking, and horseback riding. The Chugach Mountains, which form the backdrop to the town, offer appealing hiking, backpacking, mountain biking, and climbs that range from easy to technical, all within Chugach State Park and, south of town, Chugach National Forest. Visitor information for each is listed above; directions are below in the sections on specific outdoor activities. More trails and streams, barely farther afield, are covered below in the "Out from Anchorage: Turnagain Arm & Portage Glacier" section.

The best trail guide to the entire region is Helen Neinhueser and John Wolfe Jr.'s *55 Ways to the Wilderness,* published by The Mountaineers. It costs $12.95 and is available in any bookstore in the area. The best trail map of the area is published by **Alaska Road and Recreation Maps,** P.O. Box 102459, Anchorage, AK 99510, and costs $5 at sporting goods stores. It shows Anchorage roads and bike trails as well as backcountry routes in the Chugach Mountains.

EQUIPMENT You can rent most anything you need for outdoor activities. Bike rentals are listed above, under "Getting Around." You can get advice and rent kayaks, skis, snowshoes, bear-proof containers, and mountaineering equipment at **Alaska**

Mountaineering and Hiking, at 2633 Spenard Rd. (☎ **907/272-1811;** e-mail: amh@alaska.net). A block away, at 1200 W. Northern Lights Blvd., **REI** has a large store (☎ **907/272-4565**) that rents a wide range of gear, including canoes with car-top carriers, camping gear, and packs.

WALKING & BIKING

✪ TONY KNOWLES COASTAL TRAIL   Leading 10 miles from the western end of Second Avenue along the shore to **Kincaid Park,** the coastal trail is my favorite thing about Anchorage and a unique pathway to the natural environment from the heart of downtown. You can join the wide, paved trail at various points; downtown, **Elderberry Park,** at the western end of Fifth Avenue, is the most popular. From there, I've ridden my bike parallel with beluga whales swimming along the trail at high tide. Toward the Kincaid Park end of the trail, I've seen moose, or had them stop me. **Westchester Lagoon** is 10 blocks south of Elderberry Park. If you're just up for a walk, the lagoon is about 20 minutes from Elderberry, a great destination for a picnic or to feed the ducks and geese. At the lagoon, the coastal trail meets the **Lanie Fleischer Chester Creek Trail,** which runs about 4 miles along the greenbelt to **Goose Lake,** where you can swim in a cool woodland pond at the end of a hot bike ride—still, improbably enough, in the middle of the city. South, through the university campus and across Tudor Road, you come to **Bicentennial Park,** with the botanical garden and miles of dirt trails. The paved bike trails, including the Fleischer, stay well back in the trees, so you rarely see a building, and tunnels and bridges span all road and railroad crossings, so you're never in traffic.

HIKING, MOUNTAIN BIKING & BACKPACKING

✪ KINCAID PARK   Covered in more detail below, under "Nordic Skiing," Kincaid Park is an idyllic summer setting for mountain biking and day hikes. Moose sightings are a daily occurrence on the wide dirt trails that snake for about 30 miles through the birch and white spruce of the park's hilly 1,400 acres of boreal forest, often with views of the sea. Within the park, wooded Little Campbell Lake is a picturesque but little-used swimming hole and fun spot for family canoeing; there is no lifeguard.

FAR NORTH BICENTENNIAL PARK   The 4,000-acre park, on the east side of town, is a unique patch of urban wilderness, habitat for bears and moose and spawning salmon, and used by people for dog mushing and skiing in winter, and, perhaps best of all, mountain biking and day hiking in summer. The Alaska Botanical Garden, listed above, and the Hilltop Ski Area, below, are both within the park's boundaries, and you can start there for exceptional mountain biking and walks; or, even better, start at the **Campbell Creek Science Center** (☎ **907/267-1257**), an educational facility operated by the Bureau of Land Management where staff are often on hand to answer questions. To get there from downtown, take the New Seward Highway (Gambell St. downtown) south to Dowling Road, go east (toward the mountains), turn right on Lake Otis Road and left on 68th Avenue, following it to the end.

✪ FLATTOP MOUNTAIN & THE GLEN ALPS TRAILHEAD   There are many ways to the alpine tundra, intoxicating fresh air, and cinematic views of the Chugach Mountains, behind Anchorage, but the easiest and best developed are at the Glen Alps Trailhead. Even those who aren't up to hiking should go for the drive and a walk on a short, paved loop with incredible views and interpretive signs. If you are ready for a hike, you can start at the trailhead for trips of up to several days, following the network of trails or taking off across dry, alpine tundra by yourself, but usually within cell phone range. Camping is permitted anywhere off the trails.

Flattop Mountain is the most popular hike from the Glen Alps Trailhead, and a great family climb, if a bit crowded on weekends. It's a steep afternoon hike, easy for fit adults and doable by school-age children. There's a bit of a scramble at the top, easiest if you stick to the painted markers on the rocks. Dress warmly and don't go in the rain.

For a longer or less steep hike or a mountain biking trip, follow the broad gravel trail that leads up the valley from the Glen Alps Trailhead. Trails lead all the way over the mountains to Indian or Bird Creek, on Turnagain Arm, up some of the mountains along the way or to round alpine lakes in high, rocky valleys. You're always above tree-line, so you don't need to follow a trail if you have a good map. This is wonderful back-packing country.

To get to the trailhead, take New Seward Highway to O'Malley Road, head east toward the mountains, then turn right on Hillside Drive, Upper Huffman Road, then right on the narrow, twisting Toilsome Hill Drive. Bring cash or a check for a self-service day-use fee of $5.

EAGLE RIVER VALLEY & CROW PASS The Eagle River Nature Center, at the end of Eagle River road, 12 miles up Eagle River Valley from the Glenn Highway exit (☎ 907/694-2108; www.alaska.net/~ernc), is like a public wilderness lodge, with hands-on naturalist displays about the area and guided nature walks daily in the summer at 1pm. It's open in summer daily 10am to 5pm, winter Friday through Sunday 10am to 5pm. There's a $5 parking fee. The ¾-mile **Rodak Nature Trail,** with interpretive signs, leads to a viewing platform over a beaver pond. The **Albert Loop Trail** is a 3-mile route; a geology guide from the center matches with numbered posts on the way. Both have good bird and wildlife watching. The 25-mile **Crow Pass Trail,** a portion of the historic Iditarod Trail, continues up the valley into the mountains along the river, eventually surmounting the Chugach in alpine terrain, and passing near Raven Glacier before descending into Girdwood (see the "Out from Anchorage: Turnagain Arm & Portage Glacier" section, below). The nature center leads a guided 3-day hike over the trail in the summer for $165 (you bring your own food and gear). There are campsites with fire rings along the way, and a mile up the trail the center rents out a public-use cabin for $45 a night. A yurt on the Albert Loop rents for the same price. Reserve well ahead for weekends; weeknights are more readily available.

THUNDERBIRD FALLS & EKLUTNA LAKE The hike to Thunderbird Falls is an easy, 1-mile forest walk with a good reward at the end; you can see the falls without the steep final descent to their foot. Take the Glenn Highway north to the Thunder-bird Falls exit, 25 miles from Anchorage. Continuing up the gravel Eklutna Lake Road, you come to a lovely state parks campground ($10 a night, $5 day-use fee) and the beautiful glacial lake for canoeing, hiking, and really exceptional mountain biking. You can make a goal of the Eklutna Glacier at the other end. This glacial melt is where Anchorage gets much of its city water. People bottle it and sell it as "glacier water."

ARCTIC VALLEY The road to the **Alpenglow Ski Area** (☎ 907/428-1208) is a wonderful route into mountains of alpine tundra where you can romp on its soft carpet and hike or climb in any direction. Late summer berry picking is excellent. On top of the mountain to the left is an abandoned Cold War–era antimissile emplace-ment. Take Glenn Highway to the Arctic Valley exit.

OTHER OUTDOOR ACTIVITIES
DOG MUSHING In the last 20 years, sled dog mushing has become a recreational sport as well as the utilitarian activity it once was in the Bush and the professional

sport it has been for years. More and more sled dog enthusiasts are offering a chance for visitors to drive their team, or at least ride in the basket. Of course, for real mushing, or anything remotely like it, you have to be here in the winter. **Birch Trails Sled Dog Tours,** 22719 Robinson Rd., Chugiak, AK 99567 (☎ and fax **907/ 688-5713**; home.gci.net/~roxy/public/BC/BC.html), specializes in 2- to 14-mile rides, teaches mushing, and offers overnight mushing treks from their bed-and-breakfast 14 miles from Anchorage. The B&B is open year-round, with mushing in the winter only; reserve ahead. **Mush A Dog Team,** 17620 Birchwood Loop Rd. (☎ **907/688-1391**), offers a summer 1-hour tour with gold panning for $15 and winter trips by appointment. Take the South Birchwood exit off the Glenn Highway.

FISHING   There are salmon, stocked and natural, in some of Anchorage's streams and stocked trout in some lakes. Although the setting might not be the wilderness experience you've dreamed about, the 40-pound king you pull from the water under a highway bridge in an industrial area on Ship Creek may make up for it. From downtown, just walk down the hill to the railroad yard. A couple of shacks sell and rent gear in the summer. Fishing is best at or near high tide, especially at the end of the rising tide, and you'll need serious boots, preferably hip waders for the muddy banks; otherwise, you can fish from a bridge, with greater difficulty. You can also catch stocked silver salmon in Campbell Creek and Bird Creek, in the late summer and fall, and rainbow trout in many local lakes and streams. The **Alaska Department of Fish and Game** has a recorded information line with all the details on what's hot and lots of other advice (☎ **907/267-2510**); for information on regulations or more detailed advice, call, write, or visit their office at 333 Raspberry Rd., Anchorage, AK 99518-1599 (☎ **907/267-2221**).

Serious fishers will use Anchorage as a base for a ✪ **fly-in fishing trip** on a remote lake or river all your own, or to go somewhere else in the state. Several companies offer fly-in trips; two of the largest and best established are **Ketchum Air Service** (☎ **800/ 433-9114** or 907/243-5525) and **Rust's Flying Service** (☎ **800/544-2299** or 907/ 243-1595). They can take you out guided or on your own, just for the day or to stay for a while in a cabin. You can bring your own gear, or they can provide it. You don't have to be an avid fisher to enjoy one of these trips—there's nothing like the silence that falls as the floatplane that dropped you off disappears over the horizon. Prices start around $150 per person for an unguided day trip.

See chapter 2 for more ideas on how to set up a fishing vacation, especially the listing for Sport Fishing Alaska, an agency that specializes in setting up fishing trips.

FLIGHTSEEING   Small planes are the blood cells of Alaska's circulatory system, and Anchorage its heart. There are several busy airports in Anchorage, and Lake Hood is the world's busiest floatplane base. More than two dozen operators are anxious to take you on a flightseeing tour—check the visitor center for names—but the most comfortable and memorable is probably the restored DC-3 operated by ✪ **Era Aviation** (☎ **800/866-8394** or 907/266-8394). The plane re-creates the classic days of air travel—you can pretend to be Ingrid Bergman or Spencer Tracy while gazing out the oversize windows at a glacier. The daily summer flights leave from the South Airpark, off Raspberry Road, with itineraries determined by the weather: The plane has the speed and range to go where the best views are, including Mount McKinley, Prince William Sound, or Kenai Fjords National Park's Harding Ice Field. A 90-minute flight is $139 per person, or 75 minutes for $130. The route is tailored to the weather and viewing opportunities. Era also offers glacier helicopter flightseeing and glacier landings from Anchorage.

GOLF There are four courses in Anchorage and two in the Matanuska Valley, north of the city. The municipal **Anchorage Golf Course** (☎ 907/522-3363) is on O'Malley Road near the zoo, uphill from the New Seward Highway.

HORSEBACK RIDING The hilly forest trails of Bicentennial Park make lovely bridle paths in the summer. Guided rides are offered in the summer for $35 an hour by **Alaska Wilderness Outfitters** (☎ 907/344-2434), daily from 10am to 10pm. They start from the Hilltop Ski Area, on Abbott Road,

RAFTING There are several white-water rivers within a 90-minute drive of Anchorage. **Nova Raft and Adventure Tours,** P.O. Box 1129, Chickaloon, AK 99674 (☎ 800/746-5753 or 907/745-5753; www.alaska.net/~nova), is a large operator with 25-year's experience offering multiday trips all over the state, and four different half-day floats in the Anchorage area. Rafting trips ranging from relatively easygoing Class II and III rapids on the Matanuska River to the Class IV and V white water of Six-Mile Creek, for which you may be required to prove your swimming ability before you can get in the boat. Self-paddling is an option on some trips. White-water rafting always entails risk, but Nova's schedule allows you to calibrate how wild you want to get. The half-day trips range in price from $60 to $135. Children 5 to 11 can go on the calm Matanuska River float; the half-price fare is $30. Other trips are suitable only for older children and adults. You'll need a way to get to the river and may need to bring your own lunch.

SEA KAYAKING Kayaking day trips from Anchorage go through Whittier, on Prince William Sound, and I've listed two guide services in chapter 7. Anchorage-based **Crest Adventures** (☎ 800/288-3134 Lower 48 only; 907/258-3866 in Alaska; www.alaskan.com/kayak) offers day trips in Prince William Sound as well as Resurrection Bay and extended trips.

WINTER SPORTS

ICE-SKATING Westchester Lagoon, just 10 blocks from the downtown core (see "Walking & Biking," above) is a community skating paradise in the winter. When the ice gets thick enough, usually by early December, the city clears a large rink and long, wide paths on the pond, mopping the ice regularly for a smooth surface. Some years, speed skating races have used a surveyed 1-kilometer loop across the lagoon. Skaters gather around burn barrels, well stocked with firewood, to socialize and warm their hands, and on weekends vendors often sell hot chocolate and coffee. Skates are for rent at **Champions Choice,** 3700 Old Seward Hwy. (☎ 907/563-3503). Or rent skates and skate indoors at one of many rinks in town, including **Ben Boeke Ice Arena,** 334 E. 16th Ave. (☎ 907/274-5715).

DOWNHILL SKIING Anchorage has three downhill ski areas: The **Alyeska Resort,** listed in the Girdwood section, below; **Alpenglow** but a good local ski area above the treeline, in perennial financial trouble, so you should check before going (see "Hiking, Mountain Biking & Backpacking," above); and **Hilltop,** a good place right in town to learn to ski, at 7015 Abbott Rd. (☎ 907/346-2169).

NORDIC SKIING Frequently the site of national competition, ✪ **Kincaid Park** is one of the best cross-country skiing areas in the country, and with more than 30 miles of trails there's more than enough room for competitors, beginners, and those in between. Trails are groomed for skating and classical techniques. Eight kilometers are lighted in winter and open until 10pm nightly, an important feature on short winter days. Be conscious that the park gates close at 10pm, winter and summer; if you're trapped inside, you're stuck. The **Kincaid Park Outdoor Center** (☎ 907/343-6397) is open Monday through Friday from 1 to 10pm and on Saturday and Sunday from 10am to 10pm. It's a warm-up house in winter and a popular venue for weddings in the summer, as the views across the inlet are spectacular. Skiing often lasts through March; more on summertime at the park is above under "Hiking, Mountain Biking & Backpacking."

SPECTATOR SPORTS

BASEBALL   Anchorage has two semipro baseball teams—the **Anchorage Glacier Pilots** (☎ 907/274-3627) and the **Anchorage Bucs** (☎ 907/561-2827)—with college athletes playing short midsummer seasons. The quality may be uneven, but you may see diamonds in the rough: Among our famous alumni are Mark McGwire, Tom Seaver, Dave Winfield, Barry Bonds, and Wally Joyner. Check the *Anchorage Daily News* for game times. Mulcahy Stadium is at 16th Avenue and A Street, a long walk or a short drive from downtown. Tickets are cheap. Dress warmly for evening games; a blanket is rarely out of order. A weekend day game is warmer, but then you won't get to see baseball played at night without lights.

BASKETBALL   The men's basketball team hosts a major Division I preseason tournament over Thanksgiving weekend, the **Great Alaska Shootout,** and plays the regular season at the Sullivan Arena and at the University Sports Center, on campus on Providence Drive. Tickets are available from Carrs Tix (☎ **907/263-2787**).

HOCKEY   The **University of Alaska—Anchorage** fields an NCAA Division I hockey team, the Seawolves, which plays at the Sullivan Arena (see "Anchorage in the Evening," below).

3 Accommodations

Hotel rooms are priced too high in Anchorage—one reason, I'm convinced, that visitors rarely stay long in the city. I've searched for more reasonable places where you'll be comfortable—much harder to find—and concentrated on the independent hotels, which often have unique local character.

There are hundreds of **bed-and-breakfasts** in Anchorage, a reaction to the hot market for rooms and high hotel rates. You can almost always get a better room for a better price at a B&B, and you'll learn more about Alaska by meeting your hosts. I've listed a number of the best places, but a booking agency can put you together with others. **Alaska Private Lodgings,** P.O. Box 200047, Anchorage, AK 99520-0047 (☎ **907/258-1717;** fax 907/258-6613; www.alaskabandb.com), is the most established, covering the whole state and able to help with itinerary planning. Their directory of B&Bs is on the Web site, with pictures. You also can drop in the downtown office at 704 W. Second Ave. The **Bed and Breakfast Association of Alaska,** Anchorage Chapter, P.O. Box 242623, Anchorage, AK 99524-2623, runs a **B&B Hotline** (☎ **907/272-5909**), which puts callers directly in touch with B&Bs, and they publish a detailed B&B directory of members.

VERY EXPENSIVE

✪ **Hotel Captain Cook.** Fourth Ave. and K St. (P.O. Box 102280), Anchorage, AK 99510-2280. ☎ **800/843-1950** or 907/276-6000. Fax 907/343-2298. www.captaincook.com. 547 units. TV TEL. High season, $230–$250 double; $240–$1,500 suite. Low season, $125–$145 double; $135–$1,500 suite. Additional person in room $10 extra. AE, DC, DISC, JCB, MC, V.

This is Alaska's great, grand hotel, where royalty and rock stars stay. Former governor Wally Hickel built the first of the three towers after the 1964 earthquake, and now the

Chain Hotels in Anchorage

Besides the hotels and B&Bs I've reviewed, Anchorage also has the typical roster of chain hotels.

DOWNTOWN   The large **Hilton Anchorage,** 500 W. Third Ave. (☎ **800/ 245-2527** or 907/272-7411), is right at the center of downtown activities; the **Sheraton Anchorage,** 401 E. Sixth Ave. (☎ **800/325-3535** or 907/276-8700), is comparable to the Hilton, but in a less attractive area a few blocks off the downtown tourist area. The Marriot was still under construction at this writing, but will be open by 2000. An independent hotel at the same quality level is **Anchorage Hotel,** 330 E St. (☎ **907/272-4553**), in a charming and historic structure, with qualities reminiscent of a good European hotel.

Other good chain hotels downtown include the **Days Inn** (☎ **907/ 276-7226**), which has a courtesy van to the airport and many amenities; the **Holiday Inn of Anchorage** (☎ **907/279-8671**), which has a pool; the **Comfort Inn Ship Creek Anchorage** (☎ **800/228-5150** or 907/277-6887), with a tiny swimming pool, located in the railroad yard area just below downtown, and the **Clarion Suites** (☎ **907/274-1000**), across from the Federal Building, also with a small pool and suites as standard rooms.

NEAR THE AIRPORT   Good, budget rooms near the airport are rare to the vanishing point, although luxurious rooms are readily available. The lowest price, consistently acceptable rooms we could find in that area were at the **Best Western Barratt Inn** (☎ **800/528-1234** or 907/243-3131; www.barrattinn.com), a sprawling property ranging from a simple motel section to luxurious accommodations. Rates range from $119 to $179 double. Also near the airport, the new **Courtyard Marriot** (☎ **800/321-2211** or 907/245-0322) is quite fresh and attractive, with many amenities and a small pool; they charge $174 double in the summer.

---

hotel fills a city block. Inside, the decor has a fully realized (maybe a little excessive) nautical theme, with art memorializing Cook's voyages and enough teak to build a square-rigger. The standard rooms are large, with great views from all sides—you don't pay more to be higher. Request a room in the newly remodeled Tower 1. The lobby contains 16 shops, and there's a concierge, tour desks, barbershop and beauty salon, and business center. The full-service health club in the basement has a decent-sized pool and a racquetball court.

Sophisticated continental food and elaborately formal service justifies the high prices at ✪ **The Crows Nest,** the city's most traditional fine dining restaurant, on the hotel's top floor. Peasant, quail, bison and venison were on recent menus, as well as the usual seafood, beef, and lamb. All tables have stupendous views, and high-backed booths lend a sense of intimacy. The speed of service requires you set aside a full evening for a special meal—the meal unfolds gradually, with almost theatrical formality. Main courses range from $26 to $50; a five-course fixed menu is $50 per person ($70 per person with wine). **Fletcher's,** off the lobby, is an English pub serving good Italian-style pizza and sandwiches. **The Pantry** is more than a typical hotel cafe, with excellent service and interesting entrees mixed in with the more predictable choices.

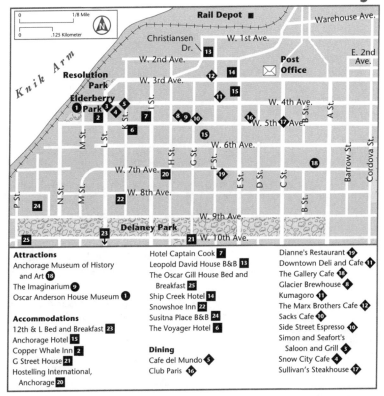

Downtown Anchorage

Rail Depot ■

Warehouse Ave.

Christiansen Dr. **13**

W. 1st Ave.

W. 2nd Ave.

E. 2nd Ave.

Post Office

12

14

W. 3rd Ave.

11

15

W. 4th Ave.

Resolution Park

Elderberry Park

1

2

4

5

7

8 **9** **10**

6

15

16

17

W. 5th Ave.

Knik Arm

M St.

L St.

K St.

I St.

H St.

G St.

F St.

E St.

D St.

C St.

B St.

A St.

Barrow St.

Cordova St.

W. 6th Ave.

W. 7th Ave.

20

19

18

W. 8th Ave.

22

P St.

N St.

M St.

24

W. 9th Ave.

Delaney Park

25

23

21

W. 10th Ave.

0 — 1/8 Mile
0 — .125 Kilometer

Attractions

Anchorage Museum of History and Art **18**
The Imaginarium **9**
Oscar Anderson House Museum **1**

Accommodations

12th & L Bed and Breakfast **23**
Anchorage Hotel **15**
Copper Whale Inn **2**
G Street House **21**
Hostelling International, Anchorage **20**

Hotel Captain Cook **7**
Leopold David House B&B **13**
The Oscar Gill House Bed and Breakfast **25**
Ship Creek Hotel **14**
Snowshoe Inn **22**
Susitna Place B&B **24**
The Voyager Hotel **6**

Dining

Cafe del Mundo **5**
Club Paris **16**

Dianne's Restaurant **19**
Downtown Deli and Cafe **11**
The Gallery Cafe **18**
Glacier Brewhouse **8**
Kumagoro **11**
The Marx Brothers Cafe **12**
Sacks Cafe **10**
Side Street Espresso **10**
Simon and Seafort's Saloon and Grill **3**
Snow City Cafe **4**
Sullivan's Steakhouse **17**

Regal Alaskan. 4800 Spenard Rd., Anchorage, AK 99517-3236. ☎ **800/544-0553** or 907/243-2300. Fax 907/243-8815. www.regal-hotels.com/anch/index.html. 248 units. TV TEL. High season, $270–$285 double; $325–$600 suite. Low season, $165–$185 double; $250–$400 suite. AE, CB, DC, DISC, EURO, JCB, MC, V.

With a good view of the floatplanes on Lake Spenard, near the airport, the large lobby suggests a big fishing and hunting lodge. There's a big patio to catch the sun and watch the planes, but the recently remodeled rooms are what's really special—decorated in a style of tasteful opulence and packed with thoughtful details, they're a delight to the eye and an invitation to relaxation. Each has a coffeemaker, fridge, hair dryer, ironing board, clock radio, modem jacks, and a Nintendo game on the TV. We were surprised to find some flaws in the housekeeping on our last check, but that could have been an isolated problem. The hotel lacks a swimming pool, but does have a health club with a spa and sauna. A courtesy van runs a regular schedule downtown, but for convenience you really need to rent a car if you stay in this area. The restaurants on-site serve a steak and seafood menu, sandwiches, and the other fare you'd expect.

EXPENSIVE

✪ **Aurora Winds Inn B&B Resort.** 7501 Upper O'Malley Rd., Anchorage, AK 99516. ☎ **907/346-2533.** Fax 907/346-3192. E-mail: awbnb@alaska.net. 5 units. TV TEL. High season, $125–$175 double. Low season, $55–$125 double. Rates include full breakfast. Additional person in room $15 extra in high season, $10 extra in low season. AE, DC, DISC, MC, V.

The rooms in this massive house far up the hillside in South Anchorage are so grand and theatrically decorated you'll feel as if you're in a James Bond movie. The upstairs living room has a white stone fireplace (one of four) and a matching white grand piano. A downstairs rec room has a gym, pool table, sauna, and theater. Each bedroom has a sitting area, VCR, and other details such as a second phone line so you can hook your computer up to the Internet and talk on the phone at the same time. Even some of the bathrooms are showplaces: Three have Jacuzzis, and one is larger than a lot of hotel rooms, with an "environmental habitat chamber." One lovely room has windows on the deck and forest on three sides. There's a large hot tub in the attractive gardens.

Copper Whale Inn. 440 L St., Anchorage, AK 99501. ☎ **907/258-7999.** Fax 888/WHALE-IN or 907/258-6213. E-mail: cwhalein@alaska.net. 14 units, 12 with private bathroom. High season, $110 double with shared bathroom, $155 double with private bathroom. Low season, $69 with shared bathroom, $79 with private bathroom. Additional person in room $10 extra. Rates include full breakfast. AE, CB, DC, DISC, JCB, MC, V.

A pair of clapboard houses overlook the water and Elderberry Park right on the Coastal Trail downtown, with charming rooms of every shape and size. There's a wonderfully casual feeling to the place. The rooms in the newer building, lower on the hill, are preferable, with cherry-wood furniture and high ceilings and, on the lower level, patios. Rooms lack TVs and phones, but in some you can get them hooked up by request.

Ship Creek Hotel. 505 W. Second Ave., Anchorage, AK 99501. ☎ **800/844-0242** or 907/278-5050. Fax 907/276-2929. E-mail: shipcrk@alaska.net. 30 suites. TV TEL. High season, $139–$149 double. Low season, $59–$79 double. Additional person in room $10 extra. Rates include continental breakfast. DC, DISC, MC, V.

With new furniture, paint, and carpet in 1999, this is a friendly little hotel of converted apartments right downtown, under the same ownership as the Snowshoe Inn (described below). The rooms are exceptionally fresh and light, and many have good water views. Each has a living room, a small bedroom, and a full kitchen. Phones have voice mail and modem ports. When we last checked, it was not a good choice for people with mobility problems, as all rooms required negotiating stairs, but they promised ramps in the future.

The Voyager Hotel. 501 K St., Anchorage, AK 99501. ☎ **800/247-9070** or 907/277-9501. Fax 907/274-0333. E-mail: rsvp@alaska.net. 38 units. A/C TV TEL. High season, $169 double. Low season, $89 double. Additional person in room $10 extra. AE, CB, DC, DISC, JCB, MC, V.

Thanks to an exacting proprietor, Stan Williams, The Voyager is just right. The size is small; the location central; the rooms large and light, all with kitchenettes; the housekeeping exceptional; the desks have speaker phones, modem ports, and extra electrical outlets; and the hospitality is warm yet highly professional. There's nothing ostentatious or outwardly remarkable about the hotel, yet the most experienced travelers rave about it the loudest. No smoking.

MODERATE

Parkwood Inn. 4455 Juneau St., Anchorage, AK 99503. ☎ **907/563-3590.** Fax 907/563-5560. E-mail: parkwood@sinbad.net. 48 units. TV TEL. High season, $99 double. Low season, $59 double. Additional person in room $10 extra. AE, DC, DISC, MC, V.

Located in midtown, somewhat convenient to the airport but not the sights, this comfortable family hotel is a converted three-story apartment building. All rooms are suites with full kitchens; larger ones go for up to $169 a night in the summer. There is no elevator, and noise can be a problem. Although completely screened by trees, the

Special-Interest B&Bs in Anchorage

Along with the other B&Bs reviewed in this section, I can also recommend the following, which cater to their own narrow niches: **Moosewood Bed and Breakfast** (☎ **907/345-8788;** www.alaska.net/~moosewd/), up in the mountains, has thought of every luxury that can be provided for vegetarians and people with disabilities. **Leopold David House B&B,** right downtown in one of the most historic houses in town, at 605 W. Second Ave. (☎ **907/279-1917;** www.Alaskana.net), has hosts who speak French, German, Polish, Russian, and Spanish. I also especially like these downtown places: **G Street House** (☎ **907/258-1717**), an elegant home hosted by a wonderful family; and **Susitna Place** (☎ **907/274-3344;** www. susitnaplace.com), overlooking Cook Inlet from atop a bluff on a quiet side street.

site is in a largely industrial area; you will need a car. Suites where smoking and pets are permitted are available; the one we visited smelled strongly of cigarettes. Others rooms are nonallergenic, and quite clean if a bit worn. The staff is friendly and competent. There's a coin-op laundry and free coffee in the lobby.

Raven House Bed and Breakfast. 3315 Iliamna Ave., Anchorage, AK 99517. ☎ **907/248-9587.** Fax 907/248-6600. E-mail: ravenbnb@alaska.net. 3 units, one with private bathroom. $85 shared bathroom, $125 private bathroom. Rates include full breakfast. AE, MC, V.

On a huge, sloping lot on the Coastal Trail in the Turnagain residential area, the house has a sleek, opulently modern style. Maxine Quist's extraordinary housekeeping helps maintain the clean lines—it's as if the place were brand new. Two nicely decorated bedrooms of medium size share a bathroom. A huge and luxuriously appointed suite downstairs has a bar, fridge, entertainment center, and two-person Jacuzzi.

✪ **Snowshoe Inn.** 826 K St., Anchorage, AK 99501. ☎ **907/258-SNOW.** Fax 907/258-SHOE. 16 units. TV TEL. High season, $99–$139 double. Low season, $59–$79 double. Additional person in room $10 extra. Rates include continental breakfast. DISC, MC, V.

This cheerful, family-run hotel on a quiet downtown street has comfortable, light, and attractively decorated rooms with bright fabrics, all perfectly clean. The building, formerly apartments, has been transformed by the energetic Zeid family, which seems to be constantly improving something. They've recently added refrigerators, microwaves, coffeemakers, VCRs, and HBO; and the paint, carpet, and furniture were new in 1999. Ten of the rooms have shower stalls, not tubs; two have Jacuzzis. I've found no better bargain downtown. Freezer and storage space and a coin-op laundry are available. No smoking.

12th & L Bed and Breakfast. 1134 L St., Anchorage, AK 99501. ☎ **907/276-1225.** Fax 907/276-1224. www.anchorage-lodging.com. 4 units. TV TEL. High season, $98 double; $128 suite. Low season, $53 double; $68 suite. Additional person in room $5–$10 extra. Rates include continental breakfast. AE, DISC, MC, V.

An architect designed this summery little B&B 6 blocks from the downtown core as his own home. Although he's gone, his work shows especially in the common areas, where the light pours though glass bricks and French doors from a walled garden rustling with weeping birches. The three rooms downstairs are smallish, but everything is well thought out, with wood floors, original contemporary art, patterned tile work in the shower stalls, and small TVs with cable mounted on the walls. The two-bedroom upstairs suite is tucked charmingly under the eaves, with skylights that open. Guests use the washer and dryer free. No smoking.

INEXPENSIVE

Hillside Hotel and RV Park. 2150 Gambell St., Anchorage, AK 99503. ☎ **907/258-6006.**
Fax 907/279-8972. 26 units. TV TEL. High season, $85–$115 double. Low season, $60–$86
double. Additional person in room $10 extra. AE, DISC, MC, V.

On a busy highway with a car dealership and self-storage business, this funny little
hotel is a friendly oasis. Rooms are generally clean and well maintained and have
features—like microwaves and refrigerators—that make them quite practical, if not
beautiful or luxurious. A gate in the RV park leads to the Lanie Fleischer Coastal Trail,
for biking or Nordic skiing. (Full hookups are $22.) There are coffee machines in the
rooms and the lobby, and a coin-op laundry is available.

A Homestead Bed and Breakfast. 6141 Jewel Lake Rd., Anchorage, AK 99502. ☎ **907/
243-5678.** Fax 907/248-6184. E-mail: jasper@chugach.net. 2 units. TV TEL. Summer $95
double; winter $65 double. Additional person in room $20 extra. Rates include full breakfast.
MC, V (5% surcharge).

This is a real 1930s homestead house built of logs, once remote but now a few minutes from the airport and Kincaid Park. Frank and Patricia Jasper have lived here more
than 30 years, and they've kept it as an authentic slice of Alaska. One of the rooms is
a charming log cabin, the other is a many-room upstairs suite with an outside
entrance. Either one is a great deal, with a feeling of rustic Alaska that doesn't compromise guests' comfort.

✪ **The Oscar Gill House Bed and Breakfast.** 1344 W. 10th Ave. (P.O. Box 200047),
Anchorage, AK 99520-0047. ☎ **907/258-1717.** Fax 907/258-6613. www.alaskabandb.
com. 3 units, 1 with private bathroom. TEL. High season, $85 double shared bathroom, $95
double private bathroom. Low season, $65 double shared bathroom, $75 double private
bathroom. Additional person in room $15 extra. Rates include full breakfast. AE, MC, V (5%
surcharge).

On the Delaney Park strip, just a few blocks from downtown, this is truly the oldest
house in Anchorage—it was built in 1913, in Knik, before Anchorage was founded,
and moved here on a barge a few years later. Oscar Gill was an early civic leader. The
house was to be torn down in 1982 but was moved to storage by a historic preservation group; Mark and Susan Lutz saved it in 1994, moving it to its present location
and, with their own labor, restoring it authentically as a cozy, friendly bed-and-
breakfast. The house is full of appropriate antiques, and manages to be both homey
and immaculate. The prices are low because the Lutzes are decent people—they book
up many months ahead, and could charge 50% more. Free bikes are available.

HOSTELS

Hostelling International, Anchorage, 700 H St., Anchorage, AK 99501 (☎ **907/
276-3635;** fax 907/276-7772), is a large place right downtown. A coin-op laundry,
kitchen, and baggage storage are available. The office is open summer daily 7:30am to
2am, winter 8am to noon and 5pm to midnight. **Spenard Hostel International,**
2845 W. 42nd Ave., Anchorage, AK 99517 (☎ **907/248-5036;** www.alaskalife.net/
spnrdhstl/hostel.html), is a friendly place near the airport, with free phones, bike and
storage rental, e-mail service, and a laundry. There are three lounges for different activities, and you can come and go 24 hours. The office is open daily 9am to 1pm and 7
to 11pm in summer, 7 to 11pm winter. Beds are $15. **Qupqugiaq Cafe, Inn and
School,** 640 W. 36th Ave., Anchorage, AK 99503 (☎ **907/563-5681**), is a special
place. The rooms, renting in summer for $49 double, are like private hostel accom-
modations, with shared phones, kitchens, and bathrooms, but quite good for what
they are. Reservations are accepted by credit card. Downstairs, the cafe is a coffee

house and community center drawing together alternative livers and idealists for music, socializing, discussion groups, and formal classes on anything from worm composting to Chinese politics.

CAMPING

Anchorage is a big city, so for a real camping experience, you need to head out of town. The State Parks' 28-site, $10-per-night **Bird Creek Campground,** 25 miles south on the Seward Highway next to Turnagain Arm, is one of my favorites. The State Parks' 56-site campground on **Eagle River** also sits in a pleasant spot, and it's well developed with paved roads and large sites with lots of privacy. It costs $15 a night. From the Glenn Highway, 12 miles from Anchorage, take the Hiland Road exit.

Within the Anchorage bowl, there are several camper and RV parks. Near the new Alaska Native Heritage Center, the nicely wooded and landscaped **Anchorage RV Park,** 7300 Oilwell Road (☎ **800/400-7275** or 907/338-7275; www.anchrvpark. com), has full services and excellent facilities; they charge $29 per night on the 195 sites. If you don't need full hookups or all the extras, the municipally owned **Centennial Camper Park,** is close by, on Boundary Road at the Muldoon Road exit from the Glenn Highway (☎ **907/333-9711** or 907/343-4474), just as you enter town from the north, with 80 dry sites, a dump station, and free showers. Camping permits are $13 a night. The **Hillside Motel and RV Park** is listed above under "Accommodations: Inexpensive."

4 Dining

DOWNTOWN

Besides these downtown restaurants, one of the most popular is **Sullivan's Steakhouse,** at Fifth and C streets (☎ **907/258-2882**); they do good steaks, and the dining room's re-creation of a jazz-age men's club is museum quality, but the prices, all à la carte, are just too high for the simple food.

EXPENSIVE

Club Paris. 417 W. Fifth Ave. ☎ **907/277-6332.** Reservations recommended. Main courses $14–$44; lunch $5.75–$15. AE, DISC, MC, V. Daily 11:30am–2:30pm and 5–10pm. STEAK/ SEAFOOD.

Walking from a bright spring afternoon, under a neon Eiffel Tower, into midnight darkness, past a smoke-enshrouded bar, and sitting down at a secretive booth for two, I felt as if I should lean across the table and plot a shady 1950s oil deal with my companion. And I would probably not have been the first. Smoky Club Paris will be too authentic for some, but it's the essence of old Anchorage boomtown years, when the streets were dusty and an oil man needed a class joint in which to do business. Beef, of course, is what to order, and it'll be done right. Full liquor license.

✪ **The Marx Brothers Cafe.** 627 W. Third Ave. ☎ **907/278-2133.** www.marxcafe.com. Reservations required. Main courses $17.50–$28.50. AE, DC, MC, V. Summer daily 5:30–10pm, winter Mon–Thurs 6–9:30pm, Fri-Sat 5:30–10pm. ECLECTIC/REGIONAL.

A restaurant that began as a hobby among three friends 20 years ago is still a labor of love, and has become a standard of excellence in the state. Dinner takes all night—you feel funny not ordering an appetizer—but you can spend the time watching chef Jack Amon pick herbs and vegetables for your meal from the garden behind the historic little building, one of the city's first houses. The cuisine is varied and creative, ranging from Asian to Italian, and every dish is an adventure. It's traditional to order the

---

Fast Food, Anchorage Style

Besides the sit-down restaurants listed below, there's lots of good take-out fast food in Anchorage. (Of course, all the franchise places also are represented.) The best, most original burgers are at **Arctic Roadrunner,** with locations on Arctic Boulevard at Fireweed Lane and on Old Seward Highway at International Airport Road. The best deli, with legendary sandwiches, is **Atlasta Deli,** in the shopping mall at Arctic Boulevard and Tudor Road; it's really a gourmet experience, with more than 100 meats and cheeses, and you can eat in. Anchorage is short on good Chinese food, but the **Fu-Do Chinese Restaurant,** at 2600 E. Tudor Rd. (☎ 907/561-6611), is better than most, and will deliver. **Omega Pizza,** 2601 Spenard Rd. (☎ 907/272-6007), has good pizza and fast delivery. **Moose's Tooth Pub and Pizzeria,** 3300 Old Seward Hwy. (☎ 907/258-2537), has been voted as having both the best pizza and the best local beer by newspaper readers. The best place to pack a picnic, or get a relaxed sidewalk cafe lunch or dinner of deli sandwiches, gourmet pizza, or Chinese food, is **New Sagaya's City Market** (☎ 907/274-6173) at the corner of 13th and I streets. It's also a wonderful gourmet grocery and community meeting place.

Caesar salad made at the table by Van, one of the founders and the host. The decor and style are studied casual elegance. One flaw: If your table is not ready, the wait is uncomfortable. Beer and wine license.

✪ **Simon and Seafort's Saloon and Grill.** 420 L St. ☎ 907/274-3502. Reservations required. Lunch $7–$15, dinner $16–$40. AE, MC, V. Mon–Fri 11:15am–3:30pm and 4:30–11:00pm, Sat noon–3:30pm, 4:30–11pm, Sun noon–10pm. STEAK/SEAFOOD.

Simon's, as it's known, is a jolly beef and seafood grill where voices boom off the high ceilings. On sunny summer evenings, the rooms, fitted with brass turn-of-the-century saloon decor, fill with light off Cook Inlet, down below the bluff; the views are magnificent. To enjoy the ambience cheaply, order a sandwich and soup in the well-stocked bar. In summer it's best to make reservations a couple of days in advance. Once there, I've never been disappointed by the straightforward salmon or prime rib, or anything else on the menu. The service is efficient and professional. Full liquor license.

MODERATE

Glacier Brewhouse. 737 W. Fifth Ave. ☎ 907/274-BREW. www.glacierbrewhouse.com. Reservations recommended for dinner. Lunch $8–$13, dinner $9–$28. AE, MC, V. High season, 11am–11pm daily; low season Mon–Sat 11am–10pm, Sun 4–9pm. GRILL/SEAFOOD/PIZZA

A tasty, eclectic, and ever-changing menu is served in a large dining room with lodge decor, where the pleasant scent of the wood-fired grill hangs in the air. They brew five hearty beers behind a glass wall. It's noisy and active, with lots of agreeable if trendy touches, such as the bread, made from spent brewery grain, that's set out on the tables with olive oil. An advantage for travelers is the wide price range—a feta cheese, spinach, and artichoke pizza is $10, crab legs $30. Not a good choice for groups, however, as it's too loud to carry on a conversation across a large table.

Kumagoro. 533 W. Fourth Ave. ☎ 907/272-9905. Main courses $11.80–$35; lunch $5.50–$18.80. AE, CB, DC, JCB, MC, V. Daily 11am–10pm. JAPANESE.

Anchorage has a lot of good, authentic Japanese restaurants, but this one, right on the main tourist street downtown, has the added advantage of convenience for travelers. My current favorite lunch anywhere is their lunch box, a large sampler of many dishes, including generous helpings of sushi and sashimi. The dining room is pleasantly low-key, with tables in rows, so you may have the opportunity to meet those seated next to you. Beer and wine license.

Sacks Cafe. 328 G St. ☎ **907/274-4022.** www.sackscafe.com. Reservations recommended for dinner. Main courses $14–$21; lunch $4.75–$9.75. AE, MC, V. Sun–Thus 11am–10pm, Fri–Sat 11am–11pm. CREATIVE/ECLECTIC.

The restaurant is currently moving to the new digs listed here. We've long enjoyed the creative and occasionally inspired cuisine at the old location. For lunch, the sandwiches are unforgettable, with choices such as shrimp and avocado with herb cream cheese on sourdough. Evening meals include experiments with Thai and other ethnic cuisines, often using fresh seafood and pasta as the canvas for the chef's creations. Art from the Decker Gallery hangs in the dining room. Best of all, it's reasonable priced—we can afford to eat there more than once a year. A new bistro/tapas menu will be added at the new location. They serve beer and wine.

INEXPENSIVE

Dianne's Restaurant. 550 W. Seventh Ave., Suite 110. ☎ **907/279-7243.** All items $4–$7.50. AE, MC, V. Mon–Fri 7am–4pm. SOUP/SANDWICH.

Located in the base of a tall, glass office building, Dianne's has developed such a reputation for great baking, soups, sandwiches, and specials that at lunch hour it's pretty well clogged with people in suits. The line at the cafeteria moves fast, however, and the bright, casual atmosphere is fun and full of energy. My first choice for a quick, healthy lunch downtown. No liquor license.

Downtown Deli and Cafe. 525 W. Fourth Ave. ☎ **907/276-7116.** All items $5–$12. AE, DC, DISC, MC, V. Daily 6am–9:30pm. DELI.

Tony Knowles made his Fourth Avenue sandwich restaurant the place to meet local politicians and people-in-the-know 20 years ago; when he was elected governor in 1994, President Clinton came for dinner. I didn't believe Clinton, however, when he said he enjoyed the reindeer stew—it's a gimmick. Stick with the generous sandwiches, simple entrees, and superior breakfasts. Prices are reasonable—especially for dinner, when downtown is short on inexpensive sit-down places—and kids are treated well. It's just the reliable place you want for a low-key meal. Some mornings, however, they're overrun with tourists and the service suffers. They serve beer and wine.

The Gallery Cafe. In the Anchorage Museum of History and Art, 121 W. Seventh Ave. ☎ **907/343-6193.** Lunch $7.50–$9. AE, MC, V. High season, Sun–Fri 9am–9pm, Sat 9am–6pm; low season, Tues–Sat 10am–6pm, Sun 1–5pm. SANDWICHES/SEAFOOD.

This is the cafe in the atrium at the museum, and it's a secret even among Anchorage residents. There's always a special of salmon or some more exotic fish, often prepared with Asian influences, and presented so beautifully you can hardly stand to mar it with your fork. Only a few restaurants in Alaska could mount a meal of this quality as a dinner entree, and they'd charge three times the price. The only flaw of the ingenious sandwiches is that the bread and croissants aren't engineered for the stress presented by the many ingredients, and tend to fall apart.

✪ **The Lucky Wishbone.** 1033 E. Fifth Ave. ☎ **907/272-3454.** All meals $3–$9.25. Summer daily 10am–11pm, winter 10am–10pm. MC, V. DINER

This Anchorage institution ("The Bone") is where the real pioneer Alaska meets families out for a delicious, not-too-greasy fried chicken dinner and famous milk shakes (try the hot fudge) and other delights from the fountain. One section of the counter is reserved for discussion of aviation and golf. When the beloved owners outlawed smoking years ago, it made the front page of the newspaper. You'll see few other tourists, as the location, among the car dealerships at the extreme east end of downtown, is too far to walk from the hotels. They have a drive-in.

Snow City Cafe. 1034 W. Fourth Ave. ☎ **907/272-CITY.** Lunch $4–$8.75, dinner $9–$13. AE, DISC, MC, V. Summer daily 7am–10pm; winter Mon–Tues 7am–4pm, Wed–Fri 7am–9pm, Sat–Sun 8am–9pm. VEGETARIAN/SEAFOOD

The food served by a friendly and efficient staff in this small, light storefront dining room is laced with interesting flavors and styles of preparation, including many vegetarian dishes. They also serve seafood, chicken, and pasta. The young people who meet here create a great sense of camaraderie even for newcomers, and those interested in backpacking, environmental issues, and the like may make new friends. The restaurant has become a primary acoustic music venue on weekend evenings, sometimes booking national performers on the verge of the big time. They serve beer and wine.

BEYOND DOWNTOWN
EXPENSIVE

✪ **Jens' Restaurant.** 701 W. 36th Ave. ☎ **907/561-5367.** Reservations recommended. Main courses $17–$25; lunch $8.50–$14.50. AE, CB, DC, DISC, MC, V. Mon 11:30am–2pm, Tues–Fri 11:30am–2pm and 6–10pm, Sat 6–10pm. Closed Jan. FRENCH

This restaurant, in a Spenard strip mall, is an improbable playground for the dean of Anchorage chefs, Jens Hansen, who closes his doors each January to go on a gastronomic working vacation to exotic places. When he comes back, he treats the faithful to his interpretations of what he learned. Other than the traditional Danish dishes served for lunch, the menu is French influenced and new every night. You'll find combinations that you've never encountered, but the cuisine doesn't go into complication for its own sake; those dishes that are best simple, such as fresh salmon, are prepared simply. While waiting for a table, sip wine from the exceptional list and sample tapas at a counter. Don't take children.

MODERATE

✪ **Campo Bello.** 661 W. 36th, Suite 10. ☎ **907/563-2040.** Main courses $11–$18; lunch $7–$11. DISC, MC, V. Lunch Mon–Fri 11am–2:30pm; dinner Tues–Sat 5–9:30pm. NORTHERN ITALIAN.

This quiet little midtown restaurant has sophisticated northern Italian cuisine and Alaskan seafood, wonderfully hospitable service, and low prices. It stands with the best of Alaska's restaurants, but charges much less than you would pay in most comparable establishments. The cuisine doesn't try to be as trendy and far-out as some, but is bold and highly flavored, creating interesting tastes mostly within the context of traditional dishes and combinations. I have met those who don't like the restaurant, but that's only because they expect the heavy tomatoes and cheese of the typical southern Italian family restaurant, which are absent here. We always head home feeling relaxed and fulfilled. The wine list is reasonably priced; they also serve exotic beer.

INEXPENSIVE

Mexico in Alaska. 7305 Old Seward Hwy. ☎ **907/349-1528.** Main courses $9–$16.75; lunch $7.95. AE, MC, V. Mon–Fri 11am–10pm, Sat noon–10pm, Sun 4–9pm. MEXICAN

The down-scale building, location, and decor camouflage Alaska's best Mexican restaurant. It's the food and the service that make it so special. The food—strictly traditional, authentic cuisine of central-west Mexico—is subtle and exciting for anyone used to the heavy flavors of American-style Mexican food. The service, carried out by the family of founder Maria-Elena Ball, goes beyond friendly—they seem really interested in sharing their love of their food and culture. The prices are low, and the dining room less than grand. To get there from downtown, take New Seward Highway (Gambell Street) south, right on Dowling Road, left on Old Seward Highway. They serve beer and wine.

Roscoe's Skyline Restaurant. 600 E. Northern Lights Blvd. (in the Sears Mall). ☎ **907/ 276-5879.** Lunch $4.50–$8, dinner $11–$20. AE, MC, V. Mon–Thurs 11am–9pm, Fri–Sat 11am–10pm, Sun noon–6pm. SOUL FOOD/SOUTHERN

Roscoe built up this large mall restaurant from a shack where he used to barbecue out back in a cutoff steel barrel. The place hasn't lost any of the authenticity or friendly, homey service in the transition, but now the dining room is comfortable and well appointed. The barbecue and fried chicken are justly famous.

COFFEEHOUSES

There are coffeehouses all over the city where people go for a cup of java and a pastry, and to meet people and engage in conversation. They've become the new town square of social interaction. My favorite is **Side Street Espresso,** on G between 4th and 5th, a meeting place for artists, radicals, musicians, and other people who want to trade ideas. **Cafe del Mundo,** at Fourth and K downtown and at Northern Lights and Denali in midtown, gathers an older crowd of businesspeople, yuppies, stay-at-home parents, and anyone else looking for a comfortable meeting place. The well-intentioned should check out **Qupqugiaq,** listed above under "Hostels."

5 Shopping

Some interesting shops are mentioned above, in the walking tour of downtown, where most galleries and gift shops are located. Before making major purchases, know what you're buying (see "Native Art—Finding the Real Thing," in chapter 2).

Many stores in Anchorage carry Native Alaskan arts and crafts. If you're going to the Bush, you'll find lower prices there but less selection. The **Oomingmak Musk Ox Producers' Co-operative,** in the house with the musk ox on the side at Sixth Avenue and H Street, sells scarves and other knitted items of qiviut (*ki*-vee-ute), the light, warm, silky underhair of the musk ox, which is collected from the tundra, combed out, and knitted in the Bush by village women. They're expensive—some caps cost over $100—but unique and culturally significant. The **Yankee Whaler,** in the lobby of the Hotel Captain Cook, at Fifth Avenue and I Street, is a small but well-regarded shop carrying Native arts. **Alaska Native Arts and Crafts,** better known as ANAC, in the post office mall at 333 W. Fourth Ave., is the traditional and original artists' outlet for authentic Native work, in operation since 1938. **The Rusty Harpoon,** next door in the yellow Sunshine Mall, at 411 Fourth Ave., also has authentic Native items, less expensive crafts, and reliable, longtime proprietors. **One People,** at 400 D St., carries folk art from all over the world, especially Native dolls, soapstone and ivory carvings, jewelry, and baskets. Farther afield, the **Alaska Fur Exchange,** at 4417 Old Seward Hwy., near Tudor Road, is a cross between an old-time wilderness trading post and a modern factory outlet. Rural residents bring in furs and crafts to sell and trade, which are displayed in great profusion and clutter. If you're in the market for pelts, go no further. Perhaps the best place for Native crafts in Anchorage is the small shop in the Alaska Native Medical Center, off Tudor east of Bragaw, where everything is on consignment from the users of the hospital. There's exceptional Native art on the walls of the hospital, too.

If you're in the market for furs, Anchorage has a wide selection and no sales tax. **David Green Master Furrier,** at 130 W. Fourth Ave., is an Anchorage institution. The **Alaska Fur Factory** is close by, at Fourth Avenue and D Street, as is the **Alaska Fur Gallery,** at 428 W. Fourth Ave., just down the block. There are others in the Anchorage Hilton Hotel and the 5th Avenue Mall. **Laura Wright Alaskan Parkys,** at 343 W. Fifth Ave., makes and sells the bright fabric coats called *kuspuks* really worn by Eskimos. Winter-wear parkys often have fur trim, but that isn't a requirement for beauty and authenticity. Most of the coats are made to order by the friendly women who work there.

There are lots of places to buy both mass-produced and inexpensive handmade crafts that aren't from the Bush. If you can be in town on a Saturday during the summer, be sure to visit the ✪ **Saturday Market** street fair, in the parking lot at Third Avenue and E Street, with food, music, and hundreds of miscellaneous crafts booths. A new Wednesday Market is planned to take place on Fourth Avenue downtown. You won't have any trouble finding gift shops on Fourth. Our favorite is the relatively classy **Cabin Fever,** at 650 W. Fourth. Other large, attractive shops include **Once in a Blue Moose**, at Fourth Avenue and F Street, **Grizzly's Gifts,** at Fourth and E, and **Trapper Jacks,** at Fourth and G. The **Kobuk Coffee Company,** at Fifth Avenue and E Street, next to town square, occupies one of Anchorage's earliest commercial buildings; it's a cozy little candy, coffee, and collectibles shop. In midtown, on International Airport Road between the Old and New Seward highways, **Alaska Wild Berry Products** is a fun store to visit. There's a chocolate waterfall and a big window where you can watch the candy factory at work. The chocolate-covered berry jellies are simultaneously addictive and rich enough to make you dizzy if you eat more than a few.

Downtown has several fine art galleries. The ✪ **Decker/Morris Gallery,** at Sixth Avenue and G Street, takes its work seriously, showing exciting and adventurous artists, even if they lack broad commercial appeal. **Artique,** 2 blocks north at 314 G St., is Anchorage's oldest gallery and has a much larger selection. Half of the gallery is given over to big oils and other gorgeous originals; the other half is chock-full of prints, less-expensive ceramics, and some mass produced or corny stuff. At Fifth and G, **Aurora Fine Arts** carries more pottery, prints, and gifts.

6 Anchorage in the Evening

THE PERFORMING ARTS

Anchorage has become an ever-more-frequent destination for major popular and classical music performers. To find out what's happening, pick up a copy of Friday's edition of the *Anchorage Daily News* for the "8" section, which includes event listings and information on the club and arts scene. Their Web site, www.adn.com, allows you to check the calendar and listings from afar. The *Anchorage Press,* the free weekly alternative paper, has a similar service, with a younger slant, at www.anchoragepress.com. **Carrs Tix** (☎ 907/263-ARTS; www.carrstix.com) is the main ticket agency covering Alaska. Their Web site is useful, and they have box offices at the Anchorage Center for Performing Arts and at Carrs grocery stores (Carrs was recently bought by Safeway, so this may change).

The arts season begins in the fall and ends in the spring, but traveling performers often come through in the summer as well, and the **Anchorage Festival of Music**

(☎ **907/276-2465**) presents a classical music series in June. The **Anchorage Symphony** (☎ **907/274-8668**) performs during the winter season. The **Anchorage Concert Association** (☎ **907/272-1471**) promotes a schedule of international-caliber music and other performing arts. And Anchorage has lots of community theater, opera, and limited professional theater, including the experimental, semiprofessional **Out North Theater** (☎ **907/279-8200;** www.outnorth.org).

Most large events take place at one of two venues. The **Anchorage Center for the Performing Arts,** at 621 W. Sixth Ave., on town square, has three beautiful theaters ranging in size from 350 to 2,000 seats. Popular music and other large-venue performances take place at the 8,500-seat **Sullivan Arena,** at 16th Avenue and Gambell Street (New Seward Highway).

✪ **Cyrano's Off Center Playhouse** (☎ **907/274-2599**) is a small theater at Fourth Avenue and D Street that presents more challenging, intimate works, poetry readings, comedy, and lectures, with many shows in the summer. The superb Bistro Bergerac is attached.

NIGHTCLUBS & BARS

For a fun, funny night out, nothing in town compares to ✪ **Mr. Whitekeys' Fly By Night Club,** on Spenard Road south of Northern Lights Boulevard (☎ **907/279-SPAM**). This drinking establishment seems to be an excuse for the goateed proprietor, a consummate vulgarian, to ridicule Anchorage in his crude, political, local-humor musical comedy shows, in which he costars with a fallen former Miss Anchorage. If you can laugh at dog poop, you'll love it. The summer show is at 8pm Tuesday through Saturday, with no smoking Tuesday through Thursday. Tickets are $12 to $18, and reservations are necessary well in advance. The bar has exceptional food, too.

Blues Central/Chef's Inn, 825 W. Northern Lights Blvd. (☎ **907/272-1341**), is dedicated to showcasing the best blues performers available, and major names come through on a regular basis. They also serve excellent beef. The huge **Chilkoot Charlie's,** at Spenard Road and Fireweed Lane (☎ **907/272-1010**), usually has Top 40 rock playing on various stages. The place is huge, but can be claustrophobic when crowded, with low ceilings and a dark, roadhouse atmosphere. The **Long Branch Saloon,** 1737 E. Dimond Boulevard (☎ **907/349-4142**), east of New Seward Highway, has country music every night and great burgers and other beef.

Humpy's, downtown at Sixth Avenue and F Street, has dozens of beers on tap, decent bar food, and live acoustic music every night. **Rumrunners,** at 330 E St., has a faithful crowd, music, and the best bartender in town, according to a newspaper poll. The **Cheechako Club,** 317 W. Fireweed Lane, is an old-fashioned Irish bar in an ancient log building; it's fun and loud. To watch a game, try the **Sports Edition,** in the Anchorage Hilton Hotel at Third Avenue and E Street. If you just want to talk, check out the **Snow Goose Restaurant and Brewery,** at 717 W. Third Ave., where you can sip their own brews on a sunny patio, or one of the hangouts listed above on the walking tour.

THE MOVIES

There are several multiplexes in Anchorage playing all the current Hollywood output; check the *Anchorage Daily News* for listings. There's no movie theater downtown, but the closest, **Fireweed Theater** (☎ **907/566-3328**), the **Century 16** (☎ **907/929-FILM**), and the **University Theater** (☎ **907/566-3335**), are all a short cab ride away in midtown. The **Capri Cinema,** 3425 E. Tudor Rd. (☎ **907/561-0064**), shows art films in a minimall.

7 Out from Anchorage: Turnagain Arm & Portage Glacier

One of the world's great drives starts in Anchorage and leads roughly 50 miles south on the Seward Highway to Portage Glacier. It's the trip, not the destination, that makes it worthwhile. The two-lane highway along Turnagain Arm, chipped from the foot of the rocky Chugach Mountains, provides a platform to see a magnificent, ever-changing, mostly untouched landscape full of wildlife. I've listed the sights in the style of a highway log, for there are interesting stops all the way along the road. It will take at least half a day, and there's plenty to do for an all-day excursion. Use your headlights for safety even in daylight and be patient if you get stuck behind a summertime line of cars—if you pass, you'll just come up behind another line ahead. Mileage markers count from Seward, the other end of the road; after you pass a milepost (116, for example), start looking for sites listed for mile 115.

Car rental is covered in the Anchorage section, above. There are many bus tours that follow the route and visit Portage Glacier (see "Getting There: By Bus" under "Essentials," above). **Gray Line** (☎ **800/544-2206** or 907/277-5581) offers a 7-hour trip that includes a stop in Girdwood and a boat ride on Portage Lake for $60, twice daily in summer.

POTTER MARSH (Mile 117)   Heading south from Anchorage proper, the Seward Highway descends a bluff to cross a broad marsh formed by water impounded behind the tracks of the Alaska Railroad. The marsh has a boardwalk from which you can watch a huge variety of birds. Salad-green grasses grow from sparkling, pond-green water.

POTTER SECTION HOUSE (Mile 115)   Located at the south end of Potter Marsh, the section house was an early maintenance station for the Alaska Railroad. Today it contains offices of Chugach State Park, open during normal business hours. A few old train cars and an interpretive display outside will briefly interest the kids. Just across the road is the trailhead for the **Turnagain Arm Trail.** It's a mostly level path running down the arm well above the highway, with great views breaking now and then through the trees. You can continue 9 miles to Windy Corner, or break off where the trails meets the McHugh Creek picnic area and trailhead, about 4 miles out.

McHUGH CREEK (Mile 111)   Four miles south of Potter is an excellent state park picnic area and a challenging day hike with a 3,000-foot elevation gain to Rabbit Lake, which sits in a tundra mountain bowl, or to the top of 4,301-foot McHugh Peak. Without climbing all the way, there are spectacular views within an hour of the road.

BELUGA POINT (Mile 110)   When the state highway department put up scenic overlook signs on this pull-out, 1½ miles south of McHugh Creek, they weren't messing around. The terrain is simply awesome, as the highway traces the edge of Turnagain Arm, below the towering cliffs of the Chugach Mountains. If the tide and salmon runs are right, you may see beluga whales. Belugas chase the fish toward fresh water. Sometimes they overextend and strand themselves by the dozens in the receding tide, farther along, but usually aren't harmed.

WINDY POINT (Mile 106)   Be on the lookout on the mountain side of the road for Dall sheep picking their way along the cliffs. It's a unique spot, for the sheep get much closer to people here than is usual in the wild; apparently, they know they're safe. Windy Point is the prime spot, but you have a decent chance of seeing sheep virtually anywhere along this stretch of road. If cars are stopped, that's probably why; get well off the road and pay attention to traffic, which still will be passing at high speeds.

You may also see windsurfers in the gray, silty waters of the Arm. They're crazy. The water is a mixture of glacial runoff and the near-freezing ocean. Besides, the movement of water that creates the 38-foot tidal difference causes riverlike currents, with standing waves like rapids. At times, rushing walls of water up to 6 feet high, called bore tides, form in the arm with the incoming tide. You need perfect timing or good luck to see a bore tide.

INDIAN VALLEY (Mile 104)   You can stop off at the Indian Gold Mine, a touristy attraction right on the road, or eat at **Turnagain House,** a good steak and seafood restaurant, open in the evening. Up the road by the restaurant is the **Indian Valley** trailhead, a gold rush–era trail that ultimately leads 24 miles to the other side of the mountains. Of course, you don't have to go the whole way, and the path, while often muddy, rises less steeply than other trails along the Arm. Indian Creek has trout and, late in the year, silver salmon.

BIRD CREEK (Mile 100)   The **Bird Ridge Trail** comes first, at mile 102, a steep alpine climb rising 3,000 feet in a little over a mile. With the southern exposure, it's dry early in the year. An excellent state campground on the right, over the water, costs $10 per night. There also is a short trail, interpretive signs, an overlook, and a platform that makes fishing easier for people with disabilities. Salmon run late June through August, and the creek becomes mobbed with anglers.

THE FLATS (Miles 96–90)   Beyond Bird Creek, the highway descends from the mountainside to the flats. At high tide, water comes right up to the road. At low tide, the whole Arm narrows to a thin, winding channel through the mud. Since the 1964 Good Friday earthquake, the Arm has not been navigable; before the earthquake, there was never much reason to navigate it. The first to try was Capt. James Cook, in 1778, as he was searching for the Northwest Passage on his final, fatal voyage of discovery (he was killed by Hawaiians later that year). He named this branch of Cook Inlet Turnagain Arm because he had to keep turning around in its shoal-ridden confines before it petered out.

TURNOFF TO GIRDWOOD (Mile 90)   This is the intersection with the road to Girdwood. The attractions of the town, covered below, are worth a visit, but the shopping center here at the intersection is not chief among them. Stop here for a rest room break and to fill your tank for the last time for many a mile.

OLD PORTAGE (Mile 80)   All along the flats at the head of Turnagain Arm are large marshes full of what looks like standing driftwood. These are trees killed by saltwater that flowed in when the 1964 quake lowered the land as much as 10 feet. On the right, 9 miles beyond the turnoff for Girdwood and across the highway from the railroad stop where you board the train for Whittier (see chapter 7), a few ruins of the abandoned town of Portage are still visible, more than 35 years after the great earthquake. There is good bird watching from the turnouts, but don't think of venturing out on Turnagain Arm's tidal mud flats. They suck people up and drown them in the incoming tide. A woman died a few years ago in the arms of rescuers who were not strong enough to pull her out of the quicksand-like mud as the water covered her.

BIG GAME ALASKA (Mile 79)   An entrepreneur fenced off 35 acres of this glacial valley to display deer, moose, eagles, owls, elk, bison, musk ox, and caribou—all injured or orphaned—in a more spacious setting than the Alaska Zoo, which has a greater variety of animals. Turn right about half a mile past the Portage train station (☎ **907/783-2025**). Visitors pick up a cassette tape and map and drive the short course looking at the animals in 3- to 5-acre enclosures. A large log gift shop is at the end of the tour. Admission is $5 for adults, $3 for children 4 to 12, with a maximum of $20 per vehicle. In summer, it's open daily from 9:30am to 7:30pm; in winter, daily 10am to 5pm.

PORTAGE GLACIER (Take 5.5-mile spur road at mile 78)   The receding Portage Glacier is a rare chance to see geologic time running faster than human time. That is to say, the name attraction at this, the most popular of all Alaska attractions, has largely melted, receding out of sight of the visitor center. (The glacier you can see is Burns.) When the center was built in 1985, Portage Glacier was predicted to keep depositing icebergs into its 800-foot-deep lake until the year 2020. Instead, it with-drew to the far edge of the lake in 1995. Even so, the $8 million the National Forest Service spent on the **Begich-Boggs Visitor Center** wasn't wasted, and neither is a trip to see where the glacier used to be. The center is a sort of glacier museum. If you're in Alaska any length of time, you'll likely be seeing a lot of glaciers, and this is an excel-lent place to learn about what you're looking at.

The center is named after Hale Boggs, who was majority leader in the U.S. House, and Rep. Nick Begich, Democrat from Alaska. They disappeared together in a small plane in 1972 during Begich's first reelection bid. The plane was never found, but Begich, even though declared dead, was reelected anyway. Later, his opponent, Repub-lican Don Young, won a special election. Today, Young still represents Alaska as its only congressman.

Several short trails start from the area of the center. Rangers lead nature walks on the ¼-mile, paved Moraine Trail up to six times a day. Another trail leads less than a mile to Byron Glacier, in case you're interested in getting up close to some ice. Always dress warmly, as cold winds are the rule in this funnel-like valley.

A **cruise boat** operated by Gray Line of Alaska (☎ 907/783-2983), under license with the Forest Service, traverses the lake hourly to get right up to Portage Glacier, ice conditions permitting; it costs $25. If this is your only chance to see a glacier in Alaska, it's probably a good choice. If your itinerary includes Columbia, Exit, or Mendenhall Glacier, Glacier Bay National Park, or any of the other accessible glaciers, you won't be as impressed by Portage.

A restaurant and gift shop called the **Portage Lodge** offers basic cafeteria sand-wiches and a variety of gift wares ranging from expensive jewelry and animal pelts to plastic souvenirs. Better meals are to be found at the **Tidewater Cafe** (☎ 907/783-2840), back at the highway junction. It's a friendly diner with grand views of the valley; the menu includes halibut, steaks, and good hot chili. There are no lodgings in Portage, but two **Forest Service campgrounds** are on the road to the visitor center, with 72 sites between them (more details are in the Chugach National Forest section in chapter 7). At the Williwaw Campground, there's also a place to watch red salmon spawning in mid-August—no fishing, though.

8 Out from Anchorage: Girdwood & Mount Alyeska

The Girdwood area—actually still part of the Municipality of Anchorage—is a small town on the threshold of turning into a major resort. Originally a mining community, and more recently a weekend skiing area for Anchorage, it still has a sleepy, offbeat character. Retired hippies, ski bums, a U.S. senator, and a few old-timers live in the houses and cabins among the big spruce trees in the valley below the Mount Alyeska ski resort. They've all got their eye on the development bonanza expected to come with the discovery of skiing here as an international attraction—but so far that hasn't hap-pened, and the town is still an authentically funky community, worth an afternoon visit even in summer. In the winter, it's a destination.

The primary summer attractions are the hiking trails, the tram to the top of Mount Alyeska, and the Crow Creek Mine, described below. In winter, it's skiing. Mount Alyeska doesn't have the size or the fame of resorts in the Rockies, but it's certainly large and challenging enough—Olympian Tommy Moe trained here. Skiers used to more crowded slopes rave about the skiing here, with views of the Chugach Mountains and, between their parted, snowy, rocky peaks, Turnagain Arm.

ESSENTIALS
GETTING THERE
A **rental car** is the most practical route to Girdwood, 37 miles south of Anchorage off the Seward Highway. The various buses that run from Anchorage to Seward and Homer, listed in those sections in chapter 7, will drop you in Girdwood. Among them, Gray Line's **Alaskon Express** (☎ **800/544-2206** or 907/277-5581) charges $25 from Anchorage to Girdwood.

VISITOR INFORMATION
The **Girdwood Resort Association** maintains an extensive Web site at **www. girdwoodalaska.com**. Check the "Anchorage" section for information by phone. In Girdwood, **Alyeska Booking Company,** on Town Square (P.O. Box 1210), Girdwood, AK 99587 (☎ **907/783-4-FUN**), takes care of booking accommodations, rafting, dog-mushing, and flightseeing trips, rentals, and so on. They also have maps and give advice for hiking and outdoor activities.

EXPLORING GIRDWOOD
Mt. Alyeska Tram. At Alyeska Prince Hotel, 1000 Arlberg Ave. (P.O. Box 249), Girdwood, AK 99587. ☎ **800/880-3880** or 907/754-1111. Fax 907/754-2200. www.alyeskaresort.com. $16 per person for the 6-minute summertime ride.

The tram isn't cheap, but I think it's worth it for anyone who otherwise might not make it to an alpine vista during an Alaska trip. (In winter, the tram is faster and comes with your lift ticket. Alaskans pay only $12 in the summer.) At 3, my son called it "the space-ship bus," and that's exactly how it feels to float smoothly from the hotel up into the mountains. At the 2,300-foot level, the tram stops at a station with an attractive but overpriced cafeteria (save greatly by buying a tram/lunch combo ticket). In the evening, the expensive **Seven Glaciers Restaurant,** so named for its view, has great food to go along with the views. Whether of not you eat, the tram presents an opportunity for everyone, no matter how young, old, or infirm, to experience the pure light, limitless surroundings, and crystalline quiet of an Alaskan mountaintop. Dress very warmly.

Crow Creek Mine. Crow Creek Rd. (off the Alyeska Hwy.), Girdwood, AK 99587. ☎ **907/278-8060.** $3 adults; children free. Gold panning $5 adults, $4 children 11 and under. May 15–Sept 15, daily 9am–6pm.

This mine opened in 1898 and operated until 1940. Today, the Toohey family has turned the paths and 14 small buildings into a charming tourist attraction where you can see the frontier lifestyle and watch the rabbits and ducks wandering around. A bag of dirt, guaranteed to have some gold in it, is provided for gold panning, and you can dig and pan to get more if you have the patience for it, which few people do. Crow Creek Road, off the Alyeska Highway, is quite rough and muddy in the spring.

ACTIVITIES
Contact information for the **Alyeska Resort,** where the skiing is located, is below under "Accommodations."

SKIING Mount Alyeska, at 3,939 feet, has 786 acres of skiing, beginning from a base elevation of only 250 feet and rising 2,500 feet. The normal season is early November to April, and it's an exceptional year when there isn't plenty of snow all winter. In 1999, skiing lasted through Memorial Day weekend. The average snowfall is 560 inches, or 46 feet. As it's near the water, the weather is temperate. Light is more of an issue, as the days are short in midwinter. There are 27 lighted trails covering 2,000 vertical feet on Friday and Saturday evenings mid-December through mid-March, but the best Alaska skiing is when the days get longer and warmer in the spring. There are nine lifts, including the tram. An all-day lift ticket costs $44 for adults, $25 for ages 14 to 17, $18 for those ages 8 to 13 or over 60, and $7 ages 7 and under or over 70. Private and group instruction are available, and a basic rental package costs $20 a day for adults, $10 for age 13 and under. There are good **Nordic trails** as well.

A **day lodge** is located at the front of the mountain, and there's a separate bar nearby. A center operated by **Challenge Alaska,** P.O. Box 110065, Anchorage, AK 99511 (☎ **907/783-2925** or 907/344-7399), allows skiers with disabilities to use the mountain without assistance, skiing down to the lift to start and back to the center at day's end. The Alyeska Prince Hotel, described below, is around the side of the mountain, where the expert North Face is served by the tram to the top.

HIKING TRAILS There are a couple of great trails starting in Girdwood. The **Winner Creek Trail** runs 5 miles through forest from behind the Alyeska Prince Hotel to a roaring gorge where Winner Creek and Glacier Creek meet; it's muddy and snowy in the spring. The winter ski trail takes a separate route, through a series of meadows, to the same destination. The **Crow Pass Trail** rises into the mountains and passes all the way over to Eagle River, after a 26-mile hike that takes a couple of days. But you can make a long day hike of it to the pass and see the glaciers, wildflower meadows, and old mining equipment. The trailhead is up Crow Creek Road, off the Alyeska Highway.

You also can explore the area in a dog sled, an exciting winter activity. **Chugach Express Dog Sled Tours** (☎ **907/783-2266**) has 30-minute to 2-hour tours ranging from $40 to $90. **Alaska Snow Safaris** (☎ **888/414-7669** or 907/783-7669) offers snow machine tours.

ACCOMMODATIONS

If you don't want to pay the rates charged by the Alyeska Prince Hotel, there are other good places to stay in Girdwood. Contact the **Alyeska Booking Company,** listed above under "Visitor Information," to find a bed-and-breakfast. **Alyeska Accommodations,** on Olympic Circle (P.O. Box 1196), Girdwood, AK 99587 (☎ **907/783-2000**), offers condos, chalets, and houses.

✪ **Alyeska Prince Hotel.** 1000 Arlberg Ave. (P.O. Box 249), Girdwood, AK 99587. ☎ **800/880-3880** or 907/754-1111. Fax 907/754-2200. www.alyeskaresort.com. 311 units. TV TEL. Summer and Christmas, $175–$450 double; $600–$1,600 suite. Winter, $175–$300 double; $500–$1,100 suite. Additional adult in room $25 extra; children stay free in parents' room. AE, DC, MC, V.

The Alyeska Resort hotel is unique in Alaska as a large, first-class hotel in a nearly pristine mountain valley. Two of the four restaurants—a cafeteria and the gourmet Seven Glaciers Restaurant—are 2,300 feet above the lobby on Mount Alyeska, at the end of a tram ride. The Japanese cuisine particularly has developed a reputation. But check to see which of the restaurants will be open when you come, as there have been long seasonal closures since the hotel opened. The accommodations and service are as close to perfect as you're likely to find in Alaska—so perfect, in fact, as to seem inappropriately solemn at times. The standard rooms are not large but have extraordinary views and lovely cherry-wood furniture, refrigerators, safes, hair dryers, and so on. The swimming pool, with a cathedral ceiling and huge windows on the mountain, has no peer in Alaska.

DINING

Chair 5. Linblad St., town square. ☎ **907/783-2500.** www.chairfive.com. Main courses $6.25–$19; lunch $5.25–$8.50. AE, MC, V. Daily 11am–midnight. SEAFOOD/BURGERS.

This is where Girdwood locals meet their friends and take their families for dinner. In the bar, Bob Dylan music accompanies a friendly game of pool while baseball plays on the TV, and men with ponytails and beards sip microbrews. In the restaurant, families sit at tables amid stained glass and not-quite-antique collectibles. Good, simple meals, welcoming service, and a pro-kid attitude make it work. Full liquor license.

Double Musky Inn. .3 mile Crow Creek Rd. ☎ **907/783-2822.** www.doublemuskyinn. com. Main courses $18–$32. AE, CB, DC, DISC, MC, V. Tues–Thurs 5–10pm, Fri–Sun 4–10pm. Closed Nov. CAJUN.

The ski-bum-casual atmosphere and rambling, cluttered dining room among the trees match the wonderful Cajun and New Orleans food in a way that couldn't have been contrived—it's at once too improbable and too authentic. Service is relaxed to a fault, and food takes a long time to arrive, but when it does it's flawless. The jambalaya was hot, but not too hot to overwhelm what else was going on. A great place for steak, too. Full liquor license.

9 Out from Anchorage: The Matanuska & Susitna Valleys

For most visitors, the Mat-Su Valley, as the area is known, will be a place to pass through on the way to somewhere else—along the Glenn Highway to Valdez or the Alaska Highway, or up the Parks Highway to Denali National Park from Anchorage. The area does have good qualities: the sweeping beauty of the Hatcher Pass area, the Matanuska and Knik glaciers, the Iditarod Sled Dog Race, the river running and fishing. There are some lovely spots and fun outdoor opportunities, but for anyone with limited vacation time, the highlights here comprise not a destination but a day trip from Anchorage or a stop on the way to the state's major attractions.

The Matanuska Valley developed from the Great Depression until the 1970s as a farming area. The New Deal relocated colonists from other parts of the country to settle the prime growing land. But as transportation links improved both within the state and outside, farming in Alaska lost in competition to shipping goods in from Seattle. Farms became subdivisions, housing a population overflow from booming Anchorage, only an hour's drive south on the Glenn Highway. With its adamantly antigovernment philosophy preventing any community planning, Mat-Su's rush of development produced the worst kind of suburban sprawl of highway-fronting shopping malls and gravel lots. The area along the Parks Highway from its start at the Glenn Highway through Wasilla to Big Lake is truly ugly, the more profoundly so for the beauty it once contained.

The entire area is enormous. The county-level government, the Matanuska-Susitna Borough, covers an area about as large as West Virginia, vaguely defined by the drainages of the Matanuska and Susitna rivers. Most of the people live in the section near Anchorage, in and around the towns of Palmer and Wasilla. In 1996, the Big

Lake area, west of Wasilla, was swept by the most costly forest fire in Alaska history, which destroyed more than 400 buildings and seared 35,000 acres of land. For the casual visitor, however, the fire's ravages are no more than a curiosity and will not affect a visit to the area.

The borough seat, **Palmer,** is a traditional small town built by the Depression-era colonists. One side of the quiet main street, Colony Way, is lined with little storefront businesses; the other is an open vista of the mountains. About 10 miles west, **Wasilla** was created mostly by a building boom of the 1970s and 1980s. The town exists primarily as a string of shopping centers along the Parks Highway, and you have to really look to find its center. The area is dotted with lakes surrounded by houses, where people water-ski and fish in the summer and snowmobile and run sled dogs in the winter. **Hatcher Pass** is in the Talkeetna Mountains on the north side of the Matanuska Valley. The Talkeetnas aren't as tall as other ranges, but they have the striking, rugged beauty of cracked rock. A historic mining site nestles up in the pass, and it's a terrific place for summer hikes and winter recreation, including Nordic skiing and snowmobiling. **Talkeetna,** at the northern end of the Susitna Valley, is covered in chapter 8, on Denali National Park.

ESSENTIALS
GETTING THERE & GETTING AROUND
You can't get around the broadly spread Valley without a car. My advice? Buy a map. The best is the widely available $5 map produced by **Alaska Road and Recreation Maps,** P.O. Box 102459, Anchorage, AK 99510.

The **Parks Highway** divides from the **Glenn Highway** about 7 miles south of Palmer on the Glenn and 7 miles east of Wasilla on the Parks. Turn left at the junction for Wasilla, Denali National Park, and Fairbanks. Go straight for Palmer, Glennallen, and the rest of the world. If you're in either Palmer or Wasilla and want to get to the other, the **Palmer-Wasilla Highway** is the direct route. The Butte area, south of Palmer, is on the **Old Glenn Highway,** which runs from Palmer to an exit on the Glenn just south of the Knik River. **Knik River Road** runs up the river from the Old Glenn.

VISITOR INFORMATION
The **Mat-Su Visitors Center,** mile 35.5 Parks Hwy., HC 01 Box 6166521, Palmer, AK 99645 (☎ **907/746-5000**), is located on the right side of the Parks Highway just after the intersection with the Glenn Highway, as you enter the area from the south. It's open in summer, daily from 8:30am to 6:30pm, fewer hours in winter. The **Palmer Visitor Center,** at 723 S. Valley Way in the center of town (☎ **907/745-2880**), has a small museum on the 1935 colony project that developed the Valley. It's open in summer, daily from 8am to 7pm, and in winter only for 1 week before Christmas.

SPECIAL EVENTS
The Iditarod Restart, on the first Sunday in March, enlivens Wasilla at the end of a long winter. The Iditarod Trail Sled Dog Race starts officially in Anchorage the day before, but then the dogs are loaded in trucks and carried to Wasilla, where the trail becomes continuous to Nome. The restart is the real beginning of the race, and the area makes the most of it.

✪ **The Alaska State Fair,** the 11 days leading to Labor Day, is the biggest event of the year for the Valley, and one of the biggest for Anchorage; it's a typical fair, except for the huge vegetables. The good soil and long days in the Valley grow cabbages the size of bean-bag chairs. A mere beach-ball-size cabbage would be laughed off the stage.

Fast Facts: The Matanuska and Susitna Valleys

Banks   You'll find several banks on the Parks Highway in Wasilla and on Bailey Street or S. Colony Way in Palmer; they have ATMs, as do most large shopping centers and grocery stores.

Hospital   The Valley Hospital is at 515 Dahlia Ave. in Palmer (☎ 907/746-8600). West Valley Medical Campus is at 950 E. Bogard Rd. in Wasilla (☎ 907/352-2800).

Police   For nonemergency business with the police, call the Palmer Police Department (☎ 907/745-4811), the Wasilla Police Department (☎ 907/373-9077), or, outside either town, the Alaska State Troopers (☎ 907/745-2131).

Post Office   In Palmer, at 500 S. Cobb St. On Main Street in Wasilla.

Taxes   Palmer levies a 3% sales tax, and Wasilla 2%. The Mat-Su borough charges a 5% bed tax on top of the sales tax.

EXPLORING THE ROADS OF MAT-SU

A trip to **Independence Mine State Historical Park,** in Hatcher Pass, combines one of the area's most beautiful drives, access to great hiking and Nordic skiing, and interesting old buildings to look at. If you're headed north to Denali National Park or Fairbanks, the rough, winding gravel road through Hatcher Pass to Willow makes a glorious alpine detour around the least attractive part of your drive. Past the mine and skiing area, the road is open only in summer and is not suitable for large RVs. Just after the Parks Highway branches from the Glenn, turn right on the Trunk Road and keep going north on Fishhook Road. From the Glenn near Palmer, take Fishhook just north of town. The state **historic site** (☎ **907/745-2827** or 907/745-3975) is the remains of a hard-rock gold mine operation that closed down in 1943. Some buildings have been restored, including an assay office that's a museum and the manager's house that's a welcoming visitor center, while other structures sag and lean as picturesque ruins. A $3 guided tour ($2 seniors and ages 10 to 18, free under 10) enters more buildings 1:30pm and 3:30pm weekdays, plus 4:30pm weekends, or you can wander with the help of an excellent walking-tour map. The visitor center is open 11am to 7pm daily in the summer, but is closed in the winter. The high Talkeetna Mountains valley the site occupies is idyllic for a summer ramble in the heather or for Nordic or Telemark skiing in winter. There are four hiking trails and two mountain biking routes in the area—ask at the visitor center. One great hike is the 8-mile Gold Mint Trail, which starts across the road from the Motherlode Lodge on Fishhook Road and ends at the Mint Glacier, where you have to turn around to hike back.

The **Musk Ox Farm,** 2 miles north of Palmer on the Glenn Highway and left on Archie Road, P.O. Box 587, Palmer, AK 99645 (☎ **907/745-4151**), raises the beasts for research and breeding, and offers tours 10am to 6pm daily in the summer season which cost $8 for adults, $6.50 seniors and ages 13 to 18, and $5 ages 6 to 12. The family-operated **Reindeer Farm,** in the Butte area (☎ **907/745-4000**), raises reindeer for pets and puts them in harness each Christmas, and has two Rocky Mountain elk and two moose. The tour teaches all about reindeer and gives you an opportunity to feed them. Take the Old Glenn Highway to the intersection with Bodenburg Butte Road and Plumley Road, going toward the butte less than a mile. It's open 10am to 6pm daily in the summer. Admission is $5 for adults, $4 for seniors, and $3 for children 3 to 11. Across the road is a great short hike to the top of the butte.

The **Dorothy G. Page Museum,** at 323 Main St. in Wasilla (☎ **907/373-9071**), preserves the early history of the area in a collection of pioneer buildings, including the recently restored Teeland's General Store, now occupied by Mead's Coffee Shop (see "Dining," below). Volunteers are often on hand to tell stories about the Valley's past, including some real area pioneers who lived and made this recent history. Several buildings are open for tours daily from 10am to 6pm in the summer, and the small museum is open daily from 9am to 5pm in the winter as well. Admission is $3 for adults, $2.50 for seniors, and free for ages 18 and under.

The **Museum of Alaska Transportation and Industry,** off the Parks Highway at mile 47, west of Wasilla, P.O. Box 870646, Wasilla, AK 99687 (☎ **907/376-1211; www.alaska.net/~rmorris/mati1.htm**), is a paradise for gearheads and tinkerers. The volunteers have gathered every conceivable machine and conveyance—13 fire trucks, for example—and fixed up to running order as many as they can. An indoor museum displays their finished masterpieces, while the 15 acres outside are crammed with future projects— trains, aircraft, fishing boats, and mining equipment—all grist for memories and imagination. It's open summer 9am to 6pm daily, winter Tuesday through Saturday 9am to 5pm. Admission is $5 for adults, $4 for students and seniors.

GETTING OUTSIDE

The Alaska Public Lands Information Center, described in the Anchorage section, is the best place for advice on the outdoors. **Rafting** in the Mat-Su is described under "Getting Outside" in the Anchorage section, earlier in this chapter. The best **hikes, skiing,** and **snowmobiling** are at Hatcher Pass, described above.

AIRBOAT TOURS   Knik Glacier Adventures, 7.5 miles up Knik River Road, HC02, P.O. Box 7726, Palmer, AK 99645 (☎ **907/746-5133**), runs twice-daily airboat tours up the river to the glacier for a cookout, often seeing bear, moose, Dall sheep, and eagles, and always taking a glacier walk. The 4-hour trip is $65 for adults, half price for children 12 and under. They also rent three rustic cabins and lead llama treks.

DOG MUSHING   The Valley is a center of **sled dog mushing,** both for racing and recreational dog driving. Raymie Reddington—son of Joe Reddington, father of the Iditarod race—offers trips up the Iditarod Trail, ranging from half an hour to several days, and will teach you to mush as well. The 30-minute ride is $35. Contact **Reddington Sled Dog Tours,** at mile 12.5 Knik–Goose Bay Road, HC 30, Box 5420, Wasilla, AK 99654 (☎ **907/376-6730**). Short summer rides are available, too. **Lucky Husky Mushing Adventures,** HC 89 Box 256, Willow, AK 99688 (☎ **907/ 495-6470; www.luckyhusky.com**) does an excellent job with their summer rides and winter rides and tours. They're located on the Parks Highway north of Willow. The summer rides include a kennel tour, and cost $24 per person, making a good stop on a drive to Denali. Winter trips are, of course, more authentic; they teach you to ride the runners, guiding the team with your voice. A half-day excursion is $175, all day $295, and a 2-day trip $695.

FISHING   The Mat-Su area has many road-accessible salmon-fishing streams and stocked lakes, as well as plenty of campgrounds to get close to the fishing. Call the **Alaska Department of Fish and Game** (☎ **907/746-6300**) for a recording with current fishing information.

HIKING   For a challenging 7- to 10-hour climb, go up 6,398-foot Pioneer Peak to the ridge below the top, with stupendous views. The trailhead is on Knik River Road, off Old Glenn Highway.

HORSEBACK RIDING   This farming country contains a lot of horses, and is one of the best places in the state for riding. Near Bodenburg Butte, **Flying G Ranch,** P.O. Box 781, Palmer, AK 99645 (☎ **907/745-7258**), offers rides in beautiful country for $25 per person per hour, $15 for children under age 7.

ACCOMMODATIONS
ON THE GLENN HIGHWAY

If you're headed down the Glenn Highway, there are two good remote lodges near the **Matanuska Glacier,** an hour from Palmer.

Majestic Valley Wilderness Lodge. Mile 114.9, Glenn Hwy., HC03, Box 8514, Palmer, AK 99645. ☎ **907/746-2930.** Fax 907/746-2931. $80 double.

This lodge offers basic rooms with private bathrooms, and serves meals with advance arrangements. While most of the rooms aren't as attractive as Sheep Mountain, there's a very comfortable cabin, and the lodge maintains its own network of groomed Nordic skiing trails—we enjoy going there for spring skiing weekends in the spectacular terrain.

Sheep Mountain Lodge. Mile 113.5, Glenn Hwy., HC 03, Box 8490, Palmer, AK 99645. ☎ **907/745-5121.** Fax 907/745-5120. 10 units. $95 double.

This historic lodge has 10 attractive mountainside cabins with private bathrooms, as well as a hostel. Their cafe has good food for a stop on your drive. Hiking trails and the private road to the glacier are nearby.

AT HATCHER PASS

Hatcher Pass Lodge. P.O. Box 763, Palmer, AK 99645. ☎ **907/745-5897.** Fax 907/745-1200. 9 units. $115 double.

Hatcher Pass has nine lovely A-frame cabins with chemical toilets right in the treeless bowl of the 3,000-foot alpine pass. Running water and showers are available in the fun, funky little restaurant. It's a great family place where, in the winter, you can ski out the front door on up to 20 kilometers of Nordic trails.

The Motherlode Lodge. Mile 14, Fishhook Rd., HC5 Box 6824-M, Palmer, AK 99645. ☎ and fax **907/746-1464.** $65 double.

Located on the road to the pass, Motherlode has good basic rooms with private bathrooms. There's a cafe, bar, and a restaurant with surprisingly sophisticated fine dining in a grand room. It's a good base for snowmobiling or hiking trips.

IN THE CENTRAL VALLEY

Bed-and-breakfasts are a good choice in the Valley. Besides those I've listed, some 30 others book through **Bed and Breakfast Association of Alaska, Mat-Su Chapter,** P.O. Box 873507, Wasilla, AK 99687 (☎ **800/401-7444** or 907/376-4461).

Alaskan Agate Inn. 4725 Begich Circle, Wasilla, AK 99654. ☎ **800/770-2290** or 907/373-2290. Fax 907/376-2294. www.agateinn.com. Apts. $125 double, rooms $95 double.

The big, comfortable apartments here come with full kitchen, while the attractive rooms have private bathrooms.

Best Western Lake Lucille Inn. 1300 W. Lucille Dr., Wasilla, AK 99654. ☎ **800/528-1234** (reservations), or 907/373-1776. Fax 907/376-6199. 58 units. TV TEL. High season, $95–$125 double; $175–$195 suite. Low season, $75–$85 double; $125–$145 suite. Additional person in room $10 extra. AE, DC, DISC, MC, V.

This well-run, attractive lakeside hotel right in Wasilla has the best standard hotel rooms in the valley. They're large and well appointed, and those facing the lake have balconies and a grand, peaceful view. Various kinds of boats can be rented for play on Lake Lucille, and flightseeing trips take off right from the dock below the lawn. There's a Jacuzzi, sauna, workout room, self-service laundry, small playground, and free coffee in the lobby. The **restaurant** is one of the best in the area, with a light, quiet dining room looking out on the water. It's open for three meals a day, with the beef and seafood dinner menu ranging from $15 to $38.

✪ **Colony Inn.** 325 E. Elmwood, Palmer, AK 99645. ☎ **907/745-3330.** Fax 907/746-3330. 12 units. TV TEL. $80 double; $160 suite. Additional person in room $5 extra. AE, DC, DISC, MC, V.

This perfect country inn occupies a lovingly restored teacher's dormitory from the New Deal Colony Project, right in the middle of Palmer. The rooms feel fresh and new, yet at the same time wonderfully old-fashioned, with rockers and comforters but also Jacuzzi bathtubs and big TVs. A large sitting room and a dining room downstairs are decorated with historic photographs that help tell the building's story. Excellent lunches and dinners are served there during the summer at the **Inn Cafe** (☎ 907/746-6118). A coin-op laundry is available. This is one of the best places to stay in southcentral Alaska, and an incredible bargain. Guests check in at the Valley Hotel, at 606 S. Alaska St., where you'll find basic rooms for very low rates.

Yukon Don's Bed and Breakfast Inn. 2221 Yukon Cir. (mail: 1830 E. Parks Hwy., Ste. 386) Wasilla, AK 99654. ☎ **800/478-7472** or 907/376-7472. Fax 907/376-7470. $95 double with shared bathroom, $115–$135 suite.

A converted dairy farm, beautiful surroundings, and a room devoted to a collection of wildlife mounts.

DINING

Some of the best restaurants in the Valley are at the Best Western Lake Lucille Inn, the Colony Inn, the Motherlode Lodge, and Hatcher Pass Lodge, described above. In Palmer, don't miss **Vagabond Blues,** 642 S. Alaska (☎ 907/745-2233), a great little coffee house with hearty soups and breads, and jazz, blues, poetry readings, and other performances on weekend nights. Sometimes nationally known acts show up in the very intimate setting. In Wasilla, **Mead's Coffee Shop** (☎ 907/357-5633) is in the historic Teeland's General Store, at the Dorothy Page Museum (see above). They serve pastries, soups, salads, and vegetarian meals, roast their own coffee, and have entertainment on weekends, as well as Internet access.

Legends at Settlers Bay. Mile 8 Knik Rd. ☎ **907/376-5298.** Lunch $8–$15, dinner $12–$27. AE, DISC, MC, V. Lunch Mon–Sat 11am–2pm, dinner Sun–Thurs 5–10pm, Fri–Sat 5–11pm. SEAFOOD/BEEF/GAME

The dining room at the Settlers Bay golf course overlooks the waters of Knik Arm and the mountains that encircle the valley. It's a casual place where families can feel comfortable and you can see your meal being cooked, but they still set an attractive table and take care over the wine-opening ritual and other professional details. The varied menu includes such exotica as elk, rabbit, boar, and duck; we can vouch for the rare, tender prime rib, generous roast chicken, and the crab cakes. You'll want to linger.

The Kenai Peninsula & Prince William Sound

The Gulf of Alaska arcs at its northern edge, forming the rounded northern shore of the Pacific Ocean, a zone of great collisions. This is where the earth's great tectonic plates collide, spewing forth froths of hot lava from dozens of volcanoes and fracturing and folding the earth with titanic earthquakes. Here the ocean's wildest weather collides with mountains jutting miles high from the sea, growing immense prehistoric ice sheets and glaciers that carve the rock into long, deep, intricate fjords. The sea proffers prodigious biological wealth on these shores, including the salmon it unleashes into the rivers in furious swarms of life that climb over the mountains and into the Interior to spawn. Nature here seems giant and superabundant, as if this magnificent arc of land and water were focusing the earth's productive energy on its lucky residents—as, in a real sense, it is.

Geography endowed this one stretch of coast with several of the world's great natural places. On the east, near Cordova, the **Copper River**'s immense, entirely unspoiled delta is the largest contiguous wetlands in the Western Hemisphere. On a day trip you're immediately alone with flocks of rare, graceful waterfowl that congregate on shallow ponds surrounded by miles of waving grass. **Prince William Sound** is a great protected sea of wooded, uninhabited islands and immense glaciers. On a recent summer day I picnicked there with my family on the beach of a deserted bay next to a stream boiling with spawning salmon. A raft of hundreds of sea otters lolled on the sunny water before us while eagles circled low overhead. **Kenai Fjords National Park** takes in bays off the open ocean where the mountains soar a mile straight from the water. Boats going there travel among humpback, gray, and orca whales; otters, seals, and sea lions; and visit swarming colonies of puffins and other sea birds. The world's biggest salmon swim up the Kenai River, on the western side of the Kenai Peninsula; and on its southern tip, **Kachemak Bay** is like a miniature Prince William Sound. The bay has wildlife and glaciers and all that, but its shores also are dotted by tiny towns with lodges, art galleries on pilings, and some of Alaska's best restaurants.

The whole region is exceptionally accessible, by Alaska standards, but the Kenai (*keen*-eye) Peninsula is especially easy to get to without the expense and exhausting travel that can make much of the state difficult. Most of what you're looking for in Alaska lies along a few hundred miles of blacktop, within reach of a rental car and perhaps a tour boat ticket: glaciers, whales, legendary sportfishing, spectacular hiking trails, interesting little fishing towns, bears, moose, and high mountains. People from Anchorage go to the peninsula for the weekend to fish, hike, dig clams, paddle kayaks, and so on, and certain places can get crowded.

There's a special phrase for what happens when the red salmon are running in July on the Kenai and Russian rivers: **combat fishing.** At hot times in certain places, fishers stand elbow to elbow on a bank, each casting into his or her own one-yard-wide slice of river, and still catch plenty of hefty salmon. The peninsula also exerts a powerful magnetic force on RVs, those road-whales that one finds at the head of strings of cars on the two-lane highways. During the summer, the fishing rivers, creeks, and beaches on the west side of the peninsula and the end of the Homer Spit can become sheet-metal cities of hundreds of Winnebagos and Itascas parked side by side. Often some local entrepreneur will be selling doughnuts or newspapers door-to-door.

Yet the decision is yours as to whether you spend time in the company of tourists. If the roadside fishing is hairy, hiking a little farther down the bank usually means you can be by yourself. In this chapter I'll describe some towns of unspoiled charm, where you can kayak virtually from your room. Being alone is easy. You can paddle among otters in Resurrection Bay; tramp over the heather in Turnagain Pass; hike, bike, or ski one of the many maintained trails in Chugach National Forest. When you're ready to come back to the comforts of civilization—or if you chose never to leave them—you'll find that aspect of the peninsula especially appealing, too: Some of the state's best restaurants and most interesting lodgings are here.

As a way of arranging the geography in your mind, think of the Kenai Peninsula as a mountainous spine of land surrounded by water, with the towns on its flanks dipping their toes in the sea. Prince William Sound, on the other hand, is a sea—far larger than San Francisco Bay; it takes more than a day to cross in a boat—and along its edges are a few towns and villages. Water is the center of the place.

Crossing Prince William Sound several years ago in a small boat, comparing a chart to the broad, sparkling water's tussocks of bedrock and trees, I thought I knew where I was—though, honestly, I didn't care that much. Then I saw one mound, close at hand, that didn't belong. It shot forth a spray of water, and a fin appeared. A humpback. We stopped the boat for pictures until the tail flipped up high, as it does when the whale is about to sound and disappear for a while. But what was that noise behind the boat? While we'd been watching the whale, a sea lion had swum up behind us. Its light-brown shape, just below the water, was the size of a large office desk, but it moved fast, shooting toward us and then circling back in the opposite direction—as fast as the shadow of a sparrow. Finally, we started up and went on our way, a warm afternoon sun on our backs as we continued east from Whittier into the big, wide, gentle Sound, thinking, "What'll we see next?"

I have a friend who has kayaked the whole Sound. He knew a place—I don't know if it's still this way—where he would camp just above a pebbled beach and wait for the moon to come out. And in the night, orcas would come, swim up on the beach, scratch their tummies on the rocks, and wriggle back into the ocean. It was their secret spot—his and the killer whales'—and they'd meet there each summer. The beach was oiled in the *Exxon Valdez* oil spill, and my friend lost the heart to kayak much after all the death he saw there and all over the Sound while trying to save birds and animals that horrible summer of 1989. But now I'm sure the oil is gone from that beach. It's time to get back out there and meet the whales.

The waters of Prince William Sound are uniquely protected and diverse. On the western side, from Whittier, there are great **tidewater glaciers** at the heads of long, narrow fjords. In the center of the Sound, there's an infinity of islands, remote beaches, and hidden bays—and not many people. On the east, near Cordova, the Sound gets

The Kenai Peninsula & Prince William Sound

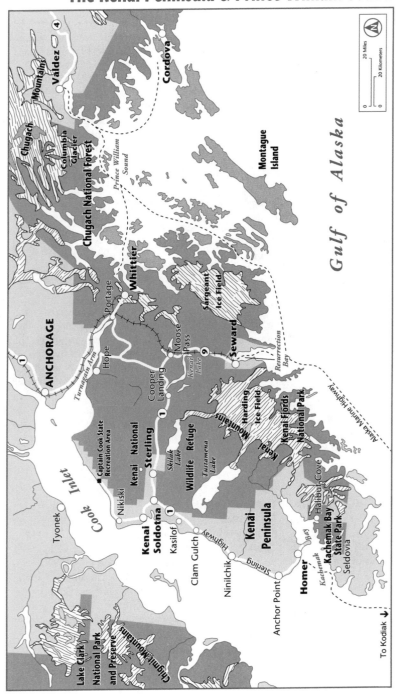

shallower and hosts millions of migrating birds. The islands and enclosing reach of the mainland keep the seas smooth in most of the Sound. That's one reason the oil spill was so devastating: These protected waters are a rich nursery, and that oil, once landed and stuck, would not soon wash away as it did out in the rougher Gulf of Alaska of Kenai Fjords National Park or Cook Inlet, on the other side of the Kenai Peninsula.

The spill coated the shores of this entire huge region and beyond, killing birds in the hundreds of thousands and damaging fish and marine mammal populations in numbers and ways that will never be known for sure. Today the oil spill is mostly history, although on its tenth anniversary scientists and subsistence gatherers still could find buried oil on some pebble beaches. Natives and longtime residents have told me that they can tell the difference in the abundance of animals compared to what was there before, and government studies support the perception that recovery is far from complete. But most everyone else will notice only that a mind-boggling abundance still remains, and on a sunny day on the water nothing could seem more remote than the technological society that could threaten such a place with crude oil.

1 Exploring the Kenai Peninsula & Prince William Sound

THE TOWNS

Kenai, on Cook Inlet on the west side of the Kenai Peninsula, is the largest town in the region. Ten miles up the Kenai River, **Soldotna** is Kenai's sister, and together they form a unit with more than 25% of the Kenai Peninsula's population of 44,000. They're also the least interesting of the peninsula's communities. **Homer,** at the southern end of the peninsula, has wonderful art and character and lots of ways to get out on the water. **Seward,** on the east side, is smaller and quieter, but also charming and a gateway to Kenai Fjords National Park.

There are three major towns on Prince William Sound. **Valdez** is an oil town, at the southern terminus of the trans-Alaska pipeline where tankers are loaded. **Cordova** is more attractive, a historic community on the eastern side of the Sound, with outdoor activities close at hand. **Whittier** is a grim former military outpost, but a convenient gateway to the protected fjords and glaciers of the western Sound.

ESSENTIALS
GETTING THERE & GETTING AROUND

Transportation networks are better developed in Alaska's Southcentral region, of which the Kenai Peninsula and Prince William Sound are part, than anywhere else in the state, making exploration easier and more flexible. Anchorage, Alaska's largest city, is the hub, with the state's only major airport. Commuter flights to other towns in the region mostly go through Anchorage, highways meet there, and Alaska Railroad trains originate at the downtown depot. The region's other transportation mode, the ferries of the Alaska Marine Highway System, serves the communities of Prince William Sound and Kachemak Bay, near Homer, and makes some stops at Seward, but does not travel to Anchorage.

BY CAR   Highways connect all the region's large towns, except Cordova. Like all Alaska's main highways, they are paved two-lane roads. A new road to be completed in 2000, built in a railway tunnel, will for the first time connect Whittier, on Prince William Sound, to the highway network (see that section, below). The Richardson Highway reaches Valdez from Anchorage through Alaska's Interior, and that route is described in chapter 9. The Seward Highway runs south from Anchorage to the Kenai Peninsula. That route is described below.

BY FERRY   The ferry system connects Whittier with Valdez and Cordova. One great 2-day circle route involves taking a car from Anchorage to Whittier, riding the ferry through Prince William Sound to Valdez, then driving back to Anchorage on the Richardson and Glenn highways. Ferries also run from Valdez to Cordova, and once a week from Whittier straight to Cordova. Unfortunately, the ferry schedule does not allow a visit of less than a few days to Cordova, unless you fly one-way. The ferry *Bartlett*, one of the smallest in the fleet, serves the Prince William Sound towns. There are no sleeping accommodations, but the boat is rarely very full and there is plenty of deck space and recliners for overnight runs. The restaurant has the best views you could hope for, and acceptable food (if short hours). The Chugach National Forest usually has rangers on board offering programs and interpretation in the observation lounge.

The ferry *Tustumena* connects Homer and Seward to Seldovia and Kodiak Island and the Aleutian Archipelago (covered in chapter 10), and also runs from Homer to Seldovia, with occasional trips to Seward, Whittier, and Prince William Sound villages as well. The schedule is not convenient for Seldovia, however, and it's much more practical to drive between Homer, Seward, and Whittier. Private passenger ferries serve the towns and remote sites around Kachemak Bay from Homer, described in that section.

BY AIR   Commuter airlines fan out from Anchorage to Kenai, Homer, Seward, Valdez, and Cordova. You can also fly an Alaska Airlines jet to Cordova, with one northbound and one southbound flight each day bound to Anchorage in one direction and Southeast Alaska and Seattle in the other. Scheduled and air-taxi services use these smaller towns as bases for the villages, carrying passengers, mail, and cargo, and to remote lodges and cabins for fishing or other outdoor activities. Valdez, Cordova, and Anchorage operators serve the Prince William Sound region. Kenai and Anchorage companies cover Cook Inlet and remote public lands such as Lake Clark National Park. Homer is the base for villages around Kachemak Bay and lower Cook Inlet bear viewing sites.

BY TRAIN   The Alaska Railroad runs from Seward north to Anchorage, with a branch from Portage to Whittier on Prince William Sound, and then farther north through the Matanuska-Susitna valleys to Denali National Park and Fairbanks, in the Interior.

Alaska Marine Highway Booking Tips

Here's a handy tip about the **Alaska Marine Highway** ferry system. While the statewide toll free number (☎ 800/642-0066) is chronically understaffed, making it difficult to talk to a real person, the staff at the office in Anchorage has less to do and usually provides quick, personal service, at ☎ 907/272-7116; fax 907/277-4829. The office is in the Alaska Public Lands Information Center, at Fourth and F streets in Anchorage (see "Getting Outside on the Kenai Peninsula & Prince William Sound," below, for complete details). In addition, the contractor who operates the ferry terminal in Homer maintains a toll-free number and Web site (☎ 800/382-9229; www.akms.com), another easy way to get into the system with a real live person. They're open Monday through Friday 7am to 5pm, Saturday 7am to 3pm, Alaska time.

VISITOR INFORMATION

Each town of significant size has a visitor information center, maps, guides, and other publications, listed as appropriate in the sections below. The peninsula as a whole also has the **Kenai Peninsula Tourism Marketing Council,** 150 N. Willow St., Kenai, AK 99611 (☎ 800/535-3624 or 907/283-3850; www.KenaiPeninsula.org), which is eager to send you a vacation planner with information on businesses in the area (call the toll-free number) and will answer other inquiries at the toll number. They are open Monday through Friday 8:30am to 5pm. The Kenai Peninsula Borough is the county-level government for the whole area. It levies a 2% sales tax, and individual towns add varying amounts of tax of their own. The more rural Prince William Sound region has only town governments.

See "Outside on the Kenai Peninsula & Prince William Sound," below, for outdoor information.

SUGGESTED ITINERARIES

BY CAR This is the easiest way to get around the region. One good itinerary of 10 days to 2 weeks would be to fly to Anchorage and spend a few days taking in the sights (covered in chapter 6). Then rent a car to drive the Seward and Sterling highways, taking plenty of time to get down to Homer, perhaps with a couple of days to stop for fishing or hiking on the way in the Chugach National Forest, in Cooper Landing, or in the Kenai/Soldotna area. In Homer, plan several days, getting out on Kachemak Bay to Halibut Cove, Seldovia, or hiking and boating in Kachemak Bay State Park. Then drive back to Whittier and take the ferry through Prince William Sound to Valdez, seeing the glaciers and wildlife on the way. Spend a day in Valdez, then drive up the Richardson Highway, perhaps making a 2-day side trip to historic Kennicott, in the spectacular Wrangell–St. Elias National Park (see chapter 9), then returning on the Glenn Highway to Anchorage or continuing up to Fairbanks, if there's time.

WITHOUT A CAR A possible 10-day carless itinerary would be to fly to Anchorage, spend a few days sightseeing there, then take the Alaska Railroad to Seward, visiting Kenai Fjords National Park by boat, with a second day in Seward in case of bad weather or for a hike or fishing. Then head back to Anchorage and fly to Cordova, taking the tour to Childs Glacier, visiting the quaint and welcoming town, and perhaps getting outdoors on a bike, a hike, a kayak, or on a fishing excursion. Then take the ferry to Valdez, spend part of a day there, and board a tour boat to see Columbia Glacier and other glaciers in western Prince William Sound, either going all the way to Whittier and taking the train to Anchorage or returning to Valdez and flying back to Anchorage. If there's time left, use Anchorage as a base for a fly-in fishing trip or take a flightseeing trip on a classically restored DC-3 over Denali National Park.

You'll need to book rental cars and hotel or lodge rooms and wilderness cabins well ahead—certainly by late April. Mid-June to mid-August is the most heavily booked, when finding any decent room can be difficult without reservations. Activities should be reserved a few weeks ahead. Reservations are not necessary for camping. Planning extra travel days because of the weather is not as critical as in Southeast Alaska, but leave plenty of time around any boating or flightseeing excursions. Reputable tour and fishing operators simply won't go out in rough water and make you miserable. If you have a backup day, you can spend the rough-weather day on shore and try again the next day. Check on weather-cancellation policies before you book any boat excursions.

I've arranged the sections below to match the ways you'll tour the region. First comes general information on the outdoors, next a road guide to the Kenai Peninsula's

Seward Highway, a section on Chugach National Forest, then the towns in the region in order of their distance from Anchorage. If you're considering taking a wildlife sight-seeing cruise, compare the sections on Seward and Kenai Fjords National Park and the section on Whittier.

2 Getting Outside on the Kenai Peninsula & Prince William Sound

PUBLIC LANDS

Most of Southcentral Alaska is protected in vast land conservation units. The towns are the exceptions, just a few beads strung along the laces of the highways. You can do everything here—or be as isolated here—as anywhere in the state or the nation, yet the towns mean comfort is closer than other parts of Alaska.

Chugach National Forest takes in all of Prince William Sound and most of the eastern Kenai Peninsula. At 5.3 million acres, it's almost three times the size of Yellowstone National Park. Anywhere else but Alaska it would be a national park, and one of the largest and most spectacular, with some of the best sea kayaking, hiking, backpacking, wildlife watching, and scenery anywhere. General information, camping, and ideas on remote areas in the Chugach are covered below, in the Chugach National Forest section. Details about National Forest areas near towns are in the appropriate town sections.

Kenai Fjords National Park, taking in the outer edge and ice cap of the Kenai Peninsula's southern side, is incomparable in its remoteness, stark beauty, and abundance of marine wildlife. Access is though Seward. On the peninsula's western side, **Kenai National Wildlife Refuge** has Alaska's most accessible wilderness lake and river canoeing as well as extraordinary fishing, with access from roads near Soldotna. Each of those areas is covered in its own section, below.

Kachemak Bay State Park offers good sea kayaking waters and wilderness hiking not connected to any road. The **Alaska Maritime National Wildlife Refuge** protects the wildlife habitat of remote islands and seashores around the state. The **McNeil River State Game Sanctuary** is a superb but difficult-to-access bear observatory. All three are covered in the Homer section, below.

VISITOR INFORMATION

The best and most central place to get outdoor information is the ✪ **Alaska Public Lands Information Center,** 605 W. Fourth Ave., Suite 105, Anchorage, AK 99501 (☎ **907/271-2737;** TTY 907/271-2738; www.nps.gov/aplic/). Since most trips to the region start in Anchorage, the center makes a good first stop. You'll be able to get guidance from residents who have spent time in the places you'll be visiting, and there are exhibits on the wildlife and outdoor opportunities in the region—even maps showing where to find various species of fish. Land agencies present information on the whole state. Pick up books and maps here, too, and buy tickets for the ferries. Summer hours are daily 9am to 5:30pm, winter Monday through Friday 10am to 5:30pm. Similar centers are in Ketchikan, Tok, and Fairbanks.

Visitor centers particular to the Chugach National Forest, Kenai Fjords National Park, and Kenai National Wildlife Refuge are included in those sections below. Visitor centers for Kachemak Bay State Park and the Alaska Maritime National Wildlife Refuge are in the Homer section.

REMOTE CABINS   Cabins managed by the Alaska Division of Parks stand in beautiful natural spots near Homer, Seward, and Valdez. (Other cabins in Chugach

National Forest are covered in that section, below.) It takes some effort to get to the cabins—either a hike to Caines Head State Recreation Area near Seward or Shoup Bay State Marine Park near Valdez, or a boat to Kachemak Bay State Park near Homer or the marine parks near Seward. For information about Kachemak Bay, contact the ranger station listed in the Homer section. For Valdez or Seward, go through the **Department of Natural Resources Public Information Center—Anchorage,** 3601 C Street, Suite 200, Anchorage, AK 99503-5929 (☎ **907/269-8400;** TDD 907/269-8411; fax 907/269-8901; www.dnr.state.ak.us/parks/parks.htm). The Web site is the most complete source of written information about the cabins, with a picture and description of each. Cabins generally cost $50 a night and can be reserved up to 6 months in advance. Call for guidance, but they'll accept the reservation only by mail or in person; the Anchorage office may have moved by the time you read this, so do call first.

OUTDOOR ACTIVITIES

FISHING   Alaska's most famous fishing stream, and the only place in the world to catch such large king salmon, is the **Kenai River,** accessible on the Kenai Peninsula from Kenai, Soldotna, and other towns along the Sterling Highway. There's also good salmon fishing virtually anywhere you choose to go in the region, depending on the time of year and the species you target. Seward is famous for silver (or coho) salmon in the fall. The most famous halibut fishing, with flat fish topping out in the 300-pound class, is from Homer, but other towns have halibut charters, too. Homer, Kenai, and Anchorage are good starting points for fly-in fishing on rivers or lakes. You can fish trout by canoe in lakes in the Kenai National Wildlife Refuge. For more fishing ideas and general information on Alaska fishing, see chapter 2.

FLIGHTSEEING   There are flight services in all the towns for flightseeing trips. If you have several people in your group, you can charter a plane and set down in some remote spot. Homer and Valdez have the most developed flightseeing operations in the region, and there's also great scenery near Seward and Cordova.

HIKING & BIKING   Chugach National Forest has short and long trails, some with historic significance, and cabins along the way, on the Kenai Peninsula and in Cordova. Some of Alaska's best remote hiking and mountain biking are found across Kachemak Bay from Homer.

SEA KAYAKING   The region has some of the best sea kayaking anywhere, rivaled in Alaska only by the Southeast area. In Prince William Sound, the best day trips and expeditions, guided and unguided, leave from Whittier and Cordova, and a Valdez operator also does paddles. Seward has competing operators taking guided day trips in Resurrection Bay, and more expensive, longer trips into Kenai Fjords National Park. Kachemak Bay, accessed through Homer, has superb protected paddling waters, and well-developed ways of getting kayakers to attractive spots.

WILDLIFE WATCHING   You have a chance of seeing whales, otters, sea lions, seals, and other marine animals on cruise or charter boats out of Seward, Homer, Whittier, Valdez, and Cordova. Bears could show up anywhere, but flights out of Homer are the region's best bet if you're dead-set on seeing one.

3 The Seward Highway: A Road Guide

The Kenai Peninsula's main lifeline is the road down from Anchorage, a 127-mile drive to Seward on a good two-lane highway, most of it through public land without development or services. Highway 1, commonly known as the Seward Highway, is the preferred route taken by most visitors to the peninsula, and a large part of those going to Prince William Sound. The highway begins at the south end of Anchorage, the only way out of town in that direction, and runs along Turnagain Arm 47 miles to Portage, where a couple of miles of tunnels take vehicles and trains under the mountains to Whittier. (See the section on Whittier below on how to do that trip.) At a fork 90 miles south of Anchorage, at Tern Lake, the **Sterling Highway** heads west to Cooper Landing, Kenai and Soldotna, and Homer, 235 miles from Anchorage. Those towns are covered in their sections, below. The Seward Highway continues 37 miles from Tern Lake through forest and past large lakes down to Seward, on the eastern side of the peninsula.

The Seward Highway is more than scenic—it's really a wonderful attraction in itself, designated a National Scenic Byway. I've written about the first 48 miles from Anchorage in chapter 6, in the section on Turnagain Arm and Portage Glacier. Use that mile-by-mile guide for the first part of your drive. As I did there, the mileage numbers I give here count from Anchorage, the direction most people drive the first time, but the roadside mileposts start in Seward. To correlate this log to the mileposts, subtract the distance listed from Anchorage from 127—so, for instance, a site listed as being 81 miles from Anchorage would be at milepost 46. There are excellent campgrounds and hiking trails all along the Seward Highway in the Chugach National Forest (covered in the next section).

Beyond the Portage Glacier turnoff, the road traverses the salt marshes to the south side of the Arm. These wetlands are good bird-watching grounds. The dead trees on the flats are leftover from before the 1964 earthquake. The area was inundated in the quake, when the entire region—the Kenai Peninsula and Prince William Sound—sank 7 feet and moved several feet laterally. Besides being the second strongest earthquake ever recorded, the '64 quake moved more land than any other. People who were here tell of their surprise to find the tide coming far higher in the days after the earthquake, until finally they realized that the land itself had sunk. Large parts of Homer, Hope, and Seldovia disappeared under the waves when the land sank.

At 52 miles from Anchorage, the highway steeply climbs through the spruce forest to the fresh, towering alpine terrain of the 1,000-foot-elevation **Turnagain Pass.** The vistas here are stupendous year-round, and if you can find dry tundra and avoid rivers, you can hike freely in any direction and appreciate the wildflowers.

The summit of the pass is 59 miles from Anchorage, where there's a pit toilet and a parking area used by backcountry skiers and snowmobilers in the winter. An avalanche near here killed five riders in the spring of 1999, so its always wise to check with the Forest Service before heading into the backcountry in the winter (see the next section).

The pass forms a continental divide, and now the road follows Granite Creek down toward the south, falling back below the treeline of stunted spruce and then popping back up into sweeping views. Arcing to the northwest after the Granite Creek Campground, the highway follows another north-flowing river, Sixmile Creek.

Seventy miles from Anchorage, the Hope Highway divides off to the north and west along Sixmile Creek while the Seward Highway continues south. Rafting companies based in Anchorage use this wild water for some of their most challenging rides (see chapter 6).

Should you choose to take the a break, you'll find **Hope** at the end of this 17-mile spur. It's a charming gold rush–era village with several hiking trails and the Porcupine Campground (the trails and campground are described in the next section, on Chugach National Forest). A few white frame buildings remain from the days when Hope was a gold-mining boomtown after a strike in 1895. Many of the newer buildings in the town center are quaint, too. Salmon run in Porcupine Creek, near the main street. Before the 1964 earthquake, the rest of the town used to stand where the creek gives way into a tidal meadow. Today, Hope's year-round population is less than 200.

The **Hope and Sunrise Historical and Mining Museum** is a one-room log cabin displaying historic objects and photographs. It's open noon to 4pm, Friday to Monday, Memorial Day to Labor Day. If you need a room for the night, the best choice is the **Bear Creek Lodge**, P.O. Box 90, Hope, AK 99605 (☎ **907/782-3141;** www.advenalaska.com/hope), with four pleasant cabins around a duck pond and two on a creek for $80 double. They have electric heat and wood stoves and share a bath-house. There's an inexpensive restaurant attached.

Returning to the Seward Highway, from the Hope intersection, we climb steeply again into the canyon of Canyon Creek, leveling out above the treeline at about 1,400 feet elevation along a series of alpine lakes in a narrow valley. The first business since the Portage Glacier, and the last for many miles, is on Summit Lake, 81 miles from Anchorage. **Summit Lake Lodge,** Mile 45.5 Seward Hwy., Moose Pass, AK 99631 (☎ **907/595-1520**), is a great old traditional log roadhouse that has been updated to house a comfortable and modern restaurant that's open every day of the year from 7am to 11pm. The food is generally good, and they take Visa and MasterCard. There's a good ice-cream counter in the log gift shop by the lake. The six-room log motel has rooms for $80 double; they have private bathrooms, but lack TVs or phones. I've often found the mountains that reach above the lake seductive for a climb, but I suspect bushwhacking through the alders up to the treeline would be hard work, and they are quite steep above. There is an unmaintained route across the highway from the lodge, but I've never attempted it.

The highway continues through similar terrain before descending into the trees again and branching at **Tern Lake,** 90 miles from Anchorage, where there's a bird-watching platform with interpretive signs and, on the west end, a picnic area. This is an unforgettable spot year-round, and a good place to get out and taste the fresh mountain air.

To the right at the intersection, the Sterling Highway leads to Cooper Landing, Kenai, Soldotna, and Homer. The Seward Highway continues to the left along a string of sparking mountain lakes, and through the little community of Moose Pass, 100 miles from Anchorage, on Upper Trail Lake. The waterwheel you see as you enter town was built just for fun. **Trail Lake Lodge,** P.O. Box 69, Moose Pass, AK 99631 (☎ **907/288-3101**), beside the lake on the left side of the highway, offers good rooms for reasonable prices and has a restaurant with a screened dining room by the water, as well as an inside dining room.

Over the next 23 miles, the highway continues past Trail Lake and Lower Trail Lake, on the left, and finally huge Kenai Lake, on the right, before entering the huge spruce trees of the coastal forest and arriving in Seward.

4 Chugach National Forest: Do-It-Yourself Wilderness

I've lived in and around the Chugach National Forest all my life, but it wasn't until well into adulthood that I had seen all its parts and appreciated its vastness and variety. Still, I doubt I'll ever really know this seemingly infinite land. **Prince William Sound,** just one of the National Forest's three parts, has 3,500 miles of shoreline among its folded islands and deeply penetrating fjords and passages. It would take a lifetime to really know all those cove beaches, climb all the island mountains, and explore to the head of every narrow bay under big rain forest trees. The **Copper River Delta** is another world entirely. Unlike the musty secrets of the Sound's obscure passages, the delta opens to the sky like a heavenly plain of wind and light, its waving green colors splashed by the airiest brushstrokes. It's another huge area: Just driving across the delta and back from Cordova is a full day trip. Finally, there's the western part of the national forest, on the **Kenai Peninsula.** This is largely an alpine realm. The mountains are steep, their timber quickly giving way to rock, tundra, and wildflowers up above. It's got remote, unclimbed peaks, but also many miles of family hiking trails, accessible fishing streams, and superb campgrounds. This is where you go in Alaska for multiday trail hikes.

The Chugach is managed primarily for recreation and conservation, although there is some logging, too. Visitors today may see large tracts of dead spruce and sometimes areas of cut timber, but these mostly are caused by a blight, the spruce bark beetle. The trees are cut in the forest and on private land to prevent fires in the standing deadwood. Logging in Prince William Sounds was slowed by the *Exxon Valdez* oil spill, when conservationists recognized the need to prevent further environmental damage to support recovery from the disaster. When Exxon was forced to pay $1 billion to a recovery fund, government trustees spent much of the money to buy back timber rights in the Sound and beyond to protect them. So far they've bought roughly as much land as is in all of Yosemite National Park—a lot of land, but only a sixth of what the Chugach already encompassed.

ESSENTIALS
GETTING THERE & GETTING AROUND
There are many ways to the Chugach National Forest. For Prince William Sound, use Whittier, Valdez, or Cordova as gateways; for the Copper River Delta, go through Cordova. Trails and campgrounds on the Kenai Peninsula generally meet the Seward or Sterling highways, or spur roads from the highways. The individual town listings later in this chapter provide details on how to get there and into the national forest. The section above describes the Seward Highway.

VISITOR INFORMATION
The most central place for information on the National Forest is the Alaska Public Lands Information Center in Anchorage, which is listed in full above under "Getting Outside on the Kenai Peninsula & Prince William Sound." For general forest inquiries, you can also call ☎ **907/271-2500** (www.fs.fed.us/r10/chugach). The national forest also has three ranger district offices, where you can get the most up-to-date local information and personal advice: **Glacier Ranger District,** Monarch Mine Road, near the Seward Highway off Alyeska Road (P.O. 129) Girdwood, AK 99587 (☎ **907/783-3242**); **Seward Ranger District,** Fourth Avenue and Jefferson Street (P.O. Box 390), Seward, AK 99663 (☎ **907/224-3374**); and **Cordova Ranger District,** Second and Browning streets (P.O. Box 280), Cordova, AK 99574 (☎ **907/424-7661**). The local offices no longer can reserve campground sites and remote cabins—for that you must use the toll free number listed below under "Accommodations." But to get information about the facilities, you'll need to go through the information center or the ranger offices.

GETTING OUTSIDE
HIKING, MOUNTAIN BIKING & BACKPACKING
Alaska's best long trails lead through the mountain passes of Chugach National Forest. A network of trails first developed by gold rush prospectors spans the Kenai Peninsula from Seward to Hope. The Iditarod Trail originally led from Seward all the way to

Nome, and you can hike parts of it on the peninsula still, although the famous race begins in Wasilla, north of Anchorage. Many shorter trails find their way to lovely mountain lakes, often with good fishing, or to the alpine terrain of clear walking above the treeline. Perhaps most remarkable, the Forest Service maintains **public cabins** on many of these trails and in other remote spots you can reach only on foot or with a boat or small plane. You can book the cabins along a trail instead of sleeping in a tent, or make a cabin your destination and spend a few days hiking or fishing from there.

I've covered trails near Cordova in that section, and some shorter hikes are mentioned below with the campgrounds under "Accommodations." Also check for hikes outside the national forest in the town sections.

The best trail guide covering the peninsula is *55 Ways to the Wilderness* by Helen Neinhueser and John Wolfe Jr., published by The Mountaineers (1011 SW Klickitat Way, Seattle, WA 98134). *Kenai Pathways,* available from the Public Lands Information Center for $4.95, contains official guidance for 25 peninsula trails, which coordinate with numbers on the excellent **Trails Illustrated** plastic map (see "Fast Facts: Alaska" in chapter 2).

RESURRECTION PASS TRAIL   This gold rush trail begins 4 miles above the town of Hope and runs over the top of the Kenai Peninsula to Cooper Landing (both towns are covered below). It's a beautiful, remote, yet well-used trail for hiking, mountain biking, Nordic skiing, or snowshoeing, rising through forest, crossing the alpine pass, and then descending again to a highway trailhead where you'll need to have transportation waiting. The 39-mile trail has eight public-use cabins, available for $35 to $45 a night. (See "Accommodations," below, for reservation information.) The cabins are well spaced to cover the trail in an easy 5 days, and those on lakes have boats for fishing. They are booked up well ahead winter and summer, but there are lots of good camping spots, too. The **Devil's Pass and Summit Lake trails** cut off from the Resurrection to the Seward Highway south of Summit Lake, shortening the route. The difficulty of doing the whole trail, by any of the entrances, is that you either need two cars or someone willing to drive you back to your starting point.

RESURRECTION RIVER & RUSSIAN LAKE TRAILS   These two connected trails begin in Cooper Landing, near the end of the Resurrection Pass Trail, and ultimately lead to Exit Glacier, outside of Seward, 33 miles away from Cooper Landing. Linked together, the Resurrection Pass and River trails took pioneers 72 miles from Seward to Hope, all the way across the peninsula. This less-used section provides access to excellent fishing and wildlife viewing (bears are common) and has a series of four cabins. Maintenance is limited, however, and at this writing two bridges were out; you should have some backcountry experience, and check with the Seward Ranger District for current information.

JOHNSON PASS TRAIL   The 23-mile trail climbs to a pair of lakes above the treeline at the 1,450-foot Johnson Creek Summit, tracing impressively narrow mountain valleys. The route, part of the Iditarod National Historic Trail, leads from Moose Pass, near Seward, to near the Granite Creek Campground, on the Seward Highway south of Turnagain Pass, so you do need transportation at each end.

LOST LAKE TRAIL & PRIMROSE TRAIL   With their fields of alpine wildflowers and small lakes, these connected trails make among the most beautiful hikes in the area. Snow lasts until late in the season up top. The upper, northern trailhead is at the 10-site Primrose Campground, on vast Kenai Lake, 17 miles from Seward off the Seward Highway on Primrose Road. The trail rises through hemlock past a waterfall about 2 miles up (look for the spur to the right when you hear water), past an old mining cabin, and then through ever smaller trees and above treeline. A Forest Service cabin is available on a 2-mile spur about 11 miles along the 15.8-mile route. The south, Lost Lake trailhead is near Seward.

FISHING

The national forest contains some of the most famous, and crowded, fishing banks in Alaska, including the **Russian River,** near Cooper Landing, with its incredible run of red salmon in July and good fishing lasting into September. Easiest access is at the Russian River Campground, just west of the village. There are plenty of other road-side salmon streams and fishing rivers and lakes in the national forest that are so remote they might never see a line all summer. Some remote lakes have Forest Service cabins for rent on their shores. The Forest Service publishes a booklet on salmon streams and another on lake fishing for trout. Most important to success is local knowledge of what's running and how to fish for it—check with the ranger offices and other visitor centers, and see "Fishing," in chapter 2.

SEA KAYAKING & BOATING

I've included information on Prince William Sound sea kayaking in the sections on Whittier, Valdez, and Cordova. The area east of Whittier, with its long fjords, glaciers, narrow passages, and Forest Service cabins, is especially appealing and popular for sea kayaking, but to get out there you need a boat ride first—the waters right around Whittier aren't as interesting. The same is true of Valdez. The local sea kayaking oper-ators can help you arrange drop-off service. Cordova has more interesting waters right near town, so you can paddle right from the boat harbor. Those who haven't done much sea kayaking should only consider a guided trip; if you're a raw beginner, start with a day trip. All three communities have operators offering rentals and guided out-ings of various lengths.

For those who aren't up to paddling, renting a skiff is a great alternative for an inde-pendent day trip. Operators in the Valdez and Cordova harbors offer rentals and fishing gear. We enjoy taking a boat out just to explore remote beaches with the kids.

ACCOMMODATIONS
REMOTE CABINS

It's hard to imagine a more authentic Alaskan accommodation than a pioneer cabin with a wood stove—a place you could stay that would give you a better feel for the soul of a wild place. The Chugach National Forest maintains more than 40 remote recreation cabins for rent to the public. The accommodations range from simple to crude—you bring your own sleeping bags, cooking equipment, and other gear, and the cabin is only as clean as the last user—but no other room you can rent has a better location or greater privacy. Cabins don't have electricity or plumbing. Some cabins are along hiking and skiing trails, others on shores where boats and kayaks can pull up, and others on remote fishing lakes accessible only by floatplane. You can stay up to a week in most, with a limit of 3 days in the Resurrection Trail cabins.

The Forest Service prints a free booklet listing the cabins with short descriptions of each. The maps are rudimentary, so you will need a detailed map such as the Trails Illustrated plastic map mentioned above under "Hiking, Mountain Biking & Back-packing," which shows cabin locations and names. Cabins rent for $25 to $45 a night, with most priced at $35 a night. Typically, the price of the cabin itself is not your major expense: You'll need a way to get there, either by plane, boat, or by having a vehicle to drive to a trailhead and then hiking. If flying, contact flight services in the nearest town (listed in the sections below) to find out the cost before you book the cabin. Flight time is several hundred dollars an hour. You can rent the equipment you'll need at the businesses listed in the Anchorage section, but you should talk to a ranger first to get details about access and what to take.

Reserve America, a company in upstate New York, took over the reservation system in 1999; I wouldn't rely on them for detailed information, only call to check availability and book your spot once you've got all the necessary guidance. Their toll free number is ☎ **877/444-6777,** TDD 877/833-6777; or with toll from overseas, ☎ 518/885-3639. In the summer, the lines are open daily 8am to midnight EST, at this writing; winter hours are daily 10am to 7pm. You can also reserve online, at reserveusa.com. They take American Express, Discover, MasterCard, and Visa, or you can reserve on the phone and then pay within 10 days by check or money order. Cabins and campground sites are available for reservation on a first-come, first-served basis. Campsites can be reserved starting 240 days ahead, cabins 180 days ahead.

CAMPGROUNDS

Don't expect anything fancy in the Forest Service campgrounds: They mostly have pit toilets and water from hand pumps, and roads may not be paved. But some of these places are truly spectacular. I've listed them in order of distance from Anchorage, but the Seward Highway mileposts count in the reverse direction. For information on campgrounds below mile 60, call the Seward Ranger District (see the top of the chapter). For the others, call the Glacier Ranger District, in Girdwood (☎ **907/ 783-3242).** Or contact **Alaska Recreation Management** (☎ **907/522-TENT;** alaskacampground.com); their Web site, still under construction at this writing, will contain campground descriptions for the entire Kenai Peninsula. Sites in a few of the following campgrounds, as noted, take reservations through the Reserve America system explained above. Camping fees are expected to go up a dollar or two soon.

Williwaw and Black Bear. Mile 4, Portage Glacier Rd. (turn at mile 78 Seward Hwy.). Williwaw $15 per night. Reservations accepted with additional fee. 38 sites. Black Bear $8 per night. 12 sites.

These two campgrounds are next to each other near Portage Glacier, along a creek where you can watch spawning red salmon in mid-August; no fishing is allowed, though. Williwaw is one of the better-developed campgrounds in the national forest, with paved roads, pumped water, and nicely separated sites.

Bertha Creek. Mile 61, Seward Hwy. $10 per night. 12 sites.

In the high country, near gold panning sites on the creek.

Granite Creek. Mile 63, Seward Hwy. $10 per night. 19 sites.

Near the Johnson Pass trailhead and gold panning on the creek.

Porcupine. At the end of the Hope Hwy. $9 per night. 24 sites.

The campground near the gold rush village of Hope is among the most beautiful in the Chugach National Forest, or the state. The sites are on a mountainside overlooking Turnagain Arm, five with sweeping ocean views. The thick trees make for privacy, but also mosquitoes. Bring repellent. Two good day hikes leave from the campground: The level 5-mile trail to **Gull Rock** makes a good family ramble, and with some effort you can scramble down to remote beaches along the way, where we've enjoyed a picnic. The **Hope Point Trail** is a stiff climb that rises 3,600 feet to expansive views. See "The Seward Highway: A Road Guide" above, for more on Hope.

Tenderfoot Creek. Mile 46, Seward Hwy. $9 per night. 27 sites.

This pleasant campground lies across Summit Lake from the Seward Highway as it passes through a narrow mountain valley above the treeline. Campsites look out on the water from a peaceful, sunny hillside. The nearby Summit Lake Lodge, described in the Seward Highway section, offers good meals, and is the only business in many a mile.

Ptarmigan Creek and Trail River. Mile 23, Seward Hwy. $9 per night. Reservations accepted, with additional fee. 16 sites.

Near the tiny towns of Moose Pass and Crown Point, the campground is at the trail-head for the trail to Ptarmigan lake, 4 miles away with only 500 feet elevation gain—a good place for a picnic or fishing for Dolly Varden char and rainbow trout. A mile away and on the other side of the highway, the Trail River Campground has 63 sites and accepts reservations.

Primrose. Mile 17, Seward Hwy. $9 per night. 10 sites.

This lovely campground lies on the edge of Kenai Lake and at the base of the Primrose Trail to Lost Lake, one of the area's most beautiful (see "Getting Outside," above). This campground is the closest to Seward that has a sense of natural isolation.

Russian River. Mile 52, Sterling Hwy., just west of Cooper Landing. $11 per night. 84 sites. Flush toilets.

This large, well-developed campground mainly serves fishermen pursuing red salmon on the river. When the fishing is good, the campground overflows and can be noisy. Reserve ahead, if possible.

Cooper Creek. Mile 50.7, Sterling Hwy. $9 per night. 26 sites. Reservations accepted.

The campground is in Cooper Landing near the Kenai River.

Quartz Creek. Quartz Creek Rd., at mile 45 Sterling Hwy. $9 per night. 45 sites. Flush toilets, boat launch.

Good lake and stream fishing are near the campground.

Crescent Creek. Quartz Creek Rd., at mile 45 Sterling Hwy. $9 per night. Flush toilets.

A couple of miles short of Cooper Landing, the campground is away from the road near the Crescent Lake trailhead.

5 Whittier: Dock on the Sound

Whittier is Anchorage's portal on Prince William Sound. Although Anchorage itself is on Cook Inlet, that muddy, fast-moving water is virtually unused for recreational boating. Whittier, on the other hand, stands on the edge of a long fjord in the north-west corner of the Sound, whose clear waters are full of salmon, orcas, and otters and bounded by rain forests and glaciers. In the past, the difficulty of getting to Whittier—through a mountain by train—helped to limit the number of people from Anchorage who would go there. Now they're paving the railway tunnel, and in the spring of 2000 visitors will be able to drive through from Anchorage to Prince William Sound in less than an hour. People in Whittier expect the whole world to arrive.

Whittier certainly has major advantages for visitors seeking to get out on the water. The water is calmer than in Kenai Fjords National Park, with seasickness rare, and the glaciers are even more numerous. One company's selling point is a **"26 glacier cruise,"** all done in a day trip from Anchorage by rail and large tour boat (see below). Prince William Sound boats also see otters and sometimes whales; Kenai Fjords tours more often see whales and see more birds. Sea kayakers also have great places to go from Whittier. Almost all of Prince William Sound is in Chugach National Forest, with its public-use cabins in lovely, remote spots on the shores (see the previous section).

On the other hand, there's little other reason to go to Whittier—unless you're on a quest to find the oddest towns in America. The majority of the 300 townspeople live in a single 14-story concrete building with dark, narrow hallways. The grocery store is on the first floor and the medical clinic on the third. The rest of the people live in one other building. **The Begich Towers,** as the dominant structure is called, was built during the 1940s, when Whittier's strategic location on the Alaska Railroad and at the head of a deep Prince William Sound fjord made it a key port in the defense of Alaska. Today, with its barren gravel ground and ramshackle warehouses and boat sheds, the town maintains a stark military-industrial character. The pass above the town is a funnel for frequent whipping winds, it always seems to rain, and the glaciers above the town keep it cool even in summer. As one young town ambassador told me when I was once on a visit, "You're thinking, 'Thank God I don't live here,' right?" The official boosters look more on the bright side: Having everyone live in one building saves on snow removal in a place that gets an average of 20 feet per winter. Kids don't even have to go outside to get to school—a tunnel leads from the tower to the school.

ESSENTIALS
GETTING THERE

BY CAR　The new road through the 2.8-mile long World War II rail tunnel to Whittier is only one lane, so you need to wait your turn to go through. The tunnel is projected to open in May 2000, and at this writing the toll and many other details had not been decided. Essentially, you'll drive the Seward Highway to Portage, follow signs for the tunnel, then pay and wait for a signal to drive through. The delay could be lengthy if you have to wait for a train or a column of cars going the other direction. Parking in Whittier also will carry a fee, as yet undetermined.

BY TRAIN　If you plan on a day trip on the Sound from a base in Anchorage—the way most people use Whittier—you can leave the car behind and take the train straight from the Anchorage depot. The **Alaska Railroad** (☎ **800/544-0552** or 907/265-2494; www.akrr.com) runs a nicely appointed daily train with a dining car timed to match the schedules of Prince William Sound tour boats. The tour boat operators offer package rates for those who take the train. Unless you have planned an activity or tour on the water, however, you'll find the 6-hour stay in Whittier is too long to just hang around there. The round-trip fare is $52 adults, $26 ages 2 to 11. The train ride is scenic and fun, but if there is more than one person along, a rental car will save you money.

It's also possible to park in Portage and take a short **rail shuttle** through the mountain, saving the cost of the tunnel toll and parking on the other end. Check with the railroad for fares and schedules, which were entirely up in the air at this writing—they plan to wait and see how many people want to drive through and how many want to ride before making those decisions.

BY FERRY　The **Alaska Marine Highway System** ferry *Bartlett* (☎ **800/642-0066,** TDD 800/764-3779, fax 907/277-4829; www.dot.state.ak.us/external/amhs/home.html) makes a 6½-hour run to Valdez several times a week, where you can drive north on the beautiful Richardson Highway, completing a circle back to Anchorage in 2 days or more. The fare is $72 for a car up to 15 feet long plus $58 for an adult passenger, with ages 2 to 11 roughly half price. The ferry also runs once a week direct from Whittier to Cordova, a 7-hour trip, or you can go by way of Valdez several times a week in roughly 15 hours. A Chugach National Forest ranger interprets the scenery in the observation lounge, and there is a serviceable little restaurant aboard. See "Exploring the Kenai Peninsula & Prince William Sound," above, for more on the ferry system.

Whittier Travel Tip

Bring any money you'll need, as Whittier lacks banking services.

VISITOR INFORMATION

The **Greater Whittier Chamber of Commerce,** P.O. Box 607, Whittier, AK 99693 (☎ **907/344-3340**), maintains a visitor center in an old railroad car near the boat harbor, where you can get a free cup of coffee to warm up from the rain, and maps, brochures, and guidance on finding a fishing charter or other ways out on the water.

GETTING OUT ON THE SOUND

Whittier is the entrance to western Prince William Sound, the area with its most protected waters up long, deep fjords and among tiny islands and passages. You're likely to see marine mammals and eagles. Glaciers lurk at the heads of many of the fjords, dumping ice in the water for the tour boats that cruise from Whittier.

TOUR BOATS

Several companies, mostly based in downtown Anchorage, compete for your business for day-trip tours to the Sound's western glaciers. Besides the incredible scenery, the water is calm and seasickness virtually unknown—for the queasy, it's a much better choice than Kenai Fjords National Park. Each operator times departures to coordinate with the daily Alaska Railroad train from Anchorage, described above, which means they have 6 hours for the trip. Some try to see as much as possible, while others take it slower to savor the scenery and wildlife sightings. Also check the Valdez and Cordova sections for tours from there.

Phillips' Cruises and Tours. 519 W. Fourth Ave. Suite 100, Anchorage, AK 99501 ☎ **800/544-0529** or 907/276-8023. www.26glaciers.com.

The 26-glacier cruise travels the Sound on a fast three-deck catamaran, counting the glaciers as they go. They charge $122 adults, $49 ages 2 to 11.

Major Marine Tours. 411 W. Fourth Ave. Suite 10, Anchorage, AK 99501. ☎ **800/764-7300** or 907/274-7300. www.majormarine.com.

This company operates a smaller, 149-passenger vessel at a slower pace than Phillips—they hit a mere 10 glaciers. They also make a specialty of their food. The fare is $99 for adults, $49 children 11 and under; the salmon or chicken buffet is $10 for adults, $5 for children.

Prince William Sound Cruises and Tours. P.O. Box 1297, Valdez, AK 99686. ☎ **800/992-1297** or 907/835-4731. www.princewilliamsound.com.

The former Stan Stephens Cruises offers a tour boat that travels between Whittier and Valdez ($119 adults, $59 children, one way), leaving Whittier each afternoon at 2:15pm. There's a 6-hour cruise from Whittier like the other operators ($109 and $54). See the Valdez section for more on the company.

Honey Charters. On the Whittier waterfront (P.O. Box 708), Whittier, AK 99693. ☎ **907/472-2493.** Fax 907/472-2491. www.honeycharters.com.

This family runs small boats licensed for only 6 to 10 passengers—the kind usually used for fishing charters called a "six-pack charter"—but they specialize in personal tours and water transportation. Instead of getting on a huge boat with a mob of people, you go where you want, get off on the beach to picnic or walk, and get really close to wildlife. A 3-hour cruise is $99 per person, 6 hours $149, with a minimum of 4 passengers and a maximum of 10. They also book fishing charters and drop off kayakers.

CRUISES

If you have more time to spend, several operators offer cruises of a few days and longer in the Sound on vessels small enough to allow exploration of its protected waters.

Cruise West. Fourth and Battery Building, Seattle, WA 98121. ☎ **800/888-9378.** www.cruisewest.com.

This is the largest of the small-ship cruise companies, offering a full package of tours and cruises statewide (see chapter 4). Their Prince William Sound trips last 3 or 4 nights aboard the 52-passenger *Spirit of Glacier Bay* and 78-passenger *Spirit of Columbia.* Fares start at $775 per person.

Discovery Voyages. P.O. Box 1500, Cordova, AK 99574. ☎ **800/324-7602.** www.discoveryvoyages.com.

For a truly intimate cruise, this company operates a classic 65-foot vessel build in the 1950s for missionary work. There are only six cabins, each sleeping two passengers. Although based in Cordova, most trips go from Whittier, with itineraries that cover just about every corner of the Sound. Their basic 5-day cruise costs $2,250 per person.

FISHING

Better than a dozen charter fishing boats operate out of Whittier, the closest saltwater fishing to Anchorage. You can get a list from the visitor center or book through **Bread and Butter Charters** (☎ **888/472-2396** or 907/472-2396; fax 907/472-2503; junebbak.com), which represents its own and four other boats. Honey Charters, listed above under "Tour Boats," has a similar service.

SEA KAYAKING

Whittier is a popular starting point for kayak trips to the beautiful and protected western Prince William Sound. Day trips for beginners paddle along the shore near Whittier, starting out with a boat ride and returning by kayak to town after exploring the coves along the shore, or visiting a bird rookery. Longer, multiday trips go by boat to even more interesting waters where you can visit fjords and paddle narrow passages.

Several businesses compete in Whittier. **Alaska Sea-Kayakers** offers 3- and 5-hour day trips, for $60 and $115 respectively, and has an office in Whittier for kayak rentals. Call ☎ **877/472-5753** for day trips, 907/472-2534 for rentals and custom tours; nova-alaska.com. **Prince William Sound Kayak Center,** P.O. Box 233008, Anchorage, AK 99523-3008 (☎ **907/472-2452** in summer or 907/276-7235 year-round), offers guided 2-hour trips starting at $65 for a single person or $50 each for a couple, and escorted trips of 2 to 4 days. The 2-day trip is $140 per person. Other companies based in Anchorage that offer guided sea kayaking and rentals from Whittier are listed under "Sea Kayaking" in chapter 6.

Experienced paddlers can plan their own trip, renting kayaks for out of Whittier for around $40 a day for a single, $60 double. Most people charter a boat to drop them off among the islands beyond the long, deep fjord in which Whittier is located. Honey Charters, listed above under "Tour Boats," offers a drop-off service. There are six Forest Service cabins in the idyllic area popular with kayakers, off Port Wells. Unfortunately, they're so popular that they often are reserved as soon as they become available, 8 months ahead. The Forest Service or Alaska Public Lands Information Center in Anchorage can tell you where to find campsites, too. For information and cabin reservations, see "Chugach National Forest: Do-It-Yourself Wilderness," above

Motel Accommodations in Whittier

Simple motel rooms are for rent at the **Anchor Inn** (☎ **907/472-2354**).

ACCOMMODATIONS

June's Whittier Bed and Breakfast Condo Suites. P.O. Box 715, Whittier, AK 99693 (☎ **888/472-2396** or 907/472-2396. Fax 907/472-2503. www.junebbak.com. 7 units with kitchens. TV, TEL. $95–$115 double. $50 each additional adult 11 and older. AE, DC, DISC, MC, V.

These seven units, located right in the Begich Towers, come with full kitchens and one, two, or three bedrooms. Some are nicely remodeled, with great views, VCRs, and other extras, while others are a bit dated but still comfortable. The friendly hostess, June Miller, charges by the person. She and her husband, Ken, also have a fishing charter and sightseeing business, Bread and Butter Charters, with two boats; they charge $160 per person for a day of fishing. Contact them for a fishing package to Whittier. They have an office on the waterfront.

DINING

The dining scene in Whittier is there for people waiting to get on boats or grabbing a sandwich while passing through, and the choice of restaurants in the shopping area at the east end of the boat harbor tends to change year to year. Last time I visited, **Orca Coffee Company and Bakery** was attractive, with great views, glass tables, and comforting odors. **Swiftwater Seafood** had a counter to order and stools for seating.

6 Seward: Gateway to Resurrection Bay & Kenai Fjords National Park

The main reason to go to Seward has always been Resurrection Bay and the access the port provides to the great mass of Alaska. The agreeable little town started life as a place to fish and to get off the boat for Alaska, then continued as a place for Alaskans and visitors to get on boats and see the bay, Kenai Fjords National Park (described below), and the marine mammals and birds that live there. With the growth of the cruise industry, Seward again is a place to get off the boat, and most cruises doing the Gulf of Alaska route start or end here, their passengers then linked by bus to the airport in Anchorage. That flow of people has brought a lot of tourist development to town, mostly of a quality that hasn't damaged the town's character.

Located by the broad fjord of Resurrection Bay, Seward is a mountainside grid of streets lined with old wood-frame houses and newer fishermen's residences. It's always been the sort of place where pedestrians casually wander across the road, hardly glancing for cars, for there likely won't be any, or, if there are, they'll be ready to stop.

The changes in town are bringing a few more cars, but most of what's new is good for Seward. The largest addition, **The Alaska Sea Life Center,** is a research aquarium that's also open to the public. Finished in 1998, the center shows off seals, sea lions, marine birds, and the scientists who are studying them in impressive exhibits. Its $50 million price tag was funded mostly by money won from Exxon after the *Exxon Valdez* oil spill, and now it dominates the waterfront in downtown Seward near a brand new hotel. Combined with Seward's excellent ocean fishing, the national park, the wonderful hiking trails, and the unique and attractive town, the new center is helping make this one of Alaska's most appealing towns for a 2-day visit.

Seward's history is among the oldest in Alaska. The Russian governor Alexander Baranof stopped here in 1793, named Resurrection Bay, and built a ship, which later sank. The town was born in its modern form in 1903, when a company seeking to build a railroad north came ashore. They failed, but Seward still was an important port. Gold prospectors had begun blazing trails from here to finds on Turnagain Arm starting in 1891, and in 1907 the army linked those trails with others all the way to Nome, finishing the Iditarod Trail. Today that route is discontinuous south of Anchorage, but you can follow it through Seward and hike a portion of it through the Johnson Pass north of town (described above in the "Chugach National Forest: Do-It-Yourself Wilderness" section).

More relevant for current visitors and the local economy, the federal government took over the failed railroad-building effort in 1915, finishing the line to Fairbanks in 1923. Until the age of jet travel, most people coming to Alaska arrived by steamer in Seward and then traveled north by rail. The train ride to Anchorage, daily during the summer, is supremely beautiful.

ESSENTIALS
GETTING THERE
Seward can be reached by all modes of transportation.

BY CAR   See "The Seward Highway: A Road Guide," above, for how to make the spectacular 127-mile drive down from Anchorage. All major car-rental agencies are represented in Anchorage.

BY BUS   The **Seward Bus Line** (☎ **907/224-3608** in Seward, 907/563-0800 in Anchorage; fax 907/224-7237) makes one trip daily, year-round, starting in Seward and going to Anchorage and back; the fare is $30 one-way. Gray Line's **Alaskon Express** (☎ **800/544-2206**), operating in summer only, instead leaves Anchorage in the morning and returns in the evening, charging $40. **Alaska Tourquest** (☎ **907/344-6667** Anchorage; 907/224-8747 Seward) charges $50 round-trip for daily service that starts in Anchorage in the morning and stops at trailheads on the Seward Highway; they also go to Talkeetna and Denali National Park. **The Park Connection,** a shuttle service operated by the Seward Windsong Lodge (☎ **907/245-0200**, see below) connects Seward with Anchorage and Denali National Park daily, running in the afternoon and evening. The fare is $39 to Anchorage, $98 to Denali, a 10-hour trip. Children are charged half price.

BY TRAIN   I think everyone should take the run between Anchorage and Seward on the ❂ **Alaska Railroad,** 411 W. First Ave., Anchorage, AK 99501 (☎ **800/544-0552** or 907/265-2494; www.akrr.com), which runs daily in summer. It's even more spectacular than the highway route, passing close by glaciers and following a ledge halfway up the narrow, vertical Placer River gorge, where it ducks into tunnels and pops out at bends in the river. The landscape looks just as it did when the first person beheld it. The train has five cars: a dining car with good deli-style food, a car with commentary, a quiet car, a dome car, and a baggage car. The railroad's young guides are well trained and provide an accurate and not overly verbose commentary. The fare is $50 one-way, $86 round-trip; children ages 2 to 11 half off. A rental car will almost always be cheaper, but the train ride is unforgettable. You can stop in Girdwood, too. The railroad also offers packages that include a boat tour of Kenai Fjords National Park, but I advise against trying to get down from Anchorage, do the park, and return in the same day; it's too much.

BY AIR   F.S. Air (☎ **907/248-9595**) serves Seward from Anchorage two or three times a day for $69 one-way, $99 round-trip.

Seward

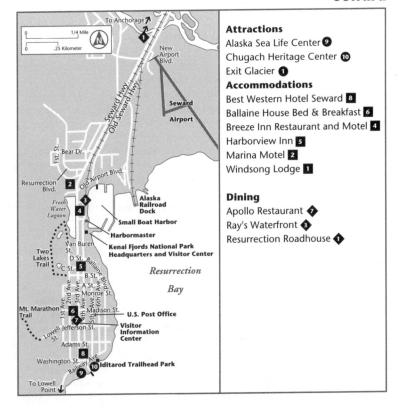

Attractions
Alaska Sea Life Center ❾
Chugach Heritage Center ❿
Exit Glacier ❶

Accommodations
Best Western Hotel Seward ❽
Ballaine House Bed & Breakfast ❻
Breeze Inn Restaurant and Motel ❹
Harborview Inn ❺
Marina Motel ❷
Windsong Lodge ❶

Dining
Apollo Restaurant ❼
Ray's Waterfront ❸
Resurrection Roadhouse ❶

BY FERRY The ferry *Tustumena,* of the Alaska Marine Highway System (☎ **800/642-0066** or 907/224-5485; www.dot.state.ak.us/external/amhs/home.html), connects Seward with Valdez (11 hours to the east), with stops by reservation in the Prince William Sound Alaska Native villages of Chenega and Tatitlek, and Kodiak (13 hours to the southwest) roughly once a week. The adult passenger fare for Valdez is $58, Kodiak $54; ages 2 to 11 are about half price. Leaving from Homer cuts off 4 hours to Kodiak. Once a month, the *Kennicott* travels from Seward to Valdez and then across the Gulf of Alaska to Juneau. The $148 fare is a bargain, but it takes more than 42 hours. The terminal is at the cruise ship dock, on the outside of the small-boat harbor.

GETTING AROUND

You can easily cover downtown Seward on foot, although a little help is handy to get back and forth from the boat harbor. If it's not raining, a bike may be the best way. **Seward Mountain Bike Shop** (☎ 907/224-2448), in a railcar near the depot at the harbor, rents high-performance mountain bikes and models good for just getting around town, plus accessory equipment. A cruiser is $12 half day, $19 full day. The **Chamber of Commerce Trolley** runs every half hour from 10am to 7pm daily in summer; it goes south along Third Avenue and north on Ballaine Street, stopping at the railroad depot, the cruise ship dock, the Alaska SeaLife Center, and the harbor visitor center. **Independent Taxi** (☎ 907/224-5000) is one of the cab companies. **Alaska Tourquest** (☎ 907/224-8747) runs shuttles around the town's sites and to Exit Glacier for $22 adult round-trip, $16 children 6 to 14 (that includes the park fee).

VISITOR INFORMATION

The **Seward Chamber of Commerce,** P.O. Box 749, Seward, AK 99664 (☎ **907/ 224-8051;** fax 907/224-5353; e-mail: chamber@seward.net), has four visitor centers. The one on the Seward Highway, near the boat harbor as you enter town, is open year-round (summer 8am to 5pm Monday to Friday, 9am to 5pm Sunday; winter closed weekends). Summer-only centers are in a kiosk at Small Boat Harbor, downtown in an old Alaska Railroad car at the corner of Third Avenue and Jefferson Street, and on the cruise ship dock. They can help with business information and last-minute help finding a room.

A handy automated voice-mail service called **Seward Information Help Line** (☎ 907/224-2424) provides information about all kinds of local services, vacancies, and reservations and can put you through directly to the businesses described on the recordings.

A local Internet provider, **Seward Internet Services,** has links to local businesses at www.seward.net/links.html.

In addition to these town information sources, don't miss the Kenai Fjords National Park Visitor Center, covered in the next section. Contacts for the Chugach National Forest are in that section, above.

SPECIAL EVENTS

✪ **The Fourth of July** is the big day of the year in Seward, when the whole town explodes with visitors, primarily from Anchorage. Besides the parade and many small-town festivities, the main attraction is the **Mount Marathon Race,** run every year since it started as a bar bet in 1915. The racers go from the middle of town straight up rocky Mount Marathon to its 3,022-foot peak, then tumble down again, arriving muddy and bloody at the finish line in town. Binoculars will allow you to see the whole thing from town, including the pratfalls of the runners on their way down.

The Silver Salmon Derby starts the second Saturday of August and runs 10 days, although the peak of silver season comes later. The chamber of commerce visitor centers can provide information.

Fast Facts: Seward

Banks   There are ATMs at the First National Bank of Anchorage, 303 Fourth Ave., and at the National Bank of Alaska, 908 Third Ave.

Hospital   Providence Seward Medical Center is at 417 First Ave. (☎ 907/ 224-5205).

Internet/E-mail   Eagle Eye Photo (☎ 907/224-2022), at the boat harbor, charges $2.50 for 15 minutes of access on their machine, and has 1-hour photo developing, too.

Police   For nonemergency situations, call the Seward Police Department (☎ 907/224-3338) or, outside the city limits, the Alaska State Troopers (☎ 907/224-3346).

Post Office   At Fifth Avenue and Madison Street.

Taxes   Sales tax is 5%. The room tax in Seward is 9%.

ATTRACTIONS IN TOWN

Besides the Alaska Sealife Center and the Chugach Heritage Center (see below), most of Seward's attractions are of the modest, small-town variety. Explore downtown with the help of a **walking-tour map** provided by one of the visitor centers.

The **Iditarod Trailhead,** on the water just east of the SeaLife Center, is where pioneers entered Alaska. Walk along the paved path from there to the park, beach, and campground. The broken concrete and twisted metal you see on the beach here are remains of the Seward waterfront from the 1964 earthquake. The campground turns into an RV and tent city in the summer—an often loud and rowdy one, unfortunately. Often you can see sea otters swimming just offshore. During silver salmon season, in August and September, it's possible to catch them casting from shore here, although you're chances are far better from a boat (see "Fishing," below).

The **Seward Museum,** at Third and Jefferson, has historical memorabilia and curiosities, and a display on the Russian ships built here in the late 18th century. Admission is $2 for adults, 50¢ for children, and it's open during the summer, daily from 10am to 5pm. The steep-roofed **St. Peter's Episcopal Church** is a delightful little chapel under the mountains at First Avenue and Adams Street.

✪ **Alaska SeaLife Center.** Railroad Ave. (P.O. Box 1329), Seward, AK 99664. ☎ **800/224-2525** of 907/224-3080. www.alaskasealife.org. $12.50 adults, $10 children 4–16, free for those under 4. Summer, daily 9am–9:30pm; winter, Wed–Sat 10am–5pm.

The center is a serious research institution and a superb aquarium of creatures from the nearby Alaskan waters. After seeing puffins dive into the water from a tour boat, here you can see what they look like flying *under* the water. Sea birds, harbor seals, and sea lions reside in three large exhibits that you can see from above or below. There are some smaller tanks with fish, crab, and other creatures, and a touch tank where you can handle starfish and other tide-pool animals. It's not as large as a big city aquarium, however, and you're not likely to spend more than an hour or two here, despite the high admission price. Programs for kids and adults happen all day. To make the most of your time, call ahead so you can catch a program on a subject that interests you.

Chugach Heritage Center. 501 Railway Ave., Seward. ☎ **907/224-5065.** Tues–Sun 10am–6pm; shows 11am, noon, 1pm, 3pm, 4pm, 5pm. Admission $8 adults, $6.50 ages 7–13, free under 7. Closed mid-Sept–May.

In the classic restored railroad depot next to the SeaLife Center, Chugach Natives and Aleuts perform a half-hour play dramatizing some of their traditional stories in a small auditorium, with impressive costumes. The gift store in the lobby carries authentic Native art and other affordable items. Call ahead, however, as changes to the program are under consideration.

GETTING OUTSIDE
Here I've described things to do out of Seward other than the national park—which includes the fjords and Exit Glacier. See "Kenai Fjords National Park," below, for that information.

BOATING & SEA KAYAKING   Introductory sea kayaking paddles stay in Resurrection Bay. **Kenai Fjords Tours** offers family kayaking at its Fox Island camp as part of its boat-tour operation. They're listed in detail in the Kenai Fjords National Park section below. **Crest Adventures** (☎ 800/288-3134 Lower 48 only; 907/258-3866 in Alaska; 907/224-3960 in Seward, summer only; www.alaskan.com/kayak) offers day trips in Resurrection Bay and the Sound and extended trips and gear rental to experienced paddlers. The Seward day trips start at **Miller's Landing** (☎ 907/224-5739), just south of town on Lowell Point Road (P.O. Box 81, Seward, AK 99664), and you can book trips there as well. The guided sea kayaking day trip costs $85, or $95 with lunch, and follows the shore toward Caines Head State Recreation Area where you can see sea otters, sea birds, and other wildlife.

Whether kayaking or not, Miller's Landing is a good place to know about if you intend to spend any time outdoors around Seward. Miller's Landing also has a camp-ground (described below), a boat launch with skiffs and sea kayaks for rent. (Skiffs are $35 for 2 hours, $130 all day; kayaks for the first day cost $30 for a single, $55 for a double, less for additional days.) In the little bait shop and grocery store a wood stove burns and a coffee pot fuels ongoing discussions on fish and boats. They'll teach you how to fish salmon and send you out on your own or on a guided charter. A water taxi operation charges flat rates to get to remote beaches and public cabins around the bay or the national park, for sea kayakers or those who just want to get off on their own.

Book **sailing charters** on Resurrection Bay through the central agencies listed under "Fishing," below. The waters are beautiful, but it's a different experience than sailing in the Lower 48—if there's any wind, it's quite chilly.

FISHING   Seward is renowned for its saltwater silver salmon fishing, and there's a harbor full of large and small charter boats waiting to take you. There's also good hal-ibut fishing. I prefer small boats because you get to know the skipper better and have more of a feeling of being out there on your own. The going rate for a guided charter, with everything provided, is around $130 per person for salmon, or up to $150 for halibut, for which the boats have to go farther. There are several central charter agen-cies, which makes life simpler for visitors. **The Fish House,** located at the Small Boat Harbor, books charters, sells and rents ocean-fishing and spin-casting gear, and carries some fly-fishing supplies. For charters, reserve ahead at P.O. Box 1209, Seward, AK 99664 (☎ **800/257-7760** or 907/224-3674). See "Boating," above, about the much less expensive option of renting your own skiff and fishing without a guide.

Bob Shaffer (☎ **907/224-3243**) is a well-recommended fly-fishing guide in Seward, charging about $100 a person.

HIKING   There are several excellent hiking trails near Seward. You can get a com-plete list and directions at the Kenai Fjords National Park Visitor Center (see the next section).

In town, the easy family walks include the beach downtown near the Iditarod Trail-head (see "Attractions in Town," above) or the flat **Two Lakes Trail,** which runs through the woods and along the ponds near town, starting from Second Avenue near B Street.

The **Mount Marathon Trail** is a tough hike to the top of a 3,000-foot mountain. The route of the famous Mount Marathon foot race is the more strenuous choice, basically going straight up from the end of Jefferson Street; the hikers' route starts at the corner of First Avenue and Monroe Street. Either trail rises steeply to the top of the rocky pinnacle and the incredible views there. Allow all day, unless you're a racer; in that case, expect to do it in under 45 minutes.

The **Caines Head State Recreation Area** has a 7-mile coastal trail south of town. Parts of the trail are accessible only at low tide, so it's best done either as an overnight or with someone picking you up or dropping you off in a boat at the far end—the Miller's Landing water taxi, mentioned under "Boating & Sea Kayaking," above, offers this service for $20 per person, one-way. The trail has some gorgeous views, rocky shores, and a good destination at the end: a promontory with the concrete remains of a World War II gun emplacement at Fort McGilvray. Three campsites are at Tonsina Point, 2 miles in, and a State Parks public-use cabin is 2 miles farther (see "Accommodations," below). At North Beach, 6½ miles from the trailhead, are two camping shelters, a ranger station, and trailheads to the fort, South Beach, and the 3-mile Alpine Trail. It's a beautiful and interesting hike. The trailhead is south of town on Lowell Point Road; pull off in the lot right after the sewage plant, then cross the road through the gate and follow the dirt road a bit until it becomes the actual trail. The state Division of Parks produces a good trail guide you can pick up free at the Kenai Fjords National Park Visitor Center at the boat harbor; ask there about the tide conditions for your hike.

SLED DOG MUSHING   The dog-driving Seavey family, including the kids, shows off their kennel off Exit Glacier Road in Seward and offers rides in summer and, for groups, in winter. A summertime ride on a cart isn't exactly the real thing, but you'll get a feeling of the dog's amazing power and intelligence. The 75-minute tour costs $29 for adults, $15 for children 11 and under. Kids love it, and husky puppies are sometimes available for cuddling, too. They call their company **IdidaRide** (☎ **800/ 478-3139** or 907/224-8607).

ACCOMMODATIONS

Connections (☎ **907/224-2323;** www.alaskasview.com) is a Seward hotel and bed-and-breakfast booking agency, and also books some tours and charters. In addition to the hotels listed below, the **Hotel Edgewater,** downtown right across from the SeaLife Center (P.O. Box 1570, Seward, AK 99664; ☎ **888/793-6800** or 907/224-2700; www.hoteledgewater.com), offers brand new luxury rooms starting at $165 double; it was opened too late for me to inspect for this edition.

✪ **Ballaine House Bed and Breakfast.** 437 Third Ave. (P.O. Box 2051), Seward, AK 99664-2051. ☎ **907/224-2362.** www.superpage.com/ballaine. 4 units, none with bathroom. $77.50 double. Additional person in room $15 extra. Rates include full breakfast. No credit cards. No children under 7.

This 1905 house near the center of downtown is a classic bed-and-breakfast, with its wooden floors, large living room, and tall, double-hung windows. It's on the National Historic Register and the town walking tour. Marilee Koszewski has decorated with antiques and handmade quilts and provides raincoats, binoculars, and other gear for outings, and will even do laundry. She also will give back the commission on boat bookings, normally amounting to a 10% discount. Some of the rooms are small, and all bathrooms are shared. No smoking.

Best Western Hotel Seward. 217 Fifth Ave., Seward, AK 99664. ☎ **800/478-4050** Alaska only; 800/528-1234 national reservations; 907/224-2378. Fax 907/224-3112. 38 units. TV TEL. High season, $183–$203 double. Low season, $69–$99 double. Additional person in room $10 extra. AE, DC, DISC, MC, V.

The rooms in a building on a downtown street are large and attractively decorated; many have big bay windows and all have VCRs, refrigerators, and coffeemakers. The view rooms on the front go for a premium. Avoid the south-facing rooms, which look out on the back of another hotel. A two-story log cabin on a cliff over the boat harbor also is part of the hotel. With a large hot-tub spa on the magnificent deck, it's one of the most beautiful and luxurious accommodations in Alaska, renting for $309 a night.

The New Seward Hotel operates out of a connected lobby with the Best Western. The rooms are smaller, older, and less expensive, ranging from $58 to $96 as a double during the summer season. Called the "New Seward" since 1945, the rooms are strictly budget lodgings.

The Breeze Inn. 1306 Seward Hwy. (P.O. Box 2147), Seward, AK 99664-2147. ☎ **907/ 224-5237.** Fax 907/224-7024. www.AlaskaOne.com/breezeinn. 86 units. TV TEL. $119–$160 double. Additional person in room $10 extra. AE, CB, DC, DISC, MC, V.

Located right at the busy boat harbor, this large, three-story, motel-style building offers good standard accommodations with the most convenient location for anyone in town for a fishing or Kenai Fjords boat trip. Many rooms have been recently updated and all have refrigerators. They operate a courtesy van. A restaurant with a full menu and a lounge is across the parking lot.

✪　Harborview Inn. 804 Third Ave. (P.O. Box 1305), Seward, AK 99664. ☎ **888/ 324-3217** or 907/224-3217. Fax 907/224-3218. www.alakan.com/harborviewinn. 36 units, 2 apts. TV TEL. High season, $109–$119 double. Low season, $49 double. Additional person in room $10 extra. AE, MC, V.

The energetic and hospitable Jerry and Jolene King family take great pride in their new inn, which grew from their bed-and-breakfast operation. And for good reason, as theirs are among the most attractive rooms in town, with lots of light, Mission style furniture, and Tlingit art based on Jolene's tribal crest. The rates are a bargain by Seward standards, and the location, midway between the Small Boat Harbor and downtown, puts both within long walking distance. Two two-bedroom apartments on the beach along Ballaine Avenue rent for the same price as the motel rooms; they're a great bargain, and perfect for families.

The Marina Motel. 1603 Third Ave. (P.O. Box 1134), Seward, AK 99664. ☎ **800/ 223-0888** or 907/224-5518. Fax 907/224-5553. 18 units. TV TEL. High season, $110–$120 double; low season $45–$55 double. Additional person in room $10 extra. AE, DC, DISC, MC, V.

This small motel across the street from the boat harbor has a nautical theme on the outside and standard rooms inside. There are two sets of rooms, with different rates. The newer, more expensive ones are larger and lighter than the older ones, but both are quite adequate. All rooms have coffee machines and refrigerators.

Seward Windsong Lodge. ½ mile, Exit Glacier Rd. (P.O. Box 221011), Anchorage, AK 99522. ☎ **800/208-0200** or 907/245-0200 in Anchorage; 907/224-7116 in Seward. www.alaska-tours.com. 72 units. High season $159 double; low season $99. Additional person in room $10 extra, children stay free. AE, DISC, MC, V.

This hotel, new in 1998, is the only one at Kenai Fjords National Park with a national park atmosphere: The four 12-unit buildings sit in a thick spruce grove, and the large new restaurant looks out on the broad, unspoiled valley of the Resurrection River. The rooms are large and feel crisp and new; all have two queen beds and rustic-style furniture. A driver is on hand to take you a few miles to town and pick you up whenever you like. The same partners operate a similar lodge at Denali, and link the two with a shuttle, listed above under "Getting There."

The **Resurrection Roadhouse** restaurant on the grounds serves seafood and other casual fine dining entrees in a dining room with a sweeping view of the Resurrection River Valley. It's certainly among the best places to eat in town. The cuisine is more varied and sophisticated than other small-town spots, and there's the advantage of a broad price range on the menu—you can order pizzas or oysters—although none of the prices will strike you as low.

CAMPING & CABINS

The Alaska State Division of Parks maintains two cabins for rent in the **Caines Head State Recreation Area,** south of town, and two in **Thumb Cove State Marine Park,** across the bay from Caines Head. Details on reserving the cabins are listed at the beginning of this chapter, under "Getting Outside on the Kenai Peninsula & Prince William Sound." It's possible to hike to the Caines Head cabins, but to get to Thumb Cove you need a boat. Water taxi service is offered by Miller's Landing (see "Boating & Sea Kayaking," above).

　Cabins in Chugach National Forest and Kenai Fjords National Park are mentioned in those sections, as are the campgrounds in the national forest, but the national park's

Other Seward B&B Options

Besides the Ballaine House, one my favorite B&Bs anywhere (see listing), try **Sea Treasures Inn** (☎ **907/224-7667**), which, although lacking traditional B&B hospitality, does offer comfortable rooms with private bathrooms for less than the price of a hotel. You can find others through the Seward Chamber of Commerce Visitor Center.

---

only campground is quite handy to Seward: Near the **Exit Glacier,** at mile 8.5 of Exit Glacier Road, the campground is on willow-covered, gravely ground that plants haven't yet reclaimed from the retreating ice. Sites are far apart and almost completely private, but lack any amenities—no picnic tables, fire grates, or anything. Snow lingers into early June. There is no fee for the nine sites, and reservations are not taken. It's open for tents only and has pit toilets and hand-pump water.

The beachfront **Iditarod Trailhead Park** on Ballaine Avenue used to be a fun place to camp, but the last time we went it was full of drunken brawlers. Until the town cleans up the situation, I wouldn't recommend it. The fee is $6 for tents, $8 for RVs, and showers are $2. It's operated by the city parks and recreation department (☎ **907/224-4055**). A quieter but poorly developed town campground is **Forest Acres Park,** among the spruce trees at Hemlock and Dimond Boulevard, just off Seward Highway near the Coast Guard Recreation Center. Fees are the same.

I found **Miller's Landing,** on Lowell Point Road south of town (P.O. Box 81), Seward, AK 99664 (☎ **907/224-5739**), more appealing. Sites are along the beach or among large spruce trees. Electric hookups are $20 a night, and rustic, sleeping-bag cabins start at $40 a night. There's lots to do here: see "Boating & Sea Kayaking," above.

DINING

For a casual lunch, we greatly enjoyed the wholesome **Miller's Daughter Bakery,** at the harbor at the corner of S. Harbor Street and Fourth Avenue. They serve sandwiches and soup in bowls of hearty hearth breads. People swear by **Smoke'n Alaska Seafoods,** at the boat harbor, where they specialize in smoked and deep fried local fish.

Besides these restaurants, see **Resurrection Roadhouse,** described above with Seward Windsong Lodge.

Apollo Restaurant. 229 Fourth Ave. ☎ **907/224-3092**. Main courses $10–$20. MC, V. Daily 11:30am–11:30pm. SOUTHERN ITALIAN/GREEK

This is a good small-town restaurant, staying in business by keeping Seward families coming back for a menu with anything they might want: Greek and southern Italian cuisine, seafood, pizza, and much else. You can order fish-and-chips or escargot. The dining room is almost all booths.

Ray's Waterfront. At the small-boat harbor. ☎ **907/224-5606**. Main courses $14–$20; lunch $6–$10. AE, DC, DISC, MC, V. 15% gratuity added for parties of 6 or more. Apr 2–Sept, daily 11am–11pm. Closed Nov to mid-Mar. STEAK/SEAFOOD.

The lively, noisy dining room looks out from big windows across the small-boat harbor, with tables on terraces so everyone can see. The atmosphere is fun and the food is just right after a day on the water. While not perfect, it's more nuanced than the typical harborside place. Most important, they don't overcook the fresh local fish—and that's really all you can ask. Full liquor license.

SHOPPING

Stop at the **Resurrect Art Coffee House Gallery,** at 320 Third Ave. (☎ 907/224-7161), in an old church that's also on the walking tour. The fine art is local, but mostly its a coffeehouse and meeting place. The **Bardarson Studio,** at 1317 Fourth Ave., at the boat harbor (☎ 800/354-0141 or 907/224-5448; www.seward.net/bardarson), specializes in Dot Bardarson's watercolor prints and also has a wonderful, welcoming attitude. There's a children's cave under the stairs and a husbands' recliner area with videos and reading matter upstairs. A shopping stop becomes an event. The **Resurrection Bay Galerie,** at 500 Fourth Ave. (☎ 907/224-3212; alaskafinearts.com), shows oils of wildlife and other Alaskan themes in a lovely old shingled house downtown—no prints, only originals. They also produce a guide to the galleries in town.

7 Kenai Fjords National Park: Primeval Sanctuary

The park is all about remote rocks, mountains, and ice that meet the ocean, and the animals that live there. For some it's a natural cathedral, and the experience of seeing the grand and rugged terrain takes on a spiritual dimension. Anyone will find the park and its surroundings impressive, and in few places are the chances better of seeing marine mammals or adding waterfowl to a birder's list. The park comprises 670,000 acres of the south coast and interior land mass of the Kenai Peninsula. The shore here is exposed to the Gulf of Alaska, whose wild, recurrent storms beat mercilessly against the mountainous shore, unbuffered by any land mass against the vast expanse of the Pacific to the south.

The geological events that formed this landscape are vast and ongoing. The steep, coastal mountains amount to a dent in the earth's crust where the northward-moving Pacific tectonic plate is colliding and adding land to the southern edge of Alaska. As the Pacific plate pushes under Alaska, it slams islands onto Alaska coast, then pulls them under into the molten layer down below. These mountains are growing measurably shorter as the earth swallows them. The 1964 earthquake dropped them by 7 feet. As your boat rides past the park's small, sharp, bedrock islands, now populated by sea birds and marine mammals, you are seeing the tips of ancient peaks that once stood far above the shore like today's coastal mountains.

It's a primeval land, entirely free of people or their mark. Its history has barely started. The fjords became a park only in 1980. In 1976, when the National Park Service explored more than 650 miles of coastline, including the park area, they didn't find a single human being. The same was true when geologists came in 1909. British explorer Captain James Cook made the first maps of the fjords area in 1778, but the coast was too rugged and rocky for him to land.

We don't know much about Native Americans who lived in the fjords. Scientists have found some areas where people lived, or at least had camps, but no one knows exactly who they were or what they were doing here. The earth—whether through earthquakes or glacial action—has erased most remains. Anthroplogists call these people Unegkurmiut, and believe they were Alutiiq, Eskimos who lived on the Pacific coast, closely related to the Chugach people of Prince William Sound and the Koniag from Kodiak Island to the south. Those groups are still around; scientists are studying the Unegkurmiut and what happened to them from the little evidence they can find on the fjord's beaches.

The mountains of the Kenai Peninsula's top are too steep for people to venture over land, so the Natives probably got around only by boat. The first mountain climbers didn't cross the Harding Ice Field, which covers most of the national park, until 1968. **Exit Glacier,** and all the glaciers of Kenai Fjords, flow from this 1,000-foot-thick ice age leftover that fills more than half the park high up in the mountains. The ice field lies in a bowl of mountains that jut straight out of the ocean to heights of 3,000 to 5,000 feet. When moisture-laden ocean clouds hit those mountains, they drop lots of rain and snow—up on the ice field 40 to 80 feet of snow falls each winter, with a water equivalent of 17 feet. Summer weather isn't warm enough to melt the snow at that elevation, so it just packs down deeper and harder until it turns into the hard, heavy ice of glaciers. No one could ever live in that land of white, where snow falls eternally, burying the snow beneath it ever deeper. So, when the U.S. Congress set the land aside as a park in 1980, it was exactly as it had been created by nature.

Nine years later, in 1989, the area's history got an ugly start. The tanker *Exxon Valdez* crashed into a rock about 150 miles to the northeast of the park in Prince William Sound and spilled almost 11 million gallons of oil. Exxon did a poor job of catching the oil before it spread, and by the end of the summer the sticky, brownish-black muck had spread over beaches in the western Sound, across the fjords, and all the way to Kodiak and the Alaska Peninsula. More than 1,000 miles of shoreline were oiled to some degree. Hundreds of sea otters and hundreds of thousands of sea birds were killed in the Sound and on the islands near the fjords. Nature scrubbed the oil off the rocks again, and you will see no evidence of it today; but scientists say many species of birds and animals haven't come back completely, and most are only starting to recover. Nonetheless, you'll still see more wildlife on a boat ride here than anywhere else I know.

Exxon paid over $1 billion to the government in penalties for the oil spill, and that money has done a lot to help the area. Most of it was used to buy land in the spill area that otherwise would have been logged, including 35,000 acres of coastal land to the national park. In Seward, the SeaLife Center (see "Seward," above) was built mostly with this money, and it contains a display on the spill. In the fjords, you can see the birds flying in the air; at the center, you can see them fly underwater, as well.

Most of the park is remote and difficult to get to. A large vessel, such as a tour boat operating out of Seward, is the only practical way to see the marine portion of the park. That's not cheap or quick, if you really want the full experience, and there are better destinations for people subject to seasickness. The inland portion is accessible only at Exit Glacier, near Seward, unless you're an experienced mountaineer.

ESSENTIALS
GETTING THERE
Seward is the threshold to the park. Exit Glacier is 13 miles from the town by road; the Kenai Fjords National Park Visitor Center is at the Seward Small-Boat Harbor; and the tour boats that visit the park leave from Seward. Many visitors try to do the park in a day, coming from Anchorage by train or road, touring the park by boat, then returning that evening. I recommend against this. To really get to the park, you need to be on an all-day boat trip—most half-day trips barely leave Resurrection Bay and hardly see the park proper. More important, a lot of the visitors I saw riding the train back to Anchorage after a 1-day marathon trip to Kenai Fjords were so tired they couldn't keep their eyes open for the extraordinary scenery passing by outside the train. A better plan is to spend a night in Seward and take in the full Kenai Fjords boat trip and Exit Glacier. See the section on Seward, above, for details on getting to and around the town.

VISITOR INFORMATION

At the **Kenai Fjords National Park Visitor Center,** Seward Small Boar Harbor (P.O. Box 1727), Seward, AK 99664; ☎ **907/224-3175;** fax 907/224-2144; www.nps.gov/kefj/), rangers answer questions and provide information on the all-important tour boats. They carry an excellent selection of books on Alaska natural history and occasionally show films. Call or drop by here for advice on Park Service cabins for rent in the fjords, guidance on a sea kayaking expedition there, or places in the area to hike and trail conditions. They're open June to August 8am to 7pm daily, September to May 8am to 5pm Monday to Friday.

SEEING THE PARK
SIGHTSEEING & WILDLIFE CRUISES

Kenai Fjords is essentially a marine park. On a boat tour, you'll see its mountains, glaciers, and wildlife. On any of the tours, you're likely to see sea otters and sea lions, and you have a good chance of seeing humpback whales, orcas, mountain goats, and black bears. Bird-watchers will see bald eagles, puffins, cormorants, murres, and various sea ducks. The farther you go into the park, the more you'll see.

Depending on the time and money you have to spend, you can choose to take a half-day trip staying generally in Resurrection Bay or a full-day trip that travels to Aialik Bay or Harris Bay, in the heart of the park. Prices are around $115 to $140 to go to Northwestern Glacier, in Northwestern Fjord off Harris Bay, an all-day trip; $100 to go to Holgate Glacier, in Holgate Arm off Aialik Bay, which takes 6 to 8 hours; and $60 for a 4-hour Resurrection Bay tour, which doesn't go to the national park at all. Children's prices are around half off.

You can shop for prices, but make sure you compare the same destinations, length of trip, and food service. Look at a map of the route. If you really want to see Kenai Fjords National Park, the boat has to go at least into **Aialik Bay** to **Holgate Glacier.** Resurrection Bay contains plenty of impressive scenery—its cliffs are as if chiseled from the mountains—but the fjords are even grander. The half-day cruises have less of a chance of seeing whales and will see puffins and other birds in lesser numbers. On the longer trips, which make it into the heart of the park proper, you will see birds and animals in greater numbers and variety. If you're lucky with the weather, you may make it to the exposed **Chiswell Islands,** which have some of the greatest bird rookeries in Alaska, supporting more than 50,000 seabirds of 18 species. The day-long trips also allow more time to linger and really see the behavior of the wildlife. Whatever your choice, binoculars will greatly enhance the trip.

An important factor in your decision is your susceptibility to **seasickness.** To reach the heart of the park, vessels must venture into the unprotected waters of the North Pacific. Large, rolling waves are inevitable on the passage from Resurrection Bay to the fjords themselves, although once in the fjords the water is calm. On a rough day, most boats will turn back for the comfort of the passengers and change the full-day trip into a Resurrection Bay cruise, refunding the difference in fare. Of course, they'd rather not do that, and the decision usually isn't made until the vessel is out there, probably after some of the passengers are already vomiting over the side. My advice is that if you get seasick easily, stick to the Resurrection Bay cruise, or take a boat tour in protected Prince William Sound out of Whittier (see the previous section), where the water is smooth. In any event, ask about the tour company's policy on turning back.

Try to schedule loosely, so that if the weather is bad on the day you choose for your boat trip, you can wait and go the next day. If the weather's bad, you'll be uncomfortable, and the animals and birds won't be as evident, or the boat may not go out at all. If you pay up front to hold a reservation on a boat—probably a good idea in the busiest months—find out the company's refund policy.

If you're shopping around, ask how much deck space there is outside so you can really see. What is the seating arrangement inside? How many passengers will be on board and how many crew members to answer questions? Is lunch provided, and what does it consist of? Another important point of comparison is if you have a ranger doing the commentary, or just the captain—some of these captains don't know when to shut up and give inaccurate information.

Most operators offer packages with the Alaska Railroad and the SeaLife Center, which may save money, but make sure you have enough time to do everything you want to do in Seward. All have offices at the Small Boat Harbor in Seward and most have an office in Anchorage, too. In addition to the operators listed in full below, **Allen Marine** (☎ **888/305-2515** or 907/276-5800) runs a 78-foot, 150-passenger catamaran; and **Renown Charters and Tours** (☎ **907/272-1961**), has smaller vessels, offering shorter, lower-priced cruises, and year-round operations.

Kenai Fjords Tours. At the Seward Small Boat Harbor and at 513 W. Third Ave., Anchorage. ☎ **800/478-8068**, 907/224-8068 in Seward, 907/276-6249 in Anchorage. www.kenaifjords.com.

This is the largest of the tour operators, with the most daily sailings. The vessels are large, which makes them steady; on the downside, the seats all face forward, like an airplane. They're professionally staffed, though when the ships are crowded, perhaps with passengers on package bus tours, the experience is somewhat impersonal. The company owns a lodge on Fox Island, in Resurrection Bay, which is a fun place to stop for lunch or dinner of grilled salmon, or even to spend the night. The food is good. An overnight package on the island costs $299 per person, $149 for children under 12, meals included. Half-day sea kayaking paddles from the island are offered for day-trippers or overnight guests: $79 to $89 per person as an add-on for overnighters, or $139 to $159, including the tour boat ride and lunch, for day-trippers. Park rangers give commentary only on the 10am and 2pm tours. They get off at Fox Island to offer programs there, so they don't continue with you into the park itself.

Major Marine Tours. 411 West Fourth Ave., Anchorage. ☎ **800/764-7300** or 907/274-7300; 907/224-8030 in Seward. www.majormarine.com.

This company pioneered first-class onboard dining and bringing along a ranger to assure high-quality commentary (the ranger stays on board for the whole trip). They don't make the long trip to Northwest Glacier, but either head into Aialik Bay to see Holgate Glacier or just tour Resurrection Bay around Seward. Instead of sandwiches or stopping for a meal, they serve a fine-dining buffet on board for $10 per person, $5 for children. I prefer their table-seating arrangement to forward-facing seats, too.

Mariah Tours. Seward. ☎ **800/270-1238** or 907/224-8623. www.mariahtours.com.

Two 45-foot vessels—much smaller than most of the other tour boats—specialize in more intimate tours, without big package-tour crowds on board. Although owned by the same Alaska Native corporation as Kenai Fjords Tours, Mariah offers longer, more in-depth trips, with the daily itinerary determined by where the captain expects the best wildlife sightings and sea conditions. They serve deli sandwiches for lunch. Smaller boats get tossed around more by the waves, but the experience is less structured.

SEA KAYAKING

For those with the money, time, and outdoor skills, it's possible to charter a seaplane or take a water taxi into the fjord and camp or stay in one of the three Park Service cabins. This is a truly remote and spectacular trip in deep wilderness rich with wildlife. I've listed the agencies that rent kayaks and offer guided custom trips and water taxis under "Boating & Sea Kayaking" in the Seward section, above, and in chapter 6, on Anchorage. Cabin rental information is below.

EXIT GLACIER

When I visited Italy a few years ago, I got to the point that I thought I'd scream if I saw another painting of the Madonna. If your trip to Alaska is long, you may start to feel the same way about glaciers. But, although relatively small, Exit Glacier really is unique, and we still enjoy visits there even as jaded lifelong Alaskans. (And I've probably seen even more glaciers than Madonnas.) You can walk close to Exit Glacier, see its brittle texture, and feel the cold, dense spires of ice looming over you. The cold air breaths down on you like an open freezer door. Approaching the glacier, you can see the pattern of vegetation reclaiming the land that the melting ice has uncovered, a process well explained by interpretive signs and a nature trail. At the same time, however, the area remains refreshingly primitive. The National Park Service's low-key presentation of the site makes it a casual, pleasant visit for a couple of hours; longer, if you do a hike. Kids enjoy the broad gravel trails, and as long as you don't let them go beyond the warning signs near the ice, there's not much trouble they can get into.

The easiest way to get to the glacier is to drive. The clearly marked 9-mile road splits from the Seward Highway 3.7 miles north of town. The second half of the road is gravel and can be dusty in summer. In winter, the road is closed to vehicles. If you don't have a car, van service is available, listed under "Getting Around," in the Seward section.

Following the road along the broad bed of the wandering Resurrection River, you'll see in reverse order the succession of vegetation, from mature Sitka spruce and cottonwood trees down to smaller alders and shrubs. It takes time for nature to replace the soil on sterile ground left behind by a receding glacier. As you get closer, watch for a sign bearing the year 1780; more signs count upward through the years, marking the retreat of the glacier through time.

An entrance booth charges a user fee of $5 per vehicle. At the parking lot, there's a simple ranger station and pit toilets. Ranger-led nature walks start here on a sporadic schedule—check at the visitor center. Often, a spotting scope is set up to see mountain goats up in the rocky cliffs. The short trail to the glacier starts here. At the glacier, the trail splits: The steep route goes up along the side of the glacier, and the easy route runs on the flat gravel at its face.

A high berm of gravel fits around its face like a necklace. This is a **moraine,** a pile of the rock the glacier gouged out of the mountains and moved here like a conveyor belt. Probably without knowing it, you've seen hundreds of moraines before all over North America, where the glaciers of the last ice age piled up debris into hills, but this is the most obvious moraine I've ever seen, and it helps you to understand how they work. Don't go beyond the warning signs; ice can fall off and crush you.

An all-day hike, 8 miles round-trip, climbs along the right side of the glacier to the **Harding Icefield**—the glacier gets its name for being an exit from that massive sheet. It's a challenging walk with a 3,000-foot elevation gain, but it's the easiest access I'm aware of to visit an ice field on foot. Because of snow, the trail doesn't open until late June or early July. The ice field itself is cold and dangerous, and there's an emergency shelter maintained by the Park Service. Don't trek out on the ice unless you know what you're doing. The Park Service sometimes guides hikes up the trail.

The **Resurrection River Trail** begins from the road just short of the last bridge to the glacier. It's a pleasant day hike, with lots of wildflowers in the fall, or the start of a long hike on the historic Resurrection Trail, leading 72 miles all the way across the Kenai Peninsula. See the section on Chugach National Forest, above, for backpacking details.

ACCOMMODATIONS

There are no hotels in the park; see the Seward section above, for choices there. The only campground in the park also is listed in that section.

Out in the kayaking waters of Aialik Bay and Northwestern Fjord, food lockers and hanging cables to keep your stuff away from bears are located at various locations, marked on a free Park Service map. You can camp anywhere, observing correct back-country precautions. Send away for a packet of information from the park. They also rent out four **public-use cabins,** three in the fjords, reachable only by boat or float-plane. One is a mile from Exit Glacier, but is open only during the winter when the road is closed. It's accessible by ski, dog sled, or snow machine. Contact the park head-quarters for a $35-a-day permit, open for reservations starting January 2 each year.

8 Cooper Landing: Road Meets River

The little roadside community of Cooper Landing, in the wooded mountain valley along Kenai Lake and the Kenai River, begins about 8 miles west of Tern Lake, where the Sterling Highway splits from the Seward Highway, and continues sporadically along the highway for about 7 miles. (The Sterling runs generally west until Soldotna, where it heads south again.) The frothing upper **Kenai River** is the community's life-line, each summer bringing the salmon that draw the visitors to fill hotels, restaurants, and the date books of guides. The **Russian River** meets the Kenai at the western edge of the community, where the mad fishing frenzy of the July red salmon season occurs. A ferry takes anglers across the river from the highway. For information on how to fish the Kenai, see "Fishing," in the Kenai/Soldotna section, below, and the essay in chapter 2.

For nonfishers, there's not much here—a couple of operators do rafting trips, and some of the accommodations could provide a romantic mountain retreat. Cooper Landing is also the starting or ending point for backpacking trips described in the Chugach National Forest section, above. Look there also for descriptions of the campgrounds.

ESSENTIALS

Cooper Landing has a post office, service stations, and small stores selling fishing gear and essentials, but it's not a center. For banking or anything else not directly related to catching a salmon, you'll have to drive to Sterling, 30 miles away to the west, or Soldotna, 44 miles away.

ACCOMMODATIONS, DINING & FISHING
UPSCALE LODGES

For those who want comforts and guided fishing and activities without worrying about the details.

Kenai River Sportfishing Lodge / Kenai Riverside Lodge and Cabins. Alaska Wildland Adventures, Sterling Hwy. along the Kenai River, P.O. Box 389, Girdwood, AK 99587-0389. ☎ **800/334-8730** or 907/783-2928. www.alaskawildland.com. No TV or TEL. $425 per person, per day for accommodations, meals, and guided sportfishing; $299 per person, per day, double occupancy, for accommodations, meals, river rafting, and other nonfishing activities. DISC, MC, V.

RV Hookups in Cooper Landing

An attractive 35-space RV park is on the site of the Kenai Princess Lodge (see review, below), with access to the facilities, charging $20 a night for full hookups. For summer, make reservations for rooms or RV sites well ahead.

Based in Girdwood, Alaska Wildlife Adventures operates this lodge between the highway and the river, with comfortable log cabins and a central bathhouse. Prices include meals, which are served in a lodge building. Clients can get either daily guided salmon or rainbow trout fishing on the river, in drift or jet boats (in which case they're dealing with the place as the Kenai River Sportfishing Lodge), or can enjoy river rafting trips and other activities other than fishing (in which case it's called Kenai Riverside Lodge and Cabins). Most visitors use it as part of a "safari" package that takes them to various outdoor activities and sites; that's described in chapter 2 under "Outdoors Tours." Their Kenai Backcountry Lodge is covered below, in the Kenai National Wildlife Refuge section.

Kenai Princess Lodge. Up the dirt Bean Creek Rd. above Cooper Landing (P.O. Box 676, Cooper Landing, AK 99572). ☎ **800/426-0500** or 907/595-1425. Fax 907/595-1424. 70 rms. $189–$209 double high season; from $79 low season. AE, DC, MC, V.

Built to service Princess's cruise ship and package-tour business, the hotel also has rooms open for independent travelers. It's the most luxurious hotel on the Kenai Peninsula. Each room is like a remote cabin, with balconies overlooking the wooded valley, wood stoves stocked with firewood, and many unique details; yet they are luxurious hotel rooms at a resort with a gym, spa, and fine restaurant. Anchorage couples use it as a romantic getaway. The hotel books guided fishing, horseback riding, tours, and other activities, and there are hiking trails nearby. An RV park is on-site (see inset, above).

MOTELS, B&BS & LESSER LODGES

Each of the accommodations listed below can find you a fishing guide or tell you where to put your line in the water.

Alpine Motel. Mile 48.2, Sterling Highway, in the heart of Cooper Landing (P.O. Box 570, Cooper Landing, AK, 99572). ☎ **907/595-1212.** Fax 907/595-1593. www.aktroutfitter. com. 12 units. TV, Tel. $85–$115 double in high season; $50–$65 low season. MC, V.

All these motel-style rooms have kitchenettes. **Alaska Troutfitters,** located right at the motel, offers guided fly-fishing for $165 to $200 a day. They also rent drift boats for $150 a day and operate a tackle store and fly-fishing school.

Alaska Rivers Co. Mile 50 (P.O. Box 827), Cooper Landing, AK 99572 (☎ **907/595-1226**).

Mostly offers guided float fishing trips, charging $125 for a full day of fishing. They also offer scenic rafting trips and rent cabins.

Gwin's Lodge. Mile 52, at the west end of Cooper Landing (HC 54 Box 50), Cooper Landing, AK 99572. ☎ **907/595-1266.**

The town's old original log roadhouse. Standing just a mile east of the Resurrection trailhead and the Russian River Campground, Gwin's Lodge convenient and has loads of character. Food in the seven-table dining room ranges from burgers to steaks and seafood. Servings are plentiful and satisfying after a hike or fishing trip. They also offer roadside small cabins and RV hookups, and have a store, tackle shop, and booking service for fishing, rafting, and other trips.

The Hutch Bed and Breakfast. Mile 48.5, Sterling Highway. ☎ **907/595-1270**. 12 units. No TV or TEL. Rooms range from $70–$100. MC, V.

This place has rooms, plus a couple of large cabins with kitchens on wheels.

9 Kenai/Soldotna & Sterling: Giant Salmon

These quintessential western U.S. towns, dominated by shopping malls and fast-food franchises facing broad highways, have a single claim to fame, but it's a pretty good claim: The largest sport-caught king salmon in the world, almost 100 pounds, came from Kenai River. The Kenai's kings run so large there's a different trophy class for the river—everywhere else in the state, the Alaska Department of Fish and Game will certify a 50-pounder as a trophy, but on the Kenai it has to be at least 75 pounds. That's because kings in the 60-pound class—enough wild muscle to fight ferociously for hours—are just too common here. Fishers prepared to pay for a charter will be in their element on the river when the fish are running hot. Catching a big king is not easy or quick, however, and success rates vary greatly year-to-year and week-to-week. For more on fishing, see chapter 2.

Those not interested in fishing will find no more than an afternoon's sightseeing in these towns. Outside town, however, you'll find plenty of outdoor activities, primarily in the lake-dotted **Kenai National Wildlife Refuge,** which has its headquarters in Soldotna. The refuge is covered in the next section.

Kenai came into being with the arrival of the Russians at the mouth of the Kenai River more than 200 years ago, but came into its own only with the discovery of oil on the peninsula in 1957. Today its economy relies on oil, commercial fishing, and, to a smaller extent, tourism. Soldotna, a smaller, newer, and even less attractive town, is the borough seat, and the primary destination for sport fishermen. Sterling is just a wide place in the road—incredibly wide, as a matter of fact, and no one is quite able to explain why such a small town needs such a big road.

ESSENTIALS
GETTING THERE

BY CAR   From Anchorage, the drive on the Seward and Sterling highways to Soldotna is 147 miles. Allow 3 hours, without stops: In summer, traffic will slow you down; in winter, speeds are limited by ice and the fear of hitting moose. Most of the major car-rental companies have offices in Kenai, at the airport.

BY BUS   The **Homer Stage Line,** P.O. Box 1912, Homer, AK 99603 (☎ **907/ 235-7009** or 907/399-1847), connects Anchorage, Homer, and points in between 3 days a week in the summer, less frequently in the winter. The fare from Anchorage to Soldotna is $35 one-way, $60 round-trip. Tickets are for sale in Soldotna at the Goodnight Inn on the highway (☎ **907/262-4584)** or in Anchorage at the ticket office at 3339 Fairbanks St. (☎ **907/563-0800)**.

BY AIR   Kenai receives several flights a day to Anchorage and Homer from **Era Aviation** (☎ **800/866-8394** or 907/283-9091).

GETTING AROUND

The area is so spread out, walking most places really isn't possible, and there's no public transportation. Everyone here owns a car, and you can rent one from most major agencies, located at the Kenai airport. If you plan only to fish, however, you may not need one, instead getting rides from your guide, host, or a taxi cab. There are several cab companies; try **Inlet Taxi Cab** (☎ **907/283-4711** in Kenai, **907/262-4770** in Soldotna).

VISITOR INFORMATION

Operated by the Soldotna Chamber of Commerce, the **Soldotna Visitor Information Center,** 44790 Sterling Hwy., Soldotna, AK 99669 (☎ **907/262-9814;** www.SoldotnaChamber.com), is located on the south side of town; drive through the commercial strip and turn right after the Kenai River Bridge. It's open Summer daily 9am to 7pm, winter Monday to Friday 9am to 5pm. Besides the unusual, they maintain notebooks full of comparative information about lodgings, camping, and other service, and will help you find a room or charter. Follow the Spur Highway from Soldotna past Main Street and look for the large, well landscaped **Kenai Visitors and Cultural Center,** on the left at 11471 Kenai Spur Hwy., Kenai, AK 99611 (☎ **907/283-1991;** www.visitkenai.com). Open Monday to Friday 8am to 7pm, Saturday and Sunday 10am to 7pm in summer; and Monday to Friday 8:30am to 5pm, Saturday 10am to 4pm in winter. This is much more than the usual collection of brochures and visitor guidance. A free two-room museum contains historic material on the arrival of Russian settlers in Kenai in 1791 and a collection of Alaska Native and pioneer artifacts. A natural history room shows animal mounts and information on public lands in the area, as well as the "King of Snags," an immense conglomeration of lost fishing lures and sticks from the bottom of the river. In the summer, they plan talks and demonstrations on cultural and artistic topics.

SPECIAL EVENTS

IN KENAI   The **Snow Goose Classic** (☎ **907/283-7989**) awards a jackpot to the person who guesses the time and date the first snow goose lands. **Alaska 2000: A Celebration of Wildlife Art** (☎ **907/283-1991**), running May through July, 2000, will show prints and paintings by nationally known artists at the Kenai Visitors and Cultural Center. **The Kenai River Festival** (☎ **907/262-9225**), in early June, has food, music, crafts, and games.

IN SOLDOTNA   The **Tustumena 200 Sled Dog Race** (☎ **907/262-4179**), held in late January, helps kick off the mushing season. **Progress Days** (☎ **907/262-9814**), in July, offers a parade, rodeo, car shows, and other festival events commemorating the completion of a gas pipeline in 1960—that's the area in a nutshell.

IN NINILCHIK   The **Kenai Peninsula State Fair** (☎ **907/567-3670**), south at mile 136 on the Sterling Highway, is in mid-August, with crafts, games, agricultural exhibits, and other country attractions, but no rides.

Fast Facts: Kenai, Soldotna & Sterling

Banks   In Kenai, the National Bank of Alaska is at the Kenai Spur Highway and Willow; in Soldotna, two banks are on the Sterling Highway commercial strip. In addition, ATMs are all over the place—in Carrs and Kmart stores, for example.

Hospital   The Central Peninsula Hospital is in Soldotna at 250 Hospital Place (☎ 907/262-4404)—from the Sterling Highway, take Binkley Street to Vine Avenue.

Internet/E-mail   Golden Tan, Hot Buns and Beans (☎ 907/283-8495; golden-tan.com) is a tanning salon, coffee house, and Internet cafe, charging $7 for the first half hour. If you're not ready for that combination, the Kenai public library, 163 Main St. Loop (☎ 907/283-4378) and the printerless Soldotna public library, 235 Binkley (☎ 907/262-4227), both offer access.

Police   Who to call for nonemergency business with the police depends on where you are: in Kenai, the Kenai Police Department (☎ 907/283-7879); in Soldotna, the Soldotna Police Department (☎ 907/262-4455); or outside city limits, the Alaska State Troopers (☎ 907/262-4453).

Taxes   In Kenai and Soldotna, sales tax is 5%; outside the city limits it's 2%.

EXPLORING KENAI

Kenai's historic sites, beach walking, and bird watching could occupy you for most of a day. Start at the visitors and cultural center mentioned above and get a copy of the *Old Town Kenai Walking Map*. Not many of the simple, weathered buildings from Kenai's life before oil remain, but those that do are interesting and lie only a few blocks down Main Street from the center, along the Cook Inlet bluff.

The **Holy Assumption Russian Orthodox Church** is the area's most significant building. The parish was founded in 1845, and the present church was built in 1895. It's a quaint, onion-domed church, brightly kept but with old icons. A donation of $1 is requested. In the tiny lobby is a fine gift shop. Several nearby buildings are interesting for their interlocking log construction. Stop at Veronica's Coffee Shop for a cup while on the tour—it's located in one of the old, cut-log buildings, with a faded sign out front. Sometimes artists work in Old Town shops in the summer.

The bluff over the beach is nearby. When the salmon are running, you can occasionally see white beluga whales chasing them upstream from here, sometimes in great numbers. To get down to the sandy **beach** itself go back up to the Kenai Spur Highway, turn to the west (left), then turn left on South Spruce Street. There you'll find a simple beach park and a place to begin a walk where it's easy to imagine the Russians' first arrival. On a calm day the beach sand and the Inlet's gray, glacial water seem to meld together into one vast shimmering plain. Walking south, the beach wraps around and becomes the shore of the Kenai River. The water is far too cold for swimming.

The mouth of the river and the wetlands of its delta make for fine **bird watching,** especially during spring and fall migrations. One of the best places to get to the tidal marshes is along Bridge Access Road, which branches from the Spur Highway. The state of Alaska has developed a viewing area near the bridge.

EXPLORING SOLDOTNA

In Soldotna, there is one modest attraction, on Centennial Park Road, behind the visitor center. The free **Homesteading Soldotna Historical Society Museum** celebrates the 50-year history of the town with a collection of cabins dating from as recently as the 1960s set among spruce trees to show what the area was like then. They house pioneer artifacts and old photographs. It's open in summer only, normally 10am to 4pm, although the volunteers may keep less consistent hours.

A family looking for something to do while a parent is off fishing may enjoy the magnificent **North Peninsula Recreation Area Nikiski Pool** (☎ **907/776-8472**), 10 miles north of Kenai on the Kenai Spur Road. Built with taxes on the oil property in the area, the facility occupies a large dome and has a 136-foot water slide, mushroom fountains of water, and a raised hot tub from which parents can watch their children play in the pool below. People travel from other towns just to swim here. Open swimming and water slide use is Tuesday through Sunday 1 to 5pm and 6 to 9pm in the summer; in the winter, they're open the same hours Friday and Saturday and Sunday 1 to 5pm. Pool admission is $3, or $6 to use the slide and pool.

FISHING

Fishing the Kenai River is the whole point of coming to the area. Check at the visitor centers for information and regulation booklets. Or contact the **Alaska Department of Fish and Game,** 43961 Kalifornsky Beach Rd. (☎ **907/262-9368** or 907/262-2737, for a recorded fishing report; www.state.ak.us/local/akpages/FISH.GAME/adfghome.htm). Serious fishers shouldn't miss that Web site. Licenses are for sale in virtually any sporting-goods store. Also, read the fishing section in chapter 2.

King salmon, the monsters of the river, come in two runs. The early run, which sometimes has been limited to catch-and-release, comes from mid-May to the end of June. These usually are the smaller fish, in the 20- to 40-pound range. The second run comes during the month of July and includes the massive fish that range up to 90 pounds. Most people fish kings from a boat, which makes them easier to catch and much easier to land. A charter averages $125 to $150 for a 6-hour, half-day trip. There are dozens of guides. Contact the visitor center in Kenai or Soldotna to get in touch with a guide; also, many hotels and lodges have their own. It's possible to rent a boat, but the river is swift and treacherous. The **Sports Den,** at 44176 Sterling Hwy. in Soldotna (☎ **907/262-7491;** alaskasportsden.com), is one of the larger charter operators, with river and ocean trips, fly-in fishing, and hunting; they also rent condos, boats, and equipment for all kinds of outdoor activities. We've found them very friendly and helpful.

The area really goes crazy when the reds join the kings in the river, mid-July to early August. You can fish red and silver salmon from the bank, although you have better chances from a boat. Silvers come in two runs. The first run is smaller, late July to late August, and the larger run arrives in September. Of course, the fish don't punch a time clock, so to know how they're running at any particular time you have to ask around. You can catch kings and silvers on lures, but reds won't strike a lure—indeed, they don't feed at all in fresh water. Fishers around here mainly use flies on spinning gear, with little lead weights to aid in casting. The fish probably don't really bite the flies, but get caught when they instinctively move their mouths. When they're thick, people catch plenty anyway. Salmon eggs work well as bait on kings and silvers, but check current regulations to determine if they're legal. Trophy-size rainbow trout and Dolly Varden char also come out of the river.

There are more than two dozen public-access points over the 80 miles of the Kenai River. A **guide brochure** with a map is available from the state **Division of Parks,** P.O. Box 1247, Soldotna, AK 99669-1247 (☎ **907/262-5581;** www.dnr.state.ak.us/parks/parks.htm); you can pick up a copy at one of the visitor centers.

For fishers interested in less competition and more of a wilderness experience, Kenai is a gateway for vast wild lands accessible by air on the west side of Cook Inlet. You can fish a stream packed with salmon all by yourself. Among others, **High Adventure Air** (☎ **907/262-5237;** highadventureair.com) has packages with fly-in cabins.

ACCOMMODATIONS
HOTELS & B&Bs

Rates at all hotels are on seasonal schedules with three, four, or even more levels linked to the salmon runs.

Daniels Lake Lodge Bed and Breakfast. 21 miles north of Kenai (P.O. Box 1444), Kenai, AK 99611. ☎ **800/774-5578** or 907/776-5578. puffin.ptialaska.net/~ducks/. 5 units, 2 with private bathroom; 2 cabins. TV. High season, $95–$110 double; $135–$190 cabins. Low season, $50–$65. 2-night minimum in cabins. Additional person in room $15 extra. MC, V.

Located on peaceful and sparsely built Daniels Lake, this lovely, relaxing place has a boat and canoe you can use for trout fishing right out the back door, among the resident ducks. The gregarious Christian hosts, with their dogs and rabbits, eagerly make friends with guests. It's not a 1-night stopover, but a place to stay for a couple of days of relaxation, closer to the Nikiski Pool and the outlet of the Swanson River Canoe route of the Kenai National Wildlife Refuge than to any town. There's an outdoor Jacuzzi and a laundry, and smoking is not permitted.

Great Alaska Fish Camp. Moose River, 33881 Sterling Hwy., Sterling, AK 99672 (in winter, P.O. Box 2670, Poulsbo, WA 98370). ☎ **800/544-2261** or 907/262-4515. Fax 907/262-8797 in summer, 360/697-7850 in winter. www.greatalaska.com. 19 cabins. Rates from $175–$249 for day trip without lodging to $3,195 for 7-day package. Rates include all meals, guide service, and travel from Anchorage. AE, MC, V. Closed mid-Oct to mid-May.

This is a full-service fishing lodge, offering bear viewing, biking, and other "ecotour" safaris as well as fishing, but located right on the highway. Guests find a bottle of wine waiting in comfortable cabins with private bathrooms. There are as many staff as guests, and they take a video for you, and provide an editing room if you want to cut the dull parts. It's located on a stretch of riverfront where the Moose River meets the Kenai, on the Sterling Highway east of Soldotna.

Harborside Cottages Bed and Breakfast. 813 Riverview Dr. (P.O. Box 942), Kenai, AK 99611. ☎ **907/283-6162.** 5 cottages. High season, $125 double. May and Sept, $100 double. AE, DISC, MC, V. Closed Oct–Apr.

On a grassy compound at the top of the bluff over the mouth of the Kenai River in Old Town, these little white cottages make the most of a perfect site. The view alone could keep you occupied all day. Although brand new, the cute little houses somehow look historic, their wood floors and wainscoting adding to the illusion. Each has a kitchen with limited cooking facilities, dining tables, and a deck with a picnic table and gas barbecue. The very competitive price includes a continental breakfast.

Kenai River Lodge. 393 Riverside Dr., Soldotna, AK 99669. ☎ **907/262-4292.** Fax 907/262-7332. www.alaskais.com/kenailodge. 25 units. TV TEL. High season, $110 double. Low season, $60 double. $240 suite. Additional person in room $10 extra. Fishing packages available. MC, V.

Overlooking the river, next to the bridge in Soldotna, this roadside motel has the advantages of well-maintained standard rooms (with refrigerators) and a great location for fishermen. The grassy front yard descends right to the water, with a barbecue where you can cook up your catch. They operate fishing charters from the hotel.

Log Cabin Bed and Breakfast. 49840 Eider Rd. P.O. Box 2886, Kenai, AK 99611. ☎ and fax **907/283-3653.** www.ptialaska.net~tedtitus. 9 units, 3 cabins. $80–$90 double. Rates include full breakfast. Additional adult in room $25 extra, child $10 extra. AE, MC, V.

Ted and Carol Titus built this huge log house specifically to be their new B&B, but with its huge common room—with a fireplace and towering cathedral ceiling—it feels more like a luxurious wilderness lodge. Located off Kalifornsky Beach Road a little south of the bridge in Kenai, the house stands over an active beaver pond, with a deck and lots of windows to watch the beavers. The upstairs rooms, which cost $10 more, are well worth it—they're large and airy. A room on the main floor has French doors to a deck over the pond. All the rooms are attractively decorated in a country style, although not all are so exceptional. In-room telephones are available, there's a Jacuzzi on the porch, and the hostess cooks a large breakfast at the time of your choosing.

Soldotna Bed and Breakfast Lodge. 399 Lovers Lane, Soldotna, AK 99669. ☎ **907/262-4779.** Fax 907/262-3201. www.SoldotnaLodge.com. 16 units, none with bathroom, and 2 separate houses. TV TEL. $140–$145 double; $280–$870 complete house. Rates include full breakfast. Additional person in room $25 extra. Fishing packages available. Open in winter by special arrangement. AE, MC, V (5% surcharge).

Right on the river, right in town, yet in a wooded setting, this exceptionally elegant inn would seem more likely to turn up in a European village than dusty Soldotna. Each room is unique, with balconies over the river or the garden, and attractive wallpaper and furnishings. There are five clean bathrooms and four separate shower rooms among the 16 bedrooms. Smoking is not permitted in the inn. The grounds slope down to the river along a sheltered boardwalk, leading to a dock where you can fish or board one of the fishing charters. The owners speak German, French, and Japanese as well as English.

CAMPING

Soldotna's appealing **Centennial Park Campground** lies atop a bluff along the Kenai River among thick spruce and birch trees. Turn right on Kalifornsky Beach Road just past the visitor center. Camping fees are $8 a night, day use $3. There is a dump station, usable for a $10 fee. **Swiftwater Park** is a similar city-operated riverside campground near the Fred Meyer grocery store and Taco Bell as you enter town from the north.

   RV parks are scattered about. **Beluga Lookout RV Park** (☎ 907/283-5999) is in Kenai's Old Town, overlooking the Inlet and the river's mouth, at 929 Mission Ave.

DINING

Franchise fast-food and burger-steak-seafood places dominate in Kenai and Soldotna. **Paradisos,** at Main Street and Kenai Spur Highway in Kenai (☎ 907/283-2222), is a good multiethnic family restaurant.

Charlotte's Bakery, Café, Espresso. 115 S. Willow, Kenai. ☎ **907/283-2777.** All items $5–$8. MC, V. Mon–Fri 7am–4pm, Sat 9am–3pm. Closed Sun. SANDWICHES.

Rich-textured bread from the bakery anchors the sandwiches, and lettuce from a nearby garden fills out the large, filling salads, but the motherly owner doesn't make a point of that—hers is not a trendy or gimmicky place. Locals fill the big wooden chairs in the bright dining room because the food is good, the service sweetly attentive, and the prices reasonable.

Sal's Klondike Diner. 44619 Sterling Hwy., Soldotna. ☎ **907/262-2220.** Lunch $4.50–$9; dinner $7–$10. AE, MC, V. Daily 24 hours. DINER.

It certainly looks corny and touristy from the outside, but Sal's turns out to be a classic Western highway diner, with huge portions, fast service, and nothing fancy that doesn't have to be. Our meat loaf sandwich and halibut fish-and-chips, served on a plastic tablecloth, were just what we wanted for a quick lunch, and our coffee cups stayed full. The children's menu is good and cheap.

✪ **Through the Seasons.** 43960 Sterling Hwy. (at intersection with Kenai Spur Hwy.), Soldotna. ☎ **907/262-5006.** Dinner $15–$22. MC, V. Summer Mon–Sat 5:30–10pm, Sun 5:30–9pm; winter Tues–Sat 5:30–9pm, closed Sun–Mon. Closed Jan. SEAFOOD/STEAK/PASTA.

The small, light dining room, with a cathedral ceiling, looks out on a birch and spruce forest despite being near the intersection of two major highways. The atmosphere, with acoustic music weekend evenings, is ferny and casual. The menu is straightforward and reasonably priced and features a variety of vegetarian selections. They experiment with various cuisines, usually successfully. Without question the best meals in the area are served here. Beer and wine license.

10 Kenai National Wildlife Refuge: Peace & Wildlife

Floating through the Kenai National Wildlife Refuge in a canoe narrows the world into a circle of green water, spruce, and birch. You can paddle and hike for days without encountering more than a few other people, your only expense the cost of your canoe and the vehicle that carried you to the trailhead. Out there with my son, I once noticed that, other than his voice, the only sounds I had heard in 2 days were the gurgling of the water and the wind shushing in the birch leaves. You rely on yourself, but your greatest tests are not overly taxing. Trail a line behind the canoe, and, when you catch a rainbow trout, land it and make a fire to cook it. Launch your body into the clear, frigid water to rinse off the sweat on a warm day. Float slowly, watching eagles circle the treetops and puffy clouds drifting like ships past your little world.

Most of the western half of the Kenai Peninsula lies within the 2 million acres of the refuge—it's almost as large as Yellowstone National Park—and much of that land is impossibly remote and truly dedicated to the wildlife. The Kenai River flows through part of the refuge, but the refuge is just a name to the fishers who pursue its salmon. (Information about the river is above, in the Kenai/Soldotna and Cooper Landing sections.)

Canoeists will be more interested in the lowlands on the west side, west of the Sterling Highway and north of Kenai and Soldotna. The lakes there are as numerous as the speckles on a trout's back—or at least that's how they appears from the air. From the ground, the region is a maze of lakes connected by trails—more than 70 lakes you can reach on canoe routes stretching more than 150 miles. It's the easiest way to real Alaska wilderness I know.

ESSENTIALS
GETTING THERE
The refuge surrounds much of the land from Cooper Landing to south of Homer and west to Cook Inlet. The Sterling Highway and roads that branch from it are the main ways to the lakes, trails, and rivers, and there is no practical way there without a vehicle.

VISITOR INFORMATION
Stop in at the **Kenai National Wildlife Refuge Visitor Center,** Ski Hill Road (P.O. Box 2139), Soldotna, AK 99669 (☎ **907/262-7021;** e-mail: R7KENWR@fws.gov), for guidance before plunging into the wilderness and to learn about the land and animals of the refuge. It's open in summer daily 8:30am to 6pm; winter, Monday to Friday 8:30am to 4:30pm, Saturday and Sunday 10am to 5pm. The U.S. Fish and Wildlife Service, which manages the refuge, maintains a small museum of the area's natural history, where a film is shown each hour in the summer. Rangers offer advice and sell books and maps without which you can't make a backcountry trip. To find the center, turn left just south of the Kenai River Bridge, taking the dirt road uphill from the building-supply store.

GETTING OUTSIDE
SPECIAL PLACES
From 1941 to 1980 the refuge was known as the Kenai National Moose Range, and its brushy wetlands are paradise for moose, rich in their favorite foods of willow branches and pond weeds. Moose like to dine while wading. Waterfowl and other birds, beavers, muskrats, and other aquatic animals are common on the lakes. People also must be partly aquatic to explore the lakes, paddling canoes across their surfaces,

pushing through lily pad passages between lakes, and frequently hiking in rubber boots between lakes while carrying the canoe and camping gear.

There are two main canoe routes, both reached from Sterling River and Swan Lake roads, north of Sterling off the Sterling Highway. The **Swan Lake Canoe Route** really is more of a network of many connected lakes. It meets Swan Lake Road twice, allowing a loop of several days, and in between adventurers can penetrate many lakes deep into the wilderness, visiting remote lakes they will have all to themselves. It's also possible to canoe through to the Moose River, and ride it back to the Sterling Highway. Getting anywhere requires frequent portages of a quarter mile or so. You can skip all the portaging by floating down the **Swanson River** to its mouth, at the Captain Cook State Recreation Area (see below), but the **Swanson River Canoe Route** also includes dozens of remote lakes that connect by portages to the upper part of the river. Both routes have many dozens of remote campgrounds—just lakeside areas of cleared ground with fire rings—and the portages are well marked and maintained with wooden planking over the wet areas.

If you go, among your most important tools will be the book *The Kenai Canoe Trails,* By Daniel L. Quick, published by Northlite Publishing Company (33335 Skyline Dr., Soldotna, AK 99669-9752). This extraordinary guide contains superdetailed maps and directions, and advice on how to plan your trip and fish and camp on your way—I've never seen a trail guide like it. The author and publisher leads guided canoe trips on the routes, calling his company **Northlite** (☎ **800/994-5997** or 907/ 262-5997; www.alaska.net/~northlit). For around $125 per person per day you get his personal attention and everything you need but your own clothes. He'll do day trips or paddles of up to a week.

Experienced canoeists don't need a guide, although, of course, you must be prepared before you go off on your own in this wilderness. I haven't provided detailed driving instructions because you'll need detailed maps to go at all. **Trails Illustrated** produces a good detailed map of the whole area, printed on plastic (see "Fast Facts: Alaska" in chapter 2 for details). Canoes and the gear to go with them, including cartop carriers, are for rent from the Sports Den in Soldotna, listed under "Fishing" in the Kenai/Soldotna section, above. But no one in the area rents camping equipment or lightweight canoes, so a better plan might be to rent everything you need, including a canoe and camping gear, in Anchorage (see chapter 6).

There's much else to do in the refuge too, including several upland hiking trails. The refuge visitor center has a free guide map, and can give guidance on where to go.

CAMPING

For car camping, away from all the fishers, the **Captain Cook State Recreation Area** is a lovely and underused seaside area on Cook Inlet, 25 miles north of Kenai on the Kenai Spur Road, at the mouth of the Swanson River. There are lots of attractive sites among large birches, trails, beach walking, a canoe landing at the end of the Swanson River Canoe Route, and lake swimming. The camping fee is $10. **Daniels Lake Lodge,** listed above under "Kenai/Soldotna," is nearby.

There are many campgrounds within the refuge, too, some of them lovely, quiet spots on the edge of uninhabited lakes, such as the small **Rainbow Lake** and **Dolly Varden Lake campgrounds,** on Swanson River Road near the start of the canoe routes. Get a complete listing from the visitor center.

11 Homer: Cosmic Hamlet by the Sea

Homer's leading mystic, Brother Asaiah Bates, maintains that a confluence of metaphysical forces causes a focus of powerful creative energy on this little seaside town. It's

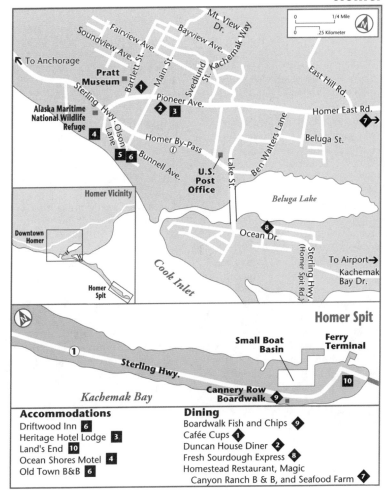

Homer

Mt. View Dr.
Bayview Ave.
Fairview Ave.
Soundview Ave.
St. Kachemak Way
To Anchorage
East Hill Rd.

Pratt Museum 1
Bartlett St.
Main St.
Svedlund St.
Pioneer Ave. 2 3
Homer East Rd. 7

Alaska Maritime National Wildlife Refuge 4
Sterling Hwy.
Olson Lane
Homer By-Pass i
5 6
Bunnell Ave.
Beluga St.

Ben Walters Lane
Lake St.

U.S. Post Office

Beluga Lake

Homer Vicinity

Ocean Dr. 8

Downtown Homer

Cook Inlet

Sterling Hwy. (Homer Spit Rd.)

To Airport →
Kachemak Bay Dr.

Homer Spit

Homer Spit

1
Sterling Hwy.
Kachemak Bay

Small Boat Basin
Ferry Terminal

Cannery Row Boardwalk 9
10

Accommodations
Driftwood Inn **6**
Heritage Hotel Lodge **3**
Land's End **10**
Ocean Shores Motel **4**
Old Town B&B **6**

Dining
Boardwalk Fish and Chips **9**
Cafée Cups **1**
Duncan House Diner **2**
Fresh Sourdough Express **8**
Homestead Restaurant, Magic
  Canyon Ranch B & B, and Seafood Farm **7**

hard to argue. Homer is full of creative people: artists, eccentrics, and those who simply contribute to a quirky community in a beautiful place. Indeed, Brother Asaiah may be the quintessential Homerite, although perhaps an extreme example, with his gray ponytail, extraordinary openness and generosity, and flowery rhetoric about "the cosmic wheel of life." Homer is full of outspoken, unusual, and even odd individualists—people who make living in the town almost an act of belief. I can say this because I'm a former Homerite myself.

The geography of Homer—physical as well as metaphysical—has gathered certain people here the way currents gather driftwood on the town's pebble beaches. Homer is at the end of the road—the nation's paved highway system comes to an abrupt conclusion at the tip of the Homer Spit, almost 5 miles out in the middle of Kachemak Bay—and believers of one kind or another have washed up here for decades. There were the "barefooters," a communal group that eschewed shoes, even in the Alaska winter—Brother Asaiah came with them in the early 1950s. There are the Russian Old Believers, who organize their strictly traditional communities around their objection to Russian Orthodox church reforms made by Peter the Great. There are the former hippies who have become successful commercial fishermen after flocking here in the late 1960s to camp as "Spit rats" on the beach. And there are even the current migrants—artists and retired people, fundamentalist preachers and New Age healers, wealthy North Slope oil workers and land-poor settlers with no visible means of support—all people who live here simply because they choose to.

The choice is understandable. Homer lies on the north side of Kachemak Bay, a branch of lower Cook Inlet of extraordinary biological productivity—the **halibut fishing,** especially, is exceptional. The town has a breathtaking setting on the Spit and on a wildflower-covered bench high above the bay. The outdoors, especially on the water and across the bay, contains wonderful opportunities. And the **arts community** has developed into an attraction of its own, drawing more artists and creating the reputation of an arts colony. There are several exceptional galleries and the Pratt Museum, which has a national reputation.

Homer gets its name from a guy named Homer, which seems fitting since it's the sort of place where first names tend to be used. Homer Pennock came to the area around the turn of the century. Miners were exploiting the low-quality lignite common on the north side of Kachemak Bay, which means "Smoky Bay," as the seams occasionally burned and created haze. The coal-fueled steamers landed at Seldovia, a metropolis at that time but today a sleepy little village. Homer people still pick up the coal that washes up on Bishop's Beach to heat their homes.

Homer began to take its modern form after two events: In the 1950s the Sterling Highway connected it to the rest of the world, and in 1964 the Good Friday earthquake sank the Spit, narrowing a much larger piece of land with a small forest into the tendril that now barely stands above the water. If not for constant reinforcement by the federal government, the Spit long since would have become an island, and Homer would hardly exist. The Spit, and the boat harbor there, are the town's vital organs; the commercial fishing and visitor industry keep it alive.

ESSENTIALS
GETTING THERE

BY CAR   At about 235 miles, Homer is roughly 4½ hours from Anchorage by car, if you don't stop at any of the interesting or beautiful places along the way. It's a scenic drive. If you take a rental car, you may want to drive it both ways, as the drop-off fees from Anchorage to Homer are high.

BY BUS   Homer Stage Line, P.O. Box 1912, Homer, AK 99603 (☎ **907/ 235-7009** or 907/399-1847), runs to Anchorage and back six times a week during the height of summer, and less frequently the rest of the year. The fare is $45, or $80 round-trip. Tickets are for sale at Quicky Mart, 1242 Ocean Dr. (☎ 907/235-2252). In Anchorage buy tickets at Seward Bus Line, 3339 Fairbanks St. (☎ 907/563-0800).

BY AIR   Era Aviation (☎ **800/866-8394**) serves Homer from Anchorage many times a day. Small air-taxi operators use Homer as a hub for outlying villages and the outdoors.

BY FERRY   The **Alaska Marine Highway System** (☎ **800/642-0066** or 907/ 235-8449; www.dot.state.ak.us/external/amhs/home.html) connects Homer to Seldovia, Kodiak, and points west along the Alaska Peninsula and Aleutian Archipelago, and Seward to the east, with the ferry *Tustumena.* The run to Kodiak takes 9½ hours and costs $48 for an adult walk-on passenger. It's a major trip, but a memorable one. A U.S. Fish and Wildlife Service naturalist rides the ferries to present programs and answer questions.

Homer on the Web

A couple of Internet sites in Homer (other than those listed under "Visitor Information") have pages of links and other community information on the area. The *Homer News* has a good site at **www.homeralaska.com**. The main Internet provider in town has links at **www.xyz.net/home**. Another is **www.NETALASKA.com.**

VISITOR INFORMATION

The Homer Chamber of Commerce Visitor Information Center, 135 Sterling Hwy. (P.O. Box 541), Homer, AK 99603 (☎ **907/235-7740;** www.xyz.net/~homer), is on the right as you enter town. In summer, staff is on hand daily from 9am to 8pm to answer questions and to hand out brochures on local businesses—and you can buy tickets for the halibut derby. Get a copy of the *Homer Tourism and Recreation Guide*, published by the *Homer News,* here or anywhere in town. It includes a useful map.

On the right side of the highway as you arrive in town, **Alaska Maritime National Wildlife Refuge Visitor Center,** 451 Sterling Hwy., Ste. 2, Homer, AK 99603 (☎ **907/235-6961;** e-mail: r7_homervc@fws.gov), is the place to stop for outdoors information wherever you go in the area. It's open in summer daily 9am to 6pm, winter by appointment. The refuge itself consists of islands off Alaska from the Arctic to near British Columbia. The U.S. Fish and Wildlife Service manages these lands for the benefit of birds and marine mammals, and people rarely set foot on their shores, but rangers in Homer also offer bird and beach walks frequently in the summer, and show natural history films and give programs at the center. Call for times.

The **Kachemak Bay State Park Ranger Station,** Sterling Hwy. 4 miles from town (P.O. Box 3248), Homer, AK 99603 (☎ **907/235-7024;** www.dnr.state.ak.us/parks/parks.htm), can help answer questions about planning a trip to the trails and beaches across the Kachemak Bay from Homer. There's valuable statewide park information on the Web site.

Call the **Kachemak Bay Birdwatchers Hotline** (☎ **907/235-7337**) to find out about recent sightings and upcoming birder events, and leave news of your own observations.

GETTING AROUND

BY CAR   The best way to get to and around Homer is by car. If you didn't bring one, you can rent a car at the airport from **Hertz** (☎ **800/654-3131** or 907/235-0734) or from **Polar Car Rental** (☎ **907/235-5998**). There are several taxi companies in town, including **CHUX Cab** (☎ **907/235-CHUX**).

BY BIKE   For strong riders, a bike is a good way around town. You do have to dodge traffic at times, and the Spit is 5 miles long, but it's a great way to experience the outdoors. Some excellent mountain biking routes are mentioned below. **Homer Saw and Cycle** (☎ **907/235-8406**), at 1532 Ocean Dr., rents mountain bikes and trailers, starting at $15 half day. They're open Monday through Friday 9am to 5:30pm, Saturday 11am to 5pm. It's wise to reserve bikes a day or two ahead, especially if an outing depends on getting one. **Chain Reaction Sports** (☎ **907/235-0750**), at 3858 Lake St., specializes in high-quality mountain bikes, and offers delivery in the Homer area for $4.

BY DAY TOUR   **Homer Tours** (☎ **907/235-0530;** www.xyz.net/~seekins/tours.htm) offers van and bus tours. A daily 4-hour tour is $40.

SPECIAL EVENTS

Homer's Winter Carnival, in mid-February, is a big community event, a small-town celebration with a beer-making contest, parade, and snow sculpture competition, among other highlights. **The Kachemak Bay Shorebird Festival,** held in early May, includes guided bird-watching hikes and boat excursions, natural history workshops, art shows and performances, a wooden boat festival, and other events. It's organized by Alaska Maritime National Wildlife Refuge and the Homer Chamber of Commerce to mark the return of the annual migration in early May. **The Kachemak Bay Wooden Boat Festival** (☎ 907/235-2141) takes place at the same time as the Shorebird Festival, and displays handmade boats from around the region and presents workshops and films. **Concert on the Lawn,** put on usually the last Sunday in July by KBBI public radio (☎ 907/235-7721), is a day-long outdoor music, craft, and food festival that brings together the whole town. **The Jackpot Halibut Derby,** lasting the whole summer long, has a top prize that has surpassed $25,000 for the biggest fish of the summer. Winning fish are in the 300-pound class, but of course you must buy your ticket before you fish.

Fast Facts: Homer

Banks   There are two banks, with ATMs, on the Sterling Highway near Heath Street.

Hospital   The South Peninsula Hospital is at the top of Bartlett Street, off Pioneer Avenue (☎ 907/235-8101).

Internet/E-mail   Homer Secretarial, 3858 Lake St. no. 316 (☎ 907/235-7766), offers Internet access by appointment, and business services. Eagle Eye Photo, 639 E. Pioneer Ave. (☎ 907/235-8525), rents computers with Internet access for $5 an hour.

Police   For nonemergency calls within city limits, call the Homer Police Department (☎ 907/235-3150); outside the city, phone the Alaska State Troopers (☎ 907/235-8239). Both have offices located across Pioneer Avenue from the intersection with Lake Street.

Post Office   On the Sterling Highway at Heath Street.

Taxes   Within city limits, sales tax is 5.5%; there's no room tax. Outside city limits you pay only the 2% Kenai Peninsula Borough sales tax.

ATTRACTIONS

Homer lacks historic buildings. The attractions of the town come from its setting—the walks on the beaches and in the hilltop meadows—and from the art the setting has inspired. A widely distributed brochure lists the galleries, including the **Fireweed Gallery** (☎ 907/235-7040) at 475 E. Pioneer Ave., the **Picture Alaska Gallery** (☎ 907/235-2300) at 448 Pioneer Ave., and **Edith Parsons Pottery** (☎ 907/235-0660) at 1520 Ocean Dr. Here are some of the best.

✪ **Pratt Museum.** 3779 Bartlett St. (at Pioneer Ave.). ☎ **907/235-8635.** www.prattmuseum.org. Admission $5 adults, $2 children ages 13–18, $1 children 6–12. High season, daily 10am–6pm. Low season, Tues–Sun noon–5pm. Closed Jan.

The Homer Society of Natural History's museum is as good as any you'll find in a town this size. The Pratt is strongest in natural history and has a small saltwater aquarium in which to see the life of Kachemak Bay close up and even touch it (after you wash your hands), but the museum also has displays of local art, history, and culture. If you're curious about all the fishing boats down in the harbor, at the Pratt you can find out about the different types of gear as well as the fish they catch. In the garden outside, you can learn to identify all the local wildflowers. The exhibit on the *Exxon Valdez* oil spill toured nationally, to acclaim. Also, the volunteers enjoy imparting local secrets about where to go, what to do, and where to eat. Starting in early June, the Pratt also sponsors the 90-minute **Historic Harbor Tour** at 3pm Friday and Saturday, a walk through the small-boat harbor to learn about the vessels and fishing industry. Tickets are $10 from the museum or the guide and include sampling from a seafood platter. Meet at the Salty Dawg Pilot House on the Spit.

Bunnell Street Gallery. 106 W. Bunnell Ave. ☎ **907/235-2662.** www.xyz.net/~bunnell. Summer Mon–Sat 10am–6pm, Sun 11am–5pm; winter Mon–Sat 10am–6pm. Closed Jan.

This nonprofit gallery, located in a perfect space in an old hardware store near Bishop's Beach at the lower end of Main Street, is one of the best in Alaska. Unlike most other Alaska galleries, which double as tourist gift shops, Bunnell was made by and for artists, and the experience is noncommercial and often challenging. You may be tempted to become a member of the nonprofit corporation that runs it, for membership comes with a one-of-a-kind plate made by one of the artists. As with all Homer art, the themes of the work tend to be fishy, and the medium and style could be anything. The gallery also puts on summer concerts, booking nationally known folk and classical performers into the most intimate of settings. Tickets are $8 to $12. Don't miss the **Two Sisters Bakery** and coffee shop next door.

Ptarmigan Arts. 471 E. Pioneer Ave. ☎ **907/235-5345.** High season, Mon–Sat 10am–7pm, Sun 10am–5pm; low season Mon–Sat 11am–6pm, Sun 11am–4pm.

Often staffed by the artists themselves, Ptarmigan Arts specializes in crafts, especially ceramics and fabrics, which are the most common media in Homer and which generally are more affordable than fine art. Occasionally you can see a demonstration by one of the resident artists, and there's always a tremendous array of work in various styles.

Sea Lion Gallery. 4241 Homer Spit Rd. (Central Charters Boardwalk). ☎ **907/235-3400.** E-mail: sealion@xyz.net. Open summer only, Mon–Sat 11am–9pm, Sun noon–6pm.

Wildlife artist Gary Lyon and his family own and staff this small gallery among the T-shirt shops on one of the boardwalks on Homer Spit. It's pleasant but a little odd to see very valuable works by Lyon and others displayed in this intimate setting. Lyon's work captures Alaska wildlife in spectacular detail, but also transforms his subjects with a distinctively dreamy vision. The rooms they rent upstairs are described under "Accommodations," below.

Norman Lowell Studio & Gallery. ☎ **907/235-7344.** Sterling Hwy. milepost 160.9 (near Anchor Point, about 12 miles out the Sterling Hwy. from Homer. Summer only, Mon–Sat 9am–7pm, Sun 1–5pm.

Lowell built his own huge gallery on his homestead to show his life's work. The immense oils of Alaska landscapes, which are not for sale, hang in a building that counts as one of Alaska's larger art museums. Admission is free, and Lowell or his wife, Libby, often host guests who walk through. Their original homestead cabin also is a museum, showing pioneer life in Alaska as it was when they originally settled here. The studio/gallery sells Lowell's paintings, which range in price from $750 to $30,000; prints start at $100.

GETTING OUTSIDE

The best **map of the Kachemak Bay area** is produced by Alaska Road and Recreation Maps, P.O. Box 102459, Anchorage, AK 99510. Available all over town, it costs around $5, depending where you buy it.

ON THE HOMER SIDE OF KACHEMAK BAY

TIDE POOLING   Exploring Kachemak Bay's tide pools is the best way to really get to know the sea and meet the strange and wonderful animals that live in it, and it doesn't cost anything but the price of a pair of rubber boots. First, check a tide book, available for free or for a nominal price in virtually any local store, or ask a local to check one for you. You need a low tide of -2 or lower, meaning that low water will be at least 2 feet below the normal low, some 25 feet below the high. Extralow tides expose more of the lower intertidal zone that contains the most interesting creatures. At a -5 tide, you could find octopus and other oddities. Also, the lower the tide, the more time you'll have to look. Keep track of the time: The tide will come in faster than you imagine, and you could get stranded and quickly drown in the 40°F water.

The best place to go in town is reached from Bishop's Beach Park, near the lower end of Main Street. Walk west on the beach toward the opening of the bay to Cook Inlet. It's at least a half-hour walk to the Coal Point area, where the sand and boulders end, and bedrock makes out from the shore. This is where you'll find pools of water left behind by the receding tide, many full of life. Explore patiently and gently—look at the animals and touch them, but always put them back as they were and be careful not to crush anything underfoot. Marine invertebrate identification keys and many other field guides are sold at **The Book Store** on the Sterling Highway next to Eagle Foods, and the Wildlife Refuge Visitors Center, above under "Visitor Information," is eager to help with advice. If you want to keep going, there's usually a sea otter raft offshore about 3 miles down the beach. Just continue walking, keeping your eyes on the water. As always with watching wildlife, binoculars will improve the experience.

HIKING   There are trails on the bench above Homer as well as across the bay at Kachemak Bay State Park (see below). The 6-mile **Homestead Trail** is an old wagon road used by Homer's early settlers. The largely informal trail is lovely and peaceful, tunneling through alders, across fields of wildflowers, and past old homestead cabins. From a hilltop meadow you can see all the way to the Inlet and the volcanoes beyond. A trailhead is at the reservoir on Skyline Drive—drive up West Hill Road from the Sterling Highway, turn right, and follow Skyline, turning left before the pond.

DRIVING OR MOUNTAIN BIKING   Several gravel roads around Homer make for exquisite drives or bike rides. Mountain bikers can use the Homestead Trail, above, too. **East End Road** goes through lovely seaside pastures, a forest, and the village of Fritz Creek, then follows the bluff line through meadows toward the head of the bay. The road eventually turns into an all-terrain-vehicle track; don't go beyond your vehicle's ability to get out. **Skyline Drive** has extraordinary views of high canyons and Kachemak Bay; drive up East Hill Road just east of Homer. The two bike shops listed above, under "Getting Around," can give you many more ideas. The best mountain biking, across the bay, is described below.

HORSEBACK RIDING   Ranchers have worked around Kachemak Bay for decades. Drive east of town on East End Road and you can see pastures full of cattle overlooking views that anywhere else would be used for resort hotels. **Trails End Horse Adventures** (☎ 907/235-6393), 11.2 miles out East End, offers trail rides and overnight trips.

ON OR ACROSS KACHEMAK BAY

Plenty of Alaska's maritime wilderness scenery—Kachemak Bay included—can wear out adjectives, but I don't know of any other place where the human element is as good a part of the picture. Along the south side of the bay, glaciers and fjords and little wooded islands are arrayed like a smorgasbord before Homer. A quick boat ride puts you there for sea kayaking, mountain biking on unconnected dirt roads, hiking in the mountains, or eating sushi in a top-flight restaurant on pilings. Or gallery hopping, or resting at a remote lodge, or studying at a nature center, or walking the streets of a forgotten fishing village. The far side of the bay has no road link to import the mundane, mass-produced world; but it does have people, and they make the landscape even richer and more enchanting than it would be alone.

There are two villages across the bay, **Halibut Cove** and **Seldovia**, each with its own services and lodgings; they are described elsewhere in this chapter, but can certainly be linked with other areas and activities. Outside of town (any town), there are three wilderness lodges and a bed-and-breakfast to use as a base, described below under "Accommodations." In addition, there are various places you can visit for a day trip or longer away from a village or lodge. That's what I cover here.

Special Places

JAKOLOF BAY   A state-maintained dock opens an area of gentle shorelines, abandoned logging roads, and inexpensive cabins to visitors who seek the wilderness but can't afford to stay at a wilderness lodge. West of Kachemak Bay State Park and east of Seldovia, the lands have roads, but they aren't connected to anything and are used as much by mountain bikers as by anyone else. You can take the Jakolof Bay Ferry, listed below, straight to the Jakolof dock. The folks there rent simple cabins, too, and the Across the Bay Tent and Breakfast, under "Wilderness Lodges" in the "Accommodations" section also has inexpensive lodgings. There's plenty to do in the area. The waters of Jakolof, Little Jakolof, Kasitsna, and Little Tutka bays, and the tiny Herring Islands, are appealing and protected for sea kayaking. Supreme mountain biking trails lead along the shore and right across the peninsula through forest and meadows for berry picking. The Red Mountain and Rocky River roads are prime routes; check with one of the bike shops or the locals to find out about dangerous river crossings and other hazards. A maintained 10-mile road west leads to the charming village of Seldovia, described below.

KACHEMAK BAY STATE PARK   The park comprises much of the land across the water that makes all those views from Homer so spectacular. The main office is at the ranger station listed under "Visitor Information" above, and a **park ranger station** in Halibut Cove Lagoon is open in summer, where there's a dock and mooring buoys for public use. The park has about 80 miles of trails; a trail guide is available from the ranger station or the visitor centers. Hike to a glacier, a mountain peak, or just over the hills to the next secluded beach. There are various campsites, three public-use cabins at Halibut Cove Lagoon, and a cabin each at Tutka Bay and China Poot Lake. Cabin permits are $50 a night and must be reserved in advance from the ranger station (reservation details are at the beginning of the chapter, under "Getting Outside on the Kenai Peninsula & Prince William Sound"). Or you can go for a day trip, walk on a beach you'll have all to yourself, in "Transportation Across the Water," or take a hike on one of the trails before being picked up at a prearranged time in the afternoon. The water taxis listed below can take you across and give you ideas on good places for beach walking, camping, sea kayaking, and hiking.

McNEIL RIVER STATE GAME SANCTUARY   McNeil River has the world's greatest known concentration of brown bears in June, July, and early August, when there's an easy meal to be had from the chum salmon trying to jump up a waterfall to return to spawn upriver. It's also among the best places in the world to watch bears, as decades of protection and wise management have taught the bears—more than 100 at a time at the height of the run—to ignore humans standing within a few yards, even while the bears go on about their business of feeding, nursing, mating, and just being bears. It's such a valuable experience that permits to visit and tent in the campground are handed out by lottery by the **Alaska Department of Fish and Game,** 333 Raspberry Rd., Anchorage, AK 99518-1599 (☎ **907/267-2181;** www.state.ak.us/local/akpages/FISH.GAME/adfghome.htm). Write to them "Attn: McNeil River" for a permit application, which must be returned, with a nonrefundable $25 fee, by late March. More than 2,000 apply annually for fewer than 250 permits. There are outhouses, and water comes from a rain barrel—it's remote camping. **Kachemak Air** (☎ **907/235-8924**), listed below under "Flightseeing," can get you there and knows where else to find bears if you can't get a permit. Mike and Diane McBride, of Kachemak Bay Wilderness Lodge (see "Accommodations" section, below), also operate a more comfortable lodging 8 miles north of the sanctuary.

Booking Agencies

The Bookie. P.O. Box 195, Homer, AK 99603. ☎ **888/335-1581** or 907/235-1581. www.alaskabookie.com.

A newer agency, this outfit books the same activities as Central Charters, but has more of an ecotourism orientation.

Central Charters. 4241 Homer Spit Rd., Homer, AK 99603. ☎ **800/478-7847** or 907/235-7847. www.central-charter.com.

This is the longest established of the booking agents in Homer. Originally the firm specialized in halibut charters, but branched out into everything that could be arranged. They have a ticket office on the right side of the Spit as you drive out.

Transportation Across the Water

The daily **Jakolof Ferry Service** (Red Mountain, Box RDO, Homer, AK 99603; ☎ **907/235-2376;** www.xyz.net/~jakolof) runs to the south side of the bay several times a day all summer with a handsome 34-foot wooden boat. The vessel can carry up to 18 passengers, mostly seated outside, and can pull right up on the beach. It's a great way to get to wilderness cabins and kayaking waters, the hiking and mountain biking roads accessible from the Jakolof Dock, Halibut Cove, Kachemak Bay State Park, and other remote points. Fares generally are under $50 round-trip, children half price, free age 3 and under—pretty much standard for a water taxi across the bay. Stop by the office on the Spit's Cannery Row Boardwalk for ideas. The Ferry Service also rents primitive cabins for $50 to $70 a night.

Many other water taxis serve the bay, booking through one of the agencies above or directly. **Mako's Water Taxi** (☎ **907/235-9055**) has been around a while and has a good reputation.

Activities

FISHING   Homer is known for **halibut,** those huge, flat bottom fish, and the harbor is full of charter boats that will take you out for the day for around $150 per person. Every day, people catch fish that are larger than they are, and halibut over 50 pounds are common. To get to where the fish are plentiful requires an early start and a long ride to unprotected waters. People who get seasick easily shouldn't go, as the boat wallows on the waves during fishing. Using gear and lines that look strong enough to pick up the boat, you jig the herring bait up and down on the bottom. Halibut aren't acrobats like salmon, and fighting one can be like pulling up a sunken Buick. One good, large operator is **Silver Fox Charters** (☎ **800/478-8792** or

907/235-8792; www.NETALASKA.com/fox). Others can be booked through one of the agencies above, or find one on the **Homer Charter Association** Web site, which has a list and links for dozens of boats, at www.xyz.net/~hca.

Salmon are fished with trolling gear year-round, not only when they're running in the streams. **North Country Charters** (☎ 800/770-7620 or 907/235-7620; www.NETALASKA.com/northcountry) and **Katmai Coastal Tours** (☎ 800/532-8338 or 907/235-7131) run those charters, as well as excursions for halibut. Also, a lagoon on the Spit is stocked with terminal run king and silver salmon by the Alaska Department of Fish and Game. These fish have nowhere to spawn, and some fishers scorn such "fish-in-a-barrel" angling. At the end of the run, snagging is permitted, which is something like mugging salmon. For more natural fishing, head back up the Sterling Highway to the Anchor River, an excellent steelhead trout stream, and the other rivers that flow west into Cook Inlet. The **Alaska Department of Fish and Game** maintains a fishing hot line at ☎ 907/235-6930. They're located at 3298 Douglas (☎ **907/235-8191;** www.state.ak.us/local/akpages/FISH.GAME/adfghome.htm).

Coal Point Trading Co., 4300 Homer Spit (☎ **907/235-3877**), will process, pack, and ship your catch as ordered.

NATURAL HISTORY TOURS   Rainbow Tours's twice-a-day **Gull Island** trip is a tremendous value: For only $20 for an adult, $10 age 12 and under, the comfortable 67-foot *Rainbow Connection* takes passengers to the Gull Island bird rookery, lingering so close to the rocks that it's possible to get a good view of the birds' nests with the naked eye. In season, you can see glaucus winged gulls, tufted puffins, black-legged kittiwakes, common murres, red-faced and pelagic cormorants, horned puffins, pigeon guillemots, and occasionally other species. The wildlife commentary on the boat is accurate and serious. The boat often continues on to drop off visitors at the Alaska Center for Coastal Studies in Peterson Bay, listed below, so you get to see quite a bit of the bay for the price of Gull Island alone. There's a snack and beer and wine bar on board. **Rainbow Tours** has an office on the Spit, at the Cannery Row Boardwalk (P.O. Box 1526, Homer, AK 99603; ☎ **907/235-7272;** www.rainbowtours.net). They also offer tours to Seldovia and fishing charters.

The nonprofit **Center for Alaska Coastal Studies** foundation is dedicated to educating the public about the sea. That means the group's emphasis isn't on making money, but on interpreting Kachemak Bay for visitors. You'll go for a daylong exploration of the Peterson Bay area: If the tides are right, the volunteers will take you on a fascinating guided tide pool walk; if not, you can take a nature walk. You decide what you want to do. There's also a lodge with saltwater tanks containing creatures from the intertidal zone and microscopes to inspect your finds. **Rainbow Tours** (☎ **907/235-7272**) books the trips and takes passengers at 9am daily on the *Rainbow Connection,* described above. At $63 per adult, $43 ages 6 to 12, it's a bargain. Pack your own lunch, as none is provided, and bring footwear suitable for hiking and beach walks. You can reach the center's office at ☎ **907/235-6667** (www.xyz.net/~cacs; P.O. Box 2225, Homer, AK 99603).

Carmen and Conrad Field both have degrees in biology and wildlife management, and deep experience with Kachemak Bay's marine biology, but what's more important is their talent at passing on their enthusiasm for the natural world. Their company, **Alaska Coastal Journeys,** P.O. Box 2094, Homer, AK 99603 (☎ **907/235-2228;** www.alaskacoastaljourneys.com), offers 3- and 5-day outdoor trips for learning: bird watching, tide pooling, watching marine mammals, collecting edible plants, and sea kayaking, mountain biking, and hiking. They also offer trips especially for families. Rates for adults start around $850.

Hermits on the Homestead

Late in October, the snow was holding back in the clouds like a strong emotion. The ground was frozen, the swamp grasses stiff, brittle, painted with frost. This was the one time of year when, with a stout four-wheel-drive truck, you could drive in to Ben's cabin. It stood on a small rise amid his hundreds of acres of swampy ground, the only spot where trees could get out of the dampness and grow. The heavy, lovingly peeled logs of the house lay horizontally amid big birch and white spruce trees. Ben had dragged these huge tree trunks from far afield, by himself, when he started his homestead nearly 40 years earlier so he could keep living trees nearer to his house.

I'm not using his real name. Ben was a private guy. He generously invited us in, offered coffee from the percolator on top of the soapstone wood stove, but it was clear that he wasn't quite sure he remembered how to talk to people—where to look, for example—and he kept mumbling and looking at my feet or the sky. He showed us around the house—the huge rocks he'd dragged in to build a foundation, the cellar where he stored his food, the collection of moose racks. Food tended to walk by each fall—he never had to go far to get his moose, and one of the biggest he shot right on the doorstep. Everything about his home was exactly the way he wanted it, the product of immense effort to make it all with his own hands. I could see plainly how he'd spent his days all these years. But I could only imagine what his nights must have been like, all alone out here—the piles of *Reader's Digest* and *National Geographic* magazines, the insistent silence.

I finally asked Ben why he'd spent his whole adult life on this homestead, so far from other people. Why not move to town, where life is easier and there's someone to talk to? Well, he said, he did work construction in the summer for cash. But I knew that was an evasion. How, I asked, did he first end up out here, in the middle of nowhere, in a huge swamp? What made him want to be off by himself when he first came out here, so long ago? Pause—check the shoes, check the sky—well, he said, it seems there was a woman. She chose the other guy.

Years ago, *U.S. News & World Report* did an article about a homesteader on the Kenai Peninsula who was a Vietnam veteran—just one of the many mad hermits from the war who had hidden off in the Alaska woods by themselves, populating the wilderness with human time bombs. The subject of the story, a well-respected member of his little homesteading community, resented the characterization, and the magazine later paid him to settle his libel suit and printed a retraction. Everyone in the area knew the article was a bunch of baloney—Alaska homesteaders are as varied as people in the city. They aren't all crazed veterans any more than they're all victims of unrequited love, although those make the best stories. What they do have in common that's unique is a willingness to invest hard physical labor every day of their lives into the things the rest of us obtain effortlessly by turning a thermostat or a faucet handle.

Alaska's homesteaders came in waves. There were the prospectors from the gold rush who stayed. Then, after World War II, GIs with families looking for broad new opportunities came north and settled more land. The counterculture movement of the 1960s brought yet another group.

Federal homesteading laws written to open the Great Plains to agriculture in the 19th century made getting land difficult and required Alaska homesteaders to do a lot of anachronistic, absurd work—like clearing large tracts for farming that could never occur. The homesteaders had to survey the land, live on it, clear much of it, and then answer any challenges about their accomplishments at a hearing. If they passed the test, they received a patent to up to 160 acres.

The laws allowing homesteading on federal lands in Alaska were all repealed by 1986, but the state government still sometimes provides land to its citizens under laws that allow homesteading, lotteries, and sale of remote land. The parcels are very remote and smaller than the old federal homesteads, and the rules still don't make it easy—for a homestead, you have to live at least 25 months on the land in a 5-year period, for example. Many families try, with a Hollywood dream of living in the wilderness, only to give up when they learn firsthand of the hardship, privations, and cold. I know from experience that I want never again to live in a home where the heating is wood or the water is in jugs, and I've never done anything approaching building a homestead. Homesteading isn't like camping. Outdoor skills won't help unless you also know how to repair engines below zero, build houses without power tools, carry all your own water and fire-wood, and live poor, largely without an income or any of the things money can buy. You have to be willing to bathe rarely, be cold in winter, and be eaten alive by mosquitoes in summer, and end up with land that isn't really worth anything.

Many successful homesteading experiences end with growing children. A couple may make it in the wilderness before having children, and kids don't care if they can take a bath, so long as the parents don't mind being far from medical care and washing diapers by hand. But when children get to a certain age, they need to go to school and be around other children. The families often expect to go back to the homestead someday, but, somehow, they rarely do. I met a couple who moved to town to educate their children; then, after they retired and the kids were through college, moved back out to their place along the railroad line north of Talkeetna. They didn't last through the winter—they'd forgotten how hard it was. Areas that were thriving little communities of neighbors in the 1950s or 1960s now are deserted, perhaps with one hermit left—like my friend Ben. Only about 160,000 acres of Alaska today—out of a total land mass of 365 million acres—show any signs of human habitation. Less than 1% is in private ownership.

My wife's parents homesteaded in the 1950s and 1960s. Her father was a World War II veteran. Today the family still has some acreage, and a treasure trove of great stories—among them the tales of my late father-in-law's feats of strength and endurance, and my wife's memory of playing with dolls as a girl, and looking up to meet the eyes of a bear that had been watching her.

But my favorite is the story of Rose and her lover. They lived in the same area in northern California where Barbara's parents grew up. Everyone in town knew the story of the red-headed beauty who had an affair with an older man. Rose's parents refused to let her marry him and ruled that the couple couldn't see each other anymore. She entered a convent, and he disappeared, never to be seen in the town again. Many years later, after moving to Alaska, Barbara's parents were boating in Kachemak Bay when they got caught by bad weather on the opposite side of the bay from Homer. On their own in an open boat and looking for shelter, they found a cabin on a remote beach of an otherwise uninhabited island. They were taken in and befriended by the hermit who'd homesteaded there for years. After warming up with a cup of coffee, they got to talking about where they'd come from and how they'd ended up in Alaska. When it came time for their host to tell his story, it was about a beautiful young woman he'd loved, named Rose.

SEA KAYAKING Silence fell as the boat pulled away from the beach, leaving us behind with the kayaks and our guide. For the rest of the day my son and I absorbed the water-reflected sunlight and glided past fancifully shaped rocks and resident sea otters around Yukon Island. We explored beaches, picnicked, raced, and discovered tiny bays too small for any other craft. At the end of the day, we had a new friend in our quietly cheerful guide, Allison O'Hara, and discovered that she'd imperceptibly taught us a lot about sea kayaking. I certainly can recommend **True North Kayak Adventures,** P.O. Box 2319, Homer, AK 99603 (☎ 907/235-0708; www.gorp.com/truenorth), which O'Hara runs with Kevin Bell. Their beginner day trips cost $125, including lunch and passage across the bay. Most kayaking day trips in Alaska towns barely get out of the small boat harbor. This trip doesn't feel so tame—it's more like a miniexpedition. They also offer more challenging overnight and multiday trips to remote waters in the area.

The protected waters, tiny islands, and remote settlements on the south side of Kachemak Bay make for perfect sea kayaking no matter whom you go with, or, for experienced paddlers, if you go on your own. Kayakers can take a water taxi across and explore at will, camping on beaches over much of the bay. Check with the Kachemak Bay State Park rangers for guidance. True North Kayak rents to experienced paddlers for $65 a day double, $45 single, with discounts for multiple days. Also see the Halibut Cove and Seldovia sections, below, for other rental opportunities.

FLIGHTSEEING There are several good air-taxis in Homer, providing access to the really remote areas of the southern Kenai Peninsula and lower Cook Inlet that you can't easily reach by boat, but **Kachemak Air Service,** P.O. Box 1769, Homer, AK 99603 (☎ **907/235-8924;** www.xyz.net/~decreeft/fly1929.htm), is really special. It offers spectacular scenic flights over the bay and glaciers starting at $90 per person. The personable Bill de Creeft, flying out of Homer since 1967, is experienced enough to qualify as a pioneer aviator; but he has nothing on his plane, a restored 1929 Travel Air S-6000-B, one of only six remaining examples of the executive aircraft, with mahogany trim and wicker seats. De Creeft also operates a DeHavilland Otter which carries fishermen, hikers, kayakers, and those who just want to see the wilderness; it also offers bear-viewing day trips on the west side of Cook Inlet.

SAILING Kachemak Bay has a predictable afternoon sea breeze, more reliable than the fluky winds of most of Alaska's coastal waters. **St. Augustine's Charters,** P.O. Box 2412, Homer, AK 99603 (☎ **907/235-7847** or 907/235-6126), offers afternoon sails and wildlife cruises, sea kayaking, Kachemak Bay State Park drop-offs, and custom trips.

ACCOMMODATIONS
HOTELS & B&BS
Along with hotels, Homer boasts some of Alaska's best B&Bs; a full list of them is available from the Homer Chamber of Commerce Visitor Center, with names and addresses. **Homer Alaska Referral Agency** (☎ **907/235-8996;** fax 907/235-2625; P.O. Box 1264, Homer, AK 99603; www.homer-referral.com) books many of the B&Bs, cottages, and apartments in town, fishing, tours, and other activities. In addition to the places I've listed, **The Sea Lion Cove,** above the Sea Lion Gallery on Homer Spit, P.O. Box 2095, Homer, AK 99603-2095 (☎ **907/235-3400** summer, 907/235-8767 winter); has two comfortable rooms with windows and a deck right over the beach where you can hear the waves roll in at night. **Cranes' Crest Bed and Breakfast,** 59830 Sanford Dr., Homer, AK 99603 (☎ **907/235-2969**), 5 miles out atop the bench behind the town, has sweeping, cinematic views you can sit and watch all day.

Motel Accommodations in Homer

Besides the hotels listed in detail below, you'll find good rooms at the **Bay View Inn,** 2851 Sterling Hwy. (P.O. Box 804), Homer, AK 99603 (☎ **907/235-8485;** fax 907/235-8716; www.bayviewalaska.com), at the top of Baycrest Hill before you come into town on the Sterling Highway, with the best view you're ever likely to find at a motel, attractive little rooms, and reasonable prices. The **Best Western Bidarka,** at 575 Sterling Hwy. (☎ **907/235-8148**), on the right as you come into town, has rooms as close as you'll find here to the standard American motel.

Driftwood Inn. 135 W. Bunnell Ave., Homer, AK 99603. ☎ and fax **907/235-8019.** netalaska.com/driftwood. 21 units, 12 with private bathroom. TV. High season, $64–$120 double. Low season, $60 double. Additional person in room $10 extra. AE, CB, DC, DISC, MC, V.

The historic building a block from Bishop's Beach and across from the Bunnell Gallery resembles a lodge or bed-and-breakfast with its large fireplace of rounded beach rock, the hot coffee pot and inexpensive self-serve breakfast in the lobby, and the owner's roving dog. The smallest rooms resemble Pullman compartments in size and configuration, but they're cute, clean, and have some real style. And they're inexpensive. Nine bedrooms share two bathrooms. Larger rooms have more amenities, but not as much charm. The walls are thin, so there's a no-noise policy during evening hours. They have an appealing 22-site RV park ($25 per night, full hookups) and a small, grassy tent area ($13 per night), plus a coin-op laundry and free coffee in the lobby.

Heritage Hotel Lodge. 147 E. Pioneer Ave., Homer, AK 99603. ☎ **800/380-7787** or 907/235-7787. Fax 907/235-2804. E-mail: heritage@xyz.net. 32 units. TV TEL. High season, $60–$90 double. Low season, $50–$60 double. Additional person in room $10 extra. AE, CB, DC, DISC, JCB, MC, V.

Homer's first hotel was built in 1948 in a log building on Pioneer Avenue. Now it's considerably larger but retains an old-fashioned feel and is a good, low-cost choice. The hallways are narrow and the rooms are not large, but they are clean and comfortable, if some are a bit out-of-date. As they differ, it's a good idea to choose for yourself. You're near the museum, downtown shops, and restaurants, but you'll have to drive to the Spit. There's free coffee in the lobby.

✪ **Land's End.** 4786 Homer Spit Rd., Homer, AK 99603. ☎ **907/235-0400,** 800/478-0400 in Alaska only. www.alaskan.com/landsendresort. 61 units. TV TEL. High season, $109–$150 double. Low season, $75–$120 double. Additional person in room $10 extra. AE, DC, DISC, MC, V.

Traditionally *the* place to stay in Homer, Land's End would be popular no matter what it was like inside because of its location at the tip of Homer Spit, the best spot in Homer and possibly the best spot for a hotel in all Alaska. It's composed of a line of weathered buildings that straggle along the beach crest like driftwood logs, but the interior has been remodeled into comfortable, modern rooms with occasionally fanciful decoration. There are 11 different classes of rooms, ranging from cute shiplike compartments to two-story affairs, and a complex rate schedule to match. The hotel is near the boat harbor, and you can fish right from the beach in front. There's free coffee and a beachfront spa.

The **Chart Room restaurant** makes good use of its wonderful location, looking out over the beach and bay, with a casual, relaxing atmosphere. The deck outside has glass wind shields, making it a warm, satisfying place to sit over coffee on a sunny day. You can watch otters, eagles, and fishing boats while you eat. Excellent chefs have passed through from year to year, so its hard to predict the quality of the cuisine. Locals discuss the current food at Land's End the way some towns talk about their baseball players. I've had simply prepared fresh seafood there that couldn't have been better.

Magic Canyon Ranch Bed and Breakfast. 40015 Waterman Rd., Homer, AK 99603. ☎ and fax **907/235-6077.** magiccanyonranch.com. 4 units, 2 with bathroom. High season, $85–$100 double. Low season, $55–$70 double. Rates include full breakfast. Additional adult in room $25 extra; additional child in room $20 extra. MC, V.

At the top of a canyon road off East End Road, the Webb family shares its charming home, 74 unspoiled acres, tree house, and sweeping views with guests, a cat, and a herd of retired llama. The air is mountain clear and quiet between the high canyon walls—one starts to relax upon getting out of the car. They serve sherry in the evening and a full breakfast in the morning. The four rooms, some nestled cozily under the eaves, are decorated in country and Victorian style.

Old Town Bed and Breakfast. 106-D W. Bunnell, Homer, AK 99603. ☎ **907/235-7558.** Fax 907/235-1503. www.xyz.net/~oldtown. 3 units, 1 with private bathroom. High season, $65–$75 double. Low season, 25% discount. Rates include breakfast. Additional person in room $15 extra. MC, V.

Artist and lifelong Homer resident Asia Freeman and her husband, Kurt Marquardt, casually host a bed-and-breakfast that combines the artiness of the excellent Bunnell Street Gallery downstairs (see "Attractions," above) and the funky, historic feel of the old trading post/hardware store that the building used to house. The wood floors undulate with age and settling, and the tall, double-hung windows, looking out at Bishop's Beach, are slightly cockeyed. Antiques and handmade quilts complete the charming ambiance. They serve a full breakfast on weekends, and during the week you get a continental breakfast at the wonderful Two Sisters Bakery, downstairs. Not a good choice for people who have trouble with stairs.

Seaside Farm. 58335 East End Rd. (right on Seaside Farm Rd.), Homer, AK 99603. ☎ **907/235-7850.** www.xyz.net/~seaside. 4 units, 9 cabins, 12 hostel beds. $55 cabin for two; $15 per person hostel bunk; $6 campsite. Additional person in room or cabin $12 extra. MC, V.

Take a step back in time—all the way to the 1960s. Mossy Kilcher's farm is populated by Morgan horses, cows, chickens, pigeons, and latter-day hippies, many of whom do chores in exchange for their room: 2½ hours of work equals a night in the hostel bunks, and 90 minutes earns a campsite in the pasture above the bay. Campers have use of an outdoor cooking and washing area, and autumn raspberry picking. Some of the primitive cabins sit in lovely, quiet places. Homer's pioneering Kilcher family spawned the singer **Jewel** (Kilcher), although you're not likely to see her around here anymore. If you can catch Mossy floating through, she'll answer any question about Homer or about birds with a breezy smile and a Swiss accent.

Ocean Shores Motel. 3500 Crittenden, Homer, AK 99603 ☎ **907/235-7775.** Fax 907/235-8639. www.akoceanshores.com. 38 units. TV TEL. High season $95–$130, low season $70–$75. Additional person in room $5 extra. DISC, MC, V. Closed Jan–Mar.

Buildings on a grassy compound overlook Kachemak Bay, with a path leading down to Bishop's Beach and nearby tide pooling, yet the location is right off the Sterling Highway as you enter town, within walking distance of downtown Homer. Rooms are fresh and bright, most with private balconies, and many with kitchens. A few less expensive rooms aren't as up-to-date and lack the stunning views, but they still have cute touches. It's a family business, and they've decorated the place with photographs and art collected over five generations in Alaska. The hospitality matches.

CAMPING

The most popular place to camp in Homer is out on the Spit. Tenters camp on the southwestern, ocean side, and RVs park around the boat harbor on the opposite side. It can be windy and sometimes crowded, and toilet facilities are minimal; but waking up on a bright, pebbled beach makes up for much. Tent campers can also go to Seaside Farm, mentioned above.

If you want hookups for your RV, there are plenty of places to go off the Spit. See the Driftwood Inn, above. **Oceanview RV Park** (☎ **907/235-3951**), at 455 Sterling Hwy., Homer, AK 99603, has 86 spaces near the downtown area with frontage on Bishop's Beach. They charge $24.95 a night for full hookups, including cable TV.

WILDERNESS LODGES

These four lodges all are based across Kachemak Bay from Homer, each in its own remote cove or bay, and each in its own market niche, from budget family travel to accommodations only the wealthy can afford. It's wise to reserve any of these the previous winter. More places to stay, some with wilderness lodge qualities, are listed below under Halibut Cove and Seldovia.

Across the Bay Tent and Breakfast. On Kasitsna Bay (P.O. Box 81), Seldovia, AK 99663 (winter P.O. Box 112054, Anchorage, AK 99511; 907/345-2571). ☎ **907/235-3633.** www. tentandbreakfast.com. 6 tents. $48 per person with breakfast, $75 with all meals. Children 6–11 half price, 5 and under free.

Like a summer camp, large canvas tents on wooden platforms stand by themselves on a steep hillside among towering spruce trees with a central house for meals, an organic garden to produce the food, an outhouse with a stained glass window, and a forest volleyball court for games. A long beachfront faces placid Kasitsna Bay—that's where water taxis drop off visitors and guided sea kayaking excursions depart ($95 per person). Up the stairs by the road, mountain bikes are for rent ($25 a day) to explore the area's network of abandoned logging roads or pedal to Seldovia. The tents have beds, but you sleep in your own bag. For families, it's an easy and inexpensive way to the wilderness.

✪ **Kachemak Bay Wilderness Lodge.** China Poot Bay (P.O. Box 956), Homer, AK 99603. ☎ **907/235-8910.** Fax 907/235-8911. www.xyz.net/~wildrnes/lodge.htm. 5 cabins. $2,500 per person, 5-day stay. Rates include all meals. Mon–Fri package only. No credit cards; checks accepted. Closed Oct 15–May 1.

I can think of no more idyllic a way to become acquainted with Alaska's marine wilderness than at this intimate, luxurious lodge, run for more than 25 years by hospitable and generous Mike and Diane McBride—I only wish it were affordable for more people, because it's a place of unforgettable experiences. The McBrides' meals are legendary, and their four cabins manage to seem rustic while having every comfort; it's easy to pretend you're the only guest. But their site, on China Poot Bay, is what's really special—it has excellent tide pooling, kayaking, a black-sand beach, and good hiking trails nearby. Experienced, environmentally conscious guide service is included for sea kayaking, hiking, and wildlife watching; outings by boat carry an extra charge.

Their **Chenik Bear Camp,** on the remote western side of Cook Inlet, near the extraordinary McNeil River State Game Sanctuary, sits in a protected lagoon among treeless hills of blowing wildflowers. This is superb wildlife habitat, especially for brown bears, and entirely untouched by human influence. Rates for the 5-day program are similar to their Kachemak Bay lodge.

Sadie Cove Wilderness Lodge. P.O. Box 2265, Homer, AK 99603. ☎ **888/283-7234** or 907/235-2350. www.sadiecove.com. 4 cabins. $150 per person per night. No credit cards.

This place reminded me of Swiss Family Robinson. Its weathered buildings of rough-cut lumber—owner Keith Iverson hauled and milled them of driftwood—climb the steep shore of the Sadie Cove fjord amid the sound of clattering water from a creek that provides the electricity and fills the wood-fired hot tub, itself an old boat set into the ground. Keith's wife, Randi, provides the softening touches and cooks the seafood dinners that complete the enchanting experience. Most activities, such as sea kayaking, fishing, and tours, are booked separately.

Tutka Bay Wilderness Lodge. P.O. Box 960, Homer, AK 99603. ☎ **800/606-3909** or 907/235-3905. Fax 907/235-3909. www.tutkabaylodge.com. 4 cabins. $300–$350 per person per night. Rates include all meals. 3-night minimum stay. MC, V. Closed Oct–Apr.

John and Nelda Osgood's personalities are reflected in the amazing place they've built—open and enthusiastic, perfectionist and safety conscious, clean-cut but truly Alaskan. On pilings and on a narrow, grassy isthmus by the green water of the Tutka Bay fjord they've put together what amounts to an upscale hotel in the wilderness, with cabins connected by long boardwalks, a deck large enough for a helicopter to land on, and a kitchen capable of producing gourmet meals. It's quite a feat—the water system alone is a wonder. There's plenty to do: tide pool walks, bird watching, hiking, berry picking, and other activities around the lodge, and you can pay extra for guided fishing, kayaking, bear viewing flights, fishing, and other outdoor experiences that go farther afield.

DINING

Homer has inspired culinary art as good as the visual art in the galleries, and today the town is second only to Anchorage in its concentration of excellent restaurants. Besides those listed here, don't miss the **Chart Room** at Land's End, described under "Accommodations," above. For good fast food in an attractive beachfront dining room, try **Boardwalk Fish and Chips** (☎ 907/235-7749), on the boardwalk across from the harbormaster's office on the Spit.

✪ **Café Cups.** 162 W. Pioneer Ave. ☎ **907/235-8330.** Reservations recommended. Lunch $6–$10; dinner $14–$21. MC, V. High season, daily 7:30am–10pm; low season daily 7:30am–3pm. CREATIVE/ECLECTIC.

The facade of the yellow house on Pioneer Avenue, with its elaborate bas-relief sculpture, is truthful advertising for the arty restaurant and creative food to be found inside. Somehow, just sitting in the small, hand-craft dining room makes you feel sophisticated. The menu specializes in surprises—ways of preparing fresh local seafood using the cooking styles of the world in ways that no one may have thought of before. The experiments seem to work (they've earned a reputation all over the state) and the prices are reasonable. Recently bought by the folks who own the Homestead, mentioned below, the service and hospitality are at once professional and warm. Beer and wine are available.

Duncan House Diner. 125 E. Pioneer Ave. ☎ **907/235-5344.** Lunch $4–$8.50. Dinner $10–$17. DISC, MC, V. Thus–Mon 7am–9pm, Tues–Weds 7am–2pm. DINER/STEAK/SEAFOOD

The locals nest on the counter stools to sip coffee and tease the waitresses, who give as good as they get—one of them is the owner. Most tables are in booths in the open dining room, which is decorated with memorabilia such as old license plates, advertisements, clocks, and the like. The hearty breakfasts and lunches are a cut above typical diner fare, and dinners include steaks, halibut, fettuccini, and other items you'd expect to find only in a fancier place. The atmosphere can be smoky.

Fresh Sourdough Express Bakery and Restaurant. 1316 Ocean Dr. ☎ **907/235-7571.** Lunch $5–$8. MC, V. High season, daily 7am–10pm. Low season, daily 8am–5pm. Closed Jan–Mar.

Ebullient Donna Maltz's organic eatery is quintessential Homer, starting with its motto, "Food for people and the planet." But there's no New Age dogma here: Sourdough Express is fun and tasty, even as it grinds its own grain and recycles everything in sight. An inexpensive menu is served all day with items such as reindeer or halibut hoagies and various vegetarian choices, and in the evening they add fine dining seafood specials. They pack lunches for outings, too. Don't miss dessert. The aptly named "Obscene Brownie," covered with espresso and ice cream, left me in a happy daze for the rest of the afternoon.

✪ **The Homestead.** Mile 8.2, East End Rd. ☎ **907/235-8723.** Reservations recommended. Dinner $17–$25. AE, MC, V. Summer daily 5–10pm, winter 5–10pm. STEAK/SEAFOOD.

The ambience is of an old-fashioned Alaska roadhouse, in a large log building with spare decoration and stackable metal chairs, but the food is as satisfying as I've had anywhere in Alaska. After a day outdoors, it's a warm, exuberant dinner house. Local paintings of marine scenes punctuate the noisy dining room. Many menu items are charbroiled, but the cuisine is far more thoughtful than the typical steak-and-seafood house, including adventurous and creative concoctions along with the simple, perfectly broiled fish and meat. Service is cordial but sometimes slow. Full liquor license.

HOMER IN THE EVENING

The **Pier One Theatre** (☎ 907/235-7333; www.xyz.net/~lance) is a strong community theater group housed in a small, corrugated-metal building on the Spit, just short of the small-boat harbor on the left. Instead of the ubiquitous gold rush melodrama and Robert Service readings, Pier One often presents serious drama, musicals, and comedy—not just schlock. They also produce dance, classical music, and youth theater events during the summer. There's generally something playing Thursday through Sunday nights in the summer. Check the *Homer News* for current listings. Tickets are available at the door, or can be reserved by phone.

There are lots of bars in Homer. The landmark **Salty Dawg** is a small log cabin on the Spit with a lighthouse on top. It's the place to swap fish stories after a day on the water.

12 Halibut Cove: Venice on Kachemak Bay

A visit to the tight, roadless little community of Halibut Cove, across Kachemak Bay from Homer, is like a dream for many visitors. All the best things about a visit to the bay are here: a boat ride, the chance of seeing otters or seals, a top-notch restaurant, several galleries and open studios with some of Alaska's best fine fishy art, and even cozy, welcoming accommodations. The settlement sits on either side of a narrow, peaceful channel between a small island and the mainland; the water in between is the only road. Boardwalks connect the buildings, and stairs reach down to the water from houses perched on pilings over the shore. The post office is on a floating dock. The pace of life runs no faster than the tide.

It's also an essentially private community. Unless you have your own boat, an excursion boat is the only way to get there. The **Jakolof Bay ferry** goes to Halibut Cove (see Homer section, above), but the main route is via the boat owned by the community's restaurant. Once there, you have to leave according to plan, as there's no business district and everything is privately owned. You're really a guest the whole time you're in Halibut Cove—the community is open for visitors, however they arrive, only between 1 and 9pm, unless you're staying at one of the lodges.

GETTING THERE

The classic wooden boat *Danny J* (book through Central Charters at ☎ 907/235-7847—full listing in the Homer section under "Booking Agencies") leaves Homer daily in the summer at noon, brings back day-trippers, and takes over dinner guests at 5pm, then brings back the diners later in the evening. The noon trip includes bird watching at Gull Island. Seating is mostly outdoors, and I wouldn't take the trip in the rain. You also take the *Danny J* if you're spending the night in Halibut Cove. The noon trip is $42 for adults, and the dinner trip is $21, but you're obliged to buy a meal at the restaurant. Kids are $21 both times; seniors $34 at noon and $18 for dinner. The same family operates a steel boat, the *Storm Bird,* which carries passengers at noon in summer, overflow other times, and runs all winter as the mail boat. Reservations and fares are identical to the *Danny J.*

ATTRACTIONS

On an afternoon trip, you can bring lunch or eat at the Saltry, described below, and then explore along the **boardwalk** that runs from the restaurant along Ismailof Island past the galleries, boat shops, and houses. There's also a barnyard where kids, who already will be in heaven, can look at rabbits, chickens, ponies, and other animals. Fine art is the major industry in this community of fewer than 100 residents, with 16 artists in residence and three galleries. The **Halibut Cove's Experience Fine Art Gallery,** P.O. Box 6468, Halibut Cove, AK 99603 (☎ **907/296-2215**), is first past the farm on the boardwalk, on pilings above the water. The airy room contains works only by Halibut Cove artists. Farther on, Diana Tillion, who, with her husband, Clem, pioneered the community, opens her **Cove Gallery** and studio to guests. Since the 1950s, she has worked almost exclusively in octopus ink, painstakingly extracted with a hypodermic needle. Alex Combs, a grand old Picassolike figure among Alaska artists, takes visitors at his studio even though he often isn't there. The building is marked by a huge self-portrait and a sign reading, "Leave money, take pottery and paintings."

ACCOMMODATIONS

The Quiet Place Lodge. P.O. Box 6474, Halibut Cove, AK 99603. ☎ **907/296-2212.** Fax 907/296-2241. 5 cabins with shared bathroom. No TV or TEL. $185 per night, double. Open Memorial Day–Labor Day. MC, V.

This family owned bed-and-breakfast sits perched on pilings that seem to climb up the side of the mainland across the water from the Saltry restaurant (see below). The five cabins, linked by stairs and boardwalks, are attractively decorated with local art and look out on the cove. They share bathrooms in the main lodge, where there's also a large rec room with a library, refrigerator, and microwave for guests. A full breakfast is served, and dinners are available 4 nights a week for $30 each. Rooms come with a row boat to get across to the Saltry and they rent kayak and skiffs from the float below the lodge, essential to explore the area. A trail out back goes to Peterson Bay tide pooling.

DINING

Saltry. On the main channel, Halibut Cove. ☎ **907/235-7847.** Lunch $10-$18, Dinner: $18-$20. MC, V. SEAFOOD.

This restaurant operates in conjunction with the *Danny J,* and sits on pilings in an idyllic setting, over the edge of the smooth, deep green of the cove's main watery avenue. You can sit back on the deck and sip microbrews and eat fresh baked bread, mussels, and locally grown salads, followed by fresh fish grilled over charcoal. Prices are on the high side, but it's hard to mind. Make reservations with Central Charters at the same time you reserve your *Danny J* tickets.

13 Seldovia: Slowing Down

The last time we visited this town of around 300 near the tip of the Kenai Peninsula, a group of children walked up to us in the empty main street and asked, in a friendly way, what we were doing there. That's how quiet Seldovia is. But early in this century, Seldovia was a metropolis, acting as a major hub for the Cook Inlet area with steamers coming and going with fish and cargo. Unconnected to the road system, the town's decline was steady until 1964, when the Good Friday earthquake destroyed most of what was left. The entire Kenai Peninsula sank, and high tides began covering the boardwalks that comprised most of the city. When the U.S. Army Corps of Engineers came to the rescue, they replaced the boardwalks with rock and gravel and erased much of the waterfront's charm. A short section of the old boardwalk that remains runs along peaceful **Seldovia Slough,** where king salmon run in early summer and a sea otter is in regular residence—you can get a close look at him, if you're patient. The other roads and trails around town make for pleasant walks. Here you can wander in and out of the forest, beach walk, see what a real Alaska fishing town is like without seeing many other tourists, and maybe see wildlife—eagles certainly and maybe bears.

ESSENTIALS
GETTING THERE

BY BOAT   The trip across Kachemak Bay to Seldovia is one of the best parts of going there. Go at least one way on the **Rainbow Tours** (☎ **907/235-7272**) boat (full listing in the Homer section, under "Natural History Tours"). You have a good chance of seeing otters, seals, sea lions, puffins, and eagles, and you may see whales. The adult fare is $45, and the boat stays 2 hours in Seldovia—long enough for most people to see the town. Bring your own lunch, however, or you'll spend most of your excursion in one of Seldovia's restaurants.

BY PLANE   You can also fly on one of Homer's air-taxis. It's a cheap way to do a flightseeing trip. **Homer Air** (☎ **907/235-8591**) is one good operator, charging $55 round-trip.

BY FERRY   The Alaska Marine Highway System ferry *Tustumena* (see "Homer," above) also visits Seldovia from Homer, but stays briefly.

VISITOR INFORMATION

Seldovia has a population, as the local slogan goes, of "307 people and a few old crabs," but there is a **Seldovia Chamber of Commerce** (☎ **907/234-7612;** P.O. Box F, Seldovia, AK 99663-0150), with a wonderful Web site, including community news, at www.xyz.net/~seldovia.

Fast Facts: Seldovia

Banks   There's no bank, and many businesses don't take credit cards. In a pinch, go to Seldovia Mart, where the cash register takes debit cards and they'll give extra cash in change.

Hospital   The Seldovia Medical Clinic (☎ 907/234-7825) is at Main Street and Anderson Way.

Police   For nonemergency service, call ☎ 907/234-7640.

Taxes   Sales tax is 5%.

ATTRACTIONS & ACTIVITIES

The **Otterbahn Trail,** built by students at the Susan B. English School, leads through woods, wetlands, and beach cliffs to Outer Beach, where there's a picnic shelter. Allow a couple of hours. Unfortunately, there are few other hiking trails, but dirt roads around town lead to some fine **berry picking** grounds, where in late summer and fall you can quickly collect enough berries for a pie. Those roads also make for intriguing and secluded **mountain biking.** There are many miles to explore without encountering another soul. You can rent bikes at The Buzz coffee shop, listed below, or rent bikes at one of the agencies listed in the Homer section and carry them across. With the lack of hiking trails, bikes really are needed to get into the woods.

The area also is good for **sea kayaking,** although not quite as appealing as the less windy areas mentioned above in the Homer section. **Kayak'atak,** P.O. Box 109, Seldovia, AK 99663 (☎ **907/234-7425**), operating out of Herring Bay Mercantile, offers rentals and guided trips. Seldovia also is considerably closer to the **halibut** grounds than Homer; drop by the **harbormaster** (☎ **907/234-7886**) for a referral.

There are several **shops** worth visiting, all on the main street. A tiny, picturesque **Russian Orthodox church** stands on the hill above the town, built in 1891. Call the Chamber of Commerce to find out how to get in.

ACCOMMODATIONS

Dancing Eagles Bed and Breakfast and Cabin Rental. On the boardwalk (P.O. Box 264), Seldovia, AK 99663 (in winter, P.O. Box 240067, Anchorage, AK 99524). ☎ **907/234-7627** in summer, 907/278-0288 in winter. Fax 907/278-0289 in winter. www.dancingeagles.com. 5 units, none with private bathroom; 1 cabin. $85 double; $125 cabin. No credit cards. Closed Oct–Apr.

The boardwalk leads to this large house, cabin, and outbuildings, all nestled on rocks and pilings above the slough and connected by their own boardwalks. Guests can use the hot tub and sauna and watch the otter who lives in the water just outside. Three rooms under the eaves upstairs are cute but very small; two other rooms are larger, as is the cabin, which has a deck, a view of the boat harbor, and its own cooking facilities. A continental breakfast is included in the price.

Seldovia's Boardwalk Hotel. 243 Main St. (P.O. Box 72), Seldovia, AK 99663. ☎ **800/238-7862** or 907/234-7816. www.alaskaone.com/boardwalkhotel. 13 units. TEL. $89–$130 double. DISC, MC, V. Closed Oct–Apr.

This Seldovia institution has light, comfortable rooms with private baths and phones. Despite the name, it isn't on the boardwalk but does stand at the top of the small-boat harbor, so rooms on the water side have a great view. They offer a $129 package from Homer, which includes a boat tour over and a flightseeing trip back—quite a deal. There's a courtesy car and free coffee in the lobby.

DINING

The Buzz Coffeehouse Cafe. At the north end of the boat harbor. ☎ **907/234-7479**. mid-Mar to mid-Sept 6am–6pm daily. CAFE/VEGETARIAN.

An espresso shop with tasty quiche, baked goods, and vegetarian dishes. They rent.

Mad Fish Restaurant. At the south end of the harbor on Main St. ☎ **907/234-7676**. Summer daily 11:30am-3pm; Sun-Thurs 5-8pm, Fri-Sat 5-9pm.

Serves fresh seafood, steaks, burgers, and vegetarian dishes for lunch and dinner daily.

14 Valdez: City in a Fjord

Big events have shaped Valdez (val-*deez*). The deep-water port, at the head of a long, dramatic fjord, first developed with the 1898 Klondike Gold Rush and the ill-fated attempt to establish an alternative route to the gold fields from here. Later, the port and the Richardson Highway, which connected Valdez to the rest of the state, served a key role in supplying materials during World War II. On Good Friday, March 27, 1964, all of that was erased when North America's greatest recorded earthquake occurred under Miners Lake, west of town off a northern fjord of Prince William Sound, setting off an underwater landslide that caused a huge wave to sweep over the waterfront, killing 32 people. The town sank and was practically destroyed. The U.S. Army Corps of Engineers rebuilt a drab replacement in a new, safer location that slowly filled with nondescript modern buildings over the next two decades. A walking tour provides the locations of a few buildings that were moved to the new town site. The construction of the trans-Alaska pipeline, completed in 1977, brought a new economic boom to Valdez and enduring economic prosperity as tankers came to fill with the oil. Then, on March 24, 1989, on Good Friday 25 years after the earthquake, the tanker *Exxon Valdez*, on its way south, hit the clearly marked Bligh Reef, causing the largest and most environmentally costly oil spill ever in North America. The spill cleanup added another economic boom.

Today, Valdez is a middle American town, driven by industry but turning to the vast resources of Prince William Sound for outdoor recreation. In town you can tour the interesting history museum and fish hatchery, and take a hike or a river float, but otherwise the city itself is short on charm or attractions for a visitor. The real reasons to come have to do with the setting—the wildlife, fishing, and sightseeing in the Sound, and the spectacular drive down the Richardson Highway.

Because Valdez lies at the end of a funnel of steep mountains that catches moisture off the ocean, the weather tends to be overcast and rainy. For the same reason, the area receives phenomenal snow falls, measured in the tens of feet. Although there is no developed skiing, Valdez attracts many "extreme" skiers for helicopter and snowcat skiing in the mountains behind town in late winter.

ESSENTIALS
GETTING THERE
BY CAR   The **Richardson Highway,** described in chapter 9, "The Alaskan Interior," is unbelievably dramatic as it crosses Thompson Pass and descends into the narrow valley where Valdez lies. Try to do the trip in daylight, in clear weather, and stop at the Worthington Glacier. This is the only road to Valdez. The drive from Anchorage is roughly 7 hours.

BY BUS   Gray Line's **Alaskon Express** (☎ 800/544-2206) runs to Anchorage daily in the summer, taking 10 hours for the trip; the fare is $68.

BY FERRY   The **Alaska Marine Highway System** (☎ 800/642-0066 or 907/835-4436; www.dot.state.ak.us/external/amhs/home.html) calls on Valdez daily in the summer with the *Bartlett,* a ferry connecting Valdez, Whittier, and Cordova. The *Tustumena* comes from Seward roughly once a week. One time-tested way to see the Sound is to put your vehicle on the ferry in Whittier for the 6½-hour run to Valdez, then drive north on the Richardson Highway. A ranger rides on board to present programs, and the ferry stops for pictures at Columbia Glacier. The fare is $72 for a car up to 15 feet long and $58 for an adult passenger (children half price).

BY TOUR BOAT   **Prince William Sound Cruises and Tours** (☎ 800/992-1297 or 907/835-4731, full listing below) offers daily summer cruises between Whittier and

Valdez, including lunch and a tour of the pipeline terminal, for $119 one-way ($59 ages 4 to 12). The boat leaves Valdez at 7:15am and leaves Whittier at 2:15pm.

BY AIR **Era Aviation** (☎ 800/866-8394 or 907/835-2636) flies many times a day each way between Anchorage and Valdez.

GETTING AROUND

BY BIKE Once you're downtown, you can walk Valdez, although a bicycle will extend your range. They're for rent at **Beaver Sports,** 316 Galena St. (☎ 907/ 835-4727), rents mountain bikes for $5 an hour and $20 for 24 hours.

BY TAXI To get to the airport, taxis are available from **Valdez Yellow Cab** (☎ 907/ 835-2500).

BY RENTAL CAR **Hertz** (☎ 800/654-3131) is the only national car-rental chain with a local office. **Valdez-U-Drive,** P.O. Box 1396, Valdez, AK 99686 (☎ 907/ 835-4402), also rents cars at the airport.

BY BUS TOUR **Sentimental Journeys,** P.O. Box 2175, Valdez, AK 99686 (☎ 907/835-4988), offers historic town tours in a 1937 bus.

VISITOR INFORMATION

The Valdez Convention and Visitors Bureau maintains a **Visitor Information Center,** at 200 Chenega Ave., a block off Egan Drive (P.O. Box 1603), Valdez, AK 99686 (☎ 800/770-5954 or 907/835-4636, or in winter 907/835-2984; www.alaska.net/ ~valdezak/). Pick up the free town map and useful *Vacation Planner.* They're open in summer daily from 8am to 8pm, and normal business hours in the winter. A booking agency, **One Call Does It All,** at 210 N. Harbor Dr. (P.O. Box 2197), Valdez, AK 99686 (☎ 907/835-4988; fax 907/835-5865; e-mail: onecall@alaska.net), reserves lodgings, fishing charters, activities, and tours in the area.

SPECIAL EVENTS

The Valdez Ice Climbing Festival (☎ 907/835-2984) is held on Presidents' weekend, in February, on the frozen waterfalls of Keystone Canyon. **The Snow Man Festival** (☎ 907/835-2330), held in early March, is a winter carnival with a food fair, ice bowling, snowman building, and a drive-in movie projected on a snow bank. **The World Extreme Skiing Championships** (☎ 907/835-2108; www.wesc.com) is held in late March or early April on the faces of mountains north of Valdez, where invited professional skiers from North America and Europe hurl themselves down near-vertical, powder-filled chutes competing in speed and style. It's an internationally recognized daredevil competition, with one death and many injuries in its history.

Three **summer fishing derbies** are organized by the Valdez Chamber of Commerce (☎ 907/835-2330), with prizes that have totaled more than $75,000. The **Halibut Derby** runs all summer, the **Pink Salmon Derby** during most of July, and the **Silver Salmon Derby** is through August until early September. Check with the visitor center or buy a ticket at the boat-rental booth in the harbor. **The Edward Albee Theater Conference** (☎ 907/835-2678) brings famous playwrights and directors to the community for seminars and performances in June. Arthur Miller, Albee, and other famous writers have met the public here in fairly intimate settings.

Fast Facts: Valdez

Banks There are two banks on Egan Drive, both with ATMs.

Hospital The Valdez Community Hospital (☎ 907/835-2249) is located at 911 Meals Ave.

Valdez

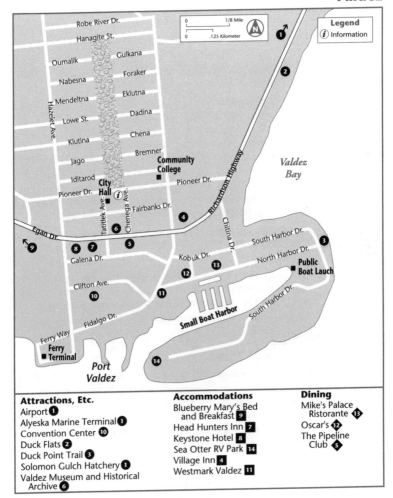

Legend
ⓘ Information

Attractions, Etc.
Airport ❶
Alyeska Marine Terminal ❶
Convention Center ❿
Duck Flats ❷
Duck Point Trail ❸
Solomon Gulch Hatchery ❶
Valdez Museum and Historical
 Archive ❻

Accommodations
Blueberry Mary's Bed
 and Breakfast ❾
Head Hunters Inn ❼
Keystone Hotel ❽
Sea Otter RV Park ⓮
Village Inn ❹
Westmark Valdez ⓫

Dining
Mike's Palace
 Ristorante ⓭
Oscar's ⓬
The Pipeline
 Club ❺

Internet/E-mail   MacCopy's, at 354 Fairbanks St. (☎ 907/835-8748), offers Internet access and fax and copying services.

Police   For nonemergency business with the Valdez Police Department, call ☎ 907/835-4560.

Post Office   On Galena Drive, 1 block back from the Egan Drive business strip.

Taxes   Valdez has no sales tax, but does charge a 6% bed tax.

ATTRACTIONS

The Valdez Museum and Historical Archive. 217 Egan Ave. ☎ **907/835-2764.** www.alaska.net/~vldzmuse/index.html. $3 adults, $2.50 over age 65, $2 ages 14–18, free for children under age 14. Summer, Mon–Sat 8am–6pm and Sun 8am–5pm; winter, Mon–Fri 10am–5pm, Sat noon–4pm.

Contains an exceptional history display that follows the story of the area from early white exploration through the oil spill. It's a little light on Alaska Native culture, but there are other museums for that. Each gallery is well designed and some are fun, like the restored bar room. There's also a saltwater aquarium and an area with transportation relics, including shiny fire engines dating back to 1886. They're working on a diorama of old Valdez, which promises to be fascinating.

The Solomon Gulch Hatchery. On Dayville Rd. on the way to the tanker terminal. ☎ **907/835-1329**. The free, self-guided tour is always open.

This place hosts one of Alaska's more impressive salmon hatchery tours, especially when the pink salmon are returning, late June through early August. The hatchery releases more than 200 million pinks each year, as well as millions of chums and silvers (or coho); and when those fish come back to spawn, it can be an awesome sight. There is no stream for the salmon to return to, so they try to get back into the hatchery, crowding together in a solid sea of fighting muscle. Seals and birds come in to feed, and you can stand on shore and watch the spectacle. (Surefire fishing is allowed up the shore—see "Fishing," below.) A self-guided walking tour leads through the hatchery and into some buildings, getting up close to tanks and pools where workers raise and breed millions of fish.

Alyeska Pipeline Marine Terminal Bus Tour. Operated by Valdez Tours, corner of Pioneer and Tatitlek sts. ☎ **907/835-2686**. $15 adults, $7.50 children, age 5 and under free. May–Sept.

The 2-hour ride begins at their office and visits the terminal where tankers carrying up to a quarter of the nation's domestic oil supply are loaded. You can't enter any of the buildings. The highlights are a chance to see the big ships and an impressive scenic overlook, the only point where you can get off the bus.

GETTING OUTSIDE
SIGHTSEEING & WILDLIFE TOURS

For most visitors, a daylong ride on a tour boat into the Sound is likely to be the most memorable part of a visit to Valdez. After passing through the long fjord of Port Valdez, the boats enter an ice-choked bay in front of **Columbia Glacier.** The Columbia is immense—3 miles across at its face and 30 miles long—and it is retreating fast, dumping thousands of ice burgs that float over miles of water in front. The smooth surface and weird white and blue shapes look like a vast Henry Moore sculpture garden—one that's been invaded by seals and other wildlife.

Environmental activist Stan Stephens started and still runs the main tour boat company, which he recently sold to the Chugach Native Corporation. Called **Prince William Sound Cruises and Tours,** P.O. Box 1297, Valdez, AK 99686 (☎ **800/992-1297** or 907/835-4731; fax 907/835-3765; www.princewilliamsound.com), its office is at the harbor in Valdez, near the Westmark Hotel. Stephens predicted and was working to prevent an accident like the *Exxon Valdez* grounding right up to the eve of the disaster, and he's still working for improved environmental safeguards for the oil companies. The company offers tours of various length to the glacier and other sites, often seeing seals, sea otters, and sea lions, and sometimes whales. Trips go to Whittier and Meares Glacier, but the primary destination is Columbia Glacier and the company's camp there, on Growler Island, where passengers get off and, on some trips, have a meal and can even spend the night and go boating. Prices range from $69 ($34 ages 4 to 12) for a 6-hour cruise to $119 to visit both glaciers and stop for lunch on the island. You can spend the night on the island for $100 per person, meals included. See "Sea Kayaking & Sailing," below for appealing options to add on a trip to Growler Island.

SEA KAYAKING & SAILING

Jim and Nancy Lethcoe are activists for the Sound, like Stephens, and possess an extraordinary store of knowledge about its natural and cultural history—they wrote the

Columbia Glacier Pros & Cons

On the plus side, it's enormous. The biggest drawback of visiting the Columbia, though, is that you won't see it calve (when ice falls off the face) because boats can't get close enough through all the icebergs. For that you must go to glaciers in the western Sound, such as Meares, but these are closer to Whittier. (Prince William Sound Cruises and Tours can take you to the western Sound from Valdez—see text.)

standard cruising guide to the Sound, as well as many other books. They guide sea kayaking, sailing, hiking, and combinations of all three in front of Columbia Glacier, and rent kayaks for self-guided expeditions. Their **Alaskan Wilderness Sailing & Kayaking Safaris,** P.O. Box 1313, Valdez, AK 99686 (☎ **907/835-5175;** www. alaskanwilderness.com), operates from Growler Island (see "Sightseeing & Wildlife Tours," above, for how to get there). That gives them a big leg up on sea kayaking operations based in towns, because they start right at a fascinating and scenic place. Options range from half a day to a week. Day trips include kayaking in inflatable boats or sailing single-person trimarans; sailing in their 40-foot yacht and then kayaking and hiking; and various combinations. Half-day kayaking or sailing is $50, full day $89 (plus the cost of getting to Growler Island), and a weeklong expedition is $1,750. They rent rigid kayaks to experienced paddlers, $45 single or $65 double.

Raven Charters, Slip C-25, Valdez Boat Harbor (P.O. Box 2581), Valdez, AK 99686 (☎ **907/835-5863;** www.alaska.net/~ravenchr/), is run by a family that lives on its 50-foot boat and take clients **sailing** and exploring the Sound. The wind tends to be light and changeable, but a sailboat makes a comfortable base for discovering interesting, isolated places. All-inclusive prices start at $750 per night for up to four passengers, or $600 for a day charter.

For kayaking right from Valdez, **Anadyr Adventures,** at 217 N. Harbor Dr. (☎ **800/TO-KAYAK** or 907/835-2814; www.alaska.net/~anadyr/), by the boat harbor, offers 3-hour kayak tours for $55, or day trips to Shoup Glacier for $139 or Columbia Glacier for $169 (with a group of four). They also lead multiday trips and rent kayaks.

Experienced kayakers and outdoors people have unlimited possibilities in Prince William Sound. One idea is to take your kayak on the ferry *Tustumena's* weekly trip from Valdez to Seward (see "Getting There," above) for the whistle stop in the village of Chenega Bay, so you can start out inexpensively in deep wilderness. The ferry stops there only when a passenger has a reservation.

FISHING & BOATING

The ocean waters around Valdez are rich in salmon and halibut. From shore, you can fish for salmon on Allison Point, along Dayville Road on the far side of the port from Valdez. Salmon here are returning to the Solomon Gulch Hatchery and are primarily pinks in July and silvers in August and September. The success rate is high when the fish are running—one wild year, fish literally jumped into boats—but it's not the most aesthetic fishing experience, right along a road with many other people. Most Alaskans I know shun fishing for pinks (see "Fishing," in chapter 2.)

To get to more isolated fishing, use one of the **fishing charters** available in the boat harbor. Halibut charters cost around $150 per person, as they have to go a long way. Half-day salmon charters are around $80, for trolling right in Port Valdez. The Valdez Chamber of Commerce (☎ 907/835-2330) publishes a *Valdez Fishing Charter Guide* including fliers from each of the charters. **Popeye Charters** (☎ **907/835-2659**) is reliable, and **Lil' Fox Charters** (☎ **907/479-0006**) also is a longtime operator. The

One Call Does It All booking agency (listed under "Visitor Information," above) books charters.

If you're up for running your own boat, they're for rent on the docks from **Valdez Harbor Boat and Tackle Rentals** (☎ 907/835-5002); a 16-foot boat costs $125 a day, plus fuel. You can get all the gear you need there. Or use the boat to explore the area, perhaps with a visit to Shoup Glacier, 20 minutes west. Renting a boat overnight, you can pull up on an uninhabited island and set up camp.

Ketchum Air Service (☎ 800/825-9114 or 907/835-3789), offers fly-in fishing starting at $199 per person, and flightseeing trips.

BIRD WATCHING & BEACHCOMBING

Between the airport and downtown Valdez, the **Duck Flats,** a tidal marsh met by a salmon spawning stream, lies along the Richardson Highway. It's a productive bird and marine habitat, busy with activity at spring and fall migrations, and a good place for bird watching or picnicking all summer at one of the two viewing areas. The National Forest Service, which has a ranger station nearby, has set up a salmon-viewing station where you can watch fish do the deed in shallow, clear water. A bird checklist is distributed by the visitor center.

HIKING & MOUNTAIN BIKING

A pleasant forest and shore walk to **Dock Point** borders the opposite side of the Duck Flats from the road, starting at the east side of the boat harbor, at the end of North Harbor Drive. It's a peaceful, natural walk close to town, with boardwalks and overlooks.

For a longer hike and perhaps an overnight, the new, state-maintained **Shoup Glacier trail** runs 12 miles west from town along the shore of Port Valdez to the glacier. The going is generally flat, and there are many places to get down to the beach. Camping is unrestricted, but be sure to bring mosquito repellent. If you plan to go all the way, reserve the state parks cabin there (details are covered at the beginning of the chapter, under "Getting Outside on the Kenai Peninsula & Prince William Sound"). The trail starts at the end of West Egan Drive.

Mineral Creek Road, off Hanagita Street, leads 6 miles along the creek up a canyon into the mountains behind town, where the gravel road gives way to a 1-mile trail to a gold rush era stamp mill. It's a good mountain biking route.

There are several other paths and bike routes in town. The visitor center can give you a list. Mountain bikes are for rent from Beaver Sports, listed above under "Getting Around."

RAFTING

Keystone Raft and Kayak Adventures, P.O. Box 1486, Valdez, AK 99686 (☎ 800/328-8460 or 907/835-2606; www.alaskawhitewater.com), takes five trips a day 4½ miles down the amazing Keystone Canyon, a virtual corridor of rock with a floor of frothing water, past the crashing tumult of the 900-foot Bridal Veil Falls. It's a wild ride, and not without risk—serious mishaps do sometimes occur. They charge $35 per person. The company also has numerous longer trips, ranging from a day to 10 days, on many of the region's rivers.

FLIGHTSEEING

There are plenty of fixed-wing operators at the airport, but I love the extra thrill of helicopters. **Era Helicopters** (☎ 800/843-1947 or 907/835-2595; www.era-aviation.com/helicoptertours) has an office and helipad downtown, near the ferry dock at Hazelet and Fidalgo. A 1-hour, $175 trip overflies Columbia Glacier and lands in front of Shoup Glacier.

ACCOMMODATIONS
HOTELS & B&Bs

Blueberry Mary's Bed and Breakfast. Blueberry Hill Rd., off West Egan Dr. (P.O. Box 1244), Valdez, AK 99686. ☎ 907/835-5015. E-mail: bmary@alaska.net. 2 units. TV TEL. $75 double. No credit cards. Closed in winter.

A lucky few get to sleep under Mary Mehlberg's handmade quilts on her feather beds, gaze at the ocean views, bake in the sauna, and breakfast on her blueberry waffles made from wild berries that grow just outside the house. She only takes parties of two or less and sometimes closes for breaks. Those who do stay here get a terrific deal on hand-crafted rooms with private entrances and a prime location.

Head Hunters Inn. 328 Egan Dr. (P.O. Box 847), Valdez, AK 99686. ☎ **888/635-2906** in Alaska only, or 907/835-2900. 5 units, 1 with private bathroom. TV. High season, $70–$80 double. Low season, $60–$70 double. Additional person in room $15 extra. AE, DISC, MC, V.

The bizarre name is owing to the beauty salon that hostess Ida Rhines runs downstairs—if no one answers at the B&B, inquire there. Once upstairs, you'll find surprisingly comfortable, immaculate accommodations. Four rooms share two bathrooms while a larger downstairs room has its own and costs $10 more. Rhines serves a huge breakfast. The inn is located right on the main street, 3 blocks from the ferry dock, and offers free rides to and from the airport. Smoking is not permitted, and you should call ahead before bringing children.

Keystone Hotel. 401 W. Egan Dr. (P.O. Box 2148), Valdez, AK 99686. ☎ **907/835-3851.** Fax 907/835-5322. www.alaskan.com/keystonehotel. 107 units. TV TEL. $95 double. Rates include continental breakfast. Additional person in room $10 extra. AE, MC, V.

This building, made of modular units, was built by Exxon to serve as their offices for the oil spill cleanup operation but wasn't completed until late summer 1989, so the company occupied it for only about a month. In 1994, after standing vacant, a new owner remodeled it into a hotel, with small rooms that mostly have two twin beds or one double bed, though some have two doubles. Select a room when you check in, as they vary in decor—some with dark paneling, some more modern. All the rooms I saw were clean and pleasant. A coin-op laundry is available.

The Lakehouse Bed and Breakfast. Nine miles from town off the Richardson Highway (P.O. Box 1499, Valdez, AK 99686). ☎ **907/835-4752.** 9 rms, 7 with private bath. $99 double, $4 each additional person. MC, V.

This place has a beautiful, secluded setting overlooking Robe Lake. The rooms vary greatly, so you must arrive early to get your pick.

Village Inn. 100 Meals Ave. (P.O. Box 365), Valdez, AK 99686. ☎ **907/835-4445.** Fax 907/835-2437. 79 units. TV TEL. High season, $129 double. Low season, $85 double. Additional person in room $10 extra. AE, MC, V.

The best standard rooms in town are here, such as you'd find in a midscale chain. They're of comfortable size and attractively decorated in southwestern colors, with features like card-activated locks that most small-town places haven't caught onto yet. The less-desirable 300-level rooms are in a half basement, where there's also an exercise room and sauna. Free coffee and a laundry are available. The **Casa Valdez Restau-**

Other Valdez B&Bs

In addition to the three B&Bs I've listed, Valdez has many others, several quite good. A binder with descriptions is available for inspection at the visitor center (see above).

A Valdez Motel

In addition to the hotels listed, you'll find standard motel rooms at the **Totem Inn,** on the Richardson Highway as it enters town (P.O. Box 648) Valdez, AK 99686 (☎ **907/835-4443;** fax 907/835-5751).

---

rant, across the parking lot, is a family restaurant with booths serving American-style Mexican food, steak, seafood, pasta, and sandwiches.

Westmark Valdez. 100 Fidalgo Dr. (P.O. Box 468), Valdez, AK 99686. ☎ **800/544-0970** (reservations) or 907/835-4391. Fax 907/835-2308. 97 units. TV TEL. High season, $149 double. Low season, $110 double. Additional person in room $15 extra. AE, DC, DISC, MC, V.

This is the only Valdez hotel on the water. There's a pleasant grassy area with tables where you can watch the boats come in the entrance to the small-boat harbor, and the office for Prince William Sound Cruises and Tours is just outside on a dock. The rooms don't all have views, however, and the quality is inconsistent. Some have dark paneling and old green bathroom fixtures, and maintenance appeared to be a problem on my inspection. It's still a decent place to stay, but overpriced at the rack rate—call ahead and ask for the "highway rate," which may save you almost half, making a good bargain. The hotel maintains a tour desk, gift shop, and fuel dock. The hotel's **Captain's Table Restaurant** has the only waterfront dining in Valdez, overlooking the harbor, with main courses ranging from $12 to $17. Unfortunately, the service was poor and the food unimpressive when we last visited.

CAMPING

Valdez is a popular RV destination. When the salmon are running, RVs can park, self-contained, at the **Allison Point** fishing area (☎ 907/835-2282) for $10 a night. The **Sea Otter RV Park,** P.O. Box 947, Valdez, AK 99686 (☎ **800/831-2787** in Alaska only, or 907/835-2787), sits on the outside of the boat harbor breakwater, with views and beachfront where you can fish for salmon or watch the harbor sea otters. They have a laundry and other facilities, and charge $20 for full hookups.

The town's **Valdez Glacier Campground** has 100 well-separated sites among alder and cottonwood trees near the airport, but the trees make it a mosquito haven. They have pit toilets. The fee is $10 a night.

The best campground in the area is the state's **Blueberry Lake Campground,** 24 miles out of town on the Richardson Highway, just below Thompson Pass. The campground is above treeline, with mountaintop views and access to limitless alpine hiking. It can be windy and cold. The small lake is stocked with trout. Fifteen private sites are $10 on a self-serve system. There are pit toilets.

DINING

I'm not really enthusiastic about any restaurant in Valdez, but you can find decent food to sustain you. I like the deep-fried fish at the **Alaska Halibut House,** a fast-food joint at Fairbanks and Meals Avenue. It's open all day. The restaurant at the **Totem Inn** (☎ 907/834-4443), on the Richardson Highway as it comes into town, is the main local hangout. The service is friendly and the food filling, the TV is always on, and coffee cups are never empty. A mural of Port Valdez on one wall seems to show the smoggy haze emitted by the pipeline terminal.

Mike's Palace Ristorante. 201 N. Harbor Dr. ☎ **907/835-2365.** Main courses $9–$25; lunch $5–$9. MC, V. Daily 11am–11pm. PIZZA/STEAK/SEAFOOD.

This is a good, family pizza restaurant, a place where Valdez residents come for a casual evening out. The calzone is good, service skilled, and everything consistent. It's a warm, cheerful place, my favorite in Valdez. Mike's also has a place in history: Capt. Joseph Hazelwood was waiting for a take-out pizza here when he slipped next door to the Club Bar for his last drink before starting the fateful voyage of the *Exxon Valdez* that hit Bligh Reef. Beer and wine license.

Oscar's. 143 N. Harbor Dr. ☎ **907/835-4700.** Lunch $6–$9; dinner $8–$29. MC, V. Daily 6am–10:30pm. BURGERS/STEAK/SEAFOOD.

The brightly lit, rather stark dining room on the waterfront is abuzz with fishers and outdoors people eating at all hours to take advantage of the endless summer days. The service is friendly and quick and the long menu includes solid diner fare and more ambitious entrees of various national cuisines, as well as ice cream, shakes, and other treats. An outdoor covered deck is pleasant on warm days, with a bar serving craft brews, including Alaskan beers.

The Pipeline Club. 112 Egan Dr. ☎ **907/835-4332.** Main courses $7.50–$23.75. AE, DISC, MC, V. Sun–Thus 5:30–11pm, Fri–Sat 5:30pm–midnight.

This traditional beef-and-seafood house is something of a time capsule from the 1970s with its very dark, cocktail ambience, booths, and at least one kidney-shaped table. Our meals showed no flaws, but were unmemorable. You can get lunch in the lounge, with its two TVs, karaoke, and golf simulator. If asked, the bartender will point out the stool where Capt. Joe Hazelwood got loaded on vodka tonics before taking command of the *Exxon Valdez*. Full liquor license.

15 Cordova: Hidden Treasure

The first time I ever went to Cordova, we arrived at the Mudhole Smith Airport in a small plane and happened upon an old guy with a pickup truck who offered to let us ride in back with some boards the 10 miles to town. The highway led out onto a broad, wetland plain—the largest contiguous wetland in the Western Hemisphere, as it happens. Our guide's voice, studded with profanity, boomed through the back window as he told us proudly about the diversity of the wildlife to be found out there. Then, absolutely bursting with enthusiasm, he leaned on the horn and bellowed, "Look at them fucking swans!" We looked; trumpeters paddling in the marsh looked back. He would have invited them along to the bar, too, if he'd known how.

Every time I've been to Cordova since, I've been taken under the wings of new friends. Although they usually don't express themselves the same way that first gentleman did, they are just as enthusiastic to show off the amazing natural riches of their little kingdom. Tourists are still something of a novelty here, for Cordova not only is off the beaten track, it's not on the track at all—there's no road to the rest of the world. Boosters call their town "Alaska's Hidden Treasure." Forgotten treasure would be more like it, for Cordova isn't difficult to get to, and—once there—the charm and attractions of the place are self-evident.

Our family has had some of our happiest times in Cordova. We spent three glorious days visiting the **Childs Glacier** and seeing the swans and geese on the delta, hiking into the mountains behind town, and boating on the Sound to meet the sea otters and sea lions, eagles and spawning salmon—and meeting no other people at all. In town, we made new friends whenever we turned around, and received hearty greetings from the old friends from previous visits. When our ferry left for Valdez, we watched Cordova shrinking behind us with a wistful hope that it would never change, that it would always stay just the way it was in that special time.

It doesn't change much. You can feel a bit like an anthropologist discovering a tribe lost to time, for Cordova has the qualities small towns are supposed to have had but lost long ago in America, if they ever did have them. Walking down First Street, you pass an old-fashioned independent grocery store, the fishermen's union hall, and Steen's gift shop, in the same family since 1909—not chains or franchises. People leave their keys in the car and their doors unlocked at night. When a friend of mine bought one of the quaint, moss-roofed, hillside houses a few years ago, he didn't receive a key—the simple reason was that the front door didn't have a lock.

Yet Cordova also possesses a surprising level of sophistication. Interesting people just want to live there. The commercial fishermen who power the economy enjoy good food and fun stuff to do. Some are politically involved and well connected, battling the oil industry to protect Prince William Sound before the 1989 oil spill and then, after the disaster (which hurt Cordova worst of all), pushing for the money won from Exxon to be spent on the Sound's environment. They want Cordova to stay the way it is—with no road. Another faction in town, the merchants and tourism workers, want a road. The debate is hot, and a few years ago a mayoral election between pro- and antiroad candidates was decided by a single vote.

This controversy has been going on for 50 or 60 years. The town's heyday was in 1911, when the Copper River and Northwestern Railroad opened, carrying copper ore down from the mine at Kennicott; it hit a low when the mine closed in 1938. Since then, boosters have been trying to get a road built on the old rail line, north along the Copper River to Chitina (that fascinating area is covered in chapter 9, "The Alaskan Interior"). The road builders have made it only about 50 miles out of town so far. From Cordova, the **Copper River Highway** provides access to the best bird watching and, in my judgment, the most impressive glacier in Alaska, as well as trails and magnificent vistas and areas to see wildlife. In town, the small-boat harbor is a doorway to Prince William Sound.

ESSENTIALS
GETTING THERE

BY FERRY Cordova is served three times a week from Valdez or Whittier by the ferry *Bartlett* of the **Alaska Marine Highway System** (☎ 800/642-0066 or 907/424-7333; www.dot.state.ak.us/external/amhs/home.html). The ferry schedule allows a 5-hour stay on Fridays—not long enough, in my view—or leaves you in Cordova for 2 or 3 days before returning (unless you fly back). You can spend that much time and more if you enjoy the outdoors. The passenger fare for the 5½-hour run from Valdez is $30, roughly half off for children. It may pay to bring a car, depending on how much time you want to spend out the road, on the delta and at the glacier. Taking a vehicle (under 15 feet) from Valdez to Cordova is $64, but, of course, you'll have to double that to get the car back to Valdez.

BY AIR Alaska Airlines (☎ 800/426-0333 or 907/424-7151; www.alaskaair. com), flies one jet daily each direction, from Anchorage to the west and Yakutat, Juneau, and Seattle to the southeast, with two more flights to Anchorage operated by **Era Aviation** (☎ 800/866-8394).

GETTING FROM THE AIRPORT & FERRY DOCK INTO TOWN The **Airport Shuttle** from the Reluctant Fisherman Hotel (☎ 907/424-3272) meets all planes and charges $9 one-way. Taxis are usually available as well from **Wild Hare Cab** (☎ 907/424-3939). Becky Chapek, who owns the local tour company, meets the ferry and will take you where you need to go for nothing.

GETTING AROUND

You can easily walk around downtown Cordova, but that's not where the most interesting sights are. To get out on the Copper River Highway, you'll need a car, bus (described below), or, if you're vigorous, a bike.

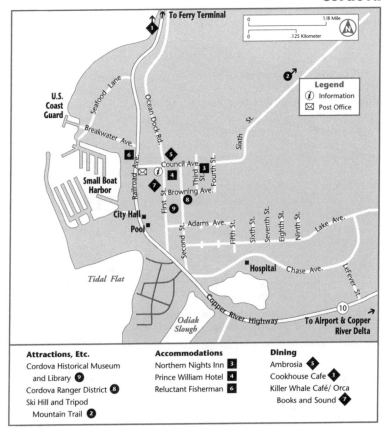

Attractions, Etc.
Cordova Historical Museum
and Library **9**
Cordova Ranger District **8**
Ski Hill and Tripod
Mountain Trail **2**

Accommodations
Northern Nights Inn **3**
Prince William Hotel **4**
Reluctant Fisherman **6**

Dining
Ambrosia **5**
Cookhouse Cafe **1**
Killer Whale Café/ Orca
Books and Sound **7**

BY RENTAL CAR Cars are for rent from the Reluctant Fisherman Hotel (listed below) for $75 a day, without mileage charges; the airport shuttle is free when you rent a car. **Cordova Auto Rentals** (☎ **907/424-5982**) rents cars, vans, and four-wheel-drive vehicles at the airport.

BY BIKE Rent bikes, kayaks, skiffs, canoes, and fishing and camping gear at **Cordova Coastal Outfitters,** at the boat harbor below the fishermen's memorial (P.O. Box 1834) Cordova, AK 99574 (☎ **800/357-5145** or 907/424-7424; e-mail coastal@ptialaska.net). They're described in full below.

VISITOR INFORMATION

A new **Cordova Chamber of Commerce Visitor Center** (☎ **907/424-7260**) is at 404 First St., north of Council Avenue (P.O. Box 99, Cordova, AK 99574). They're open Monday through Friday from noon to 6pm in summer, 1:30 to 5:30pm in winter. Besides the usual information, the center has a 60-minute recorded walking tour that you can listen to as it guides you around town. The folks at the museum and library also provide **visitor information,** at 622 First St. (P.O. Box 391), Cordova, AK 99574 (☎ **907/424-6665**). Summer hours are Monday through Saturday 10am to 6pm, Sunday 2 to 4pm; winter Tuesday through Friday 1 to 5pm. The **Cordova Ranger District** of the Chugach National Forest, upstairs in the old white courthouse at Second Street and Browning (P.O. Box 280), Cordova, AK 99574 (☎ **907/ 424-7661**), has displays and provides maps and guide information indispensable for planning outdoor activities. The rangers also will sit down and help you figure out what you want to do.

SPECIAL EVENTS

The Cordova Ice Worm Festival is a winter carnival the first full weekend in February; the big ice worm—or, to be precise, ice centipede—marches in a parade. **The Copper River Delta Shorebird Festival** (☎ 907/424-7260; www.ptialaska.net/~midtown) revolves around the coming of dizzying swarms of shorebirds—estimates range from 5 to 22 million—that use the delta and beaches near the town as a migratory stopover in early May. It's an opportunity to see immense waves of birds. The whole community gets involved to host bird-watchers and put on a full schedule of educational and outdoor activities that lasts 5 days. **The First Fish** celebration, held around May 15, marks the start of the red salmon run on the Copper River Delta, Alaska's first salmon of the year and among the very best. **The Annual Salmon and Seafood Festival** is held in late June.

Fast Facts: Cordova

Banks Two banks on First Street have ATMs, as does the Alaska Commercial grocery store at the boat harbor.

Hospital The Cordova Community Medical Center is on Chase Street (☎ 907/424-8000), off the Copper River Highway near the slough.

Police For nonemergency police calls, dial ☎ 907/424-6100.

Post Office At Railroad Avenue and Council.

Taxes Sales tax in Cordova is 6%.

ATTRACTIONS

Save some time to wander around town, possibly with the help of the **historic walking tour booklet** produced by the historic society or with the **recorded walking tour** from the chamber of commerce. Cordova is full of wonderful little discoveries to make on your own.

Stop by the **Prince William Sound Science Center** (☎ 907/424-5800; www.pwssc.gen.ak.us), a marine biology research organization located in a blue-roofed house on pilings at the north side of the small-boat harbor. There are interpretive displays to look at, and information on the marine ecosystem.

The **Cordova Historical Museum,** at 622 First St., is a well-presented one-room display with some valuable artifacts reflecting Cordova's eventful past. The three-seat kayak and other artifacts of Prince William Sound Native peoples are of particular interest. Cordova is the home of the last few Eyak, a Native people whose language now has only one speaker left. There's also a Linotype machine, an interior of a fishing boat, and photographs of fishing and historic scenes. The museum is open summer Monday through Saturday 10am to 6pm, Sunday 2 to 4pm; winter Tuesday through Friday 1 to 5pm, Saturday 2 to 4pm. Admission is $1, free under age 18.

GETTING OUTSIDE
HIKING AROUND CORDOVA

Cordova has more good hiking trails per capita than any place I know. The Cordova Ranger Station can provide you with a free trail-guide booklet with lots of ideas and maps. There are three close to town (trails farther out are listed later, in the section on the Copper River Delta).

The **Tripod Mountain Trail** begins right from town and climbs 1,255 feet over less than a mile up the first mountain back from the shore, a half-day hike with views that present the Sound and Cordova like a map below you. The trail begins at the foot of the town ski lift, on Sixth Street—take Browning up the hill.

Partway up Tripod Mountain, near the middle drop off of the ski lift, a 1-mile trip links to the **Crater Lake Trail,** which eventually joins the **Power Creek Trail** on a loop of 12 miles. An easier start for that route is the Power Creek Road—take it along the north side of Eyak Lake to the end, 7 miles from town. The creek has spawning red salmon in July and attracts a lot of bears; watch, but don't get out of your car if you come upon one. The trail follows the creek through dramatic scenery 4.2 miles to a Forest Service cabin with a great view (reserve through the system described in the Chugach National Forest section, above).

THE COPPER RIVER DELTA

The delta and its star attraction, the **Childs Glacier,** make an unforgettable day trip by car or tour bus from Cordova, but if you have a couple of days you can do more. The backwaters, sloughs, and ponds beg to be explored by canoe. Bird-watchers will be beside themselves on such a paddle, or on the boardwalks and blinds set up by the Forest Service. You can raft the rivers. There are excellent hiking trails and mountain biking routes branching from the road, and Forest Service cabins to stay in.

The delta seems to go on forever, a vast patchwork of marsh, pond, small hills of trees, and the huge, implacable gray river itself. The glacial silt it carries away—some two million tons a day—has built this 700,000 acre wetland. A well-maintained gravel road leads across it, all in Chugach National Forest, and the forest has done a good job of providing ways and places to enjoy and learn about the area. The road itself is the old bed of the Copper River and Northwestern Railroad. It leads 48 miles to the **Million Dollar Bridge.** Built by Michael Heney, a magician of a 19th-century railroad builder who also constructed the White Pass and Yukon Route in Skagway, the 200-mile Copper River line was an engineering triumph that brought the mind-boggling wealth of the Kennicott Copper Mine to ships in Cordova (more on the mine is in chapter 9, "The Alaskan Interior"). The bridge over the Copper River went up in a race against time between two surging glaciers in 30-foot-deep, fast-flowing glacial water, in winter. The bridge stood 56 years, until the 1964 earthquake knocked down one end of one of the spans, augering it into the riverbed. But you can still drive across on a jerry-built ramp and go a few miles farther on unmaintained road.

Transportation

BY CAR   Driving gives you the most freedom. The road is gravel, but it's wide and level. Beyond the Million Dollar Bridge, however, it's a rough four-wheel-drive track at best, and if you get stuck you'll be there for a long time. Pick up the road guide from the Forest Service Cordova Ranger Station, and read the highlights below.

BY BUS TOUR   **Copper River and Northwest Tours,** P.O. Box 1564, Cordova, AK 99574 (☎ **907/424-5356**), takes bus tours to the glacier several days a week during the summer. On Fridays the tour is timed to the arrival and departure of the ferry, so you can do the whole thing as a day trip from Valdez. Operated by the irrepressible Becky Chapek and her husband, Bill Myers, whose father cut ties on the Copper River line, the tours make numerous stops, spend an hour at the glacier for an excellent lunch prepared by Becky, and include a recorded narrative that's been checked for accuracy by the Forest Service and the historical society. The 6-hour trip costs $35. They also drop off hikers and bikers along the road.

BY BIKE   Mountain biking the highway is the adventurous way, camping or staying in a Forest Service cabin on the way. The drawbacks are the distances, the delta's strong winds, and a lot of road dust. Of course, you don't have to ride all the way to see lots of birds and wildlife, and there are good mountain biking routes on the delta away from the road. The 3-mile **Saddlebag Glacier Trail,** at mile 25 of the Copper River Highway, leads to a stunning vista of a glacial lake surrounded by rocky peaks. Bikes are for rent from Cordova Coastal Outfitters (see "On the Sound," below) for $15 a day.

Along the Road

Keep your eyes scanning the wetlands and mountains around you as you drive out the road. The **animals** you may see along the way include black and brown bears, wolf, coyote, moose, and mountain goats. The entire world population of dusky Canada geese nests on the delta, and you're likely to see eagles and trumpeter swans without really looking. The ranger station provides a wildlife-viewing guide and several places to stop along the way designed for bird watching. The first is a platform with interpretive signs as you leave town, as sort of an introduction to the delta; this stretch of the road is fine for bird watching.

Don't miss the **Alaganik Slough Boardwalk.** Take the 3.2-mile spur road to the right 16.8 miles out the Copper River Highway; it's marked. The sky here is big and certain while the land is ambivalent—it doesn't know if it wants to be waving grass of green and gold or shallow, shimmering ponds and tendrils of water. The road leads out to a parking lot and small, free campground, the start of the 1,000-foot boardwalk. One part leads to a large blind where you can watch the ponds and brush for birds. The other takes you above a large pond that reflects the sun and the colors of the marsh. We were speechless when we stood there one evening at sunset, even in the complete absence of birds. Often in the summer you can see breeding trumpeter swans, ducks, and grebes, and in the spring and fall migrating waterfowl and shorebirds.

The highway ends with its best attraction, the ✪ **Childs Glacier.** This is the most amazing glacier I've ever seen, and no one seems to know about it outside Cordova. The wall of ice, 300 feet tall, comes right down to the quarter-mile-wide river, where the flowing water cuts it off like a knife, eroding the base and bringing down huge chunks. As you sit on the opposite bank, the glacier on the opposite side is too large to see—it completely fills your field of vision, creating an eerie and hypnotic sense of scale. On a warm summer day, you can feel the glacier's thunder as the ice shifts, and see pieces fall off. A chunk the size of a car barely registers, but when an office-building-size hunk falls, there's a roar and gray breakers radiate out across the river. Falling glacier pieces have made waves large enough to uproot trees here, not to mention hurling a few fish around—at the Forest Service viewing and picnic area across the river, salmon have been found high up in the trees and boulders in odd places. Several years ago, such a wave injured some visitors, and now the Forest Service warns that anyone who can't run fast should stay in the observation tower. A bit farther from shore there's a campground with pit toilets.

Don't miss seeing and at least walking on the **Million Dollar Bridge,** less than a mile from the glacier viewing area. A pleasant trail connects the two, or you can drive.

Activities

HIKING   The Forest Service maintains several trails on the delta. The **Alaganik Slough Boardwalk** and **Saddlebag Glacier Trail** are mentioned above.

The **Haystack Trail,** starting on the right just past the 19-mile marker on the highway, climbs through mossy rain forest from the delta's floor onto an odd little hill. The glaciers that once covered the delta spared this bedrock outcropping. The trail is steep in places but only .8 mile in length, and it leads to an overlook.

The **McKinley Lake Trail,** at mile 21.6 on the highway, leads 2.4 miles to a lake bearing trout and red (sockeye) salmon. You can also get there by canoe from the Alaganik Slough launch point (see below). There are two Forest Service cabins, the McKinley Trail Cabin near the highway and the McKinley Lake Cabin at the lake. Each costs $35 a night and can be reserved through the national system described in the Chugach National Forest section, above.

CANOEING   The delta's canoe routes are placid and little used, leading to remote places where birds and aquatic animals rule. You can launch on Alaganik Slough at a picnic area right at mile 22 on the Copper River Highway, padding to the Forest Service cabin on McKinley Lake, or down the slough into stunningly beautiful marsh lands. The couple that runs **Cordova Coastal Outfitters** (see below, under "Out on the Sound) rents canoes for $30 a day and drops them off, and will help you decide what route to take. You can ride out on one of their bicycles and pick up the canoe already at the launch site. They rent camping gear, too.

RAFTING   The immense quantity of water draining the Wrangell–St. Elias Mountains through the Copper River Delta, and the Copper River Highway that provides river access, make this a perfect venue for rafting. **Alaska River Rafting** (☎ **800/ 776-1864** or 907/424-RAFT; www.alaskarafters.com) is well regarded by locals. Their territory means they can offer quite a range of trips, from easy floating to white water, or even rafting right in front of the Childs Glaciers. Trips last from 3 hours to all day. A 3-hour trip is $60 per person; all-day, with flightseeing, $225. Their office is 13 miles out the road, and they receive mail at P.O. Box 2233, Cordova, AK 99574.

FISHING   The delta's lakes and streams harbor all five species of Pacific salmon, as well as Dolly Varden and cutthroat trout. The Cordova Ranger Station can offer guidance and regulation booklets, and the **Alaska Department of Fish and Game** (☎ **907/424-3212**) has a Cordova office as well. See "Fishing" in chapter 2 for general guidance.

OUT ON THE SOUND

The waters of Prince William Sound around Cordova, although lacking the tidewater glaciers found in the western Sound, are calm, little used, and rich in marine life. Sea otters are so common as to no longer receive a second glance from locals, congregating in rafts of many dozens or even hundreds. Sea lions can be found predictably, too, and orcas and humpback whales are not out of the ordinary. Bird-watchers can expect harlequin ducks and many other marine birds. Getting out on the water is easy, too, either on your own or with a guide, by boat or by sea kayak.

Cordova Coastal Outfitters is a good place to start for any outdoors activities (☎ **800/357-5145** or 907/424-7424; e-mail: coastal@eagle.ptialaska.net; P.O. Box 1834, Cordova, AK 99574). Andy Craig and Seawan Gehlbach know the equipment, the skills, and the area, and they convey that knowledge with casual enthusiasm. Their booth is on the dock below the Alaska Commercial grocery store, on the south side of the boat harbor. They guide sea kayaking and rent kayaks and fully equipped boats. If your group isn't up to kayaking, **renting a boat** might be the way to go—you won't believe the sense of freedom you feel clearing the harbor breakwater to explore Orca Inlet and the bays of Hawkins Island, on the far side. Boats rent for $85 a day, fishing gear included. They also offer water taxi or guided boat tour service in the Sound and on the Copper River Delta.

The guided **sea kayaking** trip for beginners lasts 5 hours and costs $60, concentrating on wildlife sightings. A 4-hour trip for the same price paddles on Eyak Lake to see brown bears and great blue herons. They offer all-day and multiday trips, too. Single kayaks rent for $30 a day, doubles $50.

Cruises are available on larger boats. Dave Janka runs the classic wooden *Auklet,* P.O. Box 498, Cordova, AK 99574 (☎ **907/424-3428;** e-mail: auklet@ptialaska.net), a 58-foot former U.S. Fish and Wildlife Service patrol boat, to carry researchers and visitors into the Sound from Cordova, Valdez, and Whittier. He doesn't enjoy fishing and doesn't believe in hunting, so this is a wildlife and scenery experience. Within a few hours of Cordova, Janka knows where to find wildlife, and if you see whales he'll know which ones you're looking at and the history of the pod. Half days are $75 per person, and full days $115, including meals. Longer charters are available, but the accommodations on board are nautical, not luxurious. He also drops off kayakers. Other businesses offer cruises of this kind, including two listed in the Whittier section above.

Several vessels are available for fishing charters, and each offers the strong possibility of seeing wildlife. Get a referral from the visitor center, or try **Cordova Fishing Charters** (☎ 907/424-5467), offering full-day trips for $135 per person.

IN THE AIR

Cordova is all by itself, with untouched wilderness in all directions. An **airplane** or **helicopter** can get you out there for fishing, hunting, or just communing with nature. There are several Forest Service cabins in spectacular settings, accessible only by air. **Flightseeing** is available, but the most inexpensive way to do it, or to get deep into the Sound, is to take a **mail plane** to one of the villages or fish hatcheries. **Cordova Air** (☎ 907/424-3289) is the largest operator. **Fishing and Flying** (☎ 907/424-3324), located at the airport, is a friendly operation and has remote cabins for rent. Either one can fly you out to an extremely remote Forest Service cabin, where you can fish, explore, or just discover what it's like to be totally alone.

ACCOMMODATIONS

There are more establishments than those listed here (including several B&Bs). You can get a list of the others from either visitor center.

✪ **The Northern Nights Inn.** 500 Third St. (P.O. Box 1564), Cordova, AK 99547. ☎ **907/424-5356.** Fax 907/424-3291. E-mail: alaskan@cordova.net. 5 units. TV TEL. $60–$75 double. Additional adult in room $5 extra; children stay free in parents' room. AE, DISC, MC, V.

These large, charming rooms, with private bathrooms, antiques, quilts, and views, are an almost unreal value. They're upstairs in Becky Chapek and Bill Myers's historic 1906 house, a couple of blocks above the main street. Each room has been lovingly renovated, and three have kitchenettes. One room is essentially an entire apartment. There are VCRs, a coin-op laundry, and a freezer that's available for fish. The family also operates the well-run tour business in town.

Prince William Motel. Second St. and Council (P.O. Box 908), Cordova, AK 99574. ☎ **907/424-3201.** Fax 907/424-2260. www.socl.com/princewi. 16 units. TV TEL. Summer $80–$100 double, winter $5 off. Additional adult in room $10 extra; children 11 and under stay free in parents' room. AE, MC, V.

A friendly and helpful family renovated this old building into a clean, comfortable, modern motel. The lower rooms look out onto an airshaft, but that may be an advantage if you're trying to get to sleep when it's still light out. All rooms have coffee machines, microwaves, and small refrigerators, and seven have kitchenettes (these rooms go for $20 more). There's a coin-op laundry, a barbecue, and a freezer for fish.

The Reluctant Fisherman. 401 Railroad Ave. (P.O. Box 150), Cordova, AK 99574. ☎ **800/770-3272** or 907/424-3272. Fax 907/424-7465. E-mail: reluct@ptialaska.net. 50 units. TV TEL. High season, $75–$125 double. Low season, $75–$95 double. Additional person in room $10 extra. AE, CB, DC, DISC, JCB, MC, V.

Margy Johnson presides at Cordova's main hotel with limitless energy. She and her husband, Dick Borer, have created one of the best waterfront lodgings in Alaska, overlooking the small-boat harbor. The decor in the lobby, lounge, and restaurant capture the town's railroad and copper-mining history, with rich wood and pressed-copper ceilings, stained glass, and mementos of the couple's history here. The rooms are comfortable and modern, with coffee machines, VCRs, and local art. Those on the water side have good views, while an economy wing on the parking lot rents for $75 a night. There's a gift shop and travel agency in the hotel; they also rent cars and operate the $9 airport shuttle.

The ✪ **restaurant** serves the town's best dinners. Main courses of fish, steaks, and pasta range from $15 to $27. Lunch is $4 to $10. A small deck overlooks the harbor for outdoor dining. Order the Copper River king or red salmon in season, broiled—the river produces exceptionally rich fish, a real delicacy. They make it into delicious chili for lunch.

DINING

Other than the restaurants listed here, try the **Reluctant Fisherman.** Also, the **Flying Dutchman Pub and Grill,** at 531 First Street, serves good burgers, fish-and-chips, and soup at a counter overlooking the harbor. It's one of the least smoky bars in town. Some of Cordova's best lunches come from **Baja Taco** (☎ **907/424-5599**), a bus at the boat harbor with a covered dining area elevated on a small tower. The proprietor, who lives in Baja in the winter, specializes in salmon tacos here May through September. There also are a couple of other decent restaurants on First Street.

Ambrosia. 413 First St. ☎ **907/424-7175.** Main courses $5.75–$18.75; lunch $5.75–$9.75. MC, V. High season, daily 11am–11pm; low season, daily noon–9pm. GREEK/ITALIAN.

This is a comfortable Greek and Italian family restaurant with an extensive menu and pizza. It's the kind of place that stays in business in a small town: The food is reliable and the portions large, but nothing too challenging or unusual. Beer and wine license.

Cookhouse Cafe. 1 Cannery Row. ☎ **907/424-5926.** All items $5–$9. MC, V. Daily 6am–3pm, open for dinner Fri–Sat. Closed in winter. DINER.

A former cannery cookhouse on a dock with a working cannery (to find it, go out toward the ferry dock), this clean, bright cafe with bench seating has a very agreeable atmosphere. It's relaxed and airy, with high ceilings and local art hanging, but its gritty past hasn't been prettied up too much. The food, including fresh seafood and homemade bread, jam, and jelly, isn't fancy, but it's well prepared and inexpensive. You'll be tempted to linger over coffee. No liquor license and no smoking.

Killer Whale Cafe. In Orca Book and Sound, 507 First St. ☎ **907/424-7733.** All items $6–$9. No credit cards. Mon–Fri 7am–4pm, Sat 8am–3:30pm.

The food was unimpressive when we last visited, but the cafe is still worth a stop for the atmosphere in the loft above a bookstore that is a nexus of local ecopeople. Oil-spill hero Kelly Weaverling owns Orca Book and Sound, and was the only member of the Green Party to hold elective office in the United States when he was Cordova's mayor a few years ago. (He later lost to Margy Johnson, of the Reluctant Fisherman, by one vote, but refused to ask for a recount.) Order soups, sandwiches, and the like at the counter. No liquor license.

8

The Denali National Park Region

Denali (den-*al*-ee) National Park stands alone among parks in the United States: it gives regular people easy access to real wilderness. It's also got sweeping tundra vistas, abundant wildlife, and North America's tallest mountain—but other places in Alaska have equally inspiring places to see and even more animals. What makes Denali unique is that you can get there, and that your ability to do so hasn't spoiled the natural experience, as it has at so many other parks.

It's a sad truth that even the largest national parks in the Lower 48 states are too small to comprise complete ecosystems. The dream of leaving nature undisturbed is essentially lost in those places, and only through human intervention do the natural systems within the parks stay as close to their primeval state as they do—symbolized perfectly by the work of rangers at Yellowstone to drive bison back within park boundaries so they will not come to harm outside. Millions of people driving through the parks in cars adds greater interference. At Rocky Mountain National Park there's a crossing guard for big horn sheep. At Yosemite Valley and the Grand Canyon they're figuring out ways to get rid of the cars, recognizing that the vehicles themselves can spoil the experience of nature.

On the other end of the spectrum, Alaska has many parks with immense intact ecosystems unchanged from before white contact. More than two-thirds of America's national park acreage is in Alaska, taking in inconceivably huge swaths of land without roads, buildings, or landing strips. They're natural all right, but almost no one goes there. Some of these parks receive a few hundred visitors a year—only the Alaska Natives of the surrounding region and perhaps the hardiest and wealthiest outdoors people. Just chartering a plane to get out to some of these places can cost as much as most of us spend on our whole vacation. With as many people on the earth as we've got, wilderness survives only when it's rationed somehow. In most of Alaska, the rationing system is simply the expense and difficulty of getting to the wild.

At Denali, on the other hand, you can see the heart of the park for little more than it would cost you at Yellowstone. And when you get there, it's a pristine natural environment where truly wild animals live in a complete ecosystem pretty much without human interference. A single national park service decision makes this possible: The only road through the park is closed to the public. This means that to get into the park, you must ride a crowded bus over a dusty gravel road

Denali National Park

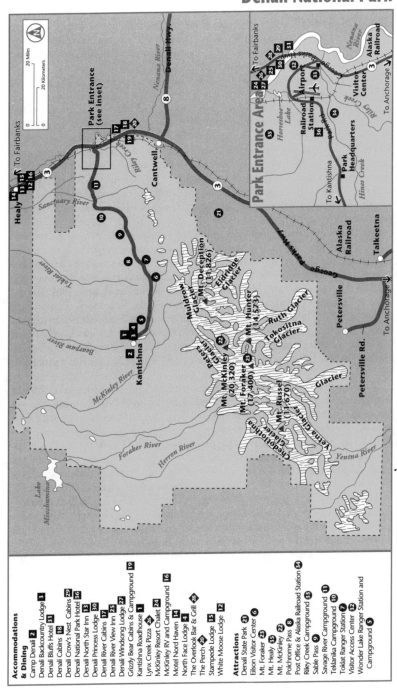

Accommodations & Dining

Camp Denali **2**
Denali Backcountry Lodge **3**
Denali Bluffs Hotel **31**
Denali Cabins **18**
Denali Crow's Nest Cabins **29**
Denali National Park Hotel **36**
Denali North Star Inn **13**
Denali Princess Lodge **30**
Denali River Cabins **17**
Denali River View Inn **25**
Denali Windsong Lodge **27**
Grizzly Bear Cabins & Campground **1**
Kantishna Roadhouse **19**
Lynx Creek Pizza **26**
McKinley Resort Chalet **24**
McKinley RV and Campground **16**
Motel Nord Haven **14**
North Face Lodge **4**
The Overlook Bar & Grill **28**
The Perch **20**
Stampede Lodge **15**
White Moose Lodge **12**

Attractions

Denali State Park **21**
Eilson Visitor Center **6**
Mt. Foraker **23**
Mt. Healy **35**
Mt. McKinley **22**
Polychrome Pass **8**
Post Office & Alaska Railroad Station **34**
Riley Creek Campground **33**
Sable Pass **9**
Savage River Campground **11**
Teklanika Campground **10**
Toklat Ranger Station **7**
Visitor Access Center **32**
Wonder Lake Ranger Station and Campground **5**

hour after hour, but it also means that the animals are still there to watch, and their behavior remains essentially normal. From the window of the bus, you're likely to see grizzly bears doing what they would be doing even if you weren't there. It may be the only $20 safari in the world.

What's even more unique is that you can get off the bus pretty much whenever you want to and walk away from the road across the tundra, out of sight of the road, and be alone in this primeval wilderness. Unfortunately, many Denali visitors never take advantage of the opportunity, which normally would cost a lot of money or require a lot of muscle and outdoor skill. Being alone under God's big sky makes many people nervous. Most of us have never been really away from other people, much less apart from anything people have made. But that's the essence of Alaska—learning, deep down, how big creation is and how small you are, one more mammal on the tundra under the broad sky. Uniquely at Denali, you can be there, and then, when you're ready to return to civilization, you can just walk to the road and catch the next bus— they come every half hour.

The Denali experience spreads beyond the park. After all, the park boundary is an artificial line—the wildlife and the scenery of the Alaska Range don't observe its significance. To the east, the **Denali Highway** runs through the same extraordinary terrain, with opportunities for hiking over the tundra and canoeing on the lakes managed by the Bureau of Land Management. To the south, **Denali State Park** and the town of **Talkeetna** provide another vantage on Mount McKinley, with the advantage of salmon fishing in the rivers and remote lake recreation. The construction of comfortable new lodges and a variety of good outdoor guides have helped make Talkeetna a popular alternative gateway to Denali. Even though it's 150 miles from the park entrance by car, Talkeetna is physically closer to the mountain than is the park headquarters.

Visitors often skip all the area's other attractions and focus instead on **Mount McKinley,** which, at 20,320 feet, is the tallest mountain in North America. It is an impressive peak, but you don't need to go to the park to see it, and in fact most people who do go *don't* see it. Summer weather patterns usually sock in the mountain by midafternoon, at least as seen from the ground in the park. Unfortunately, Denali has become a thing people feel they must do, and seeing Mount McKinley is a thing they must do when they visit Denali. Many package tours rush the park so quickly it becomes just a blur outside a window rather than an experience. If they miss the mountain, passengers may wonder why they traveled so far to stay at the ticky-tacky roadside development at the park's entrance and then ride on a bus over a bumpy road. A friend swears she overheard a tourist ask, as she boarded the train leaving Denali, "Why did they put the park way out here in the boondocks?"

The answer is there for you to find, at the bottom of the steps of the shuttle bus door.

1 Planning a Visit to the Park

ORIENTATION

The park is like a pivot in the center of Alaska, a huge slice of the Alaska Range—rock and ice robed in tundra and stunted black spruce. The total of Denali National Park and Preserve is 6 million acres, a roughly triangular polygon about 20% larger than Massachusetts. The only park entrance is 230 miles north of Anchorage and 120 miles south of Fairbanks on the paved George Parks Highway or the Alaska Railroad. Although **Mount McKinley** is visible from as far away as Anchorage, you can't see it at all from the area of the park entrance (where you will find the railroad depot and all services accessible by private vehicle), since it's on the far side of the park. A mile north on the Parks Highway, along a cliff-sided canyon of the Nenana River, hotels and restaurants have developed a kind of seasonal town on private land in the immediate area of the **park entrance.** Other services are at **Carlo Creek,** 13 miles south on the Parks, or at another gathering of roadside development 7 miles south of the park entrance, and in the year-round town of **Healy,** 10 miles north of the park entrance. From the park entrance, a road accessible only by shuttle bus leads west 89 miles through the park, past a series of campgrounds and a visitor center, and ending at the **Kantishna district,** a collection of inholdings with wilderness lodges.

WHEN TO GO & HOW FAR AHEAD TO PLAN

Crowding is relative. Once you're out in the park, Denali is never crowded. A transportation bottleneck—the shuttle system—protects the park from overuse. What makes the busy season difficult is getting through that bottleneck from the crowded park entrance into the wilderness. At that time, travelers who just show up at the visitor center without any reservations often have to spend at least a day, and often two, outside the park before they can get a seat on a shuttle bus, a campground site, or a backcountry permit. It's quite a letdown to arrive at the park for a wilderness experience and have to spend the first few hours standing in line at the always-crowded visitor center trying to buy a bus ticket for 2 days later.

The flow of visitors seems to vary greatly from year to year. Some years, you've needed **reservations** by March for July; other years, a few weeks advance planning will do. To be on the safe side, get your shuttle tickets and campsites as soon as you know the dates of your visit. Lodgings also get tight in July, but are not as critical to the success of your visit. Reserve as far ahead as you can, but don't worry about getting stuck in a dive if you don't get your first choice of rooms or cabins—there are no dives in the Denali area.

The park is populated by people beginning in mid-May, when there still is some snow; the humans migrate south again in mid- to late September, when winter is closing in. In the off-season, only a few dozen residents remain—caretakers who watch over the hotels and other buildings and sled-dog-driving rangers who patrol the backcountry. The visitor season gets into high gear in mid-June and starts to wind down in mid-August, providing a month of relative quiet and often reduced prices at the beginning of the season and another at the end. Reservations are easy at those times.

May is iffy at Denali, but fall is a wonderful time to go. The weather gets nippy at night, and there can be surprise snowfalls, but rain is less likely, and the trees and tundra turn wonderful colors. By early September, visitors are so few that the park no longer takes telephone reservations. By mid-September, private cars can drive on the park road for a few days—the park service holds a lottery to determine who will get that treat.

Another way to avoid the crowds is to book a stay in a **wilderness lodge.** Three lodges in Kantishna, listed below, have the right to carry clients to their businesses over the park road in buses and vans, avoiding the bottleneck.

SAMPLE ITINERARIES

Your park experience, and how you plan it, depends on the level of comfort you demand. Generally, the more you're willing to rough it, the closer you get to the real Denali—there are no hotels in the heart of the park.

THE HOTEL-STAY ITINERARY

Arrive by train at the park, checking into accommodations nearby—shuttles and courtesy vans will get you around. Attend a ranger talk, the *Cabin Nite* dinner-theater

The Denali Highway: The Drivable Denali

From Cantwell, 27 miles south of the Denali National Park entrance, the Denali Highway leads 133 miles east to another tiny village, Paxson, on the Richardson Highway. The little known road is a lesson in how we're influenced by labels. It runs due east from the Denali National Park border, a natural extension of the park over the Alaska Range, with scenery that's equal to and in some ways more impressive than the park's. Yet, without the national park name, the terrain along the Denali Highway is comparatively little used, even by Alaskans.

The Bureau of Land Management controls the land along the Denali Highway, and it's pretty much open for any recreational activity. The **Tangle Lakes** start a 3-day, 35-mile float trip to the Richardson Highway; there is lake canoeing here and at other series of ponds along the way, and you can see an extraordinary variety of waterfowl, including trumpeter swans, sandhill cranes, and loons. Much of the highway passes through high, alpine terrain, with views that extend infinitely into the distance and good chances of seeing caribou, moose, and black and grizzly bear. At **Maclaren Pass,** at 4,086 feet, you stand in high Alaska Range terrain of tundra and rock, with views of Maclaren Glacier. The land invites you to walk at least a little way out across it.

Simply driving the road is an experience. If traveling to Denali National Park from Anchorage or Fairbanks, consider making a return trip via the Denali Highway and Richardson Highway. The road is gravel (plans are in the works to pave it, unfortunately), but you can cover its length in under 4 hours. Small road-houses are along the way. **Biking** the road is one of the best ways to see it. Trails and remote roads from the highway offer some exceptional mountain biking and hiking routes, especially in the Tangle lakes National Register Archaeological District. There are three **Bureau of Land Management campgrounds** along the highway, and you can camp anywhere you want outside a campground.

Be sure to get the BLM's *Denali Highway Points of Interest* road guide and *Trail Map and Guide to the Tangle Lakes National Register District.* They're available at the Alaska Public Lands Information Centers in Fairbanks, Anchorage, or Tok, or directly from the **Bureau of Land Management.** Their Glennallen District Office, P.O. Box 147, Glennallen, AK 99588 (☎ **907/822-3217;** www.glennallen.ak.blm.gov/), open Monday through Friday 8am to 4pm, manages the area, and rangers there can give you guidance on where to go.

Alaskan Bicycle Adventures (described in chapter 2) leads a variety of bike tours that include the Denali Highway, generally starting from Anchorage, looping up the Parks Highway and returning south on the Richardson and Glenn highways. They provide the bikes and all the gear, as well as the van and trailer carrying the gear to make the trip comfortable. **CampAlaska Tours** (also in chapter 2) covers this ground, too, with group camping excursions.

show, or go on a short **nature walk** around the park hotel in the evening. Get to bed early, and the next morning take a shuttle bus before 7am into the park, riding to the **Eielson Visitor Center** to see the terrain and animals, and possibly to get a view of the mountain (arriving there in late morning). Now ride part way back toward the entrance before getting off the bus at a place of your choosing for a walk and to eat the bag lunch you've brought along with you (pack out all trash, of course), or take one of the **park service guided walks.** After enjoying the wilderness for a few hours, head back on the bus, finishing a long day back at the hotel. Next day try a rafting ride, flightseeing trip, or other activity near the entrance to the park before reboarding the train.

THE FAMILY CAMPING ITINERARY

Arrive at the park entrance by car with your camping gear and food for a couple of nights. (You can rent camping gear in Anchorage.) Camp that evening at the **Riley Creek campground** near the visitor center and enjoy the evening ranger program or a nature walk, or go straight to a campsite farther within the park (either way, reserve well ahead). Next day, catch a shuttle bus or camper bus well into the park for sightseeing and **hiking.** If you have another day after that within the park, you can do more hikes and have the cushion of a weather day. If staying 3 nights, you can drive your car to the **Teklanika Campground,** with good hiking on the Teklanika riverbed, and the advantage of having your home base well within the park. Finally, break camp early on the third or fourth day and return to the entrance. Add a rafting or horseback excursion at the park entrance before driving on, if you like, and possibly a night at a hotel to get washed up.

THE BACKCOUNTRY CAMPING ITINERARY

Arrive by train, bus, or car with your backpack, camping gear, and food for at least several days' hiking. Go immediately to the visitor center to orient yourself to the backcountry permit process, buy the information you need for your trek (see "Hiking the Backcountry" under "Out in the Park," later in this chapter, and choose the unit area that looks most promising. **Backcountry permits** cannot be reserved in advance, only in person for the next day, and they go fast. If you're lucky, permits will be left for the day after you arrive; more likely, you'll need to camp at the **Morino Backpacker's Campground,** 1.9 miles on the park road from the highway, and arrive at the visitor center by the 7am opening to get your permit for the following day. Now you've got another day to wait; if you've reserved a shuttle-bus seat, you can get a preview of the park and see some wildlife, or, outside the park, go on a rafting trip. The next morning you can start your backcountry hike, taking the camper bus to your unit, then traveling for up to 2 weeks in a huge area of wilderness reserved almost exclusively for your use.

THE WILDERNESS LODGE ITINERARY

For those who can afford it, this may be the best way to see Denali. The lodge will fly you in—or, if it's in Kantishna, drive you through the park—and you'll immediately be away from the crowds in remote territory. The lodges all have activities and guides to get you out into the wilderness. If you're not staying in Kantishna, you may want to schedule a day to ride the shuttle bus into the park to see the mountain and wildlife anyway, with an evening in a hotel near the park or in Healy.

THE TALKEETNA OPTION

Drive only as far as Talkeetna, about 110 miles north of Anchorage, and board a flightseeing plane from there to the park, perhaps **landing on a glacier** on Mount McKinley itself. You'll stand a better chance of seeing the mountain than anyone else, since the weather tends to be better on the south side and you won't have to go on a certain, prearranged day when the weather may be poor. You'll also save yourself hours of driving to the park and the bus ride into the park, and you'll have the pleasure of staying in a town with some character, unlike the park entrance area. But you'll miss the wildlife-viewing opportunities that can be had only on the ground in the park. (See the Talkeetna section at the end of this chapter for more info.)

2 The Essential Details

VISITOR INFORMATION

Getting the information you need to plan your visit is especially important at Denali because of the need for advance reservations. Besides the centers here, you can stop by at an interagency **Alaska Public Lands Information Center,** in Anchorage, Fairbanks, or Tok, listed in chapters 6 and 9.

The information desk at the **Denali National Park Visitor Access Center,** Denali Park Rd., ½ mile from the park entrance (P.O. Box 9), Denali National Park, AK 99755 (☎ **907/683-2294;** www.nps.gov/dena), staffed by rangers, is the easiest place to make contact with the Park Service. Since there's no park entrance station, stop here for the park map, a copy of the *Alpenglow* park newspaper, and other handouts. A small bookstore offers a limited selection on the area, and films and programs take place in an auditorium. There's a small children's area. It's open daily June to mid-Sept, 7am to 8pm; May and late September, 10am to 4pm. Closed October to April.

The nonprofit **Alaska Natural History Association,** Denali Branch. P.O. Box 230, Denali National Park, AK 99755 (☎ **907/683-1272;** www.nps.gov/dena/Anha/index.htm), publishes park information for sale at the Visitor Access Center (you can also order it before coming).

At the **Eielson Visitor Center,** on Denali Park Road, more than 60 miles inside the park (accessible only on the shuttle bus), rangers answer questions about Mount McKinley, which on clear days presents a dramatic view from the center. There are displays on wildlife and geology, and a seismograph constantly measures earthquake activity. A ranger allocates open seats on in-bound buses for passengers who want to go back on a different bus than they rode out on into the park. Picnic tables outside make a good place to eat your sack lunch before boarding the bus back. Closed October to mid-June.

ARAMARK/Denali Park Resorts, 241 W. Ship Creek Ave., Anchorage, AK 99501 (☎ **800/622-7275** or 907/272-7275; fax 907/264-4684; www.denalinationalpark. com), is the park concessionaire, operating the reservation system for the campgrounds and shuttle buses, plus three hotels, bus tours, a rafting operation, and a dinner theater you can reserve at the same numbers. They have a desk in the Visitor Access Center. The reservation system is covered below.

Destinations in Travel, P.O. Box 76, Denali National Park, AK 99755 (☎ **800/354-6020** or 907/683-1422), is a Denali-based travel agency that handles lodgings and activities other than those operated by the park concessionaire.

THE RESERVATION SYSTEM

Here's the system for reserving shuttle bus tickets and the developed campgrounds. The backcountry permit system is covered later under "Backpacking," below. This current section may look long, but paying attention to the details of the reservation system greatly improves your chances of a good visit to the park.

FOR ADVANCE RESERVATIONS

Sixty-five percent of shuttle-bus seats and 100% of campground sites (except Morino, Sanctuary, and Igloo) are offered for booking by telephone, fax, or mail, with the balance held back for walk-ins. Full payment is due within 10 days of your reservation if you don't use a credit card. Reservations by mail or fax open for the whole summer on November 1 of the preceding year. Reservations by phone open sometime in February. After that date, lines are answered Monday through Friday 7am to 6pm, Saturday and Sunday 7am to 5pm, Alaska time (4 hours earlier than eastern standard time), but at times it has been impossible to get through. By faxing, you bypass this problem and can get in before the phone lines open. Reservation forms to fax or mail are available on the Denali Web site (www.nps.gov/dena), or you can just use a blank piece of paper, making sure to include the dates, times, and campgrounds you want, plus alternate dates; the names and ages of the people in your party; and entrance and reservation fees (see "Fees" below) along with a Visa, MasterCard, American Express, or Discover Card number, with expiration and signature. You don't have to figure out the total. You can also pay by check if reserving by mail. Don't use the mail unless you're writing well ahead of the time of your trip—more than a month, certainly—as otherwise you could miss getting a reservation at all (mail to Alaska takes about 5 days from the east coast).

A **confirmation** is supposed to be sent out by mail or fax within 2 days of receipt. Take the confirmation to the "will call" desk at the visitor center when you arrive to exchange it for a camping permit and bus ticket. If you'll be arriving after the center closes at 8pm, you must call ☎ **907/683-1266** in advance to avoid losing your site or shuttle seat.

FOR WALK-INS
Phone, mail, and fax orders shut down the day before the visit starts, but walk-in reservations begin 2 days out, offering the remaining 35% of the shuttle bus seats and any leftover car camping campsites, and all sites in two primitive backcountry campgrounds, Igloo and Sanctuary. If it's a busy time of year, desirable shuttle reservations are snapped up early in the day. That means you may not get a good reservation for the day of your arrival or even the day after, only the next day after that. That's why it's so critical to reserve in advance.

On the other hand, don't despair if you arrive without reservations, as the flow of visitors rises and falls unpredictably, and it's perfectly possible you'll walk into the visitor center and get a shuttle seat on the same day.

FEES
The **park entrance fee** is $10 per family, $5 per person, good for 7 days. The is no entrance station to collect the fee, but it is automatically added to your bill when you make shuttle or campground reservations. If you have a Golden Eagle, Golden Age, or Golden Access national pass, mention it when you call in order to get your discount. In addition, a **reservation fee** of $4 is charged for each reservation session, regardless of how many different reservations you make when you call. **Campground fees** are covered below (see "Accommodations"). Another $6 fee is charged for canceling a campsite or bus ticket, which is allowable only 2 days or more in advance.

·3 Getting There
BY TRAIN
The **Alaska Railroad,** P.O. Box 107500, Anchorage, AK 99510-7500 (☎ **800/ 544-0552** or 907/265-2494; www.akrr.com), pioneered tourism to the park before the George Parks Highway was built in 1972. In the summer trains leave both Anchorage and Fairbanks daily at 8:15am, arriving at the park from Anchorage at 3:45pm and from Fairbanks at noon, crossing and going on to the opposite city for arrival at 8:15pm in each. The fare from Anchorage to Denali is $102 one-way for adults, half price for children. The full train runs only from mid-May to mid-September, with somewhat lower fares in the first and last few weeks of the season. During the winter, the Alaska Railroad runs a single passenger car from Anchorage to Fairbanks and back once a week—a truly spectacular, truly Alaskan experience.

The advantages of taking the train to Denali are that it's a historic, unspoiled route through beautiful countryside; there's a good chance of seeing moose and caribou; it's fun and relaxing; there's commentary along the way; and the food is good. There are disadvantages, too. The train is more expensive. You can rent a car for 4 days and drive up for the same price as one round-trip on the train. It's slow, adding 3 hours to a trip from Anchorage to the park, and when it's late, it can be very late. And, once you arrive, you have to rely on shuttles and courtesy vans to get around outside the park—not a big drawback, since shuttles are frequent.

The Alaska Railroad's locomotives also pull two sets of cars with full domes owned by **Princess Cruises and Tours,** 2815 Second Ave., Suite 400, Seattle, WA 98121-1299 (☎ **800/835-8907**), and **Holland America–Westours/Gray Line of Alaska,** 300 Elliot Ave. West, Seattle, WA 98119 (☎ **800/544-2206** or 907/277-5581). Each provides separate, distinct service and operates independently, as described below. You can't walk from one kind of car to another. Fares on these two operations run about 25% above the railroad's fares, but they're mainly sold, and much more advantageously priced, as lodging packages in the company's Denali hotels, for around $300 for a 1-night stay.

The Princess and Holland America cars offer a luxurious but controlled experience wherein each passenger has his or her own dome-car seat on a unique, beautifully appointed railroad car. You have assigned seats and eat during a scheduled dining seating. The cars are designed with regular forward-facing seats as well as table seating. The Alaska Railroad cars are traditional railroad cars, with seats facing forward, and you can sit anywhere you want, move between cars and stand in the breezeway between cars, and eat when you want to. The food is served in an old-fashioned dining car with tablecloths and flowers. A couple of dozen dome-car seats are available, with a 20-minute limit on staying in them—not the dome-to-yourself arrangement of the cruise-line cars. Well-trained guides provide intermittent commentary and answer questions in each car. Children will enjoy the Alaska Railroad cars more; adults can judge for themselves which approach is more appealing.

Between the two cruise-line car offerings, Princess's Midnight Sun Express Ultra Dome Rail Cars offer more headroom in the upstairs dome area and rear platforms that allow passengers to get out of their seats and enjoy the fresh air. Holland America's McKinley Explorer Railcars are all original, luxurious Budd or Pullman Standard dome cars, originally built in the early 1950s and totally reconditioned when acquired by HAL over the past 10 years. Of all the choices, however, my personal preference would be for the Alaska Railroad cars. Even if you can't sit in a dome the whole way, the windows still are large and clean, and I think half the fun of riding on a train is moving around and meeting a variety of people.

BY CAR

Renting a car and driving from Anchorage is cheaper than taking the train. The drive is about 4½ hours from Anchorage, 2½ from Fairbanks, on good two-lane highway. Many of the views along the **Parks Highway** are equal to the views on the train, but large stretches, especially in the Matanuska and Susitna valleys, near Anchorage, have been spoiled by ugly roadside development (which you don't see on the train). A long but spectacular detour around the mess leads through **Hatcher Pass** on a mountainous gravel road open only in the summer. See the "Matanuska & Susitna Valleys" section in chapter 6. Farther north from Anchorage, the Parks Highway passes through Denali State Park. If the weather's clear, you can see Mount McKinley from the pull-outs there. The state park also contains several campgrounds and hiking trails and a veterans memorial.

BY BUS

Several van and bus services inexpensively connect Anchorage and Fairbanks to Denali. Most will carry bikes and other gear for an additional fee. The **Alaska Back-packer Shuttle** (☎ 800/266-8625 or 907/344-8775; www.alaska.net/~backpack) carries passengers from Anchorage and Fairbanks to Denali in comfortable small buses that leave Anchorage from the Voyager Hotel, at Fifth Avenue and K Street and Fairbanks from the visitor center. The fare from Anchorage is $40 one-way, $70 round-trip; from Fairbanks $20 one-way, $35 round-trip. **The Park Connection** (☎ 800/208-0200 advance bookings; 907/683-1240 at Denali; 907/245-0200 in Anchorage) offers van service from Anchorage ($59 adults) or Seward ($98 adult). Children ride half price.

BY AIR

Flightseeing trips to Denali from Anchorage are listed in chapter 7. You also can charter to Denali from Anchorage or Fairbanks, although it's liable to be costly.

GETTING AROUND

If you take the train or bus, you'll find that virtually all accommodations have arrangements to get you around, although this becomes less convenient as you get farther from the park entrance. If your hotel doesn't have a courtesy van of its own, there usually is a scheduled shuttle. **ARAMARK** operates a bus that carries guests from its Denali Park Resorts hotels, a mile north and 7 miles south of the park, to the park entrance. You can use the bus even if you're not staying at an ARAMARK hotel—have the desk at your hotel call for a pickup.

If you drive to the park, you'll still need to take the shuttle bus, described below, to get into its heart, except under certain circumstances. You can drive past mile 14 on the park road only if you have a 3-day camping permit at Teklanika Campground, in which case your vehicle must remain parked at the campground for the entire 3 days; or if it is the last few days in September, and you have won a permit in a lottery that allows 1,600 cars free passage on the road. After the 4 days of permit driving are over, the road is open to anyone as far as Mile 30 until the snow flies; then it's maintained only as far as the headquarters, 3 miles from the entrance.

Bicycles have free access to the park road. For that option see "Mountain Biking" under "Out in the Park," below.

Fast Facts: Denali National Park

Banks   An ATM is located at Larry's Service Station in Healy, 12 miles north of the park. Do your banking before leaving Anchorage or Fairbanks.

Emergencies   Call ☎ 911 outside the park, ☎ 907/683-9100 within the park.

Hospital   A health clinic (☎ 907/683-2211) is located in Healy, 10 miles north of the park entrance; it's open 24 hours a day for emergencies, or normal office hours for nonemergencies.

Police   The police agency for the area is the Alaska State Troopers (☎ 907/683-2232 or 907/768-2202), which handles nonemergency calls from Cantwell, 28 miles south.

Post Office   The post office is at the park hotel, a mile within the park entrance.

Stores   The small McKinley Mercantile (☎ 907/683-9246) stands across the Denali Park Road from the train depot, about a mile inside the park entrance; it's open daily from 7:30am to 8pm in the summer. Besides convenience groceries, they have firewood, some basic camping supplies, and showers. A larger convenience store and gas station is on the Parks Highway in the Nenana Canyon area, just north of the park entrance. Do major shopping before coming to the park.

Taxes   The local bed tax is 7%. There is no sales tax.

4 Denali by Shuttle Bus

Your visit to Denali will likely revolve around your ride on the shuttle bus into the park to see the wildlife and get out for a walk in the wilderness. Some planning will make it a more comfortable ride.

CHOOSING YOUR DESTINATION

You can buy shuttle tickets to the Toklat (*toe*-klat) River, 53 miles into the park; the Eielson (*aisle*-son) Visitor Center at 66 miles; Wonder Lake at 85 miles; or Kantishna, at 89 miles (fares are on the chart, "Denali Park Road Bus Facts"). On any day trip, you have to go both ways, so you're in for a long drive. If you don't get off the bus along the way, the round-trip takes 6½ hours to Toklat, 8 hours to Eielson, 11 hours to Wonder Lake, and 12 hours to Kantishna. In choosing your destination, you need to balance your stamina, your desire to save time for a day hike, and your desire to see wildlife. There are no firm rules about where wildlife shows up, but my own observations are that in the early morning, you can often see moose and black bears on the first part of the road; in midsummer, brown (grizzly) bears seem to appear most in the higher country, beyond Toklat, which also is the best area for caribou; in the fall berry season, the grizzlies show up all along the drive. The best views of Mount McKinley show up after mile 61, also beyond Toklat. The mountain is most likely to be visible in the morning, as clouds often pile up during the day. Going beyond Eielson to Wonder Lake provides more amazing views, including the land-covered Muldrow Glacier and many classic images of Mount McKinley. There's really no reason to go as far as Kantishna unless you are headed to a lodge there. In general, I think **Eielson** is the best destination for most people, offering both the chance to see the mountain and some wildlife while leaving some time to get out and walk (I've included some ideas on where to hike below).

You won't be able to time your trip for **good weather,** as you need to book ahead, but don't despair if it rains—the sun may be out at the other end of the park. The best weather for wildlife sightings is cool overcast skies without rain. One trick of the system that allows visitors to wait for sun is to stay at Teklanika Campground. If you drive to a campsite there, agreeing to stay for 3 days, you're eligible to buy a special shuttle ticket for $21 that is good for rides deeper into the park the entire time you're staying at the campground. Or you can buy a three-trip pass from the park service for the price of two.

Denali can be a challenge for families. Young children will go nuts on an 8-hour bus ride, and often can't pick out the wildlife—this isn't a zoo, and most animals blend into their surroundings. Older children also have a hard time keeping their patience on these trips, as do many adults. The only solution is to get off the bus and turn your trip into a romp in the heather. When you've had a chance to revive, catch the next bus. Besides, just because you buy a ticket to Eielson doesn't mean that you have to go

A Few Words on the Denali Buses

It's worth noting that ARAMARK, the official concessionaire for Denali, uses only schoolbus-type buses for its Denali tours. Readers have written me that their tour operator stuck them on these buses while other visitors toured the park in luxury motorcoaches, but this just isn't so: Only ARAMARK's light buses are allowed on the park roads. So don't worry, we're all in the same boat.

It's also worth noting that the buses act a bit like mountain goats on the heights of Polychrome Pass and near Eielson Visitor Center—the road is narrow and lacks guard rails, and if you're afraid of heights it might not be at all to your liking.

that far. Also, if your child normally needs a car seat, you must bring it along on the bus, or borrow one from the park service.

ARAMARK also operates narrated bus tours, booked mostly with package visitors. The **Natural History Tour** provides just a taste of the park, going 17 miles down the park road. The **Wildlife Tour** goes to Toklat when the mountain is hidden by clouds, and 8 miles farther, to Highway Pass, when it is visible. Food is provided, but you can't get off the bus along the way, and the route skips the beautiful grizzly and caribou habitat toward the Eielson Visitor Center. The **Kantishna Roadhouse** (listed below under "Wilderness Lodges") offers a 190-mile, 13-hour marathon with lunch and a dog sled and gold panning program at the halfway mark, at the lodge. It's well done, with commentary, but you can't get off the bus along the way, and the return trip may be too rushed to stop for all wildlife sightings.

GETTING READY

Reserve your shuttle ticket for as early as you can stand to get up in the morning. This strategy will give you more time for day hikes and enhance your chances of seeing the mountain and wildlife. Many animals are more active in the morning, especially on hot days. The first bus leaves the visitor center at 5:15am, the next at 6am, and then every half hour until the 2:30pm bus, which gets back at 10:30pm. By taking an early bus, you can get off along the way for a hike, then walk back to the road and get the next bus that comes along with a spare seat. If you were to take the 5am bus, you'd have 9½ hours of slack time before you'd have to catch the last bus heading east. (To be on the safe side, don't push it to the very last bus.) The sun won't set until after 11pm May to July, so there'll be plenty of light. If you need to get back to the park entrance at a certain hour, leave yourself plenty of time, because after getting off your eastbound bus, you can't reserve seats going back the other way, and you may have to wait for a bus with room to take you.

Before you leave for the visitor center to get on your shuttle bus, you need a packed lunch and plenty of water; you should be wearing sturdy walking shoes and layers of warm and lighter clothing with rain gear packed; you should have binoculars or a spotting scope at the ready; and you should have insect repellent handy. You may also want a copy of Kim Heacox's worthwhile booklet ***Denali Road Guide,*** available for $5 at the visitor center bookstore, published by the Alaska Natural History Association, listed above under "Visitor Information." It provides a milepost commentary you can follow as you ride. ANHA also publishes guides to Denali birds, mammals, geology, and trails. If you'll be doing any extensive day hiking, you may also want to bring a detailed topographic map printed on waterproof plastic (available for $9.95

Denali Park Road Bus Facts

Bus	Purpose	Route	Frequency	Fare
ARA courtesy shuttle	Links hotels to park entrance	Hotels 1 mile north and 7 miles south and within park	Continuous loop	Free
Riley Creek Loop	Links facilities within park entrance area	Visitor Center, Riley Creek Campground, rail depot, Park Hotel	Continuous loop	Free
Camper shuttle	Access to campgrounds beyond the park entrance	From the visitor center to Wonder Lake Campground, 85 miles into the park	Several times a day	$15.50 adults, $7.75 children 13–16, free children 12 and under
Backcountry shuttle (or just "the shuttle")	General access to the park and wildlife viewing; limited commentary, depending on the driver; no food service	From the visitor center as far as Kantishna, 89 miles away through the park	Every 30 minutes to Eielson Visitor Center, every hour to Wonder Lake, less frequently to Kantishna	$12.50 to Toklat, $21 to Eielson, $27 to Wonder Lake, $31 to Kantishna; children 13–16 half price, children 12 and under free
Wildlife Tour	Seven-hour guided bus tour with lunch provided; passengers may not get off en route	From the visitor center to the Toklat River or Highway Pass, 53 to 61 miles into the park	Twice daily	$64 adults, $32 ages 11 and younger.
Natural History Tour	Three-hour guided bus tour at the edge of the park	From the visitor center 17 miles into the park	Three times daily	$37 adults, $18.50 age 11 and younger.
Kantishna Roadhouse bus	All-day bus tour to a lodge in Kantishna.	From the park entrance 95 miles to Kantishna	Once a day	$109

from the visitor center or ANHA) and a compass; if you're just going to walk a short distance off the road, you won't need such preparations.

ON YOUR WAY

There are no reserved seats on the bus, but if you arrive early you can find a place on the left side, which has the best views on the way out. Shuttle-bus etiquette is to yell out when you see wildlife. The driver will stop, and everyone will rush to your side of the bus. After you've had a look, give someone else a chance to look out your window or to get a picture. Try to be quiet and don't stick anything out of the bus, as that can scare away the animals. Of course, you have to stay on the bus when animals are present. Most buses will see grizzly bears, caribou, Dall sheep, and moose, and occasionally wolves, but, as one driver said, the animals aren't union workers, and it's possible that you won't see any at all.

The shuttle bus drivers generally offer commentary about the sights on the road, but they don't have to and haven't specifically been trained to teach about natural history. Some do a great job, some pass on inaccurate information, and some don't say much. The tour bus drivers are trained to give commentary.

A ROAD LOG

Here are some of the highlights along the road (check the visitor center or the park service information handouts to confirm times of the guided walks):

MILE 9   In clear weather, this is the closest spot to the park entrance with a view of Mount McKinley. This section also is a likely place to see moose, especially in the fall rutting season.

MILE 14   The end of the paved road at the Savage River Bridge. This generally is as far as private vehicles can go. A park service checkpoint stops anyone who doesn't have a proper permit. From the parking lot by the bridge, a simple climb over dry tundra leads to Primrose Ridge, also known as Mount Wright.

MILE 17   The portable toilets here are as far as the Natural History Tour bus goes.

MILE 29   An hour and 10 minutes into the drive, a large rest stop overlooks the Teklanika River, with flush toilets, the last plumbing until the Eielson Visitor Center. The Teklanika, like many other rivers on Alaska's glacier-carved terrain, is a braided river—a stream wandering in a massive gravel stream bed that's much too big for it. The braided riverbeds, sometimes miles wide, were created by water from fast-melting glaciers at the end of the last ice age. Each is kept free of vegetation by its river, which constantly changes course as it spreads the rock and dust debris carried down from the glaciers. Flat plains in glacial terrain usually are laid down by this mechanism.

MILE 34   Craggy Igloo Mountain is a likely place to see Dall sheep. Without binoculars, they'll just look like white dots. Manageable climbs on Igloo, Cathedral, and Sable mountains take off along the road in the section from Igloo Creek to Sable Pass.

MILE 38–43   Sable Pass, a critical habitat area for bears, is closed to people. A half-eaten sign helps explain why. Bears show up here mostly in the fall. This is the start of the road's broad alpine vistas.

MILE 46   The top of 5-mile-wide Polychrome Pass, the most scenic point on the ride, and a toilet break, 2 hours and 25 minutes into the trip. Caribou look like specks when they pass in the great valley below you, known as the Plain of Murie after Adolph Murie, a biologist who pioneered study here and helped developed the park service's scientific ethic (the name does not always appear on maps, however). Note how the mountains of colored rock on either side of the plain match up—they once connected before glacial ice carved this valley. Huge rocks on its floor are glacial erratics, plucked from the bedrock by moving ice and left behind when it melted.

MILE 53   The Toklat River, another braided river, is a flat plain of gravel with easy walking. The glaciers that feed the river are 10 miles upstream; the river bottom is habitat for bears, caribou, and wolves, and a good place for picnics. A ranger leads an up-to-2-hour hike here called the Toklat Trek—check the visitor center for times.

MILE 58   Highway Pass, the highest point on the road. In good weather, dramatic views of Mount McKinley start here. The alpine tundra from here to the Eielson Visitor Center is inviting for walking, but beware: Tundra is soft underfoot and can conceal holes and declivities that can twist an ankle.

MILE 64   Thorofare Pass, where the road becomes narrow and winding, is a good area to look for bears and caribou. Bus drivers know best where the animals are on any particular day; they exchange information among themselves.

MILE 66   The Eielson Visitor Center, the end of most bus trips, has flush toilets, a covered picnic area, and a small area of displays where rangers answer questions. Among the exhibits is one explaining why you probably can't see the mountain from this best of vantage points, just 33 miles from its summit (Mount McKinley creates its own weather and is visible only about a third of the time in the summer). There's also a seismograph on display, registering the frequent small earthquakes that accompany McKinley's prodigious growth—about an inch every 3 years. This region is a jumble of rocks pushed together by the expanding Pacific tectonic plate; the mountain, and the whole Alaska Range, are folding upward in that great collision. Starting late in June, a ranger-guided tundra walk occurs daily at 1:30pm, lasting no more than an hour. If you leave the bus here for a hike, you can get a ride back later by signing up on the standby list kept by a ranger.

MILE 68.5   The incredibly rugged terrain to the north is the earth and vegetation covering Muldrow Glacier. The ice extends to McKinley's peak, and was the early and arduous route for climbers; these days, they fly to a base camp at 7,200-feet elevation on the Kahiltna Glacier, on the south side. McKinley's glaciers, falling 15,000 vertical feet and extending up to 45 miles in length, are among the world's greatest. The Ruth Glacier has carved the Great Gorge on the south side, which is almost 6,000 feet deep above the ice and another 4,000 below—almost twice the depth of the Grand Canyon. The park road comes within a mile of the Muldrow's face, then continues through wet, rolling terrain past beaver ponds, and finally descends into a small spruce patch near mile 82.

MILE 86   Wonder Lake campground is the closest road point to Mount McKinley, 27 miles away. Some buses continue another half hour to Kantishna. The fact that McKinley looks so massive from this considerable distance, dominating the sky, is a testament to its stupendous size. You'll likely never see a larger object on this planet. From its base (your elevation here is only 2,000 feet) to its top is an elevation gain greater than any other mountain on earth. Other mountains are taller over all, but they stand on higher ground.

5 Denali on Foot: Day Hiking & Backpacking

DAY HIKING IN THE BACKCOUNTRY

One of the unique aspects of Denali is the lack of developed trails—you really can take off in any direction. I've covered some of the best hiking areas above, in "A Road Log," including Primrose Ridge, Teklanika River, Igloo and Sable mountains, and the Toklat

River. The park service, long resistant to building any trails, is giving in and recognizing trails visitors have created. There's a new path planned at Primrose Ridge and a mile-long tundra loop at the Eielson Visitor Center. A 2-mile path leads from the Wonder Lake Campground to the McKinley River Bar, which extends far to the east and west. No permit is needed for day hiking.

The broad, hard gravel flats of the **braided riverbeds,** such as the McKinley, Toklat, Teklanika, and Savage, are among the best routes for hiking in the park. **Stony Creek,** leading up a gorge to the north from the road at mile 60, is an excellent walk into the mountains. You can also hike on the tundra, of which there are two varieties: The **wet tundra** lies on top of permanently frozen ground called permafrost; it's mushy at best, like hiking on foam rubber laid over bowling balls. At worst, it's swamp. **Dry tundra** clothes the mountainsides, and generally makes for firmer footing and easier walking. The brush and stunted forest of the region are virtually impenetrable.

The major risks of hiking here relate to the weather and rivers. It can get cold and wet in the middle of summer, and if you're not prepared with warm, waterproof clothing, you could suffer the spiraling chill of hypothermia. The rivers are dangerous because of their fast flow and icy cold water. See the note on river crossings in chapter 2's "Health & Safety" section; better yet, avoid crossing any sizable rivers. Bears, which people worry most about, have never killed a Denali visitor. Tips on avoiding them are in chapter 2, and widely distributed at the park.

For a first foray beyond the trails, consider joining one of the park service guided hikes. Two daily ✪ **Discovery Hikes** last about 4 hours, with one going somewhere near the Eielson Visitor Center and another nearer the entrance end of the park. A ranger takes only 15 hikers, leading them into wilderness while teaching about the nature of the places they visit. The hikes are not too strenuous for families with school-age children, and they cost no more than the price of your shuttle ticket. You need to wear hiking shoes or boots and bring food, water, and rain gear. Reserve a place in advance, as the hikes fill up during July and you'll need to know when and where to catch the special bus. The **Toklat Trek** is an irregularly scheduled ranger-led walk in the Toklat River stream bed. The **Eielson Stroll,** at 1:30pm daily starting in early June, is a short guided stroll from the Eielson Visitor Center, at mile 66 on the park road. Check in at the visitor center for late word on all the hikes before heading out on a long bus trip.

DAY HIKING IN THE PARK ENTRANCE AREA

There are six short trails at the park entrance, weaving through the boreal forest around small lakes, and one steep and spectacular hike to the **Mount Healy overlook,** a 5-mile round trip. That trail breaks through treeline to slopes of tundra and rock outcroppings, where you can see just how small the pocket of human infestation is at the park entrance area: The Alaska Range and its foothills extend far into the distance. If you were to continue on an all-day hike right to the top of Mount Healy, you could see all the way to McKinley on a clear day. The *Alpenglow* park newspaper contains a brief guide for these trails, and you can get a natural history guide, *The Nature of Denali,* at the visitor center.

BACKPACKING

Imagine backpacking over your own area of wilderness, without trails, limits, or the chance of seeing other people. There's no need to retrace your route to get back: Anywhere you meet the 89-mile Denali Park Road you can catch a bus back to the world of people. Any experienced backpacker should consider a backcountry trek at Denali. Yes, it can be challenging. Hiking on the tundra, broken rock mountainsides, and braided rivers is tiring and it's easy to fall or turn an ankle. You must be prepared for river crossings and cold weather, know how to find your way with a map and compass, and know how to avoid attracting bears. But if you've done a backpacking trip in a less challenging area, you surely can manage it here, so long as you prepare and don't underestimate the additional time you'll need in trailless terrain. Nor do you need to trek far—you could camp just a few miles off the road and still be in a place that looks like no one has ever been there before.

You must be flexible about where you're going and be prepared for any kind of terrain, because you can't choose the **backcountry unit** you will explore until you arrive at the backcountry desk at the visitor center and find out what's available. This information, and a map of the units, is posted on a board behind the desk. Groups of four or more may have a hard time finding a place to hike, but there's almost always *somewhere* to go. You can reserve permits only 1 day in advance; you're unlikely to get one for the day you arrive, but you can reserve permits for continuation of your trip for up to 14 days at the same time. The first night of a trip is the hard one to get—for one thing, you can reserve only units that are contiguous to the park road for the first night—but after that, each night gets progressively easier. A couple of rangers are there to help you through the process. Buy the ***Denali National Park and Preserve* topographical map,** published by Trails Illustrated, available for $9.95 from the Alaska Natural History Association, listed above under "Visitor Information." Printed on plastic, the map includes the boundaries of the 43 backcountry units and much other valuable information. Also, you'll want a copy of ***Backcountry Companion,*** by Jon Nierenberg, a book selling for $8.95 that describes conditions and routes in each area, published and sold by ANHA. It's for sale at the visitor center, or you can look at a well-thumbed copy kept at the backcountry desk.

The alpine units from the Toklat River to Eielson Visitor Center are most popular. That's where you get broad views and can cross heathery dry tundra, walking in any direction. But to go far, you'll also have to be ready to climb over some rugged, rocky terrain, and the tundra itself is deceptively difficult walking—it's soft and hides ankle-turning holes. The wooded units are the least popular, since bushwhacking through overgrown land is anything but fun. The best routes for making time here and anywhere in the Alaska Bush are along the braided river valleys and stream beds. You need to be ready for stream crossings.

Before venturing into the backcountry, everyone is required to watch an **orientation film** called the *Backcountry Simulator.* It's intended to teach you how not to attract bears, but it's intimidating enough to scare you out of the park—don't let it. The park service provides bear-resistant food containers in which you are required to carry all your food. Guns are not permitted in the park; a pepper spray for self-defense from bears is allowed. You'll have to take the **camper bus** to get to your backcountry unit, at a cost of $15.50 for each adult.

Before you decide to go to Denali, however, you may want to broaden your thinking—if you're up to a cross-country hike without a trail, there are tens of millions of acres in Alaska available for backpacking that don't require a permit. Check with the Alaska Public Lands Information Center in Anchorage or Fairbanks for ideas about road-accessible alpine wilderness in Gates of the Arctic National Park, on the

Ranger Programs in the Park

Check the park newspaper, *The Alpenglow,* for ranger talks and slide shows that happen as often as several times a day at the Park Hotel auditorium, at the visitor center, and at the Riley Creek, Savage River, and Teklanika campgrounds.

Denali Highway (covered below); and in Wrangell–St. Elias National Park (in chapter 9). I've listed some great trail hikes in chapter 7, under Chugach National Forest, and in chapter 9, in the sections on Chena Hot Springs Road and the Steese Highway.

6 Biking, Fishing & Other Activities

MOUNTAIN BIKING

A bicycle provides special freedom in the park. Bicyclists can ride past the checkpoint where cars have to turn back, at mile 14 on the park road. Park campgrounds have bike stands, and you can take a bike on the shuttle or camper bus. The longest stretch on the park road between campgrounds is 52 miles. On the downside, the buses kick up a lot of dust, and bikes may not go off-road. Pick up a copy of the bicycle rules from the backcountry desk before you start. **Denali Outdoor Center,** listed below under "Attractions & Activities Outside the Park": rents front-suspension bikes for $40 a day, with discounts for longer rentals. Or shop for a better price or bike in Anchorage and bring it up with you.

SLED DOG DEMONSTRATIONS

In the winter, rangers patrol the park by dog sled, as they have for decades. In the summer, to keep the dogs active and amuse the tourists, they run a sled on wheels around the kennel, and a ranger gives a talk two to three times a day. Although there's no substitute for seeing dogs run on snow, you can get a sense of the dogs' speed and enthusiasm from this show. It was the highlight of my son's trip to Denali when he was 3 years old. There's a shortage of parking at the kennels, near the headquarters at mile 3.4 on the park road, so take a free bus from the visitor center a half our before each show. Times are listed in the *Alpenglow* park newspaper.

FISHING

Fishing is quite poor at Denali. There are grayling in some rivers, but the water is too cold and silty for most fish. Those who don't care if they catch anything, however, do enjoy fishing in this wonderful scenery. You don't need a fishing license within park boundaries, but you do have to throw back everything you catch. Bring your own gear, as it's unavailable in the park area.

CLIMBING MOUNT MCKINLEY

McKinley, because of its altitude and weather, is among the world's most challenging climbs. Summer temperatures at the high camp average 20° to 40° below zero. If you're looking here for advice, you're certainly not up to an unguided climb. A guided climb is a challenging and expensive endeavor requiring months of conditioning and about a month on the mountain. Get names of guides from the Park Service's **Talkeetna Ranger Station,** P.O. Box 588, Talkeetna, AK 99676 (☎ **907/733-2231**). The climbing season lasts from late April or early May until the snow gets too soft, in late June or early July. Climbers fly from Talkeetna to a 7,200-foot base camp on Kahiltna Glacier. About 1,000 climbers attempt the mountain annually in about 300 parties; about half typically make it to the top each year, and usually several die trying.

7 Attractions & Activities Outside the Park

FLIGHTSEEING

Getting a good, close look at Mount McKinley itself is best accomplished by air. Frequently, you can see McKinley from above the clouds even when you can't see it from the ground. Best of all, some Talkeetna operators that fly mountaineers also land

First to the Top

It's the biggest. That's why climbers risk their lives on **Mount McKinley** and why politicians fight over its name. You can see the mountain from Anchorage, more than 100 miles away. On a flight across Alaska, McKinley stands out grandly over waves of other mountains. It's more than a mile taller than the tallest peak in the other 49 states. It's a great white triangle, always covered in snow, tall but also massive and strong.

The Athabascans of Interior Alaska named it **Denali,** translated as "the high one," or "the great one," but spent little time in the immediate area, where the weather is too severe and the rivers too silty to produce much fish or game. The first white men to wander into the area were looking for gold; in 1896 a prospector named the mountain after William McKinley of Ohio, who was elected president of the United States that year. Alaskans prefer the Athabascan name, and since 1975 have petitioned to change it officially back. Ohio won't allow it. In 1980, congressmen from Alaska and Ohio compromised on the issue, changing the name of the national park to Denali but leaving the mountain named McKinley.

Alaskans still want the mountain's name changed, but the U.S. Board on Geographical Names has refused to take up the issue. They have a rule against considering an issue that is also before Congress, and Rep. Ralph Regula of Ohio has repeatedly introduced a one-paragraph bill saying the name should stay the same. The bill never goes anywhere, but just having it introduced has been enough to stop the name board. In 1999, Alaska representative Don Young brought the issue back to life with an opposing bill to change the name to Denali. He said Regula should name something in Ohio for McKinley.

The first group to try to climb Mount McKinley came in 1903, led by **Judge James Wickersham,** who also helped explore Washington's Olympic Peninsula before it became a national park. His group made it less than halfway up, but on the trip they found gold in the Kantishna Hills, setting off a small gold rush that led to the first permanent human settlement in the park area. Wickersham later became the Alaska Territory's nonvoting delegate to Congress and introduced the bill that created the national park, but the government was never able to get back land in the Kantishna area from the gold miners. Today, that land is the site of four luxurious wilderness lodges, right in the middle of the park.

On September 27, 1906, renowned world explorer **Dr. Frederick Cook** announced to the world by telegraph that he had reached the summit of Mount McKinley after a lightning-fast climb, covering more than 85 miles and 19,000 vertical feet in 13 days with one other man, a blacksmith, at his side. On his return to New York, Cook was lionized as a conquering explorer and published a popular book of his summit diary and photographs.

In 1909, Cook again made history, announcing that he had beat Robert Peary to the North Pole. Both returned to civilization from their competing treks at

visitors on the mountain itself, a unique and unforgettable experience (see the Talkeetna section, below, and see chapter 6, on Anchorage, for an air excursion from there). Small planes and helicopters fly from the park airstrip, private heliports and airstrips along the Parks Highway, and the Healy airstrip. **Denali Air** (☎ **907/ 683-2261**) has an office in the Nenana Canyon area, and flight operations at mile about the same time. Again Cook was the toast of the world. Then his Eskimo companions mentioned that he'd never been out of sight of land, and his story began to fall apart. After being paid by Peary to come forward, Cook's McKinley companion also recanted. A year later, Cook's famous summit photograph was re-created on a peak 19 miles away and 15,000 feet lower than the real summit.

In 1910, disgusted with Cook, four prospectors from Fairbanks took a more Alaskan approach to the task. Without fanfare or special supplies—they carried doughnuts and hot chocolate on their incredible final ascent—they marched up the mountain carrying a large wooden flagpole they could plant on top to prove they'd made it. But on arriving at the summit, they realized that they'd climbed the slightly shorter north peak. Weather closed in, so they set up the pole there and descended without attempting the south peak. Then, when they got back to Fairbanks, no one could see the pole, and they were accused of trying to pull off another hoax.

In 1913, Episcopal archdeacon **Hudson Stuck** organized the first successful climb to reach the real summit—and reported he saw the pole on the other peak. **Harry Karstens** led the climb (he would become the park's first superintendent in 1917), and the first person to stand at the summit was an Alaska Native, **Walter Harper.**

McKinley remains one of the world's most difficult climbs, even with modern, lightweight gear, but since 1980 the number of climbers has boomed and it's become crowded at the top. Garbage disposal is a problem. Over 1,000 people try to climb the peak each year, with about half making it to the summit; in 1970, only 124 made the attempt. The cold and fast-changing weather is what usually stops people. From late April into early July, climbers fly from the town of Talkeetna to a base camp at 7,200 feet elevation on the Kahiltna Glacier. From there, it takes about a month to get to the top, through temperatures as cold as –40°.

During the season, the Park Service stations rescue rangers and an emergency medical clinic at the 14,200-foot level of the mountain, and keeps a special high-altitude helicopter ready to go after climbers who get in trouble. They and the military spend about half a million dollars a year rescuing climbers, and sometimes much more. In 1998, a volunteer ranger lost his life trying to save a Canadian who had fallen. Including the three who died that year, 91 people have perished on McKinley over the years, mostly in falls, but also from the cold and altitude. Many others lose fingers, toes, and other parts to frostbite every year, or suffer other, more severe injuries.

About 10,000 people have made it to the top since Hudson Stuck's party. Monuments to those who never returned are in the cemetery near the airstrip in Talkeetna.

229.5 of the Parks Highway. An hour-long flight going within a mile of the mountain costs $165 for adults, $135 for children age 12 and under. **Era Helicopters** (☎ **800/ 843-1947** or 907/683-2574; www.era-aviation.com) has hourly flights for $190, including van pickup from the hotels. Their helihikes land for a 3-hour hike, for $280, and their 75-minute glacier-landing flights are $292.

RAFTING

Rafting on the Nenana River, bordering the park along the Parks Highway, is fun and popular. Several commercial guides float two stretches of the river: an upper portion, where the water is smoother and the guides explain passing scenery; and the lower portion, where the river roars through the rock-walled Nenana Canyon, and rafts take on huge splashes of silty, glacial water through Class III and IV rapids. Guides take children as young as 5 on the slow trip (although I don't know if I'd let my kid go at that age); the youngest accepted for the fast portion is age 12. White-water rafting carries risks you shouldn't discount just because a lot of people do it, as a fatal accident on the supposedly easy tour confirmed in 1999. Each session takes 2 to 2½ hours, including safety briefings, suiting up, and riding to and from the put-in and take-out points. Prices are around $50 for adults, with discounted rates for children (from $10 less to half off). **Denali Outdoor Center** (☎ **888/303-1925** or 907/683-1925; www.denalioutdoorcenter.com) is a professional operation, offering rafting trips and instruction in river techniques. There are five firms in competition, however, so you may be able to save by shopping around. When reserving, make sure to ask what kind of gear is provided: Dry suits will keep you comfortable, while you're likely to get drenched if all they give you is rain gear or Mustang floatation suits. If you're camping, plan a shower afterward, as the silt in the river water will stick to your skin and hair.

HORSEBACK RIDING

There is no riding in the park itself, but you have several opportunities in similar terrain outside its boundaries. Various companies offer rides, although the lineup of firms seem to change every year. Sixty- to 90-minute rides cost from $55 to $70. Among the operators are **Cripple Creek Ranch** (☎ **907/683-7670**) and **Denali Saddle Safaris** (☎ **907/683-1200**). Pack trips and extended journeys are available, too.

8 Accommodations

PARK SERVICE CAMPGROUNDS

I've explained how to make camping reservations above under "The Reservation System." Note the reservation fees that are added to camping fees. Only Riley Creek Campground is open after September. The rest reopen when the snow is gone, in May for all but Wonder Lake, which opens in June.

CAR-ACCESSIBLE CAMPGROUNDS

In addition to these, see **Teklanika River campground** under "Bus-Accessible Campgrounds" below, which you can drive to as long as your stay is 3 days long.

Morino Backpacker Campground. One mile from park entrance, near railroad depot. $6 per night; tents only.

This campground is simply an area of trees near the entrance where you can self-register, put up a tent, and use a port-a-potty. There's no parking, and only two people are allowed per site.

Riley Creek. Near the visitor center. $12 per site. 150 sites; RVs or tents. Campfires allowed; flush toilets, dump station.

This large campground right across the road from the visitor center is best for those who want to be in the middle of things, near the store, showers, a bus stop for the free front-country shuttle, and a pay phone. Sites are wooded with small birch and spruce

---

Keeping Clean at Denali

Keeping yourself scrubbed at Denali can be a challenge, as none of the campgrounds have showers. In the front country, campgrounds have the typical cold-water bathrooms found in the national parks. Better bathrooms are at the hotels and visitor center. Showers are at **McKinley Mercantile,** across from the railroad depot, and cost $3, with a $5 key deposit. There's no time limit or coin machine to feed. You also can take showers, even if you're not a guest, at **McKinley RV and Campground** (listed below) for $2.50. They have a token-operated laundry, too.

---

and adequately separated, but its far from wilderness camping. Reservations are relatively easy to get. The park's only sewage dump station is here.

Savage River. On Denali Park Rd., 13 miles from entrance. $12 per site. 33 sites; RVs or tents. Campfires allowed; flush toilets.

On the taiga—the thin spruce forest and tundra—this is a wonderful campground with unforgettable views. Campers can wander from their sites on some of the park's best hikes. This is the only campground you can readily drive to that's away from the activity at the park entrance.

BUS-ACCESSIBLE CAMPGROUNDS

To use these campgrounds, you'll need a camper ticket on the shuttle bus, which costs $15.50 for adults, $7.75 ages 13 to 16, free 12 and under.

Igloo Creek and Sanctuary River. On Denali Park Rd., 23 miles and 34 miles from park entrance, respectively.

These two primitive campgrounds, each with seven tent sites, offer a backcountry experience, away from cars. There's a $6 camping fee and no campfires are allowed, only stoves. Also, you can't reserve in advance, only in person at the visitor center when you arrive. Both have only chemical toilets.

Teklanika River. On Denali Park Rd., 29 miles from entrance; access by camper bus, or drive in with a minimum 3-day stay. $12 per site. 53 sites; RVs or tents. Campfires allowed; flush toilets.

This is the only car campground that's beyond the checkpoint on the Park Road. You can drive in only if you don't move your vehicle for 3 days; otherwise, take the camper bus. Sites are among the small trees of the boreal forest. The big advantage of staying here is that you begin the morning much closer to the heart of the park, cutting the time you have to spend on the bus, and one bus ticket lasts your whole 3-day stay. Using this base for 3 days, you could really explore different areas of the park in different kinds of weather.

Wonder Lake. On Denali Park Rd., 85 miles from entrance. $12 per site. 28 sites; tents only. No campfires, stove only; flush toilets.

It takes almost 6 hours to get here, but this campground by placid Wonder Lake, at the foot of Mount McKinley, puts you in the most beautiful and coveted area of the park. Sites are among a patch of spruce trees on the mountain side of the lake. Sites are tough to get.

COMMERCIAL CAMPGROUNDS

There are two commercial campgrounds in the area. **Denali Grizzly Bear Cabins and Campground,** P.O. Box 7, Denali National Park, AK 99755 (☎ **907/683-2696;** fax 907/683-2697; www.AlaskaOne.com/dengrzly), is about 7 miles south of the park entrance, and has some exposed sites and others on a hillside among small trees. Small cabins and tent cabins dot the property, too. There is a coin-operated shower. Tent sites are $16.50 for up to four people, with electrical and water hookups $6 more. A better-developed campground is 10 miles north of the park, in Healy. **McKinley RV and Campground,** at mile 248.5 on Parks Hwy. (P.O. Box 340) Healy, AK 99743 (☎ 800/478-2562 in Alaska only, or 907/683-2379) has a token-operated laundry, hot showers, and a small playground. Basic tent sites are $17.50 to $20.25, full hookups $28.75.

HOTELS

Patterns of land ownership and the furious pace of development around Denali have led to a hodgepodge of roadside hotels, cabins, lodges, campgrounds, and restaurants in pockets arrayed along more than 20 miles of the Parks Highway. There are rooms of good quality in each of the pockets, but the going rates vary widely. The most expensive rooms, and the first booked, are in the immediate area of the park entrance. Next are the hotels south of the park. Both these areas are entirely seasonal. The best deals are in **Healy,** 10 miles north of the park, where you can find a room for $50 less than a comparable room near the park entrance. Of course, if you don't have a car, it's most convenient to stay in or near the park. The other choices are to stay in **Talkeetna,** the back door to the park (described later in this chapter); at a lodge in the **Kantishna** inholding within the park; or at a remote **wilderness lodge** (covered in chapter 2). I've listed each of the choices separately. Despite their high prices, rooms can be hard to find in the high season, and it's wise to book well ahead. If you don't mind gambling, however, you can often get great last-minute deals from hotels that have had large cancellations from their package tour clients.

NEAR THE PARK

This area, sometimes known as Denali or Nenana Canyon, extends about a mile north of the park entrance on the Parks Highway, including the park hotel, which is 1½ miles within the park. Two huge hotels that primarily serve package tour passengers dominate the area, the **Denali Princess Lodge,** mile 238.5, Parks Hwy. (P.O. Box 110), Denali National Park, AK 997555 (☎ **800/426-0050;** fax 206/443-1979), and the **McKinley Resorts Chalets,** mile 238.5, Parks Hwy. (mailing address: 241 W. Ship Creek Ave., Anchorage, AK 99501; ☎ **800/276-7234** or 907/276-7234; fax 907/258-3668). If they have a cancellation, you may be able to get attractive rooms at one of these places at the last minute for a fraction of their astronomical rack rates. The McKinley Resorts Chalets also is a good place to book activities.

Since most readers are independent travelers, I've concentrated instead on smaller lodgings that cater to individual bookings. In addition to those I've listed, you'll find good standard rooms at **Denali River View Inn,** mile 238.4, Parks Hwy. (P.O. Box 49), Denali National Park, AK 99755 (☎ **907/683-2663;** fax 907/683-7433), for $134 double, and at **Sourdough Cabins,** mile 238.5, Parks Hwy. (P.O. Box 118), Denali, AK 99755 (☎ **907/683-2773**), which has comfortable little cabins in the woods below the highway for similar prices. All of the hotels in this area are open only during the tourist season, roughly May 15 to September 15.

Denali Bluffs Hotel. Mile 238.4, Parks Hwy. (P.O. Box 72460, Fairbanks, AK 99707). ☎ **907/683-7000.** Fax 907/683-7500. denalibluffs.com. 112 units. TV TEL. High season,

$179 double. Low season, $126 double. Additional person in room $10 extra. AE, DISC, MC, V.

A series of 12 buildings on a steep mountainside look down on the Nenana Canyon area from above the highway. The light, tastefully decorated rooms have two double beds, coffeemakers, and small refrigerators, and those on the upper floor have vaulted ceilings and balconies with great views. A courtesy van will take you anywhere in the area, and a coin-op laundry is available. A dining room serves simple meals for breakfast and lunch.

Denali Crow's Nest Cabins. Mile 238.5, Parks Hwy. (P.O. Box 70), Denali National Park, AK 99755. ☎ **907/683-2723.** Fax 907/683-2323. www.denalicrowsnest.com. 39 cabins. High season, $147 cabin for 2. Low season, $79. Additional person in cabin $10 extra. MC, V.

Perched in five tiers on the side of a mountain above the Nenana Canyon area, looking down on Horseshoe Lake and the other, larger hotels, the cabins are roomy and comfortable, especially those on the 100 and 200 levels. A log cabin and the warmth of the Crofoot family create more of an appropriate Alaskan feeling than the modern, standard rooms that have filled the canyon. You spend a lot of time climbing stairs, however, and despite the great views and the price, the cabins are simple, not luxurious; the rooms have shower enclosures, not tubs. They book tours and offer a courtesy van, free coffee, and an outdoor Jacuzzi. The restaurant, **The Overlook,** is recommended separately under "Dining," later in this chapter.

Denali National Park Hotel. Mile 1.5, Denali National Park Rd. (P.O. Box 87), Denali Park, AK 99755 (for reservations, contact Denali Park Resorts, 241 W. Ship Creek Ave., Anchorage, AK 99501; ☎ **800/276-7234;** fax 907/258-3668; www.denalinationalpark.com). 100 units. High season, $149 double. Low season, $109 double. Additional person in room $10 extra. AE, DISC, MC, V.

The original park hotel burned down in 1972, replaced by this "temporary" structure, cobbled together from old railroad cars and modular housing units. It will close for good in September 2001 as part of a long-term park plan; the alternative was to build a new, permanent structure, and the Park Service rightly took the opportunity instead to eliminate lodgings from within park boundaries. Despite its flawed pedigree, the doomed structure has quirky, oddly historic character beyond most of the bland, standard places outside the park. Staying here puts you at the center of park activities, with the front-country hiking trails leaving from out the back door. The rooms need remodeling, however, and have no views. There's a courtesy shuttle, coffee in the rooms, and a tour desk.

The attractive **dining room** serves large portions. The lounge, in a pair of railroad cars, has a good, campy feel. Smoking is permitted in only one of the two rail cars the hotel occupies, a fair arrangement for both sides of that debate. For fast food, the snack bar is quite adequate and probably the best place for takeout in the area. The gift shop has reasonable prices, regulated by the park service.

IN HEALY

Healy is 10 miles north of the park entrance, but a world away. It's a year-round community with an economy based primarily on a large coal mine and only secondarily on the park. It sits in a large, windy valley with a few patches of stunted trees and big, open spaces of tundra. There are many hotels and bed-and-breakfasts with rooms that cost from $20 to $90 less than those near the park. They say the water tastes better, too. On the downside, you need a car to stay in Healy.

Besides my two favorites listed below, you'll find hundreds of small, serviceable rooms with twin beds at a converted pipeline camp, the **Denali North Star Inn,** mile 248.5, Parks Hwy. (P.O. Box 240), Healy, AK 99743 (☎ **800/684-1560** or

907/683-1560; fax 907/683-4026; e-mail: DNSI@hotmail.com), for $110 double. Across the highway, the **Stampede Lodge,** mile 248.8, Parks Hwy. (P.O. Box 380), Healy, AK 99743 (☎ **907/683-2242;** fax 907/683-2243), has attractively decorated rooms, on the small side, in a renovated 1946 railroad building. They charge $90 double, in the summer. There's a reasonably priced restaurant inside serving three meals a day.

✪ **Motel Nord Haven.** Mile 249.5, Parks Hwy. (P.O. Box 458), Healy, AK 99743. ☎ **800/ 683-4501** or 907/683-4500. Fax 907/683-4503. www.ptialaska.net/~nordhavn/. 24 units. TV TEL. High season, $108–$117 double. Winter, $70 double. AE, MC, V.

This fresh little gray hotel with a red roof has large, immaculate rooms with one or two queen-size beds. They're equal to the best standard rooms in the Denali Park area and a lot less expensive. Bill and Patsy Nordmark offer free newspapers; coffee, tea, and hot chocolate; free laundry machines; and a sitting room with a collection of Alaskan books. The rooms, decorated with Alaskan art and oak trim, all have interior entrances and have been nonsmoking since construction. Up to four people can stay in the rooms with two beds for the price of a double. They'll pack a sack lunch for $8, or you can eat breakfast or lunch there from a menu of soup, salad, or sandwiches.

White Moose Lodge. Mile 248, Parks Hwy. (P.O. Box 68), Healy, AK 99743. ☎ **800/ 481-1232** or 907/683-1231. www.AlaskaOne.com/whitemoose. 12 units. TV. $90 double. Rates include continental breakfast. Additional adult in room $10 extra, additional child $5 extra. AE, DC, DISC, MC, V. Closed Oct to mid-May.

This old, low-slung building among stunted black spruce contains some unlikely finds—a small greenhouse and comfortable, cheerfully decorated rooms with flower boxes—and the breakfast consists of coffee, tea, orange juice, and pastries in the small lobby.

DENALI AREA
South of the Park

Lodgings south of the park are in widely separated pockets of private land. The first is 7 miles south of the park, and the second 14 miles south.

Denali Cabins. Mile 229, Parks Hwy. (P.O. Box 229), Denali National Park, AK 99755. ☎ **907/683-2643.** Fax 907/683-2595. www.alaskan.com/denalicabins. (In winter, 200 W. 34th Ave., Suite 362, Anchorage, AK 99503; ☎ 907/258-0134; fax 907/243-2062). 43 units. High season, $128 cabin for two; $159 suite (a larger cabin). Additional person in room $10 extra. Low season, $84 cabin for up to 4 people. MC, V. Closed mid-Sept to mid-May.

These roomy cedar cabins, arranged around a grassy compound with a pair of hot tubs, are a good choice for families. The kids may well find someone their own age to play with on the boardwalks or lawns. Also, with a cabin you don't have to worry as much about noise. The prices are high, however, for rooms that are quite basic, lacking TVs or telephones and with shower stalls instead of tubs. There's free coffee in the lobby and an inexpensive restaurant. You will need a car to get to the park.

Denali River Cabins. Mile 231, Parks Hwy. (mailing address: P.O. Box 81250, Fairbanks, AK 99708). ☎ **800/230-7275** or 907/683-2500. Fax 907/456-5212. www.denalirivercabins. com. 54 cabins. High season, $140–$150 cabin for 2. Low season, $95–$105 cabin for 2. Additional person in room $10 extra. DISC, MC, V.

These cedar cabins along a maze of boardwalks above the Nenana River feel fresh and luxurious. The sauna has a picture window on the river, and there's a Jacuzzi, free coffee and newspapers, and a comfortable lobby. They have shower stalls, not tubs, and lack closets. Those on the river, with decks over the water, are $10 more.

✪ **The Perch.** Mile 224, Parks Hwy. (P.O. Box 53) Denali National Park, AK 99755. ☎ **888/ 322-2523,** or ☎ and fax 907/683-2523. www.AlaskaOne.com/perchrest. 21 cabins, 14 with bathroom. $65–$95 cabin for 2. Additional person in cabin $10 extra. AE, DISC, MC, V.

In the trees along rushing Carlo Creek, 13 miles south of the park entrance, a variety of cabins range from large, modern units with private bathrooms to adorable if spartan little A-frames with lofts that share a bath house. There's a sense of privacy and of being out in the woods along the wooden and gravel walkways. It's an exceptional value. You will need a car to stay here. Atop a steep hill, the **restaurant and bar** is one of my favorites in the area, described below under "Dining."

WILDERNESS LODGES

For those who can afford it, a lodge allows you to experience real wilderness in complete comfort. Here I've listed the three lodges in the Kantishna district (an old gold mining inholding at the heart of the park, near McKinley) and one fly-in lodge east of the park. All are open only in the summer months. You get to Kantishna on a private bus or van over the 89-mile park road, guided by your host. Once there, you can explore the park using a special pass for shuttle rides starting in Kantishna, which costs $15.50. See the Talkeetna section, below, for other choices.

✪ **Camp Denali/North Face Lodge.** Kantishna District (P.O. Box 67), Denali National Park, AK 99755. ☎ **907/683-2290** or 907/683-1568. www.gorp.com/dnpwild. 17 cabins, none with bathroom (Camp Denali); 15 units with bathroom (North Face Lodge). $325 per person per night, double occupancy, all inclusive. Minimum stay 3 nights. No credit cards.

Uniquely at this pioneering ecotourism establishment, you can wake to the white monolith of Mount McKinley filling your window. Also uniquely, the naturalist guides here have the right to use the park road free of the shuttle system for hikes, biking, lake canoeing, bird watching, photography sessions, and other outdoor learning activities. During some sessions, nationally reputed academics and other experts lead the program. All arrivals and departures are on fixed session dates and start with a picnic on the park road on the way out. The Camp Denali cabins each have their own outhouse and share a central bath house and wonderful shared lodge rooms—it would be my first choice for anyone who can stand not having his or her own flush toilet. North Face Lodge has smallish traditional rooms with private baths. A conservation ethic pervades the operation, from the homegrown vegetables to the proprietors' efforts to preserve the natural values of private land in the park.

Denali Backcountry Lodge. Kantishna District (P.O. Box 189), Denali National Park, AK 99755. ☎ **800/841-0692** or 907/683-2594. Fax 907/683-1341. www.denalilodge.com. (In winter: P.O. Box 810, Girdwood, AK 99587; ☎ 907/783-1342; fax 907/783-1308). 30 cabins. $299 per person per night, double occupancy, all inclusive. 3-night minimum recommended. MC, V.

Thirty comfortable, modern, cedar cabins sit in rows on a deck next to babbling Moose Creek and a two-story lodge building. Guests can sit in a screened porch away from the mosquitoes and watch the day go by, or join a choice of guided hikes, natural history programs, or other activities around the lodge each day. To go out into the park, you're on your own, either on a lodge mountain bike or the shuttle, although the ride in from the entrance is treated as a safari. It's run by Alaska Wildland Adventures, which offers a variety of well-regarded ecotourism packages all over the state, including some that include a stay at the lodge.

Kantishna Roadhouse. Kantishna District, Denali National Park (mailing address: P.O. Box 81670, Fairbanks, AK 99708). ☎ **800/942-7420** or 907/683-1475. Fax 907/683-1449.

www.kantishnaroadhouse.com. (Winter: ☎ 907/479-2436, fax 907/479-2611). 28 units. $280 per person per night, double occupancy, all inclusive. AE, DC, DISC, MC, V.

This well-kept property of many buildings along Moose Creek in the old Kantishna Mining District trades on both the mining history and outdoor opportunities of the area. Some rooms are large and luxurious, while others are in smaller single cabins with lofts. The log central lodge has an attractive lobby with people coming and going—it's got more of a hotel feel and might be more attractive to an older, less active set than the other lodges in the Kantishna District. It's also less expensive and available for shorter stays. Daily activities include guided hikes, wagon rides, horseback riding, biking, and gold panning, and there's an excellent sled dog demonstration that coincides with a $109 day trip that comes out for the bus ride and lunch only.

Denali Wilderness Lodge. Wood River (mailing address: P.O. Box 50, Denali National Park, AK 99755). ☎ **800/541-9779** year-round, or 907/683-1287. Fax 907/479-4410. www.DenaliWildernessLodge.com. (In winter: P.O. Box 71784, Fairbanks, AK 99707; ☎ 907/479-4000.) 23 units and cabins. $290 per person per night, double occupancy, all inclusive. AE, DISC, MC, V.

The extraordinary log buildings were built by the late big-game guide Lynn Castle along the Wood River, and his amazing collection of mounted exotic animals from all over the world is in a sort of museum room. They don't kill the animals anymore: Now they're more valuable to look at alive, and the lodge has become an ecoestablishment, flying guests in for as little as a half day for flightseeing, horseback riding, rafting, hiking, and talks by naturalists. Stay at least a couple of days to really experience the place. This is the best place for horseback riders, with a sizable stable and one ride included in the price. The cabins, while not luxurious, are quite comfortable and have private bathrooms. The food is terrific. The location is distant from Mount McKinley, in a remote valley 30 miles east of the park entrance.

9 Dining

The large hotels all have fine dining and casual restaurants. The restaurants at the **Denali Princess Lodge** have beautiful dining rooms with great views. The **Chalet Center Cafe** at the McKinley Resorts Chalets is one of my favorites for a relaxed, inexpensive meal. It's a cafeteria serving good sandwiches and healthy dishes, in a large, light room. You can't miss the tacky highway frontage of the **McKinley Denali Salmon Bake** in the Nenana Canyon area. Although casual to the point of indifference, it can be a fun place to eat in a picnic setting, and the food is fine. A new restaurant, **The Denali Roadhouse** (☎ **907/683-2500**) was planned to open at the Denali River Cabins (see above), but not in time for me to check it out. The owners' description of a bakery-deli-bar with microbrews sounded appealing.

Lynx Creek Pizza. Mile 238.6, Parks Hwy. ☎ **907/683-2547.** All items $3.25–$22.95. AE, DISC, MC, V. Daily 11am–11:30pm. Closed late Sept to early May. PIZZERIA.

This ARAMARK-managed pizza restaurant is a center of activity for the less-well-heeled visitors to Denali, as its the only place to get a slice and a cheap beer. The food isn't anything special, and there often are lines to order, but the dining room is a low-key, relatively nontouristy place to meet young people.

The Overlook Bar and Grill. Mile 238.5, Parks Hwy., up the hill above the Denali Canyon area. ☎ **907/683-2641.** Lunch main courses $9–$15; dinner $16–$30. MC, V. 11am–11pm. Closed mid-Sept to mid-May. BURGERS/STEAK/SEAFOOD.

This fun, noisy place has the feeling of a classic bar and grill, with a vaulted ceiling of rough-cut lumber and a spectacular view of the Nenana Canyon. There are two dining rooms, one with the bar, and another, behind a glass partition, which is quieter and has tablecloths. A huge variety of craft beers is available, with several on tap. At times I've gotten superb fare here, but the last time I visited, I found the meal prices too high and the food no better than acceptable—my halibut obviously had been long frozen. All the steaks on the menu are $30.

The Perch. Mile 224, Park Hwy. ☎ **907/683-2523.** Lunch $7.50–$8.50, dinner $14–$40. Summer, daily 6am–10pm. Winter-hours vary. AE, DISC, MC, V. STEAK/SEAFOOD

The odd, knoblike hill the restaurant stands on provides reason for the name (the attractive cabins, described above, are down below). It's a friendly, family-run place serving a simple steak and seafood menu—they don't try anything fancy, but they do what they do right. The home-baked bread is noteworthy. The dining room is light, with well-spaced tables, and makes up for a certain coldness with big picture windows on three sides. It's located 13 miles south of the park.

10 Denali in the Evening

The main evening event is the concessionaire's **Cabin Nite Dinner Theater,** at the McKinley Resorts Chalets (☎ **800/276-7234** or 907/683-8200), a professionally produced musical revue about a gold rush–era woman who ran a roadhouse in Kantishna. You can buy the $39 tickets, half price under age 11, virtually anywhere in the area. The actors, singing throughout the evening, stay in character to serve big platters of food to diners sitting at long tables, doing a good job of building a rowdy, happy atmosphere for adults and kids. You go for the show, not the all-you-can-eat salmon and ribs—they try to make up for the quality with quantity. Princess Cruises and Tours puts on a similar evening show, **Mt. McK's Roadhouse Review,** in a big wall tent at the Denali Princess Lodge. The local rap says: better food, worse show. Tickets are for sale at the hotel's tour desk (☎ **800/426-0500** or 907/683-2282) for $35, or $14 for the show without the meal.

11 Talkeetna: Back Door to Denali

Talkeetna, a historic and funky little town with a sense of humor but not much happening, slept soundly from its decline around World War I until just a few years ago. Now there are paved streets (both of them), a new National Park Service building of stone, a new railroad depot, and two large new luxury lodges. It seems that while Talkeetna slumbered in a time capsule, an explosion of visitors was happening at Denali National Park. Now, not entirely voluntarily, Talkeetna finds itself enveloped in that boom.

As a threshold to the park, Talkeetna has significant pros and cons that you should take into account. On the positive side, it's closer to Anchorage; the development is much more interesting and authentic than at the park entrance; there's lots to do in the outdoors and great views of the mountain, less frequently obscured by clouds. On the negative side, a big minus: You can't get into the park from here. That means you miss the dramatic scenery, easy backcountry access, and unique wildlife viewing on the park road.

The town itself dates from the gold rush, and there are many charming log and clapboard buildings. With 15 sites of historic note, the entire downtown area has been listed on the National Register of Historic Places. You can spend several hours looking at two small museums and meeting people in the 2-block main street, then go out on the Talkeetna or Susitna river for rafting, a jet boat ride, or fishing, or take a flight-seeing trip to the national park.

ESSENTIALS
GETTING THERE

BY CAR   Talkeetna lies on a 13-mile spur road that branches from the Parks Highway 99 miles north of Anchorage and 138 miles south of the park entrance.

BY TRAIN   The Alaska Railroad serves Talkeetna daily on its runs to Denali National Park during the summer, and weekly in the winter. (See the listing earlier in this chapter.) The summer fare from Anchorage to Talkeetna is $60 one-way for adults, half price for children.

BY SHUTTLE VAN   The **Talkeetna Shuttle Service,** P.O. Box 468, Talkeetna, AK 99676 (☎ **907/733-1725** office, or 907/355-1725 cellular), runs back and forth to Anchorage for $42 one-way, $80 round-trip.

GETTING AROUND

You can walk everywhere in Talkeetna, but there are good **mountain biking** routes, too. **CGS Bicycles,** on Main Street (P.O. Box 431), Talkeetna, AK 99676 (☎ **907/ 733-1279**), is a full-service bike shop, renting mountain bikes for $15 a day and leading trail tours starting at $20 per person.

VISITOR INFORMATION

Built to serve people who aim to climb Mount McKinley, the **Denali National Park Talkeetna Ranger Station,** downtown Talkeetna (P.O. Box 588), Talkeetna, AK 99676 (☎ **907/733-2231;** www.nps.gov/dena), makes a fascinating stop for anyone curious about mountaineering. Inside the handsome river rock structure you'll find a large sitting room with a fireplace, climbing books, and pictures of the mountain—it's like an old-fashioned explorers' club. Records open for inspection cover the history of McKinley climbs. Rangers are on hand to answer questions, too. It's open daily 8am to 6pm in summer, Monday to Friday 8am to 4:30pm in winter.

   The **Denali/Talkeetna Visitor Center,** located in a tiny cabin at the intersection of the Parks Highway and Talkeetna Spur Road (P.O. Box 688), Talkeetna, AK 99676 (☎ **800/660-2688,** 907/733-2688 summer, or 907/733-2499 winter; www.alaskan. com/talkeetnadenali/), is a commercial center providing brochures and information while trying to snag bookings for the sponsoring businesses. It's the handiest commercial information stop in the region. Open daily 8am to 8pm in summer.

SPECIAL EVENTS

The Talkeetna Moose Dropping Festival, held over a weekend in mid-July, is the big event of the year, a community fair finishing its third decade as a fundraiser for the Talkeetna Historical Society (☎ **907/733-2487;** www.moosedrop.com). The main event doesn't involve dropping moose, as an aggrieved animal lover once complained, but dropping moose droppings. There's also a parade and many other events.

Fast Facts: Talkeetna

Banks   The coin-operated laundry and store at the Three Rivers gas station on Main Street in Talkeetna has an ATM.

Hospital   The Sunshine Community Health Center, at mile 4.4 on the Talkeetna Spur Road (☎ 907/733-2273, after hours 907/733-2348), is staffed by physician's assistants.

Police   The Alaska State Troopers (☎ 907/733-2256), at mile 97.8 on the Parks Highway, are just south of the intersection with the Talkeetna Spur Road.

Post Office   At the town center, near the intersection of Talkeetna Spur Road and Main Street.

Taxes   There is no sales tax. Bed tax in the area is 5%.

ATTRACTIONS & ACTIVITIES IN TOWN

Talkeetna is famous for its laid-back atmosphere and outdoors, not for activities, but there are several places to stop in to get the sense of the place. One is the ranger station mentioned above under "Visitor Information." If you come in May or June, you're sure to meet many international mountain climbers; you'll have no difficulty picking them out. The **Fairview Inn** is a historic bar with the rough edges still in place. Along Main Street, artists and craftspeople have shops where you can often find them at work. The **Talkeetna Historical Society Museum,** on the Village Airstrip a half block south of Main Street (☎ **907/733-2487**), contains artifacts and displays on the local mining history, including photographs and biographies of individual characters. It's also a good place to get community information, open daily in summer, 10:30am to 5:30pm. Admission is $1. The **Museum of Northern Adventure** is a wax museum of Alaska scenes and memorabilia, on the east end of Main Street (☎ **907/733-3999**). It's funny and corny, and great for children. Admission is $2 for adults, $1 for children.

I've found the most affecting site in town to be the **mountain climbers' memorial** at the town cemetery, near the airstrip on the east side of the railroad tracks. Besides a granite memorial of plaques for lost mountaineers, there is a small garden of monuments to many individual climbers, some in Japanese. The bodies of 34 climbers who died on the mountain have never been recovered.

GETTING OUTSIDE
✪ FLIGHTSEEING

The only way you'll get into the park from Talkeetna is by flying with one of the glacier pilots who supports McKinley climbs, which typically begin with a flight from here to the 7,200-foot level of the Kahiltna Glacier. There are several operators with long experience. The least expensive flights cost around $75 (if the plane is full) and either cruise through the Talkeetna mountains for wildlife watching or approach McKinley's south face. Rates often depend on how many are going, so if you can put together a group of four or five, or the operator can add you to a group, you can save as much as half. If you have the money and the weather is good, I'd recommend instead an extended tour that circles the mountain and flies over its glaciers, for $120 to $200 with a full plane. Best of all, in May and June you can arrange a landing on the mountain itself, just as the climbers do (the snow is too soft starting in July). The Don Sheldon Amphitheater on the Ruth Glacier is a stunning spot high on McKinley. These landings are usually treated as add-ons to the tours mentioned above, for an additional price of $20 to $40 per person. Try any of these three renowned glacier pilot operations, all operating out of the Talkeetna airport, and all with complete Web sites for comparison shopping: **K2 Aviation** (P.O. Box 545-B), Talkeetna, AK 99676 (☎ **800/764-2291** or 907/733-2291; www.alaska.net/~flyk2); **Doug Geeting Aviation** (P.O. Box 42), Talkeetna, AK 99676 (☎ **800/770-2366** or 907/733-2366; www.airtours.com); or **Talkeetna Air Taxi** (P.O. Box 73), Talkeetna, AK 99676 (☎ **800/533-2219** or 907/733-2218; www.gorp.com/flytat).

FISHING & JET BOAT TOURS

Talkeetna is at the confluence of the wild Talkeetna and Susitna rivers. **Mahay's Riverboat Service,** P.O. Box 705, Talkeetna, AK 99676 (☎ **800/736-2210** or 907/733-

2223; www.fish-world.com/mahays), is a top guide, with 2-hour tours on a unique 51-foot jet boat for $45 per person, operating several times a day from a dock near the public boat launch on the Talkeetna River. Owner Steve Mahay is legendary, the only person ever to shoot Devil's Canyon in a jet boat. Mahay offers fishing charters as well.

RAFTING

Talkeetna River Guides, on Main Street (P.O. Box 563), Talkeetna, AK 99676 (☎ 800/353-2677 or 907/733-2677; www.alaska.net/~trg/trg_dir/), offers a 2-hour wildlife river rafting tour, without white water, on the Talkeetna three times a day for $39 adults, $15 children under 12. They also offer longer trips and guided fishing.

ACCOMMODATIONS & DINING
NEAR TOWN

Besides the hotels listed in full below, good budget rooms are for rent from the **Talkeetna Motel,** at the west end of Main Street (P.O. Box 115) Talkeetna, AK 99676 (☎ **907/733-2323**). The clean, basic rooms go for $62 to $95 double. In a small A-frame they operate the TeePee restaurant, with three hearty, inexpensive meals a day in an eight-table dining room that's a slice of the old Talkeetna.

Talkeetna Alaskan Lodge. Mile 12.5, Talkeetna Spur Rd. (P.O. Box 93330, Anchorage, AK 99509-3330). ☎ **877/258-6877** or 907/265-4500. Fax 907/263-5559. www. talkeetnalodge.com. 99 units. TV TEL. Summer $179 double, winter $79 double. Additional person in room $10 extra. AE, MC, V.

Built of big timbers and river rock, this luxurious hotel was opened in 1999 by Cook Inlet Region, a Native corporation. Two miles from the town center, the lodge certainly has the town's best rooms, and promises a full set of activities, as well as continuing change for the character of the formerly low-key town. There's a restaurant and bar, and the view out the back is spectacular—when the weather is clear you can see McKinley from the patio.

Mt. McKinley Princess Lodge. Mile 133.1, Parks Hwy., Denali State Park, AK 99755 ☎ **800/426-0500** or 907/733-2900. Fax 907/733-2904. www.princesstours.com. 162 units. TV TEL. Summer $179 double, $275 suite. Spring and fall $99 double, $199 suite. Closed mid-Sept to mid-May. AE, DISC, DC, MC, V.

Finished in 1997 by the Princess Cruise Line, the main lodge building has a striking view of the mountain, only 42 miles away as the crow flies. The property isn't really near anything—100 miles south of the park entrance and about 45 road miles from Talkeetna—but, like a resort, they offer everything you need on-site and a full set of activities, including a short network of trails. The design and decoration are an inspired modernization of the classic national park style. Standard rooms are $179 a night in the high season. They're open mid-May to mid-September.

Swiss-Alaska Inn. F Street, near the boat launch (P.O. Box 565), Talkeetna, AK 99676. ☎ **907/733-2424.** 20 units. $100 double. Additional person in room $10 extra. AE, DISC, MC, V.

This place is more the essence of Talkeetna than the flashy new places above. It's a friendly family business with a small restaurant serving good, familiar American meals, plus a few German dishes. There are large, attractive rooms with oak furniture and Jacuzzis in the newer of the two buildings. The smoking rooms in the old building are clean but quite small.

A WILDERNESS LODGE

Caribou Lodge. 30 miles east of Talkeetna (P.O. Box 706) Talkeetna, AK 99676. ☎ and fax **907/733-2163.** 3 cabins. Summer $210 per person, per day; winter $175 per person per day.

The lodge sits on an alpine lake amid the tundra of the Talkeetna Mountains with Mount McKinley looming out back. The location, far from any road, offers an opportunity to live for a few days in terrain much like Denali's with only a few other people in many a mile, while hosted by a family who've made a life in this remote wilderness. They'll guide you hiking, canoeing on the lake, and watching the wildlife of the area. In the winter, come for cross-country skiing, snowshoeing, dog mushing, and snowmobiling, when the endlessly rolling hills are buried in snow. The accommodations are simple, as fits the Bush. Access is by air only—a float- or ski plane from Talkeetna is $125.

9 The Alaskan Interior

A warm summer evening in a campground; a slight breeze rustling the leaves of ghostly paper birches, barely keeping the mosquitoes at bay; the sounds of children playing; a perpetual sunset rolling slowly along the northern horizon—this is Interior Alaska. You know it's time to gather up the kids, separate them according to who belongs to whom, and put them to bed; it's 11 o'clock, for heaven's sake. But it's too difficult to feel that matters, or to alter the pace of a sun-baked day that never ends, meandering on like the broad, silty rivers and empty two-lane highways. Down by the boat landing, some college kids are getting ready to start on a float in the morning. An old, white-bearded prospector wanders out of the bar and, offering his flask to the strangers, tries out a joke while swatting the bugs. "There's not a single mosquito in Alaska," he declares. Waits for the loud, jocular objections. Then adds, "They're all married with big, big families." Easy laughter; then they talk about outboard motors, road work, why so many rabbits live along a certain stretch of highway. Eventually, you have to go to bed, leave the world to its pointless turning as the sun rotates back around to the east. You know it'll all be there tomorrow, just the same—the same slow-flowing rivers, the same long highways, the same vast space that can never be filled.

Interior Alaska is so large—it basically includes everything that's not on the coasts or in the Arctic—you can spend a week of hard driving and not explore it all. Or you could spend all summer floating the rivers and still have years of floating left to do before you'd seen all the riverbanks. It's something like what one imagines the great mass of America's Midwest once was, perhaps a century and a half ago, when the great flatlands had been explored but not completely civilized and Huckleberry Finn could float downriver into a wilderness of adventures. As it happens, I have a friend who grew up on a homestead in the Interior and ran away from home at age 15 in that exact same fashion, floating hundreds of miles on a handmade raft, past the little river villages, cargo barges, and fishermen. During an Interior summer, nature combines its immensity with a rare sense of gentleness, patiently awaiting the next thunderstorm.

Winter is another matter. Without the regulating influence of the ocean—the same reason summers are hot—winter temperatures can often drop to -30°F or -40°F, and during exceptional cold snaps, much lower. Now the earth is wobbling over in the other direction, away from the sun. The long, black nights sometimes make Fairbanks, the region's dominant city, feel more like an outpost on a barren planet, far off in outer space. That's when the northern lights come, spewing swirls of color across the entire dome of the sky and crackling with electricity. Neighbors get on the phone to wake each other and, rising from bed to put on their warmest parkas and insulated boots, stand in the street, gazing straight up. Visitors lucky enough to come at such times may be watching from a steaming hot-spring tub. During the short days, they can bundle up and watch sled dog racing or race across the wilderness themselves on snowmobiles.

Fairbanks stands second in Alaska in population, with over 80,000 in the greater area, but the Interior otherwise is without any settlements large enough to be called cities. Instead, it's defined by roads, both paved and gravel, which are strands of civilization through sparsely settled, swampy land. Before the roads, development occurred only on the rivers, which still serve as thoroughfares for the **Athabascan villages** of the region. In the summer, villagers travel by boat. In the winter, the frozen rivers become highways for snowmobiles and sled dog teams. White homesteaders and gold miners live back in the woods, too. Gold rush history is written on the land in piles of old gravel tailings and abandoned equipment, as well as in the prettier tourist attractions and historic sites. Gold mining goes on today, in small one-man operations and huge industrial works employing hundreds.

1 Exploring the Interior

More than anywhere else in Alaska, having your own car in the Interior provides the freedom to find the out-of-the-way places that give the region its character. Bus service connects Fairbanks with the Alaska Highway, including the ferry terminus at Haines or Skagway, and trains run between Fairbanks and Anchorage. But that will show you only the larger, tourist-oriented destinations. If you have the time and money, you may enjoy driving one of the remote gravel highways, or just poking along on the paved highways between the larger towns, ready to stop and investigate the roadhouses and meet the people who live out in the middle of nowhere. You'll find them mostly friendly and, often, downright odd—*colorful,* to use the polite term. As I drove an abandoned highway recently, I saw a hand-lettered sign advertising coffee. It wasn't your typical espresso stand, just a log cabin dozens of miles from the next nearest building. A squinting high plains drifter stepped out, wearing a cowboy hat on his head and a huge revolver on his hip, and asked, "Yeah?" The coffee came from a percolator warming on the wood stove, and the proprietor and I struck up a good conversation in his dark little dwelling. He just wasn't given to saying, "May I help you?" or "Have a nice day." My all-time favorite roadside sign, sighted on the Alaska Highway, stated in spray paint on plywood: "Sale—eel skins—anvils—bait." I've always wished I'd stopped in to window-shop and meet the man or woman who came up with that business plan.

Of course, not every mile of back road is scenic, nor are all the stops interesting. Driving a car through Alaska takes a long time, covers many hours of dull, brushy forest, and calls for a high tolerance for greasy hamburgers. Paved highway sections can develop frost heaves in this often-frozen land—back-breaking dips and humps caused by changing ground conditions. The gravel roads generate clouds of dust and quickly fatigue drivers, and windshield and headlights often succumb to their flying rocks.

LIKELY ITINERARIES

You can shorten your driving time by flying or taking the train to Fairbanks, then renting a car for an exploration. Renting a car one-way is a good way to go, too, if you can stand the drop-off fee. One itinerary that makes sense is to rent a car in Fairbanks, explore eastward to Dawson City, drop the car in Skagway, and then board the ferry south before flying out from Juneau, Sitka, or Ketchikan; I'd allow a good 10 days for such a plan, and expect a drop-off fee of around $300. If you prefer to return to Fairbanks, take the ferry from Skagway to Haines, then follow the Alaska Highway back. Another idea is to make a loop through Anchorage. From Fairbanks, take the Richardson Highway to Kennicott, in Wrangell–St. Elias National Park, then continue to Valdez, take a ferry to Whittier, and drive back north on the Seward Highway to Anchorage, continuing on the Parks Highway to Denali National Park and back to Fairbanks. That would take 10 days to 2 weeks, depending on how long you stayed in each place. For a shorter loop, cross through the Alaska Range on the Denali Highway, which links the Richardson and Parks highways at their midpoint. Or simply base yourself in Fairbanks and take a few days to experience the Steese or Dalton highways or Chena Hot Springs Road, perhaps with hot springs soaking, hiking, or canoeing on the way.

An especially fun way to go is with an **RV.** They're everywhere on these highways, so services are well developed even in many remote areas. An RV offers much of the freedom of camping, but sidesteps a lot of the problems of tent camping in a cool climate so far from home. Perhaps most important, it allows spontaneity. You don't have to stick so closely to an itinerary tied to hard-to-get hotel reservations. But RVs are expensive: Just the rental can cost as much staying in hotels, renting a car, and eating out for your meals. High-season rates are around $150 to $200 a day, plus the large amount of fuel you use. Campgrounds with full utility hookups cost $20 to $30 a night, or you can go self-contained at public campgrounds that cost half as much, dumping your tanks later.

Vernon Publications' *The Milepost,* a highway guide to Alaska and northwestern Canada, has long been considered the indispensable handbook for Alaska drivers. It has mile-by-mile descriptions of all the major roads and is available for sale everywhere along the Alaska Highway and at many major bookstores throughout the U.S. Most of the book, however, is taken up by advertisements that are included in the text as listings, so don't expect objective descriptions.

INTERIOR'S MAJOR HIGHWAYS

At the **Alaska Public Lands Information Center** in Tok, the first major visitor center on the U.S. side of the border on the Alaska Highway, the first question most visitors ask is: "Do you have a road map?" Then: "No, I mean a map that shows *all* the roads." The answer: "There aren't any more—welcome to Alaska." Paved two-lane highways make a triangle, connecting Tok, Fairbanks, and Anchorage, with links to the Kenai Peninsula, Valdez, and Canada. Otherwise, there are a few gravel highways reaching out a little way into the Bush, and that's it for the connected road system. Divided highways are found only in and near Fairbanks and Anchorage.

The few roads Alaska does have are long and scenic. They have route numbers, but everyone knows them by name. Elsewhere in this chapter and in the chapters on Southcentral and Denali National Park, you'll find local details on all the roads. Here, to help you choose your itinerary, I've included brief descriptions of every route on the highway system.

MAIN HIGHWAYS

ALASKA HIGHWAY (Route 2 from the border to Delta Junction) Running nearly 1,400 miles from Dawson Creek, British Columbia, to Delta Junction, Alaska, a couple of hours east of Fairbanks on the Richardson Highway, this World War II road is paved, but that doesn't mean it's always smooth. Like other northern highways, it's subject to bone-jarring frost heaves and spring potholes. Two tiny towns lie on the

Alaska portion of the road, Delta Junction and Tok. The prettiest part is on the Canadian side, in the Kluane Lake area. Driving the highway all the way to Alaska is still a real adventure, covered later in this chapter.

DENALI HIGHWAY (Route 8) I simply couldn't believe my eyes when I first drove this 133-mile gravel road. It connects the midpoints of the Parks and Richardson highways, crossing stunningly grand alpine vistas high in the Alaska Range, and provides access to a rich network of trails and mountain lakes and a good chance to see caribou, bears, moose, and waterfowl. It's popular with mountain bikers, canoers, trout fishers, and hunters. Details are in chapter 8.

GLENN HIGHWAY (Route 1 from Anchorage to Tok) This is the road you'd take if you were coming from the Alaska Highway on your way to Southcentral Alaska, including Prince William Sound, Anchorage, and the Kenai Peninsula. It connects Tok to Anchorage, 330 miles southwest. (The section between Glennallen and Tok is sometimes called the "Tok Cut-Off.") The northern section, from Tok to Glennallen, borders Wrangell–St. Elias National Park, with broad tundra and taiga broken by high, craggy peaks. That area is covered below, in this chapter. Glennallen to Anchorage is even more spectacular, as the road passes through high alpine terrain and then close by the Matanuska Glacier and along a deep valley carved by the glacier's river. That part of the road is covered in chapter 6.

PARKS HIGHWAY (Route 3) The George Parks Highway, opened in 1972, is a straight line from Anchorage to Fairbanks, 358 miles north, providing access to Denali National Park. There are some vistas of Mount McKinley from south of the park, and beautiful treeless terrain just south and north of the park, but the Parks Highway is mostly just a transportation route, less scenic than the Richardson or Glenn highways. From the northern (Fairbanks) end, the highway passes Nenana (covered in this chapter), then Denali and Talkeetna (chapter 8), and finally the towns of the Matanuska and Susitna Valleys (chapter 6).

RICHARDSON HIGHWAY (Route 4 from Valdez to Delta Junction, Route 2 from Delta Junction to Fairbanks) The state's first highway, leading 364 miles from tidewater in Valdez to Fairbanks, has lost much of its traffic to the Parks Highway, which saves over 90 miles between Anchorage and Fairbanks, and the Glenn Highway, which saves about 120 miles from Glennallen to Tok. But it's still the most beautiful paved drive in the Interior. From the south, the road begins with the heart-stopping drive through steep Thompson Pass, just out of Valdez (see chapter 7), then passes the huge, distant peaks of southern Wrangell–St. Elias National Park. North of Glennallen, the road climbs into the Alaska Range for a series of broad vistas comparable to Denali National Park, but with the addition that the road snakes along the shores of a series of long alpine lakes. Finally, it descends again to the forested area around Delta Junction and meets the Alaska Highway before arriving in Fairbanks.

SEWARD HIGHWAY (Route 1 from Anchorage to Tern Lake, route 9 from Tern Lake to Seward) The highway leaves Anchorage on the 127-mile drive to Seward following the rocky edge of mountain peaks above a surging ocean fjord. Later, it climbs through high mountain passes above treeline and passes fish-filled lakes. The section from Anchorage 50 miles south of Portage Glacier is covered in chapter 6, the remainder, to Seward, in chapter 7.

STERLING HIGHWAY (Route 1 from Tern Lake to Homer) Leading 142 miles from the Seward Highway to the tip of the Kenai Peninsula, the highway has some scenic spots, but mostly is a way to get to the Kenai River, the Kenai National Wildlife Refuge, Kachemak Bay, and the towns of Cooper Landing, Soldotna, Kenai, and Homer.

RURAL ROADS

Each of these mostly gravel roads, except for the Elliot Highway, are covered in detail later in this chapter.

CHENA HOT SPRINGS ROAD   A more civilized road into the outdoors, this paved 57-mile highway east of Fairbanks meets hiking and river routes on the way to Chena Hot Springs.

DALTON HIGHWAY (Route 11)   Built to haul equipment to the Prudhoe Bay oil fields, about 500 miles north of Fairbanks, the Dalton punctures the heart of the wilderness, crossing the Brooks Range and the North Slope.

EDGERTON HIGHWAY & McCARTHY ROAD (Route 10)   Running 93 miles east from the Richardson Highway south of Glennallen, the Edgerton penetrates Wrangell–St. Elias National Park to the historic sites at McCarthy and Kennicott.

ELLIOT HIGHWAY (Route 2 from Fox to Manley Hot Springs)   The road leads 152 miles northwest from the Steese Highway, north of Fairbanks, connecting it to the Dalton Highway, the Native village of Minto, and Manley Hot Springs, one of the least interesting of Alaska's rural routes.

STEESE HIGHWAY (Route 6)   This gravel road climbs the rounded mountains 162 miles east of Fairbanks to the Native village of Circle, on the Yukon River. It's a route to the real Alaska.

TAYLOR HIGHWAY (Route 5)   At times rough and narrow, this dirt road leads 161 miles from a junction on the Alaska Highway east of Tok to the fascinating Yukon River village of Eagle, an island in time. Portions of the road have canyon views.

TOP OF THE WORLD HIGHWAY (Yukon Route 9)   Connecting to the Taylor Highway across the Canadian border to Dawson City, a distance of 79 miles, the road rides mountaintop to mountaintop, above treeline nearly the entire way.

THE YUKON RIVER   You can't drive it, but that doesn't mean the Yukon isn't a highway. It's by far the broadest, smoothest, and longest in the state. The Yukon is navigable over most of its 2,300 miles, including all 1,900 miles in Alaska. It starts in British Columbia, leads through Yukon Territory, then crosses the Interior to its mouth, across Norton Sound from Nome. Tugs, barges, skiffs, canoes, and rafts traverse the river in the summer, snowmobiles and dog sleds in the winter. You can reach the river on the Dalton Highway 140 miles north of Fairbanks, on the Steese Highway in Circle, on the Taylor Highway in Eagle, or on the Top of the World Highway in Dawson City, Yukon Territory, and float between any of those towns—108 miles from Dawson City to Eagle, 158 miles from Eagle to Circle, and 300 miles from Circle to the Dalton Highway. Large-scale river tours run from Dawson City to Eagle, and smaller operations run on the Dalton out of Fairbanks and in Circle.

2 Outside in the Alaskan Interior

The Interior is so vast, there are plenty of ways to get away from other people and see wildlife—primarily caribou, moose, bears, wolves, foxes, and a wide variety of birds.

RIVER FLOATING   Floating any of the thousands of miles of the Interior's rivers opens great swaths of wilderness. Beginners will want to take a guided trip before venturing on their own. (See the lists of operators in chapter 2.) For Yukon River day trips, see the sections on Dawson City or the Dalton Highway. To plan your own trip, get Karen Jettmar's *The Alaska River Guide,* published by Alaska Northwest Books, P.O. Box 10306, Portland, OR 97210 (☎ **800/452-3032**), which includes details for floats on 78 rivers across the state. Also, check with the **Alaska Public Lands**

Information Center in Fairbanks, Tok, or Anchorage for guidance on setting up your trip. Among the most accessible and historic rivers in the region are the Chena, Chatanika, Yukon, and Fortymile (see the sections on Chena Hot Springs Road, the Steese Highway, Dawson City, and Eagle in this chapter, respectively).

HIKING There are fewer trails here than in Southcentral Alaska, but you'll find good trail hikes off the Steese Highway or Chena Hot Springs Road, below. If you don't need a trail, the Brooks Range beckons off the Dalton Highway. Again, the **Alaska Public Lands Information Center** can provide essential guidance before you head out. The virtues of Interior hiking are the remoteness, the animals you'll see, and the low treeline, which provides millions of acres of upland tundra. On the downside, much of the region is miserable swamp, and the mosquitoes are voracious.

MOUNTAIN BIKING Many hiking trails also are open to mountain bikes. Mountain biking is popular and well developed in Fairbanks. In addition, the Denali Highway and Denali National Park Road, described in chapter 8, are popular road routes. See "Planning an Outdoor Vacation" in chapter 2, and the Denali National Park sections for businesses leading guided rides.

3 Fairbanks: Alaska Heartland

If the story of Fairbanks's founding had happened anywhere else, it wouldn't be told so proudly, for the city's father was a swindler, and its undignified birth contained an element of chance not usually admitted in polite society. As the popular story goes (and the historians' version is fairly close), it seems that in 1901, E. T. Barnette had it in mind to get rich by starting a gold-mining boom town like the others that had sprouted from Dawson City to Nome as the stampeders of 1898 sloshed back and forth across the territory from one gold find to the next. He booked passage on a riverboat going up the Tanana with his supplies to build the town, having made an understanding with the captain that, should the vessel get stuck, he would lighten the load by getting off with the materials on the nearest bank. Unfortunately, the captain got lost. Thinking he was heading up a slough on the Tanana, he got sidetracked into the relatively small Chena River. That was where the boat got stuck and where Barnette got left, and that was where he founded Fairbanks.

Fortunately for Barnette, an Italian prospector named Felix Pedro had been looking for gold in the hills around the new trading post, and made a strike on the Tanana. On that news, Barnette dispatched his cook off to Dawson City to spread the word. The cook's story showed up in a newspaper that winter, and a stampede of hundreds of miners ensued, heading toward Fairbanks in weather as cold as -50°. Barnette's town was a success, but the cook nearly got lynched when the stampeders found out how far he'd exaggerated the truth. Much more gold was found later, however, and half the population of Dawson City came down river to Fairbanks. Barnette had made it big.

The town's future was assured thanks to a political deal. Barnette did a favor for the territory's judge, James Wickersham, by naming the settlement for Wickersham's ally in Congress, Sen. Charles Fairbanks of Indiana, who later became vice president. Wickersham then moved the federal courthouse to Fairbanks from Eagle—he loaded his records on his dog sled and mushed here—establishing the camp as the hub of the region. Wickersham's story is interesting, too—he was a notable explorer and Alaska's first real statesman as a nonvoting delegate to Congress. Houses he lived in are preserved at Alaskaland in Fairbanks and in Juneau just up the hill from the capitol building. Barnette didn't do as well in history's eyes: He was run out of the town he founded for bank fraud.

Fairbanks is Alaska's second-largest city now, with a population of about 38,000 in the city limits and 80,000 in the greater area, but it has never learned to put on airs. It sprawls, broad and flat, along big highways and the Chena—a friendly, easygoing town, but one where people still take gold and their independence seriously. They're still prospecting and mining for gold around here, fighting off environmental regulation and maintaining a traditional Alaskan attitude that it's us against the world. Fairbanks is the birthplace of strange political movements, including the secessionist Alaskan Independence Party. It's an adamant, loopy, affable place; it doesn't seem to mind being a little bizarre or residing far from the center of things. And that makes it an intensely Alaskan city, for those are the qualities Alaskans most cherish in their myth of themselves.

As a visitor, Fairbanks could strike you a couple of ways, depending on what you expect and what you like. Fairbanks could come across as a provincial outpost, a touristy cross between Kansas and Siberia. Driving one of the franchise-choked commercial strips, you could wonder why you went out of your way to come here, and the downtown area can be downright depressing. Or you could relax and take Fairbanks on its own terms, a fun, unpretentious town, full of activities and surprises, that never lost its sense of being on the frontier. There's plenty to do in Fairbanks, much of it at least a little corny and requiring some driving—sites at the University and on the Chena River, gold mining attractions north of town, and a big town park called Alaskaland. It's a terrific destination for families—my son would still be there if it were up to him—and there are good opportunities for hiking and mountain biking, and great opportunities for canoeing and slow river float trips.

ESSENTIALS
GETTING THERE

BY CAR OR RV   Fairbanks is a transportation hub. The Richardson Highway heads east 98 miles to Delta Junction, the end point of the Alaska Highway, then south to Glennallen and Valdez. The Parks Highway heads due south from Fairbanks to Denali National Park, 120 miles away, and Anchorage, 358 miles south. Exploring the region on your own requires a car. There are many rental agencies. **Avis** (☎ **800/331-1212** or 907/474-0900) is located at the airport; **Affordable Car Rentals** is at 249 Alta Way (☎ **800/471-3101** or 907/452-7341).

BY BUS   Gray Line's **Alaskon Express** (☎ **907/456-7741**) offers service 3 days a week from the Westmark Fairbanks down the Alaska Highway to Haines and Skagway (the fare is $182 and $206, respectively), with stops along the way. The **Alaska Backpacker Shuttle** (☎ **800/266-8625** or 907/344-8775; www.alaska.net/~backpack) offers daily service in comfortable small buses to Denali $20 one-way, and Anchorage $60.

BY TRAIN   The **Alaska Railroad** (☎ **800/544-0552** or 907/456-4155; www.akrr.com/) links Fairbanks to Denali National Park and Anchorage to the south, with tour commentary. The fare is $54 to Denali and $154 to Anchorage, one-way. A detailed description of the services available are in chapter 9.

BY AIR   **Fairbanks International Airport** has direct jet service from Anchorage on several airlines, with **Alaska Airlines** (☎ **800/426-0333** or 907/474-9175; www.alaskaair.com) having the most flights. Round-trip fares are typically under $200. The airport is a hub with various carriers to Alaska's Interior and Arctic communities.

GETTING TO TOWN FROM THE AIRPORT   A cab downtown from the airport is about $12 with **Yellow Cab** (☎ **907/455-5555**).

Greater Fairbanks

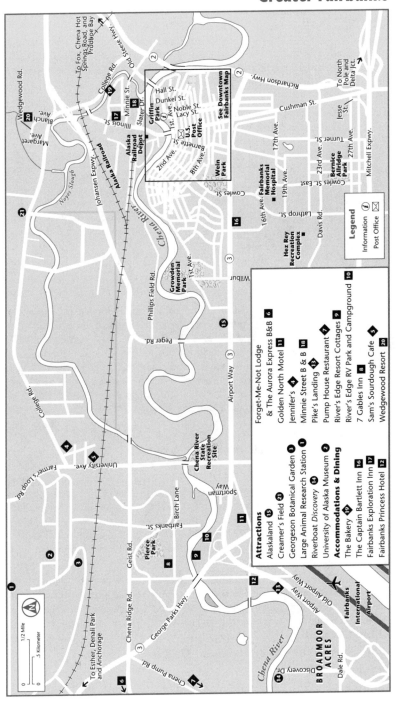

Attractions
- Alaskaland 15
- Creamer's Field 21
- Georgeson Botanical Garden 3
- Large Animal Research Station 1
- Riverboat *Discovery* 14
- University of Alaska Museum 2

Accommodations & Dining
- The Bakery 19
- The Captain Bartlett Inn 16
- Fairbanks Exploration Inn 17
- Fairbanks Princess Hotel 12
- Forget-Me-Not Lodge & The Aurora Express B&B 6
- Golden North Motel 11
- Jennifer's 4
- Minnie Street B & B 18
- Pike's Landing 13
- Pump House Restaurant 7
- River's Edge Resort Cottages 9
- River's Edge RV Park and Campground 10
- 7 Gables Inn 8
- Sam's Sourdough Cafe 5
- Wedgewood Resort 20

GETTING AROUND

It's possible to see much of Fairbanks without a car, staying in the downtown area and making excursions by bus or shuttle; but the city is designed around the car, and that's the easiest way to get around. Rental agencies are listed above. Good road maps are available free at the visitor center. The city is too spread out to use taxis much.

BY SHUTTLE   To see the widely scattered attractions without a car, try the popular **G.O. Shuttle Service** (☎ **800/478-3847** or 907/474-3847), a unique bus, van, and car system geared to independent travelers. Besides guided tours of various attractions, which cost $25, the company offers on-call shuttle service to the airport, train depot, and major attractions for flat fares of $5 or $15, round-trip, depending on the distance.

BY BUS   The lowest-cost option is the Fairbanks North Star Borough's three-route **MACS bus system,** linking the University, downtown, North Pole, and shopping areas, and some hotels. Service is every 30 minutes, at best, and virtually nonexistent on weekends. Pick up timetables at the visitor center. All buses connect at the transit park downtown, at Fifth Avenue and Cushman Street.

BY BIKE   Bicycles are for rent from **Great Land Sports,** at 261 College Rd. (☎ **907/479-8438**), a full-service bike shop.

VISITOR INFORMATION

The **Fairbanks Log Cabin Visitor Information Center,** located in a large log building at 550 First Ave., on the Chena River at the center of town, at Cushman Street, Fairbanks, AK 99701 (☎ **800/327-5774** or 907/456-5774; fax 907/452-2867; fairbanks.ptialaska.net/ or www.explorefairbanks.com), provides maps, including a road map and the good downtown walking tour map, and has a registry of available hotel rooms, as well as binders covering dozens of local bed-and-breakfasts, with information and photographs on each. The Web site contains many useful links. The center is open daily 8am to 8pm in summer, Monday to Friday 10am to 5pm in winter. When you stop by, take a look at nearby Golden Heart Plaza for a shot of civic pride.

The **Alaska Public Lands Information Center,** 250 Cushman St. (at Third Avenue), Suite 1A, Fairbanks, AK 99701 (☎ **907/456-0527;** TDD 907/456-0532; fax 907/456-0514; www.nps.gov/aplic), is an indispensable stop for anyone planning to spend time in the outdoors, and an interesting one even if you're not. Besides providing detailed information on all of Alaska's public lands and answering questions and giving advice on outings, the center has a small museum about the state's regions and the gear needed to explore them and an aquarium of Alaska sport fish. There are daily films and naturalist programs in a small auditorium. Open daily 9am to 6pm in summer, Monday to Friday 10am to 6pm in winter.

ON THE WEB   Besides the sites mentioned above and in chapter 2, **TourAlaska** (www.touralaska.org) specializes in travel information on the Interior, with a searchable database of Fairbanks businesses with Web sites, and **Fairnet** (www.Fairnet.org) is a local community network with information for visitors and residents. The **Bureau of Land Management,** which oversees much of the public land around Fairbanks, maintains an excellent site at www.ndo.ak.blm.gov.

SPECIAL EVENTS

A recording of current local happenings can be reached at ☎ **907/456-INFO.** A calendar of every local event, no matter how small, is at www.fairnet.org/agencies/fcvbcal.html.

Downtown Fairbanks

Attractions
Alaska Public Lands Information Center **9**
Early Fairbanks homes **4**
Fairbanks Community Museum **8**
Fairbanks Ice Museum **13**
Golden Heart Park **12**
Immaculate Conception Church **2**
Log Cabin Visitor Center **11**
St. Mathew's Episcopal Church **3**

Accommodations
All Seasons Inn **7**

Bridgewater Hotel **5**
Fairbanks Golden Nugget Hotel **18**
Fairbanks Hotel **14**
Westmark Fairbanks **17**

Dining
Dashing Moose Deli **10**
Gambardella's Italian Cafe **6**
Slouvaki **16**
Hot Tamales **1**
Thai House **15**

The **Yukon Quest International Sled Dog Race** (☎ 907/452-7954), held in mid-February, starts or finishes in Fairbanks (Fairbanks has the start in even-numbered years; Whitehorse, Yukon Territory, in odd-numbered years). The challenge of the 1,000-mile race is equal to the Iditarod. **The Nenana Ice Classic** (☎ 907/832-5446), held the first weekend in March, in Nenana, starts with a weekend celebration of dance performances, dog mushing, and other activities; the classic is a sweepstakes on who can guess closest to the exact date and time the ice will go out on the Tanana River (see "A Stop in Nenana," below). ✪ **The World Ice Art Championships** (☎ 907/451-8250), held in early to mid-March, brings carvers from all over the world to sculpt immense clear chunks cut from Fairbanks lakes. It's spectacular. **The North American Sled Dog Championships** (☎ 907/488-9685) cover 2 weekends in mid-March, in open and limited classes.

Lots of events happen around the **summer solstice,** around June 21. A street fair happens downtown (☎ 907/452-8671), there's a big 10K race open to walkers and people in funny costumes (☎ 907/452-7211), and the **Midnight Sun Baseball Game** hosted by the semipro Fairbanks Goldpanners (☎ 907/451-0095)—it begins at 10:30pm, and there are no artificial lights. **Golden Days,** over 2 weeks in late July, includes crafts fairs and a parade (☎ 907/452-1105). The **Fairbanks Summer Arts Festival,** on the University of Alaska Fairbanks campus (P.O. Box 80845), Fairbanks, AK 99708 (☎ 907/474-8869; www.fsaf.org/), covers 2 weeks in late July and early August. Artists of international reputation appear and offer workshops in music, dance, theater, opera, and the visual arts. **The**

Tanana Valley Fair (☎ **907/452-3750**), in early August, shows off the area's agricultural production, arts and crafts, and entertainment, and includes rides, a carnival and a rodeo.

The **Athabascan Fiddling Festival** (☎ **907/452-1825**), held in early November, draws together musicians and dancers from the Interior region for performances and workshops. **The Top of the World Classic,** late in November, brings NCAA Division I basketball teams to the University for a weekend tournament (☎ **907/474-6830**).

Fast Facts: Fairbanks

Banks   Fairbanks has numerous banks with ATMs in the downtown area and along the commercial strips; you can also find ATMs in many grocery stores. The visitor center has a complete list. Key Bank (☎ 907/452-2146) is at 100 Cushman.

Business Services   A Kinkos Copy Center is at 418 Third St. (☎ 907/ 456-7348).

Hospital   Fairbanks Memorial Hospital is at 1650 Cowles St. (☎ 907/ 452-8181).

Police   For nonemergency police business, call the Alaska State Troopers (☎ 907/452-2114) or the Fairbanks Police Department (☎ 907/459-6500).

Post Office   315 Barnette St.

Taxes   There is no sales tax. The local bed tax is 8%.

Weather   A recorded forecast is at (☎ 907/452-3553).

ATTRACTIONS & ACTIVITIES
STROLLING AROUND DOWNTOWN

If you want to explore the few sites downtown, pick up the walking tour map available at the visitor center. Among the highlights is the **Golden Heart Park,** a waterfront plaza with a fountain and a bronze of a Native family, where community events often occur. The town's most interesting building is the Roman Catholic **Church of the Immaculate Conception,** across the river on Cushman Street. The white clapboard structure, built in 1904, has ornate gold rush decoration inside, rare for its authenticity, including a pressed-tin ceiling and stained-glass windows—an appealing if incongruous mix of gold rush and sacred decor. At First Avenue near Kellum Street, east from the visitor center, **St. Mathew's Episcopal Church** is a cute old log church with a working rope-pull bell. It was founded by missionary and dog sled explorer Hudson Stuck in 1904. The original church burned; the present structure dates from 1948. At Second Avenue and Lacey Street, the **Fairbanks Ice Museum** (☎ **907/ 451-8222**) aims to show summer visitors what winter is like, with a freezer you can enter to feel the cold and artists who demonstrate ice carving. A striking high-tech slide show plays hourly, explaining the annual Ice Art Festival, and freezers contain impressive ice tableaux. Admission is $6 for adults, $4 ages 6 to 12. They're open 10am to 6pm daily in summer. At 410 Cushman Street, the former city hall contains the volunteer-operated **Fairbanks Community Museum** (☎ **907/452-8671**), with old newspapers, memorabilia, dog mushing material, and the like. Hours are 11am to 3pm Monday through Saturday.

✪ ALASKALAND

Built for the Alaska purchase centennial in 1967, Alaskaland is the boiled-down essence of Fairbanks on grounds at the intersection of Airport Way and Peger Road

(☎ 907/459-1087). It's called a theme park, but don't expect Disneyland or anything like it. Instead, Alaskaland is a city park with a theme. It's relaxing and low-key, entrancing for young children and interesting for adults if you can give in to the charm of the place. Admission to the park is free, and the tours and activities are generally inexpensive. It's open Memorial Day to Labor Day, daily from 11am to 9pm. Pick up a map and schedule when you arrive; here I've listed the highlights, but there is more to see. Depending on the pace you like to keep and the age level of your group, you could spend a couple of hours to most of a day.

The **SS** *Nenana* is the park's centerpiece. Commissioned by the federally owned Alaska Railroad in 1933, the large stern-wheeler plied the Yukon and Tanana rivers until 1952. In 1967 the *Nenana* came to Alaskaland, but was unmaintained and had nearly collapsed from rot when it was saved by a community restoration effort, completed in 1992. There are five decks of sumptuous mahogany, brass, and white-painted promenades. The wheelhouse and engine room remain well preserved, too. A tour is $5 for adults, $3 children, and goes only in dry weather—the steps and decks get slippery in rain. You can see the ground-floor cargo deck anytime without paying, and it contains an amazing set of dioramas showing all the riverside towns and villages where the boat called, modeled as they looked in its heyday.

Most of Fairbanks's history has been moved to Alaskaland. A village of log cabins contains shops and restaurants, each marked with its original location and place in Fairbanks's history. **Judge Wickersham's house,** circa 1904, is kept as a museum, decorated appropriate to the period of the town's founding. The house is less than grand—it may remind you of your grandmother's—but it's worth a stop to strike up a conversation with the historical society volunteers who keep it open. **Pres. Warren Harding's fancy rail car,** from which he stepped to drive the golden spike on the Alaska Railroad, sits near the park entrance. An exceptional **Pioneer Air Museum** is housed in a geodesic dome toward the back of the park. Besides the aircraft, some of which are open to climb into, there are displays and artifacts of the crashes of Alaska's aviation pioneers. Admission is $2.

If you have children, you certainly won't escape Alaskaland without a ride on the **Crooked Creek and Whiskey Island Railroad** that circles the park twice, with a tour guide pointing out the sights; rides cost $2 for adults, $1 for children, free under age 4. Kids also will enjoy the large **playground,** with equipment for toddlers and older children, where lots of local families come to play, and the 36-hole miniature golf course. The only carnival ride is a nice old **merry-go-round.** There's a boat landing and a mining display with a mechanical waterfall.

Tour groups generally come to Alaskaland in the evening mid-May through mid-September for the **Alaska Salmon Bake,** at the mining display (☎ 907/452-7274), and the **Golden Heart Revue,** at the Palace Theater (☎ 907/456-5960; e-mail: intrasea@polarnet.com). The all-you-can-eat halibut, ribs, or brown-sugar salmon costs $19.95, or you can get a steak for the same price. Beer and wine are available. The revue, nightly at 8:15pm, mid-May to mid-September, covers the amusing story of the founding of Fairbanks with comedy and song in a nightclub setting; admission is $12 for adults.

UNIVERSITY OF ALASKA FAIRBANKS

The state university's historic main campus contains several interesting attractions for visitors, and the administration makes a point of attracting and serving tourists. The campus is on the west side of town; look for University Avenue. A widely distributed brochure lists tours, hours, and fees. A free 2-hour **walking tour,** led by students, meets at the museum Monday through Friday at 10am, June to August except around July 4. Call ahead (☎ 907/474-7581) to confirm the time and any weather cancellations. If you don't want to take the time for a full tour, at least pick up a campus map at the museum so you can find your way around. Besides the sites mentioned below, the **Geophysical Institute** (☎ 907/474-7558) offers tours of its seismology lab, radar facility, and a talk on the aurora Thursdays at 2pm; and the **Arctic Region Supercomputing Center** (☎ 907/474-6935) shows off its big Cray machine Wednesdays at 2pm.

✪ **University of Alaska Museum.** 907 Yukon Drive (P.O. Box 756960), Fairbanks, AK 99775-6960. ☎ **907/474-7505.** www.uaf.alaska.edu/museum. June–Aug daily 9am–7pm; May and Sept daily 9am–5pm; Oct–Apr Mon–Fri 9am–5pm, Sat–Sun noon–5pm. Admission $5 adults, $4.50 ages 60 and older, $3 ages 7–17, ages 6 and under free.

A rich, interdisciplinary museum that explains the nature and culture of each of the state's regions. It's Alaska's best natural history museum, and most scholarly, with information presented at advanced as well as elementary levels. Some of the objects have a real wow factor, such as Blue Babe, the petrified Steppe Bison, and a 5,400-pound copper nugget. Don't miss the exhibit on the internment of the Aleuts (see "The Aleutians: The Quiet After War," in chapter 10). Despite the museum's small size, a curious person could spend most of a day here. The only major weakness is that it tries to do so much in too small a space and seems cluttered. A display on emission spectrums is side by side with a stuffed lynx, a woven root basket, and a broad-view aurora camera. They're working on that problem, raising money for a $20 million expansion. In the summer, catch the shows in the auditorium. UAF's scientists lead the world in the study of **the northern lights,** and their aurora show depicts and explains the phenomenon daily at 10am and 3pm; admission is $4 adults, $2 youth, $1 children. A show on Alaska Native culture is at 11am and 2pm and costs $6.50 for adults, $4 youth, $2 children.

Georgeson Botanical Garden. On West Tanana Dr. ☎ **907/474-1744.** Suggested donation is $1. May–Sept daily 8am–8pm; free guided tours Fri at 2pm.

I really enjoy the mix of science and contemplation I find at this relaxed working garden. Plots are laid out to compare seeds and cultivation techniques, usually well posted with explanatory information on the experiment; but at the same time the flowers and vegetables are spectacular, and there are peaceful memorials and places to picnic. Nearby, the barn of the university's experimental farm is open for visitors to wander through and view the cows and pigs.

Large Animal Research Station. Yankovich Rd. (drive north from campus, turn left on Ballaine Rd., left again on Yankovich). ☎ **907/474-7207.** Tours Tues and Sat 11am and 1:30pm, Thurs 1:30pm. Admission $5 adults, students $2

The university studies captive musk ox and caribou here, on a property more commonly known as the musk ox farm. Tours are given five times a week in the summer, but just walking along the fence you can see the animals behaving naturally in the large pastures. With a long lens, you can get a good picture.

COMMERCIAL TOURIST ATTRACTIONS AROUND FAIRBANKS

The Riverboat *Discovery.* 1975 Discovery Dr., Fairbanks, AK 99709. ☎ **907/479-6673.** www.riverboatdiscovery.com. Sailings at 8:45am and 2pm, with a less crowded evening sailing sometimes added. Admission $39.95 adults, $36.95 teens, $29.95 ages 3–12.

The *Discovery* belongs to the pioneering Binkley family, which has been in the riverboat business since the Klondike gold rush and whose family members still run the boat. The *Discovery* is a real stern-wheeler, a 156-foot steel vessel carrying 700 passengers on as many as three trips a day. There's nothing intimate or spontaneous about the 3½-hour ride, mostly carrying package tour passengers off buses, but the Binkleys still provide a fun, educational experience—it's doesn't feel cheap or plastic at all. After loading at a landing with shops off Dale Road, near the airport, the boat cruises down the Chena and up the Tanana past demonstrations on shore—among others, a bush plane taking off and landing, fish cutting at a Native fish camp, and a musher's dog yard (in recent years, five-time Iditarod champion Susan Butcher's yard, and she'd often show off the dogs herself). Finally, the vessel pulls up at the bank for a tour of a mock Athabascan village.

The El Dorado Gold Mine. Off the Elliot Hwy., 9 miles north of town. ☎ **907/479-7613**. Tours daily. Call for times. Admission $24.95 adults, $19.95 ages 3–12.

The Binkleys (see the *Discovery,* above) also own this working gold mine, with a train that carries visitors through a tour (including a tunnel in the permafrost) and ends with gold panning—my son ended up with enough gold to fill a plastic locket and couldn't think about anything else for a week. The whole thing takes 2 hours. The hosts of the tour are Dexter and Lynette Clark; they're real miners, perfect examples of the type—Lynette has even been involved in the Alaskan Independence Party.

Gold Dredge Number 8. 1755 Old Steese Hwy., Fairbanks, AK 99712. ☎ **907/457-6058**. Mid-May to mid-Sept, daily 9am–6pm; tours at 9:30am, 11am, 1pm, 3:30pm, and 4:30pm. Admission $14 adults, $7 children; add $6 for gold panning; add another $8 for a cafeteria lunch. To get there, go north on the Steese Expressway from town, turn left on Goldstream Rd., and again on the Old Steese Hwy.

This is the area's best gold mining historic site. The centerpiece is a 1928 gold dredge, similar to machines in Dawson City and Nome, that stands five decks tall on a barge floating in a pond it created. Huge scoops would dig from one end, the mechanism inside would digest the gold from the gravel, and then it would dump the spoils out the back—in this way, the pond and the dredge it supports crept 21 miles across the frozen ground north of Fairbanks. Many sterile areas you see in this area were created by these earth-eaters, for nothing grows on their tailings for decades after. The tour company that bought the historic site added to the dredge with museums housed in relocated gold camp buildings, showing the drab life lived by the miners and the tools they worked with. Mechanical people will be fascinated. A 2-hour tour starts with a film, then a half hour on the dredge, and finally a chance to pan for gold yourself—gold has been added to the bags of soil they give to you to sift through, so you're assured of finding some. A large cafeteria is mostly for package tour bus passengers.

North Pole. 13 miles east of Fairbanks on the Richardson Hwy.

The town of North Pole is a bedroom community to Fairbanks—but if your group is like mine was, with young fans of Santa Claus in the car, you can't be within 13 miles of the North Pole without dropping in on him. You'll find Santa hanging out at a huge gift shop and RV park just off the highway as you enter North Pole. It's called, appropriately, **Santa Claus House,** 101 St. Nicholas Dr., North Pole, AK 99705 (☎ **907/ 488-2200;** www.santaclaushouse.com), and is open year-round, with Santa on duty 11am to 7:30pm. You can also reach him by e-mail on the Web site, and arrange to have him send your child a letter. (The **Santa Land RV Park** is under different ownership; ☎ **907/488-9123.**) Other than the gift store and an opportunity for a picture with Santa, the only attraction is a pen with reindeer.

GETTING OUTSIDE

In this section, I've described the outdoor opportunities local to Fairbanks, but some other choices are barely farther afield: Make sure to look at the sections on Chena Hot Springs Road and the Steese Highway, later in this chapter.

SPECIAL PLACES

✪ CREAMER'S FIELD   At 1300 College Rd., right in Fairbanks, this migratory waterfowl refuge is a 1,800-acre former dairy farm that was saved from development in 1966 by a community fund drive. The pastures are a prime stopover point for Canada geese, pintails, and golden plovers in the spring and fall. Sandhill cranes, shovelers, and mallards show up all summer. The **Friends of Creamers Field** (☎ **907/452-5162**) operates a small visitor center with bird and history displays, open June through August Tuesday through Friday from 10am to 5pm and on Saturday from 10am to 3pm, and offers guided nature walks in summer Saturday and Wednesday at 9am and Tuesday and Thursday at 7pm. You don't need a guide, however, as I especially enjoyed the boreal forest nature walk, interpreted by an excellent booklet you can pick up at the visitor center or from a stand at the trailhead when the visitor center is closed.

CHENA LAKES RECREATION AREA   This is a wonderful and unique place for a family camping trip. A birch-rimmed lake created for a flood control project has been developed by the local government to provide lots of recreational possibilities: flat walking and bike trails; a swimming beach; fishing; a place to rent canoes, sailboats, and paddleboats; a self-guided 2½-mile nature trail; a playground; big lawns; and the terrific campground, with 80 camping sites, from pull-throughs for RVs to tent sites on a little island you can reach only by boat. In the winter, it's a popular cross-country skiing area. Drive 17 miles east of Fairbanks on the Richardson Highway and turn left on Laurance Road as you leave North Pole. For information, contact Fairbanks North Star Borough Chena Lakes Recreation Area, P.O. Box 71267, Fairbanks, AK 99707 (☎ **907/488-1655**).

ACTIVITIES

CANOEING   There are lots of places for day trips. The Chena River is slow and meandering as it flows through Fairbanks, and you have your pick of restaurants on the bank. Or you could go up Chena Hot Springs Road or to the Chatanika River, on the Steese Highway (see those sections later in this chapter). The Alaska Public Lands Information Center can provide guidance and a list of companies that rent equipment. **7 Bridges Boats and Bikes** rents canoes and kayaks for $35 per day, and provides the essential service of dropping you off at the river and picking you up at your destination for $1.50 per mile out of town, with a $10 minimum. They're at the 7 Gables Inn, 4312 Birch Lane (P.O. Box 80488), Fairbanks, AK 99708 (☎ **907/479-0751;** fax 907/479-2229; www.alaska.net/~gables7/7bridges.html).

BIKING & HIKING   7 Bridges Boats and Bikes, above, rents bicycles: street bikes are $10 a day; mountain bikes, $15. Also see "Getting Around," above. Some of the best remote trails for hiking or mountain biking are beyond town on the Steese Highway and Chena Hot Spring Road, described below, but locals also use two networks closer in. The **Skarland Trails,** at the west ridge of the University of Alaska campus, includes routes of 3 to 12 miles. North of town, on the Steese Highway, the **Birch Hill Recreation Area** also has several miles of trails. Both areas are appealing for cross-country skiing in the winter.

FISHING   Salmon fishing isn't as good as nearer the coast, where the fish are brighter, but kings and silvers are found in Fairbanks' streams. You can also fish for pike, grayling, burbot, whitefish, and various kinds of trout. You can even fish right in the Chena as it flows through town, although getting out of town and hiking a bit away from a road yields better results. The visitor center provides a brochure on where to fish and buy a license. For regulations and closures, contact the Alaska Public Lands

Information Center (under "Visitor Information," above), or the **Alaska Department of Fish and Game,** at Creamer's Field, 1300 College Rd., Fairbanks, AK 99701 (☎ **907/452-7207;** sport fish information recording 907/459-7385; www.state.ak. us/local/akpages/FISH.GAME/adfghome.htm). Guided trips by boat or plane will get you farther out into the country, where you may see wildlife, too. Check at the visitor center for current operators; going prices seem to be $250 for a boat for half a day, $450 for a full day. Lake fly-outs start at around $300 for two people.

GOLF   They may not be what you're used to at home, but in Fairbanks you can play all night under the midnight sun. The **Fairbanks Golf & Country Club** is at 1735 Farmers Loop Rd. (☎ **907/479-6555**).

WINTER RECREATION   Winters in Fairbanks can be awfully cold, but that just means you have to bundle up more (or at least that's what the locals claim). Cross-country skiing, snowmobiling, and sled dog mushing are the main participatory sports. Many local mushers offer rides; get a referral from the visitor center. There are Nordic trails at the university, and **7 Bridges Boats and Bikes,** listed above under "Canoeing," also rents snowmobiles, skis, and other winter gear. There's also a minor downhill ski area, **Moose Mountain,** 100 Moose Mountain Rd. (P.O. Box 84198), Fairbanks, AK 99708 (☎ **907/455-8362**).

ACCOMMODATIONS

Fairbanks is a popular destination in the peak summer season, and a good hotel room can be hard to find on short notice. Several establishments book up with tour groups a year ahead, then have last-minute cancellations available for independent travelers. The **Bridgewater Hotel,** 723 First Ave., Fairbanks, AK 99701 (☎ **907/452-6661;** fax 907/452-6126; www.fountainheadhotels.com), falls in this category, with good rooms right downtown. You'll also find good, reasonably priced downtown rooms at the **Fairbanks Golden Nugget Hotel,** 900 Noble St., Fairbanks, AK 99701 (☎ **907/ 452-5141;** fax 907/452-5458). The new **Comfort Inn Chena River,** 1908 Chena Landings Loop, Fairbanks, AK 99701 (☎ **800/201-9199** or 907/479-8080) has a small pool and a lovely wooded site near the river.

Fairbanks's abundant crop of **B&Bs** has grown well beyond families offering an extra bedroom—all those listed in full below were built specifically for the purpose, and differ from hotels mainly in that you get personal service from proprietors on the site. For central reservations, an Anchorage service **Alaska Private Lodgings,** P.O. Box 200047, Anchorage, AK 99520-0047 (☎ **907/258-1717;** fax 907/258-6613; www. alaskabandb.com), lists some Fairbanks B&Bs, You also can get detailed B&B information at the Fairbanks Log Cabin Visitor Information Center.

VERY EXPENSIVE

Fairbanks Princess Hotel. 4477 Pikes Landing Rd., Fairbanks, AK 99709. ☎ **800/ 426-0500** or 907/455-4477. Fax 907/455-4476. www.princesstours.com. 200 units. TV TEL. High season, $199–$209 double. Low season, $129–$139 double. $199–$349 suite. Additional person in room $10 extra. AE, DISC, MC, V.

This well-thought-out gray clapboard structure in a wooded area on the banks of the Chena, near the airport, was built to serve Princess cruise line passengers. The rooms, while not large, are trim and stylish in shades of tan, and many look out on the river. Besides the location, newspapers, data ports, and hair dryers help make it a good choice for business travelers. The lobby is attractive, and the bar and Edgewater Restaurant have a large deck. The dinner menu is short, with entree prices in the $20 to $25 range, but the food is consistent. Additional facilities include a courtesy car, health club, steam room, and tour desk.

EXPENSIVE

Captain Bartlett Inn. 1411 Airport Way, Fairbanks, AK 99701. ☎ **907/452-1888.** Fax 907/ 452-7674. E-mail: cbi@ptialaska.net. 197 units. TV TEL. High season, $140 double. Low season, $95 double. $175 suite. Additional person in room $10 extra. AE, CB, DC, DISC, JCB, MC, V.

Although it faces busy Airport Way, the Captain Bartlett succeeds in feeling like a rural Alaska roadhouse, with a log exterior, bright plantings, and historic photographs in the halls. The rooms are comfortable if, for the price, small and well worn. Only the suites have tubs and the first floor rooms are in a half basement and lack air-conditioning. All rooms have coffee machines and you can book tours in the lobby. **Slough Foot Sue's** restaurant has hearty meals for $16 to $37 for dinner, $6.50 to $9 for lunch. The lunch menu includes sandwiches and a salad bar, while dinner is beef and seafood. Patrons at the restaurant or bar can sit on a deck over the parking lot. In the **Dog Sled Saloon** ten beers are on tap and you're expected to throw peanut shells on the floor. Honky-tonk piano and sing-alongs occur in the evening.

✪ **Fairbanks Exploration Inn.** 505 Illinois St., Fairbanks, AK 99701. ☎ **907/451-1920.** Fax 907/455-7317. www.feinn.com. 16 units, 11 with private bathroom. TEL. Summer $130 double, $175 suite. Winter $69 double, $100 suite. AE, MC, V.

Executives of the Fairbanks Exploration Co. lived in these bungalows—the inn takes its name from that early gold mining operation—then left them vacant for 20 years to be rescued, lovingly restored, and made into Alaska's best historic accommodation, near the rail depot. Light streams in through screen porches and big, double-hung windows onto wood floors. There are white walls framed with varnished moldings and hung with contemporary fine art, as well as crisp period furnishings, and working fireplaces. The service is professional, offering port and sherry in the large, handsome sitting rooms in the evening and elaborate breakfasts in the morning, included in the price of the room. It's not flawless, of course—rooms can be too cool, three have only showers or lack closets, all have only one bed (you can get a roll-away in a suite), and you may have to request a TV and VCR. But you'll feel stylish the whole time.

✪ **River's Edge Resort Cottages.** 4200 Boat St., Fairbanks, AK 99709. ☎ **800/770-3343** or 907/474-0286. Fax 907/474-3665. www.riversedge.net. TV TEL. 86 cottages, 8 suites. High season $155 double. Low season $89 double. Additional person in room $10 extra. AE, MC, V.

These trim little cottages, all quite new, stand in a grassy compound along the gentle Chena River, where guests can fish for grayling. Inside, each cottage is an excellent standard hotel room, with high ceilings and two queen beds. Outside, they're like a little village, where guests can sit on the patio, watch the river go by, and socialize. The owners got the idea for the place from their RV park next door, when they noticed how their guests enjoyed visiting together in the open with their own private units to retreat to. It's perfect for families, as the outdoor areas are safe for playing and noise inside won't bother the neighbors. In the winter, business people can take both halves of a duplex at the price of one, using the other side as an office. A large restaurant sits at river's edge, with dining on a deck or inside at round, oak tables before an ornate potbellied stove. Dinner entrees are $8 to $20—steak, seafood, and down-home cooking. To get there, take Sportsman Way off Airport Way to Boat Street.

Wedgewood Resort. 212 Wedgewood Dr., Fairbanks, AK 99701. ☎ **907/452-1442.** Fax 907/451-8184. www.fountainheadhotels.com. 157 units, 294 apts. A/C TV TEL. High season, $182 double, $160 apt. for two. Low season, $105 apt. for two. Additional person in apt. $10 extra. AE, DC, DISC, MC, V.

Off College Road near the Creamer's Field Refuge, this huge, well-kept hotel sprawls across a grassy complex in eight large buildings. Seven are converted three-story

---

Other Fairbanks B&Bs

Besides the places I've described in detail in the listings, **7 Gables Inn,** 4312 Birch Lane (P.O. Box 80488), Fairbanks, AK 99708 (☎ **907/479-0751;** fax 907/479-2229; www.alaska.net/~gables7), has rooms with Jacuzzis and VCRs in a subdivision near the university, and rents canoes and other outdoor gear, with discounts for guests. **A Cloudberry Lookout Bed and Breakfast,** south of town off Goldhill Road (P.O. Box 84511), Fairbanks, AK 99708 (☎ **907/479-7334**), has rooms with great views arrayed off a four-story spiral staircase in a wooded setting.

---

apartment buildings, without elevators but with large living rooms, separate dining areas, fully equipped kitchens, air conditioners, TVs and phones with voice mail in both the living room and bedroom, and balconies. They're in the process of updating the decor and getting rid of the dark paneling, but the rooms have always been clean and comfortable. The convenience of this kind of suite is hard to exaggerate—the main difference from home is that someone else cleans up after you. Another 157 rooms, new in 1996, are large and thoughtfully designed, if somewhat antiseptic. They mostly house package tour groups in summer and are closed in winter. There are two restaurants, one with pleasant outdoor tables, sharing a brief menu (entrees $16 to $25) and are open only in the summer. A scheduled courtesy van runs to the airport and for a small fee to other sites; newspapers come to your door; and coin-op laundries are scattered around the property.

Westmark Fairbanks. 813 Noble St., Fairbanks, AK 99701-4977. ☎ **800/544-0970** (reservations) or 907/456-7722. Fax 907/451-7478. www.westmarkhotels.com. 244 units. TV TEL. High season, $149–199 double. Low season, $99–$119 double. Additional person in room $15 extra. AE, DC, DISC, MC, V.

Taking up a full block downtown, the Westmark Fairbanks—not to be confused with the seasonal and somewhat less expensive Westmark Inn on South Cushman Street—fulfills the role of the city's grand, central hotel. A recent remodel helps it hold that image, with an impressive lobby on Tenth Street, but the rooms, in a series of buildings surrounding a central courtyard, remain uneven in quality. Some are large and fresh, with new furniture, while others seemed a bit worn and dated when I visited—make a choice when you check in. Facilities include a courtesy van, tour desk, cafe, lounge, and gift shop.

MODERATE

All Seasons Inn. 763 Seventh Ave., Fairbanks, AK 99701. ☎ **888/451-6649** or 907/451-6649. Fax 907/474-8448. www.alaska.net/~inn. 8 units. TV TEL. High season, $125 double. Low season, $75 double. Rates include full breakfast. Additional person in room $25 extra. CB, DC, DISC, MC, V.

This charming and comfortable country inn stands on a pleasant residential street a couple of blocks from the downtown core. Each cozy room has its own decorative details, and the housekeeping was perfect when I visited. For socializing, a series of large, elegant common rooms connect downstairs, where you'll find a wet bar with hot drinks and a sun porch with books and games. Complimentary newspapers come with the full breakfast.

Fairbanks Hotel. 517 Third Ave., Fairbanks, AK 99701. ☎ **888/329-4685** or 907/456-6411. Fax 907/456-1792. www.alaska.net/~fbxhotl. 35 units, 11 with private bathroom. TV TEL. High season, $89–$109 double. Low season, $40–$55 double. AE, DISC, MC, V.

Four women transformed a notorious flop house into a charming art deco–style historic hotel, in the core of downtown. Although small, the rooms are light and attractively decorated, including brass beds and other period touches. Everything on the first two floors was clean and bright when I visited, but third floor "backpacker" rooms are to be avoided. The proprietors aim for the feel of a small European hotel, with that intimacy and service brimming with local knowledge. They offer a courtesy shuttle to the airport and railroad station, and rent bicycles.

✪ **Forget-Me-Not Lodge and the Aurora Express Bed and Breakfast.** 1540 Chena Ridge Rd. (P.O. Box 80128), Fairbanks, AK 99708. ☎ **907/474-0949.** Fax 907/474-8173. www.aurora-express.com. 10 units, 8 with private bathroom. $85–$150 double. Additional person in room $25 extra. Rates include full breakfast. MC, V. Closed Nov–Apr.

Susan Wilson's late grandmother appeared to her in a dream and told her there would be a train on a bank below her house, on the family's 15 acres high in the hills south of Fairbanks. So Wilson went out and got a train—a still-growing collection that includes a pair of 1956 Pullman sleepers, a locomotive, a caboose, a dining car, and a World War II hospital car—and her husband, Mike, brought it all up the mountain to install below the house, right in the spot indicated. Some cars are close to their original form, and Susan says older guests weep over the memories they bring back. Others were elaborately remodeled into small rooms on themes related to Fairbanks history. One 85-foot-long car is meant for families, with railroad-theme decor, puzzles, and toy trains. Then there's the incredible caboose, dedicated to Grandma. Three rooms in the house are sumptuous. One has a Jacuzzi and a great view. The lodge is located 6.5 miles out of town. Great Web site, too.

A Taste of Alaska Lodge. 551 Eberhardt Rd. (turn right 5.3 miles out Chena Hot Springs Rd.), Fairbanks, AK 99712. ☎ **907/488-7855.** Fax 907/488-3772. www.mosquitonet.com/~tasteak. 8 units, 2 cabins. TV TEL. $125 double, cabin $150–$200. Additional person in room $25 extra. Rates include full breakfast. AE, MC, V.

Situated atop a grassy slope on 280 acres, facing Mt. McKinley, the hand-crafted log main building feels like a wilderness lodge, but is less than half an hour from Fairbanks. You can enjoy a hot tub while taking in the view. Rooms are decorated with handmade quilts, brass beds, and other reproductions; and each has a door straight onto the grounds, where moose are often seen wandering. The cabins are especially appealing.

Minnie Street Bed & Breakfast Inn. 345 Minnie St., Fairbanks, AK 99701. ☎ **888/456-1849** or 907/456-1802. Fax 907/451-1751. www.AlaskaOne.com/minniestreet. 10 units, 6 with private bathroom. TV TEL. High season $85–$120 double, $125–$175 suite. Low season $55–$95 double, $110–$135 suite. Additional person in room $20 extra. Rates include full breakfast. AE, MC, V.

Just across the river from the downtown center, near the rail depot, two buildings around a garden courtyard contain clean, brightly decorated rooms. In a new building, there's a dining room with a high vaulted ceiling and rooms supplied with robes, alarm clocks, hair dryers, closets, custom designed carpeting, handmade quilts, and stylish furniture. The older rooms rent for less and lack some of the extras. Suites have kitchens, and one is a full one-bedroom apartment.

INEXPENSIVE

Golden North Motel. 4888 Old Airport Way, Fairbanks, AK 99709. ☎ **800/447-1910** or 907/479-6201. Fax 907/479-5766. www.akpub.com/goldennorth. 62 units. TV TEL. $69 double; $99 suite. AE, CB, DC, DISC, MC, V.

The Baer family, owners since 1971, keep the rooms in this two-story motel clean and up-to-date, making it a good bargain favored by Alaskans in town from the Bush to shop or just visit by car. The standard rooms are quite small, but the reasonably priced suites are a good choice for families. The rooms have fans, but no air conditioners. The location is near the airport. The motel provides a courtesy van to the airport or railroad station and free continental breakfast and coffee in the office.

HOSTELS

The visitor center distributes a brochure of hostels with seven listed just in Fairbanks, although none is affiliated with Hostelling International—American Youth Hostels. One of the longest established is **Grandma Shirley's Hostel,** 510 Dunbar St., Fairbanks, AK 99701 (☎ **907/451-9816**), which offers a bed with linens, towels, soap, cooking facilities, and free bicycles for $16.25 a night. The hostel is in a subdivision east of the Steese Expressway, 1½ miles from the railroad station.

CAMPING

Tent camping is a good way to go in Fairbanks, with its mild summers and ample public lands. Right in town, the **Chena River State Recreation Site** (not to be confused with the recreation "area" of the same name described in the next section of this chapter), is located where University Avenue crosses the river. Riverside sites are surrounded by birch. The self-service fee is $15 for RVs, $10 for tents. Getting a bit out of town, there are superb public campgrounds at Chena Lakes Recreation Area (see "Special Places" under "Getting Outside," above) and along Chena Hot Springs Road (in the next section).

Fairbanks has plenty of RV parks, some with full service and then some. Pick up a list at the visitor center. Among the best is **River's Edge RV Park and Campground,** at a wooded riverside bend of the Chena at 4140 Boat St., off Airport Way and Sportsman Way (☎ **800/770-3343** or 907/474-0286), with lots of services, including free shuttles and organized tours. Full hookups are $25 and tent camping $15.50. The same people operate the cottage resort and restaurant next door.

DINING
DOWNTOWN

✪ **Gambardella's Italian Cafe.** 706 Second Ave. ☎ **907/456-3417.** Main courses $9.50–$17; lunch $6–$10. 15% gratuity added for parties of 5 or more, or for split checks. AE, MC, V. Mon–Sat 11am–10pm, Sun 4–10pm. SOUTHERN ITALIAN.

Gambardella's doesn't disappoint—it's one of Alaska's best restaurants. I ordered halibut last time: very fresh, deftly seasoned, on light, rich pasta, with mixed vegetables that miraculously were all done perfectly, even mushrooms and carrots side by side. The lasagna is justly famous. Dining rooms are narrow and long, with high ceilings and well-scuffed wooden floors, and bend around a corner—pleasingly noisy but intimate at the same time. On a sunny day, eat on the patio among the hanging flowers. The service is quick and professional, the prices reasonable, and the deserts, baked inhouse, not to be missed. They serve beer and wine.

Souvlaki. 310 First Ave. ☎ **907/452-5393.** Lunch or dinner $5.25–$6.25. MC, V. Summer Mon–Fri 10am–8pm, Sat 10am–6pm. Winter Mon–Sat 10am–6pm. GREEK.

The tasty Greek cuisine here is a Fairbanks institution. Fittingly for Fairbanks, it's casual to a fault, with low prices and a varied menu to please American tastes as well. They also operate a take-out place at Alaskaland in the summer.

Thai House. 526 Fifth Ave. ☎ **907/452-6123.** Lunch $6.25–$8; dinner $9–$11. MC, V. Mon–Sat 11am–4pm and 5–10pm. THAI.

In a small storefront in the downtown area, this is a simple, family-run restaurant with authentic Thai cuisine that has made it a favorite in Fairbanks. Beer and wine license.

WITHIN DRIVING DISTANCE

Besides the restaurants listed here, there's the salmon back at Alaskaland, described above, and the Ester Gold Camp, below. Check the sections on Chena Hot Springs Road and the Steese Highway, below, for choices a little farther afield. Also, in town, near the university on University Road, **Sam's Sourdough Cafe** is a masterpiece in the art of the greasy spoon, with quick, friendly service, creative burgers, and great milkshakes. They're open 6am to 10pm, and it's a bit smoky.

The Bakery. 69 College Rd. ☎ **907/456-8600.** Lunch $4–$8; dinner $4–$15. MC, V. Mon–Sat 6am–9pm, Sun 7am–4pm. DINER.

There are an infinite number of old-fashioned coffee shops in and around Fairbanks—the kind of place where a truck driver or gold miner can find a big, hearty meal, a motherly waitress, and a bottomless cup of coffee. This is the best of the lot—which is really saying something. The sourdough pancakes are memorable, the menu long and inexpensive, the service friendly, and the quality of baked goods testified to by the number of police cars always in the parking lot. The Formica tables are worn down from years of wiping. No liquor license.

Pike's Landing. 4438 Airport Way. ☎ **907/479-6500.** Main courses $20–$55; lunch $9–$13.50. AE, DC, DISC, MC, V. Daily 11:30am–2:30pm and 5–11pm. STEAK/SEAFOOD.

The large dining room overlooking the Chena River near the airport is primarily a place for straightforward steak and seafood. It's all well prepared, with huge servings and occasional flashes of brilliance in the more sophisticated fish dishes. For an inexpensive meal, the bar serves food on the deck over the river, a pleasant choice on a sunny day. Full liquor license.

The Pump House Restaurant and Saloon. 1.3 Mile, Chena Pump Rd. ☎ **907/479-8452.** Main courses $13–$24. AE, DISC, MC, V. Daily 11am–10:30pm. STEAK/SEAFOOD.

The historic, rambling building on the Chena River is beautifully decorated and landscaped with authentic gold rush relics. Sitting on the deck, you can watch the riverboat paddle by or a group in canoes stop for appetizers and drinks from the full bar. Lunch comes from an excellent $11.50 buffet. The dinner menu is reasonably priced, with all the usual steak and fish house items. The dining rooms are large, but we found service quick.

✪ **Two Rivers Lodge/Tuscan Gardens.** 4968 Chena Hot Springs Rd. ☎ **907/488-6815.** Main courses $12–$27. AE, DISC, MC, V. Mon–Fri 5–10pm, Sat–Sun 3–10pm. STEAK/SEAFOOD/NORTHERN ITALIAN.

Inside the log lodge building, chef Tony Marsico brings interesting touches to a steak and seafood menu—such as his wonderful soups, about which he's published a cookbook. The creamy, complex king crab bisque, in a bowl of sourdough bread with a layer of cheese on top, put me in a contemplative reverie. Service is friendly but not necessarily quick—it's a place to settle in for an evening of dining. Outside, on a deck over the duck pond, a whole separate operation serves meals from a brick Tuscan oven in the open air, operating only in fine weather. Start there for appetizers, or eat a whole inexpensive Tuscan meal under the evening sun. There are full bars at both spots. The drive from Fairbanks is about 25 minutes.

SHOPPING

Fairbanks has a few good shops downtown. **Arctic Travelers Gift Shop,** at 201 Cushman St. (☎ **907/456-7080**), specializes in Native crafts, carrying both valuable art and affordable but authentically Alaskan gifts. The staff is friendly and knowledgeable, and the store has a long and excellent reputation. The **Yukon Quest Store,**

Quick Downtown Eats

For a quick lunch or takeout downtown, try the fun **Dashing Moose Deli,** at the corner of First Avenue and Cushman Street. They make good panini sandwiches. For a family pizza, try the popular **Pizza Bella** on Airport Way. For a casual Mexican meal, **Hot Tamales** (☎ **907/457-8350**) is at 112 N. Turner, just across the river from the visitor center.

---

at 558 Second Ave. (☎ **907/451-8985**), supports the incredible 1,000-mile sled dog race between Whitehorse and Fairbanks; you'll find race memorabilia and a little museum. Near the airport, at 4630 Old Airport Rd., the **Great Alaskan Bowl Company** (☎ **907/474-9663;** www.woodbowl.com) makes and sells bowls of native birch—salad bowls, of course, but also for many other purposes. They can carve up to eight nested bowls from one piece of wood. One side of the shop is a glass wall looking into the shop, where you can see workers and their power tools cutting the bowls from raw logs. **Santa's Smokehouse,** 2400 Davis Rd. (☎ **907/456-3885;** www. alaskabest.com/fish), sells delicious smoked salmon in gift packs to take home, and processes fish and game for sportsmen (take Peger Road south from Airport Road).

FAIRBANKS IN THE EVENING

Fairbanks has a lot of tourist-oriented evening activities, as well as entertainment also attended by locals. Call the 24-hour event recording of what's playing currently, or check the Web site (www.fairnet.org/agencies/fcvbcal.html), or get a copy of the *Fairbanks Daily News-Miner.* The best of the summer arts scene is at the ✪ **Fairbanks Summer Arts Festival** (☎ **907/474-8869;** see "Special Events" under "Essentials," above). There also are **movie theaters**—a large multiplex is located on Airport Way. The evening show at the **Palace Theater** is discussed with Alaskaland (see "Alaskaland," above).

The **Ester Gold Camp,** P.O. Box 109, Ester, AK 99725 (☎ **907/479-2500;** fax 907/474-1780; www.alaskasbest.com/ester), is an 11-building historic site, an old mining town that's been turned into an evening tourist attraction. The main event is a gold rush theme show at the Malamute Saloon, with singing and Robert Service poetry, nightly at 9pm; admission is $12. A "photosymphony" slide show about the aurora takes place every summer evening at 6:45 and 7:45. There's also a restaurant that serves a buffet and has mess-hall seating for $14.95 for adults, $6.95 for big kids, and $3.95 for little kids. If you have crab, it's $23.95 for adults. The gift shop is open in the evening, and there are simple, inexpensive rooms in the old gold-mine bunkhouse. A free bus is available from major hotels in Fairbanks.

The **Howling Dog Saloon,** north of town in Fox (☎ **907/457-8780**), claims to be the "farthest north rock 'n' roll club in the world." That's questionable, but the bar with the dancing dog on the roof does have a reputation for a rowdy good time—an authentic Alaskan dive with style. The music is classic rock and blues; a selection of 17 craft brews is on tap at $4 each, while regular American beer is $2.75; and there's no cover charge. Outside there are volleyball nets, horseshoe pits, and the like. The saloon usually closes for a few months in midwinter.

4 Nenana: Parks Highway Sidetrack

Although there's little to justify a special trip, you might spend a pleasant hour or two wandering the deserted streets of Nenana, a little riverside town an hour's drive south of Fairbanks, as you travel the Parks Highway to Denali National Park or Anchorage. The town has a unique memory, keeping alive a sleepy, riverbank lifestyle Samuel

Clemens might have found familiar. The Tanana River docks still serve barges pushed by river tugboats, carrying the winter's fuel and supplies to villages across the region. The Alaska Railroad still rumbles through, although it made its last stop at the depot in 1983, passing the spot where Pres. Warren G. Harding drove the golden spike marking the line's completion on July 15, 1923. (The first president to visit Alaska, Harding died soon after the trip, supposedly from eating some bad Alaska shellfish—but we don't believe that, now *do* we?)

A log cabin **visitor center** stands at the intersection of the highway and A Street, the main business street. The friendly hosts will engage you in conversation and try to entice you farther into the town. At the other end of A Street, by the river, the old railroad depot has been made, with little meddling, into a **Railroad Museum** and gift shop chock-full of Alaska Railroad memorabilia. Time seems to have simply stopped in the museum, where you'll find old documents, scales, and other items from the past era. Hours are 8:30am to 6pm daily in the summer. The golden spike is displayed outside.

A block down Front Street, along the river, **St. Mark's Episcopal Church** is the town's most historic and loveliest building; its 1905 log cabin construction remains unspoiled, even though the church is still in use. The church predates most of the town, which was built as a railroad camp. You'll probably have to track down a key to get a look inside; ask at the visitor center.

On the left of Front Street, you can see the **barge docks,** and, a block farther on the riverfront, the **Alfred Starr Nenana Cultural Center** (☎ **907/832-5520**). The center is a meeting and display venue for local art and cultural history, with a strong emphasis on the Athabaskan people of the area. Besides the museum displays—items that locals feel important to share of themselves—don't miss the **Alphonse Demien-tieff Wheelhouse Gift Shop.** Much of the Athabaskan art and craft work there is of exceptional quality, and items are displayed with biographies of their makers. Prices were very low when I visited.

Nenana's main claim to fame is the **Nenana Ice Classic** (☎ **907/832-5446**), a traditional statewide gambling event in which contestants try to predict the exact date and time of the ice breakup on the Tanana. The pot builds to over $100,000 by spring, but it's generally shared among several winners who pick the same time. The town kicks off the classic each February with a celebration that includes dancing and dog mushing races and the raising of the "four-legged tripod," a black-and-white log marker whose movement with the ice indicates that spring has arrived and that someone, somewhere, has won a lot of money. Usually it happens sometime in May. You can consult a thick book of past guesses at the visitor center.

There are **accommodations** in Nenana, but not much reason to stay. A couple of diners serve basic burgers and fries. There are a couple of shops, a library, clinic, and school, and an RV park as well.

5 Chena Hot Springs Road

The 57-mile paved road east from Fairbanks is an avenue to an enjoyable day trip or a destination for up to a week's outdoor activities and hot-spring swimming. The road travels through the Chena River State Recreation Area, with spectacular hikes and float trips and well-maintained riverside campgrounds, and leads to the Chena Hot Springs, where there's a year-round resort perfect for soaking in hot mineral springs and for use as a base for summer or winter wilderness day trips. The resort is open to people who want to rent one of the comfortable rooms or to campers and day-trippers, and it's equally as popular in the winter as in the summer (the slow seasons are spring and fall). Japanese visitors especially make the pilgrimage in winter to see the northern lights, but Americans are discovering it as well. Of all the roads radiating from Fairbanks, this short highway will be most rewarding to outdoors people, as well as providing some of the best remote lodgings accessible on the Interior road system.

The paved road leads through a forest of birch, spruce, and cottonwood, first passing an area of scattered roadside development and then following the Chena River through the state recreation area. It's a pleasant drive, around 1¼ hours from Fairbanks, but not particularly scenic. On a sunny summer weekend, the people of Fairbanks migrate to the riverside and the hiking trails; on a sunny winter weekend, they take to the hills on snowmobiles, cross-country skis, or dog sleds.

A pair of prospectors, the Swan brothers, discovered the hot springs in 1905, having heard that a U.S. Geological Survey crew had seen steam in a valley on the upper Chena. Thomas Swan suffered from rheumatism; incredibly, he and his brother poled up the Chena River from Fairbanks, found the hot springs, built a cabin and rock-floored pool, and spent the summer soaking. He was cured! More visitors followed, drawn by stories that whole groups of cripples were able to dance all night after soaking in the pools—by 1915 a resort was in operation, drawing worn-out miners and gold rush stampeders and many others as well. The resort has been in constant use ever since, and recently was bought by an aggressive new owner who is improving the fading accommodations.

ESSENTIALS

GETTING THERE   The Chena Hot Springs Road meets the Steese Expressway about 10 miles north of downtown Fairbanks. You can rent a car in Fairbanks. The resort offers rides from Fairbanks for $30 per person round-trip with a minimum of two; one-way fares are not available.

VISITOR INFORMATION   For outdoors information, check the Fairbanks **Alaska Public Lands Information Center,** 250 Cushman St. (at Third Avenue), Suite 1A, Fairbanks, AK 99701 (☎ **907/456-0527;** TDD 907/456-0532; fax 907/456-0514; www.nps.gov/aplic). It's described in the Fairbanks section, earlier in this chapter.

The **Alaska Division of Parks,** at 3700 Airport Way, Fairbanks, AK 99709 (☎ **907/451-2695;** fax 907/451-2754; www.dnr.state.ak.us/parks/parks.htm), manages the area and produces trail, river, and road guides, which are available at trailhead kiosks or from the public lands center. Contact them, also, to rent the public cabins in the area, which are described below. Call or check the Web site for information, and then reserve by mail or in person up to 6 months ahead. Full payment is required to hold the reservation.

The **Chena Hot Springs Resort** owns and operates the springs; they're discussed below.

STOPS ALONG THE ROAD

Don't miss a stop at **Tacks General Store,** at mile 23.5 (P.O. Box 16004), Two Rivers, AK 99716 (☎ **907/488-3242**). The old-fashioned country store and post office is a center of the rural community, a friendly place to stop for breakfast, lunch, or pie. One item is on the menu for each meal, but there may be a dozen or more kinds of pie, so good Fairbanks families drive out just for a slice on the weekend. You can eat in the simple dining room or picnic outside. They're open 8am to 8pm daily.

Also on the road, the **Two Rivers Lodge,** a fine-dining establishment and bar, and **A Taste of Alaska Lodge,** a bed-and-breakfast, are listed in "Dining" and "Accommodations" respectively in the Fairbanks section.

GETTING OUTSIDE: THE CHENA RIVER STATE RECREATION AREA

The recreation area takes in 254,000 acres along the river valley and over the rolling mountains of heather around it. Some of Interior Alaska's best hiking and floating are found here. *One warning:* The **mosquitoes** are brutal.

ACTIVITIES

HIKING & BACKPACKING   The best trail hikes in the Fairbanks area are in the Chena Hot Springs State Recreation Area. Backcountry camping requires no permit, and many of the trails go above treeline, so it's a good area for experienced backpackers to get into the wilderness.

The **Angel Rocks Trail** is a 3½-mile loop to a group of granite outcroppings, with alpine views. The trailhead is well marked, at mile 48.9 of the road.

The 15-mile loop of the **Granite Tors Trail,** starting at mile 39 of the road, is a bit more challenging, rising through forest to rolling alpine terrain, but the towering Tors more than reward the effort. Like surrealist experiments in perspective, these monolithic granite sentinels stand at random spots on the broad Plain of Monuments, at first confounding the eye's attempts to gauge their distance and size. They were created when upwelling rock solidified in cracks in the surrounding earth, which then eroded away into the alpine plain. Water is scarce, so bring along plenty. If you do it as an overnight, you'll find the driest ground for camping right around the Tors.

For a longer backpacking trip, the **Chena Dome Trail** makes a 29-mile loop, beginning at mile 50.5 and ending at mile 49. The 3 miles nearest the road at either end pass through forest, but the remaining 23 miles are above treeline, marked with cairns, and with expansive views, summiting 4,421-foot Chena Dome after the 10-mile mark. The trail can be quite wet and muddy in parts and steep and rocky elsewhere. Two public shelters are on the trail.

RIVER FLOATING   The Chena is an often-lazy Class I river as it flows through much of the recreation area and into Fairbanks. The faster-flowing, clearer water is found higher upstream, farther along the road. It's possible to float for days, all the way down to Fairbanks, but the road crosses the river four times and there are lots of access points, so you can tailor a trip to the amount of time you have. Get the State Parks river guide to choose your put-in. **Canoe Alaska** (☎ 907/479-5183) offers instruction and guided trips. **7 Bridges Boats and Bikes,** 4312 Birch Lane (P.O. Box 80488), Fairbanks, AK 99708 (☎ **907/479-0751;** fax 907/479-2229; www.alaska.net/~gables7/7bridges.html), rents canoes for $35 per day, and will drop you off and pick you up for $1.50 per mile out of town.

FISHING   Several of the ponds are stocked with trout, which you can keep; signs along the road mark access points. You can catch-and-release for arctic grayling in the Chena, depending on the current regulations and bait restrictions. Check with the **Alaska Department of Fish and Game,** 1300 College Rd., Fairbanks, AK 99701 (☎ **907/459-7207**).

CAMPING & CABINS

Three beautiful campgrounds with water and pit toilets lie along the road by the Chena River, managed by the Alaska Division of Parks (see "Visitor Information," above). Sites are $8 per night. Although they can't be reserved ahead, the campgrounds are unlikely to be full. The **Rosehip Campground,** at mile 27, has 38 sites, well separated by spruce and birch, with six suitable for RVs. Some sites are right on the river, and some are reserved for more private tent camping, back in the woods. The **Granite Tors Campground** is across the road from the trailhead at mile 39; it has 23 sites, seven suitable for RVs. Some sites have river frontage. The **Red Squirrel Campground,** at mile 42.8, has just a few sites on the grassy edge of a small, placid pond, where there's also a pleasant picnic area.

There are several public-use cabins in the recreation area, three of them easily accessible to summer visitors. (See "Visitor Information," above, for reservation information.) These are small, primitive cabins, and you must bring your own sleeping bags, lights, and cooking gear. You can drive to the **North Fork Cabin,** at mile 47.7 of the road. The new **Chena River Cabin** faces the river at mile 32.2. You can get to both of those by car or canoe, and they cost $35 a night. The others are $25 a night. The **Stiles Creek Cabin** is 7 miles up the Stiles Creek Trail loop, from mile 31.6 or 36.4 on the road. Check the Web site for other choices.

THE HOT SPRINGS

Our family enjoyed a relaxing outing here centered around swimming and exploring. The hot springs heat the buildings and, mixed with cold water, supply an indoor pool and a series of hot tubs and spas. A large outdoor pool is planned for completion by 2000. The existing indoor swimming pool is kept cool enough to swim, but it's small and can be overcrowded and noisy with children during the day. The locker rooms are undersized, but modern and well kept when we visited; the new owner promises they will be expanded by 2000. Having various hot tubs and spas allows you to soak at your chosen temperature, inside or outside. The facility is open daily 9am to midnight; kids are kept out from 10pm to midnight. Swim passes come with your room if you're staying at the resort; for campers or day-trippers, a day pass is $8 for adults, $6 for children and senior citizens.

All this could change under the energetic new ownership of Bernie Karl, a Fairbanks recycler who bought the resort from the state with big plans for improvement. At this writing he had added 40 attractive new rooms, but his concept of a huge, rock-walled outdoor pool had not yet come to pass.

ACCOMMODATIONS

✪ **The Chena Hot Springs Resort.** Mile 56.5, Chena Hot Springs Rd. (P.O. Box 73440), Fairbanks, AK 99707. ☎ **907/452-7867.** Fax 907/456-3122. chenahotsprings.com. 72 units, 9 cabins. High season (winter), $115–$125 double. Low season (spring and fall), $75–$95 double. Additional person in room $10 extra. AE, CB, DC, DISC, JCB, MC, V.

The resort, set on 440 acres of land in a bowl of mountains, invites a slow pace, with plenty of time spent soaking or walking, but there's plenty else to do. In the winter, the aurora viewing is exceptional here, away from city lights, and they offer Nordic skiing, snow cat and snow machine tours, skating, sled dog rides, and other activities. In the summer you can go horseback riding, rafting, hiking, gold panning, or mountain biking. The trails on-site connect to the routes in the adjoining state recreation area for extended hikes.

The rooms range from the crude, original cabins built by the prospectors who discovered the area to large new hotel rooms with television, phones, and coffeemakers. The larger cabins—not the prospectors' originals—are crude but adequate for a family or group looking for inexpensive lodgings and not particular about indoor plumbing. The lodge building contains the restaurant and bar, with a brief but sufficiently varied menu with prices only slightly above town.

CAMPING AT THE HOT SPRINGS

The resort has an RV parking area with electric hookups and two campgrounds. A tent campground with outhouses wraps itself around the bends in a creek. Dry camping is $15; with electricity, $20; and campers can use a dump station free.

6 The Steese Highway

The Steese Highway leads from Fairbanks 162 miles northeast to Circle, a village on the Yukon River about 50 miles south of the Arctic Circle (they were mistaken about the town's exact location when they named it—oh well). The historic gold rush route parallels the Davidson Ditch, a huge aqueduct and pipe that carried water to the mining operations near Fairbanks. Small-time miners and prospectors still scratch the hills. They bring their gold into the bar in Central, where they can get a shower and the current metal price is posted on the wall. **Arctic Circle Hot Springs** is out here, too, with a big, hot outdoor pool.

There are a couple of good hikes from the road, and it provides many access points to **river floats.** The clear, Class I water of the Chatanika River is perfect for family day trips or relaxed expeditions of a week or more. And the road meets two National Wild and Scenic Rivers: Beaver Creek, for trips of a week or more over easy Class I water, and Birch Creek, for more experienced paddlers. Get *The Alaska River Guide,* mentioned in "Outside in the Alaskan Interior" at the beginning of this chapter, for detailed guidance.

The Steese is paved only for the first 40 miles, and you can drive only so fast on these rural gravel roads without bouncing into a ditch. You also need to go slow so you can pull off to the side and avoid rocks thrown up by vehicles going the other direction. Consequently, you'll spend much of your day in the car going out the highway—driving both ways in one day would be absurd. On the other hand, the overnight accommodations to be had on the highway are below many people's standards, and if you're not interested in a hike, float trip, or hot springs soak, there isn't that much to do. Arctic Circle Hot Springs is the main attraction—more on that below. If you go, above all take mosquito repellent.

ESSENTIALS

GETTING THERE   The Steese begins as a four-lane expressway in Fairbanks. You can rent a car there.

VISITOR INFORMATION   The **Alaska Public Lands Information Center,** at 250 Cushman St. (at Third Avenue), Suite 1A, Fairbanks, AK 99701 (☎ **907/ 456-0527;** TDD 907/456-0532; fax 907/456-0514; www.nps.gov/aplic), can provide information on the outdoors.

The federal **Bureau of Land Management (BLM),** 1150 University Ave., Fairbanks, AK 99709 (☎ 907/474-2200; wwwndo.ak.blm.gov), manages most of the land and campgrounds. Their Web site is outstanding, with detailed information about campgrounds, trails, rivers, and even a Web cam of the view outside the office.

The **Fairbanks Convention and Visitors Bureau,** at 550 First Ave. (at Cushman Street), Fairbanks, AK 99701. (☎ **800/327-5774** or 907/456-5774; fax 907/ 452-2867; fairbanks.polarnet.com) is the best place to check for business information.

For **road conditions,** call the state hot line (☎ **907/456-7623**).

A HIGHWAY LOG

11 MILES   The Steese and Elliot highways split, the Steese heading east into hilly, wooded land. The big piles of gravel and the machinery you may see in the trees are the many-years-old remains of the environmentally destructive form of mining practiced in this region, which requires the excavation and sorting of large amounts of gravel.

28 MILES **Chatanika,** an old gold-mining settlement, has a couple of roadhouses where you can stop for a burger, a beer, and, if necessary, a room or place to park your RV. The **Chatanika F.E. Gold Camp,** 5550 Old Steese Hwy. N., Fairbanks, AK 99712 (☎ **907/389-2414;** fax 907/389-2748), is authentically unrestored, with corrugated metal walls and roof and simple rooms with a bathroom at the end of the hall for $55 to $70 as a double. Of late, the place has suffered from a short staff, and struck us as somewhat run-down. A tenth of a mile farther, **Chatanika Lodge,** 5760 Old Steese Hwy. N., Fairbanks, AK 99712-1415 (☎ **907/389-2164;** fax 907/389-2168), is a thriving and authentic roadhouse with a large bar in which to immerse yourself in local ways amid every kind of animal trophy, a collection of signed dollar bills, and 21,000 Christmas lights (we didn't count them, but the proprietor seemed honest). They serve good, simple food and rent clean rooms with TVs for $60 a night, double. It's a popular snowmobiling hangout and the scene of an **Outhouse Race** during Chatanika Days, the second weekend in March. Snowmobiles rent for $55 for 2 hours.

Beyond Chatanika, there's little more in the way of any kind of services from here to Central.

30 MILES The University of Alaska's **Poker Flat Research Range** (☎ 907/474-7558) is marked by a small rocket by the road. This is where the Geophysical Institute launches rockets to study the aurora and other high-altitude phenomena. Tours are scheduled every other Friday in the summer at 1:30pm; the cost is $5 for adults. Call to confirm before making the drive.

39 MILES The inviting state parks' **Upper Chatanika River Campground** sits on the river below a bridge on the highway, with 35 sites, pit toilets, and a hand pump for water. Camping is $8. There are grayling in the river, and it's a good spot to start or end a Chatanika float trip. State Parks produces a brochure covering the 12-hour float to the Elliot Highway, available from the Alaska Public Lands Information Center. The road is paved for another 5 miles, slowly rising along the Chatanika with some good views.

42.5 MILES A pull-out here at the McKay Creek Trailhead offers access to the **White Mountains National Recreation Area,** a 1-million-acre area managed by the BLM with some summer hiking trails, lots of rafting opportunities, more than 200 miles of winter trails with cabins, and extensive recreational gold mining.

57 MILES The old **Davidson Ditch** water pipeline is along here—it's not much to look at, just a big rusted pipe. It carried water to mining operations nearer Fairbanks. The Nome Creek Road intersects to the left, or north, then, after 6 miles, branches east and west along the creek to two campgrounds, trails, and river recreation within the BLM's White Mountains National Recreation Area. It's a well-maintained gravel way over scenic hills. The 19-site **Ophir Creek Campground** is 12 miles west of the T (18 miles from the Steese Highway), a put-in for a long float of Nome Creek and Beaver Creek. The self-service camping fee is $6. At the other end of the road, 4 miles east of the T (10 miles from the Steese), is the **Mt. Prindle Campground,** with 13 treeless sites and access to Nome Creek, floatable at high water, and a good gold panning spot. The high country beckons here by way of the 16-mile Quartz Creek Trail, open to all-terrain vehicles and hikers.

60 MILES The 12-site BLM campground at **Cripple Creek** has a ½-mile nature trail and put-in for Chatanika River floats. This is the last public campground on the highway. The fee is $6.

86 MILES   Twelvemile Summit—The drive becomes really spectacular from here to just short of Central, as it climbs over rounded, wind-blown, tundra-clothed mountaintops. There's a parking lot for interpretive signs and the lower end of the BLM's 28-mile **Pinnell Mountain Trail,** a challenging 3-day hike over this amazing terrain. (The upper trailhead is at Eagle Summit.) There are two emergency shelters on the way for protection from the ferocious weather that can sweep the mountains. Get the free BLM trail guide from one of the agencies listed above. Over the next 20 miles, the scars you see in the land are gold mines.

94 MILES   The **Upper Birch Creek** wayside is the put-in point for a challenging 126-mile wild river float trip. The take-out is at highway mile 146.

107 MILES   Eagle Summit, at 3,624 feet, is the highest place on the highway, and the best place to be on June 21 each year—the summer solstice. Although still a degree of latitude below the Arctic Circle, the sun never sets here on the longest day because of the elevation and atmospheric refraction. People come out from Fairbanks and make a celebration of it. The midnight sun is visible for about 3 days before and after the solstice, too, assuming the sky is clear. The BLM has installed a toilet and a viewing deck on a 750-foot loop trail.

CENTRAL

After descending from the mountains and entering a forest of spruce that continues to the Yukon, the road at mile 128 suddenly reaches a stretch of pavement and is surrounded by the spectral white trunks of paper birches—like a breath of fresh air after hours bouncing over gravel. You're in the friendly little gold-mining town of Central. We were made to feel like we were the first tourists ever to come this far. From Central you can turn right for the 8-mile drive to Arctic Circle Hot Springs, or continue straight on the Steese for a featureless 34-mile drive to Circle.

The big annual event is the **miners picnic** in August. The town's main attraction is the **Central Museum** (☎ 907/520-1893), which concentrates on the gold mining that has sustained the area since 1893. It's surprisingly good for a town of this size. Admission is $1 for adults, 50¢ for children; it's open Memorial Day to Labor Day, daily from noon to 5pm.

There are two restaurants, both with acceptable rural diner food. The **Central Motor Inn,** P.O. Box 24, Central, AK 99730 (☎ 907/520-5228; fax 907/520-5230), is a bit more ambitious in its menu, although smoky and dark when we visited. They serve daily from 7am to 11pm all year. Its six rooms, with TVs and private bathrooms, rent for $60 as a double. A shower is $3, and there's a coin-op laundry and a gas pump. The other establishment, **Crabb's Corner,** P.O. Box 30109, Central, AK 99730 (☎ 907/520-5599), at the corner of Circle Hot Springs Road and the Steese, has good, basic food in the bar as well as a tiny grocery, liquor store, and gas station. It seemed the cleaner of the two restaurants. Their pleasant campground among the birches costs $7 a night. Both places accept MasterCard and Visa.

Don't miss taking the 8-mile side trip to **Arctic Circle Hot Springs,** mile 8, Circle Hot Springs Rd. (P.O. Box 30069), Central, AK 99730 (☎ 907/520-5113; fax 907/520-5116). The main draw is the large outdoor pool, fed directly by the hot springs. In wintertime, Fairbanksans like to come out here for snowmobiling and to swim outdoors in subzero weather, toasty warm in the water while their hair freezes. The hotel offers massage and can arrange flightseeing and dog sledding, but it's not a center of resort activities as much as a place to taste, for a day or two, a slice of Alaska's rural past. The patched authenticity of the big, frame lodge is undeniable, confirmed by the blend of lacy antiques and simply old stuff dating from the 1940s through '60s.

The main house has 24 rooms with shared bathrooms; there are 12 cabins, some with water and some without; and five hostel cubbyholes in the eaves of the lodge. Everything is unique, but the hospitable management will try to suit your taste. Rates in the main building range from $74 to $125; cabins are $110 and hostlers pay $20. They accept MasterCard and Visa, and it's wise to reserve ahead for holiday periods. The camping area is suitable only for self-contained RVs. The comfortable dining room is open 7am to 9pm, year-round, and was serving excellent home-style meals from a short menu when we last visited.

CIRCLE

Another 34 miles past Central along the winding gravel road is a collection of log buildings and fewer than 100 people—mostly Athabascans—at the town of Circle. The Yukon flows by, broad and flat like a big field of water; it looks as if you could walk right across it, but the gray water is moving swiftly westward. As broad as it is, you can see only the nearest channel from Circle. The boat launch has a sign with facts about the river. Boaters can put in here bound for the town of Fort Yukon or the Dalton Highway to the west; the Dalton Highway bridge is 300 miles downstream. Or you can use Circle as a take-out after coming down from Eagle, 550 miles away by road but only about 158 miles and 5 days to a week over the water. **Yukon River View Motel** (☎ **907/773-8439**) offers boat tours.

You can camp free on a little patch of grass by the boat launch. The **Yukon Trading Post** (☎ **907/773-1217**), open year-round, has a cafe, store, bar, liquor store, and tire-repair shop. They serve a good burger and breakfast menu. The **H.C. Company Store** (☎ **907/773-1222**) has gas, groceries, and so on.

7 The Dalton Highway

Although it was built to service the trans-Alaska pipeline, one of humankind's largest private construction projects, the glory of the 414-mile Dalton Highway is the wilderness it passes through. Running straight through Interior Alaska to the Arctic coast, the Dalton crosses all kinds of scenic terrain, including forested rounded hills, the rugged peaks of the Brooks Range, and the treeless plains of the North Slope. This is still some of the most remote and untouched land on the globe. To the west of the highway, Gates of the Arctic National Park protects 8.4 million acres of the Brooks Range. West of the park, lands managed by the National Park Service continue, in the Noatak National Preserve, headquartered in Kotzebue, and beyond, to the ocean. This immense wilderness receives only a few thousand visitors a year.

Wildlife shows up all along the road, from grizzly bears to sport fish to songbirds. The road passes through Alaska's history of mineral extraction, too—there's the gold rush–era town of Wiseman and the current oil industry complex at Prudhoe Bay. Also, the Dalton provides Fairbanks's closest access to the Yukon River. But surely the reason most people drive all the way on the newly opened Dalton is because of where it goes, and not what's there. It goes to the very end of the earth, as far north as you can drive. It's quite a rough trip to nowhere, but a dramatic one if you have the time and endurance.

The Dalton is known to most Alaskans as the Haul Road—it was built to haul supplies to the Prudhoe Bay oilfield and the northern half of the 800-mile pipeline. It remains a wilderness route, with little in the way of human habitation along the way. Coldfoot is the northernmost truck stop in the United States. Just 15 miles up the road from Coldfoot, Wiseman now is home to about 25 people year-round. A glimpse of the past can be found at the Wiseman Trading Company, which offers a museum and tours of Wiseman. That's it for settlement until you reach the modern industrial complex at Prudhoe Bay, where you must join a shuttle or tour to see the Arctic Ocean or the oilfield.

ESSENTIALS
GETTING THERE

You can drive the highway yourself, staying in the few motels along the way or in a tent or motor home. The highway starts north of Fairbanks at mile 73 of the Elliot Highway—take the Steese Highway north from town till it becomes the Elliot. The gravel-and-dirt Dalton has a reputation for being notoriously bad, but now much of it is kept in good condition. Still, it's dusty, with soft shoulders, and flat tires are common. For **road conditions,** call the state hot line (☎ **907/456-7623**).

Driving the Dalton Highway gets you into some remote territory, and you must take **precautions.** Services are as far apart as 240 miles. Drive with your headlights on at all times. Bring at least one full-sized spare tire, extra gasoline, car tools, and spare parts. A citizens band radio is a good idea in case of an emergency. Insect repellent is an absolute necessity. Truck traffic is dominant, and there are some steep grades, a few on corners, where truckers must go fast to keep their momentum. Slow down or even stop to allow trucks to pass you either way, and be careful on bridges, as some are not wide enough for two vehicles to pass safely. Also, get well off the road for views or pictures—don't just stop in the middle as some people do.

For those who want to let someone else do the driving, several companies offer a variety of **packages,** including flights to or from Deadhorse, or flying both ways. See the "Prudhoe Bay" section in chapter 10 for details.

VISITOR INFORMATION

Fairbanks's **Alaska Public Lands Information Center,** at 250 Cushman St. (at Third Avenue), Suite 1A, Fairbanks, AK 99701 (☎ **907/456-0527;** TDD 907/456-0532; fax 907/456-0514; www.nps.gov/aplic), is the best source of information on the Dalton Highway. Rangers there have driven the road themselves. Much of the road runs through land managed by the Bureau of Land Management, 1150 University Ave., Fairbanks, AK 99709 (☎ **907/474-2200;** wwwndo.ak.blm.gov), so be sure to pick up their *Dalton Highway Road Guide,* which includes a map and important advice. For information specific to Gates of the Arctic National Park, contact the **Park Headquarters,** at 201 First Ave., Fairbanks, AK 99707-4680 (☎ **907/456-0281;** www.nps.gov/gaar). For information about businesses along the highway, try the **Fairbanks Convention and Visitors Bureau,** at 550 First Ave. (at Cushman Street), Fairbanks, AK 99701 (☎ **800/327-5774** or 907/456-5774; fax 907/452-2867; fairbanks.polarnet.com). Along the highway, there are two **visitor information centers** shared by land management agencies, one just north of the Yukon River bridge, which has no phone, and one in Coldfoot (☎ **907/678-5209** in summer).

ON THE ROAD

The bridge over the Yukon River at mile 56 is the only crossing in Alaska, and many people drive the Dalton just to get to the **Arctic Circle** at mile 115, where you'll find a colorful sign for pictures as well as a crude camping area. A number of places along the highway have incredible views, including Finger Mountain at mile 98; Gobbler's Knob at mile 132, which offers the first view of the Brooks Range; and 4,739-foot Atigun Pass at mile 245, where the road crosses the Brooks Range, winding through impossibly rugged country. The pass is the highest point on the Alaska road system, and you may find summer snow. All along the highway are opportunities to see birds and animals, including rabbits, foxes, wolves, moose, Dall sheep, bears, and caribou.

Sit still if you want to see the skittish caribou, as they may wander closer to an unmoving vehicle.

The **Wiseman Trading Co.,** a museum and general store at mile 188, offers a glimpse of the area's mining past. Ask for information in Coldfoot, at mile 175. The 4-foot-wide **trans-Alaska pipeline,** which feeds the United States up to 25% of its domestically produced oil, parallels the road all the way to Prudhoe Bay. Finished in 1977, the pipeline climbs over mountain ranges and goes under and over rivers. The final stop on the road is a fence; on the other side is the **Prudhoe Bay complex,** where the pipeline originates, and access to the Arctic Ocean, a few miles away. The only way through the gate is with a tour operator. Longer tours of the area include a trip to the ocean and viewing of the exterior of some oilfield operations, but a $25 shuttle to the water is available from the **Arctic Caribou Inn** (☎ 907/659-2368). See the Prudhoe Bay section in chapter 10 for details.

HIGHWAY SERVICES: FOOD, FUEL & LODGINGS

Among the three places offering services along the 414 miles of the Dalton you won't find anything luxurious, or even similar to budget chains.

Yukon Ventures Alaska, at mile 56, just past the Yukon River Bridge (P.O. Box 60947, Fairbanks, AK 99706; ☎ 907/655-9001), has a motel, a restaurant, a gift shop, fuel, and tire repair. The motel is a former pipeline construction camp and the food includes salmon, halibut, and Italian dishes.

The truck stop in Coldfoot, run by **Sourdough Fuel,** at Mile 175 (P.O. Box 9041), Coldfoot, AK 99701; ☎ 907/678-5201), offers a variety of services including lodging, a 24-hour restaurant, fuel, minor repairs, towing, RV hookup, laundry, a post office, and a gift shop. As at Yukon Ventures, the inn is made of surplus construction worker housing—not fancy, but the rooms are clean and have private bathrooms. The park service has a small campground.

After Coldfoot, the next service area is at **Deadhorse,** at the end of the road 240 miles north, with three hotels, fuel, restaurants, a post office, vehicle maintenance, a general store, and an airport. See the Prudhoe Bay section in chapter 10.

GETTING OUT OF THE CAR

Some of the world's most remote wilderness was opened up by the Dalton Highway. Experienced outdoors people can go it alone, but some package outdoor tours are available.

ACTIVITIES

BOATING   River tours from the Dalton Highway bridge are offered by **Yukon River Tours** (☎ 907/452-7162; fax 907/452-5063). The 90-minute trips run three times a day from June 1 to September 1 and cost $25 for adults, $15 under 12. You can buy a ticket at the bridge. The bridge also is a take-out for floats down the Yukon River.

HIKING   The road has no established hiking trails, but most of the area is open to hikers who are willing to pick their own route. Open country can be found in the alpine **Brooks Range,** north of the Chandalar Shelf at Mile 237. The tundra of the arctic's North Slope, north of the Brooks Range, may look appealing, but generally it is wet and swampy. Forests make cross-country traveling more difficult south of the shelf. A popular destination is the **Gates of the Arctic National Park and Refuge,** to the west of the road, but consider going east. The country is more open, and major rivers lie between the road and the park. Hikers who want to hike in the park without crossing the rivers can leave the road in the Wiseman area, where a short part of the road runs on the west riverbank. Topographical maps and advice on the Brooks Range area along the highway are available at the sources listed under "Visitor Information," above. Remember, this is remote wilderness; do your research, be prepared, and tell someone where you're going and when you'll be back.

FISHING The Dalton is not a top fishing area, but there are fish in streams and lakes along the highway. Many of the streams have grayling, but you'll want to hike farther than a quarter mile from the road to increase your chances. A good bet is the **Jim River area** between mile 135 and 144, where the river follows the road and fishing pressure is more spread out. Many of the lakes along the road have grayling, and the deeper ones have lake trout and Arctic char. Salmon fishing is closed along the road. For more detailed information, pick up the pamphlet "Sport Fishing Along the Dalton Highway" published by the **Alaska Department of Fish and Game,** available from the Alaska Public Lands Information Center or from Fish and Game, 1300 College Rd., Fairbanks, AK 99701 (☎ **907/459-7207**).

CAMPING

The Bureau of Land Management has several camping sites along the road, mostly just gravel pads left over from construction days. They are at:

- **Mile 60:** artesian well and outhouses.
- **Mile 98** (Finger Mountain): nice views, outhouse, and wheelchair-accessible trail with interpretive signs.
- **Mile 115** (Arctic Circle): outhouses and picnic tables, an interpretive display, and undeveloped campground.
- **Mile 136** (Prospect Creek): no conveniences.
- **Mile 180** (Marion Creek): 27 campsites, a well, and outhouses; the fee is $6.

8 The Alaska Highway

The 200 miles of the Alaska Highway from the border with Canada to the terminus, in Delta Junction, is pretty boring driving—hours of stunted black spruce and brush, either living or burned out. It's a relief when you hit the first major town, **Tok** (rhymes with Coke), 100 miles along. Don't get your hopes up, though. This is the only place where I've ever walked into a visitor center and asked what there is to do in town, only to have the host hold up her fingers in the shape of a goose egg and say, "Nothing." Another 100 miles (I hope you brought plenty of cassette tapes) and you've made it to **Delta Junction.** There's a little more to do here, but it's still not a destination. Another 100 miles, and you're in Fairbanks.

The main sources of information for the drive are based in Tok, the first town you hit after you cross the border. It acts as a threshold for the entire state. To plan the journey ahead, contact them, and see "Exploring the Interior," at the beginning of this chapter. One Web site, with many links, specializes in advice for Alaska Highway travelers: **www.alcanseek.com**.

I've arranged this section in order from the border with Canada heading west.

CROSSING THE BORDER

Remember to set your watch back an hour when crossing the border east to west—it's an hour later in Yukon Territory. Also, if you make significant purchases or rent rooms in Canada, you may be able to get a refund on the 7% goods and services tax (GST). See the section on Dawson City, below, for details.

CUSTOMS Crossing the Canadian border usually is as simple as exchanging a few pleasantries with a smiling guard, but occasionally it can get more complicated.

Firearms other than hunting rifles or shotguns may cause you problems crossing into Canada, and it's wise to call ahead if you plan to take any guns over the border. U.S. citizens don't need a visa but may need **proof of citizenship,** and a driver's license isn't adequate unless accompanied by a birth certificate, but a passport or voter's card will get you through. **Children** with their parents may need a birth certificate, children or teens under 18 unaccompanied by parents may need a letter from a parent or guardian, and children with a single parent should carry a letter from the other parent. Products you buy made of **ivory, fur, or other wildlife** will probably require special permits to be taken out of the United States, and it's easiest to have the store where you bought the item take care of it (see chapter 3 for details); there are rules concerning **animals,** as well. If in doubt, call **Canadian Customs** in Whitehorse (☎ 867/667-3943).

FROM THE BORDER TO TOK

The first 60 miles after entering the United States, the road borders the Tetlin National Wildlife Refuge. A **visitor center,** 7 miles past the border, at mile 1,229, overlooks rolling hills and lakes. It is open 7am to 7pm. The U.S. Fish and Wildlife Service also has two small campgrounds over the next 20 miles.

TOK

Originally called Tokyo Camp, a construction station on the highway, the name was shortened to Tok when it became unpopular after Pearl Harbor. Since then, Tok's role in the world hasn't expanded much beyond being a stop on the road. With its location at the intersection of the Alaska Highway and the Glenn Highway to Glennallen—the short way to Anchorage and Prince William Sound—the town has built an economy of gas stations, gift stores, cafes, and hotels to serve highway travelers.

ESSENTIALS

GETTING THERE   You're surely passing through Tok with your own set of wheels. If you get stuck for some reason, the Gray Line **Alaskon Express** (☎ 800/544-2206 or 907/883-2291) stops most days during the summer at the Westmark Inn.

VISITOR INFORMATION   There are two large, interesting visitor centers to serve highway travelers arriving at this entry to Alaska; both are located at the highway intersection that forms the town's locus. The **Alaska Public Lands Information Center,** P.O. Box 359, Tok, AK 99780 (☎ 907/883-5667; www.nps.gov/aplic), open daily from 8am to 8pm in summer and from 8am to 4:30pm in winter, has displays on the public lands and ecology of the area that provide a good introduction to the state, as well as staff to answer questions. The **Main Street Visitor Center,** operated by the Tok Chamber of Commerce, P.O. Box 389, Tok, AK 99780 (☎ 907/883-5775; www.TokAlaskaInfo.com), provides commercial information on Tok and anywhere else you may be bound on the highway. They're open May through September daily 8am to 8pm.

Fast Facts: Tok

Banks   An ATM is to be found at the bank in Frontier Foods, near the center of town, and at the Texaco station across the road from Fast Eddy's restaurant.

Hospital   The public health nurse (☎ 907/883-4101) is located at the State Troopers Building.

Police   The Alaska State Troopers (☎ 907/883-5111) police the region; they maintain an office near the intersection of the Alaska Highway and Glenn Highway.

Post Office   Across from the visitor center at the highway junction.

Taxes   There are no taxes in the region.

ATTRACTIONS

Mukluk Land, under the big fiberglass mukluk 3 miles west of town (☎ **907/ 883-2571**), is a homemade theme park that may amuse young children or even adults in a certain frame of mind; admission is $5 for adults, $4 senior citizens, $2 children and teens. It's open June to August, daily from 1 to 9pm. Gold panning is an extra $5. The **Burnt Paw Gift Shop** has a free sled dog demonstration on wheels June to August, Monday through Saturday at 7:30pm.

ACCOMMODATIONS
Hotels & Motels

The motels are numerous and generally quite competitive in Tok. Shop around, if you want to take the time. There also are many bed-and-breakfasts—check at the visitor center.

Snowshoe Motel & Fine Arts and Gifts. Across the highway from the information center (P.O. Box 559), Tok, AK 99789. ☎ **800/478-4511,** in Alaska, Yukon, and part of B.C., or 907/883-4511. 24 units. TV TEL. High season, $68 double. Low season, $48–$58 double. Rates include continental breakfast in summer. Additional person in room $5 extra. MC, V.

The 10 newer no-smoking rooms near the front are a bargain. Each is divided into two sections by the bathroom, providing two separate bedrooms—great for families. The furnishings are modern and the outside walkways are decorated with flowers.

Westmark Tok. Intersection of Alaska Hwy. and Glenn Hwy. (P.O. Box 130), Tok, AK 99780-0130. ☎ **800/544-0970** (reservations) or 907/883-5174. Fax 907/883-5178. www. westmarkhotels.com. 92 units. TV TEL. $129 double. AE, DC, DISC, MC, V. Closed Sept 16–May 15.

The central hotel in town is closed in the winter, as its clientele is primarily the package tour bus trade. It's made up of several buildings connected by boardwalks. The older rooms are narrow, without enough room at the foot of the bed for the TV, but they're comfortable and up-to-date. The new section has larger, higher-priced rooms. Ask for the "highway rate," $99 for a double. There's a "factory outlet" gift store in the lobby that sells remainders from Westmark's other shops for lower prices. A greenhouse grows huge vegetables. The restaurant serves three meals a day, with dinners in the $14 to $20 range.

Young's Motel. Behind Fast Eddy's Restaurant on the Alaska Hwy. (P.O. Box 482), Tok, AK 99780. ☎ **907/883-4411.** Fax 907/883-5023. 43 units. TV TEL. High season, $73 double. Low season, $55 double. Additional person in room $5 extra. AE, DISC, MC, V.

Good standard motel rooms occupy three one-story structures on the parking lot behind Fast Eddy's restaurant, where you check in. Eighteen newer, smoke-free rooms are the pick of the litter, but all are acceptable.

A Hostel & Camping

The **Tok International Youth Hostel,** P.O. Box 532, Tok, AK 99780 (☎ **907/ 833-3745**), occupies a three-room wall tent a mile off the Alaska Highway, 8 miles west of town on Pringle Drive. There is a shower, laundry machines, and limited cooking facilities. There are 10 beds for $10 apiece. It's closed September 15 to May 15.

Don't fail to get the 25¢ state highway and campground map from the public lands center, which includes all the public campgrounds in Alaska. The 43-site **Tok River Campground** just east of town, managed by the Alaska Division of Parks, lies along the river bottom below an Alaska Highway bridge. But if you're not ready to stop for the night, there are others along the highway which you can find on the map. There are lots of competitive RV parks in Tok. One that has wooded sites suitable for tent camping, too, is the **Sourdough Campground,** 1½ miles south of town on the Glenn Highway (P.O. Box 47, Tok, Alaska 99780; ☎ **907/ 883-5543**).

DINING

The restaurants in Tok are all of the roadside diner variety, with roughly similar prices and long hours. All are located close together on the right as you come into town from the east on the Alaska Highway. Other than the Westmark, mentioned above, the best is **Fast Eddy's** (☎ **907/883-4411**). The dining room, in dark wood and brass, is in a different league from the other diners; the service is quick and professional, and the food quite good. The **Gateway Salmon Bake** has an attractive picnic setup under big signs by the highway and a dining room, and the food is good; it's a casual experience for families. Like all salmon bakes, it's touristy, but so what? You're in Tok, after all.

FROM TOK TO DELTA JUNCTION

There's not much to look at, but you may be curious about the Bison Range as you pass the sign. In the late 1970s and early 1980s, the state tried to start a massive barley-growing project in Delta Junction, selling would-be farmers tens of thousands of acres to clear so Alaska could become the barley basket of the Pacific. Among other problems, introduced bison kept trampling the crops, so the state built another hay farm to lure the bison away from the barley farms. Meanwhile, the majority of the barley farms went bust. The landowners came out nicely, however, since they soon began receiving federal payments not to plant crops, and the payments far exceeded anything they ever made from barley. The bison are sitting pretty, too, with their own 3,000-acre farm. Who says government doesn't work? In summer, there's slim chance of seeing a bison from the road.

DELTA JUNCTION

This intersection with the Richardson Highway, which runs from Valdez to Fairbanks, is the official end of the Alaska Highway. It's an earnest little roadside town set in a broad plain between the Delta and Tanana rivers. People make their living from farming, tourism, and at a trans-Alaska pipeline pump station south of town. Nearby Fort Greely will soon close, probably to become a prison. West of town is a historic roadhouse museum, and there are several good campgrounds and lake recreation. You can spend an enjoyable half day here as a break in your travels.

ESSENTIALS

VISITOR INFORMATION   A helpful **visitor center** run by the Delta Chamber of Commerce, P.O. Box 987, Delta Junction, AK 99737 (☎ **907/895-5068;** www. akpub.com/akttt/delta.html), stands at the intersection of the Alaska and Richardson highways, in the middle of town. You can buy a certificate saying you drove the Alaska Highway. The historic **Sullivan Roadhouse** has been installed next door with an exhibit of the system of Alaska roadhouses that existed until 1926. It is open in summer daily 9am to 6pm.

Fast Facts: Delta Junction

Banks   The National Bank of Alaska has a branch right at the center of town, on the Richardson Highway, with an ATM.

Hospital   The Family Medical Center is at mile 267.2 on the Richardson Highway, 2 miles north of the visitors center (☎ 907/895-4879 or 907/895-5100).

Police   For nonemergencies, call the Alaska State Troopers (☎ 907/895-4800).

Post Office   The post office is on the east side of the Richardson, 2 blocks north of the visitor center.

Taxes   Delta has no taxes of any kind.

ATTRACTIONS & ACTIVITIES

Rika's Roadhouse and Landing, 10 miles northwest of town on the Richardson Highway (☎ **907/895-4201**), makes a pleasant stop on your drive. The state historical park preserves a log 1917 building and its lovely grounds, at the confluence of the Delta and Tanana rivers. The furnishings and museum pieces may be younger than some of the visitors, but the site as a whole, with its gorgeous vegetable garden and domestic fowl, does a good job of conveying what Alaska pioneer life was like. The roadhouse and a restaurant serving soups, salads, and sandwiches are open daily 9am to 5pm; the grounds and museum 8am to 8pm, May 15 to September 15. An impressive suspension bridge carries the trans-Alaska pipeline over the Tanana River, and boaters use the shoreline as a landing.

The lake at the **Quartz Lake State Recreation Area,** 11 miles northwest of town on the Richardson and down a 3-mile turnoff, is stocked with rainbow trout, silver salmon, and arctic char and is a popular fishing destination for people in the region. For information, contact the **Alaska Division of Parks,** at 3700 Airport Way, Fairbanks, AK 99707-4613 (☎ **907/451-2705;** fax 907/451-2706; www.dnr.state.ak.us/parks/parks.htm).

The **Delta River National Wild and Scenic River** is a float of up to 3 days for experienced canoe or raft paddlers, or an easy 18 miles on just the lower portion near town. The long version starts at Tangle Lakes, on the Denali Highway. Contact the public lands center in Tok or Fairbanks for guidance, or get a copy of the *Alaska River Guide* mentioned at the beginning of this chapter.

ACCOMMODATIONS

Hotels & B&Bs

In addition to the two somewhat idiosyncratic places listed here, you'll find inexpensive basic rooms at **Alaska 7 Motel,** 3548 Richardson Hwy. (P.O. Box 1115), Delta Junction, AK 99737 (☎ **907/895-4848;** www.alaskan.com/ak7motel).

Bed and Breakfast at the Home of Alys. 2303 Alys Ave., Delta Junction, AK 99737. ☎ **907/895-4128.** 2 units. TV. $75 double. Additional person in room $15 extra. No credit cards.

As the name says, these rooms are fully part of Henry and Alys Brewis's home, but that's good, because you wouldn't want to come to Delta Junction without meeting this fascinating couple, hearing their stories of a lifetime pioneer homesteading in Alaska, and being treated like a member of their family. Henry's parents both came to Alaska in the Klondike gold rush. The comfortable rooms look out on a yard with a greenhouse and impressive gardens, where moose often wander through. Take Brewis road off the Richardson Highway just north of town.

Big Doings in Delta Junction

The **Buffalo Wallow square dance festival** occurs over Memorial Day weekend. There's a **Buffalo Barbecue** for the Fourth of July. The biggest event of the year is the annual **Deltana Fair,** held for a weekend in late July or early August; it's a community celebration, with a parade, an outhouse race, livestock, a carnival, and games.

Kelly's Country Inn. Intersection of Richardson and Alaska hwys. (P.O. Box 849), Delta Junction, AK 99737. ☎ **907/895-4667.** www.knix.net/kellys. 21 units. TV TEL. $90 double. AE, MC, V. Additional person in room $5 extra.

This small motel, in town, has always had clean, charming rooms, and now they've got plans for a big expansion and modernization. As I saw them, some rooms had floral designs, others arched wooden ceilings, and there were lots of unexpected touches. The place is owned by real Alaska pioneers. All rooms have refrigerators and free coffee, and most have microwave ovens.

Camping

Alaska State Parks maintains five campgrounds on the rivers and lakes in and around Delta Junction and a couple of public cabins. The **Quartz Lake State Recreation Area,** 11 miles northwest of town on the Richardson and down a 3-mile turn-off, has an 80-site campground on the shallow lake; the fee is $8 a night. See "Attractions & Activities" above for contact information. To park an RV, or if you're tent camping and need a shower, **Smith's Green Acres RV Park and Campground,** 1½ miles north on the Richardson from the visitor center (☎ **907/895-4369**), is a well-developed establishment.

DINING

There are several restaurants near the intersection that defines the town. These two each accept MasterCard and Visa: The **Buffalo Center Diner** is a smoky but clean hangout for locals, with reasonable prices for roadside cafe food and an evening menu that includes a welcome break from the constant diet of beef generally found on the highway; **Pizza Bella** has a beer and wine license and reasonably priced pizza pies.

9 Dawson City: Gold Rush Destination

A gold rush scatters the seeds of civilization promiscuously. It is an irrational force of history, driven by hysterical greed for a metal that could show up almost anywhere, and its unpredictable results have the dramatic allure of madness, leaving cities behind on the landscape as if at random. Dawson City's presence at the confluence of the Yukon and Klondike rivers is just such a historic accident. Certainly, no other chain of events could have built it here, in such a remote place, nor filled it with such an extraordinary cast of characters. Today, no other town I know of as well preserves the true look and setting of a gold rush city. Being so far from the rest of the world, Dawson City never had the chance to change.

Approaching by road accentuates the town's weird isolation, especially coming from the west over the Top of the World Highway. By the third hour of bouncing over gravel road, orange midnight twilight falls to the north and a huge moon rises to the east, lighting the silhouettes of rounded mountains that stand all around in countless, receding layers, all quiet, all empty. The border to Canada is closed for the night; camping by the road, no vehicles pass in the alpine silence. Next morning, passing through Customs, you go on for 1½ hours without signs of humankind within the broad horizon, only the thread of gravel you're following. Turn another corner, and there it is. Down below, a grid of city streets at river's edge: Dawson City, once the second largest city on the West Coast of North America, and still way out in the middle of nowhere 100 years later.

Suddenly the radio's working again, bringing in an urbane situation comedy originating in Toronto. At the gravel river landing, a free car-ferry pulls up. A moment later, on the other side, there are people all over wide, straight streets, looking at well-kept old buildings. Inside a museum-like visitor center, guides dressed in period costumes are providing tourists with directions and selling them tickets to shows. Looking back at the hill across the river, at the wilderness so close at hand yet so separate, it's suddenly possible to understand the incongruity and shock of the gold rush. One hundred years ago, the world suddenly went mad and rushed to this riverbank beyond the edge of civilization and created a sophisticated city. One day it was a quiet riverbank, unknown except by the indigenous people; the next day, a city. It arrived as suddenly as it arrives in your windshield driving east on the highway.

Dawson City was the destination for some 100,000 stampeders hoping to strike it rich on the Klondike River in 1898, about 30,000 of whom actually made it here. Mining for gold and other minerals continues today, but the town's main focus is on the visitors who come to see a well-preserved gold rush boom town. Parks Canada does a good job of keeping up the buildings that make up part of the **Klondike National Historic Sites** and providing activities that bring history alive; you can easily spend 2 full days here, if you're interested in the period the town celebrates. Dawson City sometimes feels like one big museum, and it doesn't suffer from the commercialism that pervades Skagway, the other major gold rush town in the region. Low-stakes gambling in a small **casino** happens every night during the summer.

As a tourist center in a place where winter temperatures drop to -40° each winter, Dawson gets mighty quiet in the off-season. Before the last week of May or after the second week of September, you're unlikely to find any attractions open, and few other businesses. The town wakes a little for winter dog mushing and snowmobiling events, but a visit then would be without the historic aspect more people go for.

ESSENTIALS
GETTING THERE

BY CAR The main way visitors come to Dawson City is by making a long detour from the Alaska Highway. The paved Klondike Highway, also known as Yukon Highway 2, splits from the Alaska Highway a few miles west of Whitehorse, heading 327 miles north over scenic, fairly smooth road to Dawson City. For guidance on that part of the trip, get the excellent *Canada's Yukon Official Vacation Guide* from **Tourism Yukon,** P.O. Box 2703, Whitehorse, Yukon, Canada Y1A 2C6 (☎ **867/667-5340;** fax 867/667-3546; www.touryukon.com). The gravel Top of the World Highway heads west from Dawson City, crossing the border before connecting with the Taylor Highway, which leads north to Eagle and south to rejoin the Alaska Highway, 175 miles after Dawson City. The 502 miles for the detour compare to 375 miles if you stay on the pavement of the Alaska Highway. You do miss the spectacular vistas on Kluane Lake, but maybe you can see that on the way back. Below, you'll find a description of the Top of the World and Taylor highways and Eagle. The border is open 5am to 10pm Alaska time, and the road closes in winter. See the Alaska Highway section, above, for a note on Customs.

BY TOUR PACKAGE If you don't want to drive, many package tours include Dawson City. The best is probably Gray Line of Alaska's tours, with a trip to Eagle and a boat ride on the Yukon (see "On the River," below).

Dawson City

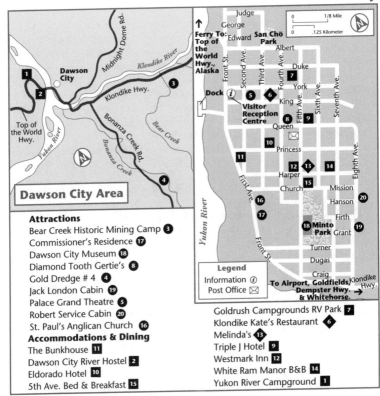

Attractions
Bear Creek Historic Mining Camp 3
Commissioner's Residence 17
Dawson City Museum 18
Diamond Tooth Gertie's 8
Gold Dredge # 4 4
Jack London Cabin 19
Palace Grand Theatre 5
Robert Service Cabin 20
St. Paul's Anglican Church 16
Accommodations & Dining
The Bunkhouse 11
Dawson City River Hostel 2
Eldorado Hotel 10
5th Ave. Bed & Breakfast 15

Goldrush Campgrounds RV Park 7
Klondike Kate's Restaurant 6
Melinda's 13
Triple J Hotel 9
Westmark Inn 12
White Ram Manor B&B 14
Yukon River Campground 1

BY PLANE   Air North (☎ 867/993-5110; fax 867/668-6224) flies round-trip from Dawson City to Fairbanks on Tuesday, Thursday, and Sunday, starting at around $300.

GETTING AROUND

BY CAR   You probably got to Dawson City in a car or RV. If not, cars are for rent from **Budget** (☎ 867/993-5644) or **Norcan Rentals** (☎ 867/993-6465). Dropping off in Whitehorse adds around $100.

BY TOUR   Gold City Tours (☎ 867/993-5175), on Front Street across from the riverboat *Keno,* offers a 3½-hour tour that includes Gold Dredge No. 4 and gold panning every afternoon in the summer for $33. They also have an airport limousine.

BY BIKE   Bikes are a fun way to get to the outlying sights for strong riders and are available for rent at the **Dawson City River Hostel,** listed below.

BY FERRY   The free **George Black Ferry** crosses the Yukon 24 hours a day from a landing at the north end of Front Street, providing a connection to the Top of the World Highway, a provincial campground, and the hostel.

VISITOR INFORMATION

Parks Canada Visitor Reception Centre, King and Front streets (P.O. Box 390), Dawson City, YT, Canada Y0B 1G0 (☎ 867/993-5566; www.harbour.com/ parkscan/khs/), is a mix of information center, museum, and theater of historic films, and is an indispensable stop. The hosts are knowledgeable and provide free maps and guides, as well as selling tickets to all the Klondike National Historic Sites tours, events, and shows. They're open daily in summer from 8am to 8pm. If you plan to do all or most of the gold field attractions, a five-tour pass the center sells for $15 Canadian is a good deal.

The **Klondike Visitors Association,** housed in the same building as the Parks Canada center, above (P.O. Box 389, Dawson City, YT, Canada Y0B 1G0; ☎ **867/ 993-5575;** fax 867/993-6415; www.hyperborean-web.com/kva/), offers information on local businesses, accommodations, and community events. Their Web page was far more informative and up-to-date than the Parks Canada site when I lasted checked.

SPECIAL EVENTS

Check the Klondike Visitor Association Web site for a complete events calendar (www.hyperborean-web.com/kva/).

The Yukon Quest International Sled Dog Race runs between Fairbanks and Dawson City, starting in Fairbanks on odd-numbered years, and Dawson in even-numbered years. It's held, naturally, in the deep cold of February. A huge snowmobile trek connects Dawson City and Tok later in the month, called **Trek Over the Top.**

The **Commissioner's Grande Ball,** in early June, is the social event of the year in Dawson City. **The Yukon Gold Panning Championships** and **Canada Day Celebrations** are on July 1. **The Dawson City Music Festival,** like a little miniature Woodstock (but better behaved), occurs in late July.

Fast Facts: Dawson City

Banks The Canadian Imperial Bank of Commerce at Second Avenue and Queen Street has an ATM. The next closest bank is 330 miles southeast in Whitehorse or 175 miles southwest in Tok.

Currency All the prices in this section are listed in Canadian dollars with U.S. equivalents. At this writing, a U.S. dollar would buy about $1.50 Canadian. Current rates are listed in the newspapers or check CNN's currency converter at www.cnn.com/travel/currency. It's wise to exchange your currency at a bank or using an ATM, or to use credit cards, rather than at a point of sale. Most Alaska businesses will accept Canadian small change at face value, but not dollar coins or bills.

Emergencies Call the Royal Canadian Mounted Police, on Front Street near Turner (☎ 867/993-5555), or the ambulance (☎ 867/993-4444).

Hospital A nursing station is located at Sixth and Mission streets.

Post Office The post office is on Fifth Avenue near Princess Street, and a historic post office, with limited services, is at Third Avenue and King Street.

Taxes You'll pay the 7% goods and services tax (GST) for almost everything, but if you're not a Canadian, you can apply to get up to $500 of it back at a duty-free shop or from Visitor Rebate Program, Revenue Canada, Summerside Tax Centre, Summerside, PE, C1N 6C6 Canada (☎ 800/668-4748 in Canada; 902/432-5608 outside Canada). Pick up a booklet containing the rules and an application from the visitor center. The rebate counts only if you spent more than $200, and only on taxes paid for goods and accommodations, not food, services, rentals, transportation, fuel, and the like.

Time Zone   Dawson City is on Pacific time, 1 hour later than Alaska. The time changes at the border.

GOLD RUSH ATTRACTIONS

Parks Canada leads a **town walking tour** from the Parks Visitor Center daily for $5. The guides are well trained and can open historic buildings you won't get to look inside otherwise. They also lend a 90-minute cassette tape version with headphones. Or you can use one of the maps they distribute to make up your own walking tour; there are interesting buildings almost anywhere you wander. Here are some of the highlights.

On Front Street, just south of the visitor center, the newly restored steamer **Keno** sits on timbers. At Third Avenue and Princess Street, **Bigg's Blacksmith Shop** is next to a gold rush–era building that is slowly sinking into the permafrost. At Front and Church streets, 2 blocks south, **St. Paul's Anglican Church** is a charming, creaky 1902 structure on the riverfront. Next door, the **Commissioner's Residence,** an impressive mansion with a wraparound porch, standing amid beautifully planted grounds, has been restored with mostly original furnishings. A tour goes through daily at 4pm for $5. In back of the house, you'll find a log building that was part of the 1897 **Fort Herchmer,** and later a jail.

The **Dawson City Museum,** on Fifth Avenue between Church and Turner streets (P.O. Box 303, Dawson City, Yukon, Y0B 1G0; ☎ 867/993-5291), is the best-presented gold rush museum I've seen. The fascinating, tin-roofed neoclassical building housed the Territorial Government from 1901 until it moved to Whitehorse, and upstairs one of the galleries still doubles as an impressive courtroom. The galleries downstairs display gold rush artifacts in a way that makes them seem immediate and alive. Guides dressed in costume lead tours further expanding on the teaching power of the objects and excellent placards. The clutter common to this kind of museum is confined to the "visible storage" gallery upstairs, where a rich collection is housed inside glass-fronted cabinets. A cafe serves soup, muffins, coffee, and tea, and there's a gift shop. Admission is $4; the museum is open Victoria Day to Labour Day, daily from 10am to 6pm. Next door is a free display of 19th-century locomotives from the short-lived Klondike Mine Line Railway, which ran 32 miles up Bonanza Creek.

The **Jack London Cabin,** at Eighth Avenue and Grant Street along the foot of the bluff, is a replica with some logs from the original cabin where London probably spent his winter in the Klondike. (The rest of the logs are in a replica in Oakland, California, where London also lived.) A small museum with a guide is at the site, and readings are given at 11:30am and 2:30pm. London found a gold mine of material for his classic adventure stories, but little gold, when he stampeded north.

Poet **Robert Service** spent more time at his cabin, at Eighth Avenue and Hansen Street, just down the road. Service wrote his ballads about the North while working as a bank clerk in Dawson City, reciting them for free drinks in the bars. Today you can hear them in tourist shows all over Alaska and the Yukon, including here on the lawn in front of the cabin. Admission is $6 for adults, $3 for children; recitals are at 10am and 3pm.

After the initial gold rush, the Rothschilds and Guggenheims financed large-scale industrial gold mining here. The remains of that amazing technical effort are preserved outside of town. **Gold Dredge No. 4,** 8 miles down Bonanza Creek Road south of town, is maintained by Parks Canada to show how these incredible earth-eating machines worked their way across the landscape, sifting gold out of the gravel; similar dredges are in Fairbanks and Nome. Hour-long tours, which circle the outside of the machine but don't go inside, take place hourly from 9am to 5pm and cost $5. Another

The Gold Rush in Context

The biggest event in Alaska history happened just over 100 years ago: the 1898 Klondike Gold Rush. If you're coming to Alaska, you'll be hearing a lot about it. Here's some of the context for the barrage of anecdotes you can expect.

Prospectors sought gold in small numbers even before Russia sold Alaska to the United States in 1867, but the Russians' main interest in Alaska was sea otter pelts, and they made few forays beyond the coast, leaving the great mass of the North and Interior unexplored. When the United States took over, Alaska had virtually no white population, and what it had was concentrated in the Southeast—in Sitka, the Russian capital, a few other Russian settlements, and at the trading post of Wrangell, which miners used as a jumping-off point for gold fields up the Stikine River in British Columbia.

After the American flag went up over Sitka, prospectors slowly worked their way into Alaska's vastness, often led or in partnership with Natives who knew the country. Called **sourdoughs** for the live yeast they carried to make their bread, these were tough wilderness men living way beyond the law or communication with the outside world. A few of them struck it rich. In 1880, a major find on the Gastineau Channel started the city of Juneau and decades of industrial, hard-rock mining there. Finds followed on the Fortymile River in 1886 (on the Taylor Highway), near Circle in 1893 (on the Steese Highway), and near Hope on the Kenai Peninsula in 1895 (on the Seward Highway). Gold slowly brought more people to Alaska, but not enough to catch the nation's attention.

In 1896, white prospector **George Carmack** and his Native partners, Tagish Charlie and Skookum Jim, found gold on the Klondike River, a tributary to the Yukon in Canada. Word traveled downriver to the gold fields in the Fortymile Country, and within 48 hours that area was empty and claims on the Klondike were being staked. The miners dug gravel from the creek that winter, and when they washed it in the spring, it yielded big hunks of solid gold, a massive discovery. They were instant millionaires in a time when a million dollars meant something.

It's hard to imagine today the impact of the news on the outside world. The economy was deeply in depression. The dollar was on a gold standard, and the scarcity of gold had caused a deflationary vise that in 1893 brought a banking collapse and unemployment of 18%. Suddenly, in 1897, a steamer arrived in Seattle bearing men from a place called the Klondike with trunks and gunny sacks full of gold. The supply of money suddenly grew and economic confidence returned. The national economy turned around on the news, and some 100,000 people set off for Alaska to get rich, too, plunging off into a trackless wilderness for which most were completely unprepared.

Contemporary Alaska marks the **Klondike Gold Rush** as the start of its history. Before the gold rush, Alaska largely remained as it had been for thousands of years, ruled and inhabited by its indigenous people. As late as 1880, the territory had fewer than 500 white residents, and only 4,000 by 1890—it was virtually empty from the point of view of those who discounted the Alaska Natives. In 1898, the stampede began, bringing an instant population. Even the mayor of

Seattle left for Alaska. Within a few years, Alaska had cities, telegraph lines, riverboats, and sled dog mail routes. About 30,000 made it all the way to Dawson City. Few of that number struck it rich, but those who built the towns and businesses to serve them did—there were suddenly saloons and brothels, dress shops and photo studios. Promoters sold a credulous public newly laid-out towns on supposed routes to the gold fields, including routes that were essentially impassable.

The **White Pass** above Skagway and the **Chilkoot Pass** above Dyea carried the most stampeders. Gold seekers arrived in the crazily lawless settlements by steamer from Seattle, got robbed and cheated, and then ferried their goods over the passes to **Lake Bennett.** (Upon completion of the railroad through the White Pass in 1901, Dyea and the Chilkoot Pass were abandoned, but Skagway lives on—see chapter 5.) The Canadian authorities wisely required each stampeder to bring a ton of supplies, a rule that undoubtedly prevented famine but made the single-file journey over the passes a miserable ordeal—prospectors sometimes had to make dozens of trips up the trail, just go get their supplies up. At Lake Bennett, the stampeders built boats, crossed the lake, and floated down the Yukon River, through the dangerous Five Finger Rapids, to **Dawson City,** a 500-mile journey from the sea.

Imagine their disappointment to find, on their arrival, that the gold claims had all been staked, and big companies were taking over. The prospectors looking to strike it rich had humbling choices. The smart ones started businesses to make money off the other stampeders, and some of them did quite well. Others worked for wages or went home. But many continued in pursuit of the next find. Their wild chase for gold drew the modern map of Alaska, founding dozens of towns. Many of these towns disappeared as soon as the frenzy cooled and now are entirely forgotten or live on only as place names, but some became real cities. **Nome** came in 1899, **Fairbanks** in 1902, **Kantishna,** now within Denali National Park, in 1905, **Iditarod** in 1908, and many others, until the rush finally ended with the start of World War I in 1914.

Even without a rush, there's still gold to be dug. Ever larger and more sophisticated machinery worked the Klondike claims and washed the gravel until the 1960s, and gold mining remains an important part of that area's economy to this day. Small-time prospectors are still looking all over Alaska and working their claims, and sometimes someone does make a significant new strike. A 1987 find north of Fairbanks, developed at a cost of $400 million, brings out more than 1,000 ounces a day.

But there's a much bigger and safer business in mining the tourist trade. The rush of visitors each summer dwarfs the numbers who came in 1898, and, in the true spirit of the event whose centennial they celebrate, the gold rush towns of Skagway, Dawson City, Fairbanks, and Nome know there's more money to be made from people than from gold.

For more on the gold rush and commemorative events, check this outstanding Web site: www.Gold-Rush.org.

7 miles up the road, the site of the original Klondike strike is marked. Parks Canada also manages the **Bear Creek Historic Mining Camp,** 7 miles up the Klondike Highway. The camp was headquarters for the company that owned the gold diggings. It's been kept as if the workers just left, including warehouses and workshops full of odd and interesting mechanical relics. The highlight is the gold room, where the gold was melted into bricks. At the end, you can watch a documentary film about the mining made before the operation shut down in 1966. The tour takes place twice daily, at 1:30 and 3pm, and costs $5.

ON THE RIVER

Dawson City is the largest town on the Yukon River after Whitehorse, and the most developed access point near Alaska. The Yukon, flowing 5 to 10 miles per hour, is a slow-paced westward-flowing highway. Two companies offer tour boat rides, and three self-guided canoe or raft floats.

Gray Line Yukon operates the new high-speed *Yukon Queen II* catamaran (☎ 867/993-5599), which runs daily from late May to early September 108 miles downriver to Eagle. The modern 115-passenger boat leaves at 8:30am for a 4-hour, narrated ride to Eagle; once there, you can eat at the cafe and visit the museum. It returns the same day, going upstream in 5 hours and serving dinner before arriving at 8pm back in Dawson City. Most passengers are on Holland America–Westours packages, but you can book a place if space is available. It's US$117 one-way, US$192 round-trip; or you can fly back. The office is across Front Street from the Visitor Reception Centre.

One popular trip is to float 3 or 4 days in a canoe or raft to Eagle and come back on the *Yukon Queen II;* there also are other more remote floats in the area, or you can keep floating down the Yukon to Circle, or even farther. A company offering gear for one-way floats to Eagle is listed in the "Eagle" section, below. The **Dawson Trading Post,** P.O. Box 889, Dawson City, YT, Canada Y0B 1G0 (☎ 867/993-5316), rents canoes and camping gear, and operates a shuttle that can drop you off on the more remote Stewart River for $175. Canoes rent for $150 a week.

ACCOMMODATIONS

In addition to the hotels listed below, there are several good B&Bs in Dawson City. The **5th Avenue Bed and Breakfast,** on Fifth Avenue next door to the museum (P.O. Box 722), Dawson City, YT, Canada Y0B 1G0 (☎ 867/993-5941), has seven rooms—basic, but fresh and well done. Three have their own bathrooms, and there are two kitchens for guests to use. The bright-pink **White Ram Manor,** at Seventh Avenue and Harper Street (P.O. Box 302), Dawson City, YT, Canada Y0B 1G0 (☎ 867/993-5772), has 10 generally small rooms with TVs, all but one with shared bathrooms; but the great feature is the large deck with a hot tub, barbecue, and picnic table, and the hospitable hostess, Gail Hendley.

HOTELS

The Bunkhouse. Front and Princess sts. (Bag 4040), Dawson City, YT, Canada Y0B 1G0. ☎ 867/993-6164. Fax 867/993-6051. 31 units, 5 with bathroom. $50 double without bathroom, $80–$95 double with bathroom. Additional person in room $5 extra. MC, V.

This is a unique place—it looks like a riverboat from the outside, and is fresh and trim, but it's intended for a budget traveler. The rooms, all no-smoking with exterior entries, have varnished wooden floors and attractive fabrics. The beds are really bunks—no bed springs. Those that share bathrooms are quite small; the bathrooms are clean, but the showers for men and women are in the same room, shielded only by stalls with doors. The rooms with private bathrooms have telephones and TVs.

El Dorado Hotel. Princess St. and Third Ave. (P.O. Box 338), Dawson City, YT, Canada Y0B 1G0. ☎ **867/993-5451.** Fax 867/993-5256. 56 units. TV TEL. $124 double; $160 suite. Additional person in room $9 extra. AE, DC, DISC, ER, JCB, MC, V.

Locals come to this year-round hotel daily to check the price of gold, posted in the lobby. The rooms are large and clean, and many have new beds, carpeting, and curtains, although some furniture and fixtures remained a bit out-of-date when I visited. There's a choice of lighter motel-style rooms in a newer building and larger rooms in a large old wood structure. All rooms have fans and coffee pots, and a courtesy car, coin-op laundry, and kitchenettes are available. The attractive but smoky **Bonanza Dining Room** has an extensive and varied menu, with entrees ranging from $17 to $23. There's a bar on the other side of the lobby.

Triple J Hotel. Fifth Ave. and Queen St. (P.O. Box 359), Dawson City, YT, Canada Y0B 1G0. ☎ **867/993-5323.** Fax 867/993-5030. 47 units, 18 cabins. TV TEL. High season, $109–$119 double or cabins for 2. Low season, $74–$79 double. Additional person in room $10 extra. AE, DC, MC, V. Closed Nov–Apr.

This rambling set of structures has three different kinds of rooms: large hotel rooms in the old, wooden main building; smallish rooms in the low-slung motel building; and cabins with kitchenettes and little porches. Some of the rooms are excellent, others nothing to brag about but still clean and serviceable. All rooms have fans and coffeemakers, and the hotel also provides a courtesy car and a coin-op laundry. The **restaurant** has a menu with a broad range of prices and varied cuisine, and they hold a popular barbecue on the deck of the lounge.

Westmark Inn Dawson. Fifth Ave. and Harper St. (P.O. Box 420), Dawson City, YT, Canada Y0B 1G0. ☎ **800/544-0970** (reservations), or 867/993-5542. Fax 867/993-5623. www.westmarkhotels.com. 129 units. TV TEL. $139–$179 double. AE, CB, DC, EURO, MC, V. Closed Sept 15–May 15.

The modern, well-run Westmark is the best hotel in town, especially the newer Jack London and Robert Service wings, where wide, well-lit hallways lead to large rooms with crisp gold rush–theme decorative touches. The older rooms are good, too, but are smaller and have older decor. All rooms have fans and clocks, and there's a coin-op laundry. Ask for the "highway rate." A patio in the grassy courtyard is the site of a daily barbecue. **Belinda's Restaurant,** with light-wood decor and well-spaced tables, is open daily from 6am to 10pm; there's also a lounge.

A HOSTEL & CAMPING

Dieter Reinmuth operates the **Dawson City River Hostel,** P.O. Box 32, Dawson City, YT, Canada Y0B 1G0 (☎ **867/993-6823**), across the Yukon from Dawson City on the free ferry. Bunks in cabins, private rooms, and camping are available, as well as a sweat lodge and cold showers. A bunk is $16 for nonmembers, a private room $32 double. He also rents bicycles and canoes for $20 a day. The wooded provincial **Yukon River Campground,** just down the road, has 98 sites; the fee is $8. The **Goldrush Campground RV Park,** at Fifth Avenue and York Street (☎ **867/993-5247**), is a conveniently located lot right downtown.

DINING

I've described restaurants at the Westmark, El Dorado, and Triple J hotels, above, and the *Yukon Lou* Pleasure Island Restaurant dinner cruise. The best place I found was **Melinda's,** at 842 Fifth Ave. (☎ **867/993-6800**), across from the Westmark. Primarily a dinner place, they specialize in Greek and Italian cuisine and also serve pizza. Reservations are recommended. **Klondike Kate's Restaurant,** in a historic building at

Third Avenue and King Street (☎ 867/993-6527), offers decent food for low prices, with a fully licensed bar. The patio is pleasant.

DAWSON CITY IN THE EVENING

Some of Dawson City's most famous and fun activities are in the evening. **Diamond Tooth Gertie's,** at Fourth Avenue and Queen Street (☎ 867/993-5575), operated by the Klondike Visitors Association, is a gambling hall and bar, with tame cabaret singing and cancan dancing floor shows. It's a fun place to go with a group. The shows, each different, play three times nightly. It's open Tuesday through Sunday from 7pm to 2am, and admission is $6 for all evening, with only those at least 19 years old admitted.

The *Gaslight Follies* is a 2-hour vaudeville show nightly at 8pm in the **Palace Grand Theatre,** a historic building at Second Avenue and King Street that has been renovated by Parks Canada. Tickets—$16 to $18 for adults, $8 for children—are on sale at the box office from 3pm. Parks Canada also leads tours through the theater at 11am daily; it costs $5 at the Visitors Reception Centre.

10 Eagle & the Top of the World & Taylor Highways

Sometime before World War I, the tiny town of Eagle got lost in an eddy in the stream of history, where it still awaits discovery by the outside world. The town was founded in 1898 as a subtle fraud, when a group of prospectors staked out the land then cleverly created a buzz in Dawson City, just upriver across the border, of a gold discovery. The federal government followed the rush, and in 1900 Judge James Wickersham chose Eagle for a new courthouse to try to bring law to the wild country. But when gold really was found in Fairbanks, the attention of prospectors and of Wickersham moved on, leaving Eagle slowly to decline to a ghost town of only nine residents by 1953. But that's where the really exceptional part of the story begins. The few remaining people recognized the value of the history that had been left behind— Wickersham's papers were still in his desk where he'd left them—and formed the historical society that today is the main activity for the town's 140 residents. Visitors can tour the courthouse, customs house, and five museums, and use Eagle for the start or end of a history-drenched Yukon River float. You'll also see the places John McPhee wrote about in his classic *Coming Into The Country.*

The reason Eagle is still so interesting is that it's still isolated, 173 dusty miles from Tok or 144 from Dawson City. It's a major side trip from the route between the two cities, which are 187 road miles apart, adding at least a day to your trip.

The **Taylor Highway** runs 160 miles north from the Alaska Highway just east of Tok to Eagle, 4 or 5 hours over a rough gravel road that's open only in summer. This is the Fortymile Country, around the past and current gold mining of the Fortymile River drainage. It's a remote country, mostly managed by the **Bureau of Land Management,** Tok Field Office, P.O. Box 309, Tok, AK 99780 (☎ 907/883-5121; wwwndo.ak.blm.gov/fortymile/FMwelcome.html). There are no services or signs of human development on the way except at the town of **Chicken,** barely a wide spot in the road 66 miles north, with gas, a couple of shops, a bar, and a cafe, but no phone. The drive does have impressive views in spots, and at mile 96 meets the Top of the World Highway, described below. That's the way more traveled. If you instead choose to go on to Eagle, you turn to the north for the last 66 miles of rough, winding road through lovely canyons and forest. That distance doesn't sound great, but at best it takes the better part of 2 hours, one-way, on this crude dirt road. There are two **campgrounds** along the Taylor, at mile 49 and mile 82, maintained by the BLM office mentioned above. The fee for each is $6. The BLM also is responsible for the **Fortymile National Wild and Scenic River,** a system with several floats of various lengths and levels of difficulty. The BLM or the public land information center in Tok can provide a river guide brochure and advice, or get *The Alaska River Guide,* mentioned at the beginning of this chapter. The BLM also produces a Taylor Highway road guide that's worth picking up.

The **Top of the World Highway,** beginning at mile 96 of the Taylor, heads 79 miles east from there to Dawson City. The Canadian part of the gravel highway is better maintained and stunningly beautiful on a clear day. You drive over the tops of mountains, treeless alpine vistas spreading far to the horizon. Just short of the border, 13 miles from the junction, there's a small roadhouse at a place called Boundary, the only habitation on the way. The border is open 5am to 10pm Alaska time. Don't forget, it's an hour later in Yukon. The road closes in winter, too. See the Alaska Highway section, above, for information on Customs.

Don't plan on making 60 miles an hour on any of these unpaved roads. In the Canadian section, most of the road is fairly broad and smooth, but speeds over 45 or so contribute to losing control or losing a headlight or windshield to a rock from a passing vehicle. On the U.S. side, the road is poorly maintained in places, and you sometimes have to go quite slowly. Part of the Taylor Highway itself was mined for gold a few years ago.

Eagle has the historic sites and the Yukon River. The **Eagle City Historical Society,** P.O. Box 23, Eagle, AK 99738 (☎ 907/547-2325), offers town walking tours Memorial Day to Labor Day, daily at 9am; the 3-hour tour costs $5. Or for the admission plus $10 more for a group, they'll do the tour any time you like, winter or summer. The guides are local people, brimming with pride and knowledge about the area. Find them at the courthouse at Second and Berry streets. In addition to the tour, a great little museum downstairs is open around the middle of the day. The tour takes you through various historic buildings loaded with the original materials left behind after the gold rush, including five buildings in the army's 1899 Fort Egbert, where Gen. Billy Mitchell had his first major assignment, in 1901 (before he was a general), to build a telegraph line to Valdez. You'll also notice the monument to Norwegian explorer Roald Amundsen, who stopped off in Eagle in 1905 during his journey through the Northwest Passage—400 miles away by dog sled—to use the telegraph.

The headquarters of the **Yukon–Charley Rivers National Preserve** is across the airstrip on the west side of town. The preserve starts a few miles downstream on the Yukon and extends almost to Circle. The National Park Service **visitor center,** P.O. Box 167, Eagle, AK 99738 (☎ **907/547-2233;** www.nps.gov/yuch/), is a good place to get information on floating the river and to register your journey. It's open Memorial Day to September, daily from 8am to 5pm, and normal business hours year-round. They also can provide lots of information on the natural history of the area and historic sites downstream.

You can start or finish a **river float** in Eagle. From Dawson City to Eagle is 108 miles and takes 3 or 4 days, and from Eagle to Circle is 158 miles and 5 to 7 days. Mike Seger's **Eagle Canoe Rentals,** P.O. Box 4, Eagle, AK 99738 (☎ **907/547-2203** in Eagle, or 867/993-6823 in Dawson City), allows you to drop off the canoe at the end of your float, and also rents rafts. The Dawson City office is located at the Dawson City River Hostel on the west side of the river next to the free ferry landing. The price, including return of the canoe, is $110 for up to 4 days to Eagle, $165 up to 5 days to Circle, and additional days are $20.

The **Eagle Trading Company,** P.O. Box 36, Eagle, AK 99738 (☎ **907/547-2220;** fax 907/547-2202), is the main business in town, with a grocery store, gas station, public showers, restaurant, and motel. Their **Riverside Cafe** is exceptionally good for the Bush, with tasty, inexpensive food and a dining room overlooking the river. The nine **motel rooms** also are surprisingly good, with TVs and phones, tubs with showers, two queen beds in each, and a rate of only $60 double.

An attractive **BLM campground** with well-wooded sites is located in the woods above Fort Egbert. It costs $6 per night. Contact the BLM for information.

11   Wrangell–St. Elias National Park & the Copper River Valley

Looking at a relief map of Alaska, you'd think the portion drained by the Copper River so overweighted with mountains as to topple the whole state into the Pacific. The Alaska Range, in the center of the state, has the tallest mountain, but this Gulf of Alaska region, straddling the Alaska-Yukon border, has more mass—the second- and fourth-tallest mountains in North America—Logan and St. Elias—and 9 of the tallest 16 in the United States. Four mountain ranges intersect, creating a mad jumble of terrain covering tens of millions of acres, a trackless chaos of unnamed, unconquered peaks. The Copper River and its raging tributaries slice through it all, swallowing the gray melt of innumerable glaciers that flow from the largest ice field in North America. Everything here is the largest, most rugged, most remote; words quickly fall short of the measure. But where words fail, commerce gives a little help: These mountains are so numerous and remote that one guide service makes a business of taking visitors to mountains and valleys that no one has ever explored before.

Ironically for such a wild land, the area's main attraction for visitors is its history. The richest copper deposit in the world was found here in 1900 by a group of prospectors who mistook a green mountain top for a patch of green grass where they could feed their horses. Instead, it was a mountain of almost pure copper, with metallic nuggets the size of desks (one is at the University of Alaska Museum in Fairbanks), trainloads of 70% copper ore so rich it required no processing before shipping, lots more copper that did need minimal processing, and much more lower-grade ore still left underground. The Alaska Syndicate, an investment group that included J. P. Morgan and Daniel Guggenheim, built the Kennecott Copper Corporation from this wealth, its name a misspelling of Kennicott, where the copper was found. To get the copper out, they paid for an incredible 196-mile rail line up from Cordova (see chapter 7), and a self-contained company town deep in the wilderness, **Kennicott.** When the high-grade ore was gone, in 1938, they pulled the plug, leaving a ghost town of extraordinary beauty that still contains machinery and even documents they left behind.

Wrangell–St. Elias National Park and Preserve now owns Kennicott and over 13 million acres across this region of Alaska. It's the largest national park in the United States by a long shot, six times the size of Yellowstone and about 25% larger than the entire country of Switzerland. The protected land continues across the border in Canada, in **Kluane National Park,** which is similarly massive. Most of that land is impossibly remote, but Wrangell–St. Elias has two rough gravel roads that allow access to see the mountains from a car, the primary of which is along the abandoned route of the Copper River and Northwestern Railroad to Kennicott and the historic sites there. It's an arduous but rewarding journey by car, requiring at least 2 days to do it right. Air-taxis, river guides, and remote lodges offer other ways into the park's untouched wilderness, mostly starting from **McCarthy,** a historic village near Kennicott. There are a few trails near Kennicott, but only for day hikes. This is a rare country that hikers and outdoors people who know what they're doing can experience completely without seeing signs of mankind.

THE KENNICOTT & MCCARTHY AREA

This is the only part of the park most visitors see, as it's the most accessible and has the most services, interesting sites, and paths to explore. It's still not easy to get to, however—that's why it's still so appealing—and there's little point in going without adequate time and planning. You can hit the highlights at Kennicott and McCarthy in one long, full day, but just getting there takes time, too. We spent three nights and could have stayed longer.

The main event is the ghost town at **Kennicott,** whose red buildings gaze from a mountainside across the Kennicott Glacier in the valley below. Now owned by the Park Service, the buildings made up an isolated company town until 1938, when it abruptly shut down. Tourists coming here as late as the 1960s saw it as if frozen in time, with breakfast dishes still on the tables from the day the last train left. Most of that was looted and destroyed in the 1970s, but when I toured the company store recently, old documents still remained, and the powerhouse and 14-story mill buildings still have their heavy iron and wood equipment. Besides the buildings, there are excellent hiking trails, including one that traverses the glacier. The town now has only a few year-round residents, but in summer there's a lodge, a couple of bed-and-breakfasts, guide services, and a Park Service meeting hall.

Five miles down the road, Kennicott's sister town of **McCarthy** served the miners as a place where they could drink, gamble, and hire prostitutes on their rare days off—the company didn't allow any frivolity in Kennicott or the bunk houses high up on the mountain. McCarthy retains the relaxed atmosphere of its past, with businesses and residents living in false-front buildings not much changed from Wild West days. More of a year-round community, McCarthy has restaurants, lodging, flight services, and other businesses.

Yet even this most populous part of the park is isolated and sparsely inhabited, with few services. You will find no banking services, real stores, gas stations, clinics, police, or anything else you're used to relying on. Phones came to McCarthy and Kennicott only within the last few years; there still are few, and none along the McCarthy Road. Bring what you need.

ESSENTIALS
Getting There
BY CAR The **Edgerton Highway** starts 17 miles south of Copper Center on the Richardson Highway, then runs east for 33 miles to the tiny, dried-up mining town of **Chitina** (*chit*-na), the last reliable stop for groceries, gas, and other necessities until you return here. Heading east, into the park, the **McCarthy Road** continues along the roadbed of the Copper River and Northwestern Railroad. It's 60 miles of narrow dirt road, rutted and liable to mud holes in wet weather, but the drive is a fun adventure. The road passes through tunnels of alders and crosses rivers on 100-year-old wooden railroad trestles, one of which spans a canyon more than 200 feet deep. There are virtually no services and no more than two or three buildings on the entire 3-hour drive. There's a good chance you won't encounter another vehicle. The road ends at a campground, parking lot, and collection of temporary business on the banks of the Kennicott River. Here you must leave your vehicle (parking costs $5 a day) and proceed across a foot bridge or two. Late in the summer the Kennicott Glacier releases a flood from an underground lake, but at other times the second channel is a dry wash and the second bridge isn't used. Hand carts are available to move your luggage across,

and on the other side you can catch a van. The place you are staying will send one, or you can buy a ticket on an **hourly van** operated by **Wrangell Mountain Air** (☎ 907/554-4411) or **McCarthy Air** (☎ 907/554-4440). Last time we visited, the going rate was $5 per person. The **Tramstation** (☎ 907/554-4401), a booth on the near side of the bridge, acts as an informal visitor center: You can pay them for parking and ask questions about the unusual transportation system; they book activities and will call a van or rent you a bicycle. They charge $25 a day for a basic bike. McCarthy is half a mile beyond the bridge and Kennicott 5 miles, so it's doable. The Tramstation also sometimes has gas and tire repair.

BY BUS   The **Backcountry Connection,** P.O. Box 243, Glennallen, AK 99588 (☎ 800/478-5292 within Alaska, or 907/822-5292), runs a van from Glennallen and Chitina to the footbridge daily in summer except Sunday, leaving at 7am and 8:30am, respectively, arriving at the bridge at 11:45am and returning at 4pm. The fare is $80 round-trip from Chitina, $99 from Glennallen, and $10 more if you return on a different day. I think a 4-hour stay would be too brief.

BY AIR   The simplest way to Kennicott and McCarthy is to fly there on one of the air-taxis, then get around on one of the vans that shuttles back and forth over 5 miles of dirt road. **Wrangell Mountain Air,** P.O. Box MXY, McCarthy, AK 99588 (☎ 907/554-4411; www.AlaskaOne.com/wma), offers twice-daily service each way for $130 round-trip. You can charter from anywhere. A five-passenger plane is $750 from Anchorage, $450 from Valdez, one-way. Another reputable operator is **McCarthy Air,** P.O. Box MXY no. 16, McCarthy, AK 99588 (☎ 888/989-9891 from outside Alaska only, or 907/554-4440; www.nevadacitysoftware.com/). Their winter address is P.O. Box 248, Cedar Vale, KS 67024 (☎ 316/758-2512). Both operators also offer charters to remote park valleys and glaciers for backcountry trips, covered below under "Getting Outside: Hiking & Backpacking." It's also possible to fly straight from Anchorage to McCarthy on the twice-weekly mail plane, operated by **Security Aviation** (☎ 907/248-2677), for $115 one-way.

Visitor Information

Park headquarters is just north of Copper Center, a mile off the Richardson Highway on the old Richardson Highway (☎ 907/822-5235; www.nps.gov/wrst), where a new visitor center is being built. Stop in to buy maps and publications or get advice from a ranger on outdoor treks. They're open Memorial Day to Labor Day, daily from 8am to 6pm; in winter, during normal business hours. You can write for information at P.O. Box 439, Copper Center, AK 99573.

The **Chitina Ranger Station** (☎ 907/823-2205) is along the most popular way to the park, in the old mining town of Chitina, 33 miles down the paved Edgerton Highway, which starts about 17 miles south of Copper Center on the Richardson Highway. The center is arranged like a reading room, with lots of material to consult, historic photographs on display, and rangers who help visitors figure out backcountry trips. There's a picnic table out front. Like almost all visitor services in the area, it is closed in winter.

The Park Service is just starting to develop **visitor services in Kennicott** itself. Usually you'll find a ranger there during the day, often giving a talk in the evening in the hall across the road from the lodge. A visitor center is planned, but hadn't gotten much beyond the idea stage at this writing.

ATTRACTIONS & ACTIVITIES IN THE TOWNS
Chitina

A town of around 50 people, Chitina has a post office and limited services, but not much to hold you. It's a desiccated outpost, with a row of historic buildings that stand empty and decaying. One stop is worth making, besides the ranger station, mentioned above: **Spirit Mountain Artworks** (☎ **907/823-2222**), where an old building has been lovingly restored into a historic landmark to house fine art and crafts. Heading a little to the west, the McCarthy Road crosses the **Copper River,** which in season is full of red salmon. It's also possible to get to fishing waters to the south, along the unfinished and abandoned Copper River Highway. Check at the ranger station for guidance.

McCarthy

McCarthy feels authentic as soon as you walk down the dirt main street between the false fronts. On a summer evening young backpackers and locals stand in the road—there is no traffic, since there are almost no vehicles—meeting and talking, carrying their glasses of beer from the lodge over to the ice cream shop, laughing loud, walking around the dogs that are having their own party. Along the street, there are flight service offices to arrange a trip out, a couple of restaurants, a lodge. Then, a street beyond, unbroken wilderness for hundreds and perhaps thousands of miles. The people here know it's unique, and everyone hopes it doesn't change. No one wants a big flood of tour bus visitors—that's why they fought the state government when it wanted to build a road bridge over the Kennicott; they prefer to have the McCarthy Road rough instead of smooth. The foot bridge should keep too many casual visitors at bay. Those who do make it are treated well—like one of the community. If you need help, you just walk up to anyone you see and he or she will help you.

The town's one formal visitor attraction is the **McCarthy-Kennicott Historical Museum,** housed in a couple of rooms and a railroad car at the edge of town. The exhibits of historic photographs help put the stories you'll hear in perspective, and there are some interesting artifacts. You'll likely be the only visitor when you arrive, so you can ask the volunteer questions you may have saved up. They're open Memorial Day to Labor Day, 10am to 6pm daily.

To learn the natural history of the area, pick up a copy of *Learning the Landscape: An Interpretive Dayhike from McCarthy to the Kennicott Glacier Face,* sold at the ranger stations for $3. It explains the botany and extraordinary geology of the area in a walking tour beginning from the footbridge.

Kennicott

This has got to be one of the world's greatest ghost towns, with some 40 buildings, mostly in condition good enough to be reused today—indeed, they still play basketball in the community hall, some buildings have become lodgings, and the Park Service may move into the store. Locals still pick rhubarb and chives from the company garden. History has the same kind of immediacy here that you get from holding an old diary in your hand, quite different from the sanitized history-through-glass that you're used to at more accessible sites. Indeed, the Park Service still needs to secure the artifacts, for when we last visited, items remained out on the ground or on store shelves that would be in museums in some places. If this were an ordinary industrial site, that would be interesting enough, but Kennicott was something well out of the ordinary: an outpost still beyond the edge of the world where men built a self-contained city almost a century ago. The hardship of the miners' lives and the ease of the managerial families' lives also presents a fascinating contrast.

You can take in a lot of it by wandering around with a walking tour booklet (available at a park service kiosk in the ghost town) and reading PS signs. They plan to open some safe buildings for self-guided tours on an official basis–currently, people just walk in at will, despite signs directing otherwise. But to see the inside of the really impressive mill building and several other remarkable structures, you need to join a ✪ **guided tour.** In the past, those have been offered by **St. Elias Alpine Guides,** P.O. Box 111241, Anchorage, AK 99511 (☎ **907/544-4445** or 907/277-6867), for $25 per person. A tour I joined lasted much of the afternoon and went into real scholarly depth on the geology and history, as well as climbing to the perilous 14th floor of the mill building. The Park Service is making changes, but some concessionaire will offer tours, and it's something not to miss.

GETTING OUTSIDE
Hiking & Backpacking

There are few trails radiating from Kennicott, for which crude maps are available from the rangers and others around town, or buy the **Trails Illustrated** (see "Fast Facts: Alaska" in chapter 2) topographic map, printed on plastic, also for sale at the ranger stations. An impressive walk or challenging mountain bike ride continues through the ghost town up the valley, paralleling the Kennicott Glacier and then its tributary, the Root Glacier. You can either climb along the Root's edge to a towering ice fall, or traverse the glacial ice itself on a trail branch. It's wise to join a group if you want to walk on the glacier, as it can be dangerous: A couple of different guides in Kennicott accept walk-ins for daily glacier day hikes and other hikes and tours. A half day on the glacier goes for around $50 a person, while all-day hikes or ice climbing lessons cost about $80 to $100. Try St. Elias Alpine Guides, listed below, or **Kennicott-McCarthy Wilderness Guides** (☎ 800/664-4537 or 907/554-4444). Another fascinating hike leads straight up the mountain behind the Kennicott buildings to the old mines and miner bunkhouses, 3,000 feet higher on the alpine tundra.

Beyond the trails, the park is endless miles of trackless wilderness—one of earth's last few places that really deserves that name. Fit hikers without the backcountry experience to mount their own expedition should join one of the guides who work in the area. **St. Elias Alpine Guides,** P.O. Box 111241, Anchorage, AK 99511 (☎ **907/554-4445** or 907/277-6867), offers day hikes, mountain biking, rafting, backpacking trips, and alpine ascents, but specializes in guiding extended trips to unexplored territory. Bob Jacobs, president of the company, stopped guiding on Mount McKinley years ago because of the crowds. He claims never to have seen another party in more than 20 years of guiding expeditions in Wrangell–St. Elias, and has led more than 30 parties of customers up previously unclimbed peaks. By definition, you can't get farther from civilization. A 2-week trek and climb, including 4 days of mountaineering instruction, is a big commitment, and costs $2,600 and up, but then, first ascents are a finite resource. The St. Elias catalogue will make anyone who loves backpacking drool. Trips begin at $775 for a 4-day Donohoe Peak trek. They are all-inclusive, but not without hardship and risk—nothing can take away from the severity of this wild country.

Hiking on your own in a wilderness largely without trails is a whole new kind of experience for experienced backpackers and outdoors people who are used to more crowded parts of the planet. You feel like an explorer rather than a follower. At times, there's a fairy-tale sense of the world unfolding around you, as fresh as creation. If you're not prepared to select your own route—a task only for those already experienced in trackless, backcountry traveling—there are various established ways through the park you can follow with a topographic map. The Park Service publishes **trip synopses** of many of the routes, and rangers will help you choose one to suit your party—although none are easy. Get a Trip Synopsis List from the headquarters. Some routes start from the roads, but a better way to go is to charter a flight into a remote valley from one of the two **air services** in McCarthy. The planes land on gravel strips, river bars, glaciers, and any other flat places the pilots know about. These companies make a business of flying out backpackers, and so have established rates for different landing sites and can help with determining a route that's right for you, as well as providing a list of supplies. You can do it for $100 per person, with at least two passengers. Or fly in to a lake or river for fishing and exploring from a base camp, and don't worry so much about how much you pack. The two operators are listed above, under "Getting There."

I wouldn't want to scare off anyone who would really be able to manage one of these trips, but people do get in trouble in the Alaska wilderness every year, and some of them don't come back. Before you head out into the backcountry, you must know how to take care of yourself where help is unavailable, including how to handle river crossings, bear avoidance, preventing hypothermia, basic first aid, and other issues. Some of this is covered in chapter 2, but you can't get all you need to know from this book. Unless you have plenty of backpacking experience in less remote areas, I wouldn't recommend starting here.

Mountain Biking

Anywhere else, the 60-mile road that leads to this area would be considered a mountain biking trail. You also can make good use of bikes between McCarthy, Kennicott, and the foot bridge. An old **wagon road** parallels the main road that connects the two towns, 4.5 miles each way; the road itself is a one-lane dirt track. Advanced cyclists can also ride the trails around Kennicott described above under "Hiking & Backpacking." Bikes are for rent at the Tramstation (see "Getting There," above).

Rafting

Many great, wild rivers drain these huge mountains, which are still being carved by enormous glaciers. The **Kennicott River,** starting at the glacier of the same name, boils in Class III rapids for some 40 minutes starting right from the footbridge at the end of the McCarthy Road. As the area lacks roads, however, most trips must include a plane ride at least one way, and that makes white-water rafting day trips here more expensive than near Anchorage or Valdez.

For just a taste of rafting, catch an hour-long float (2 hours total) right from the footbridge, traveling on glacial Class III white water a few miles down the Kennicott. **Copper Oar Adventures,** McCarthy, Box MXY, Glennallen, AK 99588 (☎ **800/ 523-4453;** 907/554-4453 summer only; e-mail: howmoz@aol.com), offers this short ride for $45 per person. They have an office at the footbridge at the end of the McCarthy Road. The Kennicott River meets the Nizina, passing through a deep, dramatic canyon; then the Nizina River flows into the Chitina River, which meets the Copper River near the town of Chitina, 60 miles from the starting point. The Copper River flows to the ocean. A float from the footbridge through the Nizina Canyon takes all day, with lunch and bush plane flightseeing back, which could include a glacier flyover. Copper Oar and St. Elias Alpine Guides (see description under "Hiking & Backpacking," above) each charge $225 for this unforgettable float and flight. They also compete on trips that continue 3 or 4 days to Chitina, for $575 to $850 per person; or 10 to 13 days, 180 miles all the way to the Copper River Delta and the sea (see "Cordova" in chapter 7), for $2,300 to $2,575 per person. I've never done that trip, but I dream about it. This is Alaska on its largest and most grandiose scale, accessible only from the banks of these great rivers.

ACCOMMODATIONS
Lodges & B&Bs

There's not a hotel room with a private bathroom for 100 miles, but the Kennicott-McCarthy area has several attractive places to stay, all thick with the history the towns represent. Besides the three recommended below, I was impressed with houses for rent behind the Kennicott ghost town. The two I saw were **Kennicott Cottage** (☎ **907/ 242-1392** in Kennicott, 907/345-7961 in Anchorage), and, right next door, **17 Silkstocking Row** (☎ **907/338-5859,** or 907/554-1717 summer only; www.alaska.net/

~lei). You can rent one room, a two-bedroom suite, or the whole three-bedroom house. The only drawback of the attractively restored houses is a lack of flush toilets or electricity, although they do have running water and showers.

Historic Kennicott Bed and Breakfast. Silk Stocking Row, Kennicott. (McCarthy no. 4 P.O. Box MXY, Glennallen, AK 99588). ☎ **907/544-4469.** 2 units, shared bathroom. $120 double. Rates include full breakfast.

The family that lives here year-round—there are fewer than 50 full-time residents in a 10-mile radius—hosts guests in a historic, unspoiled residence in the woods behind the ghost town, once the home of the family of a Kennecott Copper manager. Their warmth is infectious—the kids will try to sell you pieces of copper ore they found—giving guests a chance to make friends of people living a real pioneer lifestyle.

Kennicott Glacier Lodge. P.O. Box 103940, Anchorage, AK 99510. ☎ **800/582-5128** or 907/258-2350. In season only, 907/554-4477. Fax 907/248-7975. www.KennicottLodge. com. 25 units, none with private bathroom. $169 double. AE, DISC, MC, V. Closed mid-Sept to mid-May.

This is the area's largest and most comfortable accommodation, a first-class place that takes the edges off the isolation. The lodge accurately re-creates an old Kennicott building, with the same red-and-white color scheme, right amidst the historic structures of the ghost town. You can't get any closer to what you want to see. Guests can sip drinks on a long front porch overlooking the glacier, or relax on a lawn with the same view. The rooms are not large, and bathrooms are down the hall—although all were quite clean when we visited. Filling meals are served family style, at long tables, with a fixed menu for a fixed price (a turkey dinner was $22.50, for example). There's nowhere else to eat right in Kennicott, so plan to spend about $40 per person on food, or simply book the package that includes meals, for $127.50 per person per night. A brief tour of the ghost town comes with the room, and evening lectures take place right across the street.

McCarthy Lodge. P.O. Box MXY, McCarthy, AK 99588. ☎ **907/554-4402.** Fax 907/ 554-4404. 16 units, none with private bathroom. $110 double. MC, V. Closed Oct to mid-May.

In the relaxed village of McCarthy—you can feel the difference from buttoned-up Kennicott immediately—these small rooms are in a false-front building that you might see in an old Western movie, except that it's real and unrestored. The decor is lace and rough-cut lumber. The shared bathroom was clean when I visited.

The lodge is the main **public restaurant** in the area, an authentic Bush roadhouse. They serve breakfast from a full menu 7am to 10am, and dinner seating with a fixed menu at 7pm. Dinners range $16 to $22, and reservations are required.

Camping & Hosteling

There is no campground on the Kennicott-McCarthy side of the Kennicott River footbridge. The Park Service allows camping anywhere in the park without a permit, but there are few appropriate spots on public land (remember, much of the land along the roads is private).

The closest campground, with a hostel, is at the end of the McCarthy Road. The camping area is gravel—not very natural—with outhouses. The fee is $10, at the Tram-station. **Kennicott River Lodge and Hostel,** P.O. Box 83225, Fairbanks, AK 99708 (☎ **907/554-4441** summer, 907/479-6822 winter; www2.polarnet.com/~grosswlr), with bunks or wall tents for $25 per person, and public showers, is just up the road.

There are three campgrounds on the way to the footbridge. The most attractive is the State Parks' **Liberty Falls Campground,** at mile 23 on the Edgerton Highway, which is set among big trees at the foot of a crashing waterfall. Many of the sites are walk-ins, with wooden tent platforms and lots of privacy. The self-service fee is $10. There are pit toilets, and no running water. A mile or two beyond Chitina, across the Copper River on the McCarthy Road, a primitive **state campground** at riverside has pit toilets and dusty sites among cottonwoods. At mile 11 on the McCarthy Road, the tiny **Silver Lake Campground,** P.O. Box 28, Chitina, AK 99566, sits in a lovely, peaceful spot along the shore of a lake with Rainbow trout. Skiffs and canoes are for rent. The sites are most attractive for RVs, and there is an outhouse. The camping fee is $10.

DINING
The main restaurants in the Kennicott area are at the Kennicott Glacier Lodge and McCarthy Lodge, described above. We also enjoyed pizza and beer in a screened porch at **Taylor-Made Pizza** in McCarthy. They're open 10am to 10pm daily in the summer. There's a food stand at the footbridge, too.

SLANA & THE NABESNA ROAD
This little-visited northern portion of the park, at the divide between the Tanana and Copper River drainages, looks quite different than the terrain of fierce mountains in the Kennicott-McCarty area. There are high, craggy mountains, but also broad swards of tundra and wetlands and the small trees of the taiga, similar to Denali National Park. It's some 200 miles by road from McCarthy and Kennicott, and a drive of about 6 hours—not a good idea. Instead, consider exploring this part of the park if you're already traveling the region near the Alaska Highway.

The **Slana Ranger Station** (☎ **907-822-5238**) is in Slana, on the Nabesna Road near the intersection with the Glenn Highway's Tok cut-off, 65 miles from Tok and 74 miles from Glennallen. The Nabesna Road goes 46 miles into the park. Like the Denali Park Road, it's an avenue to see wilderness and lots of wildlife, but here you can take your own car. There's good fishing along the way—check the park newspaper for the best spots. The road can be rough, and there are a couple of river crossings that may be impassable at high water; however, you should be able to make it at least to Mile 29. Pick up a copy of the **road guide** from the ranger station or the Alaska Public Lands Information Center in Tok (see that section above). You can camp anywhere you want on park lands, but wilderness hiking is only for proficient outdoors people who know what to bring, how to handle stream crossings and emergencies, and generally how to take care of themselves far from any other person.

THE COAST
The **Yakutat Ranger Station** (☎ **907/784-3295**) is the park's back door. This is the most rugged and undeveloped approach to the park, although some people have started using the area for sea kayaking. The peaks rising from the Pacific near here are the largest coastal mountains in the world, with a vertical rise greater than the Himalayas.

12   Glennallen & the Copper River Country

The people of the Copper River Country, as this cold, arid region along the great river is known, live on homesteads and tiny settlements, and in a couple of towns near the regional hub of **Glennallen,** at the intersection of the Glenn and Richardson highways. It's a sparsely settled land for rugged outdoor activities. The volunteer-run **Copper River Visitor Center** is in a log cabin right at the intersection, P.O. Box 469,

Glennallen, AK 99588 (☎ 907/822-5555; www.alaskaoutdoors.com/Copper/); in summer it's open daily from 8am to 7pm. Glennallen has a bank with an ATM, a post office, a medical center, and government offices.

The best standard accommodations in the area are at the **New Caribou Hotel,** at mile 187 of the Glenn Highway, P.O. Box 329, Glennallen, AK 99588 (☎ 907/822-3302). The rooms are the equal of a good chain. A double is $115 in the summer. They also have economy rooms in a surplused camp for pipeline workers that was moved to this site. Although small and industrial in decor, the rooms and their shared bathrooms were clean, and a double room is only $59. The hotel's **Caribou Restaurant** is inexpensive and good for comfort food—meat loaf, roast beef, pork chops. The other place where we like to eat while passing through Glennallen is the **Tastee Freez,** a clean burger joint and local hangout with wallpaper and fine art on the walls. Besides big burgers and soft ice cream, they also serve chicken and Mexican dishes, and good milk shakes.

Fourteen miles south of Glennallen, **Copper Center** is a tiny Athabascan community on the old Richardson Highway. A historic roadhouse, the **Copper Center Lodge,** Drawer J, Copper Center, AK 99573 (☎ 907/822-3245; www.alaska.net/~ccl/), is worthy of a stop for dinner or even overnight, if it's time for a rest on your drive. Rooms in the big old log building rent for $84 a night with a shared bathroom, $94 with a private bathroom. The restaurant here has a good reputation all over the region for hearty, satisfying meals. They're open 7am to 9pm, and brag especially of their sourdough pancakes, made with starter 100 years old. Gold rush prospectors carried sourdough starter, or live yeast, always growing more so they never ran out. Alaskans sometimes track their pedigree by the lineage of their sourdough starter. The history of the lodge dates from the bizarre gold rush origins of Copper Center and Valdez, when about 4,000 stampeders to the Klondike tried a virtually impossible all-American route from Valdez over the glaciers of the Wrangell–St. Elias region. Few made it, and hundreds who died are buried in Copper Center. The original lodge was built of the stuff they left behind. The existing building dates from 1932.

Other than Wrangell–St. Elias National Park, most of the land in the Copper River Country is managed by the **Bureau of Land Management Glennallen District,** with a log cabin office in town on the north side of the Glenn Highway, P.O. Box 147, Glennallen, AK 99588 (☎ 907/822-3217; www.glennallen.ak.blm.gov/), open Monday through Friday 8am to 4pm. Information also is available from the public land information centers in Anchorage, Fairbanks, and Tok. This huge area, about the size of a midsized eastern U.S. state, is more accessible than the park, and so has outdoor recreation more people can appreciate. On the other hand, its still a rough, remote land with few high-quality visitor facilities. There are several large alpine lakes, two National Wild Rivers, many hiking trails, and five campgrounds, all reached on the Richardson, Glenn, and Denali highways. Guides are available for **rafting** and **fishing** in the rivers. Check at the visitor center or BLM office for referrals. The salmon are not as desirable this far inland as they are near the coast, as they've begun to turn red, soften, and lose oil content with their spawning changes.

The Bush 10

The Bush is most of Alaska. On a map of the state, the portion with roads and cities is really just a smallish corner. Yet most visitors—and, indeed, most Alaskans—never make it beyond that relatively populated corner. It's not uncommon for children to grow to adulthood in Anchorage, Fairbanks, or Southeast Alaska without ever traveling to the Arctic, the Aleutians, or the vast wetlands of western Alaska. The reason they don't is the same simple reason most tourists don't go to Bush Alaska—getting to the Bush is expensive, and there's not much there in the way of human activity once you arrive. Bush Alaska is one of the planet's last barely inhabited areas, where indigenous people still interact with the environment in their traditional way, and new places still remain to be explored by self-reliant outdoors people.

Although there are few people, the hospitality of those you meet in the Bush is special and warming. In Bush Alaska, where the population is overwhelming Alaska Native, it's not uncommon to be befriended and taken under wing by total strangers for no other reason than that you've taken the trouble to come to their community and are, therefore, an honored guest. Even in the larger towns, people look you in the eye and smile as you pass in the street, and if you have a questioning look on your face, they'll stop to help. Living in a small place where people know each other and have to work together against the elements makes for a tight, friendly community.

The cultural traditions of Alaska's **Native people** go beyond simple hospitality. Theirs is a culture based more on cooperative than competitive impulses, where honesty, respect, and consensus carry greater weight than in white society. Cooperation also requires slowing down, listening, not taking the lead—people from our fast-paced culture can leave a village after a visit wondering why no one spoke to them, not realizing that they never shut up long enough to give anyone a chance. The cultural differences here are real, unlike the shadows of past differences we celebrate in regions of the homogenous contiguous United States. Long pauses in conversation are normal, looking down while addressing a person demonstrates respect, punctuality is highly relative, child care is a community function, and when gifts are offered people really mean it—turning down even a cup of coffee is gauche. (For more on the culture of Alaska's Native peoples, see the appendix.)

The Native people of the Bush also have terrible problems trying to live in two worlds. There's too much alcohol and too many drugs in the Bush, too much TV, but not enough of an economic base to provide for safe drinking water or plumbing in many villages. Even in some of the relatively prosperous village hubs described in this chapter, visitors will glimpse a kind of rural poverty they may not have seen before—where prices are extremely high, and steady jobs interfere with traditional hunting and food gathering. But if you ask why they stay, you're missing something. In a world where so few indigenous cultures survive, people here are working to retain traditions that give their lives meaning while also adopting what they need from modernity. It's a work in progress, but there's no question they're slowly succeeding. They control their own land, they're building an economic base, and Native ways are being passed on to younger generations.

The world the Native people survive in is extreme in every respect—the weather, the land, even the geography. There's a special feeling to walking along the Arctic Ocean, the virtual edge of the earth, on a beach that lies between flat, wet tundra and an ocean that's usually ice. The quantity and accessibility of wildlife are extreme, too, as are the solitude and uniqueness of what you can do. Unfortunately, the prices also are extreme. With few exceptions, getting to a Bush hub from Anchorage costs at least as much as getting to Anchorage from Seattle. And once you're at the hub, you're not done. Getting into the outdoors can cost as much again. Most families and young people can't afford to make a Bush sojourn, instead satisfying their curiosity about the state's unpopulated areas on Alaska's rural highways. Most who can afford the trip usually make the most of their time and money with brief prearranged tours or trips directly to wilderness lodges. Only a few explorers head for the Bush unguided, although there are some good places to go that way—Nome, Kodiak, and Unalaska among them.

Covering the Bush also is a challenge for the writer of a book like this one. There are more than 200 Alaska villages, many lodges, camps, and guides, and a vast, undefined territory to describe. All that information would fill a larger book than this one but would be of little use to the great majority of readers. I've taken the approach, instead, of providing sections on a few **Bush hubs** that are most accessible and popular with visitors, that have modern facilities, and can be used as gateways to much more of the state for those who want to step out beyond the fringe of civilization. For more exhaustive information on even small Native villages, I recommend *The Alaska Wilderness Guide,* published by Morris Communications (☎ **800/726-4707** or 907/272-6070). The core of that book is a directory of even the tiniest villages, with the basic facts on what you'll find there.

If you find yourself in a town such as **Nome, Kotzebue, Barrow,** or **Kodiak**—hubs for outlying Native villages—there's a simple and relatively inexpensive way to get out and see how village people live: **Mail and scheduled passenger planes**—typically small, single-engine craft—make daily rounds of the villages from each hub. Without the difficulty, expense, and dubious interest of going for a longer trip to a village, you can fly out on one of these planes for a quick day trip, walk around and meet people, then fly back to the hub city on the next flight to come through. *One warning:* Don't make such an excursion in lowering weather, as you could get weathered in at a remote village. A journalist friend of mine was weathered in for more than 2 weeks on one occasion. You'll find the air-taxi operators—true bush pilots—friendly, informal, and most willing to oblige you in working out your Bush adventure. To find out where to go, just walk into the office and tell them what you're interested in seeing and how much time and money you want to spend. It's also an inexpensive way to go flightseeing.

1 Exploring the Bush

Alaska's Bush is better defined by what it's like there than where it is. For the purposes of this book, following the most convenient and common conception, the Bush is everything beyond the road system—everything north or west of Fairbanks. But there also are Bush villages in the Interior, in southcentral, and in southeast Alaska. There are even Bush villages you can drive to. After a while, you'll know a Bush community when you see one—it's a place where the wilderness is closer than civilization, where people still live off the land and age-old traditions survive, and where you have to make a particular effort to get in or out.

THE REGIONS

There are at least five commonly accepted regions in the Bush, which group easily into three:

THE ARCTIC   The Arctic Circle is the official boundary of the Arctic. The line, at 66° 33' north latitude, is the southern limit of true midnight sun—south of it, at sea level, the sun rises and sets, at least a little, every day of the year. But in Alaska, people think of the Arctic as beginning at the Brooks Range, which is a bit north of the circle, including **Barrow** and **Prudhoe Bay.** The northwest Alaska region, which includes **Kotzebue** and, slightly south of the Arctic Circle, **Nome,** also is Arctic in climate, culture, and topography. The biggest geographic feature in Alaska's Arctic is the broad North Slope, the plain of swampy tundra that stretches from the Arctic Ocean to the northern side of the Brooks Range. It's a swampy desert, with little rain or snowfall, frozen solid all but a couple of months a year.

WESTERN ALASKA   This is the land of the massive, wet Yukon-Kuskokwim Delta and the fish-rich waters of Bristol Bay. The Y-K Delta, as it's known, was never really exploited by white explorers, and the Yup'ik people who live there have maintained some of the most culturally traditional villages—in a few, Yup'ik is still the dominant language. **Bethel** is the main hub city of the delta, but holds little attraction for visitors. **Bristol Bay** is known for massive salmon runs, and avid fishers may be interested in its wilderness lodges, using **Dillingham** as a hub.

SOUTHWEST ALASKA   Stretching from the Aleutians—really a region of their own—to the Alaska Peninsula, Kodiak Island, and the southern part of the mountainous west side of Cook Inlet, this is a maritime region, like Southeast, but far more remote. The hub of the wet, windy Aleutians is **Unalaska** and its port of Dutch Harbor. **Katmai National Park** and the adjoining wild lands are the main attraction of the Alaska Peninsula, although there also are fishing lodges on the salmon-rich rivers and on the lakes to the north, including areas in **Lake Clark National Park** and **Iliamna Lake.** (The McNeil River Bear Sanctuary is included in the Homer section in chapter 7, as that's its main access point.) The lakes and west side of Cook Inlet are accessed primarily by Kenai, Homer, and Anchorage flight services for fishermen and hunters. **Kodiak** is hardly a Bush community, but fits better in this chapter than anywhere else.

GETTING AROUND

With a few exceptions for strongly motivated travelers, who can take the ferry to Kodiak and Unalaska or drive to Prudhoe Bay, getting to each town in this chapter will require flying. **Alaska Airlines** (☎ **800/426-0333;** www.alaskaair.com) jets fly to all the towns described in this chapter. Other, smaller operators serve each town as well. Throughout the chapter, I've listed the plane fare to various communities from Anchorage, based on flying coach and getting a significant discount for advance purchase and some restrictions. Full Y-class fares are more. With the way airfares fluctuate, it would be unwise to use these numbers as anything more than rough guides for preliminary planning. To get the current best fare, use a travel agent or the Internet (check the Online Directory in the appendix for tips).

Kodiak, which barely fits a chapter on the Bush, is the easiest to get to of the communities in the chapter, but it still requires either a 10-hour ferry ride from Homer or a $200 round-trip plane ticket from Anchorage. It's more similar to Southeast Alaska than to the other Bush towns listed. **Unalaska,** in the Aleutian Islands, is an interesting place to go way off the beaten path while staying in great comfort, but is short on the Native culture you may be looking for. A visit requires a $700 to $800 round-trip plane ticket. **Kotzebue** and **Barrow** are the most purely Native of the communities in the chapter. **Nome** has the advantages of Arctic surroundings easily accessible on gravel roads, but is more of a gold rush town than a Native village. **Prudhoe Bay,** at the end of the Dalton Highway, is an industrial complex without a real town associated with it. Fares range from $350 to $600 for these communities. Buying an **Alaska Airlines package tour** saves a lot of money to Nome, Kotzebue, or Barrow.

2 Outside in the Bush

The number of opportunities for outdoor solitude in the Bush are limitless. I've provided some ideas for the more popular destinations, and wilderness lodges are covered in chapter 2.

BIRD WATCHING In the Alaska Bush, serious birders can easily add to their lists birds they have scant chance of seeing anywhere else in the world. Nome, with its long gravel roads, may be the best destination for unguided trips. Unalaska is a good choice for sea birds you won't see elsewhere. Kotzebue, Barrow, and the Pribilof Islands all receive visits from avid birders in the summer.

FISHING Kodiak Island, the Alaska Peninsula, Bristol Bay, and the Lake Clark area have some of the best salmon and trout fishing to be found anywhere. I've even heard the complaint that it's too easy—at times there's not enough time waiting for a bite, and fishers' arms get too tired fighting one big salmon after another. Poor things! Access is expensive, and that's why the fishing is so good—you need to fly into a camp or wilderness lodge. The biggest halibut anywhere are caught off Unalaska.

HIKING The green hills and mountains of the Aleutians are stunningly beautiful for walks across smooth heather, free of bears and many bugs. Kodiak has some good trails. Katmai National Park is a destination for dramatic backcountry hikes.

RAFTING & KAYAKING The Noatak River and other rivers draining west from the Brooks Range are increasingly popular routes for remote float trips through massive areas of national park and conservation lands. Guided trips are available, or you can fly out of Kotzebue for an unguided trip. Less ambitious trips are guided from Nome. Kodiak provides sea kayakers with access to pristine, protected ocean waters. More guided trips are covered in chapter 2.

WILDLIFE VIEWING I'm still boring my friends with the tale of the musk ox I saw from one of the roads out of Nome. I don't know of a better place than these remote roads across the tundra for seeing unusual wildlife without getting out of a car or off a bike. Katmai National Park has incredible bear viewing, as does Kodiak, where you also can see marine mammals in abundance.

3 Kodiak: Bears, Fish & History

The habitat that makes Kodiak Island a perfect place for bears also makes it perfect for people. Runs of salmon clog unpopulated bays and innumerable, unfished rivers; the rounded green mountains seem to beg for someone to cross them; the gravel beaches and protected rocky inlets are free of people, but full of promise. But, in this respect, bears are smarter than people. Brown bears own the island, growing to prodigious size and abundant numbers, but Kodiak is as yet undiscovered by human visitors. That's a part of the wonder of the place. I'll never forget flying over the luxuriant verdure of Kodiak's mountains and the narrow string of glassy Raspberry Strait on a rare sunny day, seeing no sign of human presence in the most beautiful landscape I had ever beheld. That's something the bears will never experience, despite their superior collective intelligence.

The streets of the town of Kodiak are a discovery, too. Narrow and twisting over hills with little discernible order, they were the original stomping grounds of **Lord Alexander Baranof,** the first Russian ruler of Alaska, who arrived here more than 200 years ago—and before Baranof, of the **Koniag,** the first people who lived off the incomparable riches of the island, and who today recover their past in a fascinating little research museum. The Russian heritage includes the oldest Russian building in North America. It was nearly lost in the 1964 Good Friday earthquake, which destroyed most of the town (explaining the general lack of old buildings) and brought a 30-foot wave that washed to the building's doorstep. A marker near the police station on Mill Bay Road shows the wave's incredible high-water point.

The town still looks to the sea. Along with the Coast Guard base, fishing makes Kodiak prosperous, creating a friendly, energetic, unpolished community. Kodiak is separate from the rest of Alaska, living its own salmon-centered life without often thinking of what's going on in Anchorage or anywhere else. It's off the beaten path because it doesn't really need anything the path provides.

For the visitor, Kodiak is an undiscovered gem. When I took my family there on the ferry recently, our 3-day visit just scratched the surface of the charming, vibrant town and the easily accessible wild places. In the middle of the summer, other tourists were barely in evidence.

There are several **Native villages** on the island—a flight to one of them and back on a clear day is a wonderful, low-cost way to see remote areas of the island and to get a taste of how Alaska Natives live. **Ranches** on the road system around town offer riding and lodging. You can fly out to see the famous bears on a day trip, or stay at one of several **wilderness lodges** for wildlife watching, fishing, sea kayaking, and hunting, and even an archaeological dig you can participate in.

ESSENTIALS

GETTING THERE

BY AIR   It's a 1-hour flight from Anchorage to Kodiak on **Alaska Airlines** (☎ 800/426-0333; www.alaskaair.com). A round-trip ticket costs around $200. A **public bus** runs to the airport around the times the planes get in; call ☎ 907/486-8308 for details. A **cab,** from **Ace Mecca** (☎ 907/486-3211), runs around $13 from the airport.

BY FERRY   The ferry *Tustumena,* of the **Alaska Marine Highway System** (☎ **800/ 642-0066** or 907/486-3800; www.dot.state.ak.us/external/amhs/home.html), serves Kodiak from Homer and Seward. If you have the time for the 10-hour run from Homer—the closest port with a road—this boat ride is truly memorable. The vessel leaves land behind and threads through the strange and exposed Barren Islands. The ocean can be quite rough, and when it is, lots of passengers get seasick. A cabin is a good idea for an overnight run. The U.S. Fish and Wildlife Service staffs the trips with a naturalist. The adult passenger fare is $48, children half price. The Kodiak terminal is in the same building as the visitor center.

GETTING AROUND

The Kodiak Archipelago contains Kodiak, Shuyak, and Afognak islands, and many other, smaller islands. Kodiak is the nation's second largest island, after Hawaii's big island. The city of Kodiak is on a narrow point on the northeast side of Kodiak Island, surrounded by tiny islands. There are seven Native villages on other parts of the island. The airport and Coast Guard base are several miles southwest of town on **Rezanof Drive,** which runs through town and comes out on the other side. The center of Kodiak is a hopeless tangle of steep, narrow streets—you need the excellent map given away by the visitor center, but it's all walkable. The ferry dock is on **Marine Way,** and most of the in-town sights are right nearby. Several gravel roads, totaling 100 miles, make wonderful exploring from Kodiak to deserted shorelines, gorgeous views, pastures, recreation areas, and salmon streams. The visitors guide contains a mile-by-mile guide to each drive.

BY RENTAL CAR   Several companies rent cars, including **Budget** (☎ **800/ 527-0700** or 907/487-2220), which has offices at the airport or downtown.

BY BIKE   If its not raining, a bike is a great way to get around Kodiak, and strong riders will enjoy touring the roads out of town. Bikes are for rent at **Fifty-eight Degrees North,** a full-service bike shop at 1231 Mill Bay Rd. (☎ **907/486-3658**). Front-suspension mountain bikes rent for $35 for 24 hours.

VISITOR INFORMATION

On the ferry dock, the **Kodiak Island Convention and Visitors Bureau,** 100 Marine Way, Kodiak, AK 99615 (☎ **907/486-4782;** fax 907/486-6545; www.kodiak.org), is small, but the staff is helpful and it's a good place to start. The Web site is exceptionally good. They're open in summer Mondays 8am to 8:30pm, Tuesday through Friday 8am to 5pm, Saturday 10am to 4pm, Sunday 1 to 8:30pm; winter Monday through Friday 8am to 5pm, closed for lunch.

The **Kodiak National Wildlife Refuge Visitors Center,** Buskin River Road, near the airport 4 miles south of town (☎ **907/487-2600**), is headquarters for a refuge that covers most of the island and is home of the famous Kodiak brown bear. There are remote public-use cabins all over the refuge, reachable by chartered plane. Permits are $20, available by phone or lottery 3 months in advance. The center has interesting exhibits and is a good place to stop for outdoors information. They're open May and September, Monday through Friday 8am to 4:30pm; June through August, Monday through Saturday 10am to 4:30pm; and October through April, Monday through Friday noon to 4:30pm.

SPECIAL EVENTS

Russian Orthodox Christmas, coming about 2 weeks after the Roman Catholic and Protestant celebration, includes the **Starring Ceremony,** in which a choir follows a star in the evening to sing at the homes of church members. The late-March **Pillar Mountain Golf Classic** (☎ 907/486-4782; www.kodiak.org/kodiak/pillar/pillar. html) is played on a one-hole par-70 course that climbs 1,400 feet from tee to flag; dogs, chain saws, two-way radios, and tracking devices are prohibited, and cursing the officials carries a $25 fine. Hand saws and hatchets are allowed. The 5-day **Kodiak Crab Festival** (☎ 907/486-5557), on Memorial Day weekend, is the big event of the year and includes a carnival, parade, ultramarathon, and rubber duck race, and also the solemn blessing of the fleet and memorial service for lost fishermen. In early September, the **Kodiak State Fair and Rodeo** (☎ 907/485-4959) has all kinds of small-town contests. The **Harbor Stars** (☎ 907/486-8085), in mid-December, is a fleet parade of vessels decorated for Christmas.

Fast Facts: Kodiak

Banks   There are several banks downtown with ATMs, including Key Bank on the mall at the waterfront and National Bank of Alaska at Mission and Marine.

Hospital   The Providence Kodiak Island Medical Center is at 1915 E. Rezanof Dr. (☎ 907/486-3281).

Internet/E-mail   Sweets-N-More, 117 Lower Mill Bay Rd. (☎ 907/481-1630).

Police   The Kodiak Police Department is at ☎ 907/486-8000.

Post Office   Near Lower Mill Bay Road and Hemlock Street.

Taxes   Sales tax is 6% within city limits. The room tax inside the Kodiak city limits totals 11%, while outside the city it's 5%.

ATTRACTIONS & ACTIVITIES

A **walking tour** in the local visitors guide will show you what's available in town. The highlights include the **Fishermen's Memorial,** near the harbormaster's office at the head of the St. Paul Harbor, where a soberingly long list of Kodiak fishermen who have lost their lives at sea is posted on plaques. The warship set in concrete on Mission Way is the **Kodiak Star,** the last World War II Liberty Ship built. It was brought here as a fish processor after the 1964 earthquake destroyed the canneries, and is still in use. At Kashevarof and Mission, the **Holy Resurrection Russian Orthodox Church** was founded in 1794, although the present building dates only to 1945, when it was rebuilt after a fire. Half-hour **Native dance performances** take place June through August daily at 2pm at the Kodiak Tribal Council Barabara, at 713 E. Rezanof Dr. (☎ 907/486-4449). Admission is $15.

Alutiiq Museum. 215 Mission Rd. ☎ **907/486-7004**. Admission is $2 for adults. Summer Mon–Fri 9am–5pm, Sat 10am–5pm. Winter Tues–Fri 9am–5pm, Sat 10:30am–4:30pm.

This exceptional Native-funded and -governed museum seeks to document and restore the Koniag Alutiiq people's culture, which the Russians virtually wiped out in the 18th century. Besides teaching about Alutiiq culture in a single gallery, the museum manages its own archaeological digs (see "Getting Outside," below) and repatriates Native remains and artifacts, which researchers removed by the thousands in the 1930s. The archaeological repository now includes 100,000 objects. In 2000, this renaissance should take another step when the museum hosts a major exhibit, *Looking Both Ways: Heritage and Identity of the Alutiiq People,* which will include holdings from the Smithsonian Institution and is being organized with help from their Arctic Studies Center. The exhibit will open in May 2000 with a Gathering, a meeting and celebration by Native peoples from the entire Alutiiq region, from Prince William Sound to the tip of the Alaska Peninsula.

The Baranov Museum. 101 Marine Way. ☎ **907/486-5920.** Admission $2, free children 12 and under. Summer, Mon–Sat 10am–4pm, Sun noon–4pm. Winter Mon–Wed and Fri–Sat 11am–3pm. Closed Feb.

The museum occupies the oldest Russian building of only four standing in North America, built in 1808 by Alexander Baranof as a magazine and strong house for valuable sea otter pelts. It stands in a grassy park overlooking the water across from the ferry dock. Inside is a little museum rich with Russian and early Native artifacts. The guides know a lot of history and show 30 educational albums on various topics. The gift store is exceptional, selling antique Russian items and authentic Native crafts.

GETTING OUTSIDE
TWO RECREATION AREAS

North on Rezanof Drive a couple of miles, the **Fort Abercrombie State Historical Park** encompasses World War II ruins set on coastal cliffs amid huge trees. Paths lead to the beaches and good tide-pool walking, a swimming lake, and lots of other discoveries. The gun emplacements, bunkers, and other concrete buildings defended against the Japanese, who had attacked the outer Aleutians and were expected to come this way. A wonderful 13-site campground sits atop the cliffs among the trees and ruins. Camping is $10. The **Division of State Parks,** Kodiak District Office, 1400 Abercrombie Dr., Kodiak, AK 99615 (☎ **907/486-6339;** fax 907/486-3320; e-mail: kodsp@ptialaska.net), maintains an office here where you can pick up a walking tour brochure or, during the summer, join the Saturday night interpretive program or a guided tide-pool walk, scheduled to coincide with the tides. Or investigate the tide pools on your own, picking up an identification guide at a bookstore or the Fish and Wildlife Service visitor center. The **Buskin River State Recreation Site,** 4 miles south of town off Rezanof Drive near the Fish and Wildlife Service visitor center, has 15 sites, a hiking trail, and access to fishing. Camping is $10.

ACTIVITIES

ARCHAEOLOGY   Dig Afognak, 215 Mission Rd., Suite 212 (P.O. Box 1277), Kodiak, AK 99615 (☎ **800/770-6014** or 907/486-6014; fax 907/486-2514), operated by the **Afognak Native Corporation,** offers visitors a chance to help in scientific excavations of Koniag sites on Afognak Island, an effort by the Native group to reassemble their cultural heritage. Visitors are instructed in the natural history of the beautiful area as well as archaeology, but they're also expected to work, digging and working in a remote lab. Accommodations are in heated tents, and you have to bring your own sleeping bag. Dinner often is seafood caught in nets at the beach. A 7-day session is $1,650, including transportation from Kodiak.

BROWN BEAR VIEWING   To see Kodiak's famous bears, you need to get out on a plane or boat. The quickest way is on one of the air services making a business of finding bears, landing on the water, and watching from the safety of the plane's floats. When the salmon aren't running, many flights cross over to the east coast of the Alaska Peninsula to watch bears digging clams from the tidal flats. **Uyak Air Service (☎ **800/303-3407** or 907/486-3407) offers bear flights June through October and will give your money back if you don't see them—a safe bet for them. Flights cost

$395 per person, half price for children 12 and under with two adults. The **Karluk Lake Brown Bear Sanctuary,** owned by one of the Native corporations and operated by **Kodiak Wilderness Tours,** 1873 Shell Simmons Dr., Juneau, AK 99801 (☎ **800/ 556-8101** or 907/789-7818; fax 907/789-4228; www.ptialaska.net/~bears/), is a camp on a lake island near a river where bears congregate for the salmon run. Guests watch from a platform. They charge $799 for the shortest, overnight stay in bunkhouse accommodations, airfare from Kodiak included. Only 12 go in each tour, so you need to reserve as much as a year ahead.

FISHING   The roads leading from Kodiak offer access to terrific salmon and trout fishing. Some kind of salmon, somewhere, are available all summer. You can get a guidebook, including where to fish and the names and addresses of guides for remote fishing, from the visitor center. The **Alaska Department of Fish and Game,** is at 211 Mission Rd., Kodiak, AK 99615 (☎ **907/486-1880;** www.state.ak.us/local/akpages/ FISH.GAME/adfghome.htm). To fish the remote areas, you'll need to charter a plane to a remote public-use cabin or go to a wilderness lodge. Several boats are available for ocean salmon and halibut fishing. Check with the visitors center.

HIKING & BIRD WATCHING   There aren't a lot of trails on Kodiak, but there are some good day hikes. Pick up a copy of the *Kodiak Hiking Guide* at the visitor center for a variety of mountain climbs and day hikes from the road system. They'll also have the field-trip program of the **Kodiak Audubon Society,** with guided hikes and bird-watching trips; or write to the society at P.O. Box 1756, Kodiak, AK 99615.

HORSEBACK RIDING   The lush green hills that cover much of the island are idyllic grounds for riding. **Kodiak Cattle Co.,** P.O. Box 1608, Kodiak, AK 99615 (☎ **907/486-3705**), is one of several offering rides. They often see deer, eagles, and bears on their day trips, which start at $90 per person with a two-person minimum.

SEA KAYAKING   The Kodiak Archipelago, with its many folded, rocky shorelines and abundant marine life, is a perfect place for sea kayaking; after all, kayaks were invented here and in the Aleutian Island to the west. Several operators offer kayaking services and tours in and around Kodiak. **Mythos Expeditions,** P.O. Box 2084, Kodiak, AK 99615 (☎ **907/486-5536;** www.mythos-expeditions.com) offers intro-ductory paddles starting from the boat harbor—surprisingly complex and attractive waters for kayaking—and longer excursions of various kinds. If you're already an expe-rienced kayaker, **Shuyak Island State Park,** 54 miles north of Kodiak, is the place to go. The park is a honeycomb of islands and narrow passages in virgin Sitka spruce coastal forest. The Division of State Parks (see address under "Two Recreation Areas," above) maintains four public-use cabins, which rent for $50 a night, and distributes a free kayaking guide with route descriptions. Mythos Expeditions rents kayaks for use in the park, as well as offering custom kayaking and ecotours from a sturdy boat.

ACCOMMODATIONS

Besides the hotels listed below, you'll find good budget rooms at **Russian Heritage Inn,** 119 Yukon, Kodiak, AK 99615 (☎ **907/486-5657;** fax 907/486-4634). Below I've listed five places in town, but there also are more than 2 dozen wilderness lodges on and around Kodiak Island. See some suggestions in chapter 2; you can get a list from the visitor center, and their Web site contains links to most of them.

Best Western Kodiak Inn. 236 W. Rezanof Dr., Kodiak, AK 99615. ☎ **888/563-4254** or 907/486-5712. Fax 907/486-3430. 81 units. TV TEL. High season, $129–$139 double. Low season, $99 double. AE, DC, DISC, MC, V.

This is the best hotel in downtown Kodiak, with attractive, up-to-date rooms perched on the hill overlooking the boat harbor, right in the center of things. Rooms in the wooden building vary in size and view, although all are acceptable and have coffee-makers. There's a tour desk in the pleasant lobby. The **Chart Room** restaurant, spe-cializing in seafood and with a great view of the water, is a good choice for a nice dinner out, with entrees in the $15 to $20 range.

Buskin River Inn. 1395 Airport Way, Kodiak, AK 99615. ☎ **800/544-2202** or 907/487-2700. www.kodiakadventure.com. 50 units. TV TEL. $125 double. Additional person in room $15 extra. AE, DC, DISC, MC, V.

This quiet, well-kept hotel with standard rooms is near the airport, not the downtown sights, so it's a good choice if you're heading into the wilderness or have a rented car. Rooms on one side look out on the parking lot. It's near the wildlife refuge visitor center, a hiking trail, and the nine-hole golf course at the Coast Guard base. The Buskin makes a specialty of booking activities and offering package discounts for out-door explorations of the island. The rooms all have coffeemakers, voice mail, clocks, and hair dryers; there's a self-service laundry, and they'll pick you up at the airport. The **Eagle's Nest Restaurant** has reliable food from a complete beef and seafood menu, and a pleasant setting.

Kodiak Bed and Breakfast. 308 Cope St., Kodiak, AK 99615. ☎ **907/486-5367.** Fax 907/486-6567. www.ptialaska.net/~monroe. 2 units, both with shared bathroom. $88 double. MC, V.

Hospitable, active Mary Monroe runs this comfortable, homey place with a big, friendly dog. There is a porch to eat breakfast on sunny mornings, overlooking the harbor. Fish is often on the menu. The location is convenient, right downtown, and the entry for the bedrooms and shared sitting room downstairs doesn't require you to walk through Monroe's living quarters.

Shelikof Lodge. 211 Thorsheim Ave., Kodiak, AK 99615. ☎ **907/486-4141** or 907/486-4116. www.ptialaska.net/~kyle. 38 units. TV TEL. $65 double. Additional person in room $5 extra. AE, CB, DC, DISC, MC, V.

This economy choice right in town has large standard rooms that were recently remodeled, with refrigerators, hair dryers, and free movie channels on the TV. It's a very good deal. There's an inexpensive, windowless restaurant with a fish tank and a lounge. They offer free coffee in the lobby.

Wintels Bed and Breakfast. 1723 Mission Rd. (P.O. Box 2812), Kodiak, AK 99615. ☎ and fax **907/486-6935.** www.wintels.com. 3 units, one with private bathroom. TEL. $80–$100 double. Additional person in room $35 extra. AE, MC, V.

A long walking distance from downtown, this house stands with the ocean on one side and a lake on the other, so all rooms have water views. The owners, a family of long-time residents, can tell you a lot about Alaska and show off their mounted sea ducks and furs. The rooms are attractive, the breakfasts large, and there's a sauna and a Jacuzzi surrounded by potted plants. Laundry machines are available.

DINING

Besides the hotel restaurants listed above at the Best Western Kodiak Inn and Buskin River Inn, try these: **El Chicano**, at 103 Center St. (☎ **907/486-6116**), is a good Mexican family restaurant, with friendly service and reasonable prices. **Beryl's** is a great little sandwich and breakfast shop on a pedestrian way at 202 Center St. (☎ **907/486-3323**). It started out as a candy and ice-cream place, but now serves meals all day until 6pm. **Harborside Coffee and Goods,** at 216 Shelikof St.

(☎ **907/486-5862**), on the south side of the boat harbor, is a comfortable coffee house with soup and bagels, popular with commercial fishers and young people. **Henry's Great Alaskan Restaurant,** at 512 Marine Way (☎ **907/486-8844**), on the waterfront mall, is a popular bar and grill.

4 Katmai National Park: Natural Ferocity

Most of the land of the Alaska Peninsula, pointing out to the Aleutian Archipelago, is in one federally protected status or another, centering on Katmai National Park, which was originally set aside in 1918. Katmai (*cat*-my) lies just west of Kodiak Island, across the storm-infested Shelikof Strait. Bears and salmon are the main attractions today. **Brooks Camp,** with a campground and lodge within Katmai, is probably the most comfortable place for foolproof bear viewing in Alaska. Here, in July and September only, you can sit back on a deck and watch 900-pound brown bears walk by, going about their business of devouring the spawning salmon that contribute to their awesome size. (A brown bear is the genetic twin of the grizzly, but generally larger due to its coastal diet of salmon.) Staying the night will require you to reserve a place in the 16-space campground the previous winter (see "Reservations & Fees," below) or stay in the pricey lodge, where rooms book up over a year ahead for the bear season. You can go for a day trip, too, if you can afford round-trip airfare of around $500 and reserve a day-use permit (see "Reservations and Fees," below).

Katmai originally exploded into world consciousness in 1912, with the most destructive volcanic eruption to shake the earth in 3,400 years. When Katmai's Novarupta blew, it released ten times more energy than Mount St. Helens's eruption of 1980 and displaced twice as much matter as 1883's Krakatoa. People could clearly hear it in Juneau; acid rain melted fabric in Vancouver, British Columbia; and the skies darkened over most of the northern hemisphere. All life was wiped out in a 40-square-mile area and buried as deep as 700 feet. But so remote was the area, then still unnamed, that not a single human being was killed. The **Valley of Ten Thousand Smokes,** the vast wasteland created by the blast, belched steam for decades after. Today Novarupta is dormant, but the area is still a barren moonscape, making a fascinating day tour or hiking trip.

ESSENTIALS
GETTING THERE

The most common way to get to Katmai is through the village of King Salmon, which lies just west of the park, and then by air-taxi to Brooks Camp. The park concessionaire, **Katmailand,** with offices at 4125 Aircraft Dr., Anchorage, AK 99502 (☎ **800/544-0551** or 907/243-5448; fax 907/243-0649; www.katmailand.com), offers round-trip airfare packages of $460—a good deal. **Alaska Airlines** (☎ **800/426-0333**) is one of several operators serving King Salmon from Anchorage daily. Various air-taxis operating floatplanes make the link to Brooks Camp, including Katmailand's **Katmai Air**.

As an alternative to Brooks Camp, more and more visitors are exploring the supremely rugged wilderness on the east side of the park from the beaches along Shelikof Strait. Air-taxi operators make drops-offs and do bear viewing day trips from Homer or Kodiak (see Kodiak above, and Homer in chapter 7), and boats out of Kodiak go across for extended expeditions. In this park with more than 2,000 brown bears resident (the worlds largest protected population), it's easy for pilots to find them feeding on the tidal marshes, then land on floats for a good, close look.

RESERVATIONS & FEES

To go to the bear viewing area at Brooks Camp, you must first make a reservation and pay the use fee of $10 per person, per day. Camping costs $5 per person per night. There are only 16 sites, and they are in very high demand during the bear season in July. The crowds are less in September, but the bears are not quite as numerous. All sites become available for the entire summer on January 15. There are no limits on day-use permits, so everyone gets in. To reserve, call the **Park Service national reservation system,** which is operated by Biospherics (☎ **800/365-2267** or 301/722-1257; www.reservations.nps.gov). When the automated answering system gives you the prompt, enter **KAT#.** If reserving a campsite, make sure also to get a day-use permit. Lodge guests get their permit automatically.

GETTING AROUND

Once at Brooks Camp, there's a **bus** that carries visitors to the Valley of Ten Thousand Smokes, 23 miles by gravel road from the camp. The park concessionaire, **Katmailand,** charges $72 per person, round-trip, for the all-day excursion, plus $7 more for lunch. One-way transfers for hikers are $42.

VISITOR INFORMATION

Besides the **Katmai National Park Headquarters,** P.O. Box 7, King Salmon, AK 99613 (☎ **907/246-3305;** www.nps.gov/katm), there's also a **visitor center** at the airport in King Salmon (☎ **907/246-4250**), staffed jointly by the National Park Service, U.S. Fish and Wildlife Service, and the local government. At Brooks Camp the park service has a center where all visitors are required to attend a 20-minute orientation called "The Brooks Camp School; or, Bear Etiquette," designed to train visitors not to get themselves or the bears in trouble. In Anchorage, you can get information at the **Alaska Public Lands Information Center,** at Fourth Avenue and F Street (☎ **907/271-2737;** see the complete listing in chapter 6).

Fast Facts: Katmai National Park

Police   In King Salmon ☎ 907/246-4222. Reach the Alaska State Troopers at ☎ 907/246-3346 or 907/246-3464. Note that there are no phones or cellular service out in the park.

Hospital   The Camai Clinic, in Naknek (☎ 907/246-6155), is open during normal business hours; calls to the number go to emergency dispatchers after hours.

EXPLORING KATMAI

Katmai's famous bear viewing occurs at **Brooks Camp** when the bears are congregated near the Brooks River to catch salmon, during July and September, and maybe the last week of June or the first week of August. This is when you're assured of seeing bears from the elevated platforms near the Brooks River falls, half a mile from Brooks Camp, even on a day trip. Forty to 60 bears feed here. Other times in the summer, you might see a bear, or you might not.

The Brooks Camp area has a small park service campground, visitor center, and a lodge, located where the Brooks River flows into Naknek Lake. Unfortunately, when the area was first developed for fishing in the 1950s, the camp was placed on top of a valuable archaeological site. The archaeology is one of the attractions today, but the park service wants to move the buildings to a more suitable location in the future. The most comfortable way to stay in the camp is at the **Brooks Lodge,** operated by Katmailand (see address under "Getting There," above). The lodge has 16 units, with private bathrooms with shower stalls. To save money, book the lodge rooms as packages with air travel. The least expensive, 1-night visit is $629 per person, double occupancy, meals not included; 3 nights is $1,021. A double room without airfare is $372. The place books up a full year ahead; reservations open January of the year before the visit. Three buffet-style meals are served daily for guests and visitors who aren't staying in the lodge. Breakfast is $10, lunch $12, and dinner $22. For food, they take plastic at the lodge—American Express, MasterCard, and Visa. Also at Brooks Camp, there's a small store, the park service visitor center, and the 16-site campground. See "Reservations & Fees," above, for info on campground reservations, which should be made 6 months in advance. The rangers require special precautions to keep bears away from campers.

The rivers and lakes of Katmai lure human fishermen as well as ursine ones. Katmailand operates two lodges other than Brooks Lodge for remote fishing excursions. There also are several other lodges on inholdings along the park's huge lakes, and you can fly in for fishing or kayaking in rarely visited remote areas of the park. The park service has a list of dozens of fishing, hiking, and air guides. There is no central clearing house for remote fishing lodges, but you can find and book a good place through an agency such as **Sport Fishing Alaska** (☎ 907/344-8674; fax 907/349-4330; www.alaska.net/~sfa), listed in full under "Fishing" in chapter 2.

Backcountry hiking in Katmai means crossing a wilderness without trails, and only experienced backpackers should plan extended trips. The park service asks hikers to obtain a voluntary permit for backcountry travel, thereby clueing them in to your plans in case you need to be rescued. Anyone can walk for the day without such precaution in the desolate **Valley of Ten Thousand Smokes.** This 40-square-mile plain remains a moonscape almost 90 years after the titanic volcanic blast that buried it, little changed except that the famous plumes of smoke are gone and rivers have sliced through the debris in places to create narrow, white-walled canyons. Although it looks like a desert and is subject to dust storms, rain is common and temperatures rarely go higher than 65°F. Katmailand operates a **shuttle from Brooks Camp,** mentioned above under "Getting Around." The visitors on those tours usually stay to a short trail on the valley's rim. Longer hikes into the valley bring you into contact with more of the bizarre landforms created by the eruption.

5 Dutch Harbor/Unalaska: Aleutian Boom Town

After a lifetime of hearing how desolate the Aleutians (uh-*loo*-shuns) were, I felt a bit as though I was leaving the edge of the earth the first time I traveled to Unalaska (oon-ah-*las*-ka). Shortly after I arrived, a storm started slinging huge raindrops horizontally through the air so hard that they stung as they splattered on my face. People went on about their business as if nothing special was happening—stormy weather constantly batters these rocks that pop up from the empty North Pacific. My expectations seemed justified.

But the next day, the storm cleared like a curtain opening on a rich operatic scene—simultaneously opening the curtain of my dark expectations. Unalaska may lack trees, but it's not a barren rock—the island is covered with heather and wildflowers. Rounded mountains that invite wandering exploration rise from the ocean like the backs of huge beasts. For sightseeing, it has only a half a day's attractions, but for outdoor exploring, bird watching, and halibut fishing, few places come close.

With the protected port of Dutch Harbor so far out in a ferocious ocean habitat rich in crab and bottom fish, Unalaska has grown in two decades from a tiny, forgotten Native village to the nation's largest fishing port. The pattern of growth followed the form of the early gold rushes. There was a wild, lawless time in the 1970s when crab fishermen got rich quick and partied like Old West cowboys. Then the overfished crab stocks crashed, only to be replaced, starting in the mid-1980s, by an even bigger boom, when waters within 200 miles of the U.S. shore were rid of foreign vessels and American bottom fishing took off. Big factory ships began unloading here, and huge fish plants were built on ground chipped from the rock. Today that expansion has reached a more steady state, and more women and families are coming to town—another part of the gold rush pattern. But domestication isn't done yet. Most of the population lives in bunk houses and flies back to Seattle when the processing plants close for the season. Housing and public services still lag far behind the boom, in part because it's hard to build on the Aleutians' volcanic bedrock and there's such a lack of flat land. At the old softball field they had a rule that a home run was an out, two meant a 3-week suspension, and hitting a third merited expulsion from the league—the field was so small the balls were demolishing a woman's house who lived beyond the fence. But the town is rich enough to solve such problems: It spent $1 million for a new softball field. Unalaska may be the best current example of the American cultural phenomenon of the frontier boomtown.

Ironically, Unalaska is Alaska's oldest town as well as its newest city. The value of a good port out in the middle of the ocean was recognized from the beginning by the Aleuts. In 1759, the Russians began trading here, and fought a war with the Aleuts from 1763 to 1766, the outcome of which was slavery for the Aleut hunters and the massacre of their people. The Russians built a permanent settlement here in 1792, their first in Alaska. Unalaska also was a key refueling stop for steamers carrying gold rush stampeders to Nome a century ago, which brought an epidemic that killed a third of the indigenous population. In 1940, Dutch Harbor—the seaport on Amaknak Island associated with the town and island of Unalaska—was taken over by the U.S. Navy to defend against Japanese attack. That attack came: In June 1942, Japanese planes bombed Unalaska, killing 43. The Aleut people were removed from the islands for the duration of the war and interned in inadequate housing in Southeast Alaska, where many died of disease. The military pulled out in 1947, but the remains of their defenses are interesting to explore. Today, thanks to a 1971 act of Congress settling Native claims, the Aleut-owned Ounalashka Corporation owns much of the island.

Several sites preserve the island's history. The **Museum of the Aleutians** was completed in 1999 at a cost of $3.9 million; the old **Russian Orthodox church** is worth a look; and there are **military ruins** to see.

ESSENTIALS
GETTING THERE

BY AIR   Several operators fly to Dutch Harbor from Anchorage, including **Alaska Airlines** (☎ **800/426-0333;** www.alaskaair.com). You're likely to pay $650 to $850 round-trip. An air/hotel package makes sense and saves money—see the Grand Aleutian Hotel, described under "Accommodations," below.

BY FERRY   The **Alaska Marine Highway System** ferry *Tustumena* (☎ **800/642-0066,** www.dot.state.ak.us/external/amhs/home.html) runs once a month from Homer, leaving Tuesday night and arriving in Unalaska on Saturday morning after stopping in Kodiak and the villages along the way. The passenger fare is $242, and an outside cabin, with facilities, is $328. I don't know anyone who has actually done this long open-sea passage, but it must be an adventure. Of course, unless you want to spend only 3 hours early on a Saturday morning in Unalaska and then make the long return trip, you'll need to fly back.

GETTING AROUND

The main historic part of the town is a tiny street grid on a narrow peninsula facing Iliuliuk Bay. The **Bridge to the Other Side** (that's the official name) leads to Amaknak Island, the site of the airport, the Grand Aleutian Hotel, and the fishing industrial area of Dutch Harbor. Traveling down the road in the other direction leads a little way up into the mountains, a starting point for walks.

BY VAN TAXI   Van taxis are the main way of getting around town for the hordes of fishermen. One company is **Blue Checker Taxi** (☎ **907/581-2186**).

BY RENTAL CAR   You can rent a car, truck, or forklift from **North Port Rentals** (☎ **907/581-3880**) or a couple of other companies.

BY BIKE   **Aleutian Adventure Sports** (☎ **888/581-4489** or 907/581-4489; www.ansi.net/~advsports), in a two-story former grocery store, rents bikes for $35 a day—in good weather, that's a nice way to get around an island with only a few miles of roads.

BY TOUR   **Aleut Tours** (☎ **907/581-6001;** e-mail: akaleut@arctic.net) offers town tours in the summer, including all the major sights, with a Native guide driving the van. It lasts 2 to 3 hours, with pickup wherever you are, and costs $40. **The Extra Mile Tours** (☎ **907/581-6171**) offers similar deals.

VISITOR INFORMATION

The **Unalaska/Port of Dutch Harbor Convention and Visitors Bureau,** P.O. Box 545, Unalaska, AK 99685 (☎ **907/581-2612;** arctic.net/~updhcvb), operates out of the Grand Aleutian Hotel (see "Accommodations," below). The Web site has many useful links.

Fast Facts: Dutch Harbor/Unalaska

Banks   A Key Bank branch is near the Alaska Commercial Store.

Hospital   Iliuliuk Family and Health Services (☎ 907/581-1202) offers complete clinic services.

Internet/E-mail   At the public library (☎ 907/581-5060).

Police   The Unalaska Department of Public Safety (☎ 907/581-1233), is just above the bridge on the Unalaska side.

Taxes   Sales tax is 3%. The room tax is 5%.

ATTRACTIONS & ACTIVITIES

Unalaska's main historic site is the **Holy Ascension Cathedral.** Completed in 1896 on the site of churches that had stood since 1808, the white church with green onion-shaped domes contains 697 icons, artifacts, and artworks—a significant collection that has been continuously in use by the Aleut congregation. The congregation was founded by Fr. Ivan Veniaminov, who translated the Gospel into Aleut and has been canonized as St. Innocent. The building was not well maintained, and the buffeting of rugged weather and history put it in peril, but a $1.3 million restoration completed

The Aleutians: The Quiet After War

In 1995, the navy deactivated the secret naval base at **Adak,** in the outer Aleutian Islands, leaving only a few caretakers. Few civilians had ever seen the base, which had been hurriedly built more than 50 years before to fight back a Japanese invasion. With its closing, the book closed on a bizarre and bitter tale with few parallels in American history. The battle for the Aleutians was costly, pointless, and miserable, bringing ruin and disease to the Aleuts and death to thousands of Japanese and American soldiers. What began as a diversion became a ferocious fight for honor with little strategic meaning. When the fighting was done, it turned out that no one even wanted the land enough to stay. With the 50th anniversary of the war, Japanese and American soldiers met on the deserted islands they'd fought for and dedicated a monument. Then they left again— leaving behind the site of death and struggle to the fog, whipping wind, and migrating geese.

The Japanese attacked the islands of **Kiska** and **Attu** at the start of the Pacific war to divert the main core of the American navy away from what became the **Battle of Midway.** But the Americans had intercepted and decoded Japanese transmissions, and weren't fooled. Meanwhile, the Japanese had sent 24 ships, including two aircraft carriers, on a fool's errand to bomb the new American naval base at Dutch Harbor/Unalaska and occupy islands in the western Aleutians. Those ships could have tipped the balance at Midway, among the most important battles of the war. Instead, the Japanese met stiff antiaircraft fire in 2 days of bombing at Dutch Harbor, and, although 43 Americans were killed, the defensive function of the base was not greatly impaired.

The Japanese then took Kiska and Attu, meeting no resistance from 10 Americans staffing a weather station or from a small Aleut village whose few inhabitants were all—even the children—sent to a prison camp in Japan to mine clay for the duration of the war. About half the prisoners survived to return to Alaska.

The Americans had their own plan to remove the Aleuts, but the idea of depopulating all the islands had been turned down. Now, with the Japanese attack, it was swiftly put into effect. All the Aleuts were rounded up and put on ships. As they pulled away from their ancestral islands, they could see the glow of huge fires destroying their villages—the U.S. military had torched the villages to deny the modest assets of the islands to the Japanese, should they advance farther. With little thought given to their living conditions, the Aleuts were interned in abandoned summer camps and similarly inadequate facilities in Southeast Alaska. Shunned by the local communities and without the basic necessities of life, many died of cold and disease. The U.S. Fish and Wildlife Service took Aleut hunters to hunt furs as virtual slaves, much as the Russians had done 200 years before.

The Japanese and American military fared not much better on their new real estate. Although the Aleutians quickly became irrelevant to the rest of the war, significant resources were committed to a largely futile air and sea battle in the fog and endless storms. Flying at all was difficult and extremely dangerous, and finding the enemy in the fog over vast distances close to impossible. The Americans couldn't spare a land invasion force at first, and had to rely on bombing Kiska and Attu to punish the Japanese and try to deter a further advance up the chain. To that end, they built the base at Adak, among others, so shorter-range fighter escorts could accompany the bombers. Construction in the spongy tundra was difficult in any case, made more so by the length of supply lines.

The Japanese high command never had any intention of advancing up the chain, but also saw no reason to abandon their new Kiska air base when it was causing the Americans to exert such effort—even if it had no strategic value to either side. The Japanese concentrated on fortifying Kiska, which became a honeycomb of underground bunkers and heavy antiaircraft guns and withstood constant bombing raids from the Americans.

Finally, on May 11, 1943, almost a year after the Japanese took the islands, Americans landed on Attu, and a brutal 18-day battle for the rugged island began. The Japanese were massively outnumbered but heavily dug in. Finally, with only 800 soldiers left from an original force of 2,600, the Japanese mounted a banzai attack. Only 28 were taken prisoner—the rest were killed in battle or committed suicide. The Americans lost 549 killed, 1,148 wounded, and 2,132 injured by severe cold, disease, accident, mental breakdown, or other causes. In the end, it was the second most costly island battle in the Pacific, after Iwo Jima.

The battle for Kiska was less dramatic. The Japanese withdrew under cover of fog. After a massive bombardment of the empty island and the rallying of heavy reinforcements, the Americans landed to find that no one was there. Still, 105 American soldiers died in the landing in accidents and fire from their own forces.

After the Aleutian battle was over, American forces in Alaska declined drastically, but never went away altogether. Before the war, the absurd little Fort William Seward, in Haines, had been the totality of Alaska's defenses, with a couple of hundred men armed with Springfield rifles and no reliable means of transportation. Afterward there were large bases in several areas of the state. Military spending became the biggest economic boom the territory had ever seen, connecting it by a new road to the Lower 48 and bringing precious year-round jobs. A new wave of postwar settlers, many former GIs looking for a new, open field of opportunity, brought a population boom. The advent of the Cold War, and Alaska's prime strategic location in defense against the Soviet Union, brought ever-greater increases in military spending in Alaska. To this day, the military is one of the largest sectors of the Alaska economy, and the state has been relatively unscathed in base closures except for remote outposts like Adak.

The end of the war was more bitter for the Aleuts. Everything they had in their villages had been destroyed. Many who had survived the terrible period of internment never returned to the islands where their villages had once stood, and some of the villages never revived. Some were wiped off the map as a cost-saving measure by the bureaucrats who managed the evacuation. Aleuts who were able to return found belongings, subsistence gear, and religious icons destroyed. "When I came back to Atka after World War II, my buddy said, 'Why are you going back to the Aleutians? They say even the sea gulls are leaving there,'" villager Dan Prokopeuff has been quoted as saying. "I told him I was going because it's peaceful and quiet."

Today Atka is the westernmost village remaining in the Aleutians. On Kiska there are only ruins of the Japanese fortifications. As for Adak and the assets the U.S. military left behind, it's being taken over by the Aleut Corporation, the regional Native corporation, which hopes to redevelop it as a town.

in 1996 has left it looking bright and trim. Sitting on the edge of sparkling Iliuliuk Bay, the church and its cemetery are a picturesque cultural gem.

A new museum, to be finished after this was written, will be open for the 2000 season. The ✪ **Museum of the Aleutians,** next door to the Ounalashka Corporation in Dutch Harbor (☎ **907/581-5150;** www.aleutians.org), will contain some of the Aleuts' best artifacts anywhere, including some from North American's oldest coastal sites, on Umnak and Unalaska islands. The curators also plan to cover the town's history with World War II artifacts and other items left behind by the successive waves of occupiers. Admission is expected to be around $2; hours had not yet been set, but will be extensive in the summer. Call the visitor center for information.

Right outside the museum, an archaeological dig has unearthed more than 100,000 objects from layers of Aleut villages more than 3,000 to 5,500 years old. Work continues at the **Margaret Bay Archeological Project** (www.brynmawr.edu/Acads/Anthro/m-bay/index.html), and the scientists invite visitors to join in the work, earning college credit while digging, working to clean the artifacts in the museum, and hearing evening lectures. As the site is a stones throw from the luxurious Grand Aleutian Hotel, the bar and a comfortable bed are never far away. To volunteer, call Museum of the Aleutians Director, Rick Knecht (☎ **907/581-5150**).

There are several **World War II military ruins** around town, including some that are still in use—like a submarine dry dock that today fixes fishing boats. The activity at the port is interesting to see, too, if only for the size of the vessels and harvest and the incredible investment in buildings and equipment.

GETTING OUTSIDE

The attractive thing about Unalaska is that it's truly an island outpost, way out in one of the world's wildest and more remote oceans, with extraordinary ocean fishing, bird watching for species you can't see elsewhere, hiking, and mountain biking, yet it's also the site of a luxurious hotel and of other modern businesses. The island is out in the middle of nowhere, but it has an active, big-money economy, and that makes a difference in comfort and convenience for visitors.

ACTIVITIES

You exploit this port far out in the ocean by using it for access to **fishing** and **bird watching.** Of course, you can do both at once, with sea lions and other marine mammals thrown in. Several rare bird species nest in the area, and Asian birds occasionally drop in as accidentals. The whiskered auklet and red-legged kittiwake are among the birds commonly found around Unalaska that don't show up anywhere else. There also are rookeries with many species of birds, and you generally see lots of marine mammals, too.

FISHING   You can fly out for salmon fishing from black-sand beaches, but Unalaska has become more famous for having the largest halibut caught in the state. In 1995, a local sport fisherman caught a 395-pound halibut from an 18-foot skiff within a half mile of town; to kill the behemoth he had to beach it and beat it over the head with a rock. The next year, Fairbanks angler Jack Tragis landed the world's record halibut here, which weighed 459 pounds. If you're having trouble imagining a fish that big, drop by City Hall, where it hangs stuffed in the lobby. If you plan to fish, buy a derby ticket from the visitor center; if you break the world record you could win $100,000. Two well-reputed charter operators are Henry Olsen's **Silver Cloud Fisheries** (☎ **907/581-1823**) and John Lucking's **Far West Outfitters** (☎ **907/581-1647**). Charters are around $165 per person for a 4- to 6-hour trip, with a two-person minimum. Also check on packages with the place where you are staying, which can save money.

SEA KAYAKING   The Aleuts invented the kayak to hunt and travel, so you can bet these are good waters for either a short day trip or an overnight expedition. **Aleutian Adventure Sports,** P.O. Box 921181, Dutch Harbor, AK 99692 (☎ **888/581**-4489 or 907/581-4489; www.ansi.net/~advsports), rents kayaks and offers daily beginners' harbor tours (3½ hours, $55) as well as longer day trips and multiday expeditions. They also lead treks and volcano climbs, and rent mountain bikes.

HIKING   The island's green heather and rounded mountains of wildflowers are inviting for unguided day hiking, too. You can walk pretty much in any direction, looking at the abandoned World War II defenses; making a goal of a beach or one of the small peaks around the town; or, for the ambitious, even heading to the top of an active volcano, Mount Makushin. There are no bears and not many bugs, but there's great berry picking and beachcombing. The weather can be a threat, however, and fox holes can trip you up. As always in remote outdoor areas, you must be suitably dressed, know how to take care of yourself, and leave word of where you're going and when you'll be back. For extended hikes, go to the Department of Public Safety (see "Fast Facts: Dutch Harbor/Unalaska," above) for a travel-planning guide and to report your route on a travel plan that will assist with a search if you don't come back (not necessary if you're just going for a short ramble in the hills around town). You'll also have to pay a fee to the **Ounalashka Corp.,** at 400 Salmon Way near the Grand Aleutian Hotel (P.O. Box 149), Unalaska, AK 99685 (☎ **907/581-1276**), the Native village corporation that owns much of the island. Hiking is $5 per person per day, camping $10. They're open Monday through Friday from 8am to 5pm.

ACCOMMODATIONS

Carl's Bayview Inn. 606 Bayview (P.O. Box 730), Unalaska, AK 99685. ☎ **800/581-1230** or 907/581-1230. Fax 907/581-1880. 47 units. TV TEL. $90 double, $125 kitchenette, $150 suite. Additional person in room $20 extra . AE, DC, DISC, EURO, MC, V.

The building, in town on Iliuliuk Bay, looks a bit like a Dutch Harbor warehouse from the outside, but the eight kitchenettes and six suites inside, all newly remodeled and with every amenity, come closer to *Better Homes and Gardens,* with their pastel colors and sweeping views. The double rooms, although very clean, showed more signs of wear and are not as attractive. Only four rooms are reserved for nonsmokers. The place is owned by Democratic state representative Carl Moses, who also runs a bar and restaurant downstairs and a store and tackle shop next door.

✪ **Grand Aleutian Hotel.** 498 Salmon Way (P.O. Box 921169), Dutch Harbor, AK 99692. ☎ **800/891-1194** or 907/581-3844. Fax 907/581-7150. grandaleutian.com. 106 units. TV TEL. $150 double. $225–$250 suite. Additional person in room $15 extra. Packages available. AE, CB, DC, DISC, JCB, MC, V.

It's almost unreal to arrive in this big, luxurious hotel in a hard-driving Alaska Bush community. The Grand Aleutian is among the best hotels in Alaska, to say nothing of the Bush. For the same room in Anchorage, you'd pay considerably more. They have a courtesy van; the rooms are well designed and comfortable, many with good water views; the lobby is grand, with a huge stone fireplace; and there's a piano bar. As you walk outside into a driving gale, it's like teleporting from a big city hotel back to an exposed rock out in the North Pacific. Why build such a grand hotel in such a remote place? I don't know, but I've heard it called the "Grand Illusion." The **Chart Room** restaurant, on the second floor, allows bird-watchers to see waterfowl in the bay while dining on steak, seafood, or pasta. The menu, although brief, is Unalaska's most sophisticated. Dinner entrees range from $18 to $28. The **Margaret Bay Cafe,** downstairs, also has a good view, with a menu of grilled sandwiches and some lighter fare. When we last visited, our orders were mixed up and slow in coming, but we didn't mind because the food was good. A hamburger is $8.

The Japanese-owned UniSea fish-processing company (which built the hotel) has developed a full scope of sportfishing and birding packages to entice visitors, and booking one of those packages, including airfare, should save money over traveling independently. A 2-night package, which includes a visit to the Baby Islands to see the whiskered auklet, tufted and horned puffin, albatross, and other creatures, starts at about $1,300 per person, double occupancy. Longer packages with more birding trips are available, as well as fishing packages at about the same price.

DINING

Two of the towns best restaurants are at the **Grand Aleutian Hotel,** described above. Here's the other contender.

Tino's Steak House. North 2nd St. on Broadway. ☎ **907/581-4288.** Lunch $9–$12, dinner $16–$40. AE, MC, V. Daily 8am–11pm.

To pack in the fishers and other locals, the restaurant serves huge portions of authentic Mexican food fast, as well as steaks, a few seafood items, and lots of sandwiches and burgers. I'm told you save money but get virtually the same meal by ordering from the lunch menu—the dinner prices are on the Unalaska scale, with most over $20. My informants call it the best restaurant in town.

6 The Pribilof Islands: Birder's Paradise

The Pribilof Islands of St. Paul and St. George sit out in the middle of the Bering Sea, due north of Unalaska, teeming with marine mammals and sea birds. Some 600,000 fur seals meet at the breeding rookeries in the summer, and 2 million birds of more than 200 species use the rocks. Bird-watchers go for one of the most exotic and productive wildlife-viewing opportunities in Alaska from mid-May to August. Mid-May to mid-June is peak for sightings of Asian accidental species, July is peak for many birds and marine mammals. You can count on seeing extremely rare birds any time during the summer. Indeed, the National Audubon Society's *Field Guide to North American Birds* calls this "perhaps the most spectacular seabird colony in the world." However, the islands are extremely remote and the accommodations simple. There is only one hotel, the King Eider, which has basic rooms and shared bathrooms. There is no restaurant on the island, so, at least in the past, guests were issued food vouchers for the mess hall at the Trident Seafoods fish-processing plant, near the hotel. Three meals a day come from a buffet there, and cost $10 to $17; you settle up at the end of your stay depending on how many vouchers you used. **Reeve Aleutian Airways** (☎ 800/544-2248 or 907/243-4700; fax 907/249-2276; www.alaskabirding.com) arranges packages from Anchorage to St. Paul starting at $900 for a 2-night visit. Aleut guides carry visitors around the island in a bus. St. Paul is small, and you can walk it, too, watching birds and seals from permanent blinds. The weather is always cool and damp.

7 Nome: Arctic Frontier Town

The accidents of history deposited the streets and buildings of this lusty little town on the shore of Norton Sound, just south of the Arctic Circle in Northwest Alaska, and gave it qualities that make Nome an exceptionally attractive place for a visitor to go. For once, the local boosters' motto—in this case, "There's no place like Nome"—is entirely accurate, and that's because Nome, although itself nothing special to look at, combines a sense of history, a hospitable and somewhat silly attitude, and an exceptional location on the water in front of a tundra wilderness that's crossed by 250 miles of road. Those roads are the truly unique thing, for Nome is the only place in Arctic Alaska where a visitor can drive or bike deep into the open country, coming across musk ox, reindeer, rarely seen birds, Native villages, undeveloped hot springs, and even an abandoned 1881 elevated train from New York City. Elsewhere, you're obliged to fly from rural hubs to get so far into the Bush, a more expensive and ambitious undertaking for casual explorers.

The accidents of history have been rather frequent in Nome—history has been downright sloppy. Start with the name. It's essentially a clerical error, caused by a British naval officer who, in 1850, was presumably in a creative dry spell when he wrote "? Name" on a diagram rather than name the cape he was sailing past. A mapmaker interpreted that as "Cape Nome." The original gold rush of 1898 was caused by prospectors in the usual way, but a much larger 1899 population explosion happened after one of the '98 stampeders, left behind by an injury in a camp on the beach, panned the sand outside the tent—and found that it was full of gold dust. By 1900, a fourth of Alaska's white population was in Nome, sifting the sand. Small-time operators and tourists are still at it, and major gold mining rumbles on just outside town. A huge floating gold dredge of the kind that makes for major historic sites in Fairbanks and Dawson City sits idle on the edge of town. In Nome, it stopped operation only in recent years. There are two other, smaller dredges in town, too. Historic structures are few, however, as fires and storms have destroyed the town several times since the gold rush.

Nome has a particular, broad sense of humor. It shows up in the *Nome Nugget* newspaper and in silly traditions like the Labor Day bathtub race, pack ice golf tournament, and the Memorial Day polar bear swim. The population is half white and half Native, and the town is run largely by the white group. Some see Nome as a tolerant mixing place of different peoples, while the town strikes others as a bit colonial. Booze is outlawed in Kotzebue, the Native-dominated city to the north; but in Nome there is still a sloppy, gold rush–style saloon scene. That sort of thing is prettier as historic kitsch than when it shows up in the form of a staggering Front Street drunk.

But you can ignore that, instead taking advantage of the great bargains to be had on **Inupiat arts and crafts.** And, most important, you can use one of the pleasant little inns or bed-and-breakfasts as a base to get into the countryside that beckons, down one of the gravel roads. Nome is popular with birdwatchers, who find the roads especially useful.

ESSENTIALS
GETTING THERE

BY AIR   Flying is the only way to get to Nome. **Alaska Airlines** (☎ **800/426-0333** or 907/443-2288) flies a 90-minute jet flight either direct from Anchorage or with a brief hop from Kotzebue. The fare from Anchorage is likely to be in the range of $350 to $500, round-trip. Many visitors come on a package sold by **Alaska Airlines Vacations** (☎ **800/468-2248**), which first visits Kotzebue, starting at $494 per person, double occupancy; it is described in the Kotzebue section that follows.

GETTING INTO TOWN FROM THE AIRPORT   All taxis operate according to a standard price schedule you can get from the visitor center. A ride to town from the airport is $5. Call **Nome Cab** (☎ **907/443-3030**).

Getting Around

The town is a mostly unpaved grid along the ocean. **Front Street** follows the sea wall, **First Avenue** is a block back, and so on. A harbor is at the north end of town, and the gold-bearing beach is to the south. You can mostly walk to see this area. Three roads branch out from Nome. I've described them below, under "Getting Outside." To get out on the roads, you need to take a tour or rent a car.

BY RENTAL CAR   Several local car rental agencies operate in town; the visitor center maintains a list, with rates. **Stampede Rent-A-Car,** 157 Seppala Dr. (☎ 907/443-3838), charges $75 a day for a van or Ford Bronco, $125 for a camper. They'll deliver the vehicle to you.

BY BIKE   One-speed bikes are for rent from **Nome Outfitters** (☎ 907/443-2880), and guided bicycle day trips are available from **Bering C Bikes** (☎ 907/443-4994), about which there is more information below under "Getting Outside."

BY TOUR   Several companies offer organized tours. **Nome Discovery Tours** (☎ 907/443-2814) has the asset of talented professional actor Richard Beneville as the van driver and tour guide. He'll pick you up and drive you anywhere in the area, sharing his quirky enthusiasm and extensive knowledge of the surroundings. The highlight is the wildlife and scenery on the roads out of town. Half days are $45 per person, full days $85. **Nome Tour and Marketing,** at the Nugget Inn, at Front and Bering streets (☎ 907/443-2651), is a more traditional tour, with a dog sled demonstration and gold panning. It is timed to meet flights bringing in visitors on packages, running in the summer only, and costs $52 per person.

Visitor Information

The **Nome Convention and Visitors Bureau,** Front and Hunter streets (P.O. Box 240), Nome, AK 99762 (☎ 907/443-5535, www.nomealaska.org), is exceptionally well run, providing maps and detailed information for diverse interests, and screening videos for those interested. They're open Mid-May to mid-September daily 9am to 7pm, mid-September to mid-May daily 9am to 6:30pm.

The **Bering Land Bridge National Preserve Headquarters,** Front Street (P.O. Box 220), Nome, AK 99762 (☎ 907/443-2522), is a good source of outdoors information from the rangers who staff a desk and are responsible for a rarely visited 2.3-million-acre national park unit, which covers much of the Seward Peninsula north of the Nome road system.

Special Events

The **Iron Dog Classic Snowmachine Race** (☎ 907/563-4414), in mid-February, is the world's longest, covering the Iditarod Trail twice, a distance of 2,274 miles. Nome is the halfway point. The biggest event of the year is the ✪ **Iditarod Trail Sled Dog Race** (☎ 907/376-5155), a marathon of more than 1,000 miles that ends in Nome in mid- to late March. The sled dog racers and world media descend on the town for a few days of madness, with lots of community events planned. The activities last for the whole month; contact the Nome visitors center for a calendar. Among the most exciting vacations you could plan would be to volunteer to help run the Iditarod; call the race headquarters at the number above well in advance to get the information you need. One of the March Iditarod events, showcasing Nome's well-developed sense of humor, is the **Bering Sea Ice Golf Classic** (☎ 907/443-5162)—six holes are set up on the sea ice. The pressure ridges constitute a bad lie. Various similar silly events take place all year, including the **Polar Bear Swim,** which occurs in the Bering Sea on Memorial Day, ice permitting, and the Labor Day **Bathtub Race.** The **Midnight Sun**

Festival (☎ 907/443-5535) celebrates the summer solstice, around June 21, when Nome gets more than 22 hours of direct sunlight, with a parade, softball tournament, bank holdup, raft race, and similar events.

Fast Facts: Nome

Banks   National Bank of Alaska has a branch with an ATM at Front Street and Federal Way

Hospital   The Norton Sound Regional Hospital is at Fifth Avenue and Bering Street (☎ 907/443-3311).

Internet/E-mail   Nome Public Library, 200 Front St. (☎ 907/443-5133).

Police   The police and fire station is at Bering Street and Fourth Avenue (☎ 907/443-5262).

Post Office   Front Street and Federal Way.

Taxes   The sales tax is 4% and the room tax is also 4%, totaling 8%.

ATTRACTIONS & ACTIVITIES

Most of Nome's original buildings were wiped out by fires or by storms off Norton Sound that tore across the beach and washed away major portions of the business district. A sea wall, completed in 1951, now protects the town. An interesting **Historical Walking Tour,** produced by the Alaska Historical Commission and the Lion's Club, is available from the visitor center; it covers 20 sites, including a turn-of-the-century church and saloon, and a bust of Roald Amundsen, who landed near Nome, in Teller, after crossing the North Pole from Norway in a dirigible in 1926. Below the library, at Front Street and Lanes Way, the small **Carrie M. McLain Memorial Museum** (☎ 907/443-2566) exhibits items found on the beach and some Native artifacts. Of greatest interest are copies of the *Nome Nugget* dating from the gold rush—the price, 50¢, is still the same today, indicating just how inflated the local economy was in 1899. The museum is free and open summer daily noon to 8pm, winter Tuesday through Saturday from noon to 6pm.

In good weather, a pleasant walk is to be had southeast of town, along the **beach.** Small-time miners may be camped there, but the gold-bearing sand extends for miles more of solitary walking. You can buy a gold pan in town and try your luck, but the sand has been sifted for nearly 100 years, so don't expect to gather any significant amount of gold. The **Swanberg Dredge** you can see from here operated until the 1950s; a large dredge north of town worked into the mid-1990s. The 38 gold dredges that once operated on the Seward Peninsula crept across the tundra, creating their own ponds to float in as they went. The **cemetery,** with white, wooden crosses on top of a little hill just out of town, also is worth a look.

GETTING OUTSIDE
ON THE ROADS

The modest attractions downtown would hardly justify a trip to Nome, but the city's surroundings do. The roads provide unique access to a large stretch of the Seward Peninsula, and unlike other Arctic Bush areas, where you need to have someone take you where you want to go, all you have to do in Nome is rent a car, camper, or bike and go. There are few cars in Nome (they have to be shipped in by barge), so you won't see many other vehicles on a huge expanse of spectacular territory, with

The Dogs of Nome

Visitors come to Nome in winter mostly for the **Iditarod,** perhaps volunteering to help with the race (call the race offices, listed above under "Special Events"). If you do come when there's snow on the ground, you should take a **dog sled ride.** Check with the visitor center to find out who is currently offering them.

wildlife-viewing opportunities as good as anywhere in the state. Most of the land is managed by the **Bureau of Land Management** (BLM) P.O. Box 925, Nome, AK 99762 (☎ **907/443-2177;** www.ndo.ak.blm.gov/). The **Alaska Department of Transportation** (☎ **907/443-3444**) can provide current information on road conditions. You have a good chance to see moose, reindeer, owls, foxes, bears, and musk ox anywhere you drive, but check in with the visitor center or the **Alaska Department of Fish and Game,** at Front and Steadman streets, for where you're most likely to see animals. They can also give you guidance on fishing along the roads and a "Nome Roadside Fishing Guide."

A **Car-rental agency** is listed above under "Getting Around." Or if you don't want to drive yourself, you can go with Richard Beneville's **Nome Discovery Tours** (see "Getting Around" under "Essentials," above). Beneville knows where the wildlife is likely to be found, and the history and natural history of the area. On an all-day tour, he'll show you where to fish or take you to a gorgeous picnic spot.

ROAD HIGHLIGHTS   None of the three roads radiating from Nome has services of any kind—just small Native villages, a few dwellings, and some reindeer herders—so you must be prepared and bring what you need with you, including insect repellent. The visitor center provides a good road guide. Here are some highlights:

The **Nome-Council road** heads 72 miles to the east, about half of that on the shoreline. It turns inland at the ghost town of Solomon, an old mining town with an abandoned railroad train, known as the Last Train to Nowhere. The engines were originally used on the New York City elevated lines in 1881, then were shipped to Alaska in 1903 to serve the miners along this line to Nome. This is a great scenic spot for bird watching, and fishing is good in the Solomon River, all along the road. Council, near the end of the road, has a couple of dozen families in the summer; you have to get a boat ride across a river just short of the village.

The **Nome-Taylor road,** also known as the Kougarok road, runs north of town into the Kigluaik Mountains, 85 miles from Nome, eventually petering out and becoming impassable. About 40 miles out you reach lovely Salmon Lake, with a lakeshore campground with picnic tables, grills, and outhouses. A few miles farther, a road to the left leads to the Pilgrim Hot Springs, near the ruins of a Catholic church and orphanage. The two hot tubs are 100° to 125°F. Check with the visitor center before going, as the hot springs are privately owned and the open invitation may have changed since this writing.

The **Nome-Teller road** leads 73 miles to the village of Teller, which has about 200 residents, a gift shop, and a store. It's an opportunity to see an authentic Arctic Native village.

MOUNTAIN BIKING   The roads of Nome are a unique and wonderful ride—where else can you bike past musk oxen and reindeer? Keith Conger's **Bering C Bikes,** P.O. Box 1333, Nome, AK 99762 (☎ **907/443-4994**), offers guided bike day trips and van-supported multiday camping expeditions. Keith, a biologist, leads the tours and teaches about the ecology of the land they peddle through. He also provides equipment, advice, and transportation for those who want to **kayak** on Nome's rivers. At this writing, only one-speed bikes were for rent (see "Getting Around," above), so to go on your own you would have to bring a mountain bike from Anchorage.

BIRD WATCHING   Bird-watchers will make many discoveries out on the Nome roads, using new pages of their bird books. A bird list is available at the visitor center, and they can tell you where to look—each of the three roads has different habitat. The best times to visit for birding are right around Memorial Day, and from July to mid-August. Lana and Richard Harris were Nome's leading birders when I last visited, and the only local members of the American Birding Association. Lana can most easily be reached at the visitor center, where she now works, but the couple also maintains a **birders' hot line** on their home phone recorder (☎ **907/443-5528**); please don't call before 6am or after 10pm, Alaska time. There's a chance to see Siberian birds, and you can count on bluethroats, yellow wagtails, wheatears, Arctic warblers, and Aleutian and Arctic terns. Nome is the only place to see a bristle-thighed curlew without chartering a plane. You don't need a guide, although guided trips are available (check with the visitor center). As Lana put it, "If you haven't found a yellow wagtail, you haven't left the bar yet."

IN THE AIR

Nome is a hub for Bush plane operators. Flightseeing charters are available, or you can just fly on one of the mail-run routes out to the villages and spend a couple of hours touring for as little as $90; check how long the plane will stay in the village, as you may want to fly back with another operator to get more time. The visitor center or the flight services will help you figure it out. Among the operators are **Olson Air** (☎ **907/443-2229**) or **Cape Smythe Air** (☎ **907/443-2414**). Don't go in bad weather. You can also fly 150 miles over the International Dateline and see Russia from the air and the narrow water that divides our two nations. **Bering Air,** P.O. Box 1650, Nome, AK 99762 (☎ **907/443-5620**), specializes in these trips, which cost $150 for a 2-hour flight.

ACCOMMODATIONS

There are two main hotels in town, but the rooms are better at the smaller places listed below. The main central hotel, where package visitors go, is the 47-room **Nugget Inn,** at 2 Front St. (P.O. Box 430), Nome, AK 99762; ☎ **907/443-2323;** fax 907/443-5966). The rooms, mostly with twin beds, are smallish and have dark paneling and shower stalls instead of tubs. I cannot recommend the Polaris Hotel at all. Converted apartment lodgings are common in Nome, perhaps because the choice of restaurants is so uninspiring. A new hotel, the **Aurora Inn and Suites** (☎ **907/443-3838**), promises to be among the best in town.

Aurora Executive Suites. 157 Seppala Dr. (P.O. Box 1008), Nome, AK 99762. ☎ **800/354-4606** outside Alaska, 800/478-3838 within Alaska, or 907/443-3838. Fax 907/443-2985. 12 units. TV TEL. Summer $109 double, $125 suite. Winter $100 double, $115 suite. Additional person in room over age 6 $12.50 extra.

The standard rooms, which they call studio apartments, have kitchenettes, and the suites are two-bedroom apartments, with full kitchens and living areas. All have cable with HBO, coffee pots, and popcorn for the microwave. The building is new and more than comfortable. The same outfit owns Stampede Rent-A-Car, offering campers and other vehicles to explore the roads around Nome.

June's Bed and Breakfast. 231 E. Fourth Ave. (P.O. Box 489), Nome, AK 99762. ☎ **800/ 494-6994** or 907/443-5984; Oct–May 206/547-7826. E-mail: june@gold-digger.com. 3 units, none with bathroom. $80 double. Rates include breakfast and airport pickup. No credit cards. Closed Oct–May.

June Engstrom runs this traditional little B&B, proudly declaring, "I really am a gold digger's daughter." Her sourdough pancake starter came over the Chilkoot Trail in 1898, and she gives it and the recipe away to guests (the starter is the yeast that prospectors cultivated on the trail). The rooms are cozy, not commodious, but June's gregarious hospitality makes it special. Each has one of her handmade quilts.

Nanuaq Manor. Kings Place and Spokane St. (P.O. Box 850), Nome, AK 99762. ☎ **907/ 443-5296.** Fax 907/443-3063. 15 suites. TV TEL. $95–$175 double. AE, DC, MC, V.

These are simply light, roomy two- and three-bedroom apartments with full kitchens and their own laundry machines in buildings with permanent residents in other units. Everything was very clean and up-to-date when we visited. Two are reserved for non-smokers. Rates depend on the number of bedrooms in the apartment you use, and range up to $175 a night.

Ponderosa Inn. Third Ave. and Spokane St. (P.O. Box 125), Nome, AK 99762. ☎ **907/ 443-5737.** Fax 907/443-4149. 11 units. TV. $90–$100 double; $120 suite. Additional person in room $15 extra. AE, DC, MC, V.

Hidden in a pair of houses a few blocks back from the main drag, this inn has spacious, homey rooms in its new section. The more expensive rooms have kitchens, and the suite is a large, two-bedroom apartment. A few rooms lack phones or have only shower stalls, not tubs, and fewer amenities. There's a coin-op laundry, free coffee, and shared kitchen facilities. Unfortunately, no rooms are reserved for nonsmokers, and all the rooms we inspected had a bothersome cigarette odor.

DINING

There's not a selection of places where you'd go out of your way to dine, but you can find an adequate family meal at various establishments in Nome, all along Front Street.

There are several restaurants operated by immigrant families, offering their national cuisine and something else, often with servers who speak broken English. **Nachos,** at 503 Front St. in the Old Federal Building (☎ **907/443-5503**), has OK American-style Mexican food and good Chinese. **Milano's Pizzeria** (☎ **907/443-2924**), in the same building, serves Italian and Japanese meals, and gets good reviews for the pizza from the locals. **Twin Dragons,** on Front Street near Steadman Street (☎ **907/ 443-5552**), has made if for years with Chinese food alone, which is consistently good, although the service isn't so reliable. The other ethnic place is **Pizza Napoli** (☎ **907/ 443-5300**), a Greek/Italian combination serving good pizza and great Greek salads. It doesn't take credit cards; all the others take Visa and MasterCard

The other flavor of restaurant in Nome is the classic American greasy spoon. The ethnic restaurants mentioned above all have a way to escape the smoke; these burger habitats tend to be smoky throughout. The **Polar Cub Restaurant,** at 225 Front St. (☎ **907/443-5191**), has an extensive diner menu and prices that, for the Alaska Bush, are quite reasonable. **Fat Freddy's Restaurant,** in the Nugget Inn (☎ **907/ 443-5899**), serves more expensive fare in the evening, such as steaks and fried fish, in addition to the usual sandwiches; their prices are higher than the Polar Cub.

Fort Davis Roadhouse, on the beach about a mile east of town (☎ 907/443-2660), is more of a fine dining experience, with open views of the tundra and water, but currently it's open only on weekends.

SHOPPING

If you're in the market for walrus ivory carvings and other **Inupiat arts and crafts,** you'll find low prices and an extraordinary selection in Nome. Jim West has a legendary collection for sale, assembled in the bar room of the historic **Board of Trade Saloon** that is attached to a shop on Front Street. The **Arctic Trading Post** is more of a traditional gift shop and also has a good ivory collection, and try **Sitnasuak Ivory Shop,** also on Front Street. **Chukotka-Alaska,** at 185 West First Ave., is an importer of art and other goods from the Russian Far East, and is really worth a look. Alaska Native art you find in Nome is likely to be authentic, but still ask; see "Native Art—Finding the Real Thing" in chapter 2. See chapter 3 to find out about the special permit you need to carry ivory out of the United States.

8 Kotzebue: Big Village

Although its 4,000 residents make Kotzebue (*kotz*-eh-biew) a good-sized town, with a bank, a hospital, and a couple of grocery stores, I've heard it called a village instead. A "village," in Alaskan parlance, is a remote Native settlement in the Bush, generally with fewer than a few hundred residents, where people live relatively close to the traditional lifestyle of their indigenous ancestors. Kotzebue is a support hub for the villages of the Northwest Arctic, with jet service and a booming cash economy, but it's populated and run by the Inupiat—fish-drying racks and old dog sleds are scattered along the streets, and Native culture is thriving. It does feel like a village.

For visitors, this characteristic makes Kotzebue unique because you can see real **Eskimo culture** without leaving the comforts of jet travel and standard hotel rooms behind. Or, if you don't mind giving up some of those comforts, you can get even closer to the Inupiat way of life. For adventurous outdoors people, Kotzebue offers access to huge areas of remote public land through which you can float on a raft or canoe. **Kobuk Valley National Park,** with its bizarre black-sand dunes, **Noatak National Preserve,** and **Cape Krusenstern National Monument** are among the largest national park units in the country, and among the most sparsely visited.

It's important to realize from the outset, however, that outside of an organized bus tour, there's absolutely nothing to do in Kotzebue. As I was told, "You have to shoot something or burn a lot of gas to have any fun around here." Kotzebue is not set up for independent travelers except those of the most intrepid ilk, and they will most likely use the town as a way to get into the remote public lands. Nome offers more for the independent traveler interested in something in between an organized tour and a wilderness expedition.

The dominant business in town is the **NANA Corporation,** a regional Native corporation representing the roughly 7,000 Inupiat who live in this Northwest Arctic region the size of Indiana. NANA, which stands for Northwest Arctic Native Association, is a successful example of how the 1971 Alaska Native Claims Settlement Act gave the indigenous people control over their own destiny. With huge land and resource holdings and the cash to develop them, NANA is making money for its Inupiat shareholders and providing them with jobs in institutional catering and oil drilling, and at the Red Dog zinc mine near Kotzebue. It's the world's most productive zinc mine and employs about 400 people, half of them Native. More relevant for visitors, NANA also owns the main hotel and tourist businesses in Kotzebue.

ESSENTIALS
GETTING THERE
BY AIR   The only way to Kotzebue is by air. **Alaska Airlines** (☎ 800/426-0333; www.alaskaair.com) has several daily jets from Anchorage and Fairbanks in the summer. You'll pay in the range of $350 to $500 round-trip from Anchorage. They also fly from Kotzebue to Nome. Once in Kotzebue, there are many air-taxis and commuter lines to the outlying villages (more on that below). The cheapest and most convenient way to go to Kotzebue is to take a package offered by **Tour Arctic** and **Alaska Airlines Vacations,** described under "Exploring Kotzebue," below.

GETTING INTO TOWN FROM THE AIRPORT   The main hotel is a 10-minute walk from the airport, but there are taxis available from **Polar Cab** (☎ 907/442-2233). If you're on the Tour Arctic package, buses will pick you up at the plane and deliver you and your luggage to the hotel.

GETTING AROUND
Kotzebue is 26 miles north of the Arctic Circle on the Chukchi Sea. The town, about a mile by 2 miles in size, sits on a low spit of land extending into the shallow Kotzebue Sound. The gravel streets are on a warped grid radiating from **Shore Avenue,** also known as **Front Street,** which runs along the water. Roads extend only a few miles out of town. You can walk pretty much everywhere you need to go.

VISITOR INFORMATION
There is no town visitor center. The National Park Service staffs the **Kotzebue Public Lands Information Center** at Second Avenue and Lake Street (P.O. Box 1029), Kotzebue, AK 99752 (☎ **907/442-3760,** or 907/442-8000 for headquarters; fax 907/442-8316; www.nps.gov/noaa), providing information and displays on the immense area of protected land in the region. Employees will answer questions about the town as well. It's open in summer daily from 8am to 6pm, only sporadically the rest of the year; but the local headquarters of the park service, Fish and Wildlife Service, and Bureau of Land Management are open during normal business hours all year. The Park Service headquarters is in the post office on Shore Avenue, and the other agencies are at 120 Second Avenue.

SPECIAL EVENTS
The **Fourth of July** is something special in Kotzebue. Besides the Independence Day celebration, it's as early as you can count on all the snow being gone.

Fast Facts: Kotzebue

Alcohol Law   The sale of alcohol is illegal in Kotzebue, but possession for personal use is permitted; an election on whether to go totally dry was planned soon after this was written.

Banks   National Bank of Alaska has a branch with an ATM at the corner of Lagoon Street and Second Avenue.

Hospital   The Maniilaq Medical Center, with a 24-hour emergency room, is located at Fifth Avenue and Mission Street (☎ 907/442-3321).

Police   The Kotzebue Police Department (☎ 907/442-3351) or the Alaska State Troopers (☎ 907/442-3222).

Post Office   At Shore Avenue and Tundra Way.

Taxes   The sales tax is 6% and the room tax is $6, totaling 12%.

ATTRACTIONS & ACTIVITIES

There is only one activity in town, and it's part of an organized tour. **Tour Arctic** (☎ 907/442-3441) hosts around 10,000 visitors annually in its cultural and natural-history program, the centerpiece of which is the ✪ **NANA Museum of the Arctic.** For most people, the packages, also sold through **Alaska Airlines Vacations** (☎ 800/468-2248), are the only sensible way to go to Kotzebue. You'll learn about the Arctic and Native culture, but the tour is scripted and there are no spectacular sights on the way. Owned and operated by the Inupiat, the company's guides are real Eskimos who offer commentary for 5 hours while keeping customers comfortable, mostly in buses and indoors. A show at the museum includes children dancing, a blanket toss, and a high-tech slide show about the struggle to save Inupiat culture. The tour also includes a talk and demonstration in a tent about the clothing and survival techniques of the Eskimos. There's also a brief opportunity to walk on the tundra. Independent travelers in town for outdoor activities can attend the hour-long museum program only for $20; shows are timed to match the arrival of flights, at 3 and 6pm. The price is high, but it's the only thing to do in town.

Day trip packages are $365 from Anchorage—less than a full-fare ticket. The same tour with an overnight stay and a day in Nome is $494, double occupancy. You can choose to spend the night in Kotzebue at NANA's Nullagvik Hotel or in Nome at the Nugget Inn (at this writing); choose Kotzebue. Any of those visits will feel brief, with little time for anything but the structured tours. A 2-night trip, one each in Nome and Kotzebue, is $544, and adds more free time. Adding an excursion to the village of Kiana and a lengthy flightseeing trip over the Northwest Arctic region, including the Kobuk Sand Dunes, requires another night and an additional $350.

GETTING OUTSIDE
NEAR KOTZEBUE

Some rugged and curious travelers may want something a bit less pampered and scripted than the Tour Arctic program. **Arctic Circle Educational Adventures,** P.O. Box 814, Kotzebue, AK 99752 (in winter: 200 W. 34th Ave., Suite 903, Anchorage, AK 99503; ☎ **907/442-3509** in summer, 907/276-0976 in winter; fax 907/274-3738 in winter; fishcamp.org), offers a chance to stay at a camp similar to the fish camps where Native people spend the summer gathering food for the winter—and participate in set-net fishing, fish cutting, food gathering, and other traditional subsistence activities, as well as hiking, town tours, and bird watching. The camp on the beach 4 miles south of town is extremely rustic, and only for people who don't mind using an outhouse or sleeping in a plywood cabin. Elderhostel groups sometimes come for a week. Rates are $150 to $250 a day for the tour activities plus $95 per person per day for lodgings and meals. The season is mid-June to late August.

FLIGHTSEEING   You can get an idea of what Native villages look like and see the **Kobuk Valley National Park,** including the Great Kobuk Sand Dunes, a desertlike area of shifting 100-foot dunes, from the air by buying a round-trip seat on one of the scheduled bush planes that serve the area. **Cape Smythe Air** (☎ **907/442-3020**) charges $160 for its loop that includes Shungnak and Kobuk and overflies the dunes (make sure to tell the pilot what you want to see). For $90 you can fly a shorter, northern loop to Noatak and Kivalina, over the **Cape Krusenstern National Monument.**

INTO THE BUSH

FLOAT TRIPS   There are several remote rivers near Kotzebue with easy self-guided floating for experienced outdoors people. This is a rare chance to get deep into the Arctic on your own. The great Noatak River originates in the Brooks Range and flows 450 miles through America's largest undisturbed wilderness, in the impressive scenery of the Noatak National Preserve. The Selawik, Squirrel, and Kobuk rivers all have long sections of easy water. **Nova Raft and Adventure Tours,** listed in the Anchorage section of chapter 6, and **Equinox Wilderness Expeditions,** listed in chapter 2, both do trips in the area, although not necessarily every year. Expect to pay $2,500 to $3,000 per person, including air travel. Most river running in the region is self-guided. *The Alaska River Guide,* by Karen Jettmar, director of Equinox, published by Alaska Northwest Books (☎ **800/452-3032**), provides detailed guidance. Obviously, you should be experienced in the outdoors and in floating before heading out for a multiday trip in the Arctic. And plan ahead, arranging details well in advance with the park service and your pilot. Most visitors bring all their gear from Anchorage, but Buck Maxxon, of **Arctic Air Guides Flying Service,** P.O. Box 94, Kotzebue, AK 99752 (☎ **907/442-3030**), rents rafts and canoes for $35 a day. An experienced bush pilot, he also will fly you out; how much you pay depends on where you go, but charter rates are typically $300 an hour. You can minimize your costs by putting in or taking out at villages along the river and using scheduled air services.

JET BOATS   Lorry and Nellie Schuerch, of the village of Kiana, will take you up the Kobuk River in an enclosed, high-powered jet boat. You can visit the dunes and likely see a lot of birds and wildlife. The day trip is $300 per person. Their **Kobuk River Jets,** P.O. Box 89, Kiana, AK 99749 (☎ **907/475-2259**), also offers fishing charters for sheefish and other species, and they own the Kiana Lodge, where rooms with private bathrooms are $175 per person, with all meals.

ACCOMMODATIONS & DINING

Other than the hotel restaurant described below, dining options in Kotzebue are limited. **Mario's Pizza and Deli,** at 606 Bison St. (☎ **907/442-2666**), is a Japanese-Chinese-pizza-burger take-out place, and serves sushi. The price range is $5.25 to $12, and they don't take credit cards.

Nullagvik Hotel. Shore Ave. and Tundra Way (P.O. Box 336), Kotzebue, AK 99752. ☎ **907/442-3331.** Fax 907/442-3340. 73 units. TV TEL. $125 double. AE, DC, MC, V.

The NANA-owned hotel is thoughtfully designed and comfortably furnished. The rooms are large and up-to-date, have tables and chairs and two queen-size beds, and have windows that angle out from the building so that all get at least some ocean view. It can be startling to see Eskimo women wearing summer parkas called kuspuks cleaning in the halls. By booking with an Alaska Airlines Vacations package, you save considerable money on stays here.

The **restaurant** is clean and nicely decorated, and has a good view and excellent service—a combination found nowhere else in Kotzebue. Reindeer steak and Arctic salmon are on the menu for the tourists. Locals are more likely to order the less expensive sandwiches and beef.

9 Barrow: Way North

The main reason visitors go to Barrow is its latitude. The Inupiat town is the north-ernmost settlement on the North American continent, above the 71st parallel. Here half-liquid land comes to an arbitrary point at the north tip of Alaska. The tundra around Barrow is dotted with lakes divided by tendrils of swampy tundra no more substantial than the edges of fine lace. On this haven for migratory waterfowl, the flat, wet land and the ocean seem to merge. Indeed, for all but a few months, it's all a flat, frozen plain of ocean and land. For 65 days in the winter, the sun never rises. In the summer, it doesn't set, and the ice recedes from the shore only for the months of the brief summer. Such extreme geography is a strong attractor—people want to stand in such a place, perhaps dip a toe in the Arctic Ocean.

And then what do you do next? If you're on a package trip, you can see an Eskimo blanket toss and dancing, look at whale bones and maybe buy Native crafts, and see a few other manifestations of traditional Inupiat life amid a modern, oil-enriched town. An **Inupiat Heritage Center,** completed in 1999, exhibits and teaches about the cul-ture. Barrow is an ancient place: There are mounds right in town where prehistoric Eskimo houses stood, now the sites of major archaeological digs. But there's no need to spend the night if your only interest is sightseeing. You can do it in a day and be back in Fairbanks or Anchorage in the evening.

The village of 4,000 is culturally unique. It's ancient, and still a center of **whaling** from open boats, with a summer festival celebrating a successful hunt and distribution of the meat to the community. But Barrow also is the seat of the North Slope Bor-ough, a county government encompassing a larger area than the state of Nebraska, in which lies North America's largest oil field. The borough has everything money can buy for a local government, yet the people of the villages still must contend with crushing ice, snooping polar bears, and utter isolation.

ESSENTIALS

GETTING THERE

BY AIR   Alaska Airlines (☎ 800/426-0333; www.alaskaair.com) flies to Barrow daily from Anchorage and Fairbanks, and offers 1-day and overnight tour packages, described below. The packages are a good deal, competitive with round-trip tickets alone from Anchorage in the area of over $400, with advance purchase and restric-tions. Book them through **Alaska Airlines Vacations** (☎ 800/468-2248).

The airport is walking distance to much of the town.

GETTING AROUND

Facing on the Chukchi Sea, Barrow has two sections, lying on each side of Isatkoak Lagoon. **Browerville,** to the east, has the Inupiat Heritage Center and the Alaska Commercial store, with a food court and many services. **Barrow,** containing the offices and most businesses, is to the west. There is a **car-rental agency,** but not much of anywhere to drive. The northern tip of Alaska, **Point Barrow,** is north of the town on a spit. The road leads 6 miles in that direction to a point tour companies advertise as the "farthest north point navigable by bus," but the absolute end is farther out, beyond the road. **All-terrain vehicles** are for rent in town, if you're going to be com-pulsive about it. Gas Field Road is the only other route out of town, leading 10 miles out onto the tundra.

BY TAXI   Taxi's are handy, charging a flat $5 anywhere in town, plus $1 for each additional passenger. **Polar Taxi** (☎ **907/852-2227**) is one cab service.

BY BUS   Barrow has an extraordinary bus system. The exact location of the buses is broadcast on TV so riders can step right out the door without waiting; this saves them from standing in -40° weather in the company of polar bears. The fare is $1.

BY BIKE   Jim Vordestrasse (☎ **907/852-5211**) does bicycle rentals and tours.

BY TOUR   The main tour business in town is **Tundra Tours,** P.O. Box 189, Barrow, AK 99723 (☎ **800/882-8478** or 907/852-3900), which, with the Top of the World Hotel, is owned by the Arctic Slope Regional Corp., a Native corporation covering the region. Their tour is described below and is the same one sold through Alaska Airlines Vacations.

Visitor Information

A chamber of commerce **visitor center,** at Momegana and Ahkovak streets, near the airport, operates in the summer only, with a guide to talk to but little else. The **North Slope Borough Public Information Division,** P.O. Box 69, Barrow, AK 99723 (☎ **907/852-0215**), produces printed information about the area. On the Web, a firm called **Touch Alaska** (☎ **907/852-2236,** www.touch-alaska.com) is based in Barrow, and also produces printed visitor information.

Special Events

If the traditional bowhead whaling season has been a success, the **Nalukataq festival** in late June celebrates the event. The length of the celebration depends on the number of whales landed. Captains who land the behemoths from their open boats are held in high honor. If you're very lucky, as I was recently, you'll be there when a whale is landed, pulled up on the town beach, and butchered by the community. For another side of the community, try to catch a **softball game.** The town is mad for the games, which are often broadcast on the radio, but the short season and Arctic climate make for unusual conditions. Spectators watch from their cars, and if a ball disappears completely from sight in a puddle, runners can advance no more than two bases.

Fast Facts: Barrow

Banks   There is a bank at Agvik and Kiogak streets. An ATM is located in Browerville at the Stuaqpaq Alaska Commercial general store, inside the front door.

Hospital   On Agvik Street (☎ 907/852-4611).

Police   The borough Department of Public Safety is at ☎ 907/852-6111.

Taxes   Thanks to all that oil, there is no sales or bed tax in Barrow.

ATTRACTIONS & ACTIVITIES

For most people, it makes most sense to visit Barrow on a package because the Native cultural demonstrations are staged for the tours, and otherwise there's not much to do. Birders and outdoors people, however, may enjoy coming just to see an alien landscape and see rarely encountered birds. Also consider Kotzebue and Nome for those activities.

The new ✪ **Inupiat Heritage Center** is the town's main attraction. Completed in 1999, it is part museum, part gathering center, and part venue for living culture.

Inside is a workshop for craftsmen and a performance space for storytellers and dancers—there's a gift shop to buy the artists' output. In the museum area, the Smithsonian will exhibit its Inupiat artifacts, and you can see items recovered from the "Frozen Family," a precontact home that was found, with its occupants, in the permafrost near Barrow. If you have time, you can even join **classes** on skin sewing, carving, kayak building, or learn to speak Inupiaq. The center is open Monday through Friday 9am to 6pm, Saturday noon to 6pm, except during the midday Tundra Tours cultural show (see below). Admission is $5 adults, $2 ages 15 to 17, $1 ages 6 to 14, and free under age 6 or over age 55.

The Native-owned **Tundra Tours** (see listing under "Getting Around," above) does a competent job of presenting the town to visitors who arrive with little idea of what to expect. The tour, in a small bus, drives around the town to show off the modest sights, including the school, an Eskimo boat, the cemetery, a stop for a dip of toes in the Arctic Ocean at the farthest north point, and so on. It's interesting to drive one of the short roads out of town to find snowy owls and Arctic fox. The owls stand still out on the flat tundra like bowling pins. The tour visits the new Inupiat Heritage Center for a blanket toss and cultural presentation, with a drumming and dance performance, and a chance to buy gifts from local craftspeople. If you're choosing which town to visit, the Barrow tour has the advantage of the farthest north point, but lacks the depth and thought of the Kotzebue tour.

The day trip tour is $395, including airfare from Fairbanks, or $438 (double occupancy) to spend 1 night in Barrow at the Top of the World Hotel, giving you a chance to walk around a bit on your own. Book the tour through Alaska Airlines Vacations or with Tundra Tours at the numbers listed above. If you buy the tour separately, it's $58.

ACCOMMODATIONS

Barrow Airport Inn. 1815 Momegana St. (P.O. Box 933), Barrow, AK 99723 ☎ **907/852-2525.** Fax 907/852-2316. 16 units. TV TEL. $125 double. Additional person in room $10 extra. AE, DISC, MC, V.

These relatively economical rooms in a small, well-worn, family-operated establishment are nonetheless clean and come with at least microwave ovens and small refrigerators; nine have full kitchens.

King Eider Inn. 1752 Ahkovak St. (P.O. Box 1283), Barrow, AK 99723. ☎ **907/852-4700.** Fax 907/852-2025. E-mail: eider@barrow.com. 19 units. TV TEL. Summer $185 double. Winter $160 double. Additional person in room $20 extra. AE, MC, V.

The best rooms in town are found in this new building near the airport. With the large stone fireplace in the lobby and large seating area, it feels like a lodge. The rooms are fresh and attractive; nine have kitchenettes, stocked with microwave popcorn. There's a sauna on-site, and they'll pick you up at the airport.

Top of the World Hotel. 1200 Agvik St. (P.O. Box 189), Barrow, AK 99723. ☎ **907/852-3900.** Fax 907/852-6752. 43 units. TV TEL. Summer $179–$189 double; additional person in room $40 extra. Winter $145–$155 double; additional person in room $15 extra. AE, DC, DISC, MC, V.

This is the main hotel in town, where passengers on the packages usually stay—although for a considerably a lower rate. The lobby is decorated with a mounted polar bear and Native art, but the rooms, while clean, are simply standard, some feeling a bit cramped with low ceilings. They have either a double and twin bed or a queen-size bed; each has a fridge. Those on the ocean side rent for $10 more.

DINING

There are several decent restaurants in Barrow. Generally, they stay open very late, have TVs always on, offer free delivery, and don't offer decaffeinated coffee—I have no idea why.

Adjoining the Top of the World Hotel, **Pepe's North of the Border,** at 1204 Agvik St. (☎ **907/852-8200**), is the most famous place in town, serving large portions of familiar American-style Mexican food. The tours come here for lunch, and host Fran Tate hands out souvenirs. We found better food at **Arctic Pizza,** at 125 Apayauk St. (☎ **907/852-4222**). It's a regular pizzeria downstairs and a white-tablecloth Italian and steak/seafood place upstairs, with a gorgeous view of the Arctic Ocean and children are forbidden—they can stay downstairs and have pizza. The charbroiled halibut was excellent, and a bargain at $15.50. You'll find a menu with something for everyone in a fine dining atmosphere at **Northern Lights Restaurant,** at 5122 Herman St. (☎ **907/852-3300**). **Teriyaki House,** 1906 Takpuk St. (☎ **907/852-2276**), serves good Japanese, Chinese, and Korean food in a well-worn dining room.

For a light lunch, go to **Polar Haven Coffee Company,** on the water downtown at 980 Stevenson St. (☎ **907/852-BEAN**), a slice of Seattle in the Arctic.

10 Prudhoe Bay: Arctic Industry

The Prudhoe (*prew*-dough) Bay complex is no ordinary oil field: It's a historic and strategic site of great importance and a great technological achievement. It was built the way you'd have to build an oil field on the moon, with massively complex machinery able to operate in winters that are always dark and very, very cold. But in some ways, it might be simpler to build on the moon—here, the industry has to coexist with a fragile habitat for migrating caribou and waterfowl, on wet, fragile tundra that permanently shows any mark made by vehicles. It works, and that's quite an achievement. Workers are forbidden even to set foot on the tundra, and as you look from the edge of one of the gravel pads the heathery ground looks as undisturbed as a calm sea.

To see Prudhoe Bay, you have to sign up for a tour. Everything is behind chain-link fences and security checkpoints. The tour visits the Arctic Ocean and gives you a chance to see the tundra and touch the pipeline, but it doesn't go inside any of the buildings where the heavy-duty, high-tech equipment handles the oil and readies it for passage down the line. From the outside, these buildings and the oil wells don't look like much—just metal-sided industrial buildings. The grim town of **Deadhorse,** which serves the oil facility, is really more of an industrial yard, barely deserving to be called a town; it certainly isn't anything you'd travel to see. Frankly, I can't recommend taking the time and expense required for a Prudhoe Tour. If you're curious about the Arctic, a trip to Barrow, Kotzebue, or Nome makes more sense. (The oil companies' VIP tours, which do go inside, are fascinating, but you have to be a VIP.)

If you want to go, fly up from Fairbanks or Anchorage for the day and take the tour from Deadhorse. There's no need to spend the night if you fly, as the tour takes less than 3 hours and there's nothing else to do and nowhere else to go. Or, if you drive up on the Dalton Highway, you can engage a tour in Deadhorse, or just get a lift to the water, through the oil complex. See chapter 9, on the Interior, for information on driving the Dalton. **Alaska Airlines** (☎ **800/426-0333**) flies frequently to Prudhoe Bay. A round-trip ticket costs $550 to $750 from Anchorage. You can save money on a bus/air package, described below.

Once at Prudhoe, by whatever means, the **Arctic Caribou Inn,** P.O. Box 340112, Prudhoe Bay, AK 99734 (☎ **907/659-2368** in summer or 907/659-2840 in winter), provides visitor services, including a hotel and cafeteria, plus tours and a shuttle service to the Arctic Ocean. The 96-room hotel has accommodations starting at $95 double; rooms may not be available on Tuesday, Thursday, Saturday, and Sunday, when package tours come through (and they cost $10 more if they are). The hotel is near the airport in Deadhorse and serves as the starting point for the tours. The restaurant has a buffet for three meals a day. The hotel operates a tour to the oil complex, which costs $50; including a video, the tour lasts 2½ hours. It doesn't go inside any of the buildings, but does stop at the shore of the Arctic Ocean. The 1½-hour round-trip just to touch the ocean costs $25.

Gray Line of Alaska (☎ **800/544-2206,** or 907/277-5581 in Anchorage) operates summer trips from Fairbanks that fly one-way and drive the other over the Dalton Highway in buses. The 3-day, 2-night trip costs $775, and can be added to a longer tour or a cruise. Other tour companies offer similar services.

Appendix:
Alaska in Depth

An old photo album opens, breathing a scent of dust and dried glue. Inside, pale images speak wanly of shrunken mountains and glaciers, a huge blue sky, water and trees, a moose standing way off in the background. No family photographer can resist the drive to capture Alaska's vastness in the little box of a camera, and none, it seems, has ever managed it. Then, turning the page, there it is—not in another picture of the landscape, but reflected in a small face at the bottom of the frame: my own face, as a child. For anyone who hasn't experienced that moment, the expression is merely enigmatic—slightly dazed, happy but abstracted, as if hearing a far-off tone. But if you've been to Alaska, that photograph captures something familiar: It's an image of discovery. I've seen it on the fresh, pale faces in photographs stamped with the dates of my family's first explorations of Alaska more than 30 years ago. And then, researching this book, I got to see it once again, on my own young son's face. And I knew that, like me, he had discovered something important.

So what am I talking about? Like anything worth experiencing, it's not simple to explain. But I'll try. And, with luck, you'll know much better after you've been to Alaska.

Tour guides try to get it across with statistics. Not much hope of that, although some of the numbers do give you a general idea of scale. Once you've driven across the continental United States and know how big that is, seeing a map of Alaska placed on top of the area you crossed, just about spanning it, provides some notion of size. Alaskans always like to threaten that we'll split in half and make Texas the third-largest state. Alaska has about 600,000 residents. If you placed each of them an equal distance apart, no one would be closer than a mile to anyone else. Of course, that couldn't happen. No one has ever been to some parts of Alaska.

But none of that expresses what really matters. It's not just a matter of how big Alaska is or how few people it contains. It's not an intellectual conception at all. None of that crosses your mind when you see a chunk of ice the size of a building fall from a glacier and send up a huge splash and wave surging outward. Or when you hike for a couple of days to stand on top of a mountain, and from there see more mountaintops, layered off as far as the horizon, in unnamed, seemingly infinite multiplicity. A realization of what Alaska means can come in a simple little moment. It can come at the end of a long day driving an Interior Alaska highway, as your car climbs into yet another mountain range, the sun still hanging high in what should be night, storm systems arranged before you across the landscape, when you realize that you haven't seen another car in an hour. Or standing on an Arctic Ocean beach, it could happen when you look around at the sea of empty tundra behind you, the sea of green water before you, and your own place on what seems to be the edge of the world. Or you might simply be sitting on the sun-warmed rocks of a beach in southeast or southcentral Alaska when you discover that you're occupying only one of many worlds—a world of intermediate size, lying in magnitude between the tiny tide-pool universes of life all around you and the larger world seen by an eagle gliding through the air high above.

What's the soul alchemy of such a moment? I suppose it's different for each person, but for me it has something to do with realizing my actual size in the world, how I fit in, what it means to be just another medium-sized mammal, no longer armed with the illusions supplied by civilization. On returning to the city from the wilderness, there's a re-entry process, like walking from a vivid movie to the mundane, gray street outside—it's the movie that seems more real. For a while, it's hard to take human institutions seriously after you've been deep into Alaska.

Some people never do step back across that boundary. They live their lives out in the wilderness, away from people. Others compromise, living in Alaskan cities and walking out into the mountains when they can, the rest of the time just maintaining a prickly notion of their own independence. But anyone can make the same discovery, if he or she has the courage to come to Alaska and the time to let the place sink in. You don't have to be an outdoors enthusiast or a young person. You only have to be open to wonder and able to slow down long enough to see it. Then, in a quiet moment when you least expect it, things may suddenly seem very clear and all that you left behind oddly irrelevant.

How you find your way back to where you started is your affair.

1 Natural History: Rough Drafts & Erasures

THE SURGING ICE

In 1986, **Hubbard Glacier,** north of Yakutat, suddenly decided to surge forward, cutting off Russell Fjord from the rest of the Pacific Ocean. A group of warm-hearted but ill-advised wildlife lovers set out to save the marine mammals that had been trapped behind the glacier. Catching a dolphin from an inflatable boat isn't that easy—they didn't accomplish much, but they provided a lot of entertainment for the locals. Then the water burst through the dam of ice and the lake became a fjord again, releasing the animals anyway.

Bering Glacier can't decide which way to go. Apparently surging and retreating on a 20-year cycle, it recently reversed course after bulldozing a wetland migratory bird stopover and speedily contracted back up toward the mountains. **Meares Glacier** has plowed through old-growth forest. On the other hand, some glaciers are so stable they gather a layer of dirt where trees and brush grow to maturity. When **Malspina Glacier** retreated, the trees on its back toppled. And on a larger scale, all the land of **Glacier Bay**—mountains, forests, sea floor—is rising 1½ inches a year as it rebounds from the weight of melted glaciers that 100 years ago were a mile thick and 65 miles longer.

Yet these new and erased lands are just small corrections around the margins compared to what the earth has done before in setting down, wiping out, and rewriting the natural history of Alaska. In the last Ice Age, 15,000 years ago, much of what is Alaska today was one huge glacier. At the tops of granite mountains in Southeast Alaska, especially in the northern Lynn Canal, it's possible to see a sort of high-water mark—the highest point the glaciers came in the Ice Age. Even looking from the deck of a boat, thousands of feet below, you can see where mountain shoulders, rounded by the passage of ice, are much smoother than the sharp, craggy peaks just above, which stuck out of that incredible sheet of ice.

Some 7-year-old children worry about the bogeyman or being caught in a house fire. When I was that age, living with my family in Juneau, I learned how Gastineau Channel was formed and then went to see Mendenhall Glacier. I was told how it was really a river of ice, advancing and retreating, and with this knowledge I developed a deeper fear: ice. I was afraid that while I slept, another Ice Age would come and grind away the city of Juneau.

It's possible that a glacier *could* get Juneau—the city fronts on the huge Juneau Ice Field—but there would be at least a few centuries' warning before it hit. Glaciers are essentially just snow that doesn't get a chance to melt. It accumulates at higher altitudes until it gets deep enough to compress into ice and starts oozing down the side of the mountain. When the ice reaches the ocean, or before, the melt and calving of icebergs at the leading edge reaches a point of equilibrium with the snow that's still being added at the top. The glacier stops advancing, becoming a true river of ice, moving a snowflake from the top of the mountain to the bottom in a few hundred years. When conditions change—more snow or colder long-term weather, for example—the glacier gets bigger; that's called advancing, and the opposite is retreating. Sometimes, something strange will happen under the glacier—in the case of Bering Glacier, it started to float on a cushion of water—and it will surge forward, several feet or even dozens of feet a day in extreme cases. But most of the time, the advance or retreat is measured in inches or feet a year.

It took some time to figure out how glaciers work, and the living glaciers of Alaska, like living fossils from the last Ice Age, helped show the way. In the 1830s, scientists in Switzerland started figuring that glaciers must have shaped the valleys when they found huge rocks that obviously had moved miles from where they had once been a part of similar bedrock—called glacier ertatics. **John Muir,** the famous writer and naturalist, suggested in the 1870s that the granite mountains of Yosemite National Park had been rounded and polished by the passing of glaciers that melted long ago. He traveled to Alaska to prove it. Here, the land was still being carved by glaciers that had never finished melting at the end of the last glacial period, and he could see the shapes like those at Yosemite in the act of being created. Glacier Bay, which Muir "discovered" when guided there by his Alaska Native friends, was a glacial work in progress, as it is still today. When you visit, you'll see for yourself how the heavy blue ice and white snow are streaked with black rock and dust, called **morraine,** that was obviously gouged from mountains and left in hills at the glacial face. At Exit Glacier in Kenai Fjords National Park, you can stand on a morraine that wraps the leading edge of the glacier like a scarf, and feel the cold streaming off spires of clicking ice—it feels like standing in front of a freezer with the door open. Find another hill like that, no matter where it is, and you can be pretty sure a glacier once came that way. Likewise, you can see today's glaciers scooping out U-shaped valleys in the mountains. Fjords and valleys all over Alaska in those same shapes surely were made by the glaciers of the 50 ice ages that have covered North America in the last few million years.

Today, Alaska's 100,000 glaciers cover about 5% of its land mass, mostly on the southern coast. There are no glaciers in the Arctic because the climate there is too dry to produce enough snow. The northernmost large glaciers are in the Alaska Range, such as those carving great chasms in the side of Mt. McKinley.

The **Kahiltna Glacier** flows 45 miles from the mountain, losing 15,000 feet downhill over its course. The mountain's height creates its own weather, wringing moisture out of the atmosphere and feeding its glaciers. Will global warming shrink Alaska's glaciers? No one knows for sure, but it could make some larger if a change in climate brings greater precipitation.

THE TREMBLING EARTH

Despite my early glacier phobia, I never had a similar fear of earthquakes. Living in Anchorage, I'd been through enough of them that, as early as I can remember, I generally didn't bother to get out of bed when they hit.

It's all part of living in a place that isn't quite done yet. Any part of Alaska could have an earthquake, but the Pacific Rim from Southcentral Alaska to the Aleutians is the shakiest. That's because this is where Alaska is still under construction. The very rocks that make up the state are something of an ad hoc conglomeration, still in the process of being assembled. The floor of the Pacific Ocean is moving north, and as it moves, it is carrying islands and mountains along with it. When they hit the Alaska plate, these pieces of land, called **terranes,** dock like ships arriving, but very slowly—an island moving an inch a year takes a long time to travel thousands of miles. Geologists studying rocks near Mount McKinley have found a terrane that used to be tropical islands. In Kenai Fjords National Park, fossils have turned up that are otherwise found only in Afghanistan and China. The slowly moving crust of the earth brought them here on a terrane that makes up a large part of the south coast of Alaska.

Here's how it works. Near the center of the Pacific, underwater volcanoes and cracks that constantly ooze molten new rock are adding to the tectonic plate that forms the ocean floor. As it grows from the middle, the existing sea floor spreads, at perhaps an inch a year. At the other side of the Pacific plate, where it bumps up against Alaska, there's not enough room, so the crust bends and cracks as it's forced downward into the planet's great, molten recycling mill of magma. Land masses that are along for the ride smash into the continent that's already there. When one hits—the so-called Yakutat block is still in the process of docking—a mountain range gets shoved up. Earthquakes and volcanoes are a byproduct.

Living in such an unsettled land is a matter of more than abstract interest. The Mount Spurr volcano, which erupted most recently in 1992, turned day to night in Anchorage, dropping a blanket of ash all over the region, choking lungs and machines. A Boeing 747 full of passengers flew into the plume and lost power in all its engines, falling in darkness for several minutes before pilots were able to restart the clogged jets. After that incident, the airport was closed until aviation authorities could find a way to keep volcanic plumes and planes apart. More than 80 volcanoes have been active in Alaska in the last 200 years. Earthquakes over 7 on the Richter scale—larger than the 1994 Los Angeles quake—have occurred every 15 months, on average, over the last century. The worst of the quakes, on March 27, 1964, was the strongest ever to hit North America. It ranked 9.2 on the Richter scale, lowering an entire region of the state some 10 feet and moving it even farther laterally. No other earthquake has ever moved so much land.

There are lots of tales about what people did when the quake hit—it lasted a good 10 minutes, long enough for a lot to happen. My wife, Barbara, a 1-year-old at the time, is said to have found it hilariously funny while everyone else ran around in panic. A family friend rushed out into the street from bathing, stark naked; a neighbor who had been doing laundry when the earth started shaking met him there and handed him a pair of socks she had happened to carry with her.

The earthquake destroyed much of Anchorage and several smaller towns, and killed more than 131 people, mostly in sea waves created by underwater landslides. In Valdez, the waterfront was swept clean of people. In the Prince William Sound village of Chenega, built on a hill along the water, people started running for higher ground when the wave came. About half made it. Families were divided by just yards between those who ran fast enough and those who were caught by the water and disappeared. But the earthquake could have been much worse—it occurred in the early evening, on Good Friday, when most public buildings were empty. An elementary school in Anchorage that broke in half and fell into a hole didn't have anyone inside at the time.

But even that huge earthquake wasn't an unusual occurrence, at least in the earth's terms. Geologists believe the same Alaska coast sank six feet in an earthquake in the year 1090. Big earthquakes happen every year in Alaska, but so few people live here that most earthquakes don't bother anyone. The earth's crust is paper thin compared to the globe's forces, and, like paper, it is folding where the two edges meet. At the edge, Alaska's coast is bending down; and farther inshore, where McKinley stands, it is bowing up. The steep little rock islands you see flocking with birds at Kenai Fjords National Park are old mountain tops; the monolith of McKinley a brand new one.

THE FROZEN TUNDRA

The Interior and Arctic parts of the state are less susceptible to earthquakes and, since they receive little precipitation, they don't have glaciers, either. But there's still a sense of living on a land that's not quite sure of itself, as most of northern Alaska is solid only by virtue of being frozen. When it thaws, it turns to mush. The phenomenon is caused by **permafrost,** a layer of earth a little below the surface that never thaws—or at least, you'd better hope it doesn't. Buildings erected on permafrost without some mechanism for dispersing their own heat—pilings, or even refrigerator coils—thaw the ground below and sink into a self-made quicksand. You occasionally run across such structures. There's one in Dawson City, Yukon Territory, still left from the gold rush, that leans at an alarming angle with thresholds and lower tiers of siding disappearing into the ground.

Building sewer and water systems in such conditions is a challenge still unmet in much of Alaska's Bush, where village toilets are often "honey buckets" and the septic systems are sewage lagoons on the edge of town where the buckets are dumped. Disease caused by the unsanitary conditions sweeps the villages as if rural Alaska were a Third World country, but the government has been slow to provide the funds required to solve the problem.

Permafrost makes the land do other strange things. On a steep slope, the thawed earth on top of the ice can begin to slowly slide downhill like a blanket over a pile of pillows, setting the trees at crazy angles. These groves of black spruce—the only conifer that grows on this kind of ground—are called **drunken forests,** and you can see them in Denali National Park and elsewhere in the Interior. Permafrost also can create weird ground sometimes called **muskeg,** where shaky tussocks the size of basketballs sit a foot or two apart on a wet, muddy flat. From a distance it looks smooth, but walking on real basketballs would be easier.

The Arctic and much of the Interior are a sort of swampy desert. Most of the time, the tundra is frozen in white; snow blows around, but not much falls.

That snow melts in the summer and the water stands on the surface, on top of the permafrost, creating ponds—Alaska also is a land of 10 million lakes, with 3 million larger than 20 acres. Migratory birds arrive to feed and paddle around those shallow circles of deep green and sky blue. Flying over the Arctic in a small plane is disorienting, for no pattern maintains in the flat green tundra, and irregularly shaped patches of water stretch as far as the eye can see. Pilots find their way by following landmarks like tractor tracks etched into the tundra. Although few and far between, the tracks remain clearly delineated for decades after they're made, appearing as a pair of narrow, parallel ponds reaching from one horizon to the other.

The permafrost also preserves much older things. The meat of prehistoric mastodons, still intact, has been unearthed from the frozen ground. On the Arctic Coast, the sea eroded ground near Barrow that contained ancient ancestors of the Eskimos who still inhabit the same neighborhood. In 1982, they found a family that apparently was crushed by sea ice up to 500 years ago. Two of the bodies were well preserved, sitting in the home they had occupied and wearing the clothes they had worn the day of the disaster, perhaps around the same time Columbus was sailing to America.

Sea ice is the frozen ocean that extends from northern Alaska to the other side of the world. At the very top of the world it never thaws, but the water opens for a few months of summer along the shore. Then, in September, when the ocean water falls below 29°F, ice forms along the beach and expands from the North Pole's permanent ice pack until the two sides meet. The clash of huge ice floes creates towering pressure ridges, small mountains of steep ice that are difficult to cross. The Eskimo blanket toss—the game of placing a person in the center of a walrus-skin blanket and bouncing him or her high in the air—traditionally got hunters high enough to see over the pressure ridges so they could spot game. At its extreme, in March, the ice extends solidly all the way south to the Pribilof Islands, when it's possible to drive a dog team across the Bering Sea to Siberia. The National Weather Service keeps track of the ice pack and issues predictions you can find on the Internet (www.alaska.net/~nwsar). Crab boats like to tempt its south-moving edge in the fall and shippers look for the right moment in the summer to venture north with barges of fuel and other supplies for the coast of the Arctic Ocean—they barely have time to get there and back before the ice closes in again in the fall. Ice even interferes with shipping in Cook Inlet, around Anchorage, although the floes never form a solid pack. Walking on the downtown coastal trail, you can hear their eerie crunch and squeal as they tumble together in the fast tidal currents.

The Arctic and Interior are relatively barren biologically compared to the southern coastal areas of the state. Polar bears wander the Arctic ice pack, but they, like the Eskimos, feed more on marine mammals than on anything found on the shore. A 1,200-pound adult polar bear can make a meal of a walrus, and they're expert at hunting seal. In the summer, huge herds of caribou come north to their eastern Arctic calving grounds, but they migrate south when the cold, dark winter falls unremittingly on the region.

In Barrow, the sun doesn't rise for more than 65 days in the winter. In February, the average daily high temperature is -12°F, and the average low is -24°F. The Inupiat people learned to survive in this climate for millennia, but life was short and terribly hard. Today, they've made some sensible allowances while holding onto many cultural traditions. For example, the school in Barrow has wide, light hallways and a large indoor playground.

THE RAIN FOREST

By comparison, southern coastal Alaska is warm and biologically rich. Temperate rain forest ranges up the coast from Southeast Alaska into Prince William Sound, with bears, deer, moose, wolves, and even big cats living among the massive western hemlock, Sitka spruce, and cedar. This old-growth forest, too wet to burn in forest fires, is the last vestige of the virgin, primeval woods that seemed so limitless to the first white settlers who arrived on the east coast of the continent in the 17th century. The trees grow on and on, sometimes rising more than 200 feet high, with diameters of 10 feet, and falling only after hundreds of years. The trunks rot on the damp moss of the forest floor and return to soil to feed more trees, which grow in rows upon their nursery trunks.

Standing among these giants, one feels dwarfed by their age and size, living things of so much greater life span and magnitude than any person. Part of the mystery and grandeur also comes from the knowledge that, here at least, Alaska *does* seem permanent. That sense helps explain why cutting the rain forest is so controversial. Just one of these trees contains thousands of dollars worth of wood, a prize that drives logging as voraciously as the federal government, which owns most of the coastal forest, may choose to allow.

The rivers of the great coastal forests bring home runs of big **salmon,** clogging in spawning season like a busy sidewalk at rush hour. The fish spawn only once, returning by a precisely tuned sense of smell to the streams where they were hatched as many as 7 years before. When the fertilized eggs have been left in the stream gravel, the fish often conveniently die on the beach, making a smorgasbord for bears and other forest animals. The huge **Kodiak brown bear,** topping 1,000 pounds, owes everything to the millions of salmon that return to the island each summer. By comparison, the grizzly bears of the Interior—the same species as browns, but living on berries and an occasional ground squirrel—are mere midgets, their weight counted in the hundreds of pounds. Forest-dwelling black bears grow to only a few hundred pounds.

TAIGA & FIRE

But rain forest covers only a small fraction of Alaska. In fact, only a third of Alaska is forested at all, and most of this is the boreal forest that covers the central part of the state, behind the rain-shadow of coastal mountains that intercept moist clouds off the oceans. Ranging from the Kenai Peninsula, south of Anchorage, to the Brooks Range, where the Arctic begins, this is a taiga—a moist, subarctic forest of smaller, slower-growing, hardier trees. In well-drained areas, on hillsides and southern land less susceptible to permafrost, the boreal forest is a lovely, broadly spaced combination of straight, proud white spruce and pale, spectral paper birch. Along the rivers, poplar and cottonwood grow, with deep-grained bark and branches that spread in an oaklike matrix—if they could speak, it would be as wise old men. Where it's wet and swampy—over more and more land as you go north—all that will grow is low, brushy willow and the glum black spruce, which struggles to become a gnarled stick a mere three inches thick in 100 years, if it doesn't burn first. As the elevation grows, the spruce shrink, turning into weirdly bent ancient shrubs just before the tree line and the open alpine tundra.

Forest fires tear through as much as a million acres of Alaska's boreal forest each summer. In most cases, forest managers do no more than note the occurrence on a map. Unlike the rain forest, there's little commercially valuable timber in these thin stands, and, anyway, it isn't possible to halt the process of nature's self-immolation over the broad expanse of Alaska. The boreal forest regenerates through fire—it was made to burn. The wildlife that lives in and eats it needs new growth from the burns as well as the shelter of older trees. When the forest is healthiest and most productive, the dark green of the spruce is broken by streaks and patches of light-green brush in an ever-changing succession.

This is the land of the **moose.** They're as big as a large horse, with a long, bulbous nose and huge eyes that seem to know, somehow, just how ugly they are. Their flanks look like a worn-out shag carpet draped over a sawhorse. But moose are survivors. They thrive in land that no one else wants. In the summer, they wade out into the swampy tundra ponds to eat green muck. In the winter, they like nothing better than an old burn, where summer lightning has peeled back the forest and allowed a tangle of willows to grow—a moose's all-time favorite food. Eaten by wolves, hunted and run over by man, stranded in the snows of a hard winter, the moose always come back. In the summer, the moose disperse and are not easily seen in thick vegetation. In the winter, they gather where walking is easy, along roads and in lowlands where people also like to live. Encounters happen often in the city, until you begin to take the moose for granted. Then, skiing on a Nordic trail one day, you round a corner and come face to face with an animal that stands 2 feet over you. You can smell the beast's foul scent and see his stress, the ears pulled back on the head and the whites of the eyes showing, and you know that this wild creature, fighting to live till summer, could easily kill you.

THE LIGHT & THE DARKNESS

There's no escaping the stress of winter in Alaska—not for moose or people— or the exhilaration of the summer. In the summer in Alaska, it never really gets dark at night. In Fairbanks in June, the sun sets in the north around midnight, but it doesn't go down far enough for real darkness to settle, instead rising again two hours later. It's always light enough to keep hiking or fishing, and, in clear weather, always light enough to read by. You may not see the stars from early May until sometime in August (the climate chart in chapter 2 gives seasonal daylight for various towns). Visitors have trouble getting used to it: Falling asleep in broad daylight is hard. Alaskans deal with it by staying up late and being active outdoors. In the winter, on the other hand, you forget what the sun looks like. Kids go to school in the dark and come home in the dark. The sun rises in the middle of the morning and sets after lunch. At high noon in December, the sun hangs just above the southern horizon with a weak, orange light, a constant sunset. Animals and people go into hibernation.

As you go north, the change in the length of the days gets bigger. In Ketchikan, the longest day of the year, the June 21 summer solstice, is about 17 hours 20 minutes, in Fairbanks, 22 hours, and in Barrow, the longest day is more than 2 months. In contrast, in Seattle the longest day is 16 hours 15 minutes, and in Los Angeles 14 hours 30 minutes. On the equator, days are always the same length, 12 hours. At the North Pole and South Pole, the sun is up half the year and down the other half.

The best way to understand this is to model it with a ball and a lamp. The earth spins once a day around the North and South poles, on its axis. When the axis is upright, one spin of the ball puts light on each point on the ball equally—that's the spring and fall equinox, March 21 and September 21, when the day is 12 hours long everywhere. In the summer, the North Pole leans toward the light and the Northern Hemisphere gets more light than darkness, so during the course of one rotation each northern spot is lighted more than half the time. In winter, the Southern Hemisphere gets its turn, and more than half the Northern Hemisphere is in shadow, meaning shorter days. As you go farther north in winter, the shadow gets larger, and the day in any one spot shorter. But no matter how the axis leans, the equator is always half light and half dark, like the entire globe as a whole.

In the North, on a long, summer evening, you can almost feel the planet leaning toward the sun. The world exists under an bright, endless dome. In the winter, darkness falls as deep as space, and you can almost feel the earth's warmth wafting away into the universe as the freeze sinks ever harder in the land. Now the rainforest rivers and permafrost lakes are hard ice, the salmon are away at sea, and the bears sleep. The moose and other wintering animals burn their summer store of fat, a finite store of provisions that may or may not last. Up in the mountains, the glaciers are growing.

In the winter of 1997–98, **Lost Lake,** a fish-bearing pond in the mountains of the Kenai Peninsula near Seward, got frozen so thick and buried so deeply in snow that summer ended before the ice went out. The water went a whole year without meeting the air. As I write this, in summer 1999, we wait to see if last winter's heavy snow will melt in time for Lost Lake to reemerge by fall, or if it will spend a second year locked in ice. Like victims of a new ice age, the fish in the lake are dead, but Alaskans are rooting for the lake—its fate has even been covered in the newspaper. In the endless war between winter and summer, we're fighting for the underdog.

2 Politics & History: Living a Frontier Myth

Alaska Timeline

- **Perhaps up to 30,000 years ago** First human explorers arrive in Alaska from Asia.
- **1741** Vitus Bering, on a mission originally chartered by Peter the Great, finds Alaska; ship's surgeon and naturalist Georg Steller goes ashore for a few hours on Kayak Island, the first white to set foot in Alaska.
- **1743** Enslaving the Aleuts, Russian fur traders enter the Aleutian Islands; Aleuts are massacred when they try to revolt—their cultural traditions are eliminated, and over the coming decades they are relocated as far south as California for their hunting skills.
- **1772** Unalaska, in the Aleutian Islands, becomes a permanent Russian settlement.
- **1776–79** British Captain James Cook makes voyages of exploration to Alaska, seeking the Northwest Passage from the Pacific to the Atlantic, and draws charts of the coast.
- **1784** Russians build settlement at Kodiak.

continues

The occupations of prospector, trapper, and homesteader—rugged individualists relying only on themselves in a limitless land—would dominate Alaska's economy if the state's image of itself were accurate. Alaskans talk a lot about the Alaskan spirit of independence, yearn for freedom from government, and declare that people from "Outside" just don't understand us when they insist on locking up Alaska's lands in parks and wilderness status. The bumper sticker says, simply, "We don't give a damn how they do it outside." A state full of self-reliant frontiersmen can't be tied down and deterred from their manifest destiny by a bunch of Washington bureaucrats. At the extreme, there has even been a movement to declare independence as a separate nation so Alaskans could extend the frontier, extracting its natural resources unfettered by bunny-hugging easterners.

But just because you wear a cowboy hat doesn't mean you know how to ride a horse. In Las Vegas you find a lot more hats than horsemen, and Alaska is full of self-reliant frontier pioneers who spend rush hour in traffic jams and worry more about urban drug dealing and air pollution than where to catch their next meal or dig the mother lode. As for self-reliance and independence from government, Alaska has the highest per capita state spending of any state in the nation, with no state income or sales taxes and an annual payment of more than $1,300 a year to every man, woman, and child just for living here.

The state government provides such socialistic benefits as retirement homes and automatic income for the aged; it owns various businesses, including a dairy, a railroad, and a subsidized mortgage lender; it has built schools in the smallest communities, operates a state ferry system and a radio and television network, and owns nearly a third of the land mass of Alaska. And although the oil money that funds state government has been in decline in recent years, forcing the legislature to dig into savings to balance its books, the independent, self-reliant citizens have successfully resisted having to pay any taxes.

That conflict between perception and reality grows out of the story of a century of development of Alaska. The state is a great storehouse of minerals, oil, timber, and fish. A lot of wealth has been extracted, and many people have gotten rich. But it has always been because the federal government let them do it. Every acre of Alaska belonged to the U.S. government from the day Secretary of State William Seward bought Alaska from Russia in 1867. Since then, the frontier has never been broader than Uncle Sam made it.

Yet the whole conception of ownership didn't fit Alaska well from the first. Did the Russians really own what they sold? Alaska Natives didn't think so. They'd been living on this land for hundreds of centuries, and at the time of the purchase, most had never seen a white face. How could Russia hold title to land that no Russian had so much as explored? As Americans flooded into Alaska to search for gold at the turn of the century, and settled on some of the land, this conflict became obvious. Alaska Natives, never conquered by war or treaty, began their legal and political fight to recover their land early in the century—a fight they would eventually win.

The concept of ownership has changed in other ways, too. When the United States bought Alaska and for the next 100 years afterward, the vast majority of the state was public domain—like the Old West of frontier lore, federal land and its surface and hard-rock resources were there for the taking. They belonged to everyone, but only until someone showed up to lay private claim. Today, amid deep conflicts about whether areas should remain natural or be exploited for natural resources, federal control stands out far more clearly than it did during the gold rush, when

- **1799** Russians establish a fort near present-day Sitka, which will later become their capital; Tlingits attack and destroy the fort, but are later driven off in a counterattack; the Russian-America Company receives a 20-year exclusive franchise to govern and exploit Alaska.
- **1821** Russian naval officers are placed in control of Russian-America Company, which begins to decline in profitability.
- **1824** Boundaries roughly matching Alaska's current borders are set by treaty between Russia, Britain, and the United States.
- **1839** The British Hudson's Bay Company, surpassing Russia in trade, begins leasing parts of Southeast Alaska and subsequently extends trading outposts into the Interior.
- **1843** First overtures are made by American officials interested in buying Alaska from the Russians, so U.S. instead of British power could expand there.
- **1867** In need of money and fearful that Russia couldn't hold onto Alaska anyway, Czar Alexander II sells Alaska to the United States; Secretary of State William Seward negotiates the deal for a price of $7.2 million, roughly 2¢ an acre; the American flag is raised in Sitka, and the U.S. military assumes government of Alaska.
- **1870** The Alaska Commercial Company receives a monopoly on harvesting seals in the Pribilof Islands and soon expands across the territory (the company remains a presence in the Alaska Bush today).
- **1879** Naturalist and writer John Muir explores Southeast Alaska by canoe,

continues

discovering Glacier Bay with Native guides.

- **1880** Joe Juneau and Richard Harris, guided by local Natives, find gold on Gastineau Channel and found city of Juneau; gold strikes begin to come every few years across the state.

- **1884** Military rule ends in Alaska, but residents still have no right to elect a legislature, governor, or congressional representative, or to make laws.

- **1885** Christian missionaries meet to divide up the territory, parceling out each region to a different religion; they begin to fan out across Alaska to convert Native peoples, largely suppressing their traditional ways.

- **1897** After prospectors arrive in Seattle with a ton of gold, the Klondike gold rush begins; gold rushes in Nome and Fairbanks follow within a few years; Americans begin to populate Alaska.

- **1906** Alaska's first (non-voting) delegate in Congress takes office; the capital moves from Sitka to Juneau.

- **1908** The Iditarod Trail, a sled dog mail route, is completed, linking trails continuously from Seward to Nome.

- **1913** The first territorial legislature convenes, although it has few powers; the first automobile drives the Richardson Highway route, from Valdez to Fairbanks.

- **1914** Federal construction of the Alaska Railroad begins; the first tents go up in the river bottom that will be Anchorage, along the rail line.

- **1917** Mount McKinley National Park is established.

- **1920** The first flights connect Alaska to the rest

continues

the land's wealth was free to anyone with strength enough to take it. Alaskans who want to keep receiving the good things that government brings today equate the frontier spirit of the past with their own financial well-being, whether that means working at a mining claim or at a desk in a glass office tower. But other Americans feel they own Alaska, too, and they don't necessarily believe in giving it away anymore. They may want the frontier to stay alive in another sense—unconquered and still wild.

White colonization of the territory came in boom-and-bust waves of migrants arriving with the goal of making a quick buck and then clearing out—without worrying about the people who already lived there. Although the gold rush pioneers are celebrated today, the **Klondike rush** of 1898 that opened up and populated the territory was motivated by greed and was a mass importer of crime, inhumanity, and, for the Native people, massive epidemics of new diseases that killed off whole villages. Like the Russians 150 years before, who had made slaves of the Natives, the new white population considered the indigenous people less than human. Segregation was overcome only after World War II. Until Franklin Roosevelt became president, federal policy was to suppress Alaska Native cultures; missionaries forbade Native peoples telling the old stories or even speaking in their own languages. Meanwhile, the salmon that fed the people of the territory were overfished by a powerful, outside-owned canning industry with friends in Washington, D.C. Their abuses destroyed salmon runs. Formerly rich Native villages faced famine when their primary food source was taken away.

It was only with **World War II,** and the Japanese invasion of the Aleutian Islands, that Alaska developed an industry not based on exploitation of natural resources: the military industry. It was another boom. To this day, the federal government remains a key industry whose removal would deal the economy a grievous blow.

The fight for **Alaska statehood** also came after the war. Alaskans argued that they needed local, independent control of natural resources, pointing to the example of over-fishing in the federally managed salmon industry. Opponents said that Alaska would never be able to support itself, always requiring large subsidies from the federal government, and therefore should not be a state. As the advocates pointed out, that lack of self-sufficiency came about because Alaska did not control the resources that it could live on—it was essentially a colony, with decisions and profits taken away by the mother country. If Alaskans could control their own land, they could use the resources to fund government. The discovery of oil on the Swanson River, on the Kenai Peninsula, in 1957, helped tip the balance—here was the kind of real money that could fund a state government—and in 1959, Alaska finally became the 49th state. Along with the rights of entering the union, Alaska received a dowry, an endowment of land to develop and pay for all future government: The Statehood Act, which gave the new state the right to select 103 million acres from the total land mass of 365 million acres. Indeed, that land does pay for state government in Alaska, in the form of oil royalties and taxes—but, to this day, the federal government still spends a lot more in Alaska than it receives.

Oil revenues supported the new state and it began to start extending services to the vast, undeveloped expanse of Alaska. **Anchorage** boomed in the 1960s in a period of buoyant optimism. Leaders believed that the age-old problems of the wide-open frontier—poverty, lack of basic services, impenetrable remoteness—would succumb to the new government and new money, while the land still remained wide open. Then the pace of change redoubled with the discovery of the largest oil field in North America at **Prudhoe Bay** in 1968—land that had been a wise state selection in the federal land-grant entitlement. The state government received as much money in a single oil lease sale auction as it had spent in total for the previous 6 years. This was going to be the boom of all booms.

The oil bonanza on the North Slope would change Alaska more than any other event since the gold rush—change that came in many unexpected ways. Once, opening the frontier had only meant letting a few prospectors scratch the dirt in search of a poke of gold—nothing to make a federal case over. But getting this immense pool of oil to market, from one of the most remote spots on the globe, would require allowing the world's largest companies to build across Alaska a pipeline that, when

of the United States; aviation quickly becomes the most important means of transportation in the territory.

- **1923** Pres. Warren Harding drives final spike on the Alaskan Railroad at Nenana, then dies on the way home, purportedly from eating bad Alaskan seafood.

- **1925** Leonhard Seppala and other dog mushers relay diphtheria serum on the Iditarod Trail to fight an epidemic in Nome; Seppala and his dog, Balto, become national heroes.

- **1934** Federal policy of forced assimilation of Native cultures is officially discarded, and New Deal efforts to preserve Native cultures begin.

- **1935** New Deal "colonists," broke farmers from all over the United States, settle in the Matanuska Valley north of Anchorage.

- **1940** A military buildup begins in Alaska; bases built in Anchorage accelerate city's growth into major population center.

- **1942** Japanese invade Aleutians, taking Attu and Kiska islands and bombing Dutch Harbor/Unalaska (a U.S. counterattack the next year drives out the Japanese); Alaska Highway links Alaska to the rest of the country overland for the first time, but is open to civilians only after the war.

- **1957** Oil is found on Kenai Peninsula's Swanson River.

- **1959** Alaska becomes a state.

- **1964** The largest earthquake ever to strike North America shakes Southcentral Alaska, killing 131 people, primarily in tsunami waves.

- **1968** Oil is found at Prudhoe Bay, on Alaska's North Slope.

continues

- **1970** Environmental lawsuits tie up work to build the Alaska pipeline, which is needed to link the North Slope oil field to markets.
- **1971** Congress acknowledges and pays the federal government's debt to Alaska's indigenous people with the Alaska Native Claims Settlement Act, which transfers 44 million acres of land and almost $1 billion to new Native-owned corporations.
- **1973** The first Iditarod Trail Sled Dog Race runs more than 1,000 miles from Anchorage to Nome.
- **1974** Congress clears away legal barriers to construction of the trans-Alaska pipeline; Vice Pres. Spiro Agnew casts the deciding vote in the U.S. Senate.
- **1977** The trans-Alaska pipeline is completed and begins providing up to 25% of the U.S. domestic supply of oil.
- **1980** Congress sets aside almost a third of Alaska in new parks and other land-conservation units; awash in new oil wealth, the state legislature abolishes all taxes paid by individuals to state government.
- **1982** Alaskans receive their first Alaska Permanent Fund dividends, interest paid on an oil-wealth savings account.
- **1985** Declining oil prices send the Alaska economy into a tailspin; tens of thousands leave the state and most of the banks collapse.
- **1989** The tanker *Exxon Valdez* hits Bligh Reef in Prince William Sound, spilling 11 million gallons of North Slope crude in the worst oil spill ever in North America.
- **1994** A federal jury in Anchorage awards $5 billion

continues

completed, could credibly claim to be the largest privately financed construction project in world history. With the stakes suddenly so much higher, it came time to figure out exactly who owned which parts of Alaska—it couldn't just be public domain any longer. That wouldn't be easy—much of the state had never even been mapped, much less surveyed, and there were some large outstanding claims that had to be settled.

Alaska Natives, who had lost land, culture, and health in 2 centuries of white invasion, finally saw their luck start to turn. It wouldn't be possible to resolve the land issues surrounding the pipeline until their claims to land and compensation were answered. Native leaders cannily used that leverage to assure that they got what they wanted. In the early 1970s, America had a new awareness of the way its first people had been treated in the settlement of the West. When white frontiers expanded, Native traditional homelands were stolen. In Alaska, with the powerful lure of all that oil providing the impetus, Native people were able to insist on a fairer resolution. In 1971, with the support of white Alaskans and the oil companies, Congress passed the **Alaska Native Claims Settlement Act,** called ANCSA, which transferred 44 million acres of land and $962.5 million to corporations whose shareholders were all the Native people of Alaska. The new Native corporations would be able to exploit their own land for their shareholders' profit. In later legislation, Natives also won guaranteed subsistence hunting and fishing rights on federal land. Some Natives complained that they'd received only an eighth of the land they had owned before white contact, but it was still the richest settlement any of the world's indigenous people had received.

It was a political deal on a grand scale. It's unlikely that Natives would have gotten their land at all but for the desire of whites to get at the oil, and their need of Native support. Nor could the pipeline have overcome environmental challenges without the Natives' dropping their objections. Even with Native support in place, legislation authorizing the pipeline passed the U.S. Senate by only one vote, cast by Vice Pres. Spiro Agnew.

But there were other side effects of the deal that white Alaskans didn't like so well. After the Native settlement passed, the state—which still hadn't received a large portion of its land entitlement—and the Native corporations both had a right to select the land they wanted. There still remained the question of who would get what—and of the wild lands that Congress, influenced by a strong new environmental movement, wanted to maintain as national parks and wilderness and not give away. That issue wasn't settled until 1980, when the **Alaska National Interest Lands Conservation Act** passed, setting aside an additional 106 million acres for conservation, an area larger than California. Alaska's frontier-minded population screamed bloody murder over "the lock-up of Alaska," but the act was only the last, tangible step in a process started by the coming of big oil and the need its arrival created to draw lines on the map, tying up the frontier.

to 10,000 fishermen, Natives, and others hurt by the Exxon oil spill; Exxon appeals continue today.

- **1996** Wildfire rips through the Big Lake area, north of Anchorage, destroying 400 buildings.
- **1999** British Petroleum announces it will buy Arco, combining the ownership of more than 70% of Alaska's primary industry into one company.

When construction of the $8 billion pipeline finally got underway in 1974, a huge influx of new people chasing the high-paying jobs put any previous gold rush to shame. The newcomers were from a different part of the country than previously, too. Alaska had been a predominately Democratic state, but oil workers from Texas, Oklahoma, and other Bible-belt states helped shift the balance of Alaska's politics, and now it's solidly Republican. In its frontier days, Alaska had a strong Libertarian streak—on both the liberal and the conservative side—but now it became more influenced by fundamentalist Christian conservatism. A hippie-infested legislature of the early 1970s legalized marijuana for home use. Conservatives at the time, who thought the government shouldn't butt into its citizens' private lives, went along with them. After the pipeline, times changed, and Alaska developed tough antidrug laws.

Growth also brought urban problems, just as it has anywhere else. As the pipeline construction boom waned with completion in 1977, a boom-town atmosphere of gambling and street prostitution went with it, but other big-city problems remained. No longer could residents of Anchorage and Fairbanks go to bed without locking their doors. Both cities were declared "nonattainment" areas by the Environmental Protection Agency because of air pollution near the ground in cold winter weather, when people leave their cars running during the day to keep them from freezing. We got live television but also serial murderers.

But the pipeline seemed to provide limitless wealth to solve the problems. For fear that too much money would be wasted, the voters altered the state constitution to bank a large portion of the new riches; the politicians in Juneau could spend only half the new Permanent Fund's earnings, after paying out half the annual income as dividends to every citizen of the state. The fund now contains over $25 billion in savings and has become one of the largest sectors of the economy simply by virtue of paying out more than $800 million a year in dividends to everyone who lives at least a year in the state. All major state taxes on individuals were canceled, and people got used to receiving everything free from the government.

Then, in 1985, oil prices dropped, deflating the overextended economy like a pin in a balloon. Housing prices crashed, and thousands of people simply walked away from their mortgages. All but a few of the banks in the state went broke. Condominiums that had sold for $100,000 sold for $20,000 or less a year later. It was the bust that always goes with the boom; but even after so many previous examples, it still came as a shock to many. The spending associated with the ***Exxon Valdez*** oil spill in 1989 restarted the economy, and it continued on an even keel for a decade after, but the wealth of the earlier oil years never returned.

Meanwhile, the oil from Prudhoe Bay started running out. Oil revenues, an irreplaceable 85% of the state budget, started an irrevocably downward trend in the early 1990s. The oil companies downsized. Without another boom on the horizon, the question became how to avoid, or at least soften, the next bust. At this writing, that question remains unanswered. The governor and legislature have asked the voters to approve reducing their Permanent Fund dividends to cover a $1 billion budget gap. Conservatives say the state should just cut the budget; liberals say reducing the dividend amounts to a head tax, hitting hardest the poor people who have come to rely on the money for necessities. But a normal, graduated income tax, or even a state sales tax, appears even more unpopular. The disadvantages of individualism have become apparent in a populace that's seemingly incapable of collective sacrifice to pay for its own government.

Culture moves slower than politics or events, and Alaskans still see themselves as those gold rush prospectors or wildcat oil drillers, adventuring in an open land and striking it rich by their own devices. Even as Alaska's economy blends ever more smoothly into the American corporate landscape, Alaskans' myth of themselves remains strong. Today, the state's future is as little in its own hands as it has ever been. There may be more oil in protected wilderness areas on the North Slope, and there certainly is plenty of natural gas that could be exploited. But whether or not to explore those avenues will be decided in corporate board rooms in London and Houston, and in Congress—not in Alaska. Ultimately, an economy based on exploiting natural resources is anything but independent.

Haggling over one plot of land or another will always continue, but the basic lines have been drawn on the map. The frontier has been carved up and regulated—today it's mostly just a state of mind. Or a myth we like to believe about ourselves.

3 The People: Three Ways to Win an Argument in Alaska

NUMBER ONE: WAIT FOR SPRING

A small town in Alaska in March. Each time it snows, you have to throw shovels of it farther over your head to dig out. The air in the house is stale, and out the window all you see is black, white, and gray. Everyone's ready to go nuts with winter. It's time for a good political ruckus. No one can predict exactly what will set it off—it could just be an ill-considered letter to the editor in the local newspaper, or it could be something juicier, like a controversial development proposal. At some point, when the cabin fever gets bad enough, it almost doesn't matter what sparks the inferno. Alaskans can generate outrage about almost anything, with a ritual of charges and countercharges, conspiracy theories, and impassioned public testimony.

It's particularly amusing when some outsider is involved, thinking he's at the town council meeting in a normal political process to get some project approved, only to wind up on the receiving end of a public hearing from hell.

I'll never forget a sorry businessman who was trying to lease some land from the town of Homer. He endured hours of angry public testimony one night. He was sweating, the only person in the packed city hall meeting room wearing a tie, surrounded by flannel shirts, blue jeans, and angry faces. Finally, he stood up at his chair and, in a plaintive tone of frustration and near tears, declared, "You're not very professional as a community!" For once, no one could disagree.

He gave up. He didn't know that if he had only waited a couple of months, the opposition would dry up as soon as the salmon started running. Then most of the city council meetings would be canceled, and those that weren't would be brief and sparsely attended. If anything really important came up, the council would be smart enough to postpone it till fall. In the summer, Alaskans have more important things to attend to than government.

The sun shines deep into the night, so you can catch fish and tourists rather than sitting inside. It's the season when the money is made. The streets are full of new people, like a bird rookery refreshed by migrants. Everyone stays awake late pounding nails, playing softball, and fly-casting for reds. Office workers in Anchorage depart straight from work for a 3-hour drive down to the Kenai Peninsula, fish through the night, catch a quick nap in the car in the wee hours, and make it to work on time the next morning, with fish stories to share at the coffee machine. Sleep is expendable—you don't seem to need it that much when the sky is light all night.

In the Native villages of the Bush, everyone has gone to fish camp. Families load everything in an aluminum river boat and leave town, headed upriver and back to a time of purer cultural traditions. On the banks and beaches, they set up wall tents and spruce-log fish-drying racks, maybe a basketball hoop and campfire, too. The huge extended families work as a unit. Men gather in the salmon, and the women gut them with a few lightning strokes of a knife and hang them to dry on the racks. Children run around in a countryside paradise, watched by whatever adults are handiest.

Suddenly, August comes. For the first time in months, you can see the stars. It comes as a shock the first time you have to use your car headlights. The mood gets even more frantic. There's never enough time in the summer to do everything that needs to get done. Construction crews can count the days now till snow and cold will shut them down. Anything that's not done now won't be done until next May. Labor Day approaches as fast as 5pm on a busy business day.

As September turns to October, everything had better be done. The last tourists are gone, and T-shirt shops are closed for the season. The commercial fishing boats are tied up back in the harbor, and the fishermen prepare for vacation. Deckhands and cannery workers are already back at college. For the first time in months, people can slow down long enough to look at each other and remember where they left off in the spring. It's time to catch up on sleep, think longer thoughts, make big decisions. The hills of birch turn bright yellow, the tundra goes brick red, and the sky turns gray—there's the smell of wood smoke in the air—and then, one day, it starts to snow.

It's not the velvet darkness of midwinter that gets you. December is bearable, even if the sun rises after the kids get to school, barely cruises along the horizon, and sinks before they start for home. Nowhere is Christmas more real than Alaska, where residents sing carols with cheeks tingling from the cold. January isn't so hard. You're still excited about the skiing. The phone rings in the middle of the night—it's a friend telling you to put on your boots and go outside to see the northern lights. February is a bit harder to take, but most towns have a winter carnival to divert your attention from the cold.

March is when bizarre things start to happen. People are just holding on for the end of winter, and you never know what will set them off. That's when you'd better hunker down and lay low, watch what you say, bite your tongue when your spouse lets hang a comment you'd like to jump on like a coho hitting fresh bait. Hold on—just until the icicles start to melt, the mud shows around the snowbanks, and the cycle starts fresh.

NUMBER TWO: BE HERE FIRST

There's a simple and effective way to win an argument in Alaska—state how long you've lived here. If it's longer than your adversary, he'll find it difficult to put up a fight. This is why, when speaking in public, people will often begin their remarks by stating how many years they've been in Alaska. It's a badge of authenticity and status in a place with a young, transient population that's grown fast. No one cares where you came from, or who you were back there, and there's no such thing as class in Alaska—anyone who tries to act superior will quickly find that no one else notices. But if you haven't made it through a few winters, you probably don't know what you're talking about.

It's also traditional—although, sadly, a fading tradition—to treat strangers as friends until they prove otherwise. The smaller the town you visit, the more strongly you'll find that hospitality still alive. Visitors can find it pleasantly disorienting to arrive in a small town and have everyone in the street greet them with a smile. These traditions of hospitality and respect for experience run deepest in Alaska's **Native people.** (Alaskans use the word *Native* to mean all the indigenous peoples of Alaska.) But instead of beginning a conversation by stating how long they've lived here, Natives—who've always been here—try to find a relation with a new person by talking about where their families are from.

Theories differ about how North America was originally populated. The most widely accepted notion is that the first people arrived across a land bridge from Asia through the dry Bering Sea up to 20,000 to 30,000 years ago, in pursuit of migrating game. The bridge, up to 1,000 miles wide, would have lasted longest in the area between Nome and Kotzebue and, at its largest size, included the entire west coast of Alaska. But new archaeological discoveries have thrown doubt on the land bridge theory, suggesting a migration story that's much more complex. People who know the Arctic know the land bridge simply wasn't necessary: In the winter you can walk between Siberia and Alaska even today, and the seafaring skills of Alaska's Aleuts and Eskimos would have enabled them to travel back and forth to Asia at any time. The Siberian Yup'ik language bears strong similarity to the Central Yup'ik spoken in southwest Alaska, and the traditional stories of polar people around the globe share certain themes and incidents that cannot be coincidental. Modern Eskimos trace kin on either side of the Bering Strait. The connections among northern indigenous people suggest continuity rather than a single Ice Age event.

However and whenever the first people arrived, they quickly spread through the Americas, creating cultures of incredible complexity and diversity. Those who kept going south from Alaska were the ancestors of all the indigenous people of the hemisphere, from the Inca to the Algonquin. Those who stayed in Alaska became the Eskimos, who include the Inupiat of the Arctic, the Yup'ik of the Southwest, and the Alutiiq of the Gulf of Alaska coastline. They also became Indians: the Athabascans of the Interior and the Tlingit, Haida, and Tsimshian of Southeast Alaska and British Columbia. And seafaring

Pacific people landed in the Aleutian Chain, becoming the Aleuts, who are neither Eskimo nor Indian.

The Native groups of Alaska have a lot in common culturally, but before the white invasion, they had well-defined boundaries and didn't mix much. They didn't farm, and the only animal they domesticated was the dog—dog teams and boats were the primary means of transportation and commerce. But they generally were not nomadic, and no one in Alaska lived in igloos. Where there was no wood, houses were built of whale bone and sod; where wood was plentiful, large and intricately carved houses sheltered entire villages. Typically, a family-connected tribal group would have a winter village and a summer fish camp for gathering and laying up food. Elders guided the community in important decisions. A gifted shaman led the people in religious matters, relating to the spirits of ancestors, animals, trees, and even the ice that populated their world. Stories passed on through generations explained the universe.

Those oral traditions kept Native cultures alive. Twenty distinct **Native languages** were spoken—some elders still speak only their Native language yet today, and only one language, Eyak, is essentially extinct. The languages break into four major families: Eskimo-Aleut, Athabascan-Eyak-Tlingit, Haida, and Tsimshian (the last two are primarily Canadian). The Eskimo-Aleut language group includes languages spoken by coastal people from the Arctic Ocean to the Gulf of Alaska, including Inupiaq, in the Arctic; Yup'ik, in the Yukon-Kuskokwim and Bristol Bay region; Aleut, in the Aleutian Islands; and Alutiiq, on the Alaska Peninsula, Kodiak, and Prince William Sound. There are 12 Athabascan and Eyak languages in Alaska, and more Outside, including Apache and Navajo. In Southeast Alaska, Tlingit was spoken across most of the Panhandle. Haida was spoken on southern Prince of Wales Island and southward into what's now British Columbia, where Tsimshain also was spoken.

The first arrival of whites was often violent and destructive, spanning a 100-year period that started in the 1740s with the coming of the Russian fur traders, who enslaved and massacred the Aleuts, and continued to the 1840s, when whalers and other mariners met the Inupiat of the Arctic. There were pitched battles, but disease and nonviolent destruction of oral traditions was more influential. Christian missionaries, with the support of government assimilation policy, drove the old stories and even Native languages underground. Lela Kiana Oman, who has published traditional Inupiat stories to preserve them, told me of her memories of her father secretly telling the ancient tales at night to his children. She was forbidden to speak Inupiaq in school and did not see her first traditional Native dance until age 18.

Oman's work is part of today's **Native cultural renaissance.** It's not a moment too soon. In some villages, children know more about the geography of Beverly Hills, which they see on television, than about their own culture. Some don't share a language with their own grandparents. But schools in many areas have begun requiring Native language classes, or even teach using language immersion techniques. For the Aleut, whose cultural traditions were almost completely wiped out, the process of renewal involves a certain amount of invention. On the other hand, some traditional villages remain, especially deep in the country of the Yukon-Kuskokwim Delta, where Yup'ik is still the dominant language and most of the food comes from traditional subsistence hunting and gathering, altered only by the use of modern materials and guns.

Alaska Natives also are fighting destruction fueled by alcohol and other substance-abuse problems. Rates of suicide, accidents, and domestic violence are very high in the Bush. Statistically, virtually every Alaska Native in prison is there because of alcohol. A sobriety movement is attacking the problem one

An Alaska Glossary

If Alaska feels like a different country from the rest of the United States, one reason may be the odd local usage that makes English slightly different here—different enough, in fact, that the Associated Press publishes a separate style-book dictionary just for Alaska. Here are some Alaskan words you may run into:

break up When God set up the seasons in Alaska, He forgot one: spring. While the rest of the United States enjoys new flowers and baseball, Alaskans are looking at melting snowbanks and mud. Then, in May, summer miraculously arrives. Break up officially occurs when the ice goes out in the Interior's rivers, but it stands for the time period of winter's demise and summer's initiation.

bunny boots If you see people wearing huge, bulbous white rubber boots in Alaska's winter, it's not necessarily because they have enormous feet. Those are bunny boots, superinsulated footwear originally designed for Arctic air force operations—they're the warmest things in the world.

cheechako A newcomer or greenhorn. Not used much anymore, because almost everyone is one.

dry or damp Many towns and villages have invoked a state law that allows them to outlaw alcohol completely—to go dry—or to outlaw sale but not possession—to go damp.

Lower 48 The contiguous United States.

Native When capitalized, the word refers to Alaska's indigenous people. "American Indian" isn't used much in Alaska, "Alaska Native" being the preferred term.

Native corporation In 1971, Congress settled land claims with Alaska's Natives by turning over land and money; corporations were set up, with the Natives then alive as shareholders, to receive the property. Most of the corporations still thrive.

person at a time. One of its goals is to use traditional Native culture to fill a void of rural despair where alcohol now flows in. Politically, a "local option" law provides individual communities the choice of partial or total alcohol prohibition; it has been successfully used in many villages and towns but remains controversial in others, where repeated local option elections sometimes divide Native and white residents, with whites more often voting against prohibition.

There are social and political tensions between Natives and whites on many levels and over many issues. The lives of the city and the village share less in common than do most nations. Although village Natives come to the city to shop, get health care, or attend meetings, urban Alaskans have no reason to go to the villages. An Anchorage legislator, a life-long Alaskan, gained chairmanship of the House committee controlling rural affairs in 1999 before he made his first visit to the Bush. The most contentious rural-urban issue concerns allocation of fish and game. Some urban outdoorsmen feel they should have the same rights to hunt and fish as the Natives. The legislature has sided with them, but rural Natives have federal law on their side, and so have won the day so far. They maintain that subsistence hunting and fishing are an integral part of their cultural heritage, far more important than sport, and should take

oosik The huge penile bone of a walrus. Knowing this word could save you from being the butt of any of a number of practical jokes people like to play on cheechakos.

Outside Anywhere that isn't Alaska. This is a widely used term in print, and is capitalized, like any other proper noun.

PFD No, not personal floatation device; it stands for Permanent Fund Dividend. When Alaska's oil riches started flowing in the late 1970s, the voters set up a savings account called the Permanent Fund. Half the interest is paid annually to every man, woman, and child in the state. With more than $25 billion in investments, the fund now yields more than $1,300 in dividends to each Alaskan annually.

pioneer A white settler of Alaska who has been here longer than most other people can remember—25 or 30 years usually does it.

salmon There are five species of Pacific salmon, each with two names. The king or Chinook is the largest, growing up to 90 pounds in some areas; the silver or coho is next in size, a feisty sport fish; the red or sockeye has rich red flesh; the pink or humpy and the chum or dog are smallish and not as tasty, mostly ending up in cans and dog lots.

Southeast Most people don't bother to say "Southeast Alaska." The region may be to the northwest of everyone else in the country, but it's southeast of most Alaskans, and that's all we care about.

tsunami Earthquake-caused sea waves are often called tidal waves, but that's a misnomer. The most destructive waves of the 1964 Alaska earthquake were tsunamis caused by underwater upheavals like landslides.

village A small, Alaska Native settlement in the Bush, usually tightly bound by family and cultural tradition.

priority. Darker conflicts exist, too, and it's impossible to discount the charges of racism that Native Alaskans raise.

Alaska Natives have become a minority in their own land. In 1880, Alaska contained 33,000 Natives and 430 whites. By 1900, with the gold rush, the numbers were roughly equal. Since then, whites have generally outnumbered Natives in ever greater numbers. Today there are about 94,000 Alaska Natives—22,000 of whom live in the cities of Anchorage and Fairbanks—out of a total state population of more than 600,000 people of all races. Consequently, Alaska Natives must learn to walk in two worlds. The North Slope's Inupiat, who hunt the bowhead whale from open boats as their forefathers did, must also know how to negotiate for their take in international diplomatic meetings. And they have to use the levers of government to protect the whale's environment from potential damage by the oil industry. The Alaska Native Claims Settlement Act created a new class, the corporate Native, responsible for representing rural needs but also obliged to function as an executive for large, far-reaching business concerns. Outnumbered by white voters, Bush politicians in the legislature must be especially skilled, sticking together, crossing political boundaries, and forming coalitions to protect their constituencies.

Non-Natives traveling to the Bush also walk in two worlds, but they may not even know it. In a Native village, a newly met friend will ask you in for a cup of coffee; it can be rude not to accept. Looking a person in the eye in conversation also can be rude—that's how Native elders look at younger people who owe them respect. If a Native person looks down, speaks slowly, and seems to mumble, that's not disrespect, but the reverse. Fast-talking non-Natives have to make a conscious effort to slow down and leave pauses in conversation, because Natives usually don't jump in or interrupt—they listen, consider, and then respond. Of course, most Native people won't take offense at your bad manners—they're used to spanning cultures, and they know whites may not know how to act in a village. When I was in a village recently, I looked in confusion at a clock that didn't seem right. "That's Indian time," my Athabascan companion said. Then, pointing to a clock that was working, "White man time is over there."

Urban visitors who miss cultural nuances rarely overlook the apparent poverty of many villages. Out on a remote landscape of windswept tundra, swampy in summer and frozen in winter, they may secretly wonder why Natives stay there, enduring the hardships of rural Alaskan life when even the most remote villager can see on cable television how easy it is in Southern California. Save your pity. As Yup'ik social observer Harold Napoleon has said, "We're poor, all right, but we've got more than most people. Our most important asset is our land and our culture, and we want to protect it come hell or high water."

Alaska's Natives may be outnumbered, but they've been here a lot longer than anyone else. My money is on them.

NUMBER THREE: BE A REAL ALASKAN

Alaska's history books are full of the stories of economic booms, the people who came, what kind of wealth they were after, and how they populated and developed the land. In a largely empty place, you can make it into history just by showing up. But every wave is followed by a trough—the bust that comes after the boom—when those who came just for the money go back where they came from. Those are the times when the real Alaskans—those who live here for the love of the place, not only the money—are divided from the rest. The real Alaskans stay; the others leave. It's the perfect way to settle an argument.

Other people have other definitions of what it takes to be a real Alaskan. One definition, which I once read on a place mat in a diner in Soldotna, holds that to be a real Alaskan, you have to know how to fix a Caterpillar tractor. Similar definitions require various feats in the outdoors—hunting, fishing, or shooting—and even acts in the bar room or the bedroom. They all assume that a real Alaskan is a big, tough, white, male, bulldozer-driving type of guy. But those can be the first to leave when the economy goes down the tubes.

The first group to leave were the Russians sent by the czar and the Russian-America Company. On October 18, 1867, their flag came down over Castle Hill in Sitka in a solemn ceremony, got stuck, and had to be untangled by a soldier sent up the pole. The territory was virtually empty of Russians before the check was even signed, as Congress didn't much like the idea of the purchase and took a while to pay. The gold rush stampeders were the next to leave. The population of Nome went from 12,500 to 852 after the stampede was over. The oil years have seen the same phenomenon, as people who can't find work in the bust years pack up and leave.

But each time the boom has gone bust, enough have stayed so that Alaska ended up with more people than it had before. Over the long term, the population has kept growing dramatically. It doubled from 1890 to 1900 (the gold rush); doubled again by 1950 because of World War II and the Cold War; doubled again by 1964, with statehood and the early oil years; and doubled again by 1983, because of the trans-Alaska pipeline and the arrival of big oil. Since then, it has grown another 20%.

Each set of migrants has been similar—young, coming mostly from the West, but from other parts of the United States, too. Most people who have come to Alaska have been white—minority populations are smaller than in the nation as a whole—but there are strong minority communities in Anchorage. In Kodiak, the canneries are run by a tight Filipino community started by just a few pioneer immigrants. Today the population of Alaska as a whole is young and relatively well paid and educated. Six times as many babies are born as people die.

Historically, old people often moved somewhere warmer when they retired. Some migrate annually, spending only the summer in Alaska—they are called snowbirds. Over the years, the state government set out to keep more old people in the state, to help build the continuity and memory a community needs. Special retirement homes were built, local property-tax breaks were granted to the elderly, and the legislature created a "Longevity Bonus" entitlement whereby elders who'd been in the state at least 25 years were automatically paid $250 a month for life. When a court ruled that the state couldn't impose a residency requirement of more than 1 year for the program, Alaska began to import thousands of new elderly people who were coming north to take advantage of the handouts. Now the bonus is being phased out.

It wasn't the first time Alaska has tried to reward real Alaskans just for staying. When the Permanent Fund Dividend program started in the 1970s, to distribute some of the state's new oil riches to the citizens, it was designed to provide more money for each year of residency. A 1-year greenhorn would get $50 and a 20-year pioneer $1,000. The Supreme Court threw out the plan—apparently being a "real Alaskan" isn't a special category of citizen in the U.S. Constitution.

Alaskans have always been well paid. Until recently, the popular explanation always held that prices are higher because of shipping costs, so salaries needed to match. That's still true in rural Alaska and for some purchases in the large cities. But generally, fierce competition in the retail trade has driven prices down. Large national chains moved in all at once in 1994. Today the cost of living in Anchorage, Fairbanks, and Juneau compares to most parts of the country, and Wal-Mart has even moved into such remote towns as Ketchikan and Kodiak. Wages have gone down a little, largely because all those new retail jobs lowered average pay, but the federal government still pays a premium to its Alaskan employees, and oil workers, fishers, and other skilled workers make a very good living.

Prices for hotel rooms and restaurant meals also remain quite high. The best explanation is the seasonal nature of the economy—tourism operators need to make their full income in the summer season. The other explanation is that they'll charge what the market can bear, and empty hotel rooms are in high demand in summer.

The non-Native part of Alaska, 100 years old with the anniversary of the gold rush in 1998, hasn't had time to develop a culture of its own, much less an Alaskan accent. It's a melting pot of the melting pot, with a population made up of odds and ends from all over the United States. People tend to judge each other on the basis of their actions, not on who they are or where they came from. New arrivals to Alaska have been able to reinvent themselves since the days when Soapy Smith, a small-time con man, took over Skagway with a criminal gang and had the territorial governor offer to make him the town marshal—all in the period of a year. Everyone arrives with a clean slate and a chance to prove himself or herself, but on occasion, that ability to start from scratch has created some embarrassing discoveries, when the past does become relevant. There have been a series of political scandals uncovered by reporters who checked the résumés of well-known politicians, only to find out they had concocted their previous lives out of thin air. One leading legislative candidate's husband found out about his wife's real background from such a news story.

If an Alaskan culture hasn't had time to develop, Alaska does have traditions, or at least accepted ways of thinking—among them tolerance and equality, hospitality, independence, and a propensity for violence. In the late 1980s in Homer, there was a gunfight over a horse that left a man lying dead on a dirt road. In the newspaper the next week, the editorial called for people not to settle their differences with guns. A couple of letters to the editor shot back, on the theme, "Don't you tell *us* how to settle our differences." Guns are necessary tools in Alaska. They're also a religion. I have friends who exchanged handguns instead of rings when they got married.

The tradition of tolerance of newcomers has made Alaska a destination for oddballs, religious cults, hippies, and people who just can't make it in the mainstream. Perhaps the most interesting of the **religious groups** that formed its own community is the Old Believers, who in recent decades have built villages of brightly painted, gingerbread-like houses around Kachemak Bay, near Homer. Their resistance to convention dates from Peter the Great's reforms to Russian Orthodoxy in the 18th century, which they reject. After centuries of persecution, in Alaska they've found a place where they can live without interference—in fact, they've thrived as fishermen and boat builders. You see them around town, in their 18th-century Russian peasant dress. Even the girls' high-school basketball team wears long dresses, with their numbers stitched to the bodice.

Nikolaevsk was the first of the Russian Old Believer villages. In the public school there, they don't teach about dinosaurs or men landing on the moon—that's considered heresy. Yet other Old Believers rebelled, convinced that Nikolaevsk was making too many compromises and was bound to lose the next generation to decadent American ways. They broke off and formed another village, farther up the bay, unreachable except by all-terrain vehicle, and adhered to stricter rules. They, in turn, suffered another schism and another village was formed, farther up the bay, virtually inaccessible and with even stricter rules. The process continues. The fight against assimilation may be hopeless, as children will ultimately do as they please, but it's the Old Believers' own struggle. No one in Homer pushes them to change. No one pays any attention at all, except to buy their fish and their top-quality boats.

After several decades, it looks as if the Old Believers are here to stay. Whether they speak English or not, I'd say they're real Alaskans.

4 Critters: A Short Guide to Alaska's Wildlife

WHALES

Nothing really prepares you for the sight of a leaping humpback whale—no film or photograph, and certainly no description. It is the sort of experience that can instantaneously change the way you see the world around you, changing the sea from a familiar plain of light and motion into a hidden universe of surging giants. The whale shoots upward without warning, then seems to hang a moment and twist in the air—there's plenty of time for those facing the other direction to turn around and look—and then splashes down with a sound we once mistook for thunder when we heard it in a fog. A circle of waves spreads, large enough to rock nearby sea kayaks and even small fishing boats. Whales that surface during their feeding and cruising behavior patterns also can make you catch your breath at first, then, over extended viewing, give you a chance to understand what such a huge animal is really like—how the texture of its skin is rough yet slick, how it moves gracefully despite its incredible size.

There are several places in Alaska to see humpbacks and other whales with virtually surefire regularity at the right times of year, including waters near Petersburg or Sitka, near Gustavus and Glacier Bay National Park, and near Seward and Kenai Fjords National Park. The details are covered in each of those sections in the book. Here is some background for what you'll be seeing.

THE HUMPBACK   These migratory whales spend their summer in Alaska feeding, then swim to Mexican or Hawaiian waters for the winter, where they give birth to their young then fast until going north again in spring. The cold northern waters produce more of the small fish and other tiny creatures

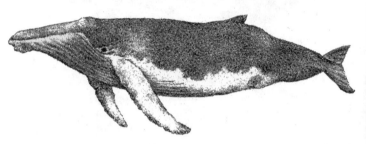

The Humpback Whale. Max. length: 53 ft.

humpbacks filter through their baleen, the strips of stiff, fibrous material that substitute for their teeth. A humpback is easy to recognize by its huge, mottled tail; by the hump on its back, just forward of its dorsal fin; and by its arm-like flippers, which can grow to be 14 feet long.

Most humpback sightings are of the whales' humped backs as they cruise along the surface, resting, and of the flukes of the tail as they dive. Humpbacks know how to weave nets of bubbles around their prey, then swim upward through the schooled fish, mouths wide open, to eat them in a single swoop, sometimes finishing with a frothy lunge through the surface. Feeding dives can last a long time and often mean you're done watching a particular whale, but if you're lucky the whale may be just dipping down for a few minutes to get ready to leap completely out of the water, a practice called **breaching.** No one knows for sure why they do this; it may simply be play. For viewers it's thrilling and, in small boats and kayaks, a little scary, even if safe; paddlers should group their boats and tap the decks to let the whales know where they are. Humpbacks are highly sensitive to noise, so keep quiet to see longer displays.

Humpbacks tend to congregate to feed, making certain spots with rich supplies of food reliable places to watch them. In Southeast Alaska the best spots include the waters of Icy Strait, just outside Glacier Bay; Frederick Sound outside Petersburg; and Sitka Sound. In Southcentral Alaska, Resurrection Bay, outside Seward near Kenai Fjords National Park, has the most reliable sightings.

THE ORCA (KILLER WHALE) The starkly defined black-and-white patches of the orca recall the sharp graphic look of the Native American art of the Pacific Northwest and Southeast Alaska. It's as if the whales were painted by their creator to reflect the speed, agility, and fierceness of the ocean's top predator. Moving like wolves in highly structured family groups called pods, and swimming at up to 25 knots (about 29 m.p.h.), orcas hunt salmon, por-

The Orca, or Killer Whale. Max. length: 30 ft.

poises, seals, sea lions, and even juvenile whales, but there's never been a report of one attacking a human being. Like dolphins, orcas often pop above the surface in a flash of a graceful arc when they travel, giving viewers a glance at their sleek shape, markings, and tall dorsal fin.

Unlike humpbacks and other whales that rely on a predictable food supply, it's not easy to say exactly where you might find orcas—you need to be where their prey is that day. Resurrection Bay and Prince William Sound both have pods often sighted in the summer; we saw a pod of orcas from the beach in Gustavus; and they could show up anywhere in Southeast Alaska waters. For cruisers coming to Alaska, a top spot to see orcas is Robson Bight, an area in Johnstone Strait (between Vancouver Island and mainland British Columbia).

THE BELUGA This small, white whale with the cute rounded beak is one of only three types that spend all their lives in cold water rather than heading south for the winter. (The other two are the narwhale and bowhead.) More likely to be confused for a dolphin than any other whale, belugas are larger and

The Beluga Whale. Max. length: 16 ft.

fatter than a dolphin and lack the dolphin's dorsal fin. Adults are all white, while juveniles are gray. Belugas swim in large packs that can number in the dozens. They're the only whale that can turn its head and one of the few with good eyesight.

Beluga feed on salmon, making the mouths of rivers with salmon runs the best places to see them. Occasionally, a group will strand itself chasing salmon on a falling tide, swimming away when the water returns. The Cook Inlet group of belugas is the most often seen: Watch the waters of Turnagain Arm while driving the Seward Highway just south of Anchorage, or watch from the beach near the mouth of the Kenai River in Kenai.

THE MINKE The smallest of the baleen whales, the minke is generally under 26 feet long and has a blackish-gray body with a white stomach, a narrow triangular head, and white bands on its flippers. Along with the humpback and (occasionally) the gray whale, it is the only baleen commonly seen in Alaskan waters.

When breaching, Minkes leap something like dolphins, gracefully reen-

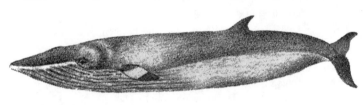

The Minke Whale. Max. length: 26 ft.

tering the water headfirst—unlike humpbacks, for instance, which smash down on their sides. Also unlike the humpbacks, they don't raise their flukes clear of the water when they dive. Minkes are easy to confuse with dolphins: Watch for the dark skin color.

LAND ANIMALS

Large mammals other than humans still rule most of Alaska. Even in the urban areas there sometimes remains a question of who's in charge, as moose snarl winter traffic and bears and wolves prey on family pets at the edge of town. For visitors, the chances of seeing the animals described below are excellent. Here are a few of the more common.

BALD EAGLE Now making a comeback all over the United States, the bald eagle always was extremely common in Alaska: In most coastal towns, a pigeon would cause a far greater stir among bird fanciers. Eagles even soar over the high-rise buildings of downtown Anchorage, and every fishing town is swarming with them. Only adult eagles have the familiar white head and tail; juveniles of a few years or less have mottled brown plumage and can be hard to tell from a hawk. Eagles most often are seen soaring on rising air over ocean or river waters, where they are likely looking for fish to swoop down and snatch, but you also can often see them perched on beach driftwood or in large trees. Haines is a prime eagle-spotting area, where thousands congregate in the fall; Sitka and Ketchikan both have raptor centers where you can see eagles in enclosures. (See chapter 5.)

Bald Eagle

Raven

The eagle represents one of the two main kinship groupings in the matrilineal Tlingit culture (the other is the raven), so eagles frequently appear on totem poles and in other Southeast Native art.

RAVEN   A member of the Corvidae family, which includes jays, crows, and magpies, the raven is found throughout the northern hemisphere and is extremely common in Southeast Alaska. You can tell a raven from a crow by its larger size, heavy bill, shaggy throat feathers, and its unmistakable voice, a deep and mysteriously evocative "kaw" that provides a constant soundtrack to the misty forests of Southeast. The raven figures importantly in Southeast Alaska Native stories, and in the creation myths of many other Native American peoples; its personality is of a wily and resourceful protagonist with great magical powers, an understandable match for this highly impressive and intelligent scavenger.

BLACK BEAR   Black bears live in forests all over Alaska, feeding on fish, berries, insects, and vegetation. In Southeast Alaska, they can be so common as to be a pest, and many communities have adjusted their handling of garbage to keep the bears out of town. Although not typically dangerous, blackies still deserve caution and respect: They stand about a yard tall at the shoulders and measure 5 or 6 feet from nose to tail. Black bears are usually black, but can also be brown, blond, or even blue—color is not the best way to tell a black bear from a brown bear. Instead, look at the smaller size, the blunt face, and the shape of the back, which is straight and lacks the brown bear's large

Black Bear

Brown Bear

shoulder hump. One of the best places to see black bears is the remote Anan Bear Observatory, reached from Wrangell or Ketchikan by float plane or boat (see chapter 5).

BROWN BEAR   Also known as the grizzly bear, brown bears are among the largest and most ferocious of all land mammals. Size depends on the bears' food source. In coastal areas where salmon are plentiful, such as Southeast Alaska or Katmai National Park, brown bears can grow well over 1,000 pounds, and even approach the 1-ton mark. The largest of all are found on salmon-rich Kodiak Island. Inland, at Denali National Park and on similar tundra landscape, where they feed on rodents, berries, insects and the like, brown bears top out closer to 500 pounds. They can also take larger prey, but that's less common. Recognize a brown bear by the prominent shoulder hump, long face, and large size; color can range from almost black to blond. Among the best places to see brown bears are Pack Creek on Admiralty Island near Juneau, at Denali and Katmai national parks, or on bear viewing floatplane excursions from Homer or Kodiak. Of these, Denali is the only inexpensive option.

MOOSE   In winter, when they move to the lowlands, moose can be a positive pest, blocking roadways and eating expensive shrubbery. In the summer, they're a little more elusive, most often seen standing in forest ponds eating the weeds from the bottom or pruning streamside willows. But even in summer gardeners can often be heard cursing these animals, which, despite their immense size, can neatly chomp the blossom off each tulip in a flower bed. The largest member of the deer family, with males reaching 1,200 to 1,600 pounds, moose are found primarily in the boreal forest that covers Interior and Southcentral Alaska. They are unmistakable. As big as a large horse, with bristly, ragged brown hair; a long, bulbous nose; and huge, mournful

Moose

Caribou

eyes, moose seem to crave pity—through they get little from the wolves and people who hunt them, and the trains and cars that run them down, and they give little to anyone in their way when they're on the move. Males grow large antlers, which they shed after battling for a mate every fall. Females lack antlers and are smaller, having one to three calves each year.

CARIBOU   Alaska's caribou are genetically identical to reindeer, but were never domesticated as reindeer were in Europe. For Inupiat and Athabaskan people, they were an essential source of food and hides, and the hunt remains a cultural mainstay. Both males and females have antlers that they shed annually. Reindeer travel the arctic tundra in herds of up to hundreds of thousands of animals, a stunning sight witnessed by only a lucky few, as the migration routes lie in remote regions. You can, however, often see caribou in smaller groups of a few dozen at Denali National Park, along the Dalton and Denali highways, and on other northern rural roads above treeline. They're skittish, so the best technique is to stop and let them approach you.

*Sitka
Black-Tailed
Deer*

Dall Sheep

SITKA BLACK-TAILED DEER   The Sitka black-tailed deer is a relatively small deer found in the coastal rain forests of Alaska. Males typically weigh in around 120 pounds, and show similarly small antlers. Both males and females sport a reddish-brown coat in summer. They can be found throughout Southeast, in the Prince William Sound and on Kodiak Island.

DALL SHEEP   Dall sheep resemble the more familiar bighorn, but are smaller, weighing up to 300 pound for males, 150 for females. Like the bighorn, males have the same curling horns, which they butt against each other to establish dominance for mating. Their habitat is the high, rocky places, where their incredible agility makes them safe from predators. Except in a few exceptional spots, such as on the cliffs above the Seward Highway just south of Anchorage on Turnagain Arm, you almost always need strong binoculars to see sheep. Denali National Park is a good place to see them in the usual way: from a great distance. Scanning the mountains, pick out white spots, then focus in on them. Often the sheep move in herds of a dozen or more animals.

MOUNTAIN GOAT   Another animal that you won't see unless you bring your binoculars, the mountain goat inhabits the same craggy mountain habitat as the Dall sheep, including the prime viewing area on Turnagain Arm. From a distance, it's easy to confuse them with female Dall sheep, but mountain goats are shaggier; have short, straight black horns (which appear in both male and female); have the typical goat beard; and have a much more pronounced hump at the shoulders.

Mountain Goat

Frommer's Online Directory: Alaska

By Michael Shapiro

Michael Shapiro is the author of *Internet Travel Planning*
(Globe Pequot Press).

Frommer's Online Directory is a new feature designed to help you take advantage of the Internet to better plan your trip. Part I lists general Internet resources that can make any trip easier, such as sites for booking airline tickets. In Part II you'll find some top online guides for Alaska, listed with an eye toward complementing the material presented in this book. Please keep in mind that this is not a comprehensive list, but rather a discriminating selection to get you started. We've awarded stars to the best sites, which are earned, not paid for (unlike some other Web-site rankings, which are based on payment). Finally, remember this is a press-time snapshot of leading Web sites—some undoubtedly will have evolved, changed, or moved by the time you read this.

1 Top Travel-Planning Web Sites

Among the most popular travel sites are online travel agencies. The top agencies, including Expedia, Preview Travel, and Travelocity, offer an array of tools that are valuable even if you don't book online. You can check flight schedules, hotel availability, car-rental prices, or even get paged if your flight is delayed.

While online agencies have come a long way over the past few years, they don't always yield the best price. Unlike a travel agent, for example, they're unlikely to tell you that you can save money by flying a day earlier or a day later. On the other hand, if you're looking for a bargain fare, you might find something online that an agent wouldn't take the time to dig up. Because airline commissions have been cut, a travel agent may not find it worthwhile spending half an hour trying to find you the best deal. On the Net you can be your own agent and take all the time you want.

Online booking sites aren't the only places to book airline tickets—all major airlines have their own Web sites and often offer incentives, such as bonus frequent flyer miles or Net-only discounts, for buying online. These incentives have helped airlines capture the majority of the online booking market. According to Jupiter Communications, online agencies such as Travelocity booked about 80% of tickets purchased online in 1996, but by 1999 airline sites (such as

What You'll Find at Frommers.com

Of course, we're a little biased, but we highly recommend Arthur Frommer's Budget Travel Online (**www.frommers.com**) as an excellent travel-planning resource where you'll find indispensable travel tips, reviews, monthly vacation giveaways, and online booking.

Subscribe to Arthur Frommer's Daily Newsletter (**www.frommers.com/newsletters**) to receive the latest travel bargains and inside travel secrets in your mailbox every day. You'll read daily headlines and articles from the dean of travel himself, highlighting last-minute deals on airfares, accommodations, cruises, and package vacations. You'll also find great travel advice by checking our Tip of the Day or Hot Spot of the Month.

Search our Destinations archive (**www.frommers.com/destinations**) of more than 200 domestic and international destinations for great places to stay, tips for traveling there, and what to do while you're there. Once you've researched your trip, you might try our online reservation system (**www.frommers.com/book-travelnow**) to book your dream vacation at affordable prices.

www.ual.com) were projected to own more than half of the online market, with online agencies' share of the pie dwindling each year.

WHEN SHOULD YOU BOOK ONLINE?

Online booking is not for everyone. If you prefer to let others handle your travel arrangements, one call to an experienced travel agent should suffice. But if you want to know as much as possible about your options, the Net is a good place to start, especially for bargain hunters.

The most compelling reason to use online booking is to take advantage of last-minute specials, such as American Airlines' weekend deals or other Internet-only fares that must be purchased online. Another advantage is that you can cash in on incentives for booking online, such as rebates or bonus frequent flyer miles. Online booking works best for trips within North America—for international tickets, it's usually cheaper and easier to use a travel agent or consolidator.

Online booking is certainly not for those with a complex international itinerary. If you require follow-up services, such as itinerary changes, use a travel agent. Though Expedia and some other online agencies employ travel agents available by phone, these sites are geared primarily for self-service. And remember, the descriptions below are true at press time, but the pace of evolution on the Net is relentless, so you'll probably find some advancements by the time you visit these sites.

Credit-Card Security on the Net

Far more people look online than book online, partly due to fear of putting their credit cards through on the Net. Though secure encryption has made this fear less justified, there's no reason why you can't find a flight online and then book it by calling a toll-free number or contacting your travel agent. To be sure you're in secure mode when you book online, look for a little icon of a key (in Netscape) or a padlock (Internet Explorer) at the bottom of your Web browser.

LEADING BOOKING SITES

Cheap Tickets (**www.cheaptickets.com**)

Essentials: Discounted rates on domestic and international airline tickets and hotel rooms. Sometimes discounters such as Cheap Tickets have exclusive deals that aren't available through more mainstream channels.

Registration at Cheap Tickets requires inputting a credit-card number before getting started, which is one reason many people elect to call the company's toll-free number rather than book online. One of the most frustrating things about the Cheap Tickets site is that it will offer fare quotes for a route, and later show this fare is not valid for your dates of travel—other Web sites, such as Preview Travel, consider your dates of travel before showing what fares are available. Despite its problems, Cheap Tickets can be worth the effort because its fares can be lower than those offered by its competitors.

✪ Expedia.com (**expedia.com**)

Essentials: Domestic and international flight, hotel, and car-rental booking; late-breaking travel news, destination features and commentary from travel experts; deals on cruises and vacation packages. Free registration is required for booking.

Expedia makes it easy to handle flight, hotel, and car booking on one itinerary, so it's a good place for one-stop shopping. Expedia's hotel search offers crisp, zoomable maps to pinpoint most properties; click on the camera icon to see images of the rooms and facilities. But like many online databases, Expedia focuses on the major chains, such as Hilton and Hyatt, so don't expect to find too many one-of-a-kind resorts or B&Bs here.

Once you're registered (it's only necessary to do this once from each computer you use), you can start booking with the Roundtrip Fare Finder box on the home page, which expedites the process. After selecting a flight, you can hold it until midnight the following day or purchase online. If you think you might do better through a travel agent, you'll have time to try to get a lower price. And you may do better with a travel agent because Expedia's computer reservation system does not include all airlines. Most notably absent are some leading budget carriers, such as Southwest Airlines. (Note: At press time, Travelocity was the only major booking service that included Southwest.)

Expedia's World Guide, offering destination information, is terribly weak—it takes a lot of page views to get very little information.

Preview Travel (**www.previewtravel.com**)

Essentials: Domestic and international flight, hotel, and car-rental booking; Travel Newswire lists fare sales; deals on cruises and vacation packages. Free one-time registration is required for booking. Preview offers express booking for members, but at press time this feature was buried below the fold on Preview's reservation page.

Preview features the most inviting interface for booking trips, though the wealth of graphics involved can make the site somewhat slow to load. Use Farefinder to quickly find the lowest current fares on flights to dozens of major cities. Carfinder offers a similar service for rental cars, but you can only search airport locations, not city pickup sites. To see the lowest fare for your itinerary, input the dates and times for your route and see what Preview comes up with.

In recent years Preview and other leading booking services have added features such as Best Fare Finder, so after Preview searches for the best deal on your itinerary, it will check flights that are a bit later or earlier to see if it might be cheaper to fly at a different time. While these searches have become quite sophisticated, they still

---

Note to AOL Users

You can book flights, hotels, rental cars, and cruises on AOL at keyword: Travel. The booking software is provided by Preview Travel and is similar to Preview on the Web. Use the AOL "Travelers Advantage" program to earn a 5% rebate on flights, hotel rooms, and car rentals.

---

occasionally overlook deals that might be uncovered by a top-notch travel agent. If you have the time, see what you can find online, and then call an agent to see if you can get a better price.

With Preview's Fare Alert feature, you can set fares for up to three routes and you'll receive e-mail notices when the fare drops below your target amount. If it does, you'll get an e-mail telling you the current fare.

Priceline.com (www.priceline.com)

Even people who aren't familiar with too many Web sites have heard about Priceline.com. Launched in 1998 with a $10 million ad campaign featuring William Shatner, Priceline lets you "name your price" for domestic and international airline tickets and hotel rooms. In other words, you select a route and dates, guarantee with a credit card, and make a bid for what you're willing to pay. If one of the airlines in Priceline's database has a fare that's lower than your bid, your credit card will automatically be charged for a ticket. You can't say what time you want to fly—you have to accept any flight leaving between 6am and 10pm on the dates you choose, and you may have to make one stopover. No frequent flyer miles are awarded, and tickets are nonrefundable and can't be exchanged for another flight. So if your plans change, you're out of luck. Priceline can be good for travelers who have to take off on short notice (and who are thus unable to qualify for advance purchase discounts). But be sure to shop around first—if you overbid, you'll be required to purchase the ticket and Priceline will pocket the difference between what it pays for a ticket and what you bid.

Travelocity (www.travelocity.com)

Essentials: Domestic and international flight, hotel, and car-rental booking; deals on cruises and vacation packages. Travel Headlines spotlights latest bargain airfares. Free one-time registration is required for booking.

Travelocity almost got it right. Its Express Booking feature enables travelers to complete the booking process more quickly than they could at Expedia or Preview, but Travelocity gums up the works with a page called "Featured Airlines." Big placards of several featured airlines compete for your attention—if you want to see the fares for all available airlines, click the much smaller box at the bottom of the page labeled "Book a Flight."

Some have worried that Travelocity, which is owned by American Airlines' parent company, AMR, directs bookings to American. This doesn't seem to be the case—I've booked there dozens of times and have always been directed to the cheapest listed flight—for example, on Tower or ATA. But this "Featured Airlines" page seems to be Travelocity's way of trying to cash in with ads and incentives for booking certain airlines. (*Note:* It's hard to blame these booking services for trying to generate some revenue—many airlines have slashed commissions to $10 per domestic booking for online transactions, so these virtual agencies are groping for revenue streams.) There are rewards for choosing one of the featured airlines. You'll get 1,500 bonus frequent flyer miles if you book through United's site, for example, but the site doesn't tell you about other airlines that might be cheaper. If the United flight costs $150 more than the best deal on another airline, it's not worth spending the extra money for a relatively small number of bonus miles.

On the plus side, Travelocity has some leading-edge techie tools for modern travelers. Exhibit A is Fare Watcher E-mail, an "intelligent agent" that keeps you informed of the best fares offered for the city pairs (round-trips) of your choice. Whenever the fare changes by $25 or more, Fare Watcher will alert you by e-mail. Exhibit B is Flight Paging—if you own an alphanumeric pager with national access that can receive e-mail, Travelocity's paging system can alert you if your flight is delayed. Finally, though Travelocity doesn't include every budget airline, it does include Southwest, the leading U.S. budget carrier.

FINDING ACCOMMODATIONS ONLINE

While the services above offer hotel booking, it can be best to use a site devoted primarily to accommodations because you may find properties that aren't listed on more general online travel agencies. Some accommodations sites specialize in a particular type, such as bed-and-breakfast inns, which you won't find on the more mainstream booking services. Other services, such as TravelWeb, offer weekend deals on major chain properties, which cater to business travelers and have more empty rooms on weekends.

All Hotels on the Web (www.all-hotels.com)

Well, this site doesn't include all the hotels on the Web, but it does have tens of thousands of listings throughout the world. Bear in mind that each hotel listed has paid a small fee of ($25 and up) for placement, so it's not an objective list but more like a book of online brochures. Also see Hotels and Travel on the Net (**www.hotelstravel.com**), which claims to offer discount booking on more than 100,000 hotels and other accommodations in more than 120 countries.

Go Camping America (www.gocampingamerica.com/main.html)

An extensive listing of RV parks and campgrounds for the United States (and some Canadian provinces), organized by state. The listings include dates of operation, number of sites, hookup availability, tent sites, and modem access. Some campgrounds offer "online brochures" which, like printed brochures, put the best possible face on a place.

InnSite (www.innsite.com)

B&B listings for inns in all 50 U.S. states and dozens of countries around the globe. Find an inn at your destination, have a look at images of the rooms, check prices and availability, and then send e-mail to the innkeeper if you have further questions. This is an extensive directory of bed-and-breakfast inns but only includes listings if the proprietor submitted one (note: it's free to get an inn listed). The descriptions are written by the innkeepers and many listings link to the inn's own Web sites, where you can find more information and images. Also see Bed and Breakfast Channel (**bedandbreakfast.com**).

Places to Stay (www.placestostay.com)

Mostly one-of-a-kind places in the United States and abroad that you might not find in other directories, with a focus on resort accommodations. Again, listing is selective—this isn't a comprehensive directory, but can give you a sense of what's available at different destinations.

✪ TravelWeb (www.travelweb.com)

TravelWeb lists more than 16,000 hotels worldwide, focusing on chains such as Hyatt and Hilton, and you can book almost 90% of these online. TravelWeb's Click-It Weekends, updated each Monday, offers weekend deals at many leading hotel chains. TravelWeb is the online home for Pegasus Systems, which provides transaction processing systems for the hotel industry.

LAST-MINUTE DEALS & OTHER ONLINE BARGAINS

There's nothing airlines hate more than flying with lots of empty seats (well, maybe they hate competition more, but that's another story). The Net has enabled airlines to offer last-minute bargains to entice travelers to fill those seats. Most of these are announced on Tuesday or Wednesday and are valid for travel the following weekend, but some can be booked weeks or months in advance. You can sign up for weekly e-mail alerts at airlines' sites (see the appendix) or check sites such as WebFlyer (see below) that compile lists of these bargains. To make it easier, visit a site (see below) that will round up all the deals and send them in one convenient weekly e-mail. But last-minute deals aren't the only online bargains—other sites can help you find value even if you can't wait until the eleventh hour.

✪ 1travel.com (www.1travel.com)
Deals on domestic and international flights, cruises, hotels, and all-inclusive resorts. 1travel.com's Saving Alert compiles last-minute air deals so you don't have to scroll through multiple e-mail alerts. A feature called "Drive a little using low-fare airlines" helps map out strategies for using alternate airports to find lower fares. And Farebeater searches a database that includes published fares, consolidator bargains, and special deals exclusive to 1travel.com. *Note:* The travel agencies listed by 1travel.com have paid for placement.

BestFares (www.bestfares.com)
Budget seeker Tom Parsons lists some great bargains on airfares, hotels, rental cars, and cruises, but the site is poorly organized. News Desk is a long list of hundreds of bargains but they're not broken down into cities or even countries, so it's not easy trying to find what you're looking for. If you have time to wade through it, you might find a good deal. Some material is available only to paid subscribers.

Go4less.com (www.go4less.com)
Specializing in last-minute cruise and package deals, Go4less has some eye-popping offers. You can avoid sifting through all this material by using the Search box and entering vacation type, destination, month, and price.

LastMinuteTravel.com (www.lastminutetravel.com)
Travel suppliers with excess inventory distribute unsold airline seats, hotel rooms, cruises, and vacation packages through this online agency.

Moment's Notice (www.moments-notice.com)
As the name suggests, Moment's Notice specializes in last-minute vacation and cruise deals. You can browse for free, but if you want to purchase a trip, you have to join Moment's Notice, which costs $25.

Smarter Living (www.smarterliving.com)
Best known for its e-mail dispatch of weekend deals on 20 airlines, Smarter Living also keeps you posted about last-minute bargains on everything from Windjammer Cruises to flights to Iceland.

✪ WebFlyer (www.webflyer.com)
WebFlyer is the ultimate online resource for frequent flyers and also has an excellent listing of last-minute air deals. Click on "Deal Watch" for a roundup of weekend deals on flights, hotels, and rental cars from domestic and international suppliers.

Watch the Clock for Savings

While most people learn about **last-minute air specials** from e-mail dispatches, it can be best to find out precisely when these deals become available and check airlines' Web sites at this time. To find out when deals become available, check the pages devoted to these specials on airlines' Web pages. Because these deals are limited, they can vanish within hours, sometimes even minutes, so it pays to log on as soon as they're available. An example: Southwest's specials are posted at 12:01am Tuesdays (central time). So if you're looking for a cheap flight, stay up late and check Southwest's site at that time to grab the best new deals.

TRAVELER'S TOOLKIT

Veteran travelers usually carry some essential items to make their trips easier. Following is a selection of online tools to smooth your journey.

ATM Locators. Visa (www.visa.com/pd/atm/), MasterCard (www.mastercard.com/atm)
Find ATMs in hundreds of cities in the United States and around the world. Both include maps for some locations, and both list airport ATM locations, some with maps. Remarkably, MasterCard lists ATMs on all seven continents (there's one at Antarctica's McMurdo Station). *Tip:* You'll usually get a better exchange rate using ATMs than exchanging traveler's checks at banks.

✪ **CultureFinder (www.culturefinder.com)**
Up-to-date listings for plays, opera, classical music, dance, film, and other cultural events in more than 1,300 U.S. cities. Enter the dates you'll be in a city and get a list of events happening then—you can also purchase tickets online. Also see Festival-Finder (**www.festivalfinder.com**) for the latest on more than 1,500 rock, folk, reggae, blues, and bluegrass festivals throughout North America.

Intellicast (www.intellicast.com)
Weather forecasts for all 50 states and cities around the world. Listings are in degrees Celsius.

✪ **MapQuest (www.mapquest.com)**
Specializing in U.S. maps, MapQuest enables you to zoom in on a destination, calculate step-by-step driving directions between any two U.S. points, and locate restaurants, hotels, and other attractions on maps.

Net Café Guide (www.netcafeguide.com/mapindex.htm)
Locate Internet cafes at hundreds of locations around the globe. Catch up on your e-mail, log on to the Web, and stay in touch with the home front, usually for just a few dollars per hour.

Tourism Offices Worldwide Directory (www.towd.com)
An extensive listing of tourism offices, some with links to these offices' Web sites.

The Travelite FAQ (www.travelite.org)
Tips on packing light, choosing luggage, and selecting appropriate travel wear.

Trip.com: Airport Maps and Flight Status (www.trip.com)
A business travel site where you can find out when an airborne flight is scheduled to arrive. Click on "Guides and Tools" to peruse airport maps for more than 40 domestic cities.

Check E-Mail at Internet Cafes While Traveling

Until a few years ago, most travelers who checked their e-mail while traveling carried a laptop, but this posed some problems. Not only are laptops expensive, but they can be difficult to configure and can incur expensive connection charges—and they're attractive to thieves. Thankfully, Web-based free e-mail programs have made it much easier to check your mail.

Just open an account at a free-mail provider, such as **Hotmail** (hotmail.com) or **Yahoo! Mail** (mail.yahoo.com) and all you'll need to check your mail is a Web connection, easily available at Net cafes and copy shops around the world. (We've listed Internet cafes under "Fast Facts" throughout this book.) After logging on, just point the browser to www.hotmail.com, enter your username and password and you'll have access to your mail.

Internet cafes have become ubiquitous, even in many small Alaskan towns, so for a few dollars an hour you'll be able to check your mail and send messages back to colleagues, friends, and family. If you already have a primary e-mail account, you can set it to forward mail to your free-mail account while you're away. Free-mail programs have become enormously popular (Hotmail claims more than 10 million members) because they enable everyone, even those who don't own a computer, to have an e-mail address they can check wherever they log on to the Web.

2 Top Web Sites for Alaska

ONLINE GUIDES TO ALASKA

360 Alaska (www.360alaska.com)
Slide shows and panoramic views of many of Alaska's leading attractions. Sound files accompany the images, enlivening this site.

Alaska or Bust (www.alaskaorbust.com)
This site combines links to about a dozen local visitors' bureaus with an extensive directory of options for accommodations (including camping), sightseeing, restaurants, travel agencies, and more.

Alaska Division of Tourism (www.commerce.state.ak.us/tourism/homenew.htm)
Official information including a statewide calendar of events, printed publications you can order online, current weather, and tips, attractions, and accommodations.

Alaska Internet Travel Guide (www.alaskaone.com/travel)
A wide-ranging guide with hundreds of links to Alaska-related Web sites. Among the categories: accommodations, activities, featured attractions, parks, and many others. Use this guide to find Web sites of hotels, outfitters, and tour companies.

Alaskan Cabin, Cottage and Lodge Catalog (www.midnightsun.com)
An extensive directory of lodges organized by region. Some listings have links to properties' Web sites and e-mail.

✪ **Alaskan.com (alaskan.com)**
Though this isn't solely a tourism directory, it has dozens of categories suited for tourists, including lots of outdoor activities, all sorts of accommodations options, and transportation links. This is a terrific gateway to specialized Web sites for all aspects of touring Alaska.

Alcanseek (www.alcanseek.com)
This site is modeled after the Yahoo! search engine, with categories getting more specific as you drill down. Travel Center links are in the left column, including guides to cities, parks, and transportation options.

Tour Alaska (www.alaskanet.com/Tourism/index.html)
Hundreds of links to Alaska accommodations, outfitters, and tour companies. Select the category you're interested in and click on the Search button to scan the database.

Welcome to Alaska (www.travelalaska.com)
This site welcomes visitors with images of Native Alaskans and their music, and goes on to offer virtual tours, trip planning advice, and live images from Anchorage, Valdez, and Fairbanks.

Wild-Eyed Alaska (www.hhmi.org/alaska)
Imagine watching a bald eagle close up, or peeping into a puffin's burrow. Well, thanks to the magic of tiny surveillance cameras, you can get a glimpse of Alaska wildlife online. According to this site, the animals become accustomed to the cameras, and you can see sample images through the Net. The sound files require software you can download for free.

THE GREAT OUTDOORS

✪ **Alaska Outdoor Adventures (www.alaskan.com/outdoors/outdoors.htm)**
Listing hundreds of outfitters by categories, this is a terrific site to start planning guided outdoor excursions. Among the more than 2 dozen categories: backpacking, bear viewing, fishing, mountain climbing, kayaking, and photography.

Alaska Outdoors (www.alaskaoutdoors.com/index.html)
A yellow pages–style directory for all sorts of outdoor activities, from sportfishing to river rafting.

Alaska State Parks (www.dnr.state.ak.us/parks/units/index.htm)
While Alaska's stunning national parks may be better known, there are numerous state parks that are equally worth visiting. This regional index links to pages for about a dozen state parks, with plans to add more in the future. Among the parks covered at press time: Captain Cook State Recreation Area, Kodiak Area State Parks, and Alaska Chilkat Bald Eagle Preserve.

Alaska State Park Cabins (nutmeg.state.ak.us/ixpress/dnr/parks/index.dml)
Alaska State parks offers over 40 cabins, typically for $25 to $50 a night. These cabins are in over 15 state park units, as far north as Fairbanks and as far south as Ketchikan. Get cabin descriptions, fees, and availability online.

Bureau of Land Management (www.ndo.ak.blm.gov/)
This Department of the Interior agency manages much of Alaska, and has an excellent Web site.

Ecotourism in Alaska (www.alaska.net/~awrta)
More than 200 environment-sensitive outfitters are listed here, along with advice for getting the most out of your time in Alaska's wilderness. Sponsored by the Alaska Wilderness Recreation and Tourism Association.

✪ **Great Outdoor Recreation Pages: Alaska (www.gorp.com/gorp/location/ak/ak.htm)**
GORP is the leading online directory of outdoor attractions and activities. This site includes lively feature stories on topics ranging from the midnight sun to salmon, as well as reams of advice for exploring America's largest state.

Note to Readers

If you come across any Web sites you think should be included in future directories, feel free to send an e-mail to **frommers@idgbooks.com**—please put the term "Online Directory" in the subject field.

National Park Service: Alaska Parks (www.nps.gov/parklists/ak.html)
Links to park service pages for more than a dozen Alaska national park and recreation areas, including Denali, Glacier Bay, and Kenai Fjords. Use this page as a jumping-off point to park pages, which list top attractions, visitor information, accommodations and camping facilities, and tips on getting around.

National Weather Service Alaska Region Headquarters (www.alaska.net/~nwsar/)
This page has links to every conceivable forecast, weather map, and historical climate summary.

GETTING AROUND

Alaska Marine Highway—Alaska State Ferry (www.akferry.com)
This site will tell you everything thing you need to know about the ferry system, including summer and winter schedules, fares, and ship specs. If you choose to take the ferry, you can buy your tickets online, and you'll get confirmation via e-mail within 24 hours.

AlaskaPass (www.alaskapass.com)
The AlaskaPass Travelpass allows unlimited travel on ferries, railroads, and buses in Alaska, the Yukon, British Columbia, and Washington State. Buyers receive a handbook containing schedule information, an accommodations directory, and discount coupons for tours and side trips. Learn more on the Web site.

Alaska Railroad (www.akrr.com)
Itineraries and images for some of the greatest rail journeys remaining in the United States. Explore Alaska's vast frontiers from the comfort of a window seat.

Bell's Alaska Travel Guide (www.alaskan.com/bells)
A mile-by-mile guide of Alaska's highways, as well as information on the Alaska Marine Highway. The site includes in-depth descriptions of towns, highways, history, accommodations, camping, railroads, fishing, visitor attractions, and what to see and do.

Index

FROMMER'S® COMPLETE TRAVEL GUIDES

FROMMER'S® DOLLAR-A-DAY GUIDES

Australia from $50 a Day
California from $60 a Day
Caribbean from $70 a Day
England from $70 a Day
Europe from $60 a Day
Florida from $60 a Day

Hawaii from $70 a Day
Ireland from $50 a Day
Israel from $45 a Day
Italy from $70 a Day
London from $85 a Day
New York from $80 a Day

New Zealand from $50 a Day
Paris from $85 a Day
San Francisco from $60 a Day
Washington, D.C.,
  from $60 a Day

FROMMER'S® PORTABLE GUIDES

Acapulco, Ixtapa &
  Zihuatanejo
Alaska Cruises & Ports of Call
Bahamas
Baja & Los Cabos
Berlin
California Wine Country
Charleston & Savannah
Chicago

Dublin
Hawaii: The Big Island
Las Vegas
London
Maine Coast
Maui
New Orleans
New York City
Paris

Puerto Vallarta, Manzanillo
  & Guadalajara
San Diego
San Francisco
Sydney
Tampa & St. Petersburg
Venice
Washington, D.C.

FROMMER'S® NATIONAL PARK GUIDES

Family Vacations in the
  National Parks
Grand Canyon

National Parks of the
  American West
Rocky Mountain

Yellowstone & Grand Teton
Yosemite & Sequoia/
  Kings Canyon
Zion & Bryce Canyon

FROMMER'S® GREAT OUTDOOR GUIDES

New England
Northern California

Southern California & Baja
Washington & Oregon

FROMMER'S® MEMORABLE WALKS

Chicago
London

New York
Paris

San Francisco
Washington D.C.

FROMMER'S® IRREVERENT GUIDES

Amsterdam
Boston
Chicago
Las Vegas

London
Los Angeles
Manhattan

New Orleans
Paris
San Francisco

Seattle & Portland
Vancouver
Walt Disney World
Washington, D.C.

FROMMER'S® BEST-LOVED DRIVING TOURS

America
Britain
California

Florida
France
Germany

Ireland
Italy
New England

Scotland
Spain
Western Europe

THE UNOFFICIAL GUIDES®

Bed & Breakfast in New England

Bed & Breakfast in the Northwest

Beyond Disney

Branson, Missouri

California with Kids

Chicago

Cruises

Disneyland

Florida with Kids

The Great Smoky & Blue Ridge Mountains

Inside Disney

Las Vegas

London

Miami & the Keys

Mini Las Vegas

Mini-Mickey

New Orleans

New York City

Paris

San Francisco

Skiing in the West

Walt Disney World

Walt Disney World for Grown-ups

Walt Disney World for Kids

Washington, D.C.

SPECIAL-INTEREST TITLES

Born to Shop: France

Born to Shop: Hong Kong

Born to Shop: Italy

Born to Shop: New York

Born to Shop: Paris

Frommer's Britain's Best Bike Rides

The Civil War Trust's Official Guide to the Civil War Discovery Trail

Frommer's Caribbean Hideaways

Frommer's Europe's Greatest Driving Tours

Frommer's Food Lover's Companion to France

Frommer's Food Lover's Companion to Italy

Frommer's Gay & Lesbian Europe

Israel Past & Present

Monks' Guide to California

Monks' Guide to New York City

The Moon

New York City with Kids

Unforgettable Weekends

Outside Magazine's Guide to Family Vacations

Places Rated Almanac

Retirement Places Rated

Road Atlas Britain

Road Atlas Europe

Washington, D.C., with Kids

Wonderful Weekends from Boston

Wonderful Weekends from New York City

Wonderful Weekends from San Francisco

Wonderful Weekends from Los Angeles

FROMMER'S CITY-TO-GO

Keeping You Connected on the Road...

Frommer's and Palm Computing, Inc. have teamed up to bring you all the convenience of a Frommer's guide in the form of the Palm VII™ connected organizer.

Whether you're in New York City on business or wandering the streets of San Francisco for leisure, let Frommer's City-To-Go be your guide. With listings for the best restaurants, accommodations, nightlife, sightseeing and shopping highlights in most major U.S. cities at your fingertips, you'll have the ideal pocket-sized travel resource wherever you go.

For more information about Frommer's City-To-Go and the new Palm VII™ organizer, visit www.palm.com.

Frommer's City To Go is a trademark of IDG Books Worldwide, Inc.
Palm VII is a trademark of Palm Computing, Inc., 3Com Corporation, or its subsidiaries.

WHEREVER YOU TRAVEL, *H*ELP IS NEVER FAR AWAY.

From planning your trip to providing travel assistance along the way, American Express® Travel Service Offices are always there to help you do more.

Alaska

ANCHORAGE
American Express Travel Service
700 G Street
Suite 128
(907) 274-5588

American Express Travel Service
5011 Jewel Lake Road, Suite 104
(907) 266-6600

American Express Travel Service
5530 E. Northern Lights Blvd.
Suite 05
(907) 333-8585

EAGLE RIVER
American Express Travel Service
11409 Business Blvd. #4
(907) 694-2169

FAIRBANKS
American Express Travel Service
400 Cushman Street
(907) 452-7636

KODIAK
American Express Travel Service
Building N-38, 6th Avenue
(907) 487-2500

American Express Travel Service
202 Center Street
Suite 103
(907) 486-6084

NOME
American Express Travel Service
Front Street
Old Federal Building
(907) 443-2211

do more AMERICAN EXPRESS®

Travel

www.americanexpress.com/travel

**American Express Travel Service Offices
are located throughout the United States.
For the office nearest you, call 1-800-AXP-3429.**

Listings are valid as of December 1999.
Not all services available at all locations. © 1999 American Express.